Strategy

Sustainable Advantage and Performance

G. Page West III
Wake Forest University

Charles E. Bamford
Queens University of Charlotte

SOUTH-WESTERN
CENGAGE Learning™

Australia • Brazil • Japan • Korea • Mexico • Singapore • Spain • United Kingdom • United States

SOUTH-WESTERN
CENGAGE Learning™

Strategy: Sustainable Advantage and Performance

G. Page West III

Charles E. Bamford

Vice President of Editorial, Business: Jack W. Calhoun

Vice President/Editor-in-Chief: Melissa Acuña

Sr. Acquisitions Editor: Michele Rhoades

Developmental Editor: Jennifer King

Marketing Manager: Nathan Anderson

Marketing Coordinator: Suellen Ruttkay

Sr. Marketing Communications Manager: Jim Overly

Associate Content Project Manager: Jana Lewis

Manager of Technology, Editorial: Pam Wallace

Media Editor: Danny Bolan

Frontlist Buyer, Manufacturing: Sandee Milewski

Production Service: S4Carlisle Publishing Services

Compositor: S4Carlisle Publishing Services

Sr. Art Director: Tippy McIntosh

Internal Designer: LouAnn Thesing

Cover Image: ©Shutterstock

Permissions Manager: Mardell Glinski-Schultz

Photo Researcher: John Hill

For product information and technology assistance, contact us at **Cengage Learning Customer & Sales Support, 1-800-354-9706**

For permission to use material from this text or product, submit all requests online at **www.cengage.com/permissions** Further permissions questions can be emailed to **permissionrequest@cengage.com**

Exam *View*® is a registered trademark of eInstruction Corp. Windows is a registered trademark of the Microsoft Corporation used herein under license. Macintosh and Power Macintosh are registered trademarks of Apple Computer, Inc. used herein under license.

Cengage Learning WebTutor™ is a trademark of Cengage Learning.

Library of Congress Control Number: 2009923261

International Student Edition ISBN-13: 978-1-4390-4130-7
International Student Edition ISBN-10: 1-4390-4130-X

Cengage Learning International Offices

Asia
cengageasia.com
tel: (65) 6410 1200

Australia/New Zealand
cengage.com.au
tel: (61) 3 9685 4111

Brazil
cengage.com.br
tel: (011) 3665 9900

India
cengage.co.in
tel: (91) 11 30484837/38

Latin America
cengage.com.mx
tel: +52 (55) 1500 6000

UK/Europe/Middle East/Africa
cengage.co.uk
tel: (44) 207 067 2500

Represented in Canada by Nelson Education, Ltd.
nelson.com
tel: (416) 752 9100 / (800) 668 0671

For product information: **www.cengage.com/international**
Visit your local office: **www.cengage.com/global**
Visit our corporate website: **www.cengage.com**

Printed in Canada
1 2 3 4 5 6 7 13 12 11 10 09

Preface

If you are a strategy professor, instructor, or student, you're probably asking yourself, "What makes this textbook unique in a crowded field of strategic management texts?" As we were developing this text, we carefully considered that question, too. We wanted to create something special, something that was sure to enable instructors to teach strategy effectively while engaging students with realistic and practical information.

Specifically, we decided to incorporate several key innovations in this textbook:

- Integrating content throughout the book, relying upon important strategy concepts (value chain, resource based advantage) as the primary integrating mechanisms.
- Relating each content area to a set of contemporary strategic imperatives introduced in the first chapter: Opportunity Recognition and Value Creation.
- Devoting a full chapter to performance.
- Integrating emerging content within the traditional outline of strategic management, rather than grafting on new chapters.
- Providing guidance on practical use and application of important strategy concepts (e.g., steps to conduct an industry analysis, how to conduct a resources analysis).
- Using small companies as well as large companies for illustrations, and using examples that students are familiar with and find interesting.
- Using fresh examples, heavily drawing upon current events.
- Adopting a writing style that is student-friendly and accessible.

We briefly explore some of these innovations in detail on the following pages.

Innovations in This Textbook

Integration Across the Chapters

The textbook uses "value chain" and "resource-based advantage" as core integrating mechanisms. These two perspectives require students to consider how firms create value on a sustainable basis. This approach offers several advantages. First, the combination enables a broader discussion of organizational stakeholders, corporate social responsibility, and organizational goals. Economic value and social value are each perceived as legitimate organizational goals, and therefore this approach embraces a wide range of organizations including not-for-profits and those with specific social goals. This approach allows the strategic management course to be applied to these sectors, where student interest is rapidly growing. But these more contemporary ideas cannot exist in isolation from the essential sustainability goal of strategic management.

The value chain focus facilitates the discussion of industry entry approaches as well as the discussion of how value is created in different ways at different stages of an industry's or company's evolution. Finally, the issue of value creation is seen as a critical ongoing strategic challenge in industries characterized by dynamic, revolutionary change. Therefore the tension that exists between mandates for change versus the need for continuity can be highlighted. We emphasize the importance of coordinating mechanisms across the value chain, routines, and other intangible dimensions, which in turn helps make resource-based advantage more practical and more understandable. Conclusions from industry analysis can be evaluated in the context of value adding activities and resource-based capabilities, as can business-level strategies, competitive dynamics, diversification, organizational structuring, and internal control and performance monitoring. All of the material throughout the text is related through these two integrating perspectives.

For the students we also explicitly introduce two strategic imperatives in Chapter 1 that we revisit throughout the book: the value creation imperative and the opportunity recognition imperative. We position strategic management today as occurring in a dynamically changing context: the real challenge of sustainability has to do with superior performance now and in the future.

Chapter on Performance

This new text emphasizes—in fact spotlights—performance as a key outcome focus of strategic management. No other strategy textbook does this. We seek to encourage the perspective that strategy demands a capability in moving back and forth between the conceptual and the practical, including the performance that results. Students must understand that strategic decisions and actions translate to financial effects. Our observations are that faculty want students to conduct financial analyses of companies for class discussions and projects, yet texts and teaching materials do not provide explicit content to assist in this teaching effort (other than the usual appendix containing financial ratios). By addressing this important topic early in the book (Chapter 2), faculty will have an easier time in drawing upon financial analysis throughout the course and in asking students to consider performance implications in class discussions.

Integrating Emerging Content into Chapters

Emerging content in strategic management is thoroughly integrated into existing frameworks. For example, you will not find a separate chapter on International Strategy. Instead, this material is integrated into a chapter on growth, since it represents one of many options for firms to pursue in the development of their business. You will not find that Entrepreneurship is separated out in its own chapter, because it is not a separate function or process in any organization. Instead, the challenge of new value creation enables the instructor to deal with the ongoing entrepreneurial challenge at any stage of a company or industry. Other chapters covering material such as entry strategies, competitive dynamics, corporate strategy, and implementation all relate back to foundational material in earlier chapters on value chain and resources. We believe that this integrative approach makes the field of strategic management more understandable to students and allows instructors to more easily draw on the critical foundations.

Theory to Practice

This book is strongly grounded in strategic management theory, but it also has a very practical bent. Students are increasingly being pushed to translate their education into practical, growth-oriented efforts within the companies that have hired them. While many students still go to work for large, diversified companies, even these companies are demanding a more practical and innovative orientation by their employees. This reality makes it incumbent on textbooks to accomplish what students actually need: strategy as a practical and applicable means for use immediately after graduating college (as well as among senior management), and content that is readily applicable to all businesses.

We want our students to be able to take these ideas and use them, easily. So you will find that most chapters provide guidance on actually putting the ideas to use (e.g., steps to conduct an industry analysis, how to do a resource analysis) along with examples of how to do so. Our classroom tests have found this works!

Engaging Style

Finally, this book overcomes the biggest complaint by students and faculty about many strategy books—that they are very dry and uninteresting for students to read. The writing for this book strikes a balance between providing very strong, theory-based arguments and a style that is engaging for students. We often use the first person plural "we." We view learning about strategic management as a journey we are embarking on alongside our students, rolling up our sleeves and working hard together to understand this fascinating field. We also make liberal use of companies and industries that students can relate to in order to provide plenty of translation of ideas to practice (e.g., music industry, Xbox 360, Starbucks, Target). How do we know our style works? We've classroom tested it for two years. Students have overwhelmingly responded favorably to the writing style of this book.

Recurrent Ideas Across Chapters

We have already emphasized how we use "value chain" and "resource-based advantage" as integrating mechanisms across all the chapters in the book. This allows the professor to build cumulatively as the semester goes on, showing how later concepts relate to earlier ideas, and allows the student to understand strategic management as a set of related ideas and concepts rather than a series of discrete frameworks.

There are other ideas carried across the chapters in this book that will aid the professor in teaching strategy. These include the following:

- **Strategic Moves.** Appearing in nearly every chapter are very short vignettes that build on the discussion of the chapter to that point, and then pose questions for students to consider further. The remainder of the chapter seeks to provide further information to help provide the answers. These Strategic Moves vignettes spark more active engagement by the students so that they can drill down deeper into the situation. They also provide excellent material for follow-up class discussions.

- **How To....** Nearly every chapter concludes with a section on how to actually use the framework or ideas that the chapter has developed. What are the steps in conducting an industry analysis? How does one construct strategy maps? How do you do a value chain analysis? How do you actually perform a resource analysis? What are the steps to take in pursuing an acquisition? Kurt Lewin said, "There is nothing so practical as a good theory." We quite agree, and practical applications are highlighted in the text's margins with an Action Steps icon.

- **Leadership and Ethics.** Often strategic leadership and ethics are each dealt with in their own chapters in strategy textbooks. But not here. Leadership and ethics are evident in all aspects of strategic management, such that the consideration of any type of strategic situation or analytical framework synthetically and simultaneously calls up these ideas. Therefore, throughout the book you will find small graphics in the margins of the text where issues of leadership and ethics appear prominently. This reminds the students that these dimensions are an ongoing part of every aspect of the field.

Support Materials

Make It Yours custom case program. We have aligned cases from the leading case providers to each chapter in this text, and through the authors' own research have developed the most commonly used and recommended cases for teaching Strategy. From this list instructors can easily create a comprehensive and cost effective case-based learning solution. To review and select from this comprehensive case listing please visit us online at www.cengage.com/custom/makeityours/BamfordWest1.

A full set of supplements is available for students and adopting instructors, all designed to facilitate ease of learning, teaching, and testing.

Instructor's Resources. Instructors will find all of the teaching resources they need to plan, teach, grade, and assess student understanding and progress at their fingertips for *Strategy: Sustainable Advantage and Performance*. These supplement offerings include:

- **Instructor's Manual**—This valuable, time-saving Instructor's Manual streamlines course preparation with its presentation of chapter outlines, teaching suggestions and lecture notes, and answers to all chapter questions.
- **Testbank**—The *Strategy: Sustainable Advantage and Performance* Testbank in ExamView software allows instructors to create customized tests by choosing from True-False, Multiple Choice, and Short Answer/Essay questions for each of the book's 12 chapters. Ranging in difficulty, all questions have been tagged to the text's Learning Objectives and AACSB standards to ensure students are meeting the course criteria.
- **PowerPoint Slides**—A comprehensive set of PowerPoint slides will assist instructors in the presentation of the chapter material, enabling students to synthesize key concepts.

Premium Web site. Students will receive access to additional study aids and self-evaluation tools free with the purchase of a new *Strategy: Sustainable Advantage and Performance* 1e text. Available to students will be PowerPoint study slides, key term flashcards, and interactive quizzing, as well as a guide to case analysis, which will allow students to instantly gauge their comprehension of the material. The quizzes are all tagged to the book's Learning Objectives and AACSB standards.

Product support Web site. The *Strategy: Sustainable Advantage and Performance* product support Web site at www.cengage.com/international enables instructors to download files for the Instructor's Manual, PowerPoint slides,

Video Guide, and a robust Teaching with Cases Resource Center. Through the Product Support Web site, students can access the Learning Objectives and flashcards.

WebTutor on BlackBoard and WebTutor on WebCT. Available on two different platforms, *Strategy: Sustainable Advantage and Performance* WebTutor enhances students' understanding of the material by featuring the Opening Cases and Video Cases, as well as e-lectures, the Glossary, and study flashcards.

DVD. Instructors can bring theoretical concepts to life with the current and relevant video cases available on the *Strategy: Sustainable Advantage and Performance* DVD. Each videocase is correlated to the book's sections, and discussion questions and answers tied to each video case can be found in the Instructor's Manual.

Acknowledgments

We would like to acknowledge the many people who have contributed to this effort. Our thanks to:

Terry R. Adler, Ph.D., New Mexico State University

Brent Allred, The College of William & Mary

Joe S. Anderson, Northern Arizona University

Sonny Ariss, Ph.D., University of Toledo

Samuel DeMarie, Iowa State University

Thomas J. Douglas, Southern Illinois University, Edwardsville

Scott E. Elston, Iowa State University

Robert E. Ettl, Stony Brook University

Dr. Charles R. Fenner, SUNY–Canton

Debora J. Gilliard, Metropolitan State College

Ari Ginsberg, New York University

Barbara A. Good, Ursuline College

Marcellina Hamilton, SUNY–Canton

Jay J. Janney, University of Dayton

Sal Kukalis, California State University Long Beach

Joseph W. Leonard, Miami University

Paul Mallette, Colorado State University

James Randall Martin, Florida International University

Elouise Mintz, Ph.D., Saint Louis University

Michael L. Monahan, Frostburg State University

J. L. Morrow, Jr., Birmingham–Southern College

Fred P. Newby, D.B.A., Sullivan University

Daewoo Park, Xavier University

Ralph W. Parrish, University of Central Oklahoma

John K. Ross III, Texas State University

Amit Shah, Frostburg State University

Paula S. Weber, Saint Cloud State University

We would also like to acknowledge our families. They put up with our constant yammering about "the book" over all the time it was being written and revised. They were wonderful to allow us (sometimes with not so sweet comments) to miss family time and the Friday night movies with popcorn so that we could revise Chapter 6 one more time.

And finally, we would like to acknowledge our students. For the last two years we have been testing chapters of our book on our students. We told them we were doing this. We asked for their feedback, and they gave it to us—both positive and negative. Our students were extremely helpful through this, and through their help we know we have a book that students will enjoy using more.

About the Authors

G. Page West III, Ph.D.

Dr. Page West is Professor of Strategy and Entrepreneurship and the BB&T Fellow in Capitalism and Free Markets at Wake Forest University. He earned his B.A. in Economics at Hamilton College, an MBA at The Amos Tuck School of Business Administration at Dartmouth College, and a Ph.D. in Strategic Management at the University of Colorado at Boulder. Prior to earning his Ph.D. he held positions in marketing and new business development for 17 years at consumer packaged goods companies including General Mills and Celestial Seasonings, and consulted with Westinghouse and other technology companies. He also started up his own food manufacturing company, raised venture capital, and expanded the business to a national level.

At Wake Forest he has taught undergraduate and graduate Strategic Management, Entrepreneurship, International Entrepreneurship, Capitalism and Free Markets, and Shakespeare on Management. His experience includes teaching management in London, UK, and he is a regular visiting faculty member of École de Management in Bordeaux, France. He has won awards for innovative teaching three times, and was recently named as the most influential professor by Wake Forest business school alumni.

His research focuses on top management teams and the evolution of strategy in new ventures. He has published articles in *Journal of Management*, *Journal of Management Studies*, *Journal of Business Venturing*, *Entrepreneurship Theory and Practice*, *Journal of Technology Transfer*, *Journal of Small Business Management*, and *International Journal of Organizational Analysis*.

Page is married to his college sweetheart. They have five children ranging from 18–30 years old, and recently became grandparents. He enjoys hiking the Colorado high country and researching family genealogy.

Page West

Charles E. Bamford, Ph.D.

Dr. Chuck Bamford is the Dennis Thompson Chair of Entrepreneurial Leadership at Queens University of Charlotte. He earned his A.S. degree at Northern Virginia Community College, a B.S. degree at the University of Virginia, an MBA at Virginia Tech, and a Ph.D. in Strategy & Entrepreneurship at the University of Tennessee. During a twelve-year span prior to pursuing his Ph.D. he held positions managing Business Analysis (Mergers & Acquisitions, Dispositions, and Small Business Consulting) for Dominion Bankshares Corporation (now Wells Fargo Corporation). Other positions during his business career included Director of Corporate Training, Systems Analyst, COBOL programmer, and full time instructor in the early 1980s at Virginia Western Community College.

Chuck has taught courses in Strategic Management and Entrepreneurship at the undergraduate, graduate, and executive levels. His teaching experience includes courses taught at universities in Scotland, Hungary, and the Czech Republic. Prior to joining Queens University he held positions as an Associate Professor at Texas Christian University and at the University of Richmond. He teaches Executive MBA courses at Texas Christian University, The University of Notre Dame, and at Queens University of Charlotte.

Chuck has won fourteen individual teaching excellence awards during his career, including six Executive MBA Teacher of the Year Awards. He is also a Noble Foundation Fellow in Teaching Excellence.

His research has been published in the *Strategic Management Journal, Journal of Business Venturing, Entrepreneurship Theory & Practice, Journal of Business Research, Journal of Business Strategies, Journal of Technology Transfer,* and *Journal of Small Business Management.*

Chuck is married and has three children, ranging from 12–25 years old. In his spare time he is an avid sailor and writer of fiction.

Chuck Bamford

To Linda for her steadfast love, belief, and support. And to Dale for his inspiration to make a difference in the lives of students.

G. Page West III

To Yvonne, Rob, Sean, Mo, and Bill for your support and love in my daily life. I can't thank you enough.

Charles E. Bamford

Brief Contents

Table of Contents

Introduction: Strategy, Performance, and Direction

Look around you. Read the headlines in today's *Wall Street Journal*. Some companies succeed wildly, while others fail miserably, and most fall somewhere in between. Why is this? Why do some companies perform better than others even in the same industry, and why do some companies achieve superior performance over the long run? That's what this book is about.

There are a lot of textbooks about strategic management. So why have we elected to write yet another one? As students, you know the problems with many textbooks you have been required to read during your time in college:

1. Relatively dry, long-winded, and often oriented toward the memorization of content.

2. Generally out of touch with the reality that most of you are interested in or will be dealing with when you enter the business world, because the texts largely draw upon examples that spring from the highest management levels of the world's largest organizations.

3. Impractical, with so little effort made to show how you can actually put important concepts and frameworks into practice immediately.

No wonder so many students recommend "get rid of the textbook" in end-of-semester course evaluations!

We're trying to solve these kinds of problems with this new textbook. Using a fresh writing style, contemporary examples of companies you've heard about, good theory that is honed in practical management, and a sincere attempt to show you how to actually apply the ideas about strategy, we think you'll appreciate the difference. We hope you will give us feedback on this new text, so that we can continue to make improvements. Let us know what you like and what you don't. Tell us where you think something is confusing, tell us when you read something that you enjoyed or gave you new insight. Write your local congressman! (Just kidding.)

The first section of this book covers both the beginning and the ending of Strategy. Chapter 1 will tell you about Strategy itself and provide a roadmap for where the book will take you during the semester. Then Chapter 2 drills down into Performance, which is what senior managers (and everyone else in the organization) should be working toward. Superior performance is THE outcome, the end-result of great strategy. We begin with this ending precisely because it is so important. Then in Chapter 3 we go back to the beginning, where you'll read about crafting the strategic vision and the mission for how to get where you want to go (hint: Performance).

We look forward to working with you collaboratively to better understand Strategy.

Strategy

LEARNING OBJECTIVES

1 Identify and discuss the importance of the two strategic imperatives facing every company today.

2 Define the essential characteristics of strategy, and review the five critical questions encompassed by it.

3 Explain how the field of strategy today has evolved out of its historical roots.

4 Connect the concept of strategy with vision, ethics, and leadership.

5 Describe an effective process for developing and implementing strategy.

Sirius XM Satellite[1]

Today's Sirius-XM radio was originally founded as two separate organizations more than twenty years ago. XM Radio began in 1988 as American Mobile Radio Corporation, and Sirius was founded in 1990 as Satellite CD Radio Inc. Both companies were formed to provide broad multichannel, digital, satellite-based radio service for customers in the United States.

In 1997 American Mobile received the first satellite digital audio radio license and contracted with Boeing Satellite Systems to build and launch two satellites. Over the next four years, the company changed its name to XM Satellite Radio, held an initial public offering of its stock, signed licensing agreements with various media providers, and prepared for the March 2001 launch of its first satellite (Rock) followed in May by its second satellite (Roll). In September 2001, XM officially launched its service. Sirius Satellite Radio launched its service in July 2002, and the two companies competed fiercely until their merger in July 2008.

For both companies, launching a successful satellite radio business was much more involved than simply competing for customers. New digital signal processing technology was developed. Suppliers of new types of chips had to be identified, and a complete satellite system developed and launched. Consumers could not receive satellite broadcasts on any existing radio, so each company forged receiver technology relationships with electronics manufacturers such as Sony and distribution arrangements with retailers such as Best Buy and Circuit City. XM struck agreements with General Motors and BMW to offer its satellite radio in new vehicles, while Sirius struck deals with Chrysler, Mercedes-Benz, and Freightliner trucks. These were expensive undertakings. By the time its service began, XM had raised over $1.5 billion in debt and equity, while Sirius had raised nearly $2.5 billion.

Each company carefully considered the adoption of different business models—charging subscriptions, selling advertising, or some combination of both. There had never been a business like this launched before, so there was no telling in advance which model would work best. Allowing advertising would generate revenue faster, but it would then seem more like everyday radio and also interfere with the kind of value for consumers that the founders had originally envisioned. By not allowing advertising each company would need to invest heavily to develop a subscription base, requiring them to compete with other forms of discretionary entertainment spending by consumers.

Neither iPod nor MP3 technology existed at the time of XM's or Sirius's founding. The only way customers could listen to the music of their choice was to bring along a selection of CDs or cassette tapes. So-called "free radio" was broadcast locally, using analog technology and continually interrupted by the need to broadcast commercials in order to generate revenue. However, this industry changed dramatically shortly after the two companies committed to satellites as a means of delivering radio content. The *Wall Street Journal* reported that "many people are simply having iPod adapters installed in their cars and skipping satellite altogether, a concept that was barely on the horizon when the industry was young." Both companies had tried free trial subscriptions, reduced rate receivers, preinstalled radios on new vehicles as well as cut-rate programs for the first year of operation.

Faced with very slow growth in subscribers, the two companies made a series of tactical moves to dramatically change their fortunes. In October 2004, Sirius announced that shock jock Howard Stern would be moving from CBS radio under an agreement that would potentially cost Sirius more than $500 million over five years. This was followed by deals with the National Football League ($220 million over seven years), the National Basketball Association, and the English Premier League. At the same time, XM concluded deals with Major League Baseball ($650 million over eleven years), Oprah Winfrey ($55 million over three years), and the National Hockey League. After more than six years of frustration, the two companies merged in 2008 to form one company in an effort to create an economically viable organization. The proposed merger was carefully examined by the Federal Trade Commission for possible monopolistic practices.

Case continued from page 5

Traditional broadcast competitors complained that one company would control 100 percent of satellite radio; XM and Sirius management countered that the definition of the industry and competitors was considerably broader than just "satellite." The combined entity is now trying a series of moves to encourage customers to switch to satellite radio. Sirius XM is offering à la carte packages that range from $7 to $17 a month, new receivers, and a plan to turn on all dormant devices with a small selection of free stations.

When formed, the combined company had a stock price of almost $2.50. Less than six months later it was trading for less than $0.14. The company needed to raise almost $800 million to cover debt repayments and operations during 2009. Goldman Sachs predicted that the company would lose more than $500 million in 2009 even as sales climbed above $12 billion. Just before being forced to enter the clutches of bankruptcy protection in early 2009, Liberty Media (owner of DirecTV) scooped up the company in a last-minute deal, squeezing out attractive terms while also thwarting their longtime opponent, who controlled Dish Network, from expanding into satellite radio.

XM-Sirius raises many issues and questions that are tied directly to strategy and are therefore the purpose of your studying this field:

Questions

1. What constitutes a "good" strategy?
2. What are the appropriate outcomes of an effective strategy?
3. How might you approach a business the size and complexity of Sirius XM?
4. Under what circumstances does it make sense for a company to merge with or acquire another company?
5. Over what time horizon does strategy play itself out?
6. How do you drive a company into the future within the constant day-to-day scrutiny of Wall Street analysts?
7. Who should be involved in setting strategic direction and making the key strategic decisions for a company?
8. How much difference can one person at the top of the organization make in its strategy and performance?

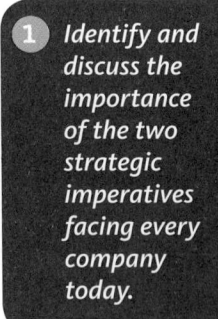

1 *Identify and discuss the importance of the two strategic imperatives facing every company today.*

TODAY'S STRATEGIC IMPERATIVES

Once upon a time, before the 1970s, companies sought to achieve performance amidst fairly stable markets. Back then, markets were fairly well defined (e.g., a phone provided voice telephone service), barriers to entry to markets were fairly robust, competitors basically understood one another and respected each other's turf, disruptive innovations occurred infrequently, and people in business kept fairly sane work hours.

Today, the game has changed and the rules are very different. Advances in technology occur rapidly and make even the smallest competitor a nuisance to the large, incumbent firm. It's hard to know how to accurately define an industry (e.g., a phone is a camera is an e-mail device is a portable music player is a Web browser). Globalization and the relative ease of forging alliances create situations where even geographically remote firms will compete in your own backyard for your most prized customers. Customers have come to expect more from all companies, pushing the essential value frontier of greater features and customization for lower and lower prices. The pace of work has escalated because we are now in a global environment. Although the financial markets close in New York at the end of the workday, they are open nearly

24/7 because of the Tokyo, Hong Kong, and London exchanges. When you attend a trade show in Chicago, a visitor to your booth uses his cell phone to snap a picture of the new product that your company is proudly displaying. Within forty-eight hours, halfway around the world, a possible competitor has "dummied up" a similar new product in its low-cost manufacturing facility and added the item to its price list. Our colleague Richard D' Aveni coined the term *hypercompetition* to describe today's competitive environment.[2] Jack Welch, former CEO of General Electric, described the 1980s as "white knuckle" competition but said the next decades would be even worse.

These ideas about intense competition amidst rapidly changing and evolving circumstances have tremendous implications for strategic management today. We believe that every aspect of the practice of strategy today—analysis, formulation, implementation, and evaluation—must embrace two imperatives in light of the new competitive context:

1. *Opportunity recognition imperative*
2. *Value creation imperative*

These two imperatives are the cornerstones of this textbook, and should be the lens through which you examine the various aspects of the field. Because industries, technology, globalization, and competition evolve so rapidly, every company must excel at **opportunity recognition**—the critical need in business to identify and exploit where the market is heading. In this environment, companies must constantly position themselves to search for, identify, and embrace new opportunities that may ultimately replace their existing business. Rapid change tends to make every new product or service obsolete much faster than in the past. Few companies can rest on the laurels of what they accomplished five years ago or even last year, because hungry new competitors—both small and large—will seek to imitate what made them so successful. The downside of rapid technological advances, increasing opportunities to partner with other firms to gain complementary capabilities, and the fluidity of international financial institutions is that competitors now have the tools to go after lethargic companies whose management is rewarding themselves for past performance by basking in the sun at a villa on Grand Cayman.

The upside is that such change produces many new opportunities that are ripe for pursuit. The problem that most successful companies have is that they become set in their ways of doing things and looking at things. The challenge for management, then, is to build an organization and a process that will proactively search out new opportunities, bring them to the table, and embrace experimentation on new products or services. The constant tension that will exist between managing the existing business and supporting new business development efforts will require exceptional management talent.

Creating new business in the face of ever-changing industry and competitive contexts brings to light the **value creation** imperative. Successful companies are like machines: once they figure out how to do something well, they refine the process and "institutionalize" it so they become better and better at it. Now along comes a new type of business direction that requires value to be created in fundamentally different ways, challenging the status

Opportunity recognition The critical need in business to identify and exploit where the market is heading.

Value creation The primary goal of strategy. The value created is widely accounted for by all the stakeholders of the company.

quo (and likely upsetting a lot of people who made the company so successful under the old way of doing things). Value creation is a central theme in this book, and we will unpack it more carefully in Chapter 5. Companies must recognize that, as markets change, the process of creating perceived value will also change. In order to flourish and prosper, companies must be willing to commit to learning how to create value in new ways. Companies today have to understand who their new customers are going to be, what new values these customers will increasingly appreciate, and how to make money creating and delivering those new values. As we shall see, however, value creation embraces many stakeholders—not just customers—in a company. Therefore, many opportunities are presented to management as ways to uniquely create value, which is the foundation of sustainability.

How Does This Relate to Me?

This is a great question to ask, right here at the beginning of the course. You will be graduating soon, and the likelihood that you will immediately become the president of Sirius XM, GE, Boeing, or any of the other large companies we will mention throughout this book is slim to none. Yet strategy is not something that is decided upon or occurs at only the very top of the organization. Strategy permeates every aspect of an organization. In fact, every part of an organization is a reflection of its strategy. People throughout every company are essentially involved in its strategy. Take a look again at the Sirius XM story. Research and development, supplier relationships, retail relationships, customer marketing, content providers, finance: both separately and in combination, each of these functional areas is central to the company's effective market entry and successful performance. No matter where you go to work or in what function you work, you will be involved with company strategy.

Perhaps you will not go to work in a large corporation after you have graduated, but instead find employment in a small business or your family's business. After all, more than 99 percent of all business organizations in the United States are small businesses (defined as having fewer than 500 employees), and they employ fully 50 percent of the U.S. workforce. These types of companies generate most of the job growth in the United States because they are responsible for the lion's share of new technological innovation, export, and GDP.[3] The person who understands strategy in a sophisticated manner is better prepared to succeed in the small business environment.

② *Define the essential characteristics of strategy, and review the five critical questions encompassed by it.*

WHAT IS STRATEGY?

Strategy may be one of the most overused and misused terms in society today. Everyone has a "strategy" for virtually every activity in their lives. These range from those that might truly contain legitimate elements of a strategic decision to those that are completely inaccurate uses of the term. Here are a few common examples:

- A strategy for obtaining a career goal. Realizing that only those individuals with line experience appear to obtain the top spots in the company, Joe requests a transfer from his staff analyst position into a much lower level line position in one of the plant operations.

His hope is to develop his operational skills and prove his ability to handle the mainstream functions of the company.

- A strategy for getting to work in the morning. Hadley faces a tough commute each day because of the traffic snarls and construction around her house. Each morning she listens to the traffic reports before leaving and uses one of more than a half-dozen routes that she has mapped out to get her to the office.

- A strategy for waking up on time. Primarily because William has missed his 8:00 class four times this semester, he has decided to set two alarm clocks. One on his bedside table is a normal buzzer alarm. The second is a timer across the room that automatically cranks up the James Brown song "I Feel Good" on his iPod.

- A strategy for developing an innovative product. Realizing that their new battery and miniaturization technique for employing GPS technology might have many uses, Jennifer and Jim—the founders of FindemRightNow, Inc.—decide to evaluate each potential market before employing an engineering design firm to mold the technology into its marketable configuration.

- A strategy to be # 1 in the industry. This type of proclamation has been heard many times over the years from a variety of well-known companies. The ownership of "first place" in an industry (whatever that really means) is actually an outcome, and offers no insight about the ways in which the company intends to operate.

A term that describes everything can describe nothing very well. Strategy is much more than any simple set of activities designed to obtain some desired end. Let's first talk about what strategy is generally, then we will define it in more specific terms. In general terms you can think of **strategy** as the overall concept for how a company organizes itself and all its activities in order to conduct business successfully, outperform competitors, and deliver superior returns to its shareholders. As the Sirius XM story at the beginning of this chapter illustrates, a company's strategy has implications for every functional area across a company. That is, the efforts in each functional area (marketing, operations, finance, etc.) should reflect and support the central idea about how a company intends to conduct business and compete. But the concept of strategy is more than just how a business coordinates all its activities; it is also about performing better than competitors and delivering superior returns. Some companies may be well-coordinated across their functional areas, but are beat up by competitors in the marketplace and earn only average or below-average returns. We are interested in how to win when we talk about strategy.

Strategic management is the process through which strategy is developed, executed, and evaluated. There are typically four stages of the strategic management process: analysis, formulation, implementation, and evaluation. *Analysis* includes examining and understanding the industry in which you want to compete, and looking carefully inside the company to understand what its unique competitive strengths are and how it organizes its activities to create and deliver value. It is through the analysis process that companies often discover new opportunities or threats, and begin to realize how they

Strategy The overall concept for how a company organizes itself and all its activities in order to conduct business successfully, outperform competitors, and deliver superior returns to its shareholders.

Strategic management The process through which strategy is developed, executed, and evaluated. There are typically four stages of the strategic management process: analysis, formulation, implementation, and evaluation.

can organize or reorganize to create new value. *Formulation* is the stage in which management articulates its vision and mission, outlines its goals and objectives, and decides upon a particular type of strategic approach to take. Of course, formulation depends on good, strong analysis. *Implementation* is where the rubber hits the road. In this stage, the formulated strategy is put into practice through the decisions that companies make about how to allocate resources, how to structure the organization and motivate employees, and which types of tactics, programs, and activities the company actually engages in. Strong implementation efforts call for consistency of effort across all the functional areas of a company. The fourth part of the strategic management process is *evaluation,* an activity that actually occurs throughout each of the first three stages. By creating a system of evaluation that operates continuously, management is able to respond more rapidly when actual results begin to diverge from what they had expected in the formulation stage.

This general description of strategy and strategic management is helpful only up to a point. We need to get more specific and detailed. As a field of study and a matter of business practice, strategy now has specific meaning as a set of well-grounded approaches and a set of implementation frameworks that can be applied in a variety of business settings. We define strategy as a field that deals specifically with the following five critical questions:[4]

1. **Why are firms different?** Why do some firms perform better than others? Strategy concerns the creation of a position of advantage over other companies in a competitive marketplace.

2. **How are competitive differences sustained?** Strategy is focused on sustaining a superior position in the market over an extended period of time.

3. **What is special about strategic decisions?** Strategy deals with a handful of decisions that rise above specific functional concerns.

4. **What is the nature of strategy in a multibusiness firm?** Questions 1 and 2 are fundamentally about a *single* line of business. Today, however, many companies are diversified, owning and operating many different kinds of businesses. The top execs at headquarters cannot possibly know every detail about all the different lines. So what kinds of issues do they deal with and what kinds of decisions do they need to make?

5. **How is strategic effectiveness measured?** Examining summary financial performance measures is the most frequently used method of assessing strategy. However, many executives understand that strategy must also consider other stakeholders, and that both qualitative and quantitative measures are required.

Why Are Firms Different? Creating Competitive Advantage

Strategy requires a basic understanding of a business that is often absent. This happens in part because, as mentioned earlier, the term strategy is used in so many different ways. There is a central economic logic to the way a business operates that should provide a clear idea about how superior profits are earned. Top managers are often focused on their own area's affairs and the immediate issues that are pressing them on a day-to-day basis, taking attention away from the central logic for the company. Even if an effective understanding of the business is well understood by its people at the top, it is rarely translated down through the organization's hierarchy. A typical Q & A session with middle managers can often sound something like this:

Q: Why are you in business?
A: To make money!

Q: How much?
A: As much as we can.

Q: When do you have to earn this money?
A: We have quarterly goals that we need to make so that our financial statements will look good.

Q: How will you meet those goals?
A: By selling as much as we can!

Q: Have you considered starting up an Internet business?
A: NO!

Q: Have you considered getting into the insurance business or owning a casino?
A: NO!

Q: Why not?
A: Because that's not what we do!

Q: What do you do?
A: We sell as much as we can of our products.

Q: Would you do something illegal?
A: NO!

Then you are **NOT** in business to make as much money as possible! The strategy of a business is not to make money! It is not to be #1 in the industry. No one will buy your products because you want to make money. Money and market share are the *results* of an effective strategy. Companies are in business to provide something of value to customers in a manner that will yield substantial, positive returns to the organization. Yet, this simple truth gets lost in the minds of employees who are focused on the next quarter's bottom line. This misunderstanding occurs most often because senior management has failed to distinguish performance from the fundamental logic that guides how the business should operate.

Strategy is about the approach a company takes to the market that places it in a superior position relative to its competitors. Conventional economic theory assumes that any advantage for one firm will be quickly imitated by its competitors and thus neutralized or negated by natural market forces—the result being that all firms in an industry will eventually look and act alike. And yet the reality—that there are many different types of firms in any one industry—is obvious to us all. Why are firms different, given what we know about economic theory? Strategy is fundamentally about developing a dominant logic for how the company should uniquely operate, focusing its attention and investments on that unique model, and ensuring that all parts of the organization are working consistently in support of that model. Sound strategy enables a company to create differences between itself and other companies, in ways that are valued in the marketplace. When companies create value in unique and compelling ways, then markets respond and the results for the company will include market share and profits.

Consider the situation in which Blockbuster currently finds itself. Blockbuster was extraordinarily successful for a substantial period of time in building an international chain of movie rental stores that took advantage of the growing interest in new technologies (VCRs and home theater equipment), which together enabled a quality movie experience at home. Blockbuster created tremendous value for its suppliers (studios) and its customers in a unique fashion. Taking advantage of the market created by Blockbuster, a number of other movie rental competitors entered the market using alternative strategies. Hollywood Video, Wal-Mart, and others entered the rental market by undercutting Blockbuster's pricing and offering DVDs for sale at sharply reduced prices. Netflix entered the industry much later with a mail-order system that lacked late fees and advertised an unlimited number of movies to be viewed per month for a set monthly fee. Blockbuster senior management attempted to address the growing competition by addressing their perceived competitive weaknesses. They did this by attempting to match what other competitors were doing. This involved:

1. Eliminating late fees, not because they were not profitable (they were) and not because of customer complaints (complaints were insignificant), but simply in response to a start-up business (Netflix) that was using the tactic to enter the DVD rental market. This move had the effect of dramatically cutting profits without providing any discernible advantage.

2. Allowing customers to keep their rentals as long as they wished, eventually buying the rental movie if they held it out long enough. This left many store shelves empty as the sophisticated logistical system that had led to the predictability of rental times, upon which the business had originally been built, fell apart.

3. Investing heavily in a mail-order rental system. Once again responding in a reactive manner, this move put them in the position of being a slow follower in an arena that did not take advantage of their enormous physical neighborhood retail presence.

4. Giving over valuable store space to the rental of games for children. This put them in direct competition with a whole new industry without the competitive advantages that they enjoyed with the movie industry (where they obtained films months prior to general release to the public).

Although Blockbuster and its system of video/DVD rentals originally created value, the onset of low-priced "bricks and mortar" operations as well as new online video retailers eroded its competitive advantages. While the company stumbled with competitive matching moves, the root causes of its crisis still existed. Good strategic decision making involves a systematic approach to developing a unique set of resources and capabilities that set the company apart from its competitors in a way that is compelling for both suppliers and customers. Blockbuster was endowed with some significant resource advantages in its early years, but new competition has forced it to refocus the business in a manner that will once again create valuable competitive differences.

One of the central concepts of this book is a focus on value creation and the **value chain**—"a systematic way of examining all the activities a firm performs and how they interact...." in order to find a basis for competitive advantage.[5] We will be further discussing how the unique creation of value can deliver superior performance.

How Are Competitive Differences Sustained? Long-Term Orientation

Strategy is also about getting from the present to the future, about mapping out a direction for the longer term, which takes into account an always-evolving market and smart competitors. When we understand that strategy is about the longer term, we come to realize that many everyday uses of the word strategy are incorrect, because they often refer to short-term actions or short-term results. Strategy is also about the *sustainability* of competitive advantage over a period of time. In today's global marketplace we are often witness to rapid changes in technology, economic conditions, and competitive actions. Under these circumstances when so much is constantly in flux, how is it possible to have a long-term orientation? An essential part of strategy is therefore the vision the company develops, in the context of all past, present, and anticipated future moves of its competitors, customers, suppliers, and other known and unknown stakeholders. While this might seem to be an environment in which a longer-term approach is of little value, the simple fact is that the *need for strategy* (the title of this chapter!) is even greater as a consequence of these rapidly evolving marketplace conditions. Otherwise, companies will find themselves bouncing along haphazardly based on decision-making that in a simple fashion barely responds to the next immediate fire.

Distinguishing between strategies and tactics is critical to successfully implementing a strategy. Imagine an NCAA Final Four basketball tournament in which the national championship is decided by only one point at game's end. What enables one team to win at that moment, in that game, is how they and

Value chain Provides a systematic way of examining all the activities a firm performs and how those activities interact with each other to find a basis for competitive advantage.

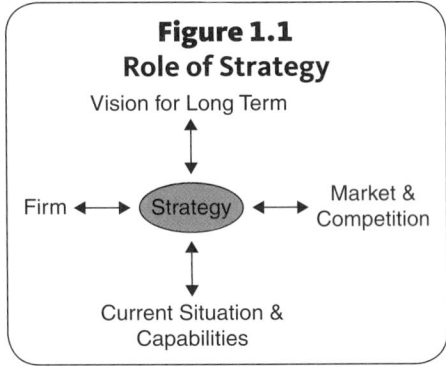

Figure 1.1
Role of Strategy

Vision for Long Term

Firm ← → Strategy ← → Market & Competition

Current Situation & Capabilities

their coach *tactically* deal with the other team's plays and players. The *strategy* for the winning team, however, was determined much earlier when the coach's vision for how this group of players could compete effectively was put into practice. The combination of years of experience in a competitive arena, complete knowledge of the competitors, experience in recruiting new high school players, hiring coaches with specific skills and understanding, and thorough new training regimens—is what puts a team in a position to win.

Figure 1.1 captures the sense of these first two important dimensions of strategy.

Strategic Moves
Competition in Commercial Aircraft Manufacturing

In May 2006, Boeing rolled its last 717 model off the aircraft assembly line in Long Beach, California. The Boeing 717 was a continuation of the McDonnell Douglas MD-95 model, which itself was based on the Douglas DC-9 that first took to the skies in 1965. The 717 and its earlier predecessors were 100-seat models designed for regional transportation and routes between cities that did not require large-capacity aircraft. The Long Beach factory opened in 1941 and produced almost 10,000 airplanes for the World War II effort, and then converted to commercial airplane construction thereafter. The 717 was the last plane this facility would manufacture, after having been operating for 65 years.

During the same month, Boeing and its chief competitor, Airbus Industries, faced critical decisions that would affect their rivalry for years into the future, their suppliers, the airlines who are their customers and us as the traveling public. Boeing needed to decide whether to ratchet up the development schedule for its potentially lucrative 787 model (The Dreamliner) in order to preempt the new Airbus 350 model that was in development, or create a "stretch" version of the 787 to better compete with the larger Airbus A380, which was scheduled to roll out the next year. Ratcheting up the schedule to get into production sooner might put significant pressure on their suppliers, thereby raising costs, causing shortages, and cutting profitability. Developing a stretch 787 would cost more in the short run, but might also blunt Airbus should this market grow quickly. Airbus needed to decide whether to significantly redesign its A350 model to better compete with the 787 that was already taking an enormous share of the midsize 200–300 seat market preorder sales. In combination with the fact that the A350 was already two years behind schedule, further delays would more than double its development price from $5 billion to $10 billion. Because of the long development cycle and the length of years that new models are in service, in the airline business "such strategic moves usually occur only once or twice in a decade."[6]

This vignette illustrates important dimensions of strategy: the long-lasting effects that strategic decisions can have, and the nature of decisions made early on that lead to significant differences between competitors. Whereas the Boeing 717 model was effective over a forty-year period, now both Boeing and Airbus seek sustainable competitive positions in the future through the development and introduction of new classes of planes. The Douglas manufacturing and assembly facility had an effective life span of more than half a century.

Will Google, Microsoft, or Apple be able to sustain competitive advantage for another forty to fifty years?

What Makes Strategic Decisions Special?

The commercial aircraft manufacturing story brings us to the third critical dimension that describes strategy. We would like to develop the ability to separate the kinds of decisions and actions that are truly strategic from those that are not. Deciding how to get up in the morning or get to work on time may be important, but those decisions and plans are not strategic, in part because they are not fundamentally dealing with the question of sustainability or long-term outcomes. Additionally they are also not strategic because they do not exhibit the critical characteristics that define a strategic decision.[7] **Strategic decisions** are different from other types of decisions in that they:

1. Are ill-structured and nonroutine
2. Significantly affect the subsequent actions of the entire organization
3. Involve a significant commitment of resources (broadly defined)
4. Are difficult to reverse both economically and politically
5. Are easily identified with the success or failure of the organization

Ill-structured and nonroutine situations. Though companies are continuously reviewing their strategy, executing it, and monitoring their strategic progress, decisions on major new strategic initiatives are not made on a regular basis. Making a significant decision on strategy is unlike the decision a brand manager at Procter & Gamble might make regarding a new advertising campaign. The design and execution of new ad campaigns occurs with some regularity in a packaged goods company and there is a generally prescribed method for managing and implementing these efforts. This is simply not true for major strategic decisions. Here we are talking about the need to confront unique and changing market conditions and competitive circumstances for which there is often no historical record of similar types of decisions. Furthermore, beyond generic advice, company executives find that there is little off-the-shelf information readily available. Strategic decision making deals with a level of ambiguity not only about conditions in the present but also about how decisions made today will affect the company years down the road. This is actually what makes the practice of strategy so exciting and interesting: the opportunity for the decision maker to use intuition, creativity, and analysis—a combination of art and science.

Affects subsequent actions. Strategy is also unique in the field of management for other reasons. First, it is integrative because effective strategy requires that all of the functional areas of a business (marketing, finance, production, etc.) act in ways that consistently support the overall approach to the market. A company's strategy may, for example, involve continuous innovation and new product development. Nevertheless, should the finance function not support the investment spending in R&D, or if the production department refuses to allow for adequate test production runs in the factory, then the overall approach is likely to fail. Strategy requires internal consistency across all functions in a company. Indeed, a clear statement (mission and/or vision) and understanding about the strategy of the company is one of

Strategic decisions
Strategic decisions exhibit five characteristics: 1) are relevant to ill-structured and nonroutine situations; 2) significantly affect the subsequent actions of the entire organization; 3) involve a significant commitment of resources; 4) are difficult to reverse both economically and politically; and 5) are easily identified with the success or failure of the organization.

the most important means of ensuring that all functional areas consistently support one another in the implementation of strategic direction in all of their individual activities.

Significant commitment of resources. Because outstanding accomplishments rarely come from small efforts or small initiatives, strategic decisions most often involve significant commitments of resources. To create unique competitive differences that are well valued in the marketplace, as well as to sustain those differences over time, a company must commit itself to a challenging path. When Amazon.com first started up, it relied upon publishers to warehouse and ship books that Amazon customers were ordering online. As the volume of business increased, however, shipping times and quality control suffered. It became clear to Jeff Bezos (founder and CEO) that publishers did not share his view of what constituted quality customer service. Amazon was positioning itself on customer service, information, and rapid results. Amazon made the decision to build and operate its own regional distribution warehouses, fully stocked with their best-selling books. The effort cost the company tens of millions of dollars, and once set in motion could not be pulled back without severe penalties. The effort ensured the quality of service Amazon promised, distanced itself from its competitors, and helped launch the company on an unparalleled growth trajectory.

Difficult to reverse. Suggested by the discussion earlier of long-term sustainability, strategic decisions have a long-lasting impact on the company and the competition in the market. Strategy is not like riding a bicycle, where you know immediately if you have erred because you fall down and scrape your knee. Strategy is more like navigating a high-speed oil supertanker far out at sea: you turn the rudder to change direction, but because of the inertia and the size of the ship, the turn may take many miles to complete. Decisions made today to move forward with strategic investments will not usually manifest themselves as results until many years down the road.

Identified with success or failure. It is for the reasons just described that strategic decisions have the greatest impact on a company's performance. They involve huge commitments of resources over long periods of time. They focus attention on specific opportunities, meaning that other possible opportunities are passed up. These focused commitments are designed to create a unique and sustainable competitive position. Strategy sets the goals of the overall organization as well as establishes how all the functional areas will work both individually and together. This is not to say that functional area issues and decisions are unimportant. Quite to the contrary, when a problem occurs within a functional area, it is because it can affect strategy for the company—and therefore all the other functions that must be seamlessly integrated—that overall company performance may be put at risk.

What Is the Nature of Strategy in a Multibusiness Firm?

Corporate strategy
The strategy involved in managing multiple business units under the same corporate banner.

A completely unique issue in strategy involves the issue of **corporate strategy**, that is, the efforts involved in operations that manage multiple business units under the same corporate banner. Corporate-level strategy is fundamentally concerned with acquiring, managing, and divesting various business units in an effort to create a portfolio that attains economic returns in excess of what the individual business units could produce on their own. This is done primarily through resource sharing and efforts to achieve economies of scale and scope within the organization. Corporate-level strategy had been studied since the inception of the field, and today is often defined by the relatedness of a company's diversification efforts. 3M Corporation (formerly Minnesota Mining & Manufacturing Company) was founded in 1902 by a group of businessmen to exploit abrasive mineral deposits. The company struggled to find a successful business combination, frequently changing the company's concept and product mix. On the basis of several successful product launches in the 1920s, 3M began to acquire other promising businesses with the help of a set of wealthy investors. Today 3M has over 69,000 employees, sales in excess of $20 billion, and operates companies in six different business segments: Consumer and Office; Display and Graphics; Electronics and Tele-communications; Safety, Security, and Protection Services; Health Care; and Industrial and Transportation. 3M management oversees the entire opera-tion from St. Paul, Minnesota, and regularly acquires and divests various components of the business. Corporate-level strategy is a distinct area in the field of strategy and will be covered in detail in Chapter 10.

How Is Strategic Effectiveness Measured?

Because the nature of strategic decisions focuses attention on the performance of the company, companies employ **metrics**—qualitative and quantitative measures that allow the firm to measure the effectiveness of its business strat-egy. The customary manner in which the effectiveness of strategy is assessed is by financial performance metrics. These often include measures such as return on equity (ROE) or one of its components such as profitability.

Even more important than simple return measures, the assessment of strategic effectiveness usually involves a measure or set of measures that compare how well a company did *relative to* its competitors in the industry. Figure 1.2 shows performance, defined by a profitability metric (net income divided by sales revenue) for key competitors in the retail grocery store in-dustry in 2006. The average for the industry during the period was only about 0.83 percent, because the grocery store business has never been very profitable in percentage terms. Publix and Whole Foods both far exceed the industry average, while Pathmark and A&P stores both significantly trail the industry. Whole Foods is an example of a strategically high-performing company partially because it is by definition delivering "above-average prof-itability" as a result of its business model. An above-average profitability metric means that Whole Foods is more attractive to financial markets, and most likely has superior cash flows that allow it to reinvest back in its busi-ness to further enhance its position and growth.

There are several other types of metrics used to gauge effective strategic performance, such as profitability and ROE. A CEO also pays attention to the financial markets' response to the company's performance, since stock prices and debt ratings can significantly impact how and when a company

Metrics Qualitative and quantitative measures that allow the firm to measure the effectiveness of its business strategy.

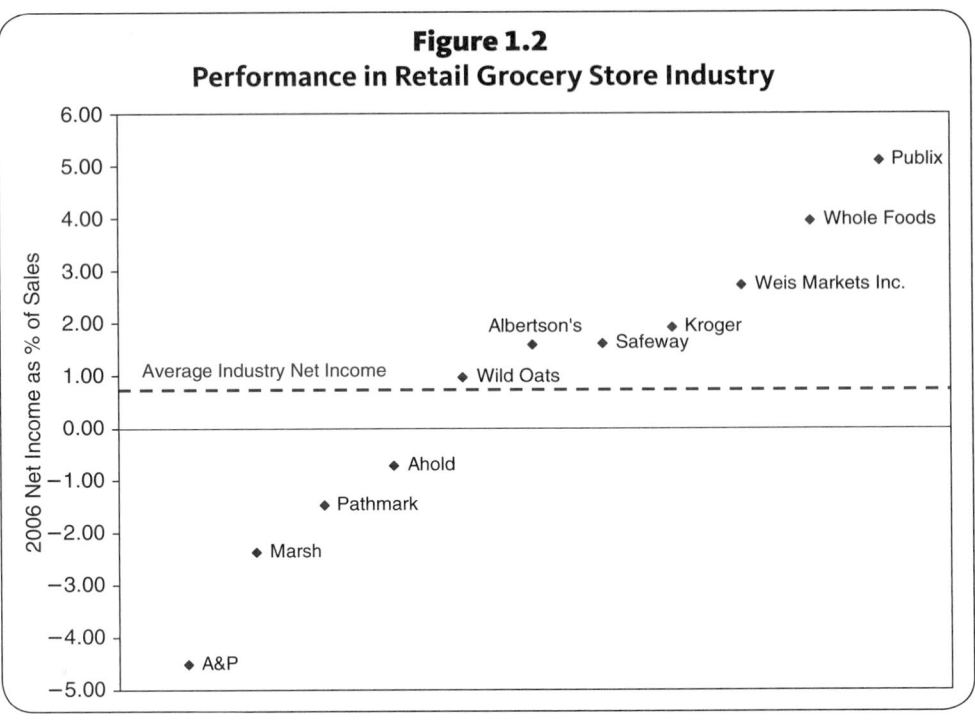

Figure 1.2
Performance in Retail Grocery Store Industry

can raise capital. Increasingly, corporate executives are considering how well their companies create value for a variety of stakeholders. In the next chapter we will further explore dimensions of performance, including financial and nonfinancial measures.

The essential goal of strategy is the creation of competitive advantages that can be developed, refined, and dynamically maintained such that the company will achieve **superior performance** relative to its competitors. Superior performance refers to outcomes that exceed the average for the industry in which the company competes; those firms whose performance is average or below average are less attractive. This kind of relative evaluation allows the firm to compare its most important measures of performance against those of its direct competitors. The strategy approach to performance emphasizes an evaluative system that rewards those who are capable of moving their organization consistently beyond the average expectations in the industry. In Chapter 4 we will further discuss the nature of strategy and above-average returns.

Superior performance
As used in the field of strategy, refers to performance outcomes that exceed the average for the industry in which the company competes.

3 *Explain how the field of strategy today has evolved out of its historical roots.*

HISTORY OF THE FIELD OF STRATEGY

How did the field of strategy get to this point, in which it is defined by the five questions just discussed, and where both opportunity recognition and value creation are absolutely imperative for any company? While there might be some disagreement regarding the roots of the field, the field had its foundation

2,500 years ago with **Sun Tzu** and his writings in *The Art of War*. This succinct text consists of thirteen chapters that helped codify many of the fundamental concepts of strategy that are still important today. These include:

1. A complete understanding of the nature of the competitive marketplace is the first step in a winning campaign.

2. A deep understanding of the mindset of your competitors and how they might react to various new moves enables you to anticipate competitive challenges.

3. The realization that preparation, understanding, and a deep commitment to excellence allows one to anticipate and preempt competition. An organization that is focused on its business, that is constantly refining and improving its ability to compete with attention to the finer details, and one that is on the cutting edge of best practices in its competitive arena may prevent others from even attempting to compete. Therefore victory (in its most pure form) is defined as never having to enter battle.

4. An evaluation of the resources and capabilities of your organization will point out the best ways to compete and win.

Reading Sun Tzu through the lens of business provides many insights about the most basic nature of strategy analysis, formulation, and implementation. An illustration of the chapter content of Sun Tzu's book is included in Figure 1.3.

Sun Tzu never actually used the term "strategy." The seeds of strategy and strategic management in business were sown nearly one hundred years ago, as economies moved out of the industrial revolution and into an era of big business. The development of large industrial giants such as Standard Oil of New Jersey led to antitrust legislation in the United States that aimed to ensure free market competition and to labor legislation to protect the rights of workers. As legislation sought to create a level playing field in competitive markets, large companies began to look internally for sources of advantage over competitors. In the early 1900s, **Frederick Taylor** conducted "science of work" time-and-motion studies that helped identify more efficient production processes and ideas about structure and hierarchy. These studies contributed to the creation of a more effective organization in progressively larger companies. Mass assembly lines, pioneered by Henry Ford in the 1930s and thus nicknamed "Fordism," contributed to even greater efficiencies and a lowering of costs in manufacturing.

In 1962 a Harvard professor, Alfred Chandler, catalogued the growth and administrative changes which had occurred over the previous fifty years at four giant pillars of industry at the turn of the twentieth century (General Motors, Sears, Standard Oil, and Dupont).[8] As these companies grew, top executives found that they were increasingly removed from day-to-day business activities. The complexity of their businesses and the sheer number of activities made it virtually impossible to manage in the same ways as they had in the past. Chandler explained how senior managers discovered new roles for themselves making long-term decisions about the direction of their diverse

Sun Tzu Author of *The Art of War*, an ancient Chinese book on military strategy.

Frederick Taylor Father of the "science of work" time and motion studies that helped identify more efficient production processes and ideas about structure and hierarchy.

Figure 1.3
Strategy Excerpts from *The Art of War* (Sun Tzu, 500 B.C.)

Chapter & Title	Quotation and Interesting Strategy Points
1 Estimations	"Warfare is a great matter to a nation; it is the ground of death and of life; it is the way of survival and of destruction, and must be examined." • Calculation and rational thought are keys to success. • Important factors to evaluate include moral influence, leadership, competitive arena, and plans. • *Example:* In contrast to other commercial banks, BB&T has avoided significant credit risk by rational analysis and objective evaluation of its loan applications.
2 Waging War	"When doing battle, seek a quick victory. A protracted battle will blunt weapons and dampen ardor . . . If the army is exposed to a prolonged campaign, the nation's resources will not suffice." • Continuous battling depletes resources and makes you vulnerable. • *Example:* When Microsoft decided to compete in the Internet browsing business against Netscape, it offered its Internet Explorer software for free, seeking to drive Netscape out of business quickly.
3 Planning	"To gain a hundred victories in a hundred battles is not the highest excellence; to subjugate the enemy's army without doing battle is the highest of excellence. Therefore, the best warfare strategy is to attack the enemy's plans, next is to attack alliances, next is to attack the army. . . ." • *Example:* After September 11, 2001, the United States initiated a series of security policies designed to detain suspected terrorists and ferret out terrorist plans before they could be implemented.
4 Disposition	"One who is free from errors directs his measures towards certain victory, conquering the defeated." • Preparation, experience and an attitude toward success is critical. • *Example:* Wal-Mart successfully expanded into urban markets building on their experience and organizational innovations learned in rural areas.
5 Strategic Power	"What enables the masses of the Three Armies invariably to withstand the enemy without being defeated are the unorthodox and the orthodox." • Doing just the orthodox makes you a player in the industry, but to win you must also do the unorthodox very well. • Over time, the unorthodox becomes the orthodox and you must find another competitive advantage to keep winning. • *Example:* Best Buy first achieved success through scale and efficiency as a big box electronics retailer. Others imitate this approach now, so Best Buy began changing the playing field by targeting service and distinctive customer programs as new points of competitive advantage.

(continued)

Figure 1.3
Strategy Excerpts from *The Art of War* (Sun Tzu, 500 B.C.)

Chapter & Title	Quotation and Interesting Strategy Points
6 Vacuity & Substance	"In order to prevent the enemy from coming forth, show them the potential harm. In order to cause the enemy to come of their own volition, extend some apparent profit." • Erect barriers to entry that keep potential competitors away. • Form alliances or joint ventures with competitors to achieve shared goals. • *Example:* Pharmaceutical companies seek patent protection on new drugs to prevent competitors from selling them. Competitors United Airlines and Continental agreed to share schedules and mileage programs to increase passenger volume on each carrier.
7 Military Combat	"Accordingly, if the army does not have baggage and heavy equipment it will be lost; if it does not have provisions it will be lost; if it does not have stores it will be lost." • Failure is guaranteed without the right resources, effectively organized. • *Example:* Pets.com and other dot coms traded on Internet interest, but had few unique and valuable resources to forestall competitors. Atari pretty much invented the video game category in the 1970s but failed because it lacked sophisticated game programmers in the 1980s. Skybus failed in 2008 because it lacked financial resources needed to deal with soaring aircraft fuel costs.
8 Nine Changes	"One who commands the army but does not know the techniques for the nine changes, even though he is familiar with the five advantages, will not be able to control men." • Know the competition and the competitive environment. • *Example:* Howard Schultz successfully grew Starbucks because he lived and breathed specialty coffee experiences.
9 Maneuvering the Army	"If orders are consistently implemented to instruct the people, then the people will submit." • Communication of mission drives coordinated effort. • *Example:* Disney's mission "to produce unparalleled entertainment experiences" is known and practiced daily by its employees. It so epitomizes excellent customer service that other companies visit Disney to learn how they, too, can improve.
10 Configuration of the Terrain	"When the general regards his troops as young children, they will advance into the deepest valleys with him. When he regards the troops as his beloved children, they will be willing to die with him." • Vision instills passion in the organization. • *Example:* CEO Stanley Gault's vision of an "aisle of Rubbermaid" propelled the company to develop and successfully introduce dozens of new products.

(continued)

Figure 1.3
Strategy Excerpts from *The Art of War* (Sun Tzu, 500 B.C.)

Chapter & Title	Quotation and Interesting Strategy Points
11 Nine Terrains	"When the soldiers and officers have penetrated deeply into [enemy territory], they will cling together. When there is no alternative, they will fight." • Where significant exit barriers exist, competitors will retaliate and fight viciously. • *Example:* As automobile sales flatten out, Ford, General Motors, and Chrysler compete vigorously to sell vehicles so they can keep their plants operating.
12 Incendiary Attacks	"Implementing an incendiary attack depends on the proper conditions. . . ." • Know when to attack and when to wait. • *Example:* The entry of discount airlines to new markets prompts the legacy carriers to lower fares in order to prevent passenger loss. In the 1980s Ronald Reagan spent vigorously on a military buildup; economically unable to match this buildup, the Soviet Union collapsed.
13 Spies	"The means by which enlightened rulers and sagacious generals moved and conquered others, that their achievements surpassed the masses, was advance knowledge." • Importance of prospective information that guides the future. • *Example:* When Staples opened its first stores in Boston, it collected detailed data on customers and their spending, allowing the company to quickly develop a "real estate model" for expansion down the eastern seaboard.

enterprises. They made investments and modified organizational structures to increase the efficiency with which each operated. Chandler called these long-term plans "strategy," the first time the term was used to describe business processes. The term derives from two Greek root words, *strat* and *egos,* meaning "general of the army," or more directly from the combined ancient Greek word *strategos,* meaning "art of the general."

The popular model for strategy in the 1960s and 1970s included the concepts of "policy" and "long-term planning." Policies were simply guidelines within which managers could make decisions. **Long-range planning** came to be very popular; almost every firm of any size instituted an annual long-range planning exercise. The mainstay of this exercise was the budget process, where programmed actions essentially remained the same but new, updated numbers were plugged in for the next year. Consequently, long-range planning became more of an extrapolation of the past than a real look to the future. This complacent business approach and a belief that the U.S. economy defied all models ran headlong into a strong group of rising global businesses headquartered outside of the United States.

Beginning in the early 1970s American industry suffered a number of significant environmental jolts, which have forever changed the way business interprets and implements business strategy. The first of these was the 1973

Long-range planning
A traditional approach to planning used before 1980 that often simply extrapolated into the future what the company had done well in the past.

Arab oil embargo, which resulted in gas prices increasing roughly 35 percent overnight, from under 40¢ per gallon to 55¢ per gallon on average nationwide (Figure 1.4), with significant shortages and prices over $1 per gallon in many local areas. Much as in the early 1940s, people easily recall one- to two-hour waiting lines at gas stations because gas was so scarce. It had taken over forty years for gas prices to rise from 21¢ to 38¢ per gallon, but only five more years before prices topped $1 nationwide in 1979. Americans started questioning the wisdom of buying large, gas-guzzling automobiles, opening the door for a host of foreign competitors who were already trying to enter the market with smaller fuel-efficient cars. Honda, Toyota, Datsun (now Nissan), and other international car companies aggressively sought a foothold in the U.S. market. In 1973 foreign companies had a tiny percentage of the U.S. auto market, but within ten years their market share increased to over 35 percent. The rapid decline in the U.S. automobile industry caused a significant rethinking by American business about how to sustain superior performance in a new global environment, and it had an enormous cascading impact in other industries (steel, rubber, parts, and other industries). U.S. auto manufacturers never foresaw this as a possibility; they had simply been extrapolating past trends into the future, never really considering a situation where competitive conditions might change so dramatically and so rapidly. Moreover, a relatively complacent industry took nearly five years to bring a new automobile model to market as U.S. companies tried to maximize the "life" of the previous models. A rapid response to the new competitive threats was virtually impossible.

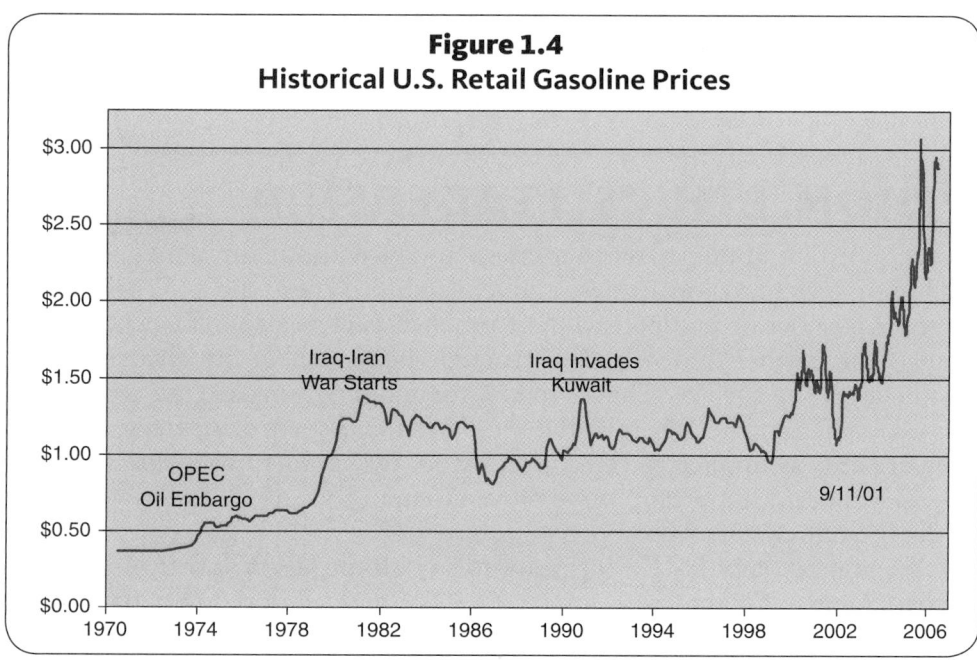

Figure 1.4
Historical U.S. Retail Gasoline Prices

Source: zFacts.com.

Figure 1.5
U.S. Industry Gains & Losses, 1978–1985

Industry type	Share Gains	Share Losses
Raw materials	27	23
Manufacturing	18	28
Consumption	38	46
	83	97

Source: Porter, Michael E. 1990. *Competitive Advantage of Nations.*

Michael Porter
Leading proponent of the move from long-range planning to strategy. His two early books on the subject, *Competitive Strategy* and *Competitive Advantage,* described competitive strategy as "positioning a business to maximize the value of the capabilities that distinguish it from its competitors."

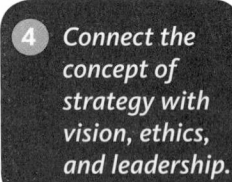

4 *Connect the concept of strategy with vision, ethics, and leadership.*

At the same time, a fundamental shift was beginning to occur in the sources of industrial growth. There was an economy-wide move toward more of a service and technology-based economy that shifted the emphasis away from heavy manufacturing. Ready access to information and markets diminished the value of proximity and made foreign competition even more viable. Consumer tastes increasingly appreciated better quality and superior service. An aging U.S. manufacturing infrastructure compromised the ability of many companies to deliver these real values, while foreign competitors could do so more easily with their newer plants built in the aftermath of World War II. From the early 1970s until the mid-1980s in industry after industry, American firms lost out competitively to international firms. During this period, more than half of all U.S. industry categories lost market share (Figure 1.5).

U.S. firms had been like the proverbial frog in the pot of slowly heating water: they had been fairly content in their positions and had not recognized the change going on around them and the need to jump out as the water temperature rose. Traditional planning largely downplayed external competitive forces and most often consisted of doing no more than what had worked in the past.

The field of strategy as we know it today was thus born, when people in industry and professors in business schools realized that newer approaches were required for companies to develop and maintain competitive advantage as a means to deliver superior performance. A number of important books and articles published during the 1970s began to articulate the kinds of ideas we now teach in strategy, ideas that might have helped American companies avoid their declines in the previous decade.[9] In his seminal 1980 book *Competitive Strategy,* **Michael Porter** described competitive strategy as "positioning a business to maximize the value of the capabilities that distinguish it from its competitors."[10]

VISION, ETHICS, LEADERSHIP

We cannot talk about or teach strategy today without simultaneously considering issues of vision, ethics, and leadership. Where the goal of effective strategy is superior competitive performance and superior financial performance, these other dimensions of strategic management are always lurking just beneath the surface. That is to say, these dimensions are not always discussed explicitly when we talk about a particular aspect of strategy, however they are always implicit in the conversation. It's smart to be aware that they are relevant and important as we move along in this book, and as you move along in your careers.

We will actually have a lot more to say about vision shortly—in fact, a whole chapter (Chapter 3). Suffice it to say here, though, that part of the problems encountered by U.S. companies in the 1970s was a lack of vision. Mere extrapolations from the past, combined with a sort of complacent attitude about what changes the future might bring, led to the situation described earlier. The contemporary view of strategy that has since emerged now emphasizes the need to sustain competitive differences over time. In turn, a longer-term view is called for to help guide the company and its employees in the right direction. More importantly, calls for today's strategic imperatives of opportunity recognition and value creation demand that companies be forward-looking and anticipate dynamic changes in the business environment while at the same time leveraging what they do best. As we will describe later, articulating vision (and mission) is one effective means for helping to bridge between the present and the future.

Recent headlines about mismanaged companies such as Enron, WorldCom, and Tyco, and the 2008 financial markets crisis fueled by factors such as unusual mortgage lending activity and baffling credit default swaps, trigger cries about the ethical behavior of senior executives. But ethics in strategy covers a far broader range of behaviors than strange accounting techniques or mysterious financial innovations. Externally, managers need to carefully consider decisions such as advertising to children, manufacturing in offshore locations where sweatshops are prevalent, or how "green" a company should be in its business practices. Internally, we need to carefully consider decisions such as how fairly employees are treated and provided opportunities, what kinds of healthcare benefits are provided, or how personal data is secured. Many strategic decisions concern initiatives or actions that may be technically legal and highly effective from a competitive point of view, but which may be morally challenged. Throughout the chapters in this book you will occasionally encounter the graphic symbol to the right, indicating an ethical issue. These will be points in our discussion of strategy where dimensions of ethics surface, and where you will need to balance different factors that enter into the decision situation.

ETHICS

Every aspect of strategy and the strategic management process depends on effective leadership. No doubt you have already read about dimensions of leadership—such as setting direction, establishing goals, making decisions and allocating resources, building culture, engaging in symbolic behavior—in some of your other courses. Articulating vision and establishing ethical guidelines are also part of the responsibility of strategic managers. However, there is also an interesting contradiction about strategy: that senior management often knows less about what is really working (or falling apart) in their company than do people further down in the organization. The closer you get to dealing with competition, the closer you get to dealing with customers, the closer you get to the actual operations in your company, the more aware you will become of the two strategic imperatives mentioned earlier: opportunity recognition and value creation. Because you will be closer to "the action," you will notice details and nuances that senior management cannot possibly comprehend from 30,000 feet. You will have a strategic responsibility to feed this information up the line when and where you see the company doing exceptionally well or poorly, and when and where you see new opportunities emerge that the company can pursue. You will be on the "firing line," where the balance often plays itself out in real terms between ethical behavior and actions that further increase competitive advantage or financial performance. You can exert strategic leadership, even at your lower level, to help others articulate and further develop these ideas. Today, every employee in an organization has a strategic leadership role to play.

STRATEGIC MANAGEMENT PROCESS

5 *Describe an effective process for developing and implementing strategy.*

So far we have briefly reviewed the history of strategy in business and why it became so important. We have also described the characteristics and chief concerns of strategic decisions, and how these are very different from other areas of management that you may have studied already. The strategic management process is what the rest of this book is about—a concise and practical guide to analyzing, formulating, implementing, and evaluating strategy. Figure 1.6 provides a blueprint of how the rest of the book is organized to present the topics critical to the strategic process.

What you might notice first about Figure 1.6 is that Chapter 2 is on the right side of the figure, traditionally indicating the end. You might be asking yourself, why would the authors begin the book at the end? We do so to emphasize the need for keeping our eye on the ball. The "ball" is superior performance, the fundamental goal of strategic management. So to emphasize superior performance as the ultimate goal, we concentrate on it in our next chapter, before we describe more specific details about how to achieve it in subsequent chapters.

After considering performance, we move into the processes of analysis and formulation (Chapters 3–7). But as the circular arrow in the center of this block

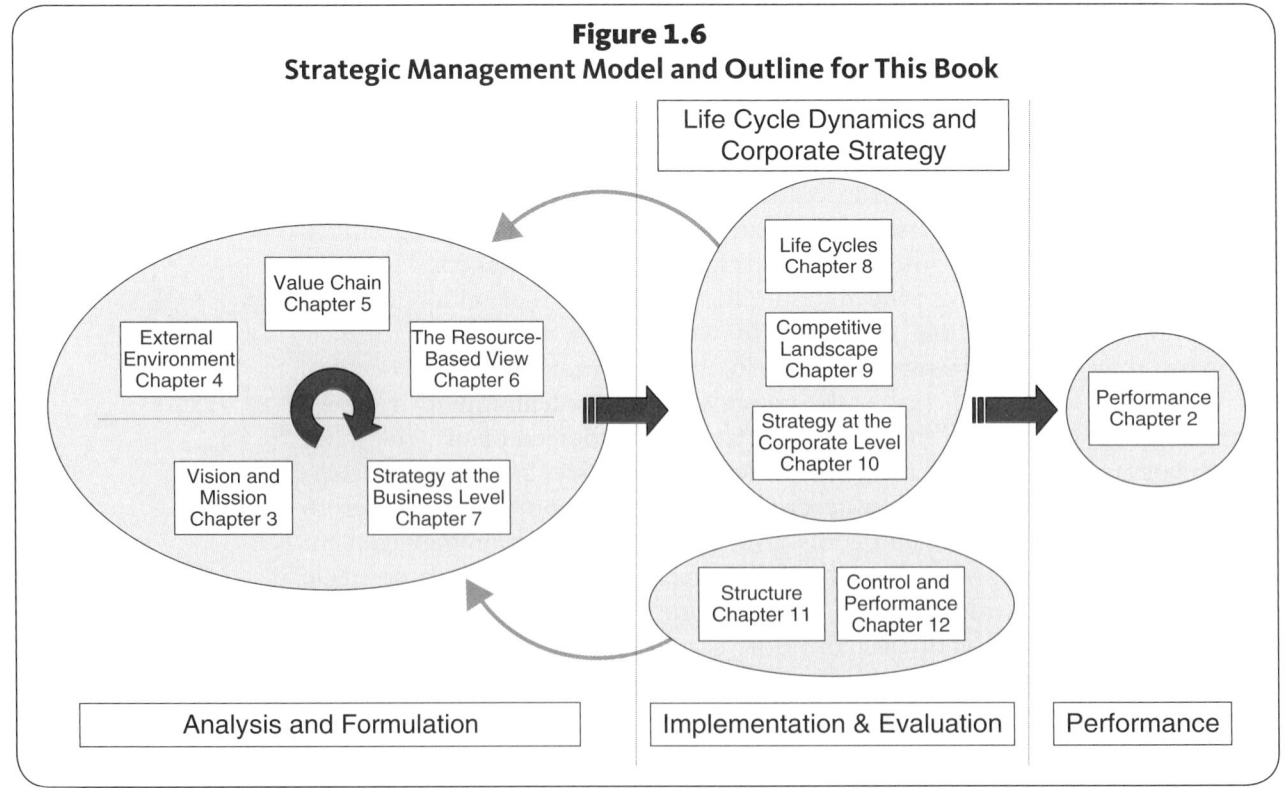

Figure 1.6
Strategic Management Model and Outline for This Book

of chapters suggests, there should be a constant cycling back and forth between analysis and formulation. The final chapters of the book (Chapters 8–12) present topics necessary to the processes of implementation and evaluation, and ultimately lead to the desired outcome of superior performance.

Analysis and Formulation

As indicated by the circular arrow in the middle of the left group of chapters in Figure 1.6, the processes of analysis and formulation are not strictly sequential. For instance, even though a high degree of analysis might be required before a company's effective vision and mission can be solidly established, a company needs to formulate a vision and mission statement to effectively sum up what the company is all about. Therefore, before getting into a discussion of the analysis process (Chapters 4–6), mission and vision are covered in Chapter 3. This chapter describes the necessity of establishing a vision that guides the company into the future, a mission statement that enhances day-to-day consistency and coordination of activities in support of the vision, and objectives that represent tangible targets for a company and its employees to work toward.

The analysis chapters yield a more detailed understanding of what works in a particular competitive environment and why, while helping us understand how well our company's activities and resources are suited to the competitive environment. Often, the industry a company competes in or how a company competes is a reflection of an earlier choice that management made about its long-term direction.

Types of analysis. Every attempt to grapple with strategy formulation and implementation relies upon a strong foundation of analysis. A detailed analysis of industries and competitors (Chapter 4) enables a solid understanding of the competitive context, how it is evolving, and what competitive dimensions appear to be growing in importance. This analysis also offers insight into the intentions of key competitors. Understanding this broader industry and competitive context contributes to a better understanding of how a particular company will be able to effectively compete. The analysis process described will begin with an external analysis at the industry level, and then drill down into the company of interest.

The "internal analysis" of the company encompasses two perspectives. The first is the value chain (Chapter 5), which is a central theme to effective strategic management in this book. Value chain analysis takes into account two sets of activities that create value and offer the potential for competitive advantage: 1) activities transacted between the company and its suppliers and customers, and 2) activities transacted within the walls of the company. It will be pointed out that companies themselves are an organized set of activities that participate in a chain of value-adding activity across an industry. We will also learn that products and services produced by a company are simply a manifestation of sets of activities that occur within the company. Therefore, if we are interested in the source of competitive advantage in a market, we need to carefully examine how value is created by a company through the activities it engages in. We will also examine when it makes strategic sense for a company to outsource important value-creating activities instead of performing them in house.

The second internal analysis method is **resource-based analysis** (Chapter 6). This is an exciting and relatively new area of study for strategy that offers the opportunity to better understand how to develop a *sustainable* competitive advantage. While the value-chain perspective in Chapter 5 helps answer the first key question about strategy (Why are firms different?), the resource-based perspective in Chapter 6 helps answer the second question (How are competitive differences sustained?).

One final comment on the analysis chapters: Recall from the earlier discussion that strategic decisions are special for a variety of reasons. The nature of strategy—dealing with ill-structured situations, uncertainty, and making decisions for the long term—will necessarily require decision makers to "make bets." Strategists must make decisions and investments today whose payoff is often far down the road; it's simply the nature of this area of management. When a strategic decision is made, the decision maker is essentially building on a logic that he or she has developed about cause and effect in the marketplace, saying "If we do X now and over time, then Y will occur in the future." The best way to build that logic is through strong, foundational analysis. This enables decisions to be made, based not upon "I hope this will work," but based upon "I have developed a sufficient case to believe that this will work for my company."

All of which brings us back once again to the need to take the results of analysis and use them to formulate business-level strategies (Chapter 7)—and thus the iterative process indicated by the circular arrow in Figure 1.6.

Formulation. In Chapter 7, we consider business-level strategic approaches to the marketplace and competition, focusing especially on low-cost and differentiating approaches. Having now analyzed the industry and a company's internal resources and value-creating activities, and taking into account its long-term vision, we are now in a position to formulate a precise and actionable approach to building a business, engage competition, and produce superior returns.

As previously mentioned, managers must not approach analysis and formulation as sequential stages in the strategic management process, but rather must constantly be cycling back and forth between these elements. The competitive environment is dynamic, and so changes in factors affecting whole industries or new initiatives by competitors may make previously hatched approaches or existing sets of resources less relevant going forward. Similarly, new resources we develop or new initiatives we put into play in our company may shake up an industry and competitors, calling for our own re-analysis of this dimension.

Implementation: Strategy in the Marketplace

Will all of the effort put into analysis and formulation be successful for the company in developing sustainable competitive advantage? The

Resource-based analysis An approach to an organization that examines its current resources and capabilities in an effort to find those that will provide the company with value-generating competitive advantages.

answer you will often hear is "It depends." What does effective strategic performance depend on? It depends on the evolving contexts that confront the company in the marketplace, and this next section explores some of these contexts. Chapter 8 explores interesting strategy issues that occur in different stages of the life cycle of both companies and industries. The resources, activities, and strategic approach of a young company are likely to be very different from those of an established competitor in the same industry. In fact, there are specific market entry strategy issues that confront new ventures and young companies that existing companies need not worry about. Similarly, there are differences in strategic approaches that make sense, depending on the nature of the industry itself. What works in a young, growing industry may not work well at all when that same industry begins to mature. What works in fragmented industries may not be appropriate for consolidated industries. Finally, this chapter tackles what to do when the industry or the company enters a mature stage and additional growth is required. Here we explore ways to redefine the value chain as a way of uncovering new growth opportunities. One especially important area for potential growth may be international expansion, and so here we look carefully at the unique challenges presented by this type of expansion.

After having completed an industry and competitive analysis and having formulated a vision and strategy, what do you do when your competitors start taking actions in response to your moves? Chapter 9 explores the many possibilities of competitive dynamics. For those students who enjoy gaming and sports, there are some very interesting parallels here to your out-of-class activities.

Chapter 10 concerns itself with a different avenue for growth, specifically growth achieved by buying or merging with other companies. This is a chapter on corporate strategy, that is, the strategic management of a company that owns and operates more than one type of business. Mergers and acquisitions (or their "divestitures" counterpart) are often front-page news. It is important to understand what motivates this method of growth, critical dimensions of the acquisition process, and how to manage a diversified company.

Implementation and Evaluation

The missing piece in so many discussions of strategy is the practical internal implementation of the plan and its ongoing evaluation. A well-developed strategy involves the coordination of a tremendous number of areas within the organization, including its structure, systems, internal control procedures, values, and performance metrics. Chapters 11 and 12 examine these critical steps in ensuring the success of a successful strategy.

Iterative Processes

The model in Figure 1.6 makes the strategy process appear to be linear and sequential, where one step logically follows another and where one cannot take a step until others before it have been completed. As noted earlier, this is not really the case. For the purposes of studying strategic management, particularly for the first-time student, it is easier to lay the process out as we have done in Figure 1.6. However, please note that there are arrows feeding from the Marketplace and Implementation/Evaluation sections back to Analysis and Formulation. This is one way of suggesting that there is a "continuous dialogue" that occurs among portions of this process. As we read earlier in this chapter on strategic imperatives, the nature of markets today requires that the strategy process be synthetic and integrative across all the areas pictured in the process diagram. Therefore, the creation of strategy is both intentional and emergent. We conduct analyses, draw conclusions, lay plans, and implement those plans with programs and actions. Yet the nature of markets and competition will change the context in which we did our planning and require us to make modifications as we go along. At the same time, if we are prepared, we will recognize new opportunities that changing markets expose, and we will elect to make modifications in our plans to take advantage of them.

CHAPTER SUMMARY

We began this chapter with a discussion of the real meaning of strategy. The field of strategy is generally defined as addressing five critical questions in business:

1. Why are firms different?
2. How are competitive differences sustained?
3. What is special about strategic decisions?
4. What is the nature of strategy in a multibusiness firm?
5. How is strategic performance measured?

A review of the history of strategy from its earliest foundations with Sun Tzu to its emergence following the 1970s demonstrated how firms needed to think more clearly about how to create and sustain valuable differences versus their competition, and therefore how to achieve superior performance. The need for strategy is even greater in the twenty-first century with the advent of technology, globalization, ease of access to financial markets, and other macro-economic trends. Increasingly, as a result of these forces, strategy must concern itself with two imperatives:

1. Opportunity recognition imperative
2. Value creation imperative

Superior performance depends upon these capabilities. The structure of this book follows a model for strategic planning. We must recognize that strategy planning and implementation requires continuous monitoring of the competitive environment and constant reevaluation and adjustment of plans.

KEY TERMS

Corporate strategy (p. 16)

Frederick Taylor (p. 19)

Long-range planning (p. 22)

Metrics (p. 17)

Michael Porter (p. 24)

Opportunity recognition (p. 7)

Resource-based analysis (p. 28)

Strategic decisions (p. 15)

Strategic management (p. 9)

Strategy (p. 9)

Sun Tzu (p. 19)

Superior performance (p. 18)

Value chain (p. 13)

Value creation (p. 7)

SHORT ANSWER REVIEW QUESTIONS

1. How might your understanding of other areas of business (finance, accounting, marketing, management, and information systems) be affected by your ability to apply the concepts of strategy?

2. Describe five types of strategy decisions in which ethical concerns must also be accounted for. Search the Internet for a business article that discusses this type of decision for a real company.

3. Who are Sun Tzu, Michael Porter, and Frederick Taylor?

4. What strategic concept encompasses a detailed understanding of the processes within an organization?

5. What do you expect to be able to do after you finish this course in strategy?

6. Why is opportunity recognition such an important concept in strategy?

7. If you were asked for some advice about how strategy can help a business develop and grow, what are the areas in which you would suggest that strategy could make a difference?

8. What elements help distinguish a strategic decision from one that is tactical?

9. How has strategy evolved over the past forty years?

10. What are some measures of an effective strategy?

11. How was strategy operationalized during the early part of the 1900s?

12. Who uses strategy in a typical company?

13. Imagine that you have arrived back home from your first class in strategy and you receive a call from your father asking you about your class. How would you explain to him what strategy is?

14. Why is being better than average in an industry an important strategy concept?

GROUP EXERCISES

1. Ford Motor Company is facing some significant strategic dilemmas. The most compelling is for the company to find a means of creating a value for its product. Consumers buy Ford cars on a daily basis and yet the company cannot achieve a profit. Form a group of three to five people and answer the following questions:
   a. How is Ford different from Toyota, General Motors, Chrysler, and Honda?
   b. How might you take those differences and make them the centerpiece of the business?
   c. How should Ford measure its success?

2. Oil prices have significantly affected every business. Business models that were highly profitable when gas prices were lower have been completely upset by higher gas prices. Form a group of three to five people and address the following:
   a. Are some businesses not affected by the price of oil?
   b. How have the airlines tried to cope with the new higher prices of fuel?
   c. What would you suggest as a sustainable strategy for profitability in the trucking industry?
   d. Assuming that there are always new ways for companies to charge more for what they provide, what would you suggest to the owner of an independent trucking company?

3. Blockbuster has been significantly challenged by mail rental businesses such as NetFlix and by discount retailers such as WalMart that sell DVDs at low prices. In your group discuss the following:
   a. What are the critical resources that made Blockbuster successful in the past?
   b. How do these resources assist and/or constrain the company's approach to the market going forward?

REFERENCES

[1] Is Sirius falling to Earth? *BusinessWeek,* November 3, 2008, 86; Sirius unveils raft of options for programs, *Wall Street Journal,* October 3, 2008 (www.wsj.com); Sirius XM sends signals of change, *Wall Street Journal,* September 15, 2008 (www.wsj.com); Until recently full of promise, satellite radio runs into static, *Wall Street Journal,* August 15, 2006, A1; Steve Finlay, XM Radio ventures beyond audio services, *Ward's Dealer Business,* July, 2005, 39 (7): 8; Steve Finlay, XM Radio looks beyond audio, *Ward's Auto World,* June 2005, 41 (6): 18; Noel Bussey, Can satellite radio become a serious medium? *Campaign (UK),* January 27, 2006, (4), 17; Tom Lowry & Paula Lehman, Grudge match, *BusinessWeek,* August 21/28, 2006, 86–87; Edwards, Cliff, Taking XM Out for a Stroll, 14, August 2006, 18; Record Companies Sue XM Radio for Copyright Infringement, *The Computer & Internet Lawyer,* September 2006, 23 (9), 38; Wildstrom, Stephan, Copyrights and Wrongs, *BusinessWeek,* 3, July 2006, 24; XM Radio (www.xmradio.com); Sirius Satellite Radio (www.sirius.com); Two upstarts vie for dominance in satellite radio, *Wall Street Journal,* March 30, 2005, A1–A9; XM Satellite director resigns after expressing cost concerns, *Wall Street Journal,* February 17, 2006, A3.

[2] R. A. D'Aveni, 1994, *Hypercompetition,* Free Press: New York.

[3] S. Venkatraman, 2004, Regional transformation through technological entrepreneurship, *Journal of Business Venturing,* 19 (1): 153–167; G. P. West & C. E. Bamford, 2005, Creating a technology-based entrepreneurial economy: A resource-based theory perspective, *Journal of Technology Transfer,* 30 (4): 433–451.

[4] R. P. Rumelt, D. E. Schendel, & D. J. Teece (eds.), 1994, *Fundamental Issues in Strategy,* Boston: Harvard Business School Press.

[5] M. E. Porter, 1985, *Competitive Advantage: Creating and Sustaining Superior Performance,* Free Press, 33.

[6] D. Michaels & J. L. Lunsford, Jet makers reach crossroads, *Wall Street Journal, May 12,* 2006, A4.

[7] Schwenk, C.R. 1988. "The Essence of Strategic Decision Making," Lexington Books, New York, NY.

[8] A. D. Chandler, 1962, *Strategy and Structure,* Cambridge, MA: MIT Press.

[9] K. R. Andrews, 1971, *The Concept of Corporate Strategy.* Homewood, IL: Irwin; C. W. Hofer & D. Schendel, 1978, *Strategy Formulation: Analytic Concepts,* New York: West Publishing; R. E. Miles & C. C. Snow, 1978, *Organizational Strategy, Structure, and Process.* New York: McGraw-Hill; H. Mintzberg, 1977, The strategy concept I: Five P's for strategy, *California Management Review,* Fall: 11–24; H. Mintzberg, 1978. Patterns in strategy formation, *Management Science,* 24 (9): 934–948; R. P. Rumelt, 1974, *Strategy, Structure, and Economic Performance,* Cambridge, MA: Harvard University Press.

[10] M. E. Porter, 1980, *Competitive Strategy: Techniques for Analyzing Industries and Competitors,* Free Press, 47.

CHAPTER 2

Performance

LEARNING OBJECTIVES

1. Explain the value of using both financial and nonfinancial performance dimensions to measure strategy effectiveness.

2. Describe the relationship between financial performance and a sustainable competitive advantage.

3. Use financial analysis to examine company strategy.

4. Explain the economic logic of industries and companies.

5. Examine and explain the interaction between strategy formulation and financial analysis.

34

2006 was a "tough, sloppy" year for U.S. airlines and for the traveling public. In the United States, four of the "legacy" airline carriers operated under Chapter 11 bankruptcy (Delta, Northwest, United, and US Airways), reflecting an industry that had lost $35 billion and laid off 150,000 workers in the years since September 11, 2001. Fuel costs skyrocketed with the surge in oil prices, challenging all carriers to deal with rising costs. American Airlines avoided bankruptcy by yanking pillows out of planes, cramming more seats into coach class, experimenting with charging customers for soft drinks (something that rapidly became the norm in the industry), and working with unions and management to shed unnecessary costs. Legacy carriers in the United States felt increased competitive pressure from the expansion of low-cost carriers such as Southwest Airlines and JetBlue Airways. U.S. carriers that relied upon profitable overseas routes were also assaulted by upstarts like Eos Airlines and MaxJet Airways, who attempted to steal market share in the lucrative business-class segment. Amidst this backdrop, merger talk dominated headlines in the second half of the year. Fresh off its merger with America West, US Airways emerged from bankruptcy and made an unsolicited bid to acquire Delta in an attempt to grow larger and improve operating efficiency. United Airlines considered a deal with Continental, and Northwest was considered a possible target by several carriers (Northwest was acquired by Delta in 2008). Speaking of the proposed Delta merger, US Airways CEO Doug Parker stated, "The airline industry remains extremely fragmented with substantial levels of excess capacity. . . . Our industry stands at a crossroads. We can continue down the current path of boom and bust uncertainty, or we can chart a new course."

Financial performance of the U.S. airlines was mixed during 2006. Northwest Airlines lost money, even though it enjoyed one of the highest load factors[2] in the industry. On the other hand, Southwest Airlines was the most profitable airline despite its low load factor. Although Southwest was the most profitable airline, its larger rival Continental Airlines delivered superior return on equity to shareholders, at 105.9 percent versus Southwest's 7.3 percent.

2006 Selected Airline Financial Performance						
	American	**Continental**	**JetBlue**	**Sky West**	**Southwest**	**US Airways**
Revenue (millions)	$22,563	$13,128	$2,363	$3,115	$9,086	$11,557
Net income (millions)	$231	$367	−$1	$146	$499	$404
Net income %	1.02%	2.80%	−0.04%	4.69%	5.49%	3.50%
Earnings per share	$0.98	$3.53	−$0.01	$2.30	$0.61	$3.32
Stock price range	$18.24–34.30	$16.74–46.29	$8.93–15.60	$20.88–30.44	$14.61–18.20	$28.30–63.27
Stock price 12/31/06	$30.23	$41.25	$14.20	$25.51	$15.32	$53.85
Return on equity	n/a	105.9%	n/a	12.4%	7.3%	41.7%

The traveling public experienced significant headaches. Domestic ticket prices rose because fewer seats were available as the airlines cut back on their schedules. New security procedures that banned carry-on liquids created long lines and short tempers at airports. Since new security prompted customers to check more bags, lost baggage plagued many airlines; system wide mishandled baggage reports increased by 10 percent over 2005 levels and 37 percent over 2004. Overbooking by airlines resulted in a 14 percent increase in passenger "bumping" off flights in 2006 versus 2005. Flight delays increased over previous years, and major winter snowstorms at the end of the year caused hundreds of flight cancellations with thousands of missed connections.

Case continued from page 35

2006 Selected Airline Operating Performance								
	American	**Continental**	**Delta**	**JetBlue**	**North-west**	**South-west**	**US Airways**	**United**
SMs (millions)*	108,999	52,203	83,885	27,418	48,549	91,316	34,050	84,829
Load factor	82.0%	84.4%	78.6%	82.0%	82.8%	72.9%	78.1%	82.0%
Cost per ASM (cents)	12.61	13.44	13.86	7.72	14.17	8.69	15.72	13.24
On-time arrival	76%	75%	76%	72%	75%	81%	77%	76%
Average delay (mins.)	12.7	13.4	10.8	15.1	11.3	8.4	10.5	13.3

*Available seat miles

Questions

1. Since all domestic airlines confront identical industry conditions, why did certain airlines enjoy superior financial performance?

2. What did Continental excel in that allowed it to produce an industry-leading return on equity?

3. How was Southwest able to report positive financial results despite one of the lowest industry load factors?

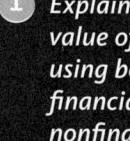

1 Explain the value of using both financial and nonfinancial performance dimensions to measure strategy effectiveness.

FOCUS ON PERFORMANCE

In the first chapter we highlighted the need for strategy in today's competitive and ever-changing world, and we discussed several questions that help us understand critical dimensions that define the nature of strategy. Throughout that discussion we often used terms or expressions that referred to performance. These included expressions such as "superior performance," "substantial positive return," and "above average profitability." This is because performance is one of the key outcomes of interest for students who are studying strategy and for managers who are responsible for formulating and implementing a company's strategy. Refer back to Figure 1.6 in the first chapter, and you will see that performance is both the culmination of the strategy model and the starting point for continual refinement. In fact, such importance is placed on performance as the critical outcome measure of strategy that we locate this chapter on performance right in the beginning of this book.

Sound strategy helps to create a position of sustainable competitive advantage in the marketplace, the results of which should be superior performance. Recall that strategic decisions involve *nonroutine situations* calling for a *significant commitment of resources and effort* that affect the *entire organization* over the *long run*. When managers are called upon to make such decisions, they must be able to reason that the company's subsequent performance will justify their resource investments and spending commitments. A consistent pattern of decision making that doesn't result in positive firm performance is usually a signal that it is time to replace those making such fine decisions. So as you study strategy this semester by examining company cases and situations, you should always be considering the performance implications of their strategic moves and actions. By discussing performance early in the study of strategy, we have learned that students will be far more insightful about and discriminating in their company evaluations.

Customary Performance Dimensions

There are three aspects of performance that are important to consider from a strategy point of view (Figure 2.1). First, since strategic decisions and actions involve virtually the entire organization, the types of performance measures we pay the greatest attention to are those that reflect the company's efforts as a whole. A marketing department may be interested in market share gains or advertising effectiveness as key performance outcomes, and a finance department might work toward an optimal capital structure or lowering the company's cost of

> **Figure 2.1**
> **Key Strategy Performance Dimensions**
> Summary performance
> Relative to competition
> Over the long run

capital as an outcome. However, at the strategic level we are interested in summary accomplishments of the entire company that roll up and include these functional area effects, as well as the performance in other functional areas. Since strategy requires consistency and coordination across all functions, the key performance measures of interest should be those that reflect the impact of integrated efforts across the entire company.

Second, the kinds of performance measures we will pay the greatest attention to are those that can be compared to other companies. As mentioned in the first chapter, the goal of strategy is to produce superior performance, and strategists are by definition relativists. Reporting that net income per employee increased by 3 percent over last year is interesting; however, realizing that the comparative group average in the industry was up only 1.2 percent makes the result remarkable and indicates a significantly better approach. In Figure 1.5 in the last chapter we saw that, although its 3.6 percent profitability by itself did not appear astounding, Whole Foods exceeded the retail grocery store industry average by a multiple of four and bested most of its competitors. Relative to competition, the company was doing very well. Therefore, it is especially helpful to consider key performance measures that can be easily compared to other companies.

Finally, since the nature of strategy is about commitment and sustainability, the kind of performance measures we pay the greatest attention to are those that reflect the company's long-term commitment. There is normally a long lead time between strategic investments and the outcomes of those investments. Imagine, for example, the commitment by Wal-Mart to begin using RFID chips on all merchandise flowing through its massive distribution system. This required a long-term investment in technology and infrastructure by both the company in its own warehouses and stores, as well as parallel commitments by companies that sell to Wal-Mart.[3] It may be misleading to evaluate performance over a short period of time, simply because the time between this strategic investment and its strategic impact can be substantial. A more complete view of strategic performance, therefore, would require assessing whether a company is delivering superior returns consistently over time. In this sense, measuring performance over longer periods of time provides better information on the outcomes of strategic decisions and actions. Using performance measures that implicitly or explicitly incorporate dimensions of a company's long-term commitments are simply more insightful. For example, a financial measure such as return on equity (ROE) evaluates current period profitability with reference to the company's equity basis (which ordinarily does not exhibit short-term variability). Profitability measures (such as net income percentage) report on current period activity, but implicitly take into account manufacturing infrastructure that produces efficiency, asset investments that must be depreciated, and the interest burden associated with long-term debt.

Emerging Performance Dimensions

Despite the Whole Foods example and others that emphasize financial measures of performance, effective strategy demands careful consideration of other, sometimes more qualitative, dimensions of the strategic performance question. Whole Foods creates more than just economic value for its shareholders. The success of the company has created markets for organic and natural foods that were previously underdeveloped. This effort has served to legitimize producers of these foodstuffs such that even Wal-Mart is now offering organic fruits in their superstores. In this way the company has helped create value upstream for its suppliers. There is also a social benefit to communities in which Whole Foods stores are located, as consumers in these areas are now provided with shopping choices previously unavailable to them. Since the company sponsors cooking and health seminars as part of its operations, additional noneconomic benefits accrue to communities in which the company locates stores.

One of the more recent moves by companies that benefit both society and the organization is the effort at becoming a "green" organization. Using natural light, installing natural power generation, eliminating waste, and selling products that are made in a sustainable way lead to significant benefits for society and are rapidly being seen as a means of competitive advantage for companies.[4]

These ideas emphasize that strategy is about value creation that can take many forms—economic, cultural, social, and knowledge-based—and that is not just for the benefit of those with formalized economic interests in or claims on a company. In the past many businesses have largely been managed with a very transactional view of their relationships and with an intense focus on enhancing profitability for shareholders to the exclusion of other goals. This approach has occasionally led to what we now consider abuses of the public good, such as the belching smokestacks in heavy industry, the use of underpaid children in Honduras for clothing manufacturing, untreated animal farm runoff in the Southeast, or the tearing down of a neighborhood health clinic to make room for a parking garage for corporate executives in the skyscraper next door.

Today a more holistic view of business exists, a view that recognizes that business operates in both a competitive and social context. In this more emergent view, firms consider performance with respect to a broader range of **stakeholders**. Stakeholders are those individuals or groups who have an interest in or an influence on the business and operations of a company. They generally fall into two categories—internal stakeholders and external stakeholders (Figure 2.2). As awareness of stakeholder issues has become more prevalent over the last decade, a vibrant debate has sprung up as to whether firm performance should be focused purely on financial measures or on a broader selection of measures that account for stakeholder interests. This debate implies that profitability and stakeholder performance may be at odds with each other; however, there is growing realization that addressing broader stakeholder goals may also further the financial goals of most companies.[5] For instance, Toyota's groundbreaking efforts on the Prius hybrid automobile not only responded to society's concerns about the impact of automobile exhaust on global warming, but also catapulted the company to the forefront of the industry as gas prices rose and the more efficient car was sought. Microsoft embarked on a drive to enhance information technology education in community colleges across America. This effort provides much-needed resources to schools in a time of constrained state and federal spending, and also responds to the company's long-term need to hire a large number of new advanced-trained IT graduates.

Taking into consideration the interests of a range of stakeholders is consistent with the two strategic imperatives we discussed in the first chapter: the opportunity recognition imperative, and the value creation imperative. Supporting the more enlightened view that business organizations and society are mutually dependent on each other, new trends that are emerging in society and industry can represent opportunities for both existing and new businesses. Some companies have started up with social objectives stated explicitly, in addition to ordinary corporate profitability objectives, and by doing so create a valued connection with consumers that goes beyond merely the benefits of the products they sell. Newman's Own started in 1982 with the goal of selling a few bottles of salad dressing and donating whatever profits they might earn to charity. The company attracted considerable consumer attention and has grown dramatically. Over the past two and a half decades it has donated in excess of $200 million to thousands of charities worldwide. Ben & Jerry's similarly attracted a broad following and achieved phenomenal economic performance by combining an economic mission ("sustainable financial basis of profitable growth") with a social mission ("initiating innovative ways to

Figure 2.2
Stakeholders

Internal
- Employees
- Managers & officers
- Board of directors
- Stockholders

External
- Suppliers
- Unions
- Creditors
- Customers
- Governments
- Communities
- Interest groups

LEADERSHIP

Stakeholders
Individuals or groups who have an interest in or an influence on the business and operations of a company. They fall into two categories—internal stakeholders and external stakeholders.

improve the quality of life locally, nationally and internationally"). Reporting on their efforts, CEO Walt Freese writes:

> How are we doing? This seventeenth annual Social and Environmental Assessment report is our answer. From my perspective, 2005 was a year of success across all three parts of our Mission Statement, with a particularly strong economic performance. Our overall domestic sales increased by nearly 13% over 2004; Ben & Jerry's Scoop Shop franchise network opened 96 new stores and grew sales volume by 29%; and our international sales achieved a truly impressive 22% growth rate. . . . We also had a strong year with respect to our Social Mission in 2005. Here's a quick sampling. We bought more than half of our ingredients and raw materials from suppliers aligned with our company's values—such as family farmers and Fair Trade certified coffee producers. We used the power of our brand to draw national attention to important causes: preserving the Arctic National Wildlife Refuge, fighting global warming and supporting family farms. In the environmental arena, we met every one of the goals at our manufacturing plants to improve efficiency and reduce waste, and we offset 100% of our greenhouse gas emissions. In global markets, as well as the U.S., we built dozens of relationships with groups who are working for sustainable communities, environmental health, and economic and social justice.[6]

The integration of corporate financial performance and corporate social performance goes beyond simply attracting like-minded customers. Increasingly, companies are finding new ways to make a difference in socially important issues as they go about the day-to-day activities that have to do with their core business. Both Nestlé and Ben & Jerry's help to preserve small-scale farming by sourcing raw materials for manufacturing from small family farmers, while Sysco's reliance on small family farms also ensures the provisioning of fresh, locally grown produce for their foodservice and restaurant supply operations. Marriott provides job training for chronically unemployed workers, which helps the communities in which Marriott does business and also aids the company in its recruitment of entry-level workers.[7]

Finally the increasing application of the principles of strategic management in the nonprofit sector, as well as in government, has also heightened attention to nonfinancial measures of organizational performance. Since by definition these organizations do not produce profits and do not have shareholders, we must deal with important questions about how to measure their performance. In both these instances the key to measuring performance is to focus on the values appreciated by the organization's various stakeholders. Profits in ordinary businesses are an outcome measure reflecting successful value creation that results in a greater number of new customers and/or greater purchasing by existing customers. Similarly, for nonprofits and governments, performance measurement should begin with how well stakeholders are being served. Some nonprofits have very focused missions, in which case the summary performance measures that report how well the entire organization has functioned are relatively easy to describe and measure. America's Second Harvest, the largest national charitable food donation network, collects and distributes food to people in need at community kitchens, food pantries, homeless shelters, Kids Cafe, senior centers, soup kitchens, and youth programs. Their performance is measured by tonnage of donations and distribution, and by the proportion of cash donations received, which are devoted to programs rather than to administration (the "charitable commitment rating"). Figure 2.3 illustrates performance measures for valued donor and receiver stakeholders for this relatively focused nonprofit organization.[8] In contrast, any government entity is likely to have a far more complex network of stakeholders—individual citizens, interest groups, businesses, arts and entertainment organizations, schools, municipal employees, etc.—so that gauging performance would likely require an array of measures relevant to all these stakeholders.

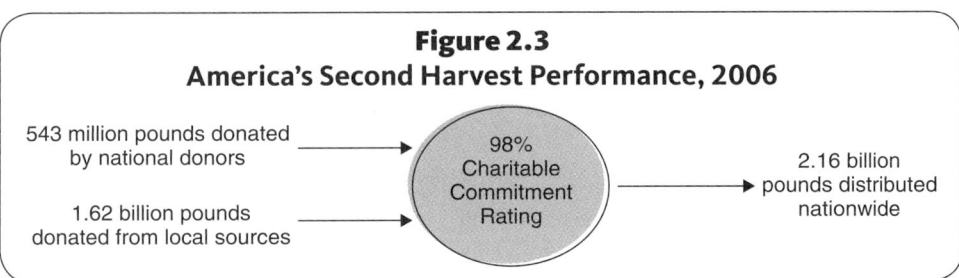

Figure 2.3
America's Second Harvest Performance, 2006

543 million pounds donated by national donors

1.62 billion pounds donated from local sources

98% Charitable Commitment Rating

2.16 billion pounds distributed nationwide

FINANCIAL PERFORMANCE AND COMPETITIVE ADVANTAGE

Having made the case that strategy should be assessed by a balance of both customary financial and emerging nonfinancial measures, we turn back now to more carefully examine aspects of financial performance and their relationship with strategy. Once again we begin with the premise that effective strategy is connected with superior financial performance—that is, something more than what the average competitor achieves. **Normal profit** may be viewed as the minimum return earned by a company that is necessary to attract and secure the owners' inputs. In other words, when people invest in a company and become shareholders, their expectation is that the return they will earn through their investment is at least equal to the kind of return they could earn on average by investing elsewhere in the marketplace at the same level of risk. Otherwise, why would they invest in this company? Long ago, however, economist Alfred Marshall distinguished **economic profit** from normal profit.[9] Economic profit represents the *residual income* above and beyond normal profit that accrues to owners, deriving from the prowess of management in planning, supervision, and control. Residual income associated with economic profit occurs when a company's return on equity (ROE) is greater than its cost of equity capital.[10] This is precisely the logic behind the focus of CEOs (and strategy students)

Normal profit The minimum return earned by a company that is necessary to attract and secure the owners' inputs. Generally defined as the cost of equity capital multiplied by the amount of shareholder equity.

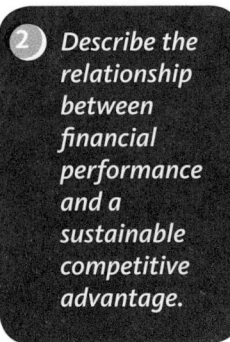

② Describe the relationship between financial performance and a sustainable competitive advantage.

Economic profit The residual income above and beyond normal profit that accrues to owners, deriving from the prowess of management in planning, supervision, and control.

on ROE as one of the key strategy performance indicators. If a company produces higher ROE than the average in the marketplace, without incurring any additional risk, then the company is earning economic profit—or as we usually refer to in strategy, above-average profitability.

In turn, we must now ask, in practical terms, how can strategy impact a company's return on equity? To answer this question, we need to break ROE down into its component parts. Figure 2.4 decomposes ROE into three different ratios: profitability, asset productivity, and financial leverage. When these three ratios are calculated for any company and multiplied together, the resulting product is the return on equity percentage for the company. The three ratios provide the significant insight that there are different ways in which superior returns can be created, either through a focus on any one area or through some combination of areas within the company. Illustrating this, the figure provides a breakdown of ROE in 2006 for two of the airlines that were profiled in the opening vignette of this chapter. Here we see that Southwest's 5.5 percent profitability ratio was much better than Continental's; however, Continental's financial leverage of 32.6 far exceeded that of Southwest and contributed to its stellar ROE in a very tough and competitive airline market environment. Unfortunately, there is always another view of any move. In this case, that high leverage ratio (meaning assets secured through debt financing) could disproportionately harm the company if interest rates increased significantly.

Since strategy performance is gauged "over the long term," as we said earlier in this chapter, we need to be very careful about looking at just one year. Figure 2.4 derives ROE for Continental and Southwest for just 2006, and it looks as if Continental's performance is superior. However, viewing a longer time period provides a better measure of the sustainability of superior performance. For the nine years leading up through 2006—a period that included both expansion and contraction in the U.S. economy—Southwest's ROE was 10.01 percent while Continental's was only 8.93 percent. This is because Southwest managed to stay profitable during the post–September 11 decline in airline traffic, whereas Continental was unprofitable during four years of this period. An excellent question to ask here is, why was Southwest able to sustain its performance while Continental and other airlines were not? To understand Southwest's strategy and the source of its superior performance, we have to dig deeper into the company.

Figure 2.4
Decomposing Return on Equity (ROE)

	Profitability	x	Asset Productivity	x	Financial Leverage	=	ROE
	$\dfrac{\text{Net income}}{\text{Sales}}$	x	$\dfrac{\text{Sales}}{\text{Assets}}$	x	$\dfrac{\text{Assets}}{\text{Shareholder equity}}$	=	$\dfrac{\text{Net income}}{\text{Shareholder equity}}$
Southwest	5.49 %		0.639		2.087		7.32 %
Continental	2.80 %		1.161		32.588		105.94 %

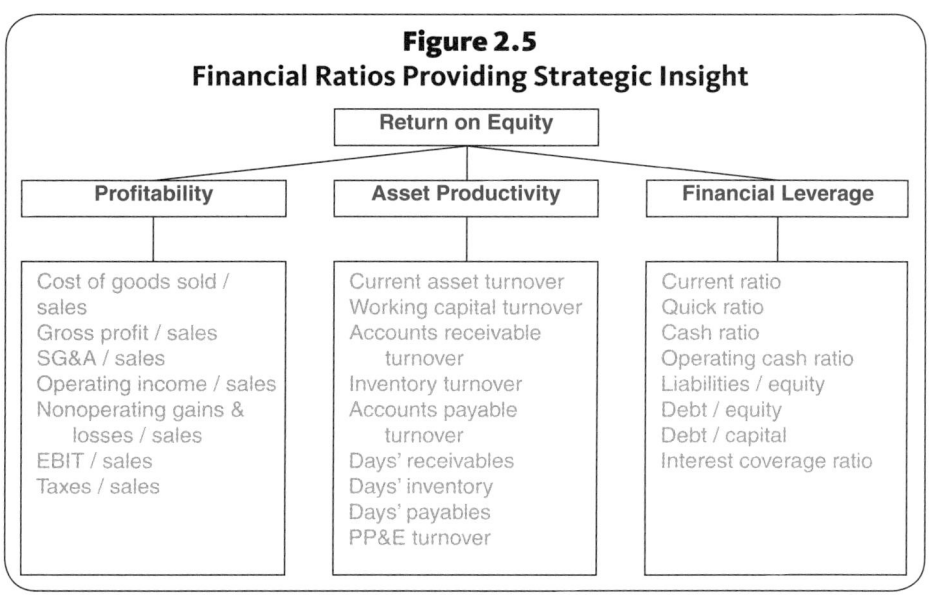

Figure 2.5
Financial Ratios Providing Strategic Insight

Return on Equity		
Profitability	**Asset Productivity**	**Financial Leverage**
Cost of goods sold / sales Gross profit / sales SG&A / sales Operating income / sales Nonoperating gains & losses / sales EBIT / sales Taxes / sales	Current asset turnover Working capital turnover Accounts receivable turnover Inventory turnover Accounts payable turnover Days' receivables Days' inventory Days' payables PP&E turnover	Current ratio Quick ratio Cash ratio Operating cash ratio Liabilities / equity Debt / equity Debt / capital Interest coverage ratio

The decomposition of ROE into its component ratios can be taken further to provide greater ammunition for the strategist. There are many financial ratios that can be used to develop an even more refined view of the sources of advantage within each of the three components. Figure 2.5 lists many such subcomponent ratios that are helpful in both assessing company performance relative to other companies, and in identifying advantages that can be leveraged and areas that might suggest management attention. Remembering that all performance evaluation is relative to our competitors' performance, we may see that a company's profitability is lower than that of its competitors. An examination may reveal that the sources of that inferior position can be traced back to cost of goods sold; selling, general, and administrative costs (SG&A); or some other nonoperating characteristics of the business. These areas might then receive a greater focus by management in order to improve profitability and overall return on equity. Appendix A to this chapter provides a review of financial ratios that may be helpful in analyzing companies and their strategic performance. Use these ratios when you examine cases and companies in your strategy course.

So far the measure return on equity has been highlighted as being particularly important, because of its direct relationship to the strategy goal of superior performance. However, there are other market-based measures of performance that are also used by CEOs, analysts, and strategy students to quantitatively assess how well companies are performing. While there are a variety of other such measures, three seem to be used most frequently: sales revenue growth, returns to common stock, and some measure of a company's market value such as market capitalization.[11]

Revenue growth is generally of great interest to the senior executives of most companies. The ability to grow a company's revenue demonstrates that the company continues to develop relationships with existing and new customers, is able to expand into new geographic territories, and is staying relevant to the marketplace. Unfortunately, revenue growth often occurs at the expense of growth in profitability, since the factors that generally drive up sales (e.g., more advertising, investment in new product development, building a more effective sales force) often add expenses that diminish the bottom line. So there is a certain yin and yang quality to sales growth and ROE (which depends on the profitability ratio). Senior managers who can increase both sales *and* profitability simultaneously are highly regarded, since in practice this does not happen very often (only 9 out of 1,077 companies in a recent McKinsey survey achieved this feat).[12]

Common stock returns and market capitalization are the other two measures of firm performance that are commonly mentioned. **Common stock returns** take into account both the dividends paid by a company to its shareholders as well as increases in the price of the shares. Abnormally high returns, relative to common stock returns for competing companies, are desirable and indicative of high-performing companies. A well-known and popular business book, *Good to Great*, used abnormally high returns as the starting point for examining the strategic moves of those special companies. The eleven companies (out of 1,435 analyzed) that formed the basis of the book were identified by examining this type of performance metric over long periods of time.[13]

Market capitalization, defined as the market value of outstanding shares of stock, also depends on stock price and characterizes the total value of the company. While both these measures provide perspective on the performance of a company, they also reflect investors' anticipation of future performance and assume that all available information is reflected in the stock price. Investors partially base their evaluations of companies on traditional metrics such as ROE and revenue growth rates. Yet we have recently witnessed times when an "irrational exuberance" (an unaccountable and unsupported opinion that things will keep getting better and better) among investors drives stock prices so high that they bear absolutely no relationship to a company's fundamental economics (e.g., the "dot bomb" era). Since a purely market-based evaluation of a company's performance might be misleading, it is always important to evaluate companies using several measures.

Common stock returns
Take into account both the dividends paid by a company to its shareholders as well as increases in the price of the shares.

Market capitalization
The market value of outstanding shares of stock. Stock price multiplied by all outstanding shares.

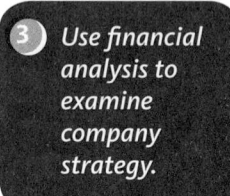

3 *Use financial analysis to examine company strategy.*

INSIGHTS FROM DETAILED FINANCIAL ANALYSIS

The chapters that follow in this textbook will provide useful frameworks for analyzing industries and competition, and for formulating and implementing company strategy. But be forewarned! Industries and competition do not always exist exactly as the textbook models say they should (even those in this textbook!), and companies don't always operate exactly as strategic management "theory" would suggest that they should. Moreover, although companies often make statements about their strategies and discuss broad strategic initiatives in shareholder meetings or analysts' conference calls, they generally do not "publish" great detail about their strategies because they do not want to reveal their deepest and most critical thinking to their competitors. Strategy should be articulated to and understood by important external constituents, but not so much revealed that it can be easily imitated. So how can we determine what a company's strategy really is, what is really at the core?

Financial analysis of companies and competitors is a tool that should be used in parallel to the forthcoming frameworks you will read about in this textbook. This is because, as companies implement their strategies, their implementation results in patterns of asset allocations and interrelated activities that ultimately manifest themselves in financial results. The key to utilizing strategic financial analysis is that the patterns revealed by the numbers demonstrate what companies are really doing and how they are actually operating in the marketplace, regardless of what they *say* they are doing. In combination with the strategy frameworks we will be developing in later chapters, we can then effectively induce what their actual and intended strategies really are. Another way of thinking about this is that a company may state what its overall strategic approach will be, but the numbers show what they are actually doing. It should come as no great surprise to anyone that Wal-Mart pursues a low-cost strategy; we hear about it all the time, from them in their ads as well as from others. But you can really understand how the company makes this an effective strategic approach by carefully examining their financial statements. Here is where we can see what they are actually doing that makes their approach so successful.

Current Financial Statements

Financial statements paint a picture about how companies are operating. A quick example can illustrate this quite easily. Figure 2.6 (a) provides both income statement and balance sheet information for three types of well-known national retail chains—a supermarket, a drug store, and a department store. Without the labels (the three chains are labeled A, B, and C), we have to examine the financial detail to determine which is which. At the outset we can make a couple of obvious comments and draw preliminary inferences. Chain A produces higher net income on only one-third the sales revenue of Chain B while using an asset base that is roughly two-thirds that of Chain B. At the same time, Chain C is producing more than twice the net income of Chain B using roughly the same size asset base. It appears as if Chain B conducts business in a low-margin industry, is experiencing significant operational issues, or is facing strong competition. Apparently size or scale is less important for the industry in which Chain A competes, since it is more profitable on a much lower revenue base. All three companies carry considerable inventories and have significant investment in physical infrastructure (property, plant, and equipment) that is financed by varying combinations of long-term debt and equity. Chain B, however, has a far lower level of receivables than the other two chains, especially in light of its high annual sales revenue.

Figure 2.6 (a)
Financial Data for Three Retail Chains (in millions)

	Chain A	Chain B	Chain C
Income Statement			
Revenues	$13,402	$38,426	$37,006
Cost of goods sold	8,639	26,370	27,105
Depletion expense	334	933	589
Gross profit	4,424	11,113	9,312
Selling, general & admin (SG&A)	2,963	9,729	7,293
Operating income	1,416	1,384	2,020
Interest expense	79	419	130
Taxes	504	288	684
Net Income	**842**	**561**	**1,220**
Balance Sheet			
Assets			
Cash & short term investments	287	373	513
Receivables	1,652	351	1,840
Inventories	2,238	2,766	5,720
Other current assets	90	213	320
Property, plant & equipment	4,543	9,097	3,953
Other assets	353	2,756	2,816
Total Assets	**9,153**	**15,757**	**15,161**
Liabilities & Shareholders' Equity			
Accounts payable	830	2,152	2,468
Short term debt	108	753	595
Income taxes payable	167	124	0
Other current liabilities	529	709	1,504
Long term debt	1,046	5,605	1,594
Other liabilities	185	745	652
Total Liabilities	3,196	10,837	6,829
Equity & retained earnings	5,957	4,920	8,223
Total Liabilities & Equity	**$9,153**	**$15,757**	**$15,161**

It is often difficult to get a clear picture when comparing companies of different sizes. So a more useful view can be developed by converting the financial statements to **common-sized statements**. This is done for income statements by setting revenue for each company equal to 100 percent, and for balance sheets by setting each side of the balance sheet to 100 percent. Figure 2.6 (b) shows the common-sized statements for the three retail chains. In addition, selected financial ratios provide further insight. It can now be observed that Chain C has the highest cost of goods sold as a percentage of sales, but makes up for this slightly through its lower SG&A expense.

Chain C's inventories represent fully 37 percent of its assets, significantly higher than its investment in property, plant, and equipment. This sounds like a chain that carries relatively more expensive merchandise and possibly operates out of relatively less expensive retail space. Chain C may be operating out of generally smaller stores than the other two chains, or it could be engaging

Common-sized statements A method of financial analysis that facilitates comparisons between different-size companies. For income statements set revenue for each company equal to 100 percent, and for balance sheets set each side of the balance sheet to 100 percent.

Figure 2.6 (b)
Common-Sized Data for Three Retail Chains (%'s) & Selected Ratios

	Chain A	Chain B	Chain C
Income Statement			
Revenues	100.0	100.0	100.0
Cost of goods sold	64.5	68.6	73.2
Depletion expense	2.5	2.4	1.6
Gross profit	33.0	29.0	25.2
Selling, general & admin (SG&A)	22.1	25.3	19.7
Operating income	10.6	3.6	5.5
Interest expense	0.6	1.1	0.4
Taxes	3.8	0.8	1.9
Net Income	**6.3**	**1.5**	**3.3**
Balance Sheet			
Assets			
Cash & short term investments	3	2	3
Receivables	18	2	12
Inventories	24	18	37
Other current assets	1	1	2
Property, plant & equipment	50	58	26
Other assets	4	19	19
Total Assets	**100%**	**100%**	**100%**
Liabilities & Shareholders' Equity			
Accounts payable	9	14	16
Short term debt	1	5	4
Income taxes payable	2	1	0
Other current liabilities	7	8	10
Long term debt	10	31	10
Other liabilities	6	10	5
Total Liabilities	35	69	45
Equity & retained earnings	65	31	55
Total Liabilities & Equity	**100%**	**100%**	**100%**
Selected Financial Ratios			
Current assets/current liabilities	2.44	0.87	1.83
Inventory turnover (x per year)	3.86	9.97	4.74
Receivables collection period (days)	44.99	3.33	18.14
Total debt/total assets	0.11	0.36	0.13
Net income/sales (Profitability)	0.063	0.015	0.033
Sales/total assets (Asset productivity)	1.46	2.44	2.42
Total assets/equity (Financial leverage)	1.54	3.20	1.83
Net income/equity (Return on equity)	14.13%	11.41%	14.70%

in a higher degree of leasing. Chain C turns its inventory over 4.7 times per year, while Chain B's inventory—the lowest of the three chains in percentage terms—turns at almost 10 times each year. What kind of merchandise would we hope and expect to be turning more frequently—clothing, drugs and sundries, or food? There are also very different receivables collection periods for the three companies. Chain B's average collection period is just over 3 days; it is almost a pure cash or immediate transaction business. On the other hand, Chain A's collection period is 45 days, suggesting that it extends credit to its customers; and at 18 days collection Chain C looks as if its business may be about half cash and half credit. Already, we should be starting to think about these observed differences: Chain C with smaller stores and expensive inventory that turns slowly, versus Chain B with large investment in plant and low value inventory that turns over rapidly. The sum of these differences, in fact, describes the kinds of different operating characteristics that we should expect to see across three types of retail chains:

Chain B—Supermarket chain (Safeway)

- large stores with sophisticated furnishings (freezers, coolers, bakery) with heavy investment in warehousing and transportation logistics
- lower priced, everyday merchandise that sells through quickly
- largely a cash, debit card, or credit card business
- competing with other chains to ensure low prices and thin margins

Chain C—Drug chain (CVS Caremark)

- smaller stores than supermarkets or department stores
- higher priced merchandise because of carrying costs of expensive medications
- combination of cash as well as payments from insurance company reimbursements for medications sold

Chain A—Department store chain (Kohl's)

- large stores with basic display furnishings
- moderately priced merchandise
- customers rely heavily on department store credit cards for payment

Interestingly, although the supermarket develops less than half the net income percentage of the drug chain and less than one quarter the net income percentage of the department store chain, its return on equity is still reasonably close to these other two organizations. This is because B also exhibits superior asset productivity (2.44) as well as strong financial leverage (3.20), so that in combination its ROE is fairly competitive with other retailers.

Trend Analysis

In the preceding example we have examined three companies at a point in time, using the financial data from one year's performance. The differences we observe between companies can illustrate different approaches to the marketplace. As we found when we looked at ROE over several years instead of just one year, however, it can also be helpful to evaluate the financial statements of a company over a series of years. Figure 2.7 provides five years of historical financial data, from 1997 through 2001, for a company you probably know

Figure 2.7
Financial Data for Amazon.com (in millions)

	2001	2000	1999	1998	1997
Income Statement					
Revenues	3,122	2,762	1,640	610	148
Cost of goods sold	2,323	2,106	1,349	476	119
Gross profit	799	656	291	134	29
Selling, general & admin (SG&A)					
Fulfillment & marketing	512	594	413	133	40
Technology	241	269	160	46	13
All other	457	657	323	64	8
Operating income (loss)	(412)	(864)	(606)	(109)	(33)
Interest & other income (loss)	25	(112)	47	14	2
Interest expense	(139)	(131)	(85)	(27)	0
Net Income (loss)	**(567)**	**(1,411)**	**(720)**	**(125)**	**(31)**
Balance Sheet					
Assets					
Cash & marketable securities	997	1,100	706	373	125
Inventories	144	175	221	30	9
Other current assets	67	86	85	21	3
Fixed assets	272	366	318	30	9
Goodwill & other intangibles	80	255	730	179	0
Other assets	78	152	411	16	2
Total Assets	**1,638**	**2,135**	**2,472**	**648**	**149**
Liabilities & Shareholders' Equity					
Accounts payable	445	485	463	113	33
Other current liabilities	476	490	276	49	11
Long term debt	2,156	2,127	1,466	348	76
Total Liabilities	3,077	3,102	2,205	510	120
Stockholder equity	4	4	3	3	1
Additional paid-in capital	1,463	1,338	1,196	299	64
Other equity	(45)	(16)	(51)	(1)	(2)
Retained earnings	(2,861)	(2,293)	(882)	(162)	(34)
Total Liabilities & Equity	**1,638**	**2,135**	**2,472**	**648**	**149**

quite well—Amazon.com. The financial trends in evidence here provide insight into what the company was actually doing as it grew from a very small online retailer into a much larger, dominating dot.com powerhouse.

We could spend considerable time picking apart these statements, as you should when you conduct your own strategic analysis of a company. But let's highlight a couple key areas that go to the heart of this company's business and its successful growth trajectory. First we observe that the company's gross profit increased from 19.5 percent in 1997 to 25.6 percent by 2001. This may mean that the company has been able to raise its prices to consumers during this time, or that it is receiving more favorable prices from its suppliers. We know that the retail book business is fairly competitive and that Amazon was seeking to drive more buyer volume to its Web site, so it is not likely it was raising its prices. Instead, the much greater volume of business they were doing by 2001 ($3 billion in sales versus $148 million only five years earlier) suggests they struck agreements with suppliers (likely facilitated by a higher volume of business).

How did the company manage to grow so quickly? The statements tell us they were making massive investments in fulfillment and marketing, technology, and administrative support. These investments helped make their Web site especially attractive and easy to use (for example, their "One-Click" checkout innovation), helped drive consumers to their Web site, and made sure there was sufficient staff to support the added business. In 1999 and 2000 the company's intangibles increased considerably, indicating it was purchasing other companies and/or booking significant technological innovations onto its balance sheet.

A closer look at the balance sheet data reveals startling increases during this period of time in a number of categories. As the company's business volume grew, it began to build its own inventory and distribution warehouses to make sure ordering customers received their books quickly. So we see that fixed assets skyrocketed in one year from $30 million to over $300 million. How could the company afford to make such large investments in warehousing, marketing, and technology? It continued to lose money throughout this period, as illustrated by its net loss of hundreds of millions of dollars each year! Its growth was financed by both long-term debt and the sale of additional shares of stock (paid in capital); both categories combined to provide the company $2.8 billion in cash between 1998 and 2000.

At this point you have to ask yourself, why would anyone invest in shares of a company that was losing so much money every year, a company that had not produced positive ROE at any time in its history and wasn't likely to for the foreseeable future? This is a really great question, and one which many people were asking in 1998 and 1999. The company's success—and the investor's return—would depend critically on the market and the company's strategy in that market. These are areas we will be tackling in the next few chapters. Stay tuned!

Strategic Moves
Narrow Range of ROE Measures

Throughout this book we will periodically introduce questions or provide interesting company stories that ask you questions that build further on the material the chapter has just covered.

Many of the financial ratios appearing in Figure 2.6 (b) exhibit a wide range across the three companies. But ROE stays within a fairly narrow range.

1. Why do you suppose this would be the case?

2. Why wouldn't we see greater variability in ROE?

Discuss this with other members of your class. We will explore the answer to this question in the next chapter on Industry and Competitive Analysis.

The preceding retail example has illustrated two key learning points about how strategy and financial performance mirror each other:

1. Strategy is implemented by taking actions and operating in the marketplace in certain ways, which result in certain financial performance characteristics; and
2. Financial performance characteristics reveal the way in which a company is operating in the market, which follows from the company's strategic direction and decisions.

It is important to emphasize that merely understanding how a company operates does not provide perfect insight into the company's strategy, which was described in the first chapter as the coordinating pattern of decisions and investments affecting the entire company over a long time period. Yet analyzing a company's operations and financial performance provides evidence about and insight into the higher-level thinking that guides the company. It also provides significant insight into whether the company is actually pursuing the strategy that it claims to be. Strategy is about action and the commitment of resources. A stated strategy that is not backed by sufficient investment and supportive actions is not a strategy at all.

ECONOMIC LOGIC AND OPERATING CHARACTERISTICS

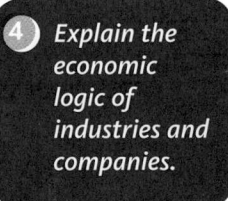

4 *Explain the economic logic of industries and companies.*

If you step back from a detailed analysis of financial statements, you can often discover that there is a core **economic logic** that helps in understanding a successful company's strategic thinking and operational execution. Economic logic is the means by which the successful company seeks to generate a return that is greater than what competitors earn and greater than its cost of capital.[14] The economic logic for warehouse club retailing, such as Sam's Club stores, can be described as being "pile it high, mark it down, and move vast quantities." Successful retailers whose strategies embrace this logic are likely to develop healthy ROE by increasing the asset productivity component as a consequence of sales throughput. In contrast Saks Fifth Avenue's approach might be characterized as "merchandise beautifully, pamper the clientele, and charge premium prices." Such operations are relatively less interested in asset productivity and more interested in profitability as a route to superior ROE. Although Sam's and Saks Fifth Avenue compete in different industries, in some industries sufficient strategic variety exists that we might witness very different economic logics being used by different competitors. In grocery retailing, Wegman's and Whole Foods have a very different economic logic in mind (premium quality, wide variety of selection, higher prices) when compared to Food Lion (commonly needed household foods priced to sell).

In other industries conditions may exist where a core economic logic drives all competitors to a great extent. For example, commercial banks have historically earned profits by focusing on "net interest margin," the difference

Economic logic The means by which the successful company seeks to generate a return that is greater than what competitors earn and greater than its cost of capital.

between interest rates they pay to borrow capital and the interest rates they charge to lend that capital out. Online discount stock brokers such as e*Trade and online auctions such as eBay earn extremely small fees on each of their transactions, and therefore seek to drive up their sheer volume of transactions. This is a low-margin, high-volume economic logic. In several technology-based industries (e.g., inkjet printers, gaming, computer operating systems), the logic for competing often involves establishing a broad "installed base" of users while earning little in the process of doing so. Having established the base, returns are then earned through future transactions that installed base users must engage in (e.g., replacement ink cartridges, buying additional games for the game platform). None of these overarching economic logics dictate exactly what strategy any individual competitor in an industry must follow or how they are to operate. Yet once we understand the economic logics that tend to operate in an industry, we have a better chance of accurately diagnosing the strategy of a particular company in which we are interested.

Along with the core economic logic that helps to frame a company's approach in an industry, strategy analysis should also pay close attention to important operating characteristics that describe how well the company addresses the economic logic at play. In the commercial airline industry, which was profiled at the beginning of this chapter, the economic logic reflects an industry that has become commoditized and therefore where the combination of low costs and high passenger volume might be the key to success. What drives profitability for every carrier are low costs per available seat mile flown, in combination with passenger load factors (although that model is in the process of changing with their new efforts to charge for everything that used to be included with a ticket). These two operating characteristics are closely watched by the financial news media, because they are so critical to airline profitability, and thus they command great attention from senior managers in charge of strategy. Referring back to the tables in the opening vignette of the chapter, Southwest Airlines has a lower load factor than the other airlines listed, yet it also has the lowest cost per available seat mile of any of its major competitors. Though the low-cost-high-volume economic logic applies to every carrier in the industry, it does not dictate a particular strategic approach. In this case Southwest achieves its low-cost position through a combination of exceptionally strong human resource practices that create a coherent workforce, fast gate turnarounds at airports, use of identical Boeing aircraft to save on maintenance costs, crew training, crew availability and downtime, routes that take passengers to less expensive airports near major cities, and other unique investments the company has made. In Chapters 5 through 7 we will learn more about designing unique and sustainable strategic approaches, such as those developed by Southwest.

Every industry has combinations of operating characteristics that provide insight on how well competitors are faring. Important operating characteristics in retailing include, among others, sales per square foot of retail space and same-store sales increases (for stores open at least one year). Wholesaling and distribution companies are interested in metrics such as warehouse turns and percent of complete orders shipped/received on time. The cable

TV industry pays close attention to net subscriber additions, churn (the tendency of subscribers to drop out quickly), average revenue per subscriber, cash costs per subscriber, and average minutes of use per subscriber. Your analysis of companies and industries will be aided by researching important operating characteristics that are consistent with the economic logics you have identified. This might include standard measures of performance as well as measures that are unique to the strategy they are pursuing.

STRATEGY PLANNING

5 *Examine and explain the interaction between strategy formulation and financial analysis.*

The important connection we have made in this chapter between strategy and performance is a two-way street. By that we mean that the student of strategy should strive to develop an ability to go back and forth between strategy and its financial outcomes. Financial statements can be revealing about strategy, while a type of strategy should result in certain patterns in financial statements (Figure 2.8).

Most of what we have just covered illustrates how the analysis of financial statements can reveal dimensions of important strategic behavior. This is because, as we mentioned earlier in this chapter, strategy really involves a pattern of asset allocations and inter-related activities that ultimately manifest themselves in financial results. It is nice to have a statement of the company's strategy that the financial media and analyst communities can consume. However, a company's strategy is given real force when the company *acts*—when it organizes itself to support its pronouncements, when it pursues a segment of a particular industry that matches its investments, and when it commits resources to specific projects and initiatives. The allocation of resources and the activities that people in the company engage in are often below the radar of competitors and the financial community in specific terms, but ultimately reveal themselves in financial statements. So understanding a company's strategy through financial statement analysis is sort of like what Yogi Berra once said: "You can observe a lot by watching."

At the same time, we want to emphasize that excellence in strategy *formulation* also requires excellence in financial analysis. When you are the architect of a new strategy for your company, it means that the company will need to act in new ways in organizing itself and allocating human, physical, and financial resources. Every strong strategic plan will project out

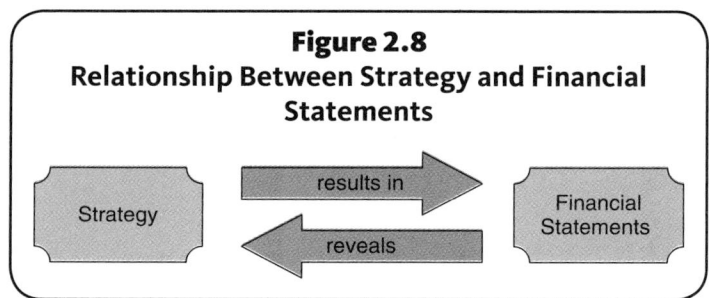

Figure 2.8
Relationship Between Strategy and Financial Statements

what these new activities and resource allocations will look like financially. In addition, every strong strategic plan will ensure that desired outcome of "above-average profitability" or "superior performance" will be the financial outcome realized. Remember, though, as we mentioned in Chapter 1 and also illustrated by the earlier Amazon.com example, that the financial outcome of superior performance will often involve long time horizons.

CHAPTER SUMMARY

Performance (both quantitative and qualitative) is the key outcome of interest for those studying strategy and managing strategy. Three dimensions of performance are important: 1) summary measures that reflect the impact of integrated efforts across the entire company, 2) measures that can be compared to competitors, and 3) measures that account for longer periods of time. Return on equity (ROE) is the most common performance measure used by executives. ROE can be broken down into three component ratios that provide insight on company profitability, asset productivity, and financial leverage; each of these components may be further broken down into additional financial ratios to provide more specific information about sources of strengths and weaknesses.

Other financial dimensions are also used frequently to assess performance resulting from strategy (stockholder returns, market capitalization, sales revenue growth). Nonfinancial performance dimensions account for two other important considerations: 1) the realizations that companies may create social, cultural, and knowledge value in addition to economic value; and 2) the emerging view that there are a variety of stakeholders (internal and external) who have interests in a company. Whereas debates have existed in the past as to whether companies should be single-mindedly focused on providing returns to shareholders, the emerging view suggests that attention to stakeholders can create profitable new growth opportunities for companies and strengthen existing franchises.

Insight can be gained about company strategy through three methods: 1) detailed financial statement analysis, often using common-sized statements to compare competitors; 2) identifying the economic logic(s) that may operate within an industry as a means of framing how companies operate; and 3) identifying and evaluating important operational characteristics that portray how well companies appear to be addressing economic logics. Together, these techniques can provide a better understanding of the nature of a company's strategy.

KEY TERMS

Common-sized statements (p. 46)	Economic logic (p. 51)	Market capitalization (p. 44)
Common stock returns (p. 44)	Economic profit (p. 41)	Normal profit (p. 41)
		Stakeholders (p. 39)

SHORT ANSWER REVIEW QUESTIONS

1. What are nonfinancial performance measures?
2. How would you determine what strategic approach a company is actually pursuing?
3. What three methods provide the greatest insight into company strategy?
4. Why is revenue growth such a critical performance measure?
5. What is the most common performance measure used by executive management? Why? What components make this particular measure so useful?
6. How do financial ratios provide insight into a company's true strategy?
7. What three dimensions of performance are most critical?
8. Explain the performance considerations necessary when we involve stakeholder's desired outcomes.

GROUP EXERCISES

1. Examine the last five years of annual financial statements from a public company that you think you already know fairly well from your own personal experiences (for example, Blockbuster or Starbucks).
   a. Discuss the possible meanings of patterns you observe in the income statements.
   b. Discuss the possible interpretations of patterns you observe in the balance sheets.
   c. Use the financial ratios in Appendix A to compare the company to its closest competitor.
   d. What differences do you now observe about the company's strategic approach to the market, as compared to observations from your personal experiences?
   e. Do you believe this company is achieving superior performance?
2. Choose a nonprofit organization that you are interested in. Examine its publications and documents to determine how it measures its performance.
3. Nobel prize winner Milton Friedman claimed many years ago that the only business of business is to earn a profit for its shareholders. In 2008 successful businessman Bill Gates, founder of Microsoft, advocated corporations to practice "creative capitalism" where they use their capabilities to "do good" while not sacrificing "doing well" for shareholders. The public outcry for greater corporate social responsibility is great. In your group discuss whether

you believe corporations should focus only on economic performance for shareholders, or should they also address broader social and community concerns in their day-to-day activities and goals.

4. In 2008 Exxon Mobil (XOM) came under intense public scrutiny because it had reported $11 billion in net income in each of its preceding quarterly statements, at the same time that gas prices were rising to over $4 per gallon for the American public. Some political candidates were recommending a tax on excess oil company profits. According to Thomson Financial, XOM's net income represented 11.3% of revenues, its corporate tax rate was 48% (paid $30 billion during 2007 fiscal year), and its return on equity was 9.36%. Discuss whether you think it would be prudent for government to place additional financial regulation on oil companies.

REFERENCES

1 Several sources were used for this vignette. S. McCartney, 2007, A report card on the nation's airlines, *Wall Street Journal*, February 6: D1; M. Trottman, 2006, Airline CEO's novel strategy: No bankruptcy, *Wall Street Journal*, April 17: B1; K. Wingfield, 2007, A dogfight in business class, *Wall Street Journal*, January 25; International Airline Transport Association (http://www.iata.org/index.htm); U.S. Department of Transportation (http://www.dot.gov); Thomson One Banker (http://www.thomson.com/solutions/financial). Financials reflect 12-month performance through 2006.

2 Load factor is calculated by dividing the number of revenue passenger miles flown by the number of available seat miles.

3 G. McWilliams, 2007, Wal-Mart's radio-tracked inventory hits static, *Wall Street Journal*, February 15: B1.

4 E. L. Plambeck, 2007, The greening of Wal-Mart's supply chain, *Supply Chain Management Review*, July 1, 2007.

5 M. E. Porter & M. R. Kramer, 2006, Strategy and society, *Harvard Business Review*, 84 (12): 78–92.

6 http://www.benjerry.com/our_company/about_us/social_mission/social_audits/2005_sear/sear05_1.0.cfm.

7 Porter & Kramer, op. cit.

8 America's Second Harvest annual report, 2006.

9 A. Marshall, 1890, *Principles of Economics*, London: Macmillan Press.

10 Using the capital asset pricing model, the cost of equity capital for a company depends on the company's sensitivity to market risk (which is captured by the company's β). When we discuss economic profit, we refer to the ability of a company to earn above-average returns without requiring shareholders to assume enhanced risk (higher β). In this case the company earning economic profit produces an ROE that is greater than the expected return using the capital asset pricing model.

11 B. S. Chakravarthy, 1986, Measuring strategic performance, *Strategic Management Journal*, 7: 437–458; G. G. Dess & R. B. Robinson Jr., 1984, Measuring organizational performance in the absence of objective measures: The case of the privately held firm and conglomerate

business unit, *Strategic Management Journal*, 5: 265–273; M. Lubatkin & R. E. Shrieves, 1986, Towards a reconciliation of market performance measures to strategic management research, *Academy of Management Review*, 11 (3): 497–512.

[12] J. Devan, M. B. Klusas, & T. W. Ruefli, 2007, The elusive goal of corporate outperformance, *The McKinsey Quarterly*, May (http://www.mckinseyquarterly.com).

[13] J. Collins, 2001, *Good to Great*, New York: HarperCollins Publishers.

[14] D. C. Hambrick & J. W. Fredrickson, 2001, Are you sure you have a strategy? *Academy of Management Executive*, 15 (4): 48–59.

Financial Ratios Useful in Strategy Analysis

Profitability

Measure	How to calculate it	What it means
Return on equity	Profitability × Asset productivity × Financial leverage	Profitability of shareholder investment
Profitability	Net income / Sales	Company profitability per dollar of sales
Asset productivity	Sales / Assets	Dollars of sales generated per dollar of assets used
Financial leverage	Assets / Shareholder equity	Dollars of assets employed per dollar of equity raised
Return on assets	Net income / Assets	The profitability of assets employed by the firm
Operating profit margin	Operating income / Sales	The profitability of ongoing operations of the firm
Gross profit margin	Gross profit / Sales	Gross profit percentage for each dollar of sales

Liquidity—Short Term

Measure	How to calculate it	What it means
Current ratio	Current assets / Current liabilities	The ability to meet current obligations
Quick ratio	(Current assets—Inventory) / Current liabilities	The ability to meet current obligations without relying on selling inventory to do so
Cash ratio	Cash / Current liabilities	The ability to meet current obligations relying only on current cash position
Inventory to working capital	Inventory / (Current assets—Current liabilities)	How much of working capital is tied up in inventory

Liquidity—Long Term

Measure	How to calculate it	What it means
Total debt ratio	(Assets—Shareholder equity) / Assets	Reveals percentage of balance sheet tied up in debt
Debt-to-assets ratio	Total debt / Assets	Reveals percentage of assets financed by debt
Debt-to-equity ratio	Total debt / Shareholder equity	Ratio of borrowed funds to funds provided by shareholders
Long-term debt to equity	Long-term debt / Shareholder equity	Ratio of long-term borrowings to equity contributions
Times interest earned (coverage ratio)	EBIT / Interest	The ability to meet interest payments
Cash coverage ratio	(EBIT + Depreciation) / Interest	Ability to meet interest payments using operating cash

Shareholder Returns

Measure	How to calculate it	What it means
Dividend yield	Dividend per share / Current market price per share	Return to common stockholders through dividends
Dividend payout ratio	Dividend per share / Net income per share	An approximation of profits returned to investors versus those kept to reinvest in the business
Price-earnings ratio (PE)	Current market price per share / Earnings per share	How much investors are willing to pay per dollar of current earnings
Market capitalization	Current market price per share $\times$ Total shares outstanding	Total value of all the company's stock at current stock market prices

Activity Ratios

Measure	How to calculate it	What it means
Inventory turnover	Sales / Inventory	The number of times a firm sells its inventory each year
Asset productivity	Sales / Assets	Sales generated per dollar of assets used
Fixed asset turnover	Sales / Fixed assets	Sales generated per dollar of fixed assets used
Capital intensity	Assets / Sales	The dollar investment in assets needed to generate each dollar in sales (this is the inverse of Asset Productivity ratio)
Accounts receivable turnover	Annual credit sales / Accounts receivable	The number of times each year a company collects on credit sales
Receivables collection period	Accounts receivable / Average daily sales	How long it takes for the company to collect payment for sales

CHAPTER
3

Vision
and Mission

LEARNING OBJECTIVES

1 *Examine how vision and mission statements can be used to provide effective direction for a firm.*

2 *Describe the process of developing a vision and a vision statement.*

3 *Explain the steps involved in developing an effective mission statement.*

4 *Name five techniques for communicating vision and mission.*

Google and Wal-Mart[1]

"Google and Wal-Mart are the business world's version of yin and yang." Google is a high-growth, high-revenue, extremely high-margin company. Three thousand employees produce annual sales of $5 billion (at the current run rate), or $1.67 million per worker. Cash flow is greater than $500,000 per worker per year. The typical Google worker possesses a very high IQ, and about half of their employees hold advanced degrees in science or engineering, most from elite universities. Google makes every effort to seek out the best and the brightest, even asking to see prospective employees' SAT scores.

In many ways, Wal-Mart appears to be the opposite of Google. It is the world's largest company by sales—$285 billion—but its profit of $10 billion is typical of low-margin retail. Wal-Mart possesses the world's largest workforce of 1.3 million people who generate $190,000 in sales apiece. Cash flow and profits per Wal-Mart worker are very small—only $16,000 and $6,700, respectively, or about 3 percent of those of their Google counterparts.

Google and Wal-Mart have become huge successes, each in their own very different ways. But the two have the following in common:

- Each company has a simple *mission*. Wal-Mart's is "always low prices." Google's is "to organize the world's information and make it universally accessible and useful." These companies know who they are.
- The brand and the mission statement of each are aligned. Picture Google and Wal-Mart in your head. There's no confusion about what these companies do. Neither is there confusion for their employees.
- Each company's offerings are dirt-simple to use. Shopping at Wal-Mart does not take a heroic intellectual effort. But neither does using Google, even though the search engine behind the curtain is the product of a prodigious intellectual feat.
- Both companies are technology leaders. The previous editor of *Forbes*, Jim Michaels, likes to call Wal-Mart the world's preeminent tech company. It pioneered the use of bar-code scanners, slick supply chains, and inventory management tweaked to local purchasing preferences. The Bentonville, Arkansas, giant never sleeps. Now Wal-Mart is pushing into RFID chips. Wal-Mart's aggressive use of technology puts the lie to a recent *Harvard Business Review* article, "IT Doesn't Matter," that says it's okay to sit back and let others lead. Google, meanwhile, continues to attract the best tech brains in Silicon Valley.
- Both companies exploit the cheap revolution. Google's search engine runs on 100,000 cheap servers and a form of free Linux software. Wal-Mart searches the planet for low-cost production. It buys 10 percent of the goods China exports to the United States.

1 *Examine how vision and mission statements can be used to provide effective direction for a firm.*

STRATEGIC DIRECTION

We will learn in the chapters to come that each organization must possess a set of resources and capabilities (Chapter 6) that will allow it to achieve extraordinary and sustainable returns. One way of doing this that we will emphasize is through the value chain of the organization (Chapter 5), which involves tight coordination and internal consistency of activities across the company. The ability to coordinate all of those activities is critical. It is also imperative that we have a deep understanding of the competitive environment, our company's position in that environment, and how we may profit from that position. But at the same time we face these complicated challenges, we must consider whether *where* we compete and *how* we intend to compete are consistent with the *direction* we choose to take for our company, and whether everyone in the company is pulling in unison in that direction.

Getting all or even most of the individuals in a corporation to move in generally the same direction is infinitely more difficult than "herding cats." Without a true understanding of a company's guiding purpose, people—like cats—will tend to wander wherever each thinks it is best to go. A **mission statement** can be defined as a brief statement that summarizes how and where the firm will compete in the present, whereas a **vision statement** presents a more compelling, overarching image of the organization in the future that motivates employees to focus their actions toward a common point.

Students and managers often get mission and vision confused. Mission statements have a significantly more bounded nature than broader, longer-term vision statements. Think about it this way. Imagine you are a secret agent working for an intelligence agency, such as Maxwell Smart working for Control. You and Agent 86 are sent on a mission to recover from KAOS a secret encoder that is key to how the Cone of Silence works. This mission is actually part of a grander long-term vision to reduce and ultimately destroy KAOS and its influence. Mission has to do with what we do in the immediate moment, and how we go about doing it based on our current strengths and capabilities. "Sorry about that, chief!"

The combination of both statements provides fundamental guidance by laying out the unique purpose of the organization and its defining competitive approach.[2] Defining the mission and vision for a business are two of the most difficult, yet equally most critical, elements in any company's long-term success. In fact, some have referred to the creation of vision and mission statements as a "wicked problem" because the problem is ill-formulated, the process can involve many people with conflicting values, and the result has ramifications for the whole business system.[3] What constitutes a good mission and vision statement? How can these statements be developed? What impact will an effective set of statements have on the overall strategy and performance of the business?

Before we proceed to the details of developing effective mission and vision statements, let's consider a larger question first: Why does it matter whether a company has a defined mission or vision statement? The majority of employees at any company come to work every day with the intention of working hard, doing something of real value for their company, and finding a personal and professional sense of accomplishment. What motivates employees to do their work? It is unrealistic to believe that a paycheck is their primary motivation. The question is, what is the glue that binds employees' collective actions on a daily basis into a consistent and unified effort for the company? This is the purpose of mission and vision statements.

Business, by definition, is a place of coordinated action that cannot be effectively accomplished by the individual. However, studies have consistently demonstrated that significant differences of opinion exist among senior-level executives about both strategic goals and the means to accomplish them.[4]

Mission statement
A brief statement that summarizes how and where the firm will compete in the present.

Vision statement
More compelling and overarching than the mission statement, an image of the organization in the future that motivates employees to focus their actions toward a common point.

Mere consent to others' goals, or worse, disagreement about goals and the means by which to achieve them, will have a cascading negative effect on employee behavior across the company. Employees left without a clear corporate direction will intuitively and explicitly try to guess what their bosses really want them to do. A sobering question for senior management is: "Does the company have any confidence that what employees are doing on a day-to-day basis is consistent with senior management's overarching goals for the organization?"

Evidence from industry suggests that the resounding answer to this question in many cases is *NO!* Only about half of the Fortune 500 companies have developed and published comprehensive mission statements. Of those companies, some have added loads of superfluous elements to their mission statements, hoping to satisfy as many stakeholders as possible without upsetting others. Roughly 5 percent of the Fortune 500 has neither a mission nor a vision statement, but they do have written values or principles. Most surprising, after years of admonitions about the value of mission statements, fully 25 percent of the world's largest companies have no written statement at all that would serve to guide their organizations.[5]

Providing Direction and Purpose

Why is any company in business? To some this may sound like a foolish question, but as we pointed out in Chapter 1, companies most certainly are *not* in business just to make money. As appealing as it may be to believe this, customers will never purchase a product or service just because the company needs to make money. Imagine the company's mission statement that would accompany such a goal:

Mission

Because our fiduciary responsibility is to maximize shareholder value, we strive to make the most money possible within the legal constraints of the countries within which we do business.

Without a doubt, all employees would understand their task each day. The employees would simply explain to customers, suppliers, and fellow employees that since the organization must make as much money as possible, this is why they are: 1) charging more for the same value or providing less for the same price, 2) requiring pay, benefit, or work condition concessions, 3) demanding reduced prices for raw materials, etc. It is not the employees' fault; they are simply pursuing the mission. Furthermore, this mission statement would be so generic as to be applicable (albeit poorly) to virtually every company in the world, because any type of technically legal business activity would be acceptable.

Similarly, a company is not in business to meet its "fiduciary responsibility to maximize shareholder value," since once again this provides no direction for the company's employees and therefore provides no unifying reason for its existence. Profitability and shareholder value are the *results* of a strategically focused organization, not its reason for being. Customers purchase a product or service because of the value they receive in exchange for the money and time invested. The reason that companies are in business is to provide a product or service that creates value for customers, who in turn are willing to profitably compensate them for their efforts.

An organization exists to create and deliver value in ways that an individual cannot accomplish alone in free-market transactions. We call a company an "organization" because everything it does involves the orchestration of the efforts of more than one individual. The most pressing issue that develops as the organization grows is one of coordination and consistency of effort toward a common purpose. As was pointed out many years ago by Henry Mintzberg in his definitive book *The Structuring of Organizations,* the issue of coordination is the continual struggle to get more and more employees' efforts focused on the mission of the organization.[6] All employees have a series of routines and tactics they use to handle situations on a day-to-day basis. These routines and tactics should be guided by the set of objectives that reflect each employee's job description and upon which each employee is compensated. In turn, their objectives are arrived at as a subset of the strategic plans of the organization, and those plans are a direct result of the mission that company wishes to accomplish. Vision initiates the whole process by laying out the compelling, overarching focal image guiding everyone in the organization in a certain direction. A mission statement then provides guidance on what the company does in the present. Therefore, vision and mission statements help to answer two basic questions for every employee in an organization:

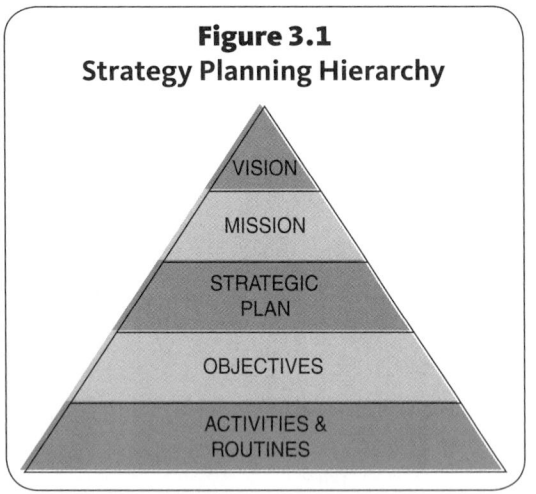

**Figure 3.1
Strategy Planning Hierarchy**

1. What am I expected to be doing today? Answer: Mission statement, which characterizes how the company competes in today's market.
2. Why are my co-workers and I expected to act this way? Answer: Vision statement, because this is what we want the company to become.

Figures 3.1 illustrates the relationship between vision, mission, and activities.

2 *Describe the process of developing a vision and a vision statement.*

VISION AND VISION STATEMENTS

Whereas the mission defines specifically what the organization does in the present, the vision is the desired future state of the organization. What is the organization's purpose and why should everyone who works for the organization care? The vision of the organization (sometimes referred to as the statement of purpose) helps define the long-term future for the company, which management guru Peter Drucker described as "what should our business be."[7] Figure 3.2 lists the elements that characterize effective vision statements.

The benefits of having a shared vision can be remarkable. Employees can not only execute on a daily basis more easily if there is a collective understanding of where they are supposed to be headed, but they can also better imagine for themselves how they will be rewarded through the accomplishment of the vision. When members of an organization are inspired and see how their individual efforts can work toward a grand future, their collective efforts can make a powerful difference. On January 11, 1987, the Denver Broncos football team fell seven points behind the Cleveland Browns late in the fourth quarter of the AFC Championship game. Gaining possession of the ball on their own two-yard line with 98 yards to go to tie the game, quarterback John Elway announced in the offensive huddle that the Broncos "now had them right where they wanted them." After "The Drive"[8] in which the team marched up the field and tied the game, which led to an overtime win, members of the offensive line commented that the vision of superiority that Elway implanted had inspired and enabled them to rise to the challenge. Yet another compelling example of how vision motivates occurred on October 15, 1415, when King Henry V of England confronted the French army in Agincourt, France. With only 5,000 to 6,000 soldiers against an estimated 20,000 French soldiers, the odds were against the English. Henry delivered his visionary "band of brothers" message to his troops, later immortalized by Shakespeare (Figure 3.3), and his troops went on to defeat the French in what is regarded as the most lopsided military victory in history.[9] Henry's vision inspired his troops to imagine themselves years later as old men, when others would still recount their heroism in victory at Agincourt.

Designing a vision is an exercise that balances foresight with a deep understanding of the company's present resources. On the one hand, senior management wishes to establish long-term direction that will require the company to grow significantly beyond its present position and capabilities. On the other hand, the vision cannot afford to imagine a future that is simply unattainable, given current capabilities and position. Designing a vision thus brings together many of the skills you will be reading about in the following chapters. Topics include diagnosing industry driving forces that will forever change the nature of competition, building strong value chain activities that identify emerging opportunities, appreciating the enduring core values that are a part of the organization and its culture, and realistically appraising the company's current resource positions. Through this process the vision should establish an event horizon that guides current practices within the company. There should be a specific and discernible endpoint in mind—for example, the goal line, living to old age, etc.—that is at the horizon but is not further than the eye can see. So, the vision statement encourages the organization

Figure 3.2
Effective Vision Statement Elements

Incorporates foresight
Provides event horizon
Connects with current capabilities
Incorporates enduring core values
Is short
Is memorable

Figure 3.3
Henry V's Speech at Agincourt, 1415

"That he which hath no stomach to this fight,
Let him depart; his passport shall be made
And crowns for convoy put into his purse:
We would not die in that man's company
That fears his fellowship to die with us.
This day is called the feast of Crispian:
He that outlives this day, and comes safe home,
Will stand a tip-toe when the day is named,
And rouse him at the name of Crispian.
He that shall live this day, and see old age,
Will yearly on the vigil feast his neighbours,
And say 'To-morrow is Saint Crispian:'
Then will he strip his sleeve and show his scars.
And say 'These wounds I had on Crispin's day.'
Old men forget: yet all shall be forgot,
But he'll remember with advantages
What feats he did that day: then shall our names.
Familiar in his mouth as household words
Harry the king, Bedford and Exeter,
Warwick and Talbot, Salisbury and Gloucester,
Be in their flowing cups freshly remember'd.
This story shall the good man teach his son;
And Crispin Crispian shall ne'er go by,
From this day to the ending of the world,
But we in it shall be remember'd;
We few, we happy few, we band of brothers;
For he today that sheds his blood with me
Shall be my brother; be he ne'er so vile,
This day shall gentle his condition:
And gentlemen in England now a-bed
Shall think themselves accursed they were not here,
And hold their manhoods cheap whiles any speaks
That fought with us upon Saint Crispin's day."

Shakespeare, *Henry V*, Act IV, scene 3

to significantly stretch its strategic capabilities, in order to achieve a valuable and secure position in an unfolding future. The event horizon presents a motivational, attainable goal that is true to the vision statement. The former CEO of Rubbermaid articulated the vision for the company as being able to go into any supermarket and walk down an "aisle of Rubbermaid." Can you imagine an entire aisle of Rubbermaid products in a store? It sounds a bit funny to us, but to employees it crystallized in their minds what they wanted the company to become, and it led to significant and effective innovation and new product introductions over the next few years.

Typically the time horizon for a vision statement will be something close to a decade. This makes sense when we think about the fulfillment time required for ongoing strategic initiatives, which can often take three to five years to pan out (recall the character of strategic decisions discussed in Chapter 1). This means that the event horizon is beyond the more immediate boundary that marks the longer-term outcomes of current strategic initiatives and in all likelihood beyond what can be accomplished with current capabilities. Setting an event horizon thus requires management to consider carefully not only how external forces will shape competitive markets, but also how current capabilities may be enhanced or supplemented to develop a portfolio of possibilities. Figure 3.4 captures the sense of this discussion. Here a company builds on two of its resource positions as it engages in strategic initiatives that are estimated to have A and B as outcomes. The horizon for the company's vision, however, extends well beyond outcomes A and B, to fuzzy sets of possibilities that might build further on A or B and the resource positions that led to them.

Examples of successful visioning such as this can further illustrate the nature of longer-term horizons. President John F. Kennedy propelled NASA in the 1960s with his very clear and well-articulated vision of putting a man on the moon and returning him safely to earth within the decade. In his speech to Congress on May 21, 1961, he resolutely laid out his stretch goals for the United States while recognizing its current technological capabilities, and asked us to imagine how proud we would all feel in such an accomplishment (Figure 3.5). Management author Jim Collins referred to this type of statement as a "*BHAG,*" that is, a Big, Hairy, Audacious Goal.[10]

A more recent example of vision is the case of Amazon.com, which started up as a new business named Cadabra.com in 1994. As an Internet startup in the dawn of the Internet age, the original vision espoused by founder Jeff Bezos was to be the "biggest bookstore"—quite a stretch for a small technology company that relied on book distributors for its merchandise. After the company's business took off in the late 1990s, Bezos established an updated vision as "earth's most customer-centric company...a place where people can come to find and discover anything they might want to buy online."[11] Since then, Amazon has been reinvesting in technology to deliver superior online selling performance, as well as establishing relationships with providers of a tremendous variety of merchandise.

As suggested earlier, vision statements should be memorable and inspiring to everyone throughout the organization. Though politicians and Shakespeare are accustomed to using "words, words, words"[12] in their inspirational passages, vision statements for organizations should be short. Whirlpool Corporation has a simple, but compelling vision: "Every home...Everywhere. With pride, passion, and performance." The vision sets forth an event horizon for the business that can easily be used as a guidepost for current activities and tactics. Other examples are presented in Figure 3.6.

Developing the Vision

Developing a vision for the organization is a process that can be full of ambiguity. There is no one way to develop an effective vision statement, although there are clearly methods that seem to assist in the process. Gaining buy-in from the entire organization is crucial in the initial development process, however. This is not to say that everyone in the company has a great sense of what

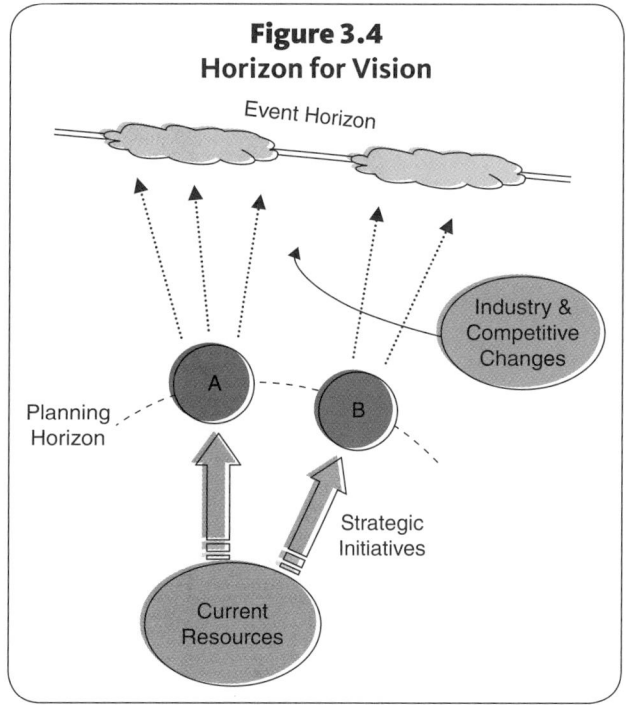

Figure 3.4
Horizon for Vision

Event Horizon

Industry & Competitive Changes

Planning Horizon

A   B

Strategic Initiatives

Current Resources

Figure 3.5
John F. Kennedy's 1961 Speech

"Finally, if we are to win the battle that is now going on around the world between freedom and tyranny, the dramatic achievements in space which occurred in recent weeks should have made clear to us all ... the impact of this adventure on the minds of men everywhere, who are attempting to make a determination of which road they should take.... Now it is time to take longer strides—time for a great new American enterprise—time for this nation to take a clearly leading role in space achievement, which in many ways may hold the key to our future on earth. I believe we possess all the resources and talents necessary....I believe that this nation should commit itself to achieving the goal, before this decade is out, of landing a man on the moon and returning him safely to the earth....But in a very real sense, it will not be one man going to the moon—if we make this judgment affirmatively, it will be an entire nation. For all of us must work to put him there."

Figure 3.6
Effective Vision Statements

Company	Vision
Microsoft (a)	To enable people and businesses throughout the world to realize their full potential.
Microsoft (b)	There will be a personal computer on every desk running Microsoft software.
Continental Airlines	To be recognized as the best airline in the industry by our customers, employees, and shareholders.
Avon Products	To be the Company that best understands and satisfies the product, service, and self-fulfillment needs of women—globally.
EMC	To create the ultimate information lifecycle management company—to help our customers get the maximum value from their information at the lowest total cost, at every point in the information lifecycle.
Oxford Health Plans	We will be a catalyst in redefining access to quality care and the leader in our market for the delivery of a better healthcare experience.

the vision should be, but it is to suggest that everyone should have input on the values that are reflected in the long-term direction. As Jim Collins suggests, leaders at the top cannot "set" or "install" organizational values; values can only be discovered.[13] This can be approached through a solicitation to the whole organization for direct input, yet in large companies with many employees this process may result in a deluge of communication that becomes difficult to sift through for meaningful content.

Instead, another more effective method used to bring together core values as well as an understanding of present capabilities is to compose a small group of five to seven people who embody the deeply held values of employees. If employees are asked to nominate the group, often the result is a group of individuals that employees look up to because they stand as exemplars for the company's important values and knowledge. Together with top management, the group should consider several critical questions to generate a compelling vision:

1. What do we hold to be "true" and meaningful in our business, factors that should never change as we go forward?
2. What does it mean to work in this organization? After ten more years what would I want to look back upon and be proud of for having worked in this organization?
3. At the core, what are we particularly good at doing? What is our core competence, and what extraordinary resources do we possess?
4. What are the compelling changes and opportunities in the competitive environment that we should be taking advantage of?
5. Where should our company be in ten years?

The Lena Pope Home was established in the 1930s in Fort Worth, Texas, as a place for all foster children to feel welcome. Lena H. Pope developed a place where high expectations were set. They wish to equip their youth with an education, job skills, and in some cases, rehabilitation. However, they also want a place that teaches integrity, personal responsibility, fairness, and good citizenship.

Today, their efforts have expanded to include both children and their families. Last year they served more than 20,000 families. They are running a foster care agency, a counseling operation, and they run an extensive school program for kids no longer welcome at the public schools, they teach courses in family preservation as well as assist in adoptions.

By 2008, the organization had grown to a point where it was financially independent and the leading provider of services to children and their families in the Dallas-Fort Worth Metroplex. The Board of Directors was faced with the imminent retirement of their outstanding, long-term Director. The Board also recognized that the agency had grown to employ hundreds of people in many different areas. In order to ensure a smooth transition and to get the whole organization on a path moving forward, they embarked upon an effort to reset the organization for the coming decade.

They wanted a new mission statement that encompassed who they were now, and they wanted a singular vision statement to use as guidance for the employees and the community.

Their Web page site is: http://www.lenapopehome.org.

QUESTIONS

1. Given what you've read about the organization, how do you view their overarching aim?

2. Given what you've read about the organization, write a vision statement for the Lena Pope Home, Inc.

3. How do you suggest they address the needs of the many stakeholders that they work with?

These questions spur the development of a vision statement that can be used by every individual in the course of his or her daily interactions. The actual writing of the statement is an iterative process, attempting to capture the richness of a company in a statement that is short, memorable, and inspiring.

MISSION STATEMENTS

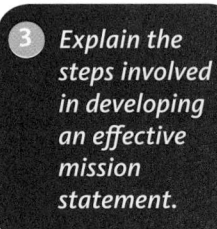

3 *Explain the steps involved in developing an effective mission statement.*

The firm's mission helps the corporation by targeting its current efforts in specific arenas and on specific opportunities. No business can or should attempt to serve up all things to all people. Instead, the business needs to focus on those areas where it possesses extraordinary resources and creates value in ways that competitors cannot. A consistent pattern of history over the past thirty years has shown that corporate performance improves as firms focus their resources and capabilities on a narrower, not broader, set of activities.[14] The firm's mission helps the business achieve this type of focus because it serves to specify what the company does best in its competitive industry. In a wonderfully related manner, a well-developed mission statement also helps the business stay away from areas that opportunistically sound promising, but which actually take the business away from its principal focus. Take note of the fact that as a business diversifies into other areas of competition, it loses focus on its core area of business. If that occurs, history suggests that there are always singularly focused companies in any market that are ready to capitalize on the fragmentation of effort that results.

Developing a Mission Statement

The mission statement is the vehicle that captures the immediate purpose of the company and its unique way of fulfilling that purpose. The process of developing an effective mission statement requires that the top management team simultaneously align five key criteria (Figure 3.7). These criteria can be further described as follows:

1. Short. Does it fit on a coffee mug?
2. Simple. It has to be something that everyone in the company can easily learn and understand.
3. Company-Specific. A mission should tell everyone exactly what the company does and by definition it will tell them what the company does not do.
4. Actionable. It has to be able to guide every individual in the company each and every day.
5. Measurable. The company should be able to develop a metric for every part of the statement.

These five criteria are not sequential, but an overall design that companies should try to achieve. Let's look at each of these criteria in more detail.

Keep It Short

We recognize that there are two schools of thought in creating mission statements—keeping them short and succinct, or using them to summarize many desirable elements of what a company is all about. We prefer keeping them short, since such statements are more easily remembered and therefore more easily relied upon for day-to-day actions and decisions.

Some of the most often mentioned historical guides used in developing a mission statement have suggested a long list of items that must be included in order to create a comprehensive mission statement. This advice holds that a mission statement must include many or all of the following elements:[15]

1. Customers
2. Products/Services
3. Geographic Markets
4. Technology
5. Concern for Survival/Growth
6. Philosophy
7. Public Image

**Figure 3.7
Elements of
Effective Mission
Statements**

Short
Simple
Company specific
Actionable
Measurable

8. Employees
9. Distinctive Competence

As you can readily see, the effect of this suggestion is to create a list so inclusive that the statement will be found to be completely acceptable to every constituency inside or outside of the company. As a result, however, some company mission statements have become multisentence or even multiparagraph tomes that are geared to avoid conflict rather than guide employees. The practical result of this approach has been mission statements that could not be easily recalled—even by individuals with a photographic memory—and therefore could not be acted upon. An all-encompassing mission statement that cannot be easily recalled and used by employees is simply an exercise in frustration, expense, and occasionally outright derision by employees.

Does it fit on a coffee mug? This may be the single most important element of a well-designed mission statement. It is not an essay that describes everything that a company has done or might do, such that the organization can cover every single avenue of potential profit. An effective mission statement is best described as a short, direct statement that precisely encapsulates what approach the organization takes as it seeks to accomplish its purpose.

One of the truly outstanding companies in the United States is Caterpillar. Unfortunately, this manufacturer of enormous earthmoving equipment has a mission statement that fails virtually every tenet of effective mission statement development. Consider the following:

Caterpillar. *Caterpillar will be the leader in providing the best value in machines, engines and support services for customers dedicated to building the world's infrastructure and developing and transporting its resources. We provide the best value to customers. Caterpillar people will increase shareholder value by aggressively pursuing growth and profit opportunities that leverage our engineering, manufacturing, distribution, information management and financial services expertise. We grow profitably. Caterpillar will provide its worldwide workforce with an environment that stimulates diversity, innovation, teamwork, continuous learning and improvement and rewards individual performance. We develop and reward people. Caterpillar is dedicated to improving the quality of life while sustaining the quality of our earth. We encourage social responsibility.*

The Caterpillar mission statement certainly encompasses every aspect of potential influence for the business. It has the look and feel of a checklist with a series of statements that, while not objectionable, are not going to be remembered by the staff of the organization. An effective mission statement does not explain in detail how the mission will be done. However, it does state the purpose of the company and the basic approach the company will use to accomplish that purpose. An effective modification of the Caterpillar mission might look something like this:

Caterpillar (revised). *Caterpillar is the leading manufacturer of machines, engines and support services for customers dedicated to developing and building the world's infrastructure.*

It simply states the mission of the organization. It is easily recalled, and leaves the detailed means of attainment up to the experts within the organization.

Another clear example from an excellent company is as follows:

Halliburton Company. *The world needs energy resources and commercial and industrial facilities to fulfill the need of its communities in a safe and environmentally sound manner. Halliburton Company is dedicated to leading the way in meeting this need through demonstrated excellence in providing a broad spectrum of services and products for finding and developing energy resources; designing, constructing, operating and maintaining facilities; and protecting the environment. We will afford our employees opportunities to contribute to our Company's success. Through their skills and abilities, we will continuously improve the quality of services and products we supply our customers. We will provide a fair return for our shareholders and good opportunities for our business partners and suppliers, and be good citizens of our communities.*

Reading carefully, we can see that this statement contains a smorgasbord of ideas. While everyone within the organization would be hard pressed to find something they would disagree with, neither would they be able to remember or execute against this lengthy statement. What might be the alternative to some of these statements? While not perfect, a rewrite for this large conglomerate organization might be:

Halliburton Company (revised). *Halliburton is the leader in a broad spectrum of services and products aimed at finding and developing energy resources as well as designing, constructing, operating and maintaining facilities used in energy production.*

Keep It Simple

A well-designed mission statement has to be something that everyone in the organization can learn and understand. A mission statement that does not incorporate shared language and meaning for all employees has little value to the organization. Learning and understanding require that the statement be relatively simple. The senior management team needs to ensure that the words and concepts employed in the statement are straightforward and have a clear meaning to all who hear or read them. If you saw the movie *Pirates of the Caribbean*, you may recall the entertaining language at play when Captain Barbossa replies tongue-in-cheek to his upper class captive, "I'm disinclined to acquiesce to your request," pauses for moment, and turns back to his captive and says, "Means 'NO.'"

Consider the following corporate mission statement from a very focused and successful company, which certainly meets the first criteria of keeping it short but fails on the dimension of simplicity:

Waste Management. *To maximize shareholder value, while adhering to the laws of the jurisdictions within which it operates and observing the highest of ethical standards.*

Try to imagine the vast group of truck drivers being told to use this mission statement in the course of their daily pickups. "Adhering," "jurisdictions," and "ethical standards" are all fine concepts and yet are of little value on a day-to-day basis to most employees. Why is Waste Management in business? Why would a customer want to use them? What are their resource-based advantages? Where do they attain extraordinary returns in their value chain? As an employee, what exactly is there to take from this? What are the alternatives? Don't all corporations (or should we say, *shouldn't* all corporations) adhere to the laws? Would any corporation suggest that they will minimize shareholder value? We're being a tad facetious here to make an important point. It is not to suggest that Waste Management isn't a fine organization; it is simply to suggest that the true mission of the organization is not what is stated in the mission statement, and this lack of focus does not help the organization move consistently toward a goal. The use of terms that have no meaning to the employees, suppliers, customers, or the investing community provides inadequate direction, opening up the possibility to both an unfocused future and a group of employees who will "interpret" the mission of the organization in different and possibly creative ways.

The ability to learn and understand a mission statement requires that it be written in such a manner that virtually everyone can obtain significant meaning from it and know how to apply it. Take a look at the following short, simple, and effective mission statement:

Parker Hannifin. *To be the leading supplier of precision miniature fluid control products.*

Keep It Company-Specific

There are occasions where a short and simple mission can also miss the mark of being company-specific:

J.P. Morgan Chase. *To create exceptional value for our clients, employees and investors by delivering our deep, broad and integrated capabilities.*

We hesitate to guess what the daily result of this statement would be if it were used to make daily decisions. These ideas are so vague that few could possibly understand what the company does or how employees are to conduct themselves for the company to achieve its goals. This mission is not company-specific. Without the name we attached to it, this could be a statement about virtually any company.

Mission statements that stay at too general a level are like the mass mailings that show up in your mailbox from aspiring political candidates. They seek to curry favor with the entire population. Everything seems so agreeable; who could disagree? Just as the mailings provide no precise definition of the candidates or even what political parties they actually belong to, these types of statements provide virtually no clear definition of the company in question. A mission statement that is not clear and specific to the company invites continual questions as to purpose and direction.

One of our favorite companies (primarily because of its focus and quality leadership) nonetheless has a mission statement that would actually prevent employees and others from learning or understanding what the company seeks to achieve. AmeriCredit is one of the leading companies in subprime (individuals with less than stellar credit records) automobile lending and yet their mission statement reads:

AmeriCredit. *To create value for our stakeholders by constantly improving our services, investing in innovative solutions and information-based strategies, and promoting a culture of teamwork, excellence and integrity.*

Upon a first reading one would be inclined to believe that they had read the mission statement of a software company or a Web-based business. You could easily take this mission statement and apply it to virtually any organization, anywhere in the world, and while it would be equally useless, it would nonetheless be perfectly applicable.

Other well-known and respected companies also suffer from this type of ineffective mission statement writing. Take a look at some of the following mission statements:

Merck. *The mission of Merck is to provide society with superior products and services by developing innovations and solutions that improve the quality of life and satisfy customer needs, and to provide employees with meaningful work and advancement opportunities, and investors with a superior rate of return.*

Albertson's. *Guided by relentless focus on our five imperatives, we will constantly strive to implement the critical initiatives required to achieve our vision. In doing this, we will deliver operational excellence in every corner of the Company and meet or exceed our commitments to the many constituencies we serve. All of our long-term strategies and short-term actions will be molded by a set of core values that are shared by each and every associate.*

If all you had in front of you were these mission statements, how might you know what these companies actually do? How might these statements help anyone in their organizations to make decisions? These statements are certainly not disagreeable, but in fact could be interchangeably attached to virtually any company anywhere in the world. There appears to be nothing outside of their "opportunity space." It is not unusual to read comments from corporate executives that state that one of their goals is not to close any doors on any opportunity. This is an unrealistic view of strategy and is counter to the weight of more than thirty years' worth of studies and consulting practice showing that strategic focus is one of the most important factors in company success.

One of the primary goals of an effective mission statement is, therefore, its ability to allow (often empower) employees at all levels to use their directed judgment in the execution of their daily responsibilities. Employees are constantly faced with decisions that may have both an individual as well as a cumulative strategic impact. An effective mission statement tells everyone exactly what to "DO" and therefore, by omission, what "NOT TO DO." The focus within the mission statement must go beyond a laundry list of areas covered in the business; instead it should be narrowly defined as "an organization's unique and enduring purpose...."[16] Consider the following mission statement:

Autoliv. *To create, manufacture and sell state-of-the-art automotive safety systems.*

Every employee, customer, and supplier knows exactly what Autoliv does and does not do. If an employee is approached by a vendor with an interesting new product that might improve the sound quality within an automobile, the employee knows instantly that this product is outside the stated purview of the company. Management has made the decision to focus their time, energy, and resources upon the creation, manufacture, and sale of state-of-the-art automotive safety systems. This focus prevents the company from wasting valuable time and resources pursuing areas outside of its core competence.

Keep It Actionable

One of the measures of a high-quality mission statement is its ability to guide every individual in the company each and every day. Virtually every employee is faced with a large number of decisions in their daily jobs. Therefore, an effective mission statement needs to be actionable for every employee. An effective mission is one grounded in specificity, creating a bounded business model that allows every company to be the best at some aspect of their business. The mission statement must highlight and focus the energy of all the employees upon the direction that the top management team believes is best for the business.

The Parker Hannifin mission from earlier in this chapter achieves just that. It takes extraordinary care to develop a statement that can guide the entire organization and at the same time be effectively utilized by every employee of the company, regardless of their level in the organization. Imagine the customer service employee who every day deals with customers calling in with concerns and complaints. If the mission statement of the organization is a long, multiparagraph affair that essentially says "we do it all," or if it is like so many statements and simply extols the employees to "maximize shareholder value," then how is the customer service employee to act? As we said previously, what is most likely to happen is that they will simply do their best, given some mix between their own common sense and the admonishments of their immediate superior. An effective statement is one that helps the employees make active decisions in the moment without always having to refer every decision up the chain of command. A mission statement that comes fairly close to simultaneously achieving all of the components that we have thus far discussed is the one for Southwest Airlines.

Southwest Airlines. *The mission of Southwest Airlines is dedication to the highest quality of customer service delivered with a sense of warmth, friendliness, individual pride, and company spirit.*

Reading this mission statement, some of you may argue that it could be applied generically to just about any organization. Although Southwest is clearly an airline company, they view the business as one of customer service. Virtually every aspect of the activities performed by employees on a day-to-day basis are focused on providing exceptional service to the company's customers.

Keep It Measurable

The final element of an effective mission statement is a bit more complex and time consuming than the previous four. The mission statement is only as valuable as it is practical. While all corporations have a set of metrics to evaluate the organization as a whole, the metrics developed from an effective mission statement focus the company's efforts upon its unifying approach to gaining competitive advantages.

Many mission statements exhibit one of three types of performance dimensions: 1) "feel-good" goals, 2) specific financial goals, or 3) general financial or vague market goals. Feel-good goals—such as "provide employees with meaningful work and advancement opportunities"—contained in mission statements tend to be ineffective. This is because they focus on qualitative dimensions that cannot be measured; if they cannot be measured, they are of little help in providing direction for the company. In contrast, highly specified financial goals appear to lock management and employees into specific targets, potentially compromising strategic actions that are better suited for sustained performance. Financial performance goals are ethically neutral and therefore may lead to a distortion in the activities of employees. Employees may have compelling reasons to achieve financial targets regardless of the strategic impact on the company. This is not unlike the challenges faced by public companies in managing toward short-term earnings targets. General financial goals or vague market goals are also not very helpful in connecting mission statements to performance. This is because it is difficult to connect specific actions and practices that fulfill a mission to such fuzzy goals.

Studies strongly suggest that alignment between a well-written mission statement and the firm's performance evaluation system helps to magnify the impact on performance of the mission statement.[17] Metrics of this sort generally fall into two categories, those that are quantitative and those that are qualitative. A good rule of thumb is to develop seven metrics with approximately four being quantitative and three being qualitative. Since we emphasize the importance of action at the individual level that is facilitated by an effective mission statement, some of the quantitative metrics should presumably be tied to the firm's personnel performance evaluation system. For example, since innovation is central to the mission of 3M Corporation, each employee is encouraged and expected to devote a percentage of his or her workweek to investigating new business ideas. The actual time percentage spent by each employee in this area can be captured on an individual basis, and then aggregated to a departmental, divisional, or corporate level.

A great check on the quality of a mission statement is to note whether metrics can be designed to measure each and every part of the mission. Consider the following mission statement:

New York Times. *Enhance society by creating, collecting and distributing high quality news, information and entertainment.*

This well-designed mission statement allows for the development of metrics (performance measures) that will provide an effective measure of their success at achieving their mission. The *New York Times* aims to do three things (create, collect, and distribute) across three areas (high-quality news, high-quality information, and high-quality entertainment) in order to accomplish one goal (enhance society). All of these can then be translated into a mix of qualitative and quantitative metrics given the top management's interpretation about what constitutes high quality. Examples might be:

1. Number of high-quality news articles written by *NY Times* staff writers divided by the total number of news articles appearing in the *NY Times*. This could be measured daily.
2. Perception of the quality of articles in *NY Times*.
3. Number of *NY Times*–written articles that are picked up by other news sources.

The metrics designed for the *NY Times* will be unique to that organization and truly measure how it is succeeding in its mission.

Take a look at the following different mission statement from an office products manufacturer:

Steelcase. *Our mission is to provide the world's best office environment products, services, systems, and intelligence ... designed to help people in offices work more effectively.*

Steelcase does one thing ("provide," which can be defined as producing, outsourcing, or simply purchasing for resale) that can be defined quite widely across four areas of expertise (products, services, systems, and intelligence) aimed at one area (office environments) with one goal (helping people work more effectively). The specificity of the items appearing in the statement not only focuses employees on sets of activities, but also provides substantial opportunity for the development of metrics.

Well-Designed Mission Statements

Combining all of these qualities into an effective mission statement is both an art and a science. Figure 3.8 shows several examples of well written mission statements.

No mission statement is ever perfect, and everyone in the organization will have their own ideas of how the five concepts presented might best be articulated. However, the effort made to design a quality mission statement has a high potential payoff for the business that undertakes its creation.

Figure 3.8
Examples of Mission Statements

Company	Mission Statement
H&R Block	To help our clients achieve their financial objectives by serving as their tax and financial partner.
Host Marriot	To be the premier hospitality real estate company.
Collins & Aikman	To be recognized as a leading-edge automotive systems supplier and an innovator of world-class NVH (noise, vibration, harshness) and acoustic technologies.
MGM Mirage	To design and operate an unmatched collection of resort-casinos and provide unsurpassed service and amenities to our guests.
AMGEN	To be the world leader in the developing and delivering of important, cost-effective therapeutics based on advances in cellular and molecular biology.

Strategic Moves
Lena Pope Home Inc., Part 2

The Lena Pope Home management and employees met in a multiday session to evaluate their key value drivers and talk about who they were and who they wanted to be in the future. The organization determined that the following four areas constituted their potential competitive advantage:

- Exceptional Value
- Reputation for Excellence
- Complete Continuum of Care
- When No One Could – LPH Did

With this decided, the group designed the following mission statement:

Lena Pope Home is committed to creating a future of hope for children and families through an effective continuum of behavioral healthcare services to strengthen families and develop resilient children.

QUESTIONS

1. How well does their new mission statement meet the five criteria established for effective mission statements?
2. What would you change in their mission statement and why?
3. How would you suggest they use this mission statement?

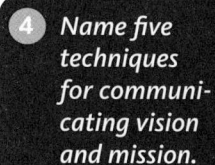

4 *Name five techniques for communicating vision and mission.*

COMMUNICATING THE VISION AND MISSION

The best vision and mission statements are of little value if they are not communicated to all employees. Following the tenets of good practice, this communication should be in as many forms as are available. Employees learn in different ways and it is crucial that they learn and incorporate the vision and mission into their everyday processes at work. An organization's culture and means of interacting are not consistent throughout a company and therefore, the means of communicating must be tailored.[18] Furthermore, organizations have their own sub-unit communication systems that generally vary by area. The key is to increase the solidarity within the organization. It is the responsibility of senior management to ensure that the vision and mission are both known and used by their employees. This can be done in a number of ways:

1. Creating Narratives—One of the newer means of embedding the vision and mission in an organization is the use of one of the oldest communication techniques known to humankind—storytelling. Telling stories that point to the understanding and use of the vision and mission is an extremely effective method of relaying important, actionable concepts. A story allows the listener or reader to visualize the situation and the result. Individuals have a much higher recall level with good stories than they do with bulleted items, lists, or verbal presentations.[19] When Sony was developing the first music CD in 1982, they took a prototype to Stevie Wonder at his Los Angeles home. He was enamored with the sound quality and excited about its possibilities for sound reproduction. This story was repeated throughout Sony, inspiring further commitment to the new direction. In another case, Sony founder Akio Morita said "I'll leave Sony if we don't do the Walkman," a story that was repeatedly told throughout the company, which mobilized the entire organization to become the first mover in the portable listening device field.[20]

2. Role Models—Management has a profound ability to affect the actions of their employees by serving as a role model in the embodiment of the vision and mission. Strong, consistent actions by top management demonstrating to all employees that the vision and mission are the measures by which they evaluate their actions provides direct and compelling evidence of its importance to all employees.

3. Specific Short-Term Objectives—Translating the loftier and more general direction provided by the vision and mission into specific, short-term objectives clarifies the actions expected of individual employees and provides a quick reinforcement that employees are headed in the right direction. Simplicity and focus are crucial. We will discuss this and the techniques available in detail in Chapters 11 and 12.

4. Personalizing the Vision and Mission—Employees are encouraged to develop their own vision and mission that are consistent with the ones developed by the organization. The ability to personalize the vision and mission for themselves not only has the effect of internalizing what is needed, it also acts as an effective check to ensure that senior management has developed a set of statements that is effective with the organization's employees.

5. Create Objects that Display the Vision and Mission—Placing the vision and mission on a coffee mug and distributing one to every employee has been used as a communication device to set the stage

for constant reinforcement of the company's approach to business. Printing the vision and mission on posters, banners, and/or plaques that can be prominently displayed helps reinforce their importance to the future of the organization.

Medtronic is a leading medical device company that specializes in cardiac and spinal products. The company's common goal is to restore health, alleviate pain, and extend life in partnership with the medical community. To this end, one of the founders of the company had a medallion cast with the image of a patient rising from the operating table. Every new employee, when he or she is hired, is presented a medallion by a member of the senior management team at a ceremony. Employees are encouraged to keep the medallion at their desk to remind them of the goal of the organization.[21] The organization celebrates its ability to accomplish this mission with events throughout the year and honors employees who exemplify their approach to this business. It is part of what separates them in a very competitive field.

CHAPTER SUMMARY

This chapter has focused on: 1) Understanding the importance of an effective vision and mission for an organization; 2) Developing the criteria for evaluating and writing these statements; and 3) Practicing the process of developing them. Truly great companies have developed an effective vision and mission that provides direction and accountability for their businesses.[22] As in much of strategy, the process, evaluation, and use of both a vision and a mission statement is a combination of both art and science. The ability to apply the science and practice the art provides a strong foundation for your business career.

Effective vision statements incorporate six elements: 1) Incorporate foresight; 2) Provide an event horizon; 3) Connect with current capabilities of the organization; 4) Incorporate enduring core values; 5) Be short; and 6) Be memorable.

Effective mission statements incorporate five criteria in their design. They can be evaluated by their simultaneous accomplishment of the following characteristics: 1) Be short; 2) Be simple; 3) Be company-specific; 4) Be actionable; and 5) Be measurable.

KEY TERMS

Mission statement (p. 62)

Vision statement (p. 62)

SHORT ANSWER REVIEW QUESTIONS

1. Describe how a mission statement can encourage ethical behavior in a company.
2. How are vision and mission statements best communicated to the employees in an organization?

3. How does a company's sustainable competitive advantages guide its vision and mission?
4. What is a BHAG?
5. How can you make a mission statement actionable?
6. Why is it important to keep a mission statement short?
7. How would you suggest a company create narratives for its vision and mission statements?
8. What criteria should be kept in mind for writing an effective vision statement?
9. How would you evaluate a mission statement?
10. How is a vision statement used in organizations?

GROUP EXERCISES

1. Using the information presented in this chapter, create a vision statement for your business school.
   a. How well did the process work?
   b. Who else would you include if you were to do this again?
   c. What might you do differently if you were to try this again?
   d. How accurately does your vision statement present the school and its future?

2. Have your team agree on five large, publically traded companies. Using the Internet, try and determine the vision and/or mission statement.
   a. How many were you able to find?
   b. Evaluate each vision/mission on how well it meets the criteria laid out in the chapter.
   c. Do you have any excellent statements? Any horrible ones? Which are they and why did you evaluate them as such?
   d. For the companies that had poor vision/mission statements, write an improved one.

3. Take a look at the following list of mission statements. Match them to the company listed at the end of the exercises.

   Company # 1

   Our Mission—We are a global family with a proud heritage passionately committed to providing personal mobility for people around the world. We anticipate consumer need and deliver outstanding products and services that improve people's lives.

   Company # 2

   Use our pioneering spirit to responsibly deliver energy to the world.

   Company # 3

   To provide society with superior products and services by developing innovations and solutions that improve the quality of life and satisfy customer needs, and to provide employees with meaningful work and advancement opportunities, and investors with a superior rate of return.

Company # 4

OUR MISSION is to be a leader in the distribution and merchandising of food, health, personal care, and related consumable products and services.

Company # 5

To create exceptional value for our clients, employees and investors by delivering our deep, broad and integrated capabilities.

Company # 6

To continually provide our members with quality goods and services at the lowest possible prices.

Company # 7

Guided by relentless focus on our five imperatives, we will constantly strive to implement the critical initiatives required to achieve our vision. In doing this, we will deliver operational excellence in every corner of the Company and meet or exceed our commitments to the many constituencies we serve. All of our long-term strategies and short-term actions will be molded by a set of core values that are shared by each and every associate.

Company # 8

We will become the world's most valued company to patients, customers, colleagues, investors, business partners, and the communities where we work and live.

Possible Answers:

Albertson	JPMorgan Chase
Bear Stearns	Kroger
ConocoPhillips	Merck
Costco	Pfizer
ExxonMobil	Safeway
Ford	Sam's Club
General Motors	Toyota
GlaxoSmithKline	Wachovia

REFERENCES

1 R. Karlgaard, 2005, YingYang, Big Bang. *Forbes*, March 14, 2005, 175 (5): 33.

2 J. A. Pearce & F. David, 1987, Corporate mission statements: The bottom line, *Academy of Management Executive*, 1 (2): 109–116.

3 J. E. Conklin & W. Weil, 1997. *Wicked Problems: Naming the Pain in Organizations*. Washington, DC: Group Decision Support Systems Inc.

4 For perspectives on top management team disagreement see Bourgeois, 1980, Performance and consensus, *Strategic Management Journal*, 1: 227–248, or Eisenhardt, Kahwajy, & Bourgeois, 1997, How management teams can have a good fight, *Harvard Business Review*, 75 (4): 77–85.

5 Many of the largest corporations in the world are highly diversified in unrelated businesses. It may be that these corporations refrain from offering a corporate mission statement because such statements should be focused. Evidence suggests, however, that many operating divisions of such diversified corporations still do not have mission statements.

6 H. Mintzberg, 1978, *The Structuring of Organizations*, Prentice Hall.

7 P. Drucker, 1974, *Management: Tasks, Responsibilities, Practices,* New York: Harper & Row.

8 http://www.profootballhof.com/history/decades/1980s/the_drive.jsp.

9 J. Barker, 2006, *Agincourt: Henry V and the Battle That Made England*. New York: Little, Brown.

10 J. Collins, 2001. *Good to Great*. New York: HarperBusiness.

11 Amazon.com investor relations (http://phx.corporate-ir.net/phoenix.zhtml?c=97664&p=irol-faq).

12 W. Shakespeare, *Hamlet*, act 2, scene 2.

13 J. Collins, 1996, Aligning actions and values, *Leader to Leader*, 1: 19–24.

14 L. E. Palich, L. B. Cardinal, & C. C. Miller, 2000, Curvilinearity in the diversification-performance linkage: An examination of over three decades of research, *Strategic Management Journal*, 21: 155–174.

15 F. R. David & F. R. David, 2003. It's time to redraft your mission statement, *Journal of Business Strategy*, 24 (1): 11–14; R. D. Ireland & M. A. Hitt, 1992, Mission statements: Importance, challenge, and recommendations for development, *Business Horizons*, 35 (3): 34–42; J. A. Pearce & F. R. David, 1987, Corporate mission statements: The bottom line, *Academy of Management Executive*, 1 (2): 109–116.

16 C. K. Bart & M. C. Baetz, 1998, The relationship between mission statements and firm performance: An exploratory study, *Journal of Management Studies*, 35 (6): 823–854.

17 Ibid.

18 R. Goffee & B. Jones, 1996, What holds the modern company together? *Harvard Business Review*, November–December 1996: 133–148.

19 G. Shaw, R. Brown, & P. Bromily, 1998, Strategic stories: How 3M is rewriting business planning, *Harvard Business Review*, May/June 1998 (Reprint # 98310).

20 S. A. Buckler & K. A. Zien, 1996, The spirituality of innovation: Learning from stories, *Journal of Product Innovation Management*, 13 (5): 391–405.

21 http://www.medtronic.com/corporate/mission_medallion.html#mm.

22 J. C. Collins & J. I. Porras, 1991, Organization vision and visionary organizations, *California Management Review*, Fall: 30–52.

Analysis

In the first three chapters of this book we have laid a foundation for understanding strategic management. The first chapter outlined the nature of strategy as the direction in which the firm is going reflected in an ongoing stream of decisions that management must make about long-term investments. Through its strategy the firm seeks to achieve a level of performance that is superior to competing firms in the short term and offers the potential to sustain performance differences over time. We also discussed the two fundamental imperatives that impact every strategic management process today. These are "value creation" and "opportunity recognition." The dynamic nature of world markets makes it exceedingly difficult to sustain superior levels of performance. This context makes developing and executing strategy, as well as achieving a sustainable performance difference, both complex and challenging.

Chapters 2 and 3 provided a set of "bookends" for the strategic management process. In the beginning management needs to develop a vision for the direction the company is heading, and a mission that describes how it is going to get there. The ending that strategy seeks is superior performance, and we discussed ways in which the performance of companies is gauged.

Given this, you are probably still asking yourself "What is strategy, really? What the book has done so far is provide an outline, but it hasn't really described it in detail." Somewhat akin to trying to describe a kitchen chair by saying "it's a wooden thing, with spindles that run vertically and horizontally for support, and by the way, you sit on it when you eat your breakfast."

Let's get specific. The next four chapters of the book take up the challenge of how to develop strategy and a sustainable competitive advantage. There are two basic steps in the design and development of a strategy: 1) examine the industry and your competitors in order to develop a deep understanding of the market and how your firm must operate within it in order to be successful; 2) examine your own company in order to develop a list of activities and capabilities that potentially provide competitive advantage.

INDUSTRY MODEL: EXTERNAL ANALYSIS

This model originates from a branch of Economics called Industrial Organizational Economics, and focuses on the economic structure of an industry. Attractive industries are those where the conditions are favorable for a company to earn above-average returns. An industry's attractiveness as a place to do business is largely determined by industry characteristics outside the company. These characteristics suggest key factors that any strategic approach

External
Environment
Analysis

Attractive
Industry

Strategy
Formulation

Assets,
Skills

Strong
Implementation

Superior
Returns

should address, and in turn the strategic approach requires the company to assemble or develop certain kinds of assets and skills. According to this approach, effective implementation of the strategy using these assets and skills would then lead to superior performance.

Here's an example of this approach. Mt. Tabor High School has a very strong sports program that has enabled it to earn numerous county and state awards. This generates significant alumni and community support for the school. However, its programs have largely stayed in the traditional sports programs: football and soccer in the fall, basketball during winter, baseball during spring. What other sports should it expand into? Lacrosse is a fast-growing spring sport across the state and the region. The lacrosse "industry" looks attractive in part because competition is not yet fierce and because the equipment needs represent barriers to entry for other schools that are not as well endowed as Mt. Tabor. For the present time, lacrosse appears to be attractive as a place for the school to play in—a place where it can develop a program and win simultaneously.

The Industry Analysis methodology is covered in Chapter 4, along with several means of analyzing specific competitors.

COMPANY MODEL: INTERNAL ANALYSIS

The second approach is with a detailed examination of the company. This model begins with: 1) a detailed analysis of the entire business via a value chain analysis; 2) an examination of the company's current resources and capabilities; and 3) a determination of which resources and value-adding activities are truly extraordinary, providing a foundation for sustainable competitive advantage. The result of this analysis will suggest a type of strategic approach that leverages the resources and activities, which in turn suggests the kinds of industries or businesses to get into (those that will leverage the company's existing skills). Successfully implementing this approach in new circumstances will lead to superior returns for the company.

By example, Mt. Tabor High School also decided to enter into the field hockey arena. Like lacrosse, this is a fast-growing competitive arena for area high schools. However, the rationale for moving into field hockey was that coaches and players could borrow heavily from the training and coaching techniques that were behind the very successful soccer program at the school, and use the athletic fields in the fall, which were only used for spring sports. Since the competitive dimensions of field hockey in many ways resemble the competitive dimensions of soccer, the school believed it could successfully leverage its skills, capabilities, and physical resources into this new arena.

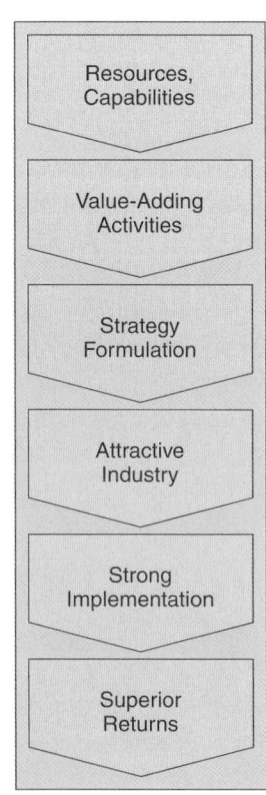

Resources,
Capabilities

Value-Adding
Activities

Strategy
Formulation

Attractive
Industry

Strong
Implementation

Superior
Returns

Chapter 5 covers the Value Chain and its associated analysis techniques, while Chapter 6 explores Resources and the associated application of a resource-based analysis.

FORMULATING A STRATEGIC APPROACH

Chapter 7 puts the three chapters together in a discussion of Business-Level Strategies as ways to approach the marketplace. Specific strategic approaches must respond to the requirements dictated by industry conditions, but must also build on sets of activities or resources and capabilities that enable a company to create and deliver value in a superior fashion to competition. At the same time, managers must have a sense of strategic trajectory that accounts for anticipated dynamic changes in the industry and competition, but that also builds and follows a vision for the company. We will therefore learn that strategic management is a blend of science and art, a complex and fascinating undertaking that is the heart and soul of any successful enterprise.

External Environment

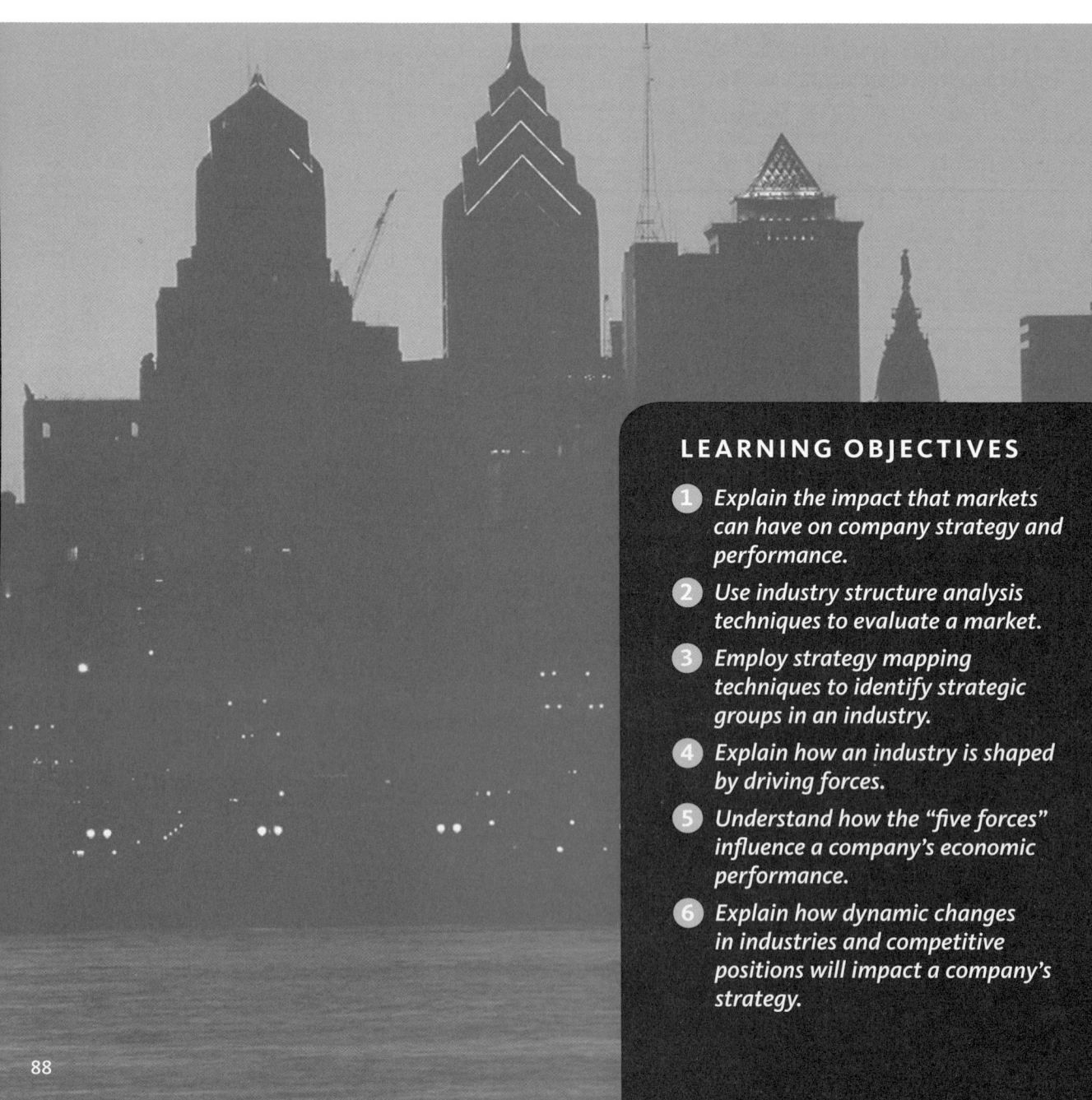

LEARNING OBJECTIVES

1 *Explain the impact that markets can have on company strategy and performance.*

2 *Use industry structure analysis techniques to evaluate a market.*

3 *Employ strategy mapping techniques to identify strategic groups in an industry.*

4 *Explain how an industry is shaped by driving forces.*

5 *Understand how the "five forces" influence a company's economic performance.*

6 *Explain how dynamic changes in industries and competitive positions will impact a company's strategy.*

Championship Foods

Traditionally food manufacturing has been an industry that has experienced a very high level of entrepreneurial activity. This is because the barriers to entry have been fairly low. Nearly everyone has a grandma who has passed down a special food recipe, so coming up with a unique and tasty food product idea has never been a problem. In addition, everyone has access to a "manufacturing plant"; it's called your kitchen at home with a sink, refrigerator, stove, and ingredients easily accessible.

Championship Foods started off exactly this way in 1988, with a recipe for prepared chili that was "to die for." The company intended to sell its chili in supermarkets, shelved next to Hormel and other canned products. Championship Chili was made with fresh ingredients and high-quality beef, and it was packed in glass jars to exude homemade quality. Who would buy canned chili when Championship was available?

The company encountered significant market forces that made it exceedingly difficult to earn profits. While beef, seasonings, and spices are readily available from a variety of suppliers, glass is not. Glass manufacturing is heavily concentrated, while glass users are not. Glass suppliers charged exorbitant prices for their products, and Championship had no recourse.

On the other end of the spectrum, buyers were also fairly concentrated. Championship started business in Denver, where only three supermarket chains controlled roughly 85 percent of the market. Because Championship had few alternatives for distribution, and because the supermarket buyers entertained many possible new products to place in their stores, Championship was forced to pay "slotting allowances" to gain initial shelf space. The company was also required to participate in each chain's special advertising and display programs on a regular basis.

The food industry is characterized by intense rivalry. Just look at the ads on TV every day, and notice the volume of coupons that appear in local newspapers on Wednesdays and Sundays. To create consumer awareness, trial, and repeat purchases, Championship had to play the game where rules were set by the likes of General Mills, Procter & Gamble, Kraft, and other large food manufacturers. Hormel and other chili manufacturers were also not happy about Championship entering the market, and the company experienced competitive retaliation when its products appeared on store shelves.

THE NATURE OF MARKETS AND OPPORTUNITY FOR COMPETITIVE ADVANTAGE

We continue our discussion of strategic management with a chapter on the external analysis of markets. Why do we begin here? First, because every company exists in a market of some sort, and as the chapter's opening stories illustrate, there are varying market forces exerting influences on companies. These forces pressure every company to behave in certain ways in order to be successful, and to not behave in other ways. Second, when we think about achieving "competitive advantage," which is the goal of strategic management, we are acknowledging that there are many companies that may be competitively close to our business. Sets of competitors, in fact, help to define markets. Abraham Lincoln once said, "If we can know where we are and something about how we got there, we might see where we are trending—and if the outcomes which lie naturally in our course are unacceptable, to make timely change."[2] Understanding the market in which a company competes will be helpful in guiding the company in its strategic direction and choices.

But let's first step back in time a bit earlier than Lincoln, to the eighteenth century and economist Adam Smith. You will probably recall from one of your first economics courses that he wrote *Wealth of Nations*. To Adam Smith what created the successful functioning of an economy was the pursuit by each individual of self-interest:

> "...and by directing industry in such a manner as its produce may be of greatest value, he intends only his own gain and he is in this, as in many other cases, lead by an invisible hand to promote an end which was no part of his intention. By pursuing his own interest he frequently promotes that of society more effectually...."[3]

Here and elsewhere in his book we find Smith arguing that there is an efficiency in markets that is guided by the aggregated pursuits of individuals. Resources are efficiently allocated, and the demands and needs of the marketplace are met.

If it is true that markets can efficiently allocate resources and meet demand through the actions of individuals, then why do businesses even exist? The answer, of course, is that businesses can do a number of things that individuals cannot. They can achieve administrative efficiency and more easily organize the specialization of labor. They can gain access to capital unavailable to individuals and therefore have the ability to construct large facilities and achieve economies of scale and scope that isolated individuals cannot achieve. In today's world business firms can also shield managers and employees from some of the liabilities of the business itself as well as from the risks taken on by the firm's investors.

In Chapter 1 we pointed out that strategy concerns itself with five basic questions, two of which are particularly relevant here: 1) why are firms in an industry different—that is, why are some firms more successful than others;

and 2) how and why are those differences between successful and unsuccessful firms sustained over time? The slight deviation we have taken here into Adam Smith and the nature of markets provides us with a very important starting point for exploring these questions. Adam Smith and two centuries of economists have focused on the efficiency of markets in allocating resources and meeting demands, with **perfect competition** as an elegant concept that illuminates this efficiency. In contrast, the ability of firms to create sustainable differences versus other firms is only possible because of the *failure* of perfectly competitive markets.

Let's explain this carefully. Recall from your economics courses the characteristics that describe perfectly competitive markets: all firms are identical, produce exactly the same products, and no firm earns any profits at all. This is because in perfectly competitive markets every firm enjoys perfect information about what is going on in the industry, there are no costs associated with making adjustments in how or what a firm produces, and there are no costs for new firms to enter the industry. If Billy Bob's Barbeque somehow figures out how to make a better sauce and starts generating more business as a result, in a perfectly competitive market all the other barbecue places would see this change instantaneously and just as instantaneously imitate it exactly. Why wouldn't they? Why would they allow Billy Bob to generate more business and profit, if they can produce exactly the same award-winning sauce? As soon as one firm has figured out how to make more money, in a perfectly competitive market all the other firms will immediately imitate that recipe for success. In addition, because there are no costs to enter the industry, if someone on the outside observes that the barbecue sauce companies are making money while they are not, then they will enter the industry to participate in the profit-making. This process will continue until all the profits have been competed away. As the economists say, the market equilibrates at the point where once again all firms are virtually identical and no firm is making any profit.[4]

Perfect competition is on one end of a continuum of types of markets. Commodities markets and trading are an example of a market that closely resembles perfect competition. The other end of the continuum is the exact opposite of perfect competition. Instead of lots of firms, which are all identical and none of which is earning a profit, there is one firm and it earns all the profits. This is called a **monopoly** (Figure 4.1). Here one company owns all of the business in an industry. Without the policing effect of an efficient market populated by competitors, the monopoly firm can usually charge what it wants for its products or services. Because it is the only game in town, it can likely extract economic concessions from its suppliers that lower its costs and raise its profits even further. Monopoly companies may be protected in many ways from new firms entering the industry and from substitute products or services taking away their customers. Local gas and electricity utility companies and cable TV providers are examples of monopolies that have been historically protected through government regulation. Another example might be Microsoft, which enjoys a huge installed base of users of its operating system on personal computers, making it difficult for other software companies

Perfect competition
A situation of little or no differentiation between competitors and one in which there is virtually perfect information available to market participants.

Monopoly A situation where a single firm virtually constitutes the entire industry.

Figure 4.1
The Range of Markets

Perfect Competition	Type of market	Monopoly
Zero profit	Potential Profit per Firm	All the profits

Greater competitive advantage

to be successful in this market. Although it now experiences more competition than before, it has been targeted by both the U.S. government and the European Union for its monopolistic position and the aggressive business practices it engages in with the market power it exerts.

Competitive advantage is therefore possible when there is a *failure* of perfectly competitive markets. In a perfectly competitive market, no firm has or can gain a competitive advantage and no firm earns profits. In a monopoly market, one firm exerts market power and one firm earns all of the profits. If we think about the goal of strategy as being the creation of sustainable differences between companies that result in higher profits, then we see that the possibility for competitive advantage and profits are more likely when our company exists in a market that is at a point on the continuum further away from perfect competition and closer to the monopoly position.

In September 1996, a possible merger was initiated between Staples and Office Depot in the office supplies industry. The Federal Trade Commission prevented the merger from going through, because the combined company would have been too monopolistic and would have possessed too much market power. The FTC came into existence in the early years of the twentieth century in order to regulate and prevent precisely this type of powerful business combination. To do so they often examine the structure of industries and how industry structure can increase or reduce competition. In the 1970s Harvard Business School professor Michael Porter proposed that instead of using principles of industry structure analysis to prevent monopolies from developing, the very same principles could be productively used by companies to guide them in the development and management of their strategies.[5] Companies want to be careful about not getting too close to the endpoint of the market continuum and creating a monopoly, because that would likely draw the wrath of the FTC and generate a huge regulatory backlash. However, the great insight of the industry analysis view is that a firm can generate competitive advantage and earn above-average profits if it uses tactics to move the market further away from perfect competition. How does it do this? In Chapters 5 through 7 we will explore how companies can develop specific types of activities and resources to create value uniquely. The strategic approaches that depend on these activities and resources will often involve consciously creating "barriers to entry" to the industry that a company competes in to prevent new companies from entering the industry, as well as "barriers to mobility" that make it difficult for other companies already in the industry to imitate what the company is doing. By creating these kinds of barriers, the company makes the industry less perfectly competitive. Sustainable competitive advantage is then possible when companies figure out how to take advantage of this type of imperfect market.[6]

STRUCTURE—CONDUCT—PERFORMANCE

2 Use structure industry analysis techniques to evaluate a market.

The structural analysis of an industry will allow us to develop clear insight about two characteristics of the industry that are helpful to a company in developing and executing its strategic approach. The first is an understanding about how businesses earn above-average profits while the second is how businesses identify and utilize key success factors.

Potential for Above-Average Profits

Industry analysis is a means by which we examine whether the nature of competitive forces makes an industry attractive or unattractive. In industries that are less perfectly competitive, the potential is greater for a company to earn superior returns. At this point one might ask, "Why is this important, since my company is already in an industry? Whatever that industry is, we just have to deal with it." The answer is that companies often make strategic choices to participate in an industry or not. Today most large companies operate in several industries, and companies are often engaged in acquisitions that may diversify their operations further into new industries (we will discuss this in depth in Chapter 10).[7] Not every industry is equally profitable; see Figure 4.2 for example. The prepackaged software industry has earned the highest return on invested capital over the seventeen-year period presented. Microsoft, a competitor in this industry, has amassed huge sums of cash as a consequence of its very profitable operations, and has used that cash to acquire other companies. While Microsoft might be interested in participating in the delivery of entertainment to the home, the profitability of the cable TV industry is well below the national average. Therefore, its route to get into home entertainment delivery would in all likelihood not involve starting up or acquiring a new business unit in this industry. When your grandfather took you fishing, he may have told you that "it's best to fish where the fish are." In this case it is generally better to participate in industries where there is a strong likelihood of earning profits rather than in industries where the average profitability is already depressed.

Key Success Factors

If your company is going to participate in an industry, **industry analysis** can provide guidance on how it should be done. The structure of every industry

Industry analysis
Means by which we examine whether the nature of competitive forces makes an industry attractive or unattractive.

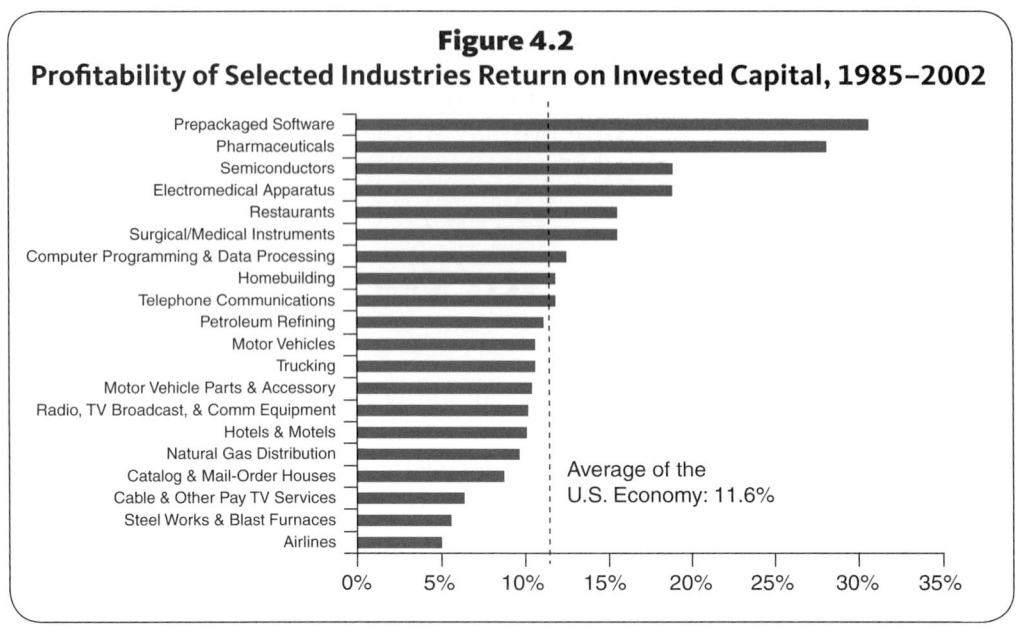

Figure 4.2
Profitability of Selected Industries Return on Invested Capital, 1985–2002

Average of the U.S. Economy: 11.6%

imposes constraints on and defines options for firms competing in it. For example, an agricultural business operating in the wheat market could not (in general) charge higher prices than the current market rate for wheat, because wheat is bought and sold as a commodity, with a virtually identical product readily available from many competitors. A company manufacturing PCs and laptops cannot afford to forgo innovation and product line upgrades, because its suppliers push new technology and its customers demand continual progress. In any industry there will always be a small number of key factors that characterize how to navigate the challenges that the industry presents. These **key success factors (KSFs)** are "rules of thumb" for operating that reflect the structural conditions of the industry. The KSFs identify the aspects of business that each company must pay attention to—and make strategic investments in—if it is to be successful in the industry. Think about an industry in the same way you might think about a game such as *Grand Theft Auto 4*, one of the most popular video games today produced by Rockstar North. The game operates a certain way, and there are actions that players must follow in order to help the main character, Niko, advance through the game and accomplish the primary mission of locating and dealing with a former acquaintance who betrayed his army unit. Side missions are possible and may be entertaining to the player, but pursuing these can increase the player's "wanted level" from the police and distract the player from accomplishing the primary mission in the game. Just as focusing on the main "location" missions in this game increases the likelihood of moving to higher levels, focusing on the key success factors in an industry also increases the odds of success for the company.

Key success factors (KSF) "Rules of thumb" for doing business in an industry that reflect the structural conditions of the industry.

We now see that the potential to earn superior returns in an industry partially results from the structure of the industry. We also see that the structure of an industry will suggest that there are certain fundamental basic rules, which are referred to as key success factors. These ideas help explain what is commonly known as the Structure-Conduct-Performance (SCP) paradigm in strategic management. SCP was historically used to describe the performance of entire industries, but has now become one of the foundations in strategic management for improving company performance.[8] The SCP perspective tells us that the structure of an industry helps determine rules for competing, forcing companies to conduct their business according to the rules. The company's conduct refers to its strategic approach and the types of strategic investments it makes (like manufacturing infrastructure or field sales force development) that support its approach. If the conduct of the company aligns with the KSFs suggested by the current structure of the industry, and presuming the company is effective in its actions, then the company's performance should be enhanced.

DEFINING AN INDUSTRY

3 *Employ strategy mapping techniques to identify strategic groups in an industry.*

Before we move on to analyzing an industry, we need to be clear what we mean by an "industry." An industry can generally be defined as a group of productive, profit-making, or value-creating enterprises[10] that draw upon related suppliers of various sorts, develop different kinds of customers, and compete with each other. Economists like to further narrow this definition by focusing on two types of possible substitutions: 1) substitutions for the consumption of a company's output, and 2) substitutions in supply/inputs to the company's production process.[11] A firm is included as a competitor in an industry if its products or services present alternatives for other companies' products or services

Zale Corporation was founded in 1924 by brothers Morris and William Zale in Wichita Falls, Texas. Using a pitch that included buying jewelry with "a penny down and a dollar a week," the Zale brothers grew their business as a place that was affordable to the average American family. Their tag line for the past fifty years has been "The Diamond Store." The company sold relatively inexpensive jewelry using a strategy that presented jewelry as good, better, and best in an effort to up-sell customers. Through acquisitions and growth, Zale Corporation now has seven distinct operations:

- Zales Jewelers
- Zales, The Diamond Store Outlet
- Gordon's Jewelers (high-end jewelry)
- People Jewelers
- Mappins Jewelers
- Bailey Banks & Biddle (high-end jewelry)
- Piercing Pagoda (mall-based jewelry for teens)

Net sales in 2004 were approximately $2.3 billion, which was a modest increase over the previous year's $2.2 billion. Competitors included virtually every major market supplier of jewelry:

Wal-Mart	Tiffany	Signet	Saks
QVC	Sears	JCPenney	May
Federated	Friedman's	Helzberg Diamonds	Target

Zale's target customer is the male shopper between the ages of twenty-five and sixty-five whose annual income averages between $40,000 and $75,000. Its best seller is the diamond solitaire, and most of its stores are in malls. Sales at Christmas 2004 were extremely disappointing for the second year in a row and the board of directors demanded some significant strategic action. Christmas is when the company books almost half of its sales and virtually all of its profit for the year.

QUESTIONS

1. What is your assessment of the market?
2. What characteristics and dimensions of this industry do you think will affect Zale's strategy?
3. Who would you consider your primary three or four competitors?

in the eyes of customers. If a price rise in another company's product would cause someone to buy your company's product instead, then the other company is considered a competitor (Figure 4.3). This is usually how we think about competition. However, competitors may also exist on the supply side of what a company does. Imagine a high-tech firm located in Silicon Valley, for example, that is seeking to expand its business and needs to hire well-trained programmers. Although the software that the company intends to produce is different from that offered by Apple, Oracle, and other software developers, the company must still compete with these companies for the trained people that will ensure its success. So a firm is also included as a competitor in an industry if it uses similar raw materials or employs similar production methods as other companies,

**Figure 4.3
Defining an Industry**

Similar Inputs → Competitors → Similar Outputs

even if the final products produced are not similar for consumers. In this case, since the company already competes with other companies for production inputs, it might then easily compete for customer business by producing similar products if the lure of potential profits is great enough.

It is important to recognize that industries can be defined differently, depending on who's doing the talking. For example, Staples and Office Depot sought the office supplies market as encompassing competitors as diverse as Circuit City (who largely sells audio and video equipment) and Wal-Mart (who largely sells general merchandise and food). On the other hand, the FTC defined the industry very narrowly, including only "one-stop-shop" office supply stores like Office Max and the local mom-and-pop shops that traditionally sold these goods. The narrowest industry definitions ordinarily involve the group of competitors who produce similar outputs *and* utilize similar inputs.

Sometimes industry definitions can be very confusing. For example, what industry classification do cell phones exist in? Until the mid-1990s it seemed very clear that cell phone manufacturers and cell phone service providers competed in the telephone industry, that is, in local and long distance calling. But consider the graphic that appeared in a national business magazine just a few years later, describing the multiple functions that cell phones now serve in multiple industries (Figure 4.4)[12] If a company is in the cell phone business today (equipment or service), it is not entirely clear how it might draw the boundaries around the industry. Here's another example: consider the "home entertainment" industry. Not long ago this industry included manufacturers of various kinds of equipment such as stereos, TVs, VCRs, and DVD players. But within the last few years technology has now enabled a host of new types of firms to go after the consumer home entertainment dollar. These include new equipment manufacturers as well as content providers: video game manufacturers, Internet-based gaming sites, video on demand from cable, downloadable music and video from Apple, Internet sites, and even your cell phone service provider. How to define the boundaries of an industry can be complicated, and can affect the kinds of conclusions drawn from an industry analysis.

As we shall see later on, an industry definition is very important to come to grips with. Broadly defined industries will usually require companies to engage in a variety of value-creating activities (Chapter 5) that depend upon developing broad and deep resource positions (Chapter 6) in order to be successful. Broadly defined industries usually encounter international competition or require international development, which of course place additional demands on companies. Narrowly defined industries, in contrast, allow companies to focus their efforts and resource investments more carefully. So the definition of the industry has implications for the boundaries of the competing firm and the kinds of capabilities it has to develop.

Basic information on virtually any industry can be obtained from the Internet, library, or data search engines. This data gathering should start with locating the **NAICS code** (North American Industry Classification

NAICS code (North American Industry Classification System) Generated by the U.S. government in an effort to gather, track, and publish data on specific industries (http://www.census.gov/epcd/www/naics.html).

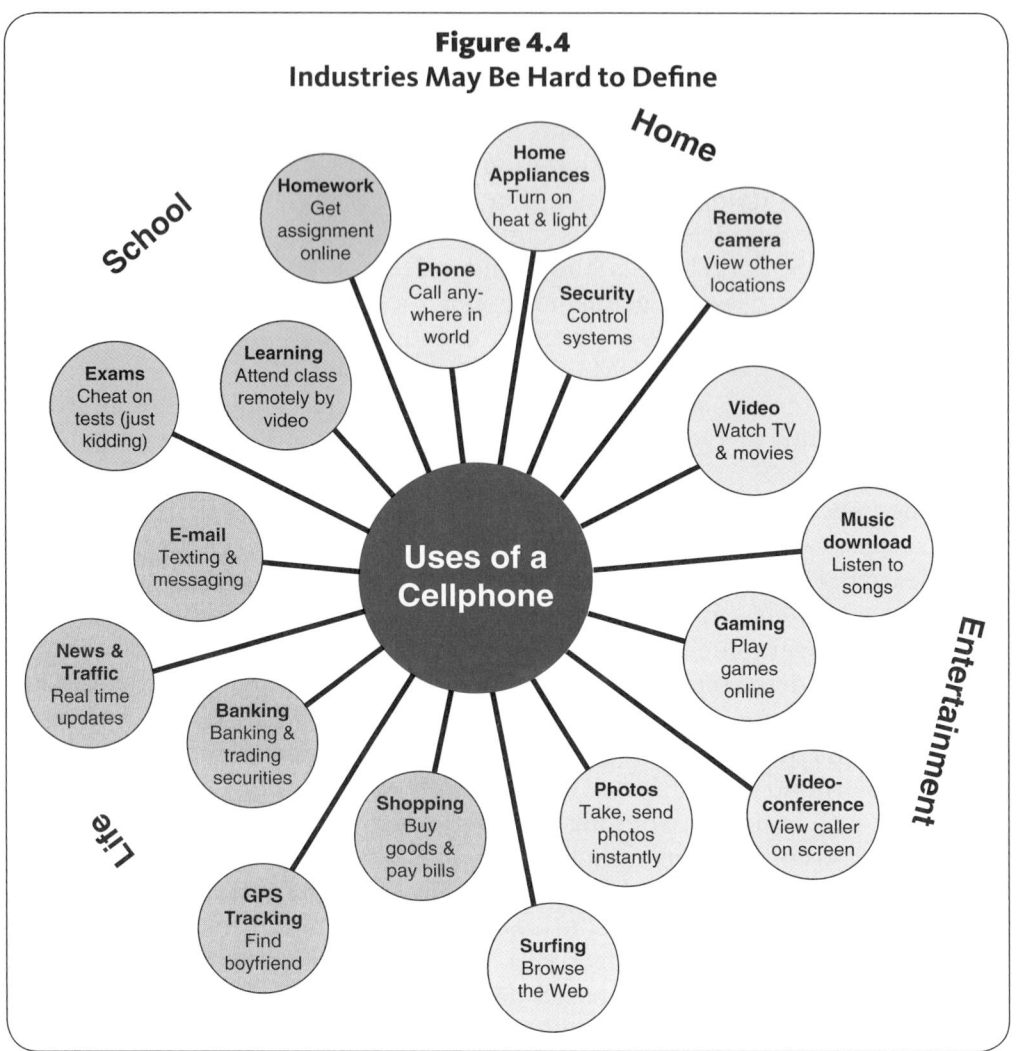

Figure 4.4
Industries May Be Hard to Define

School · *Home* · *Entertainment* · *Life*

Uses of a Cellphone

Homework Get assignment online

Home Appliances Turn on heat & light

Remote camera View other locations

Phone Call anywhere in world

Security Control systems

Exams Cheat on tests (just kidding)

Learning Attend class remotely by video

Video Watch TV & movies

Music download Listen to songs

E-mail Texting & messaging

Gaming Play games online

News & Traffic Real time updates

Banking Banking & trading securities

Shopping Buy goods & pay bills

Photos Take, send photos instantly

Video-conference View caller on screen

GPS Tracking Find boyfriend

Surfing Browse the Web

System) for the industry. An NAICS code (formerly known as a SIC or Standard Industrial Classification Code) is generated by the U.S. government in an effort to gather, track, and publish data on specific industries.[13] The code can vary from two to seven digits; the more digits, the more specific the industry classification. Figure 4.5 illustrates the NAICS classifications in which the office supplies industry (code 45321) is found, where Office Depot and Staples compete.

While there are many ways to obtain this code, there are two relatively simple means available. The first is to consult the list of NAICS codes available from the U.S. government (either at a library or on the Internet).[14] The second is to locate either your company or a public company that might be a direct competitor to your business and simply use their NAICS code to look up overall industry data on the industry (via *Dun & Bradstreet, Lexis/Nexis*, etc.).

At an aggregated national level the data gathered on a firm's industry has some value; however, it is the rare business that draws customers equally from all parts of the United States. Most of the data available will be on a national basis, but provides little understanding of the local, regional, or territory-specific competitive environment. The national industry may be doing very poorly while in a local area there may be few competitors or the industry is doing very well. Effective analysis requires a definition of the industry that is broad enough to be inclusive of all potential competitors, but not so broad as to negate effective evaluation. It is one part of the art of strategic management.

Figure 4.5
NAICS Codes for Office Supplies Industry

Code	Classification
45	Retail trade
453	Miscellaneous store retailers
4532	Office supplies, stationery, gift stores
45321	*Office supplies & stationery stores*
45322	Gift, novelty & souvenir stores

GENERAL ENVIRONMENT

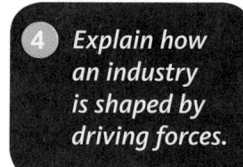
4 *Explain how an industry is shaped by driving forces.*

It is important to recognize that every industry is surrounded by a rich array of **exogenous** (meaning "outside" factors) **forces** in the general environment that have the ability to impact the growth of the industry and the nature of competition. These "driving forces" are conditions and trends in the general environment that no one company can change, but that every company in the industry must incorporate into its planning. Driving forces can have a variety of significant effects on an industry and the competition within it:

- Increase or decrease demand
- Increase or decrease supply or supply alternatives
- Create opportunity to provide greater value to customers
- Create higher costs for suppliers or buyers
- Create higher costs for rivals
- Lower barriers to entry and elevate the threat of new entrants
- Create a wider pool of potential substitutes

Strategy Acronym: STEEPG

Driving forces
S Social
T Technological
E Economic
E Environmental
P Political/Legal
G Global

These possible effects need to be figured into your analysis of the industry, because they suggest ways in which the nature of the industry may change over time.

Consider driving forces as equivalent to trying to drive on a really steep grade in a car or a four-wheel drive vehicle. No matter where you're trying to go, the grade is so steep that it will affect your direction and your speed, and if it is steep enough you may not get where you're trying to go. Therefore an

Exogenous forces
Forces outside the control of the business.

Figure 4.6
STEEPG: Driving Forces in the General Environment

Social

Demographic
- Population size & trends
- Age structure
- Geographic distribution
- Ethnic composition & segment growth
- Income distribution

Psychographic & Cultural
- Lifestyle
- Entertainment
- Convenience
- Women in workforce
- Work/home balance

Technology
- Discoveries in basic science
- Governmental support for R&D
- Broader availability of new technologies

Economic
- Inflation & interest rates
- General economic conditions—growth vs. recession
- Capital market availability
- Unemployment rates
- Exchange rates for currency translations

Environmental
- Increasing pressure for sustainable approaches
- Increasing attention to externalities of pollution
- Greater scrutiny about accessing natural resources

Political / Legal
- Antitrust laws & philosophy of enforcement
- Tax laws
- Legislation on corporate governance (Sarbanes Oxley Act, 2002)
- SEC regulations
- Labor related issues—minimum wage, health insurance, pension coverage
- Patent laws & changes
- Social expectations that can lead to political and legal initiatives

Global
- Political events
- Consolidating institutions—OPEC, European Economic Community
- Emerging markets—consumption, supply, finance
- Cultural sensitivities—moderating vs. escalating
- Terrorism and security issues

easy way to remember these forces is by using the acronym STEEPG, which is the combination of the first letters of each of the driving forces: social, technological, economic, environmental, political/legal, and global. Figure 4.6 provides a comprehensive list that categorizes types of driving forces in the general environment, with key dimensions for each category. While a comprehensive study of the various dimensions of these forces could take up an entire book by itself, we will highlight a few of these more carefully below to provide a sense of how powerful they may be.

Social driving forces are of two varieties: 1) demographic, and 2) psychographic, or cultural. Basic demographic structure and changes can have a dramatic impact on the nature of competition within industries. The clearest example of this impact is illustrated by your parents' generation, the often-discussed "baby boomers," which refers to U.S. citizens born in the years 1946–1964 (Figure 4.7). During this time U.S. birth rates spiked, creating a large new demographic segment defined by age. As this segment has aged through the decades, it has dramatically affected demand in an array of industries, including soft drinks, education, real estate, vacation homes, automobiles, investments, and now retirement planning. But it is the *combination* of basic demographics and the "psychographic," or cultural, factors that have affected industry growth, decline, and competition. For example, the first minivan was introduced by Chrysler in the 1980s, just as baby boomers were entering the lifestyle years of having their own families with young children. In contrast to other automobile manufacturers, Chrysler sensed the opportunity for a new kind of passenger vehicle by doing psychographic customer research rather than traditional demographic studies, in order to identify lifestyle needs of potential buyers.[15] During the same time period Sony and BMW made great headway in U.S. markets because this generation began to value "high status" possessions such as Walkman portable tape players and engineered imported cars. One other major cultural factor is worth mentioning, that of women in the workforce. Today 59 percent of women in America are in the workforce. Where this has resulted in a family with two working adults, it has had an economic effect in the form of higher disposable income per family and has led to the dramatic changes in industries as diverse as daycare and luxury vacations.

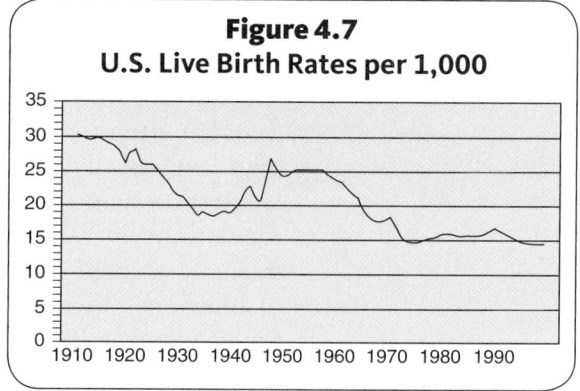

Figure 4.7
U.S. Live Birth Rates per 1,000

In the example mentioned earlier about the home entertainment industry, technology advances in microchip design, fiber optics, file compression algorithms, and many other developments have enabled new companies to begin competing with the traditional equipment manufacturers. These types of technological developments most often originate in other firms outside the industry or are discoveries made in science and research laboratories. Yet the new developments will diffuse throughout the economy and be used productively within many different industries. This can change the nature of competition.

ETHICS

Environmental factors are increasingly seen as driving forces in many industries today. It might seem that these effects would be most pronounced in basic manufacturing and in the kinds of suppliers that manufacturers rely upon for raw materials. So we read about pollution control equipment requirements on smokestacks and in runoff from factories that use large amounts of water. However, environmental concerns are expressed in ways that affect us in our daily lives, as well. For example, Hewlett Packard and other companies that provide laser and inkjet toner cartridges now include recycling instructions and mail-back envelopes in every package they sell. The Environmental Protection Agency issued a report that clears the way for lawn mowers, watercraft, and other users of small gas-powered engines below 50 horsepower to meet tougher emissions standards.[16] Engineering these more stringent standards into small engines will raise the cost of manufacturing these products and we will likely see higher prices in stores. On the plus side, of course, our back yards and lakes will have much cleaner air as a result!

Political and legal forces can come and go, but their presence is always felt. During the 1990s there was relatively less attention on antitrust issues than has been the case at other times in recent history. On the other hand, a high level of mergers and acquisitions by U.S. firms during the same decade led to the issuance of new Financial Accounting and Standards Boards (FASB) regulations in 2001 that governed how the combining of two businesses must be treated by the accounting profession. FASB eliminated "pooling of interests" as an acceptable method of accounting for business combinations, which allowed companies to add together the book values of their net assets without indicating which entity was the "purchaser" and which was the "purchased." When this method was used, investors often had difficulty telling who was buying whom or determining how to evaluate the transactions. Instead, FASB favored the "purchase method" of accounting for mergers. With the purchase method, one company is identified as the buyer and records the assets of the company being acquired on its books at the price it actually paid. This led to greater transparency for investors. One of the most comprehensive, frame-breaking pieces of legislation to directly affect business in recent times was the passage of the **Sarbanes-Oxley Act (SOX)** in 2002. This legislative initiative responded to violations of financial reporting by Enron, WorldCom, and other companies by imposing stiff new demands on companies and their auditors to ensure that published financial statements are accurate.

ETHICS

In addition to explicit political and legal forces, we add a final dimension to this category that has been increasingly important for companies to pay attention to: social expectations that could become political and legal initiatives. SOX is an example of a social concern about business that was institutionalized into a body of law, largely because companies were often perceived as acting in ways detrimental to their shareholders. There is a whole class of social issues that falls into this gray area, such as environmental concerns, offshoring jobs to countries with lower wage rates, or privacy and data protection issues. A survey by *McKinsey Quarterly* found an overwhelming

Sarbanes-Oxley Act (SOX) The legislative initiative enacted in 2002 that imposes stiff new demands on companies and their auditors to ensure that published financial statements are accurate.

majority of their readers felt that corporations needed to take on a wider role in dealing with these issues, something that goes beyond simply producing returns for their investors.[17] The implied **social contract** that businesses have today with the communities and societies within which they exist has become a standard that is embraced by the public and will most likely result in greater regulation that affects how industries function.

FIVE-FORCES ANALYSIS

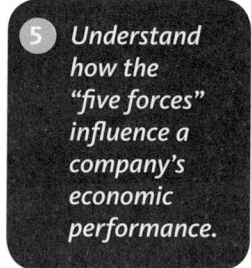

5 Understand how the "five forces" influence a company's economic performance.

An analysis of the industry is possible once the industry has been defined and we gain a better understanding of the forces in the general environment that can affect it. There are a number of techniques available to perform this type of analysis, with five forces and competitive mapping being the most popular.

The Harvard Business School professor we mentioned earlier, Michael Porter, developed the five-forces model in the 1970s to examine the five main structural elements in any industry; Figure 4.8 provides a summary of these forces. This model expands the way we think about competition. Untrained, one might view only direct competitors and their competitive success as the primary determinant of the economic performance of a company. However, the **five-forces model** explicitly acknowledges the roles that new entrants, substitutes, buyers, suppliers, and rivalry also play in this equation. In the process of considering the five forces, every effort should be made to evaluate the extent to which each force influences how the industry is either more or less profitable for the set of competitors. Five-forces analysis is used as a strong first step in understanding how one industry compares to another.

Threat of New Entrants

Industries that tend to be profitable (see Figure 4.2) are attractive to companies outside the industry because they see the possibility of entering the industry and participating in the profit-making. New entrants may take the form of either startup companies going into business for the first time, or existing companies that decide to grow by entering new markets. Existing companies are the most challenging new competitors when they enter an industry since they may possess a set of capabilities and financial resources that allow them to enter in a big way. Regardless of whether they are a start-up or an existing company, new entrants will tend to expand industry capacity as they seek to sell goods and services to the same customers currently being serviced by the **incumbent firms**. Expanded capacity has the tendency to lead to downward pricing pressure on industry competitors for several reasons: 1) each company wants to ensure that its existing capacity continues to be fully utilized; 2) companies feel the overwhelming need to grow sales regardless of industry dynamics; 3) companies may mistakenly believe that market share is of primary importance; and 4) greater availability generally leads buyers to look for bargains. Competition for the same customers will lead to higher levels of marketing, sales, and promotional expenses by all competitors as the requirements for differentiation continually increase (i.e., the "why should I buy from you?" question). Finally, unless new entrants to an industry can significantly expand overall industry revenue, the **profit pool** that is

Social contract Implied relationship between businesses and the communities in which they operate.

Five-forces model A model originally created by Michael Porter to examine the various aspects of the competitive environment. The model consists of new entrants, substitutes, suppliers, buyers, and rivalry.

Incumbent firms Established firms in the industry.

Profit pool Generally the amount of profit available in the industry in a particular period of time.

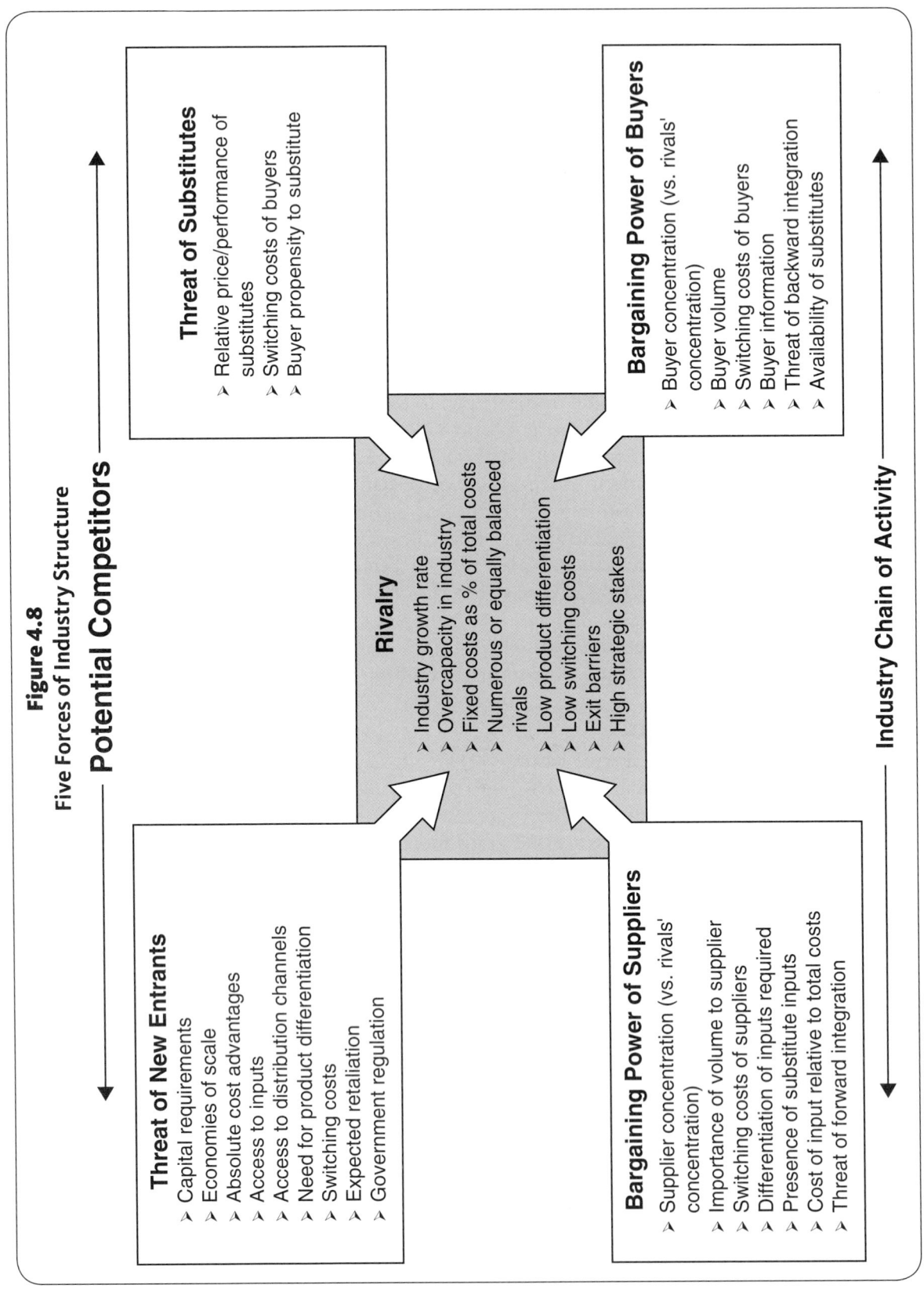

Figure 4.8
Five Forces of Industry Structure

Potential Competitors

Threat of New Entrants
- Capital requirements
- Economies of scale
- Absolute cost advantages
- Access to inputs
- Access to distribution channels
- Need for product differentiation
- Switching costs
- Expected retaliation
- Government regulation

Threat of Substitutes
- Relative price/performance of substitutes
- Switching costs of buyers
- Buyer propensity to substitute

Rivalry
- Industry growth rate
- Overcapacity in industry
- Fixed costs as % of total costs
- Numerous or equally balanced rivals
- Low product differentiation
- Low switching costs
- Exit barriers
- High strategic stakes

Bargaining Power of Buyers
- Buyer concentration (vs. rivals' concentration)
- Buyer volume
- Switching costs of buyers
- Buyer information
- Threat of backward integration
- Availability of substitutes

Bargaining Power of Suppliers
- Supplier concentration (vs. rivals' concentration)
- Importance of volume to supplier
- Switching costs of suppliers
- Differentiation of inputs required
- Presence of substitute inputs
- Cost of input relative to total costs
- Threat of forward integration

Industry Chain of Activity

available in any given year will be spread across a greater number of competitors, on average reducing the potential profits available to any one company. Therefore, the combination of a greater number of competitors, lower prices, and increased expenses diminish the potential for the existing firms in the industry to generate revenue and profits.

This threat of new entrants is considerably reduced if substantive barriers can be erected in the industry. Existing competitors may attempt to reduce the threat of new entrants by building entry barriers to raise the costs to start business in the industry. In turn, higher entry costs prompt potential entrants to question whether they can afford to enter the industry, or make sufficient profits once they have entered. On the flip side, current competitors must weigh the cost of erecting barriers with the potential downside of additional competitors. There are several significant varieties of barriers to entry (Figure 4.9) and we discuss each of these next.

Figure 4.9
Threat of New Entrants

Threat of New Entrants
➤ Capital requirements
➤ Economies of scale
➤ Absolute cost advantages
➤ Access to inputs
➤ Access to distribution channels
➤ Need for product differentiation
➤ Switching costs
➤ Expected retaliation
➤ Government regulation

Capital requirements. Starting up a new business in an industry generally involves a significant commitment of capital. For example, in a manufacturing industry a new entrant would need to invest in a manufacturing facility, production assembly line, tools and dies, as well as build inventories of raw materials and finished goods. Depending on the industry, this can involve a huge outlay. The restaurant industry experiences a very high level of new entrants, and yet establishing even one restaurant location can be costly. A typical stand-alone Krispy Kreme outlet, which makes only doughnuts and coffee, might cost $1.5 million or more to build. If a company wanted to compete against Best Buy in the home electronics retailing industry, the inventory alone to set up and stock a comparable-sized store would cost millions of dollars. In our experience, students often believe that it would be fairly easy to set up an Internet business by developing a Web site fairly quickly. However, the kinds of Web-based businesses that promise the potential for sustainable advantage will usually involve spending an initial investment upwards of $250,000 to develop a sophisticated Web site, back-end database, and the programming that smoothly integrates the two.

Economies of scale. In some industries the ability to compete will depend on whether a company can produce its product or service at a cost that is low enough to offer low competitive prices. Low costs are sometimes achieved because companies produce on a large scale where the benefits of volume translate directly to unit cost reductions. Economies of scale characterize many industries, including automobiles, packaged consumer products, and computer manufacturing. They are often achieved as a direct result of huge investments in physical infrastructure, which raises the initial capital requirements (e.g., barrier to entry) mentioned earlier.

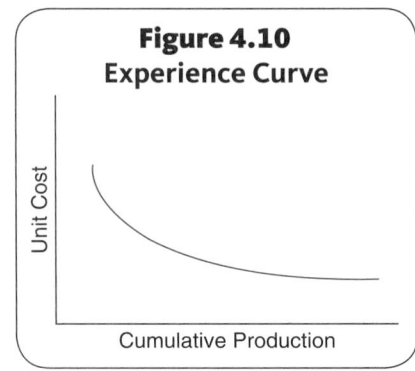

Figure 4.10
Experience Curve

Unit Cost

Cumulative Production

Absolute cost advantages. New entrants may be deterred from entering an industry if the incumbent firms in the industry enjoy a cost advantage that comes only from having been in the industry for a while. The usual type of absolute cost advantage derives from what is known as the **experience curve**, in which cost reductions per unit produced are based upon cumulative production over time (in contrast to economies of scale, in which unit cost reductions are associated with volume during a fixed time interval). With greater experience the company learns about subtle and not-so-subtle new procedures that can contribute to cost reductions. Figure 4.10 diagrams the classic experience curve relationship. It is important to note that the entry barrier of experience holds only if the learning that comes through experience cannot be easily appropriated by new entrants through hiring away a competitor's employees, purchasing machinery or equipment that incorporates the refined production practice, or somehow copying what the competitor is doing. A second type of absolute cost advantage occurs when an existing competitor has developed a unique and proprietary design for a product or manufacturing process that may be obvious to others, but which is protected through patents. In this case a new entrant would have to invent a new way to produce a particular product, and often this will involve significantly greater expense.

Access to inputs. Barriers to entry exist when raw materials or important inputs are not available to potential new entrants. A group wishing to start a new hamburger restaurant needs a good-quality, high-traffic location. However, the best street corner locations in your community might already be occupied by other businesses (or by McDonald's itself!). Once these prime corner locations are occupied, then there are simply no more available. Moving from the mundane to the sublime, the DeBeers Company has nearly exclusive access to South African diamond mines, making it exceedingly difficult for any other potential competitor to gain access to the raw materials.

Access to distribution channels. Companies that desire to enter an industry may discover that they are unable to gain access to customers. If a new company wanted to introduce a cola- or lemon-flavored soda into the soft drink industry, for example, it would need to find a bottler to mix its concentrate with water and CO_2, bottle it, and distribute it. However, the major bottlers and canners are contractually locked into long-term deals with existing soft drink competitors and are therefore prevented from bottling competing cola or lemon soda products. In other cases, access to distribution may be difficult because prospective customers simply place limits on the number of companies with whom they do business. In the food business, supermarkets have limited shelf space and are only interested in carrying proven products that will sell quickly. In the financial industry, companies often provide a limited set of mutual fund alternatives to employees for investing through their retirement programs, so other financial firms seeking to offer new mutual funds may be excluded from consideration.

Experience curve
Cost reductions per unit produced that are based upon cumulative production over time (in contrast to economies of scale, in which unit cost reductions are associated with volume during a fixed time interval).

Switching costs. Customer resistance to new entrants may also arise due to the costs to switch to the new competitor's product or service (both real and perceived). The costs involved in changing buying habits include the real costs of time, price, new buying patterns, inventory turnover, and customer service as well as perceived costs, including reputation, history, market image, and comfort. Many folks who began using personal computers in the early 1980s have been forced to learn a continuing series of newer word processing, spreadsheet, and systems packages throughout the years. Switching from Edline to WordStar to VolksWriter Deluxe to WordPerfect to Microsoft Word was a painful, slow process that appeared necessary to be able to enjoy the benefits of writing on computers. Today it would be quite difficult to convince those same customers to switch to a new word processing package as both the real and perceived costs to switch from Word would appear enormous.

Consider the switching costs related to changing soft drinks. There are virtually no real switching costs involved. Actual consumers do not have to learn how to open the can or bottle in a new way, swallowing is unchanged, the purchase price is virtually identical, and availability is not an issue. For the retailer who stocks soft drinks, the same size cans and bottles require no new handling in their warehouses or stores, and promotional displays are built the same way as before. However, there are enormous *perceived* switching costs involved in convincing a Coke drinker to move to Pepsi and vice versa. Take a look at a typical advertisement by these two rivals. The advertisements focus exclusively on perceptions, not on their quality ingredients, extraordinarily clean environments, nor on their Rocky Mountain Spring Water! Similarly, for most retailers the strength of long-term supply relationships with Coca-Cola and Pepsi may make it difficult to switch out to Uncle Jethro's Wicked Cola or some other new concoction.

Real switching costs can take many forms. For instance, those individuals who live near and fly out of Atlanta or Dallas generally fly on Delta or American Airlines, and by doing so accumulate mileage under Delta's SkyMiles or American's Advantage programs. These programs encourage customers to remain loyal to the airlines, and create real switching costs for those customers when they consider flying on another airline. A Platinum traveler on Delta has priority boarding, a high chance for upgrading to first class on many flights, and a reduced membership fee for the Delta Room Club. Each of these items has a real, tangible value that would have to be overcome by a competitor for a traveler to switch to another airline.

Need for product differentiation. In most industries, existing competitors have carefully crafted a brand image and reputation that helps generate a continuing customer base. One of the key elements of strategy is the positioning of the business in a space that differentiates it in the mind of customers relative to the businesses' competitors. Similarly, in established industries new entrants most often find they must effectively differentiate each of their products or services. Often this will involve major marketing and sales expenditures on advertising, promotion, sales force development, and penetration in order to create a unique positioning in the minds of customers.[18]

Government regulation. "Big Brother"—in the form of federal, state, and local government—can have an enormous effect on the propensity for new firms to enter an industry. In order to enter the food manufacturing industry, every new entrant must at a minimum be in compliance with FDA rules or may be required to have all of the new firm's products, packaging, and processes approved in advance and regularly inspected by USDA. Starting a restaurant requires that the new business meet all state and local health regulations, submit to regular inspections, and post those results in the public view. All of this takes significant time and expense, which is only indirectly related to the reason that customers patronize the business. Every industry has its own unique set of regulations, required licenses, and personnel to ensure compliance. If the costs of starting a new business are onerous, then the rate of new entrants will be dramatically reduced. Despite the enormous operational advantages to the use of nuclear power, new power stations in the United States have been at a virtual standstill since the late 1970s. The primary reason has been government regulation. Those wishing to build, operate, attain fuel rods, and then dispose of those same fuel rods face an almost Herculean set of regulations and regulators. The impact of the government regulation has been crushing to the growth of the industry in the United States.

When new start-up companies are possible new entrants, regulation by various countries' governments can be a significant constraining force. Whereas in the United States it takes an average of about five days to complete five procedures to start up a new company and costs only 1.5 percent of average personal income, government regulations in some other countries are onerous and can significantly impede foreign new-venture competition. For example, in Greece new companies must complete fifteen separate steps that take thirty-eight days on average, at a cost of nearly 25 percent of average personal income.

Expected retaliation. New entrants in any established industry should not expect existing competitors to sit idly by and watch another company compete for their customers. Retaliation by existing competitors is increased when the following conditions exist: 1) there is a history of such retaliation in the industry; 2) the existing competitors have deep pockets and plenty of resources to devote to more intense competition; 3) the existing competitors have already sunk significant costs in building infrastructure or establishing a market position, and a loss of business would create financial pressures; and 4) the industry is not growing quickly, meaning that any business for a new entrant must come from an existing competitor. In April 2006, low-cost carrier JetBlue Airlines announced that they would begin daily nonstop service from Charlotte to New York City's LaGuardia Airport beginning in July 2006. Tickets went on sale for the equivalent of half the current market price of the major airlines flying out of Charlotte. Within two weeks all of the major airlines announced dramatic fare reductions to NYC in a bid to retain their customers. When Tiger Woods broke into the professional golf circuit and started winning tournaments by out-driving other pros off the tee and showing pinpoint short-club accuracy, what did the other pros do? They increased their physical training regimens and began spending longer hours in practice. His entry changed the game.

Threat of Substitutes

Substitutes are products or services that perform the same function or meet the same need as the products or services in the industry under study, but which are produced using different raw materials and inputs. The classic example that economists use is coffee, tea, and sodas; the competitors to Starbucks or Folgers would be other brands of coffee, whereas Lipton tea and Coca-Cola would be viewed as substitutes. The availability of substitutes can have two impacts on industry competition and profitability. First, they establish a price ceiling for products and services in the industry; exceeding the ceiling would prompt customers to take flight to the substitute products that are available. Second, substitutes can prompt the competitors in an industry to ramp up their marketing and promotional efforts to stem the outflow of customers. Together these put pressure on competitors in the industry to keep prices low and to spend more to attract and retain customers, which can depress sales and profits in the industry. Today bottled water and sports drinks, as substitutes, have significantly impacted the traditional soft-drink industry, which in 2005 experienced its first volume decline in U.S. sales in twenty years.[19]

Three factors determine how strong the threat of substitutes will be for an industry. These include: 1) the relative price/performance of the substitute products; 2) the switching costs for the buyer to obtain and use the substitute; and 3) buyers' propensity to try substitute products or services. Substitution tends to increase when the substitute's price is equal to or lower than prices of incumbents and the value to the buyer is equal to or greater. In this case the value to buyers can sometimes be satisfied more economically by turning to companies outside the industry. If the costs for buyers to switch to substitutes are also fairly low, then even greater pressure may be exerted on the competitors' ability to generate sales, as buyers then have even less reason to remain loyal. Finally, although many buyers and consumers maintain loyalty to companies and brands, today there appears to be a greater psychological willingness to experiment and try alternatives. Often this willingness to experiment with substitutes springs from characteristics of the relationship between companies and their customers, going far beyond mere product or service characteristics. Figure 4.11 offers additional examples of increasing substitution.

Whereas the threat of new entrants will usually depend on the attractiveness of the industry, an increase in the threat of substitutes depends on the dynamics of *other* industries. Competitors should watch for warning signals that pressure from substitutes may be increasing. For example, in the early 1990s the soft-drink aisle in most supermarkets contained beverages on one side and snacks and chips on the other side. By the late 1990s the aisle had become the "beverage" aisle, with soft drinks on one side and bottled waters on the other. It was obvious that consumers were flocking to bottled waters, and beginning to drink them instead of soft drinks. The major soft-drink companies all made the move to add bottled water to their product offerings. Warning signs that companies in substitute product industries might be getting more aggressive include production capacity increases, significant accumulations of cash, merger

Substitutes Products or services that perform the same function or meet the same need as the products or services in the industry under study, but which are produced using different raw materials and inputs.

Figure 4.11
Threat of Substitutes

Factors Increasing Substitution	Examples
High relative price/performance	Making airline reservations online, compared to using a travel agency.
	Downloading MP3 music to your iPod, compared to buying CDs in music stores.
Low switching costs	Soft-drink companies used corn syrup as a sweetener instead of sugar, because it required no changes in operations.
	Consumers can now buy electricity for their homes from wind farms, by merely signing a form and sending it in to their power company.

and acquisition activity, as well as significant technological changes. The addition of production capacity signals that substitute producers might want to get more aggressive in pricing and marketing in order to fully utilize available capacity. In addition when profits are growing, such companies might consider investing additional marketing dollars to broaden their customer base.

Bargaining Power of Buyers

Buyers affect the profitability of the industry's competitors with their purchase choices. The profitability levels in any industry are determined by the bargaining power that buyers have in purchasing goods and services offered. Buyers may affect profitability by demanding that competitors spend money to deliver other valued dimensions such as enhanced product quality, extended payment terms, promotional support, and other services. Buyers will often pit competitors against one another in order to negotiate the best terms possible. The ability of buyers to extract various economic concessions depends on the variety of factors shown in Figure 4.12.

Buyer concentration. It is important to remember that an industry analysis is an examination of the *structure* of the entire industry. This reminder is very important when we talk about the bargaining power of buyers that may result from buyer concentration. Here we are not discussing the bargaining power that any one buyer (such as Wal-Mart) may have with its suppliers;

Figure 4.12
Bargaining Power of Buyers

➢ Buyer concentration (vs. rivals' concentration)
➢ Buyer volume
➢ Switching costs of buyers
➢ Buyer information
➢ Threat of backward integration
➢ Availability of substitutes

instead we are referring to the structure of buyers as an entire group. A high level of buyer concentration means that there are just a few major buyers in an industry, and each one on average commands a significant share of the market. Under these circumstances competitors have few meaningful alternative places to sell their products. Furthermore, the loss of any one buyer to a competitor would create a dramatic shift in the industry: the company would lose significant sales and market share, which would be entirely taken up by a direct competitor. These conditions make it likely that buyers would be able to exert significant pressure on the companies in this industry to either reduce prices or provide additional services, or both.

Buyer concentration can be measured in one of a couple ways. A relatively easily calculated measure of concentration is simply referred to as the **concentration ratio**, which is the percentage of market share in the industry owned by the largest buyer firms. The U.S. government often looks closely at the concentration ratio of the largest four firms, known as CR_4. If this measure is less than 40 percent, then it suggests the industry is very competitive, with no buyer owning a very large market position. Concentration ratios are the "quick and dirty" method for determining concentration, but the measure is incomplete because it captures only the largest firms in the industry. In its place, the Herfindahl-Hirschman Index (HHI) is often used, because it provides a more complete portrayal of industry concentration. The HHI uses the market shares of all the firms in an industry to calculate a measure that can range from 0 to 10,000 (see Figure 4.13 for how to calculate the concentration ratio and HHI). The FTC uses HHI as a guideline for evaluating mergers. An HHI between 1,000 and 1,800 signals moderate concentration, while an HHI exceeding 1,800 reflects an industry that is considered highly concentrated. A merger of Staples and Office Depot would have produced an HHI greater than 5,000, while as the opening case illustrates, the HHI for the supermarket buyers in Denver for Championship Chili was greater than 2,600. In these two examples companies selling to these highly concentrated groups would be subject to intense bargaining power of buyers.

Buyer volume. Similar to buyer concentration, if buyers purchase a high percentage of goods and services produced by companies in the industry, it means that the producing companies cannot afford to lose that business. Under these circumstances buyers have the potential to demand additional services, changes, and/or price concessions.

Switching costs of buyers. In a similar manner to the earlier discussion about switching costs under the "Threat of New Entrants" section, as switching

---

Figure 4.13
Calculating Concentration

Concentration Ratio

The concentration ratio uses the formula:

$$CR_m = s_1 + s_2 + s_3 + \cdots + s_m$$

where m is the number of firms to be examined, and s_j is the market share of the jth firm.

Evaluation of CR_4:

< 40	very competitive industry
40–70	moderately concentrated
> 70	highly concentrated

Herfindahl-Hirschman Index (HHI)

The HHI uses the formula:

$$HHI = s_1^2 + s_2^2 + s_3^2 + \cdots + s_n^2$$

where n is the number of firms in the industry, and s_j is the market share of the jth firm.

Evaluation of HHI:

< 1,000	very competitive industry
1,001–1,800	moderately concentrated
> 1,800	highly concentrated

Increases in HHI by more than 100–200 raise serious anti-trust concerns in markets where HHI is greater than 1,800.

Concentration ratio
The percentage of market share in the industry owned by the largest firms.

costs (both real and perceived) go down, the relative power of the buyers is increased. With lower costs there is less to keep buyers loyal to incumbent producers. In the past it was really a pain to switch cell phone service providers because you could not keep your cell number and would then have to let everyone know that your number had changed. Today the new "portability" law means that the cost of switching from one provider to another has been significantly reduced and therefore buyer power has been increased.

Buyer information. The advance of technology has dramatically increased the power of buyers. Whereas most buyers were previously limited in their knowledge of competitive pricing, product availability, and comparisons of the features of competitive products, the advent of technology has created an empowered buyer. Until the mid-1980s, for example, food manufacturers used to conduct their own research on product sales and market shares in supermarkets using third-party research firms like A. C. Nielsen, and would then present their findings to supermarket category buyers. With the advent of UPC scanning technology and personal computers, supermarket buyers could capture data instantaneously about sales in their stores, and they in turn presented this to the salespeople who called on them. Today the roll-out of RFID (radio frequency identification) technology allows even greater information about sales, inventory levels, product locations, and more. Information asymmetry refers to a situation where either the buyer or the seller has information that gives that party a competitive advantage in the sales transaction. As the availability of good buyer information increases, so does the buyer's power.

Threat of backward integration. Buyers may decide to simply produce the product or service that was previously being purchased from someone in the industry. Frustration with the current companies in the industry, an excess amount of buyer cash, a desire to control the whole process, ego, and a host of other factors may encourage a particular buyer to integrate a business backward by developing or acquiring capacity in the industry. This is particularly true if buying organizations observe that the competitive rivals in an industry are earning attractive levels of profits and returns. This is one reason why many supermarket chains now produce and stock their own "private label" food products.

Figure 4.14
Bargaining Power of Suppliers

➢ Supplier concentration (vs. rivals' concentration)
➢ Importance of volume to supplier
➢ Switching costs of suppliers
➢ Differentiation of inputs required
➢ Presence of substitute inputs
➢ Cost of input relative to total costs
➢ Threat of forward integration

Bargaining Power of Suppliers

Similar to buyers, suppliers have the ability to exert their own power upon the competitors in an industry. This power manifests itself in price pressures, availability issues, services provided, and speed of technological advancement. Figure 4.14 presents a list of factors that can impact supplier power.

Supplier concentration. The same methods of concentration analysis are performed for supplier concentration analysis as they are for the buyer analysis. As the number of suppliers becomes more concentrated in a few businesses, the more they will be able to control the interactions between the producers and themselves. Intel and AMD, for example, have manufactured a majority of the computer chips used as the "brain" in personal computers for the past three decades. This power has allowed them to set the pricing, availability, and features available to the many manufacturers of personal computers. Several businesses have attempted to enter this business with the strong backing of the personal computer manufacturers; however their success has been limited.

Importance of volume to supplier. As the volume of material that producing businesses buy from the suppliers increases, the importance of the suppliers to the businesses increases. A common theme in the business press is one of reducing the number of suppliers and forging long-term relationships with a few suppliers. While this does provide an element of control to the process, those selected suppliers are also in an increasingly powerful role relative to the company they supply.

Presence of substitute inputs. Businesses work very hard to develop their products with particular inputs going into the final product. In cases of supply disruption, raw material shortages, or supplier efforts to raise prices, the presence of effective substitutes will dampen the impact of that supplier's power. For example, though the perfect input for fueling your car as it is currently manufactured is a petroleum oil derivative, corn-based ethanol is proving to be a powerful substitute as traditional gas prices rise.

Cost of input relative to total costs. The power of suppliers is increased as the cost of the input increases relative to the total cost of the product or service produced. If the suppliers' input is 25 percent of the value of the total product produced, then suppliers will have significantly more leverage when compared to an industry where the suppliers' part is worth only 1 percent of the final value of the product. This is especially true if substitutes for the input are not available.

Switching costs of suppliers. Once again, the cost to switch suppliers (both real and perceived) is a factor in the power of the supplier. The more companies in an industry tie their operations to certain types of supplies or highly specified inputs, the more power such suppliers have with these companies. In today's market, many companies are tying their operations very closely with select suppliers in order to get guaranteed just-in-time deliveries, advanced access to new technology, more favorable pricing, guaranteed prices, and first options on products. Supplier management is a two-edged sword since the higher degree to which producers lock themselves in to suppliers, the greater leverage such suppliers will then have to exact economic concessions from the producers.

Threat of forward integration. Just as buyers have the ability to integrate backward to replace their suppliers, suppliers have the ability to integrate forward and become a competitor to the businesses that they may still supply. Honda has produced engines for many small pieces of power equipment. In addition, they now sell their own line of lawn maintenance equipment and portable generators. Similarly, Home Depot acquired one of the major plumbing supply operations in the United States. This supply business is one of the main sources from which plumbers have historically purchased items for their own business. In addition, Home Depot now offers plumbing services to its customers, thus moving into the business of the plumbers.

Intensity of Rivalry

The intensity of competition among rivals varies from industry to industry. Although we often read that many organizations believe they are in a chaotic, intense, cost-conscious, highly competitive industry, the fact remains that not all industries experience the same level of intensity. Each industry or industry subset should be evaluated with a set of criteria (Figure 4.15) that may then be used to understand the intensity of competition. Recall that it is important to define the industry and the rivals in it; the most important rivals are those companies who are in direct competition with a company for its customers *and* for the same types of supplies or inputs to production. This may or may not be the entire industry as defined by the government or the popular press.

Industry growth rate. Every industry has a rate of growth that ranges from negative to explosively positive. While one might believe that either of the extremes would lead to more intense rivalry amongst competitors, the simple fact is that slowing or negative industry growth rates lead to destructive patterns of corporate behavior and dramatically increase the rivalry. Consider the U.S. automobile industry during periods of average-to-poor growth in sales. If one of the auto manufacturers wants to increase sales revenue over its previous year, in a flat or declining industry the *only* way to do this is to take business away from one of its competitors. In contrast, when an industry is enjoying fast growth in revenue dollars and units shipped, then an individual company may also increase sales without necessarily having to take it from a competitor. In growth markets all companies may grow and prosper, but in a stagnant or declining market companies will become extremely aggressive in either trying to grow their business or prevent declines.

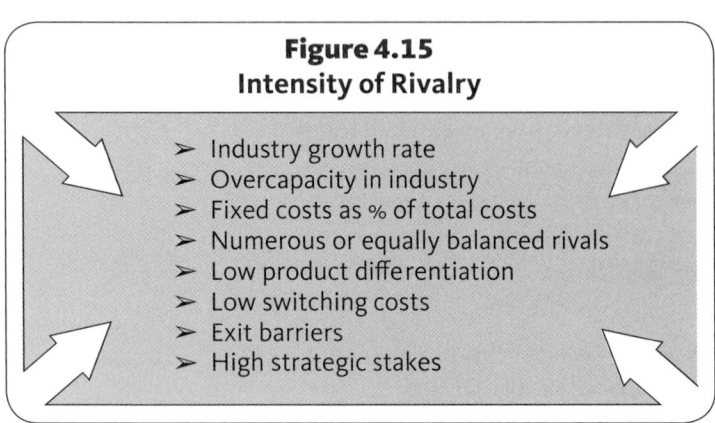

Figure 4.15
Intensity of Rivalry

➤ Industry growth rate
➤ Overcapacity in industry
➤ Fixed costs as % of total costs
➤ Numerous or equally balanced rivals
➤ Low product differentiation
➤ Low switching costs
➤ Exit barriers
➤ High strategic stakes

Industry capacity. The sheer capacity of the industry has a significant effect upon industry rivalry. Throughout the 1980s, many firms spent billions laying fiber optic cable in a bid to take advantage of the cutting-edge needs of an expanding Internet. Within several years the bubble burst as cable supply far outstripped demand. By 2001, utilization rates ran around 40 percent and prices dropped almost 80 percent as cable operators tried competitively low rates in order to generate enough business to pay back the investment they made in laying the fiber optics.[20] The same dynamic is true in the auto industry. Here excess plant capacity as well as fixed union contracts represent huge financial burdens. So U.S. manufacturers have repeatedly turned to intensely competitive "employee pricing" and "dealer rebate" schemes in order to generate sales and keep the plants producing and the paid union workers making cars.

Industries with too little capacity to meet the buying desires of customers will find that there is less industry rivalry relative to an industry where there is dramatic overcapacity. Where industry demand exceeds industry capacity, rivals do not need to turn to intensely competitive tactics. If we were to examine the narrow industry subsegment of electric cars, for example, we would find that consumer demand far exceeds industry supply. So in 2006 while Ford was discounting F-150 pickups trucks and General Motors was discounting Impala four-door sedans, Toyota did not discount the Prius, which sells very close to MSRP (manufacturer's suggested retail price).[21] The situation spiraled out of control by late 2008, when auto sales were dropping by double-digit percentages every month.

Numerous or equally balanced rivals. Another means for evaluating the relative intensity in the industry is to examine the source of sales in the industry. A widely fragmented market with lots of competitors leads to practices that are detrimental to the success of any one company. Dry cleaners appear on virtually every corner of every populated area in the United States. Price changes and competitive moves to differentiate oneself in this industry are quickly copied by all the other companies in the immediate area. Similarly, rivalry can become intense even in fairly concentrated industries with only a few major players, such as the personal computer manufacturing industry. Here price changes and moves to differentiate oneself are also quickly copied by competitors in an effort to maintain market share. The key point here is that relative equality among competitors—whether in a fragmented or concentrated industry environment—tends to make those competitors fight against each other to a greater extent as each seeks to develop a superior position.

Product or service differentiation. The degree of separation between the offerings of different companies has a significant impact upon the intensity of rivalry. In industries where the competitors have been able to establish a significant level of differentiation among their products, the intensity of rivalry is sharply reduced. Charlotte, North Carolina, is like so many other communities across the United States in that it has several member-only country clubs within the area. While each offers its members golf, tennis, and restaurant privileges, each has effectively carved out its own unique clientele and specialty offerings within this regional industry. There is a healthy competition among the various clubs, but the level of rivalry is quite low. In contrast, the New York City health and fitness club industry competes intensely for working professional memberships. These clubs all provide Stairmasters, elliptical equipment, free weights, Nautilus, aerobics, Pilates classes, juice bars, and socializing areas. Like dry cleaning stores, health clubs in the city are often just around the corner. Because of the similarities, therefore, each company competes very hard to acquire and retain members.

Switching costs. Similar in fashion to each of the other four competitive threats, switching costs have an impact on the intensity of rivalry. When products or services are nearly identical and switching costs to buyers are low, competitors fight fiercely to keep their existing customers and attract new customers. This leads to rivals expending significant resources in marketing, promotions, price concessions, innovation, and other costly initiatives that reduce their profitability.

Exit barriers. High costs to exit a business cause competitors to perform in ways that are often counterproductive to both company and industry performance. Exit barriers can exist in the form of fixed manufacturing plants, long-term contracts, costly infrastructure, ownership of basic inputs, governmental limitations, or specialized and unique assets, sometimes complicated by declining markets in which there are simply no buyers. However, exit barriers can also be perceived, and perceived barriers can be just as compelling. These include a long history in the industry, prior decisions or statements by senior management that would look questionable in the face of exit, nostalgia, a desire to protect a community and the employees, as well as a stubborn desire to prove that the business is still viable. The combination of real and perceived exit barriers causes competitors to fight very hard to maintain their business. Eastern Airlines fought a losing battle in a postregulated world in the 1980s. The major airlines have extremely high fixed costs and a strong need to fill seats on each plane that takes off. As new, low-cost carriers entered the market and other established airlines were able to negotiate cost-effective contracts with their workers, Eastern suffered with a pre-deregulation high cost structure, a debilitating inability to

Strategic Moves
Zale Corporation, Part 2

In early January 2005, CEO Mary Forte decided to move the entire Zales Jewelers operation more upscale. Experience at her previous positions at QVC, Federated Department Stores, and most recently as the head of the Gordon's unit at Zales had led her to believe that moving upscale was a key to success. In this case she reasoned that her primary competition had moved in on the low-end and was seriously impacting the ability of Zales to differentiate itself. She ended the traditional system of discounting heavily at the holidays, changed out a significant portion of their line of jewelry, ended their old tag line, instituted a new one, "Be Brilliant," and began a system of buying better quality diamonds directly from suppliers and thereby bypassing the traditional middle-man system.

The big change occurred during 2005 in preparation for final quarter sales.

QUESTIONS

1. What is your assessment of the new strategy?
2. Do you believe this approach will be successful?
3. Will this approach work to counter some of the forces in the industry?

work with their labor unions, and a series of highly publicized crashes. Despite all this, the airline continued to fly unprofitably until 1991 before it was finally forced to cease operations.[22] High exit barriers impacted the business decisions and were a significant influencing factor in the industry.

EXTENDING INDUSTRY ANALYSIS

Conclusions on Industry

Having gone carefully through the five forces, and having considered driving forces from the external environment, it is now possible to draw together some conclusions from those observations and to put those conclusions to practical use. Recall that there are two types of conclusions that should be drawn from this analysis: 1) the attractiveness of the industry, and 2) the identification of key success factors.

Industry attractiveness. Each of the five forces will exert influence on an industry that either enhances or detracts from the potential for any individual company to earn above-average profits. Summarizing the effect of all of the five forces at one time provides a clearer picture of the industry. The "Five Forces Analysis Checklist" in Figure 4.16 provides a convenient means to create this summary. Every factor within each of the five forces should be evaluated with an indication as to whether the effect of the factor is strong or weak on that force in the industry being evaluated. Having profiled each of the factors provides the backdrop for making an informed judgment about how each of the five forces affects potential profitability in the industry. Developing judgments about the strength of each of the five forces allows for the drawing of a conclusion about the attractiveness of the industry as a whole. The industry appears attractive when the five forces work in a way that insulates the profit-making potential of the business. It looks much less attractive when the five forces indicate that profits for the rivals in the industry are being siphoned off to suppliers, buyers, new entrants, and substitutes, or because the intense rivalry among competitors causes all of the companies in the industry to spend at higher levels and commit additional resources in order to compete (Figure 4.17).

Key success factors. We mentioned earlier in this chapter that key success factors (KSFs) are like the "rules" of the industry; they indicate the kinds of activities that every company needs to focus on in order to succeed. Unlike external driving forces, which affect an entire industry and which no company can impact, the KSF-related activities are critical dimensions that companies can affect through their strategic investments. The extent to which companies pay attention to KSFs and succeed in addressing them will distinguish the winners from the losers in an industry.

Every industry will have its own unique set of KSFs, and in each industry there are likely to be no more than four to six such factors. While there are a vast number of competitive factors within any industry, KSFs are those that are the most critical to success. Because the KSFs are a "short list," it is important to understand that not every company in an industry will be forced to compete in exactly the same way in order to succeed. In fact, one of the most challenging

6 Explain how dynamic changes in industries and competitive positions will impact a company's strategy.

Figure 4.16
Five Forces Analysis Checklist

	Strong	Weak
Threat of new entrants is low when		
Capital requirements	★	
Economies of scale	★	
Absolute cost advantages	★	
Access to inputs		★
Access to distribution		★
Need for differentiation	★	
Switching costs for buyers	★	
Government regulation	★	
Expected retaliation	★	
Threat of substitutes is low when		
Relative price/performance		★
Switching costs of buyers	★	
Buyer bargaining power is low when		
Buyer concentration		★
Buyer volume		★
Switching costs of buyers	★	
Buyer information		★
Availability of substitutes		★
Threat of backward integration		★
Supplier bargaining power is low when		
Supplier concentration		★
Importance of volume to supplier		★
Presence of substitute inputs		★
Differentiation of inputs required		★
Cost of input relative to total costs		★
Switching costs of suppliers	★	
Threat of forward integration		★
Intensity of rivalry is low when		
Industry growth rate	★	
Overcapacity in industry		★
Fixed costs as % of total costs		★
Product differentiation	★	
Informational complexity	★	
Switching costs of buyers	★	
Numerous or equally balanced competitors		★
Strategic stakes		★
Exit barriers		★

Equifinality Multiple means to achieve success.

and interesting aspects of strategic management is that strategic variety not only exists within most industries, but also that there is **equifinality**—the concept that there are many means to achieve success. That is, despite the fact that there are only a limited number of KSFs, companies compete quite successfully for industry profits in many different ways. KSFs provide guidance for being strategically competitive, but do not dictate specific actions that companies must take. In ancient history it used to be said that "all roads lead to Rome." Here in the twenty-first century, the roads are the KSFs: they guide companies to the destination of superior performance. Companies vary in the roads they may take, the chariots and horses they use, the training of the charioteers, and the speed or deliberation in their journeys.

Having conducted a five-forces analysis, identifying KSFs becomes a more straightforward exercise. There are two key questions to answer in this identification process (Figure 4.18):

1. *How is value created for customers in this industry?* In the five-forces analysis earlier we considered the conditions under which customer bargaining power is increased, with the result being that customer power may actually diminish the profitability of competitors in the industry. Though the power of customers in the industry can negatively impact industry profitability, it is important to remember that customers are the fundamental source of revenue and profit for companies. Customers in any industry will prize certain product or service features and characteristics over others. They will also value a certain type of relationship with a company that provides them with products or services. Carefully defining the values that are most appreciated by customers will lead a company to take actions to deliver those critical values. Earlier, for example, we mentioned that consumers increasingly demand that cutting-edge technology be incorporated into the PCs and laptops they use. To deliver on this value, PC and laptop manufacturers must engage in continuous innovation. In the fast food business consumers value convenience, which has led companies like McDonald's and Burger King to develop expertise in real estate site selection for the new restaurants in order to ensure that each new restaurant is centrally located and easily accessible to their customers.

2. *What are the critical dimensions of rivalry that enable a company to successfully compete in delivering values to customers?* This question should be addressed as a multifaceted problem to be solved with the best combination of approaches. What is it that the company will have to do in order to compete effectively and survive in the industry? The other way to phrase the question is "what are the factors that will cause the company to fail if we do not attend to them?" Five-forces analysis goes a long way toward addressing these questions. The threat of new entrants often prompts existing competitors to either create or increase economic barriers to entry or to establish stronger brand reputations that will differentiate their products. This might lead existing competitors to build larger manufacturing facilities or to increase the amount they spend on advertising and image development. The pressure on costs from suppliers as well as on prices from buyers, and

Figure 4.17
Potential to Earn Superior Returns in Industry

Five Forces	Good Potential	Poor Potential
Threat of new entrants	Low	High
Threat of substitutes	Low	High
Bargaining power of buyers	Low	High
Bargaining power of suppliers	Low	High
Intensity of rivalry	Low	High

Figure 4.18
Identifying Key Success Factors

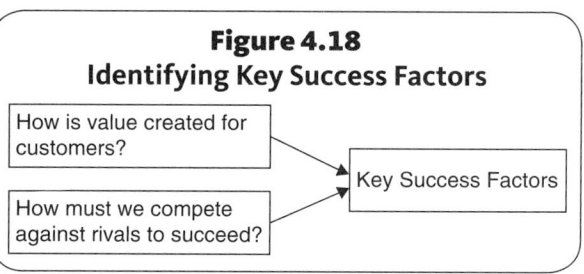

potential substitutes, generally causes companies to seek ways to develop a low cost structure so that they can offer more competitive pricing.

Answering these questions completely often requires a process of thinking through the reasons that lie beneath the surface dimensions that might be initially identified. We have already noted that in the PC industry customers value the opportunity to shop for cutting-edge technology, which in turn means that PC manufacturers must focus on innovation as a fundamental KSF. However, the customer desire for innovation is balanced by the desire to have technology that is also manufactured around a commonly accepted standard. Standardized product offerings allow customers to comparison shop more easily among competing models, instill confidence that the technology will work well, and ensure the customer that the product can be repaired easily if something goes wrong. There are two implications derived from the parallel need for innovation and standardization in the PC industry. First, companies must find ways to produce standardized models inexpensively, because their competitors will be producing to the same standards, and price competition will likely be fierce. This suggests that cost management is an important KSF in this industry. Second, companies must seek to move their models incorporating new technology standards into the marketplace quickly, suggesting that speed to market is also a KSF.

Changes in key success factors. By answering these two questions posed earlier, we should be able to identify a short list of KSFs for any industry. Before moving on, however, we want to emphasize that industries change over time and therefore the important KSFs might also change. This is especially true as an industry matures and its growth rate of new customers or revenues begins to flatten out, or as the presence of viable substitutes becomes increasingly important. The U.S. automobile industry has seen a continuous evolution of KSFs over the last seventy-five years, moving from purely low cost and basic functionality, to style and design, to quality and performance, and now to economical performance. General Motors and Ford—including their unionized workforces—have remained so mired in models of business dating back to the 1960s and 1970s that they failed to recognize a fundamental shift in the kinds of KSFs that were emerging in the 1980s and 1990s. Poor anticipation of major shifts that generate new sets of KSFs have led these competitors into "critical condition" and at this writing it is unclear if any kind of radical surgery (cutting jobs and costs) or other measures can save the patients.[23] Therefore, the ability to identify changing and emerging KSFs helps a company to better anticipate possible threats to its existing business.

By the same token, a company can identify new opportunities through its efforts to better anticipate the changes in KSFs that its industry will be experiencing. Recall that in Chapter 1 we discussed "opportunity recognition" as one of two key strategic imperatives. By answering slightly reworded questions in Figure 4.18, a company can potentially develop insight about new opportunities before its competitors do. The questions now become "what kinds of value should be created for customers in the future?" and "how will we need to compete against rivals to succeed?" Companies that develop regular activities and routines to constantly ask and answer these questions can do a better job of scoping out significant opportunities and threats. We will have much more to say about threats, opportunities, and activities in the next chapter.

Competitive KSF Analysis

Identifying key success factors that are currently important in the industry is an important step that allows for the evaluation of each primary competitor along each KSF dimension. This is best completed by looking at how well each primary competitor addresses the KSFs that distinguish between success and failure in the industry. A comparison of competitors on each KSF dimension highlights the relative positions of strength in the marketplace. This is important on many levels, not the least of which is that companies need to be careful about making strategic moves that attack a competitor's position of strength. You will recall from Chapter 1, where we paraphrased lessons from the ancient writings of Sun Tzu, that this was one of the lessons he taught. Attacking the strength of a competitor is an attempt to win based upon the competitor's strengths and experience rather than based upon the unique capabilities of the company doing the attacking. Comparative analysis also reveals relative positions of weakness in the marketplace and thus reveals possible areas of exploitation through strategic moves. This sort of comparative analysis was central to Sun Tzu's beliefs about how to succeed.

The goal of a competitive KSF analysis is to produce a table that resembles that in Figure 4.19. Here the KSFs we have just identified are listed across the top, and the chief competitors in the industry are listed down the side. This type of analysis requires us to evaluate the strength or competency of each firm on each of the KSFs. In evaluating each firm it is very important not to "guesstimate" or simply "eyeball" how well or how poorly the competitor does on a particular dimension. This analysis should be based on hard facts and data, not simply upon opinions and subjective evaluations. Since the KSFs are the critical dimensions that distinguish success from failure in the industry, basing strategic decisions on factual evidence will be particularly helpful. In contrast, basing important strategic decisions on estimates and opinions may lead a company to under- or overestimate a particular competitor.

Here is an illustration. We have referred to the PC manufacturing industry several times in providing examples for aspects of industry analysis. We have suggested that innovation is a KSF in this industry. The question, then, is how innovative are competitors in this industry? We need to measure innovation somehow, and there are several ways we might consider:

- R&D spending each year
- R&D spending as a percentage of revenue

Figure 4.19
Competitive KSF Analysis Table

	Key Success Factors			
	KSF #1	KSF #2	KSF #3	KSF #4
Firm A				
Firm B				
Firm C				
Firm D				

- Number of new models introduced each year
- Degree of improvement in performance characteristics of new models

Dollars spent on research and development (R&D) each year is an industry standard means of assessing the level of commitment that companies are putting into discovery and innovation. However, there is a wide variation in size, with some companies (e.g., Hewlett Packard) being significantly larger than other companies competing in this industry, and therefore simply having more dollars available to spend on discovery. In fact, during 2005 HP spent $3.5 billion on R&D, while Apple Computer spent only $534 million. It looks like HP is outspending Apple by a ratio of nearly 7-to-1. Another way of evaluating innovation, therefore, is to "common-size" R&D spending by looking at it as a percentage of sales revenue. A different picture emerges: during 2005 HP spent 4.0 percent of sales on R&D, and Apple spent 3.8 percent—nearly the same. It is likely that the R&D spending for each company is spread across multiple product lines—printers and instrumentation for HP, and iPods for Apple. However, we are particularly concerned with how innovation impacts the PC industry. So perhaps a more salient metric to evaluate—and one that would be more relevant for customers like Best Buy and Circuit City or for competitors—is how many new PC models each firm introduces in a given period of time. While R&D information is generally available on the Internet by accessing an annual report, data on models introduced are not. These are data that require careful investigation to obtain, such as interviewing purchasing managers at Best Buy and Circuit City or finding and reviewing historical price lists of the companies. Once again, however, Dell and HP are significantly larger than Apple or Gateway. One might expect that larger companies with broader lines would tend to introduce a larger number of new models during any given period. Therefore, a fourth possible measure for innovation is one of relative degree, that is, how much have new models improved in computing performance over existing models? Here one might examine specific operating characteristics of new PCs such as increases in speed, capacity, or size relative to power.

This brief discussion illustrates that selecting the best metrics to evaluate companies on KSF dimensions involves choosing among a range of options. While there is no one best set of metrics, each tends to lead the company to a slightly different conclusion. The best choices will usually be the type of measurement techniques that are best aligned with the needs and desires of the core customers.

Strategy Maps and Strategic Groups

Strategic group A group of businesses competing for virtually the same customers in virtually the same manner.

We can take the analysis of competition one step further by using KSFs to provide greater insight on strategic positions within an industry. "Mapping" the position of competitors in an industry allows for the identification of important strategic groups. A **strategic group** is a collection of companies that tend to behave in relatively the same way strategically by focusing on the same subsets of KSFs. They therefore occupy positions in an industry that are close enough to each other that they become primary competitors with each other. A competitive KSF analysis (Figure 4.19) can help identify companies that are very similar to each other on key competitive dimensions. However, a **strategy map** is a visual tool that takes this one step further by revealing competitors' relative positions and competitive advantages. A strategy map is created by using a pair of the identified KSFs as axes in a graph, and then plotting the companies on the graph according to their measures for each of the KSFs.

Constructing strategy maps. Let's use the PC manufacturing industry once again to illustrate the creation of strategic maps and the identification of strategic groups. There are several steps in the process:

1. Identify the KSFs in the industry and, as objectively as possible, measure each competitor on these dimensions. Earlier, for instance, we identified that two of the KSFs in the industry are innovation and low-cost manufacturing. Choose two of the KSFs and plot the competitors in the industry in a graph using these dimensions as the axes (Figure 4.20). By convention we put the "desirable" condition for each KSF toward the outer end of each axis, so in this case "Low" for Unit Cost (an objective measurement of the Low Cost KSF) is toward the right end of the axis. This makes the upper-right portion of each graph the most desirable part of the graph to be, in this case low unit cost and highly innovative. Note that no company currently occupies that position in "strategic space." It can be seen that Dell is pushing the frontier of low-cost production with an average level of innovation, while Apple is significantly higher on the innovation dimension but less advanced in unit cost manufacturing.

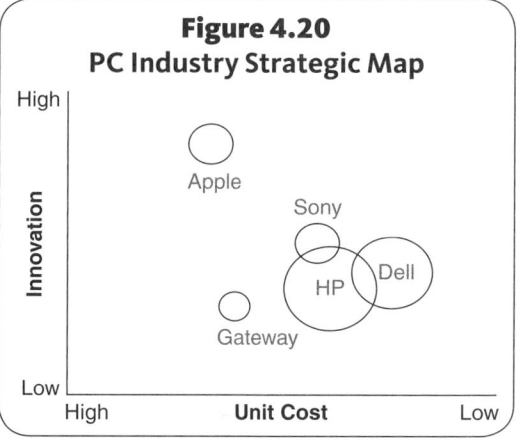

Figure 4.20
PC Industry Strategic Map

2. At the point where competitors are located on the graph, draw circles for each competitor. The size of the circle should represent the relative size of the competitor, in either market share of the industry or annual revenue. In Figure 4.20, for instance, PC manufacturers are represented by circles whose size approximates market share for each company; thus HP is slightly larger than Dell and four to five times the size of Apple.

3. Assess the presence of strategic groups. In this example, Sony, Dell, and HP make up a strategic group because they are extremely close to each other on these two critical strategic dimensions in the industry. Dell and Sony should be most concerned about the way in which HP will be competing in the marketplace, because HP tends to create value for customers in much the same way and represents a greater threat to take business away from them. So HP is the competitor that threatens them the most. Dell would be much less concerned about Apple, who appears to compete more on the dimension of innovation and less on the cost/price dimension.

Strategy map A two-dimensional map showing where competitors are positioned using a quantitatively defined set of criteria.

4. Use other combinations of KSFs to draw additional maps. With four KSFs identified in an industry, there will be only five possible graphs to draw using combinations of any two KSFs. Other graph combinations can also be revealing about industry competition. For example, in the PC industry a graph showing Unit Cost versus Speed to Market might also portray a strategic group made up of Sony, Dell, and HP. This finding should elevate the attention paid by any one of those competitors to the other two, because it reinforces the relationship seen in Figure 3.20.

5. Make sure that KSFs provide unique information. Sometimes industry KSFs turn out to be highly correlated with each other. Figure 4.21 is a strategic map of the fast food industry in which Food Quality and Low Costs were previously identified as KSFs. The alignment of all the companies along the negatively sloping diagonal indicates that there is a high degree of correlation between food quality and unit costs: the lower the unit costs, the lower the food quality. Therefore the addition of Food Quality to the list of industry KSFs does not impart any new information that is not already captured by the Low Cost KSF. If Food Quality similarly aligns with other KSFs identified in the industry analysis, then it should be removed from the list of KSFs, because it does not distinguish between success and failure any better than the other KSFs do.

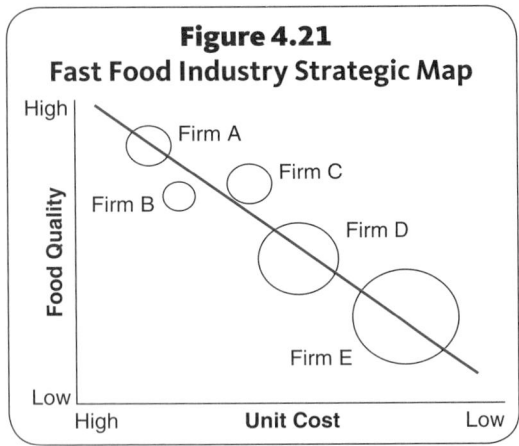

Figure 4.21
Fast Food Industry Strategic Map

Identifying strategic trajectories. Another advantage of strategy maps is that they can be used to illustrate the trajectories of strategy development that have occurred in an industry. A single strategy map is similar to a photo: it is a static view that is a representation of the industry at a defined point in time. A series of strategy maps developed over time would be like a movie, showing the dynamic character of the industry over a period of time. This type of dynamic view would help illuminate the historical trajectories that competitors have taken throughout this period of time.

Building further on the PC industry strategy map developed earlier, Figure 4.22 now provides a dynamic view of the changes in strategic position over time for two key competitors in the industry. A few years ago Apple Computer was an innovative company, as it has been since its founding in the 1970s. A few years ago Dell was superior to Apple on the Unit Cost KSF, but was inferior to Apple on the Innovation KSF. Over time Dell has worked diligently to continue lowering its unit cost structure, and its trajectory from the past to its present-day position illustrates its accomplishments. At the same time, it has only marginally improved its Innovation position since it relies heavily upon Intel, Microsoft, and other suppliers of subassemblies for its basic PC models.

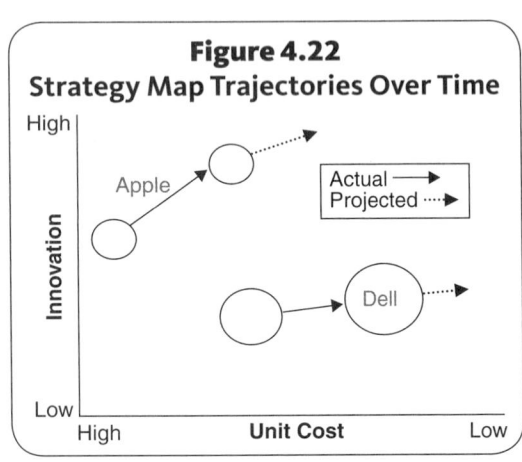

Figure 4.22
Strategy Map Trajectories Over Time

In contrast, Apple has continued to push an innovation agenda, evidenced by its introduction of the Cube, the G3, and the MacBook Air. Apple has also recognized the need to become more price competitive, which has caused it to make substantial improvements in its unit cost dimension. The dark arrows in Figure 4.22 illustrate the trajectories each company has followed over the last few years.

These historical trajectories are manifestations of the intended strategic approach each company has taken in the marketplace in order to improve its competitive position. To pursue these trajectories each company has made strategic investments in certain resources and activities that allow it to make significant progress. In Chapter 6 we will discuss in some detail the nature of these types of resource investments and how they can lead to competitive advantage. The point that should be emphasized here is that such investments are major commitments by a company and, like most strategic decisions, are not easily reversed. They are "sticky," meaning that once you build a capability for innovation, that capability will stick with you for a long period of time.

Past strategic intentions are indicators of future strategic direction. Because the strategic investments made by each company are indicative of strategic intention and are sticky, it is reasonable to expect that each company will continue to move in a similar direction. In Figure 4.22 the dotted-line arrows suggest the direction that each company will move in the near future, assuming each will continue to build on past strategic investments. Anticipating the direction in which one of your competitors will move can be extremely helpful. To achieve further reductions in unit cost, for instance, Dell can expect that Apple will be evaluating a range of strategic options that will help fulfill this intention. Since PC manufacturing costs have been well-connected with economies of scale, one option that Apple may consider would be a way to make their PCs more attractive to a wider audience. It should come as no surprise, then, that in early 2006 Apple developed its own software enabling users to run Windows and Windows-based software on its Apple computers.[24] This instantly makes the Apple computing platform a viable option for tens of millions of computer users who would experience significant switching costs to give up the Windows environment in order to use an Apple.

Identifying strategic opportunities. The strategy map can also be a useful tool for identifying new opportunities for strategic distinction. In Figure 4.20 Sony appears to be competing directly with both HP and Dell, two larger companies in the PC business. Direct competition seldom has positive results for smaller companies, simply because the smaller company has fewer resources at its disposal to fight the good fight (another lesson from Sun Tzu). This is one of the reasons why competitors frequently score goals in lacrosse or ice hockey when a player on a team has to sit out in the penalty box. Additional resources generally lead to higher performance. So what options are available for Sony to compete, while at the same time trying to remove itself from a battle of attrition? The map in Figure 4.20 suggests that opportunity for Sony lies in the space in the upper-right corner. The anticipated trajectories Dell and HP appear to be taking are primarily to the right, as they pursue an agenda of unit cost reductions. Therefore, Sony might consider making new strategic investments in innovation capabilities, which would create strategic separation from Dell and HP and allow them to move into a currently unoccupied part of the "strategic space."

Effect of industry boundary definitions. Earlier in this chapter we discussed the difficulty that can arise in defining the precise boundaries of an industry. Similarly, industry boundary definitions can make a difference in how strategy maps are interpreted. Let's assume that we are conducting an industry analysis of the pizza industry, and that two of the KSFs that have been identified are Quality and Convenience. Figure 4.23 portrays a hypothetical strategy map of the industry. Pizza Hut, Domino's, and Papa John's dominate the industry and constitute a strategic group of companies that court the consumer in much the same way. Brick Oven is a sit-down restaurant producing high quality pizzas, while Pizza Spinners is the local late-night place that students call only if everything else is closed. We also plug in DiGiorgio's Pizza, which is purchased in supermarket frozen food sections, simply to acknowledge that this brand is also a competitor of delivery and restaurant pizzas.

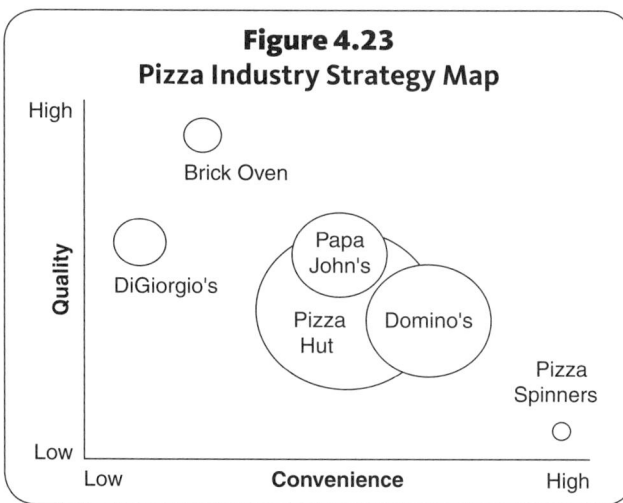

Figure 4.23
Pizza Industry Strategy Map

A broader industry definition can lead to a very different view of the main competitive strategic group. In fact, consumers often choose pizza instead of some other type of fast food, and vice versa. So if the industry analysis is broadened to account for the wider variety and values that consumers seek when they make choices, a different strategy map emerges. Figure 4.24 illustrates the strategy map when the industry definition is broadened to "fast food." In this instance we observe that McDonald's and Burger King have been added to the map, and they appear to compete for the consumer in precisely the same manner as do the delivery pizza restaurants. Consequently, Domino's must worry about not only the competitive efforts of Papa John's in producing quality pizzas and delivering them in a timely fashion. They must also worry about McDonald's efforts to provide higher quality foods more broadly available through their convenient drive-up windows or directly via the McPizza. Presumably the broader definition of the industry would also have implications for relative strengths on other KSFs, such as Price/Value.

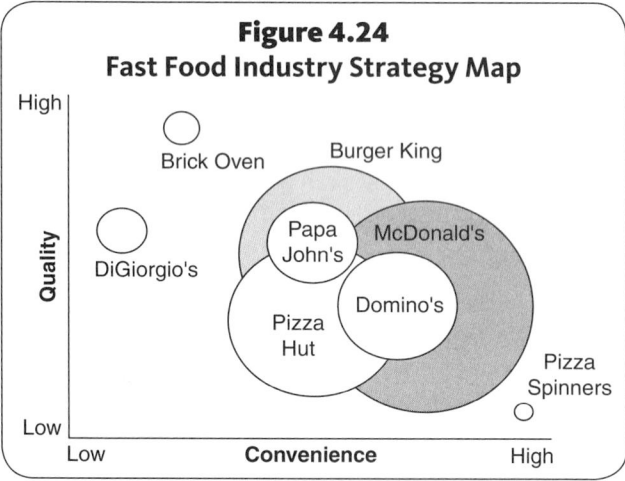

Figure 4.24
Fast Food Industry Strategy Map

In January 2006, CEO Mary Forte was forced to resign amid disappointing sales. Zales dropped to Number 2 in the market behind Signet for the first time in their long history. Zale Corporation installed board member Betsy Burton as the interim CEO. Ms. Burton founded several business ventures, including Supercuts Inc. (a wide-market, discount hair salon). She has quickly moved the entire Zales Jewelry operation back to its roots, re-instituting "The Diamond Store" campaign, and returning to their traditional mix of products. This is the same strategy that caused the previous CEO to look for a change because of falling sales.

QUESTIONS

1. Can Zales Jewelers return to their former position in the market?
2. Should they do this?
3. What would you recommend Zales do in response to the original issue given the results over the past two years?

CHAPTER SUMMARY

Industry analysis as a tool provides some objective evaluation of where an industry as a whole stands on a continuum that ranges from a perfectly competitive market to one that is a monopoly. In perfectly competitive markets (which are rare), it is difficult for any company to earn superior profits. Imperfect markets are characterized by the potential to sustain differences between companies, which can lead to superior profits. The examination of five structural forces of an industry provides insight on the potential for companies to earn profits. These forces include the threat of new entrants, threat of substitutes, bargaining power of buyers, bargaining power of suppliers, and the intensity of rivalry among competitors. The stronger each of these forces is, the lower the potential for the target company to earn superior returns.

Through industry analysis, inferences may be drawn about the critical strategic dimensions of competition that distinguish between successful and unsuccessful companies. These are referred to as key success factors (KSFs). KSFs can be used to evaluate the relative strengths and weaknesses of competitors in the industry as well as to construct visual strategy maps, which may reveal groups of companies that compete in very similar ways.

Industry analysis involves the following steps:

1. Define the industry of interest. Narrow industry definitions involve companies whose inputs are very similar, whose geographic markets are similar, and whose customers are very similar.

2. Examine the five forces in the industry to understand how the structure of the industry affects the potential to earn profits. Each force is evaluated through a series of characteristics that will indicate whether profits for competitors are insulated or may be drawn off.

3. Examine the general environment for exogenous forces that will affect the industry and every company in it. These forces include social, technological, economic, environmental, political/legal, and global forces.

4. Complete the five-forces analysis checklist. Draw conclusions about the attractiveness of the industry for earning profits.

5. Identify key success factors by answering two pivotal questions: 1) how is value created for customers; and 2) how must we compete in order to succeed?

6. Determine the appropriate way to measure companies in the industry on each of the KSFs.

7. Complete the competitive KSF analysis table, in order to easily compare companies on the KSF dimensions.

8. Draw strategy maps using paired combinations of KSFs. Identify strategic groups of closely competing companies. Identify historical trajectories of competitors, as well as anticipated direction of future development.

9. Change the industry definition used, and re-examine KSFs and strategy maps for new insights on the nature of competition.

KEY TERMS

Concentration ratio (p. 111)

Equifinality (p. 118)

Exogenous forces (p. 99)

Experience curve (p. 106)

Five-forces model (p. 103)

Incumbent firms (p. 103)

Industry analysis (p. 93)

Key success factors (KSF) (p. 94)

Monopoly (p. 91)

NAICS code (p. 97)

Perfect competition (p. 91)

Profit pool (p. 103)

Sarbanes-Oxley Act (SOX) (p. 102)

Social contract (p. 103)

Strategic group (p. 122)

Strategy map (p. 123)

Substitutes (p. 109)

SHORT ANSWER REVIEW QUESTIONS

1. What are the types of absolute cost advantage, and how do they impact the five forces?
2. The general environment impacts industries and companies. Explain how the Internet has affected competitive rivalry and the attractiveness of the airline industry.
3. What factors help limit the entry of new competitors into an industry?
4. Name the elements that impact the competitive rivalry of an industry and explain their impact.
5. How can we use the five-forces model to examine industries?
6. In what ways do suppliers impact the competitiveness of an industry?
7. What criticisms do you have of the five-forces model? What does it not explain that you believe is important in competitive strategy?
8. How would you explain buyer concentration?
9. How are NAICS codes utilized in industry analysis?
10. What are the three factors that determine how strong the threat of substitutes will be for an industry?
11. What elements help us define an industry?
12. How do substitutes affect an industry's competitiveness?
13. How do key success factors (KSF) inform us about a particular market?
14. Provide examples of real switching costs.
15. What did Adam Smith have to say about efficient markets?
16. What are perceived switching costs?

GROUP EXERCISES

1. Classifying a company is the first step in analyzing an industry. Take five businesses that are close to the university and use the NAICS classification system to classify each. Try to get the code as specific as possible.
   a. How difficult was it to get the classification code to five digits?
   b. What other businesses fall under the same classification code?
   c. What insights does this classification provide you in your analysis of a particular company?
2. Take one of the businesses that you used in Exercise #1 and develop a five-forces analysis for the industry in which it competes.
   a. What conclusions can you reach about the competitiveness of the industry?
   b. What areas of the industry concern you most?
   c. What aspects of the industry appear to provide the best opportunities for those already in the industry?
   d. What conclusions have you reached about the general competitiveness of this industry?

3. Take the same business for which you developed a five-forces map in Exercise #2 and create a strategic map for the industry in which it competes.
   a. What conclusions can you reach about the industry's KSFs?
   b. What recommendations would you provide a company that wished to enter this industry?

REFERENCES

[1] Thomas, P. 1996. Office Max sees opportunity in plight. *Wall Street Journal*. September 9.

[2] Basler, R. P. (ed.). 1953. *Collected works of Abraham Lincoln*. Piscataway, NJ: Rutgers University Press.

[3] Smith, A. 1977. *An inquiry into the nature and causes of the wealth of nations*. New York: Dutton.

[4] Technically, the economists would say that the market equilibrates when the firm's marginal revenue equals its marginal cost. Since every firm is identical, this means that no firm is earning a profit. At this point there would be no inducement for firms to change what they are doing or for other firms to enter the industry.

[5] Porter, M. E. 1980. *Competitive strategy*. New York: Free Press.

[6] Goodman, R. A., and M. W. Lawless. 1994. *Technology and strategy: Conceptual models and diagnostics*. New York: Oxford University Press.

[7] Porter, M. E. 2003. *The U.S. Homebuilding Industry and The Competitive Position of Large Builders*. Presentation at Centex Investor Conference, New York.

[8] Saloner, G., A. Shepard, and J. Podolny. 2001. *Strategic management*. New York: John Wiley.

[9] Newspaper Association of America. 2005. 2005 Specialty retail profile—Zale Corporation. Kannon consulting; Zimmerman, A., and K. Hudson. 2006. Lost sparkle: Chasing upscale customers tarnishes mass-market Jeweler. *Wall Street Journal*. June 26. www.zalecorp.com; Bernstein, D. 2000. Is Zale a jewel for next year? December 22. www.TheStreet.com.

[10] We distinguish between profit-making and value-creating enterprises for the moment. Value-creating enterprises might include for-profit companies that produce economic value, but a broader view will include nonprofits as well because they create social value. Nonprofits also exist in industries, and compete with other firms for resources and customers.

[11] Scherer, F. M., and D. Ross. 1990. *Industrial market structure and economic performance* (3rd ed.). Boston: Houghton Mifflin.

[12] Lewis, P. 2004. Broadband wonderland. *Fortune*. September 20: 191–198.

[13] See http://www.census.gov/epcd/www/naics.html.

[14] See http://www.sec.gov/info/edgar/siccodes.htm.

[15] West, G. P., III, and J. O. DeCastro. 2001. The Achilles heel of firm strategy: Resource weaknesses and distinctive inadequacies. *Journal of Management Studies* 38(3): 417–442.

[16] EPA. 2006. Cleaner small engines are safe. March 17. http://www.epa.gov.

[17] Bonini, S. M., L. T. Mendonca, and J. M. Oppenheim. 2006. When social issues become strategic. *McKinsey Quarterly* (2): 20–32.

[18] Ries, A., and J. Trout. 2000. *Positioning: The battle for your mind* (3rd ed.). New York: McGraw Hill.

[19] Terhune, C. 2006. Coke attempts to paint it 'black.' *Wall Street Journal*. April 1: A2.

[20] Kalla, S. 2001. Fiber glut: It's real. *Network Fusion News*. September 10. http://www.networkworld.com/forum/2001/0910faceoffyes.html.

[21] See http://www.edmunds.com.

[22] Wikipedia, 2006. http://en.wikipedia.org/wiki/Eastern_Airlines.

[23] Loomis, C. J. 2006. The tragedy of General Motors. *Fortune*. February 20: 59–75.

[24] Mossberg, W. S. 2006. Boot camp turns your Mac into a reliable Windows PC. *Wall Street Journal*. April 6: B1.

Value Chain

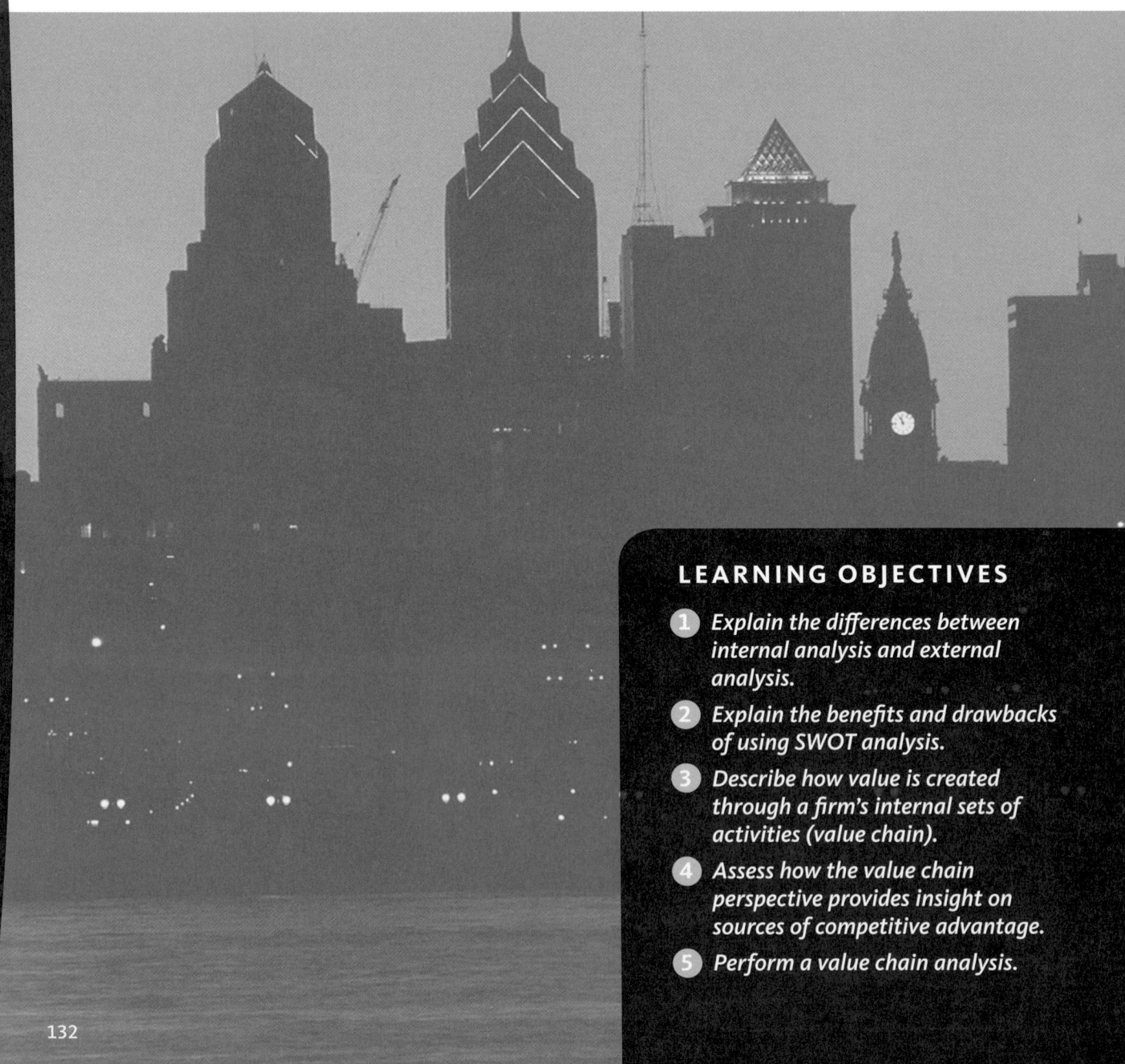

Less than a decade ago, the travel agency industry was a vibrant, fast-growing industry. The large "baby boom" generation was aging into peak traveling years, and their growing disposable income allowed them to travel more often than their parents did. Travel agencies reaped the advantage of these trends, since airlines sold tickets only over the phone, and complicated trip planning services were not available elsewhere.

The advent of the Internet and PC technology changed how value is created in this industry. Whereas previously the travel agency was the primary intermediary between the airlines and customers, now both airlines and online travel sites (such as Expedia and Priceline) can reach customers both effectively and efficiently. Figure 5.1 illustrates the new value chain in the industry. For incremental costs far lower than what travel agencies used to charge in commissions, airlines and online travel sites can book and deliver airline tickets much faster.

By 2000 e-tickets already accounted for over 60 percent of all airline ticket volume, and online travel sales had risen from $400 million to over $15 billion. Since travel agencies had previously booked 67 percent of domestic airline travel and 80 percent of international airline travel, these new developments had dire implications for the industry. Between 1997 and 2002 the number of U.S. travel agencies declined from over 29,000 to under 22,000, and employment in the industry dropped from 183,000 to 147,000.

The declines continue in this industry today.

Questions

1. If your family owned and operated a travel agency business, what initiatives would you recommend that they undertake in order to survive and grow?

2. How is value created by online services compared to the airlines' own ticketing operations, and why wouldn't the airlines themselves simply offer the same benefits?

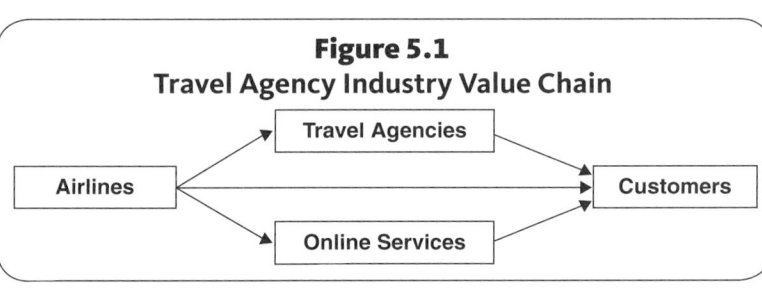

Figure 5.1
Travel Agency Industry Value Chain

INTERNAL ANALYSIS VERSUS EXTERNAL ANALYSIS

In the last chapter we had a chance to explore the impact of industry structure on the strategies of firms and their ability to earn profits. Out of the analysis of the five industry forces, we are able to draw conclusions about key success factors and driving forces. These factors and forces partially determine how firms must act if they are to succeed. Key success factors can also be used to plot the locations of competitors on a strategic map, determine if there are groups of companies that seek to compete in similar ways, provide insight on the trajectories that companies are following strategically, and identify both potential threats and opportunities.

Despite the insight gained about competitors and firm strategy through industry analysis, understanding strategy requires us to go to a much deeper level. As you may recall from Chapter 4, different industries exhibit very different levels of profitability. Industry analysis helps us understand why some industries tend to be more profitable than others. However, this is only part of the picture. The pharmaceutical industry enjoyed one of the highest average levels of returns between 1985 and 2002. However, we see in Figure 5.2 that there is tremendous variation in the performance of companies within this industry. Usana (which manufactures drug-related products) earned stellar returns, GlaxoSmithKline and J&J earned strong returns, while Boston Scientific and Schering earned far below the average for the industry. Figure 5.3 demonstrates that variations in performance also hold true in a super-competitive industry characterized by low returns, such as the passenger airline industry.

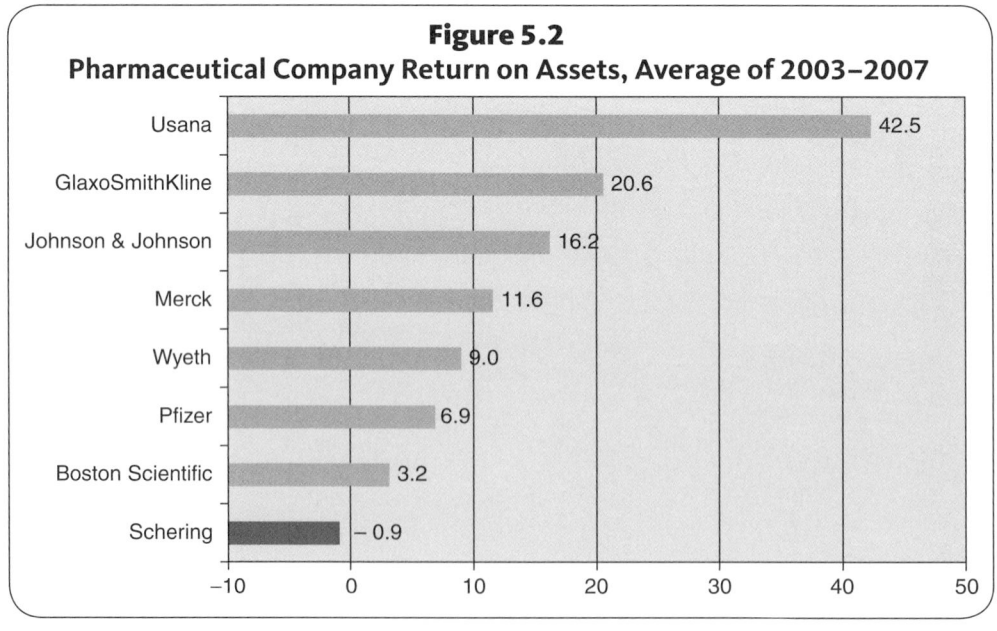

Figure 5.2
Pharmaceutical Company Return on Assets, Average of 2003–2007

Company	ROA
Usana	42.5
GlaxoSmithKline	20.6
Johnson & Johnson	16.2
Merck	11.6
Wyeth	9.0
Pfizer	6.9
Boston Scientific	3.2
Schering	– 0.9

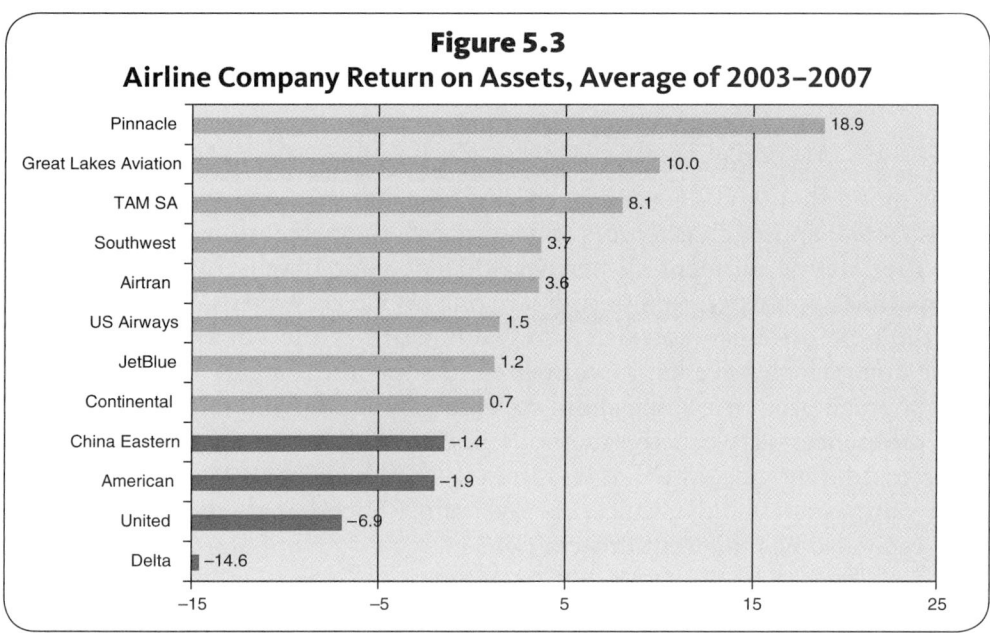

Figure 5.3
Airline Company Return on Assets, Average of 2003–2007

Pinnacle	18.9
Great Lakes Aviation	10.0
TAM SA	8.1
Southwest	3.7
Airtran	3.6
US Airways	1.5
JetBlue	1.2
Continental	0.7
China Eastern	−1.4
American	−1.9
United	−6.9
Delta	−14.6

Some sophisticated strategy research has demonstrated that industry structure and conditions can explain only a small portion of the variance in the performance of firms within an industry.[1] In fact, only about 20 percent of the differences in performance among firms within an industry can be explained using the tools of industry analysis. While that insight is critical and important as a starting point for all strategy analysis and planning efforts, it is simply not enough! As strategic managers we need to develop more than 1-in-5 odds of being successful in the marketplace. Much more of the performance differences between companies in an industry can be understood by looking *inside* the companies to examine what they do, what they fail to do, and how they operate. Through "internal analysis" of companies it is possible to gain much greater insight into the sources of competitive advantage that enable them to occupy leading (or lagging) positions in an industry, and to better understand what strategic paths they will follow based on their activities and resource investments. This can be accomplished by delving deeply into companies in order to better answer the key questions we posed in Chapter 1: why do some firms perform better than others, and why are those differences sustainable over a long period of time? It's to the internal analysis of firms that we now turn our attention.

There are three basic methods for conducting an internal analysis that will provide insight into a company's strategic potential: resource-based analysis, SWOT analysis, and value chain analysis. Resource-based analysis is a very popular topic among many strategy professors and professionals, and it deserves separate focus as a technique. The next chapter of this book (Chapter 6) takes up resource-based analysis, primarily because it builds upon ideas in this chapter about the value chain.

The focus of this chapter is on SWOT and value chain. There is a big distinction between these two internal analysis methods. SWOT provides a snapshot of what a company *is*, while the value chain provides perspective on what a company *does*. When asked what music you are listening to today, you share information that is both momentary and dependent upon your mood that day. That music choice describes you at a point in time, just as a SWOT approach attempts to summarize the perception of a company's situation at the moment. When we look at your playlist we can see how many times you listen to a particular song and get a pretty good perspective on the type of music you listen to the most. It is the patterns of behavior over time, which have led to your present state and suggest a future path of development, that the value chain seeks to capture. So you might think about the differences between the methods like the differences between a photograph and a movie: SWOT is a static view of a company at a point in time, and value chain is a dynamic view over time. Each has its uses and benefits, but each also has inherent drawbacks.

2 *Explain the benefits and drawbacks of using SWOT analysis.*

SWOT

There is hardly a firm of any size or age that is not familiar with the concept of SWOT, and it is important for you to be familiar with it as well. SWOT consists of four categories: strengths, weaknesses, opportunities, and threats. **SWOT analysis** has been taught in business schools for over thirty years. Almost without exception, every large corporation will go through an annual or biannual strategic planning process. SWOT analysis is on the front end of that process in nearly every case. Like fireworks on the 4th of July, it is a familiar—and therefore comfortable—process to anyone involved in strategic planning. As testimony to its ubiquitous nature, a simple Google search for the term "SWOT analysis" turns up over 2 million hits!

LEADERSHIP

> **Strategy Acronym: SWOT**
>
> **S** Strengths
> **W** Weaknesses
> **O** Opportunities
> **T** Threats

SWOT analysis A form of analysis, resulting in a listing of a company's strengths, weaknesses, opportunities, and threats. It is a static view of the company at a particular point in time.

SWOT is usually conducted by a team. Several individuals representing various functions in a company will convene to discuss and agree upon the strengths and weaknesses inherent in their company, and to identify the opportunities and threats that the company faces. The initial conversations are designed to identify these characteristics and can happen at different levels of management. Sometimes senior management will participate, while in other circumstances a middle management team will do the initial work and then present their ideas to senior management for approval. The result of a SWOT analysis is usually a list of factors that the team agrees on as being most important for management to consider as a very early first step in the formulation and adjustment of their strategic plans.

Strengths and weaknesses are ordinarily thought of as characteristics of the company, while opportunities or threats are ordinarily construed as either elements of the competitive environment or outside factors, such as the driving forces discussed in the last chapter. In fact, the output of the KSF analysis and strategic mapping exercises done in an industry and competitive analysis (Chapter 4) can be an important input into the process of identifying areas of potential threat (e.g., encroaching competitors on a particular KSF or in a strategic group) and opportunity (e.g., uncontested space in a strategy map). Figure 5.4 shows a typical SWOT analysis, in this case for a manufacturing company that is creating a Web site to sell directly to its end users.

Figure 5.4
Manufacturing Company SWOT Analysis

Strengths	Opportunities
• Product quality and reliability. • Superior product performance. • Flexible manufacturing capacity. • Staff with end-user experience & perspective. • Possess lists of heavy-user customers. • Strong innovation capability for new products. • Achieved superior industry certifications. • Good information systems support. • Experienced management team.	• New products desired by customers. • Few competitors in international markets. • Suppliers are generally unhappy with manufacturers. • New capabilities enabled by advances in technology.
Weaknesses	**Threats**
• Customer service unproven. • Products do not cover full range. • Small size relative to competition. • No direct marketing experience. • Limited distribution capacity for all markets. • Sales force thin. • Limited access to outside financing. • Poor long-term planning; greatest attention on short-term needs.	• Pending legislation on safety and standards. • Unclear if recent market growth reflects fad or long term trend. • Possible cannibalizing core business. • Retention of management and staff. • Vulnerable to reactive attack by major competitors.

SWOT Benefits

Easy to understand and use. One of several benefits that arises to companies that use SWOT analysis is that it is a fairly simplistic method of internal analysis that nearly everyone can understand with little formal training. For this reason it is easy for management to involve a broad cross-section of departments and employees in the process. Although companies ordinarily do not extend SWOT involvement to the lower levels of a company's hierarchy—such as production line workers, salespeople, and customer service reps—the simplicity of the method does at least offer this potential. This may actually be a missed opportunity for many companies because these employees on the "firing line" are often the first to observe how well or how poorly certain company initiatives are faring, or how customers might react. Therefore they tend to have early, first-hand knowledge about potential strengths and weaknesses.

Alignment. Matching up items that are identified in a SWOT analysis can be helpful in determining whether a company is prepared for and properly aligned to deal with looming threats and opportunities. Here the management team compares each of the elements with the other three to make judgments of the following kinds:

- Will our strengths play into emerging opportunities?
- Are there emerging threats that might marginalize our existing strengths?
- Do our weaknesses seriously compromise the company, even though it has strengths?
- Can our strengths overcome looming threats?

As an illustration, let's take a brief look at 3M. 3M is widely recognized as being an innovative company, a success story they have created because they have institutionalized innovation throughout their business practices. Reflecting its "primary and defining strategy of organic growth through innovation,"[2] the company has a stated goal that it seeks to develop 40 percent of its sales from new products introduced within the last four years. In fact, they encourage all employees to take 15 percent of their time—nearly one full day each work week—to experiment with new ideas. So innovation has become a virtue for the company, but it has implications for the nature of opportunities they are realistically able to pursue. In 2005 the company achieved $21 billion in worldwide revenue. So achieving the 40 percent new business goal sets a target of $8 billion in revenue over the next four years from products that do not exist today. This is larger than the revenue of roughly half the companies in the S&P 500! With this goal in mind, 3M can pursue only large business opportunities. Smaller opportunities (like the original Post-It Notes product line) are likely to be passed over, because the company would need to start up scores of such smaller businesses in order to reach their revenue goals. This example illustrates that matching strength to opportunity can reveal appropriate development direction.

Suggests overall direction. Occasionally management teams will use the matching process to develop overall guidance for the direction of the company. This is accomplished through the use of a **TOWS matrix** (which is a great strategy acronym, but in this case does not stand for anything except SWOT spelled backwards!). Figure 5.5 shows a TOWS matrix that provides general guidance for what direction a company might take. When new opportunities present themselves, for example, the company may decide to expend efforts to overcome existing weaknesses instead of leveraging its current strengths. If threats are looming, the company may focus

Figure 5.5
TOWS Matrix

	Opportunities	Threats
Strengths	Use strengths to take advantage of opportunities	Use strengths to avoid threats
Weaknesses	Take advantage of opportunities by overcoming weaknesses	Defensive measures to minimize weaknesses and avoid threats

greater attention on defensive actions to protect the downside from some combination of threat and apparent weakness. In the 3M example above, we saw that its large size prevented 3M from pursuing smaller new business opportunities. One possible way to overcome a weakness associated with large size would be to spin off a new product development group into a separate operation that is unconstrained by size, such as Hewlett-Packard did in the 1980s with its inkjet printer division. Freed from corporate policies and constraints, that division became very successful with new technology and today brings home the lion's share of HP's revenue.

Competitive analysis. With SWOT, the management team may also begin to make comparisons between its company and competitors. This would involve a process similar to the Key Success Factor competitive comparisons discussed in the previous chapter. Having identified a list of strengths and weaknesses, the team would need to decide how to accurately measure each SWOT item using accessible data and information. In this way an objective assessment would reveal the relative strengths and weaknesses of the company versus its competition. Comparisons such as these might lead to decisions to further invest in strength-building initiatives, or to find ways to minimize areas of weakness that competitors might take advantage of.

Strong starting point. Perhaps the greatest value gained by identifying the SWOT components is that the process provides a starting point for in-depth discussion and analysis of company strategy and competitive position. Preparing a SWOT list is a first step to focus attention on critical components. Then management needs to engage in a deeper conversation about the nature of its business and its competitive environment.

Potential SWOT Drawbacks

Results in a laundry list. One of the key dangers in a SWOT analysis is that the list of items identified across the four categories becomes very large. This can often occur because the items on the list are usually based upon the opinions of the team members, without supporting data or critical analysis.

TOWS matrix A matrix that arrays a company's strengths and weaknesses against its opportunities and threats, providing general direction.

Since teams are ordinarily composed of managers from different functions in the company, each functional area would like to see its own critical issues included in the list. Other team members may not have sufficient expertise to judge whether function-specific issues are important enough, and so inclusion tends to occur more than exclusion. The result is that a SWOT list can include an immense number of items. For instance a SWOT analysis done for the City of Burnet, Texas, produced 83 items in the four categories,[3] while an Iowa State University SWOT analysis contains 43 items.[4] Figure 5.4 shows a more typical list of items generated by a manufacturing company that is considering starting up its own Web site for sales directly to competitors. When the list becomes even this long, it becomes very difficult to use in practice. Try to imagine the challenge for 6–7 key team managers from different departments in a company trying to substantively address up to 25 important issues each year as part of the planning process, while at the same time taking care of their ongoing daily departmental management responsibilities.[5] With long lists it is hard to know where to focus.

Over simplification. The items that are listed in SWOT often tend to sound fairly general, lacking the kind of specificity that creates meaning. Where "new product development capability" is listed as a strength, for instance, the generality of the item tends to disguise what is really behind this successful business practice. Is the company strong in this dimension because they are excellent at sourcing new ideas, excellent at translating ideas from concept to actual product, able to move through the process very quickly, or adept in their marketing and sales methods for introducing new products to the market? A manufacturing company in North Carolina listed "new product development capability" as one of their strengths even though sales from products introduced in the past four years accounted for less than 1% of sales. General descriptions often hide more than they reveal. In addition, the guidance provided by the use of the TOWS matrix also tends to be fairly general, not focusing on specific products, services, or operations. Finally, the method provides little guidance on the appropriate balance of effort that should be devoted to different cells in the TOWS matrix.

Definitions may vary. In many cases it is not clear to management whether a particular item represents a strength or a weakness, or perhaps both. 3M's size clearly presents a strength for the company in that size confers market power, better access to financial markets, and other advantages. However size also represents a weakness since the company is unable to pursue the smaller business opportunities that once made it successful, and is not particularly agile in responding to sudden competitive moves. If size is both a strength and a weakness simultaneously, the management implications may be difficult to determine. In the case of Disney, their CEO Michael Eisner masterminded the company's revival in the early 1990s. His imagination and management skills represented a significant strength for the company. Later on he underwent quadruple bypass surgery at a time when there was no executive succession plan in place, and then his fight with board members over company direction paralyzed the company. Strength or weakness? Hard to tell.

Are they relevant? Simply because a company has a particular strength does not mean it can effectively compete in its industry. If a company's strengths or weaknesses have relevance for the key success factors in the industry, then attention devoted to them can be important. However business history is rife with examples of companies which developed amazing strengths that were incredibly irrelevant for their industries. Sharper Image, which finally went bankrupt in 2008, originally thrived on its knack and pizzazz in sourcing and presenting high-tech personal gadgets such as ion air purifiers, jogging watches, and nose hair trimmers (!). Unfortunately, the kind of creative force that was the foundation of the business became irrelevant to consumers and retailing in the 2000s.

Static view. The most discouraging part of SWOT is that the list developed during each planning cycle only provides a picture of the company at a fixed point in time. In the process of creating the list there is little attention devoted to understanding why or how a company came to possess a certain strength or develop a certain weakness to begin with. Without developing an understanding of cause-and-effect, management is not provided with guidance on what kinds of steps to take going forward. From one planning cycle to the next it is not uncommon to find new strengths appear and previously held strengths disappear. A company conducts its strategic planning biannually, and in successive plans has identified the strengths pictured in Figure 5.6. Items A, B, and F remain strengths consistently over this period, but C has morphed into something slightly different as C*. Meanwhile new strengths E and G have appeared and D has for some reason dropped off the list. As time goes by and companies encounter changing market conditions with evolving competition, it is not unusual to witness these kinds of changes in perceived strengths taking place.

A dynamic view of a company's strategic potential is more appropriate and more useful. As strategic managers we are interested in understanding not only that strengths and weaknesses may exist, but also what it is that creates strengths and prevents weaknesses from developing, which in turn will allow us to develop competitive advantage. If we understand how actions and activities undertaken

**Figure 5.6
Strengths in Successive SWOT Analyses**

Year 1		Year 3
A	→	A
B	→	B
C	→	C*
D		
	→	E
F	→	F
	→	G

The Greenbrier resort has stood in the mountains of West Virginia for more than a hundred years. Founded as a haven for those seeking the healing powers of the nearby White Sulphur Springs, the resort really came into being as more than a hotel when the C&O Railroad purchased the property in 1910. Today the enormous property has more than 700 rooms, 10 lobbies and a complete conference center. The resort boasts three championship golf courses, tennis courts, a spa, and more than 6,500 acres of land. The Greenbrier has been awarded the AAA Five Diamond status since the inception of the award and is one of only three properties to have earned this distinction for 33 consecutive years.

During good times, the resort has prospered as a destination resort for the rich and famous as well as families looking for an elegant vacation getaway. Among the more interesting features of the resort is the vast underground bunkers built to house the President and Congress in the event of a national emergency.

While not easy to travel to, one of the real appeals to the resort is its relative proximity to major cities in the eastern United States.

QUESTIONS

1. What are the Strengths and Weaknesses of the resort?
2. What are the Opportunities and Threats for the resort?
3. How would you suggest they take advantage of their Strengths and minimize their Weaknesses?
4. How would you suggest they take advantage of their Opportunities and minimize their Threats?

Value chain A concept that emphasizes that a company is an organization of interrelated activities designed to create value for stakeholders, and that the derivation of superior performance is better understood by focusing on what a company actually does.

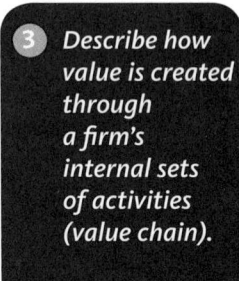

3 *Describe how value is created through a firm's internal sets of activities (value chain).*

in the past result in our current strategic position, then we can make better judgments about the effects that our current actions and activities will have going forward. This is the vital distinction between SWOT and the value chain perspective, to which we now turn.

VALUE CHAIN

Much like SWOT, the concept of the value chain was first explored in strategic management about thirty years ago, when management scholars started thinking about the sets of activities that are combined by a company to form a successful "business system." The **value chain** provides "a systematic way of examining all the activities a firm performs and how they interact …" in order to find a basis for competitive advantage.[6] In the first chapter of this textbook, we stressed that the value chain is one of the core concepts at the heart of effective strategic management. As a method of internal analysis, exploring the value chain requires us to go significantly deeper into a company than does the SWOT approach. The basic rationale of the value chain is that some types of activities are observed when a company competes one way, while other sets of activities are observed when another company competes in a different way. Therefore through the value chain we move below summary ideas about a company's strong or weak points; instead, we examine the nature of activities performed in or by the company, and we estimate how such activities are able to uniquely create value in the industry vis-à-vis competitors.

Industry and Company Value Chains

The value chain concept recognizes that a company is one of many entities that participate in an entire chain of value-adding activity within any given industry (see Figure 5.7). When you open up a can of soda at home, it is because a complex array of integrated activities has taken place across an industry or industries that provide you this enjoyment. The chain of activities starts with basic raw materials and extends all the way to the finished product in your hand. Consider just the can itself: from mining bauxite ore, to the smelter, to mixing aluminum with manganese and magnesium, to extruding and roll casting aluminum sheets, to cutting and forming cans, to filling them with soda on a high-speed production line (that in itself is a complicated process involving multiple parts of an industry), to packed 24-count cases loaded onto pallets and shipped in semi-trucks, and then finally distributed to your supermarket. The travel agency vignette demonstrates that an identical product or service may be provided through one of several different sets of industry-wide activities. In this case an electronic airline ticket and other travel reservations can be sourced directly from an airline carrier, purchased through an online intermediary such as Orbitz.com or Priceline.com, or procured through a travel agency where the traveler can meet in person with a travel consultant to discuss personal plans and preferences. Each method involves a different set of activities, but each results in a similar outcome for the traveler.

In addition to value chain activities across a single industry or multiple industries, there are value chain activities within each company competing in the industry. Although we may tend to think about competing companies

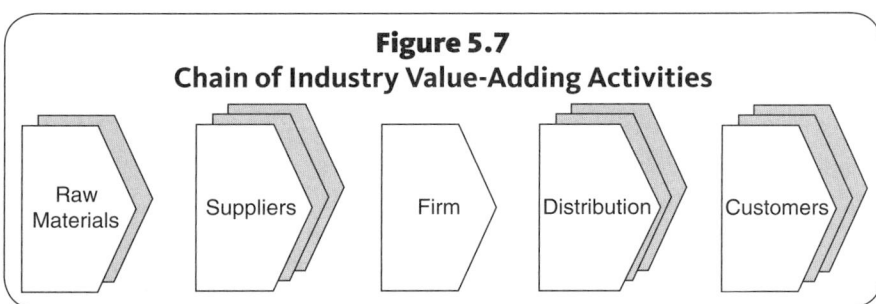

Figure 5.7
Chain of Industry Value-Adding Activities

Raw Materials · Suppliers · Firm · Distribution · Customers

in terms of the products or services that we see them providing, the value chain concept instead focuses on the different sets of activities that ultimately lead to the production of their products or services. This is the great insight about strategy that the value chain perspective provides: that a company is nothing more than a set of organized activities, and that products or services are simply the outcomes of the activities that have led to their creation. When we refer to a company as an organization, occasionally we might be referring to an organization of people, such as through departmental structure and hierarchy. However, at a very simple foundational level a company is structured so that employees *act* in certain ways. It is their activities that describe how a company actually conducts its business and produces products or services.

It is relatively easy to observe examples of how different activity sets define the differences between competitors and their approaches in an industry. In the photo finishing business Kodak has long been known for its focus on producing high-quality paper that was used by camera shops to print pictures. With the advent of digital photography, Canon—previously known for its strengths in plain paper copiers and printers—entered the camera market and encouraged end users to print pictures on Canon printers. In response Kodak developed the Easy-Share camera-printer docking combination, and is rapidly expanding its photo kiosks in drug stores and other retail locations nationwide. In book retailing the activity sets that distinguish Amazon.com from "bricks and mortar"–based Barnes & Noble are quite dramatic. Figure 5.8 provides other examples that illustrate how competitors' strategic approaches are characterized by different activity sets.[7]

Figure 5.8
Company Value Chains Differ

Industry	Company & Value Chain Activity	Company & Value Chain Activity
Book retailing	Barnes & Noble bricks 'n mortar stores	Amazon online retailing
Business education	Harvard real professors in physical classrooms	University of Phoenix directed self-education diplomas by mail
Personal computers	Dell modular design mass customization JIT manufacturing	Apple proprietary design limited model selection
Movie rental	Blockbuster neighborhood stores movies and games	Netflix convenience by mail
Steel	Arcelor-Mittal blast furnaces large volume from iron ore	Nucor electric arc furnaces mini-mills using scrap
Food retailing	Whole Foods exceptional quality organics & naturals	Food Lion acceptable quality wide selection

Looking carefully within any company, we can differentiate between two kinds of important value-adding activities. When we mention "Toyota," most people will think of certain models of cars and trucks; when we say "Starbucks," it calls to mind something like a "vente latte double shot no whip skim extra hot" (yikes!). When we used Priceline.com as an example earlier, we tend to think of the inexpensive ticket we were able to get on their Web site. That is, most people naturally tend to associate companies with their products and types of services. Along the bottom of the company value chain diagram in Figure 5.9 are "primary activities." These are the activities engaged in to actually produce the tangible products and services that come to mind when a company's name is mentioned. If we walked into a Pepsi facility, we would expect to see these activities on the bottom of the figure taking place: ingredients and packaging materials coming in the back warehouse door, the high-speed lines queuing and filling cans, preparing the finished goods for shipping, and so on. We also regularly observe the Pepsi trucks delivering product to local stores, and we see their ads on TV with their most current "hip" pitch person.

In contrast, in the top half of Figure 5.9 are what have been called "support activities." These include much of the white collar work done in companies such as finance, information systems, human resources, legal work, research and development, and purchasing efforts. When we consider any type of company and its products or services, we generally do not think too much about the people performing these so-called support functions despite the fact that those jobs are generally more coveted by new college graduates. When we step into the Pepsi plant, we are struck with the furious production activity going on before our eyes, not with what the person in the corner office is working on.

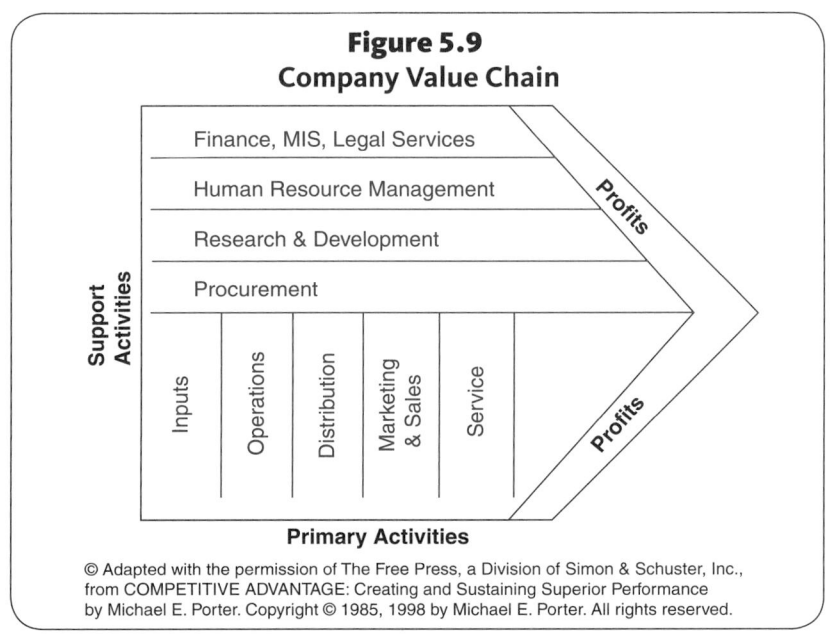

Figure 5.9
Company Value Chain

Support Activities
- Finance, MIS, Legal Services
- Human Resource Management
- Research & Development
- Procurement

Primary Activities
- Inputs
- Operations
- Distribution
- Marketing & Sales
- Service

Profits

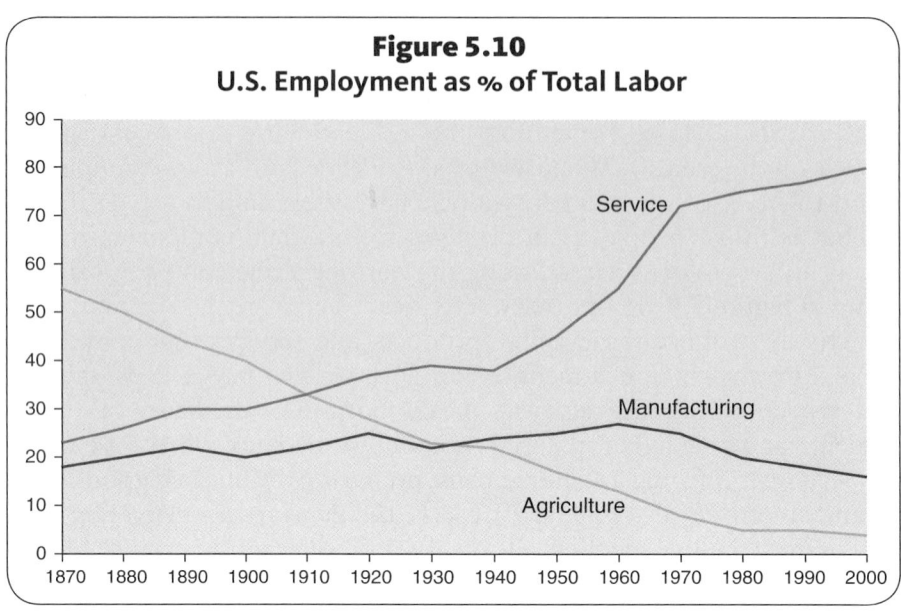

Figure 5.10
U.S. Employment as % of Total Labor

Which type of activities—primary or support—do you think are more important from the standpoint of strategic management? One perspective on this comes from a study on employment in the United States conducted a few years ago, examining the importance of both manufacturing and service jobs in America. Whereas manufacturing jobs involve handling physical objects, service jobs involve "anything…that could not be dropped on your foot."[8] Service activities include such areas as finance, HR, purchasing, research, design, engineering, administration, and legal, even in traditional manufacturing companies. Figure 5.10 reproduces the results of this study.[9] In a dramatic shift from earlier in the twentieth century, by 2000 manufacturing activities constituted less than 20 percent of U.S. employment while service activities represented over 75 percent. Service activities—including primarily all the activities in the top half of the company value chain in Figure 5.9—are where employment is concentrated. Here, and in the coordination that must occur between support activities and primary activities, is where significant strategic value is truly added.[10]

Value Chain Benefits

Illustrates derivation of strengths and weaknesses.
We pointed out earlier that the list of strengths and weaknesses is likely to change over time, but that SWOT does not substantively explore the reasons behind such changes. The value chain perspective can answer these questions because it is the activities that a company undertakes that lead to positions of superiority (strength) or contribute to positions of weakness. Examining the activities therefore focuses attention on the causes of internal strengths and weaknesses. For example, "we are particularly strong in new products because of how well our marketing research and R&D staff works together to move new ideas rapidly into development and production."

Dynamic. One of the most important differences from SWOT is that the value chain approach focuses more on what a company does, not what a company is. Consistent with the idea of a business system, the activities that take place within companies are often organized and systemized ways of conducting affairs. When companies are successful, like a well-oiled machine they seek to reproduce and fine-tune on an ongoing basis the actions they took that made them successful. For these reasons the actions that lead to success tend to persist over periods of time. If companies are not successful, then they try to change the ways they conduct business in order to find more effective methods. When weaknesses that have developed remain stubbornly persistent, it is likely that a company's actions are perpetuating them. So a focus on the activities—patterns of behavior over a period of time—has a dynamic quality to it that the static SWOT approach invariably misses.

More predictable path of development. When the analysis focuses on how patterns of activities result in performance, it becomes much easier to predict—at least in the near term—what future developments will take place for a company. If it is true that examining activities helps develop a cause-and-effect understanding of successes and failures, then that same logic can be used productively to look ahead. Since managing strategically involves setting goals and objectives for the future, an understanding of the effects of actions and behaviors can guide goal setting. This understanding can also reveal gaps that exist between goals that have been set and the predicted results of activities the company currently engages in.

Spotlights internal synchronization and consistency of effort. One of the hallmarks of strategic decisions discussed in Chapter 1 is that they significantly affect all parts of the organization. Coordination across departments and functional areas (marketing, finance, operations, etc.) is integral to effective strategic management. While many activities highlighted in a value chain analysis will occur within these functional areas, the value chain explicitly recognizes the need to evaluate how those various activities are coordinated with other departments, so that the company accomplishes the required level of cross-department integration and consistency of effort in its approach to competitive markets. Therefore identifying and managing the coordinating activities become extremely important. This dimension will be further discussed in the next section.

Provides more actionable information for managing strategy. With attention on the day-to-day activities that occur within a company as the means to understand how competitive strengths are developed, it should come as no surprise that value chain analysis can be very useful as a tool of management. Since the analysis has drilled down to the level of actions that departments and people take, decisions to enhance strengths or correct weaknesses can focus on specific activities. By breaking down a conceptual strength (such as "new product development capability") into specific sets of activities that lead to this competitive advantage, management has more actionable information that can guide investments made to enhance the process.

Potential Value Chain Drawbacks

Depends on information systems to provide useful data. It is nice to be able to break down a company's overall strengths into sets of activities that in combination or in sequence produce a positive outcome. Yet the risk remains that these contributing activities are described in only general terms, and this does not go far enough to understand the company's approach relative to competition. Remember from Chapters 1 and 2 that the goal of strategic management is to be different from and better than competitors. The provision and use of objective information is required to draw informed conclusions. One NASCAR team worked diligently to reduce the pit time for its driver, which makes a significant contribution to overall race standings. Yet by collecting metrics to evaluate their improvements relative to their competition, they discovered that competing teams had also reduced their pit times. Moreover, the team that thought it had achieved competitive superiority on this dimension employed a greater number of pit crew workers to accomplish the reduced time, and so the cost/benefit comparison with its competitor looked even worse. A company may conclude, for instance, that its new product development capability is strong because it moves through the R&D process quickly (from idea to finished product). However, more data is needed to have confidence that this conclusion is warranted. Is the development time, in fact, faster than what competitors have been able to engineer? Is the development time compressed because the company overspends on staff and resources in this area, relative to competition? Even though competitive information may not always be easily available, the company must use data to develop metrics that provide hard evidence supporting preliminary conclusions. **Activity-based costing**, which students have often been exposed to in early accounting classes, can be helpful in developing internal cost and performance metrics.

More focus internally, less focus on market. One of the positive features of SWOT is that it explicitly recognizes market threats and opportunities as components of its analysis. With value chain analysis there could be a tendency to simply focus inwardly on activities and behaviors of the company, and not account for the nature of the marketplace. It is not uncommon to find that companies perform sets of activities in certain ways "because they have always done it this way," or because these activities have contributed to past successes and have therefore been reinforced over time. In the 1990s, the pigments manufacturing division of Ciba-Geigy had significantly reduced their costs per ton produced while maintaining product quality. Yet they later discovered that they were losing market share because competition had moved to more adeptly respond to escalating customer requirements by producing higher quality at even lower costs, leaving Ciba-Geigy behind.[11] Value is defined in the marketplace, and the market is constantly shifting based on technological advances, changing customer preferences, and dynamic competition. When companies consider the activities they engage in as part of the "value chain," attention must remain focused on how the marketplace continues to shape the meaning of value.

Activity-based costing
A managerial accounting method used to assign all direct and indirect costs to a particular activity.

VALUE CHAIN AND COMPETITIVE ADVANTAGE

4 Assess how the value chain perspective provides insight on sources of competitive advantage.

Value Creation

Companies must create value and then capture value in order to develop competitive advantage. What is value, and how is it created? This simple question is really at the very heart of effective strategic management. **Value creation** occurs when some other party appreciates something that we do for him or her and is willing to execute a profitable transaction with us as a result. Value is thus defined in the marketplace through transactions between willing buyers and willing sellers; it is not defined by either party in isolation from the other. In his California kitchen, Wally Amos created a special recipe for chocolate chip cookies that people loved and which he developed into the Famous Amos brand that has flourished for over 25 years. In contrast, Fortune 44 was a Colorado company that developed sensational tasting fortune cookies, only to discover that few people appreciated a great-tasting fortune cookie enough to buy them. The company went out of business very quickly.

There are several basic ways in which value can be created. The most obvious way to create value appreciated by others is to provide greater benefits to them for the same price they have been accustomed to paying previously. Panel (a) in Figure 5.11 illustrates that Company Y has created value in this fashion, compared to Company X. For example, in 2005, for no extra annual fee *The Wall Street Journal* added a "weekend edition" delivered on Saturdays to its regular subscribers. In the same year Blockbuster changed its return policy to "no late fees" without increasing its basic movie rental fee.

Another means to create value involves just the opposite of these examples, by providing exactly the same benefits as always but at a price that has been reduced below what is normally paid. In panel (b) of Figure 5.11 Company Q has somehow figured out how to deliver to its customers precisely the same benefits they have always received, but at a lower price than Company P still charges (presumably reflecting that Q has discovered ways to effect cost savings). At the dawn of the "browser wars" in the 1990s, Microsoft gave away Internet Explorer for free while Netscape continued to charge customers for its software.

Panel (c) of the figure combines elements of both these basic methods for creating value. In this case Company T has raised its prices over what is normally paid, but it delivers significantly greater benefits than does Company S;

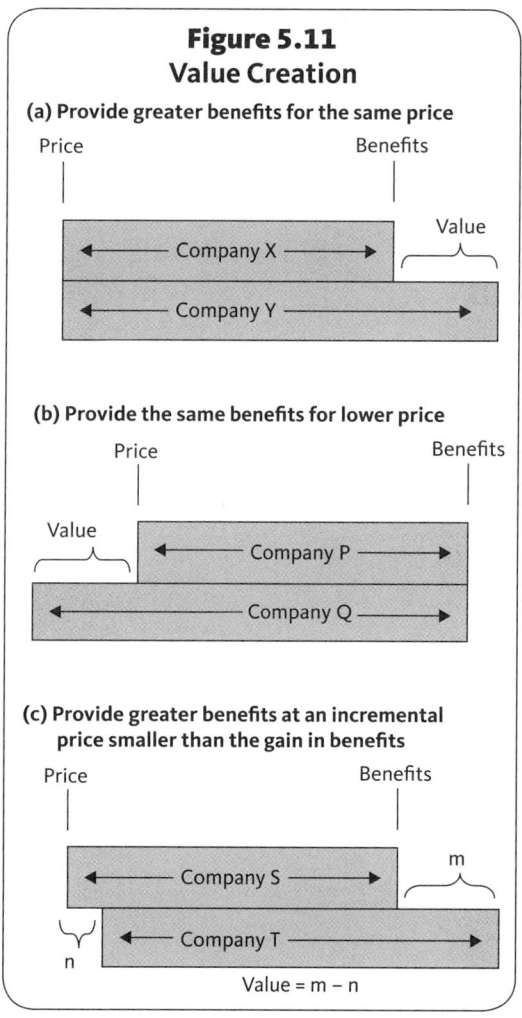

**Figure 5.11
Value Creation**

(a) Provide greater benefits for the same price

Price   Benefits

Company X

Company Y   Value

(b) Provide the same benefits for lower price

Price   Benefits

Value

Company P

Company Q

(c) Provide greater benefits at an incremental price smaller than the gain in benefits

Price   Benefits

Company S   m

Company T

n

Value = m − n

Value creation When some other party appreciates something that we do for them and is willing to execute a profitable transaction with us as a result.

here the value created by T is the difference between **m** and **n** in the figure. For corporate customers Dell preloads not only software but also inventory "tag" information on both its PCs and the customer's inventory database, charging $100 more for this service but also creating up to $200 savings per PC for the customer. Apple's iPod also falls into this category. Commanding roughly 75 percent of the MP3 player market, iPods are certainly more expensive than other products. Yet clearly the Apple product is the player of choice because the capabilities of the device, its design, internal software, and the iTunes song library deliver significantly greater benefits to customers that more than offset its higher price.

There is a fourth method of value creation that is not illustrated in the figure. It is also possible to create value by broadening access to benefits to a wider audience, without sacrificing the benefits delivered to existing customers. For many years Coors beer was not distributed east of the Mississippi River—a decision made by the company for both operational and marketing reasons, but one which also created a sort of mystique about the brand. In 1981 national distribution was initiated, spreading the highly desirable western brand to those in the east who had never before tried it. eBay becomes more valuable to existing customers when its network of users expands, since it provides everyone a more efficient auction environment, through a greater selection of merchandise and a larger group of potential buyers. Often the value created by broadening access involves building a new type of customer base or reaching out to new geographic markets, such as was the case with the Coors expansion.

ETHICS

However, value can also be viewed as a social good, unrelated to products and services provided by companies. Facebook.com provides a social network for ever larger numbers of people, whose access only enhances the usefulness of the network. Several states have, over the years, managed to reduce unemployment and its associated governmental cost by connecting unemployment applicants with a local jobs database. Value is created for taxpayers because government spending can then be redirected to other vital needs, and value is created for unemployed workers who get connected with potential employers. General Electric initiated a new program labeled "Ecoimagination Vision." As explained by CEO Jeffrey Immelt, "We will establish partnerships with our customers to tackle the most pressing environmental challenges and double our research spending to develop the products and services they want. And we will use these technologies to improve our own energy efficiency and environmental performance. Increasingly, for your business, 'green' is green."[12] In this last statement the profit motive is plainly evident. Yet the benefits of environmentally conscious methods of manufacturing turbines, compressors, locomotives, and other industrial equipment will be enjoyed by the population at large and especially the communities in which GE locates factories.

Although ordinarily value creation is discussed in the context of what companies are able to do for their customers downstream in the industry, it is also appropriate to consider value creation possibilities *upstream* for suppliers. A company can create value for suppliers in several ways, and then capture that value to enhance its strategic position relative to its competitors. For example, research and development may identify a new manufacturing process that reduces costs previously borne by suppliers in providing highly specified raw material inputs. Another alternative may be that a company will outsource a particular function to a supplier that takes advantage of the supplier's own unique capabilities. Toshiba, for example, uses United Parcel Service for pickups and redeliveries in its laptop warranty repair service. Finding that its laptop customers valued "speed" when needing repairs, Toshiba worked with UPS—where speed is a valued organizational process—to outsource the actual laptop repair operation. Now laptop customers are pleased because repair time has been reduced, and value is created for supplier UPS by delivering new business to them.[13] A new venture often confronts suppliers who are hesitant to do business with an unproven, risky enterprise. However the promise of providing access to entirely new end users is a significant value because it can accelerate supplier growth. On a larger scale Whole Foods has provided precisely this type of broader market access to organic foods manufacturers, whose increased volume and greater efficiencies have now resulted in cost savings for Whole Foods.

Value Capture

For a company to gain competitive advantage it must be able to capture the value that is created. Assume that Company Y in Figure 5.11 has, in fact, figured out a way to provide greater benefits than Company X or the rest of its competitors without charging a higher price. Building on the logic of perfect competition explored in Chapter 4, we might expect that the other competitors will observe what Y is doing and then imitate it. In this way any kind of advantage gained from providing greater benefits will be competed away over some period of time. How, then, is value captured? To capture value a company must perform a set of activities that is superior to the way in which its competition acts. In addition, the company's set of activities must be **idiosyncratic**, meaning that they must be unique. To perform a set of activities in a unique fashion also means that competitors will not be able to imitate that set of activities, or cannot imitate them very easily or very inexpensively. Therefore, **value capture** occurs when a company creates value by acting in ways that its competitors cannot or will not act.

What portions of a company's value chain activities are difficult or impossible for a competitor to imitate? Once again, turn to the company value chain diagram in Figure 5.9. In most cases the primary activities associated with the actual production of a manufactured item or a service can be reproduced because they are more observable to outsiders. Although the Coca-Cola secret recipe has been the subject of much speculation and news over the years, any food technologist could easily identify its chemical makeup with commonly available analysis equipment. Knowing the formulation, an exact imitation of the product could be reproduced. With sufficient financial backing, a scale-efficient canning line could also be installed that replicates the manufacturing process for the finished product. Indeed, Sam's Choice Cola was released to the market in 1991 and although sold only in the Wal-Mart

Idiosyncratic Unique to the company (and hopefully of value), which cannot be reproduced by a competitor or imitated very easily.

Value capture When a company creates value by acting in ways that its competitors cannot or will not act.

chain, has done exceedingly well as a generic brand.[14] Similarly, competitors in the coffee business can closely imitate the physical characteristics of a typical Starbucks shop, the roast of its coffee, and its other beverage selections. These characteristics are more tangible, and can be reverse-engineered and reproduced fairly easily.

Value chain activities that are far less obvious to outsiders and competitors, and therefore far more difficult to imitate, are the support activities. These are unobservable, so that competitors can only surmise how research and development operates, what kinds of human resource practices are employed, the nature of internal financial controls that provide for sound management, or the policies and procedures used by a purchasing department to ensure higher quality inputs and/or lower costs. If a company hires exceptional employees to staff these support domains, and if the company develops particularly effective ways of operating within each of these domains, then it increasingly insulates the company from competitive imitation.

Taking this line of reasoning one step further, the greatest source of value capture resides in the *coordination* and *linkages* that exist between and across elements of a company's value chain. Consistent with the nature of strategy, to the extent that a company can tightly organize, coordinate, and orchestrate *all* of its value-adding activities into a unified, consistent approach to the marketplace, the more it ensures that its value chain is idiosyncratic and not subject to imitation. Hackensack University Hospital reduced the time it takes to treat heart attack patients by 30 percent and has a mortality rate for heart attacks 2 percent below the national average. It has achieved these results because of an intense effort to review and establish new cross-functional procedures and coordination.[15] In the $89 billion electronic manufacturing services industry, 77 percent of manufacturing is done outside the United States in order to take advantage of low-wage countries. However Plexus, a Neenah, Wisconsin, company, generates 69 percent of its revenue from components manufactured in the United States. The company uniquely specializes in low-volume production of a high mixture of items. To do so requires tremendous coordination across its internal and external value chains in order to achieve both flexibility to change quickly and inexpensively as well as maintain some control over costs.[16]

Even if a competitor were to hire away a top executive and his or her staff (which has occasionally happened in various industries), the effectiveness of that individual or staff will be impaired in their new organization because the nature of their relationships with other departments will be different. The aspects that work toward coordination and consistency of approach throughout any organization—factors such as culture, communication systems, personal relationships established among employees, long-held cross-organizational routines—are impossible for competitors to observe and extremely difficult for competitors to duplicate. We will talk more about these types of intangibles as critical "resources" in the next chapter.

Value Creation and Capture Through Opportunity Recognition

Implicit in the notion of value creation and capture is that a company is able to identify an opportunity to provide greater benefits for customers or suppliers, or discover ways to reduce costs and prices. There are a great many ways in which new ideas and opportunities are brought to the surface in organizations.[17] Competitive advantage, however, arises to the extent that some company in an industry is more successful in this process than others, and to the extent that its methods for achieving a higher success rate cannot easily be imitated.

The sets of activities through which companies may excel in opportunity recognition include the following: 1) through internal coordination within the company value chain, 2) through external relations downstream with customers and upstream with suppliers, and 3) through other external relations and "boundary-spanning" activities that enhance the company's ability to anticipate emerging trends and industry/competitive dynamics.

The first approach—relying on internal activities and processes—is the traditional approach. Many companies have extremely vibrant and well-funded internal research and development efforts underway. Occasionally, centralized R&D efforts have been broken up into physically separated "skunk works" units in order to shed some corporate policy guidance and loosen up development teams. A trend through the 1990s has been to increase the level of cross-departmental coordination on new developments, such as through cross-functional teams involving R&D, marketing, operations, and purchasing to simultaneously provide input rather than sequentially examine new ideas. These methods parallel value capture methods that focus on the linkages across internal company value chain activities.

Working upstream with suppliers and downstream with customers has proved successful for some companies. An investment in activities that regularly feeds back customer preferences and feeds forward supplier ideas can stimulate further internal development activity. Paralleling value-capture methods that work across the industry value chain, investments in these activities can work to combine customer needs identification, supplier research, and the company's own knowledge. Procter & Gamble has instituted just such a "connect and develop" program that produces over 35 percent of the company's innovations and billions of revenue dollars. Through this program they develop new ideas that arise from bringing together information from seventy "technology entrepreneurs" who identify emerging consumer needs with the 50,000 R&D workers employed by fifteen major suppliers.[18]

The third approach involves boundary-spanning outside the industry. In this fashion companies identify emerging competitive, technological, environmental, economic, and social trends that are estimated to have a significant impact on their business or industry. Ideas that spring from such broad, prospective activities may often result in small internal efforts to prototype new products or services that could respond to the emergent industry environment. Early prototyping activities enhance the potential for

Value chain analysis
A method that identifies value-creating activities in a company, categorizes them into important subsets, develops information to understand how the activities create value and what their costs are, and pinpoints opportunities for enhanced value creation and cost reduction. It is a dynamic view of a company's activities.

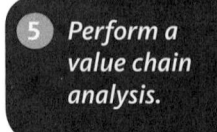

5 *Perform a value chain analysis.*

a company to better anticipate and successfully take advantage of significant changes. The types of activities associated with these efforts are often the most challenging to undertake in any organization, because they are intentionally focused on identifying opportunities that do not exist in the present and products or services for whom a customer base has not yet developed.[19] Yet as described in Chapter 1, the nature of industries and markets today suggests that these prospecting capabilities are of growing importance. The ability to create and capture value depends to an increasing extent on the activities that companies structure to develop prescience about their industries and to use such prescient knowledge productively.

CONDUCTING A VALUE CHAIN ANALYSIS

There are five significant results of a **value chain analysis**. First, the company creates a better understanding of the complete set of value-creating activities it engages in—sort of a roadmap of all the steps it takes to manifest a product or service for its customers. Second, it helps clarify how the activities in different functional areas of the company (marketing, purchasing, production, customer service, etc.) are either working in synch in support of a common strategic approach or may be working at odds with each other. Third, a strong analysis will identify how much of a contribution is made by some of those intangible service activities performed in the company (the top half of the value chain diagram in Figure 5.9), and how important is the intangible coordination activities among departments. Fourth, this type of analysis can shed light on how and where in the company the creation and capture of value can be enhanced and/or where costs can be lowered without sacrificing value. Finally—and again reflecting the strategic imperatives mentioned in Chapter 1—value chain analysis can provide actionable information on the extent to which the company engages in activities that are specifically designed to help recognize and move on new opportunities emerging in the competitive environment. If we think about a company as an organization of activities designed to create and capture value, then this type of analysis focuses our attention on what the company actually does that makes a difference in achieving superior performance.

There are three primary steps in a value chain analysis:[20]

1. Identify the value chain activities.
2. Evaluate their value-creating properties and cost characteristics.
3. Identify improvements that allow the company to capture greater value.

Step 1: Identify Value Chain Activities

The first step is to identify key value-creating activities throughout the organization. Every functional area of the company should be part of this process since, as we have argued earlier, value is created through activities and there are important activities performed in all departments throughout the organization. Therefore a value chain analysis is one means for understanding how higher-level strategic goals and direction are translating to day-to-day behavior in each functional area.

We are not suggesting that we identify and analyze every single activity performed by every single employee! Looking at the millions of such activities goes way too far. There are some guidelines that help us focus on particular kinds or particular categories of activities. The important activities to pay attention to are those that exhibit any of the following characteristics:

- They represent a significant percentage of operating cost;
- What enables the activity to be performed or what it costs to perform the activity is different from what's involved in other activities in the company;
- The activities are performed by competitors in different ways (competitive analysis on key success factors, strengths and weaknesses is critical!); or
- The activities appear to have great potential to create strategic differences from competition.

Occasionally, these guidelines may focus our attention on a discrete department or function within a company, such as purchasing or marketing, because it is a big operation or because the company is generally known to be particularly good at performing these functions. More often than not,

**Figure 5.12
Activities
Associated with
Advertising**

Develop brand
positioning
statement

Develop
alternative
ad layouts

Write
advertising
copy

Test ad
layouts with
consumers

Coordinate
final ad
production

Develop media
placement
plan

Buy media

Evaluate
readership &
response

however, simply considering an aggregation of activities at a summary functional level will be inadequate for the outcomes we seek in this type of analysis. There is too much going on within an entire department or function; we need to drill down further. Just as we described earlier how "new product excellence" can be the result of a whole series of different kinds of activities, departmental or functional excellence in all likelihood comes from subsets of activities within its sphere.

Let's say, for example, that we believe our company's reputation for excellence in its marketing actually springs from the effectiveness of its advertising. We receive feedback that our advertisements are superior, that they generate high levels of readership, and that consumers cut out our coupons and use them at a higher rate than industry averages would suggest. Value chain analysis would then prompt us to break down the activities associated with advertising, in order to identify more precisely what we do and how we do it so well. Figure 5.12 provides a view of the chain of value-adding activities in this one area within the marketing function. Now we are able to focus in more carefully on what contributes to great advertising, which in turn contributes to great marketing and our ability to out-compete other companies.

Step 2: Evaluate Activities' Value Characteristics and Costs

In the earlier discussion of potential drawbacks to the value chain we mentioned that information systems are required to provide useful data. This is especially true when we seek to understand the cost- and value-creating characteristics of various activities. The typical company does not readily capture specific enough cost information, for example, on the activities in the advertising function outline in Figure 5.12. Yet this type of detail can be especially revealing.

Figure 5.13 shows how helpful it can be to identify important categories of activities as suggested in Step One, and to capture essential cost information about those categories. The information is from a manufacturing company whose key strategic position in the marketplace depends on custom manufacturing of unusually complicated electronics components and a very tight relationship between its sales force in the field and the customers. Before the company ever begins a custom production run of an item, there is a sort of a dance it engages in between the customer, sourcing, and buying the parts needed for the customer's special order, receiving the various parts, and testing and preparing them for use in production. The astute student will recognize that sales and purchasing are both functions that exist in the top half of value chain diagram (you can't "drop them on your foot"), while receiving and testing is on the lower half in the primary activities sector. So this is a company that has to coordinate well across value chain sectors in order to do well in its market.

The left side of Figure 5.13 shows the traditional accounting treatment for the personnel and minor supplies and overhead expenses that

Figure 5.13
Manufacturing Firm Value Chain Analysis (000s)

Traditional accounting		Value chain analysis		
Salaries	$177,400		Field sales purchase orders	$72,300
Benefits	56,325	Sales	Purchase order processing	24,500
Supplies	36,600		Expediting delayed orders	13,500
Fixed costs	11,275			
			Sourcing suppliers	68,000
	$281,600	Purchasing	Issuing supplier orders	36,000
			Tracking supplier order status	7,500
			Receiving & handling	8,300
		Receiving	Resolving supplier quality	24,300
			Reissuing supplier orders	10,700
			Preparation for production	16,500
				$281,600

are involved in these efforts. These costs would usually get rolled up into a corporate income statement, but they do not tell us anything at all about the essential activities performed by the company. However, company management thought carefully about the categories of activities that were important in their business, and then used an activity-based costing system to produce the figures on the right side. The "Sales" category is really a combination of field sales and internal sales office activities (which themselves are a subset of the Marketing and Sales department). "Purchasing" is a subset of activities within the Procurement department that relate specifically to these types of custom orders, and "Receiving" is also a subset of activities within the entire warehousing function. None of these categories of activities would appear on any regular financial statement. Yet the combinations and categorizations reveal not only where the greatest costs lie but also where there may be opportunities to enhance value capture.

Each activity performed by a company presumably creates value and involves costs, and hopefully many activities will have value-capturing characteristics (meaning that they are unique and cannot be imitated very easily). To better understand how each activity creates value and what determines its cost, we can evaluate it by considering two different kinds of drivers—**executional drivers** and **structural drivers** (Figure 5.14). Executional drivers are derived from the execution of the business activities—involving people, systems, routines, culture, and coordination—and usually have a fairly important learning dimension to them (i.e., get better over time). Structural drivers are derived from the strategic choices made about the underlying economic logic and structure of the business—such as the scale and scope of its operations, the complexity of its products or services, and its use of technology. Executional and structural drivers can be sources of either value

Executional drivers
Performance and cost dimensions of activities that are derived from the execution of the business activities—involving people, systems, routines, culture, and coordination—and usually have a fairly important learning dimension to them.

Structural drivers
Performance and cost dimensions of activities that are derived from the strategic choices made about the underlying economic logic and structure of the business—such as the scale and scope of its operations, the complexity of its products or services, and its use of technology.

enhancement or cost reduction, and sometimes both simultaneously. In Chapter 7 when we more carefully describe generic strategies, which depend on the value chain ideas we're covering here, we will spend considerably more time discussing the nuances of these types of drivers.

Step 3: Identify Improvements That Allow the Company to Capture Greater Value

The categorization and cost itemization of value chain activities in the previous step ordinarily make this final step much easier, and sometimes almost obvious. For example, in the company profiled in Figure 5.13, management learned that $24.3 million was spent annually in checking the quality of received parts from suppliers, and nearly $11 million on efforts to reorder from suppliers whose received material did not meet specification. Management realized that by investing a bit more in the effort to source quality suppliers to begin with, the company would save costs later on, orders could go into production sooner, and customers would be shipped final product more quickly. Management also realized that an investment in more sophisticated enterprise management software would lead to reduced costs in order processing and tracking, and again lead to smoother flow of orders to manufacturing.

There are five basic questions to ask during this step of value chain analysis. These reflect the ways in which value can be created, shown earlier in Figure 5.11 and its discussion:

1. Can we increase benefits in this activity (or subset of activity), holding costs constant?
2. Can we hold benefits constant while reducing costs?
3. Could we reduce assets required for this activity, while holding both benefits and costs constant?
4. Would a further investment in assets improve the company's ability to either create benefits or improve costs?
5. Can we expand the scale or scope of our activities to a broader audience without sacrificing benefits or costs to our current sets of stakeholders?

Outsourcing
When activities that are essential in producing a company's products or services are provided by other companies on a contractual basis.

It may be that, through identifying sequences of value creating activities, we also realize that **outsourcing** is a possibility for some activities—that is, they could be handled effectively by other companies. We need to be careful about the decisions used to determine whether activities—even minor sets—are outsourced to others, since they could have important strategic consequences. We will return to the topic of outsourcing in Chapter 7, when we describe more carefully the types of strategies companies can follow and the key value chain activities choices they make for each.

CHAPTER SUMMARY

Internal analysis can improve our understanding of why there are performance differences between companies in an industry. By examining carefully what a company does, what it fails to do, and how it operates, one can better identify the sources of strengths (and weaknesses) that enable it to occupy a leading (or lagging) position in an industry. SWOT tends to provide a perceptual snapshot of a company at a point in time. Value chain analysis is a more dynamic view because it exposes causes and effects, draws our attention to the critical concepts of value creation and value capture, and provides important insights on sources of competitive advantage by focusing on unique activities that cannot be imitated by competitors.

The value chain concentrates on activities conducted within a company. Primary activities are those we can easily observe, and are associated with the more tangible aspects of products and services that a company produces. Support activities involve the efforts of company employees and management behind the scenes, including functions such as human resources, research and development, finance and accounting, procurement, and administration. Coordinating activities are those that seek to ensure strategic consistency across the company by tightly linking activities across different functional areas of the value chain and making sure they are mutually reinforcing. The uniqueness that provides a foundation for competitive advantage often resides in support and coordinating activities.

Companies may prosper by creating value for customers, for suppliers, and for broad stakeholder groups such as communities. Value can also be created through company processes that more effectively detect emerging opportunities and take advantage of them before competitors. Sustained superior returns resulting from these efforts depend on the uniqueness of a company's value-creating activities.

Value chain analysis is a three-step process that helps management identify and understand the subsets of critically important activities in a company. By identifying and categorizing important sets of activities, and by understanding their value creation and cost characteristics, managers are in a better position to explore how to create and capture greater value and/or how to reduce costs and prices without sacrificing benefits.

Chapter 6 will further explore internal analysis by discussing the relationship of resources to sustainable competitive advantage. One of the principal characteristics of strategic resources is that they create value. We will return to value chain analysis in Chapter 7 on Business Level Strategies, which can be better understood as coordinated sets of value-adding activities.

KEY TERMS

Activity-based costing (p. 148)

Executive drivers (p. 157)

Idiosyncratic (p. 151)

Outsourcing (p. 158)

Structural drivers (p. 157)

SWOT analysis (p. 136)

TOWS matrix (p. 139)

Value capture (p. 151)

Value chain (p. 142)

Value chain analysis (p. 154)

Value creation (p. 149)

SHORT ANSWER REVIEW QUESTIONS

1. How is opportunity recognition enhanced with the use of value chain analysis?
2. What are the big differences between the primary and secondary activities?
3. What are some of the structural drivers?
4. What elements constitute a value chain?
5. What are some of the executional drivers?
6. What are some negative characteristics of SWOT?
7. How is a value chain analysis best conducted?
8. What are some positive characteristics of SWOT?
9. How do you use a TOWS matrix?
10. How can SWOT be effectively used in organizations?
11. What can you reasonably expect to result from a value chain analysis?
12. What does SWOT stand for?
13. Where is the best place to look for value in an organization? Why?

GROUP EXERCISES

1. Draw a value chain for a manufacturing company, such as Dell Computer. Be sure to include industry value chain relationships as well as internal value chain activities. Highlight activities that you believe help insulate Dell from competitive threats.

2. Draw a value chain for an Internet-based company such as Google. Who are the suppliers? Who are the customers? What activities do you imagine Google has engaged in to become the world's premier search engine, and what must they do to sustain this position?

3. Draw a value chain for your business school. Are students to be considered as part of the supply network or part of the customer network? What value chain activities does your business school engage in to develop competitive advantage?

REFERENCES

[1] Rumelt, Richard R. 1991. "How much does industry matter?" *Strategic Management Journal* (12): 167–185.

[2] 3M Annual Report, 2005.

[3] http://www.angeloueconomics.com/growingburnet/Reports/SWOT_Report.pdf.

[4] http://www.iastate.edu/~strategicplan/2010/process/docs/swot.shtml.

[5] For perspective on the capacity to manage in complex environments, see: Miller, George A. 1994. The magical number seven, plus or minus two: Some limits in our capacity for processing information. *Psychological Review* (101)2: 343–352.

[6] Porter, Michael E. 1980. *Competitive strategy.* New York: Free Press.

[7] Porter, Michael E. 1985. *Competitive advantage.* New York: Free Press.

[8] Quinn, J. B. 1988. Technology in services: Past myths and future challenges. In B. R. Guile and J. B. Quinn (eds.), *Technology in services: Policies for growth, trade, and employment.* Washington, D.C.: National Academies Press.

[9] Quinn, J. B. 1992. *Intelligent enterprise.* New York: Free Press.

[10] There is considerable evidence that significant strategic value is added by support activities and the coordination that occurs between primary and support activities. For example, the Gartner Group recently reported that worldwide spending in 2006 on information technology was estimated to include $682 billion for technology services, but only $485 billion for manufactured hardware and software (which both include significant support activity components). In the strategy press over the last few years there has been significant attention paid to "knowledge" management and other intangible resources that underlie the manifestation of services and products by successful companies. See Blackler, F. 1993. Knowledge and the theory of organizations: Organizations as activity systems and the reframing of management. *Journal of Management Studies* 30(6): 863–883; Grant, R. 1996. Toward a knowledge based theory of the firm. *Strategic Management Journal* 17: 109–122; Winter, S. G. 1987. Knowledge and competence as strategic assets. In D. J. Teece (ed.), *The competitive challenge,* 159–184. New York: Harper & Row. Quinn argues that the "manufacturing-services interface is now the key to most manufacturing organizations." See Quinn, J. B. 1992. *Intelligent enterprise.* New York: Free Press.

[11] Pascale, R. 1997. *Nothing fails like success.* Princeton, NJ: Films for the Humanities and Sciences.

[12] http://ge.ecomagination.com.

[13] Friedman, Thomas. 2005. *The world is flat.* New York: Farrar, Straus and Giroux.

[14] *Discount Store News.* 1993. Sam's Choice climbs beverage brand list—Wal-Mart's Sam's American Choice beverage brand. October 4.

[15] Szabo, L. 2006. Hallmark of quality care: Efficiency. *USA Today,* October 20: 3B.

[16] Bulkeley, W. 2005. Plexus strategy: Smaller runs of more things. *Wall Street Journal.* October 8: A1.

[17] Baron, R. 2006. Opportunity recognition as pattern recognition: How entrepreneurs "connect the dots" to identify new business opportunities. *Academy of Management Perspectives* 20(1): 104–119.

[18] Huston, L., and N. Sakkab. 2006. Connect and develop. *Harvard Business Review,* March: 58–66.

[19] For a fuller discussion of this challenge, see Christensen, C. 1997. *The innovator's dilemma.* Boston: Harvard Business School Press.

[20] This section draws on material from Shank, J. K., and V. Govindarajan. 1993. *Strategic cost management.* New York: Free Press; See also Hammer, M., and J. Champy, 1993, *Reengineering the Corporation,* HarperBusiness: New York. See also Grant, R. M., 2005, *Contemporary strategy analysis* (5th edition). Malden, MA: Blackwell.

The Resource-Based View

In 1995 Phil and David Kavanagh, brothers from England, started the Classic Car Club. The brothers believed that banks practiced age discrimination by denying loans to young people who wanted to buy classic cars. Looking for a way for young people to be able to drive "cool cars," the brothers formed the Classic Car Club (CCC).

CCC started with three dozen members, ten cars, and one location in London. By 2005 it had four hundred members, forty cars, and a waiting list for its London location. In the meantime the Kavanaghs began to franchise their business to others in England. Across its six locations in England, the club now has two thousand members.

The club's following can be attributed to its unusual "rental" system. Unlike car companies that charge excessive prices for young drivers, or feature only relatively new, unexciting cars, the club operates on a points system, similar to many timeshare plans. Members receive a fixed number of points for the year and use them to rent the cars of their choice. The 750 annual points are good for about thirty to forty days of use a year. Cars are divided into six "bands," based on their value and desirability. For instance, a 1991 Mini Cooper is a Band One, while a Ferrari 348 is a Band Six. The Ferrari is assigned six points. Drive it on a weekday in December, and it will only cost twelve points. Drive that car on a Saturday, and it costs you twenty-four points. Drive it on a Saturday in July, it costs you ninety-six points.

Classic Car Club also works to maintain its club atmosphere, with a clubroom in each franchise, and it features monthly events for members only—as well as a few open weekends a year. The club's managers try to encourage the members to drive different cars, not just the Band Sixes. Many of the managers were originally members, and they believe that the point of the club is to try a wide variety of cars, something most people would not be able to achieve on their own.

Prospective members submit a character reference and have their driving records examined. If accepted into the organization, members must pay a total of £4,250 their first year, including a one-time joining fee and their annual dues. Although many of the club's London members are professional men age thirty to forty-five, it is becoming more diverse, appealing to couples and single women.

The club's next move was to franchise in the United States. Fees are higher in the United States due to insurance costs: a $1,500 joining fee and $7,500 in annual dues. The Manhattan branch opened in 2005, with branches planned in Miami and Los Angeles. The U.S. branches will be able to maintain an inventory of any cars that the managers wish. However, Kavanagh will work with U.S. franchise owners on their selections by developing a list of "must-haves," such as a Porsche 911 Turbo, a Series III Jaguar E-Type, and a Ferrari 308, as well as "classics" like the 1966 Mustang Fastback. As more members join each location, the fleet will be updated. The club seeks to maintain a certain member-to-car ratio, so that there is a reasonable chance to get the desired car on the desired dates. The club's challenge is to appeal to Americans, despite higher membership fees.

Questions

The Kavanaghs recognized an opportunity, had the financial resources, and utilized an existing rental point concept to provide unique cars for those individuals who ordinarily were prevented from enjoying them.

1. What unique factors did the founders bring together to start this business?

2. How would you classify the industry in which this business competes?

3. What are the value-adding activities their company performs that deliver competitive advantage?

4. What happens to this business now that large car rental firms, such as Hertz or Avis, have begun to offer high-end cars for rent?

In the previous two chapters we developed the reasoning and analysis techniques for examining the external environment, as well as how to use value chain analysis to understand the means by which a business can create a unique and valuable position for itself in the industry. In this chapter we will extend both of these approaches by outlining a very practical framework for developing a competitive advantage for a business. We will drill down deeper into the nature of business in order to understand the reasons for how and why a particular strategy has the ability to be successful. Here we focus on the resources that provide the foundation for the firm to succeed in the market. We will see that the careful identification and analysis of a *narrow* set of resources provides a business with the *broadest* possible opportunity to succeed in the marketplace and to sustain that success over time.

1 *Demonstrate how to categorize and compare the types and characteristics of company resources, which can generate competitive advantage.*

THE CHARACTERISTICS OF RESOURCES

The resources of an organization are truly at the foundation of the development of its sustainable competitive advantage. The "resource-based" approach was originally suggested almost fifty years ago, and has been carefully and more fully developed over the last twenty years by a number of strategic management scholars.[2] The approach contains a fairly well-developed theoretical framework, but has often been difficult for business people to implement in practice. This chapter will clearly lay out the principles behind the approach, and most importantly will provide a method for how to use it in practice.

Ordinary and Extraordinary Resources

At the outset we need to make a distinction between resources as contemplated by this approach and the way we might normally consider assets possessed by a firm. Whereas assets are typically thought of as those items listed or accounted for in the firm's balance sheet, the resource-based approach contends that not all such "accounting" assets are strategically important to the firm. As an example, the office desks and chairs of any business are indeed assets of the firm accounted for in its financial statements; however, these physical office furnishings do not represent a foundation upon which the firm can develop and sustain a competitive advantage. Having the finest, most ergonomically correct, Italian leather chairs and handcrafted desks may feel good, but few customers are going to pay the company more for their products (assuming the desks and chairs are not the product being sold) because its back-office operation has those accessories.

In contrast, the resource-based approach concentrates on resources of the business that have the potential to be strategically important. There are two types of resources that have the potential to be strategically important: tangible resources and intangible resources. **Tangible resources** are physical assets such as equipment, buildings, land, furniture, human resources, money, and patents. Tangible assets are relatively easy to identify, and are generally easy (albeit sometimes quite expensive) to acquire. While this list

Tangible resources
Physical assets such as equipment, buildings, land, furniture, human resources, money, and patents.

also includes items that may have no strategic value, in some instances physical assets do indeed provide the business with a strategic foundation. For instance, it may be possible that ergonomic Italian leather chairs are found to improve employee morale and job satisfaction to such a level that it directly leads to enhanced customer service and firm performance (this might be quite a stretch). More often, though, special manufacturing equipment or facilities, patents, and other customized operational assets[3] are the kinds of tangible resources with strategic importance. **Intangible resources** are those assets that are not physical in nature but are often more critical to the success of the business. Intangible assets include such things as relationships with key suppliers and other businesses, the culture of the organization, processes or routines within the organization, as well as the knowledge and skills of the senior management team or other key employees. The skills and experience of founders, for instance, is often cited as a key intangible asset in the development of new ventures.[4]

To this distinction between tangible and intangible resources, we need to also distinguish between ordinary resources and extraordinary resources. Embedded in all the thinking about resources is the fact that some of them are necessary simply for the business to operate legitimately in an industry, while others are truly unique to the business and help set it apart from its competitors. Many (if not most) of the resources possessed by a firm are **ordinary resources**, those that the firm must possess in order to be a credible contender in the industry. If you operate a sit-down restaurant, then you must have refrigerators, food preparation equipment, food preparers, serving staff, utensils, plates, napkins, condiments, a cash register, a credit card transmitter, telephones, a building to operate within, computers, some office furniture, lighting, a payroll system, a business license, and so on. These constitute the absolute minimum resources that must be in place for the business to be considered a restaurant; however, they provide no distinctive competitive advantage to the firm. Other than curiosity, customers are provided with no compelling reason to spend their money at this restaurant. Similarly, many of the capabilities of the business as well as the skills of the founders and employees are simply required to operate the restaurant. Serving safe food to customers that meets the cleanliness standards of the industry may be done very well by the new restaurant; however, the standard expectation of most customers is that every restaurant possesses this capability. Thus, while necessary to compete in this industry, this capability alone is not sufficient to be a source of sustainable competitive advantage.

Please don't presume by this observation that these ordinary resources and capabilities are not important. Quite the contrary! They must be developed and they must be developed well, or at least as well as the standard in the industry. A restaurant that barely clears its health inspection and receives a low grade may indeed operate. However, the general expectation of most customers of this industry is that restaurants have an "A" rating from the health department; a restaurant receiving something less than that "A" rating is likely to negatively impact the performance of the company. Investment in the ordinary resources of a particular industry is a necessary

Intangible resources
Those resources/ capabilities that are not physical in nature, including such things as relationships with key suppliers/ businesses, the culture of the organization, the history of the business to date, and perhaps most importantly, the skills of the founders.

Ordinary resources
Those resources or capabilities that are required just to be considered a business in an industry.

condition to operate, although they alone are not sufficient to develop a competitive advantage.

To create a sustainable competitive advantage with the associated opportunity to earn substantial returns, some of the resources that the business possesses must be **extraordinary resources**. These are resources that either individually or in combination with each other:

a. Provide the business with the opportunity to produce extraordinary economic returns;

b. Are unique in the industry;

c. Allow the business exclusive access—to either suppliers or customers—for some period of time;

d. Cannot be easily matched by another business in the short run; or

e. Cannot be easily transferred to or appropriated by another business.

There must be a reason why customers would consider giving their business to a different company. For most people it is far more convenient to continue in their established patterns of behavior than it is to change those patterns. Customers are often not willing to switch unless there is a compelling reason to do so. A company's extraordinary resources can create exceptional value and become the source of that motivation to change. Why would a customer choose one restaurant over another? Why will customers come to the new business rather than go to a well-known competitor? Will the restaurant have a unique atmosphere, type of cuisine, level of service, or entertainment when compared to other restaurants? Will its cost structure allow for prices to be set significantly lower than those of the competitors, while still providing comparable value on other dimensions that customers appreciate? Will access to the business location be more convenient? If it is only going to do the same thing that other firms do, why would anyone switch to the business? The strategic focus of any company in an industry, therefore, is to identify and develop extraordinary resources that enable the firm to offer an improvement in value to its customers and other key stakeholders. Extraordinary resources are at the foundation of value creation *and* value capture, and offer the opportunity to achieve financial gains in excess of ordinary returns produced in a particular industry. Figure 6.1 presents characteristics that help distinguish between ordinary and extraordinary resources.

The descriptions of extraordinary resources in Figure 6.1 prompt us to recall the discussions in Chapter 4 about imperfect markets and barriers to entry or imitation. Whether tangible or intangible, extraordinary resources are not readily available in competitive markets. Any industry in which firms have been able to develop and utilize extraordinary resources is one that will tend away from the perfectly competitive markets endpoint (Figure 4.1), where some firms are likely to be able to earn superior returns.

Five Key Dimensions of Extraordinary Resources

How can one determine if resources are ordinary in nature, or if they are extraordinary and provide a foundation for sustainable competitive advantage? While various strategy textbooks and articles provide somewhat

Extraordinary resources Those resources or capabilities that are believed by the management of a business to be simultaneously rare, durable, relatively nonsubstitutable, nontradable, and valuable.

Figure 6.1
Differences Between Ordinary and Extraordinary Resources

	Tangible (Hard assets; on balance sheet)	Intangible (Soft assets; not on balance sheet)
Ordinary (Necessary to compete, but not sufficient for advantage)	Easily viewed Easily purchased	Easily recognized Well known routines Able to learn easily
Extraordinary (Provide basis for competitive advantage)	Difficult to acquire Uncommon in industry Possibly immobile	Difficult to identify or understand Difficult to evaluate May require time to learn May require experience to understand

different approaches, in general five elements help answer this critical question. This is the VRIST framework. You might remember it more easily by thinking about the Latin word *verist,* meaning "truth," because any resource that exhibits all five characteristics is truly extraordinary. Such true resources represent a foundation for the business's strategy.

Strategy Acronym: VRIST
Extraordinary Resource Dimensions

V	**Valuable**	It is Valuable
R	**Rare**	It is Rare
I	**Imitation**	It is difficult to Imitate
S	**Substitution**	It cannot be Substituted for
T	**Tradable**	It cannot be Traded for

Is it valuable? Only those resources that have the ability to create value for the company might qualify as extraordinary. In assessing value creation, the truly extraordinary resource must help the company in at least one of several possible ways (Figure 6.2). These mirror the value chain discussion in Chapter 5: 1) lower its cost structure relative to competitors for a particular product or service; 2) provide enhanced product or service benefits to customers while maintaining parity on costs and prices; 3) provide the ability to charge more for its products/services and more than offset any related cost increases; or 4) enhance the company's ability to reach target customers more effectively or attract additional customers more efficiently than competitors. Over the years the major soft drink companies have discovered ways to reduce

Figure 6.2
Ways to Create Value

Accomplish this	While providing this
Lower costs	Parity on product/service features
Add features	Parity on costs and prices
Increase revenue	Revenue increases more than cost increases
New customers	Undiminished value to existing customers

their production costs for a typical can of soda, which has led to price declines at retail (in constant dollars) for these products. Supermarkets and their customers (us) are thus able to buy the same can of soda today at a price that is less than what was paid twenty years ago. At the heart of this effort were the design, procurement, and operational planning resources of these companies that led to mega-scale canning facilities and ultra-high-speed canning production lines. Another example is a small retail convenience store chain that had decided to create the "World's Cleanest Bathrooms." They invested heavily in the design and maintenance system of their bathrooms and then raised the prices on virtually every item in the store. Customers stopped in to use the "clean bathrooms" and were inclined to pick up convenience items there rather than loading the kids back in the car and heading to another location. Their sales volume and profits shot up during the next year, easily paying for the upgrades and providing a continuing value proposition for the company.

Is it rare? Each potentially extraordinary resource must be evaluated for its uniqueness relative to the competitors in the industry. Is the resource or capability relatively unique for your competitive industry? The question of rarity should be answered using research and objective data, although occasionally qualitative judgments may be necessary. If the management team finds that the resource or capability does not qualify as rare within the industry then it should be categorized as ordinary. Krispy Kreme Doughnuts went public in April of 2000 with a number of rare tangible and intangible resources including, among others, its brand name, its heritage in the southeastern United States, in addition to a unique recipe and doughnut making system that utilized proprietary machinery. These resources were unique in the industry and provided a potential competitive advantage to the company. In contrast, one of the reasons McDonald's restaurants are so popular is the general customer perception that they have cleaner food preparation operations and eating areas than other fast food operations. Their cleaning standards have, in fact, been incorporated into their franchise manual so that every McDonald's restaurant follows virtually identical procedures. Yet these standards are not actually rare, evidenced by the incorporation of similar procedures at Burger King, Wendy's, and other national fast food restaurants. As in our discussion of switching costs from Chapter 4, when we consider the elements of the resource-based approach we should consider whether each may be categorized as either real or perceived. A resource that is *perceived* as rare can be just as powerful as a real resource that is rare. The cachet of a brand name is a perception by consumers, and yet may provide a significant resource-based advantage for the firm that simultaneously meets all five of the VRIST criteria.

Is it difficult to imitate? If you have determined that a particular resource is valuable and rare, then the next step is to determine whether some other company might be able to easily imitate it. If it can be imitated, how perfectly can it be copied? One obvious means to prevent imitation is to obtain **intellectual property protection** for the resource, such as through a patent or trademark. Trademarks protect names and graphic designs associated with a company from being copied. Patents may be granted to unique, nonobvious products and business processes. These make it illegal for a competitor to "reverse engineer" a product and then turn around and produce exactly the same thing in exactly the same way. Qualcomm invented and patented computer chips providing CDMA (code division multiple access) technology for digital cell phones, which has become a worldwide industry standard; no other company has been able to infringe on their rights, and every cell phone equipment provider that utilizes CDMA must pay Qualcomm a royalty.

More often than not, however, resources that cannot be imitated involve unobservable routines or processes with a company; they are "behind the scenes" from the physical product produced or service provided. Boeing re-engineered its aircraft design system in the 1990s, so that all future commercial aircraft are designed entirely using electronic means with no paper blueprint drawings ever produced. This was an enormous undertaking because each of their airplanes incorporates 3 million parts and critical aerodynamic features with extremely small tolerances. In turn, this digital conversion made electronic sourcing with thousands of worldwide suppliers much easier. Airbus, unable to observe this process, also began to move in this direction but has had to reinvent the process for themselves, taking years to do so.

Intellectual property protection A legal means of protecting those tangible and intangible assets that are unique to the organization. This is accomplished through patents, copyrights, trademarks, and trade secrets.

Consider the organ transplant "industry." In 2006 there were over 3,000 Americans waiting for heart transplants, but there are only 135 heart transplant facilities nationwide. Why don't more hospitals and their cardiac surgery units get into this field? The answer is that "imitation" of successful practice here is incredibly difficult. These facilities must be pre-approved by hospital boards of directors as well as federal and state health care regulatory agencies, stocked with incredibly expensive diagnostic equipment and specially developed clean areas in a hospital, and staffed by transplant-trained doctors and medical staff, whose surgical techniques and skills cannot be imitated and cannot be easily learned.

Can it be substituted for? Every resource that a company determines to be potentially valuable, rare, and not subject to quick or easy imitation should be evaluated for close substitutes. Whereas earlier in Chapter 4 we said substitutes referred to products or services offered by potential competitors, here substitution means other resources that can provide comparable value-creating benefits. So a resource substitute is something that meets the same basic need being satisfied by a company's resource. As with the question of rarity, it is seldom that tangible resources cannot be easily substituted. Retail or corporate location, machinery, equipment, and raw materials are all usually substitutable. Amazon developed and patented its "One-Click" method for customers to use in buying books and merchandise; however, other online retailers have developed similar systems that allow customer information to be retained and called up easily at the time of purchase.

So substitution most often applies to intangible resources. General Electric's Superabrasives Division competes with DeBeers in industrial diamonds and cutting tools. GE discovered that DeBeers had invented a new process that yielded higher quantities of industrial diamonds, thus lowering their costs and allowing them to price more aggressively in the marketplace. There was no practical substitute for this process that GE could put into place; their only hope was to imitate what DeBeers had already accomplished, and this took a long time. Occasionally, however, it is possible to substitute for intangible resources. For instance, new executives can be hired to replace those who depart from a top management team and in some cases improve the performance of the team. The "brand management" system of marketing was developed by Procter & Gamble in the 1960s, but other consumer packaged-goods companies (e.g., General Mills, Kraft) developed their own "product management" systems that work equally well in the marketing of consumer products.

From this discussion it should become clear that the questions of imitation and substitution begin to focus our attention on the *durability* of advantage that any developed resource might confer. We will return to the question of durability in the following section.

Can it be traded for? Once again, for those resources that are simultaneously valuable, rare, not subject to imitation, and not easily substitutable, the business must consider tradability (or transferability) of the resource. How mobile is it? Can it be purchased somehow by another company, and if so will there be a loss in the short- or long-term value-creating benefit of that resource? Is the resource most valuable in a particular geographic location? A potentially extraordinary resource has increased value to your company if it is also difficult to transfer. In the 1970s and early 1980s John Sculley was president of PepsiCo, after having been promoted up through the organization. He was well known for his marketing acumen; in fact he oversaw the initiation of the Pepsi Challenge, which enabled Pepsi to begin gaining market share from Coca-Cola in U.S. supermarkets. In 1984 Sculley was hired away from Pepsi to become chairman of Apple Computer, while founder Steve Jobs' responsibilities were stripped away. The Apple board believed that Sculley could bring the same kind of marketing success for their company that he had engineered in the soft drink business. However, his tenure at Apple was marked by suboptimal product development plans, failed market launches (e.g., the Newton PDA), and increasing division and dissension within the company. It appeared that the success at Pepsi had been a combination of Sculley and the team of individuals involved, the culture of the company, the cooperation they fostered, and the unique procedures and knowledge base of all the other employees at that company. The Apple board had deemed that this resource could be imported into their growing company, when in reality it was a nontransferable combination of people, culture, and systems.

Figure 6.3 summarizes these concepts and provides further examples of each.

Connecting Extraordinary Resources to Sustainable Advantage

The five criteria shown in Figure 6.3 are used to determine whether or not resources are extraordinary also help describe why extraordinary resources are the foundation of a competitive advantage that is sustainable. In the Introduction to Section B it was pointed out that there may be no unique strategic positions possible for competitors in an industry simply as a result of conducting an industry analysis, because the information that feeds into such analyses is commonly available to all companies. A firm's competitive advantage thus depends on the development or possession of an idiosyncratic resource or set of resources that cannot be easily developed or acquired by other firms.

Three of the criteria discussed above—rare, nontradable, and nonsubstitutable—characterize a resource that is *unique* to the business and that cannot be appropriated by potential competitors. These characteristics confer the possibility to develop an immediate competitive advantage because no competitor has the resource nor can they buy it or substitute for it.

We understand, however, that—while no advantage lasts forever—all businesses wish for their advantage to last as long as possible. Practice would suggest that there are two ways to examine and predict the *durability* of advantage. First, the anticipated time lag between the development of a particular competitive advantage and the point where a competitor will be able to closely match that advantage creates a window where the business can

Figure 6.3
Extraordinary Resource Criteria

Criteria	Key Question	Illustrations
Valuable	Does the resource lead to a product or service that creates value?	Your company has a staff of *highly traveled and experienced agents* who custom design premium vacation travel. Customers regularly pay five times the cost of doing it themselves to have your company create the whole package and deliver a total vacation.
		Paul Newman created a nonprofit organization, The Hole-in-the-Wall Gang, that provides terminally ill children a no-cost camp experience. Mr. Newman's *reputation* enabled the nonprofit to attract an extraordinarily high level of philanthropic giving to support its mission.
		Firm XYZ has developed a targeted method to access a consumer population very active in outdoor activities. Their consumers provide *feedback information* about camping equipment that XYZ shares with its suppliers to assist suppliers in future new product development efforts.
Rare	How unique is the resource?	After years of research and investment, your organization has developed a new *diagnostic process* for detecting with 99% accuracy that your computer's hard drive is about to fail.
Imitation	Is it difficult or costly to imitate?	Your programmers have just implemented a new Web site that is innovative because it relies on a *novel, nonobvious method* allowing users to access a public database. Although competitors will be able to view your approach immediately through the Web site, you have *patent protection* possibilities that would prevent anyone from replicating your method for a specified period of time.
Substitution	How easily can competitors develop a strategically equivalent resource?	Your firm has an in-house staff of process engineers that enable you to take designs to production in a very efficient manner. However, there are *process engineering consulting companies* that can be hired to accomplish essentially the same task.
		Ride the Rockies Inc. worked out an *exclusive agreement* with the National Park Service allowing them to run downhill bike tours in Rocky Mountain National Park.
Tradeable	How mobile is the resource?	A restaurant whose business depends on drive-through traffic manages to snag the *last remaining corner location* along the busiest commercial route in town.

earn extraordinary returns. Second, if a competitor would be required make huge investments and devote great amounts of management attention in order to achieve the same result, then the competitor may not be able to earn an adequate return on its investment or may believe that too much attention would be diverted away from its existing business. Keeping competitors at bay increases the potential for durability and therefore the ability to earn extraordinary returns in comparison to the industry.

Because the question of durability is so central to sustainable competitive advantage, it is important to know about the three primary sources of durability:[5]

1. *Historical conditions.* The ability to develop unique resources often depends on **historical conditions**—the time and place in which businesses locate, begin, or grow. For example, real estate entrepreneurs Richard Peery and John Arrillaga began buying California farmland in the early 1960s, subsequently converting it into industrial use and office space. Their original plot of farmland is known today as the corner of Maude and Mathilda Avenues in downtown Sunnyvale, the center of Silicon Valley. Peery-Arrillaga Properties is one of the largest commercial real estate firms in North America, and the two founders are regularly listed among the world's wealthiest individuals.[6] By virtue of the time period in which they were acquiring the land and their specific location, Peery and Arrillaga were able to acquire vast land resources, locking up the "supply" of land and preventing other would-be real estate developers from becoming involved.

2. *Causal ambiguity.* **Causal ambiguity** exists when the link between a business's resources and its competitive advantage is poorly understood. If the linkage is poorly understood, then potential competitors are likely to have a difficult time trying to imitate the "recipe" for success. We might think about causal ambiguity as what occurs when we try to instruct people in how to ride a bicycle when they have never done so before. We can describe the mechanics of peddling and steering but there is a tacit component that is impossible to describe,[7] such as the relationship between speed and turning or understanding how to ride safely on a gravel surface. Experience is necessary to understand how superior performance is achieved, but what is learned from the experience cannot be completely written down or easily communicated to others. For example, General Electric is famed for its ability to produce business leaders. It is more than the GE University experience or their system of rotating managers between businesses. What creates this capability cannot be completely explained and competitors have a very difficult time trying to reproduce it.

   You should recognize that there is a sort of paradox about this notion of causal ambiguity.[8] Just as it makes it difficult for a competitor to understand the foundation of your company's strong

Historical conditions
The ability to develop unique resources often depends on the time and place in which the business began operations.

Causal ambiguity
A condition that exists when the link between a business's resources and its competitive advantage are poorly understood.

competitive position, it may also be difficult for your management team to identify why it is doing so well. Resource positions are not always obvious, even to those who benefit from them. In fact, one of the challenges of growth and development is the accurate internal identification of the kinds of resources that your company can build upon effectively. We will return to the challenge of identifying resources in a few minutes.

3. *Social complexity.* Here the business's resources may result from **social complexity**, a phenomenon that cannot be systematically managed or influenced. For example, Apple's iPod resulted from a socially complex design/product development process. Highly trained engineers worked closely with designers in a culture that values the unique and exceptional. Other companies may be able to hire away the engineers for their technical or design skills, but the integrated combination of the team, culture, and environment cannot be easily reproduced elsewhere. Social complexity may also extend upstream or downstream to relationships that ventures develop with their suppliers or customers, where the business relationship regarding product or service transactions is further cemented by other personal and social relations.

The astute student will also see that the criteria for assessing whether a resource is "valuable" ties back directly to the discussion in Chapter 5 about the value chain. Resources are *valuable* if they enable the company to implement an approach that achieves superior performance. If the company is unable to utilize a particular resource to earn above-average returns, then while it may be potentially interesting, the resource cannot be classified as extraordinary and does not represent a foundational component for competitive advantage. It is not uncommon to have a particular resource meet all four of the other criteria previously mentioned, and yet be unable to create strategic value by increasing revenues, reducing costs relative to competitors, obtaining more customers, or delivering added benefits for the same price. If a firm performs an activity that is rare, durable, nontradable, and nonsubstitutable, but not valuable relative to competition, then no economic advantage can be garnered. Figure 6.4 illustrates that the five critical dimensions of extraordinary resources, if fulfilled, create conditions of *value, uniqueness,* and *durability* that together confer sustainable competitive advantage.

The identification and creation of value, in part, depends upon differences in expectations about how resources may be utilized. In the real estate example mentioned earlier, Peery and Arrillaga purchased land that was thought by most investors

Social complexity
Resources that may result from a socially complex phenomenon, something that cannot be systematically managed or influenced.

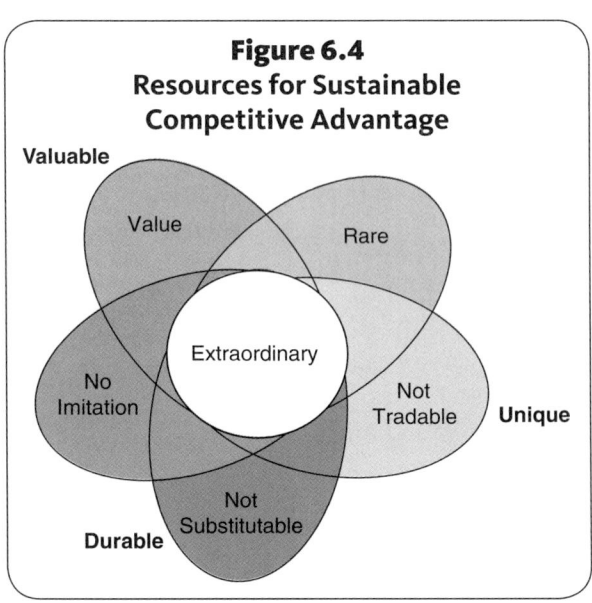

Figure 6.4
Resources for Sustainable Competitive Advantage

Valuable

Value

Rare

Extraordinary

No Imitation

Not Tradable

Unique

Not Substitutable

Durable

to be useful only for farming. The real estate entrepreneurs had a different concept in mind about possible uses for the land and the significantly higher revenue potential that the land appeared to represent. In another case illustrating differences in assessment of value, startup Championship Recipe Foods utilized newly developed food production technology in a novel way. Whereas its special process had been developed to assure more consistent flavor in canned vegetables, Championship relied on the process for its prepared beef chili. The new venture was unique in its ability to introduce prepared beef products into supermarkets packaged in glass jars, which consumers significantly preferred over the canned varieties produced using traditional canned beef processing techniques.

One of the central premises of this text is that both opportunity recognition and value creation are strategic imperatives for all companies in the twenty-first century (Chapter 1). The preceding discussion on differing expectations about value creation potential illustrates precisely where these two imperatives come together. Superior and sustainable performance requires more than luck in happening to come upon a new idea that builds on resources exhibiting the five VRIST criteria including value. Strategic management today involves anticipating markets and then creatively using new and already developed resources to take advantage of emergent trends. The next step involves structuring the organization and its internal processes to regularly generate new business ideas and new resource possibilities that can create future value. Managing growth will be covered later on in Chapter 8, and structuring the organization will be covered in Chapter 11.

The identification of extraordinary resources should guide any business in its investments and strategic development. To reiterate, those resources and capabilities that are ordinary must be *done* and *done well,* but they need not be done any better than the average for the industry. Having stunning office chairs may be nice, but it is probably not going to create strategic value for the company. However, those resources that are truly extraordinary should receive the attention and investment by the management team. These become the foundational core upon which to develop competitive advantage. Over-investment in the ordinary dimensions of the business will distract attention needed at the critical strategic core, and have the potential to siphon much-needed funding and time into areas that are not capable of yielding superior economic returns for the business. These ideas allow students and managers to see the strategic management of business as a balancing act, using the financial and human capital available to develop ordinary resources that must be in place just to conduct business, while dedicating as much funding and attention as possible to the extraordinary resources that have the capacity to deliver competitive advantage and sustainability.

Types of Extraordinary Resources

The earliest writings in strategy discussed three basic types of resources that firms might rely upon in their development of strategy: physical capital, financial capital, and human capital. The word "capital" in these categories was an extension of even earlier economic thinking about the "factors

Figure 6.5
Categories of Resources

Resources	Examples
Knowledge	Unique knowledge about a potential opportunity Prior industry experience Prior new venture startup experience
Social	Informal networks to gain business & startup knowledge Formal industry and value chain networks—industry leaders, suppliers, customers
Human	Prior relevant management experience Credibility Functional area expertise
Financial	Access to seed stage & growth capital Relationships to support cash flow management Access to institutional capital for later stage development
Organizational	Ability to organize the chaos of new ventures: administrative systems, task systems, policies Departmentalization Coordination expertise & combining expertise Methods to articulate complex resources & capabilities Ability to share & routinize capabilities in other parts of the new venture
Technology	Intellectual property claims Unique/special manufacturing process or physical equipment
Physical	Manufacturing facilities & location Access to suppliers Access to customers

of production" used by manufacturing firms. Strategic management theory and analysis have since evolved considerably, increasingly recognizing service-based enterprises and the importance of knowledge in all types of business. Strategists now recognize an expanded list of resource categories (Figure 6.5). As we move forward into the analysis of resources for businesses, it is helpful to keep these categories in mind as a guide.

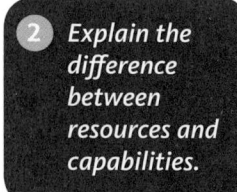

2 *Explain the difference between resources and capabilities.*

RESOURCES AND CAPABILITIES

Thus far in this chapter we have referred solely to the idea of "resources." Many strategy professors and people in business, however, often refer to "capabilities" as well as resources. Having presented the five criteria that help determine if resources are extraordinary, we are now in a position to more carefully examine the difference between these two frequently used concepts. Extraordinary resources represent the raw materials of a business, a foundation upon which the competitive advantage of the business may be built. As can be seen from the Apple iPod example, exciting new products are really the result of intermediate level **capabilities** that exist between the identified extraordinary resources and the products actually sold in the marketplace. Capabilities may be thought of as sets of tightly integrated activities, organizational skills, and internally developed routines that rely on extraordinary resources and that allow the company to create value in a fashion superior to other companies.[9] In this case the intermediate level includes a new product development team that works extremely well together. The new product development capability, however, is a result of extraordinary resources of the firm at a deeper, foundational level, such as their recruiting process for engineers and a culture that emphasizes design and technical excellence. An extraordinary resource meets all of the VRIST criteria.

This development team capability might be leveraged in multiple ways, such as creating multiple types of new products (e.g., video iPods, home entertainment centers) or by working with various types of customers (consumers, schools, government, business). Thus we see that resources and combinations of resources lead to the development of firm capabilities, which in turn represent a platform from which multiple approaches to the marketplace may be pursued.[10] In this case Apple intends to leverage its resource-based capabilities to produce additional products and entertainment gadgets that will enable the company to "colonize rooms throughout the home."[11]

Figure 6.6 captures the sense of this relationship between resources, capabilities, and business performance. The figure indicates that extraordinary resources are the foundation upon which capabilities are built, and that together these enable the business to introduce products or services in order to generate superior performance. Interestingly, this perspective also suggests that ordinary resources are important only if they are built on a foundation of extraordinary resources and capabilities, a point made earlier in this chapter.

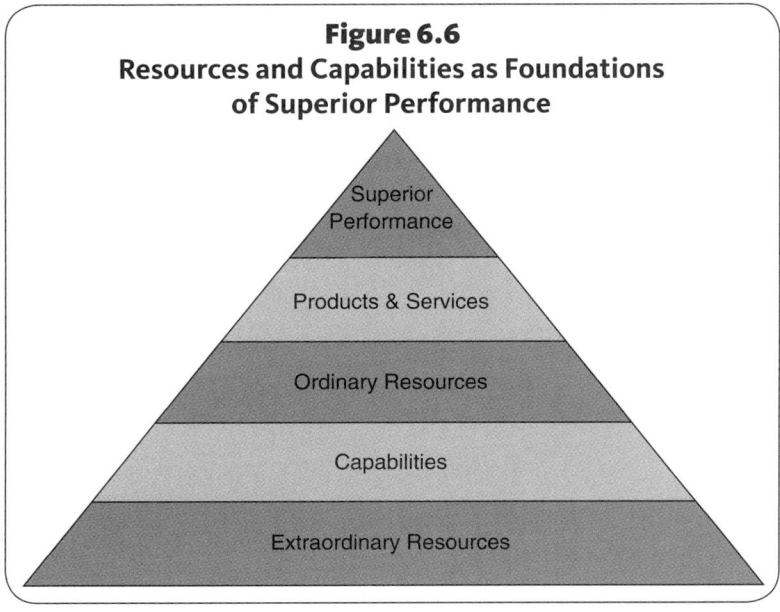

Figure 6.6
Resources and Capabilities as Foundations of Superior Performance

- Superior Performance
- Products & Services
- Ordinary Resources
- Capabilities
- Extraordinary Resources

Capabilities Sets of tightly integrated activities, organizational skills, and internally developed routines that rely on extraordinary resources and that allow the company to create value in a fashion superior to other companies.

This idea can be extended further by suggesting that the accumulation of ordinary resources and the development of products or services are often not even possible unless the proper strategic foundation has been laid. For example, investors and venture capital firms are often unwilling to support a new venture unless there has been some very clear thinking about the sources of sustainable competitive advantage. Similarly, top management teams and boards of directors of established firms would be remiss in their shareholder responsibilities if they decided to embark on a major new direction without significant attention devoted to the question of sustainability and its foundation.

The combination of resources and capabilities at the base of a business again prompts us to return to the value chain model explored in Chapter 5. The value chain discussion highlighted the critical importance of the coordination of activities across both the internal and external value chains of the business. A product development process, such as that which existed for the Apple iPod, is a capability that involves an entire coordinated set of

Strategic Moves
Starbucks, Part 2

Everywhere Starbucks looked in 2007–2008, they were being attacked. McDonald's announced that they would be putting in the exact same coffee drink machines that Starbucks had used for the past few years and would be offering drinks for substantially less. Neighborhood coffee businesses were sprouting up wherever there was a Starbucks, and the declining world economy prompted consumers to think twice about high-priced goods. Starbucks was not growing as it wished.

Facing this situation, Howard Schultz wrote an open letter to the entire organization about commoditization and the need to make Starbucks unique in the market. He acknowledged that most of the decisions the company had made to handle growth had been for the right reasons, but that the sum of the decisions was a dilution of Starbucks cachet. They had moved to automated machines, vacuum-packed coffee, and cookie-cutter store designs. While he didn't specifically mention it, the company had also started providing hot lunch sandwiches, which put them in direct competition with fast food restaurants.

He told the employees, "I have said for 20 years that our success is not an entitlement and now it's proving to be a reality. Let's be smarter about how we are spending our time, money and resources. Let's get back to the core. Push for innovation and do the things necessary to once again differentiate Starbucks from all others."

QUESTIONS

1. What can Starbucks do to reverse the trend toward commoditization?
2. What are their resources and capabilities, and based on these, what new avenues would you suggest for Starbucks?

value adding activities. In this instance, research and development worked closely with both procurement and operations internally, as well as with upstream suppliers of components. The legal staff developed relations with artists and music labels, and worked carefully with programmers to create digital music protocols that would protect copyrighted material. The marketing team developed plans for selling iPods through new channels of distribution. These types of connections and coordination in the value chain are valuable, unique, and durable, giving rise to a sustainable competitive advantage. For this reason Apple continues to dominate this market with a 70+ percent market share, and sales of iPods have contributed mightily to the company's profits, stock price, and shareholder returns. The ability to understand and manage these connections, once developed or learned, has also become a valuable capability for the business that should continue to be generative of competitive advantage in the future.[12]

PUTTING IT ALL TOGETHER

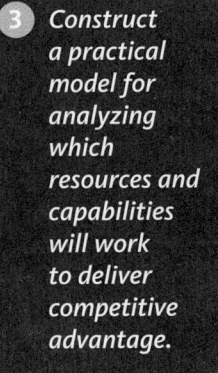

3 *Construct a practical model for analyzing which resources and capabilities will work to deliver competitive advantage.*

Although a few illustrations of the ideas about resources and capabilities in this chapter have been provided, the treatment of this important strategic concept often stays at a very conceptual level in most classroom and boardroom discussions. In this chapter we want to bring the ideas closer to practice so that they can be used as a standard tool by students of strategic management.

Resource-Based Analysis Method

A **resource-based analysis** approach allows each resource or capability to be examined for its potential to provide the business with a competitive advantage. We are looking for those extraordinary resources or capabilities that will provide a focus for the business. As a tool for identifying and evaluating the resources and capabilities of the business, resource-based analysis has the advantage of providing management with a practical methodology for discerning the real foundations for a sustainable competitive advantage. This methodology has four basic steps that should be proceeded through sequentially:

1. Develop a listing of all resources and capabilities, including those that are tangible and those that are intangible;
2. Divide those resources and capabilities into two additional categories of ordinary and extraordinary for the industry in which the company competes. Ordinary resources are those that must be done, done well, but no better than the standard for the industry.
3. For those resources and capabilities that appear to be extraordinary, use the five-point VRIST framework to determine which are truly extraordinary:
    a. Valuable
    b. Rare

Resource-based analysis A methodology and theoretical approach that examines the functioning of the business in terms of whether a product/service simultaneously meets the criteria of rare, durable, nonsubstitutable, and valuable.

c. Difficult to imitate

d. Cannot be substituted for

e. Cannot be traded for

4. For those resources and capabilities that pass all of the five points, develop the means to leverage these extraordinary positions.

Developing a resource and capability list. The best method to accomplish this task involves gathering together the key decision makers in the organization. This group will develop a complete list of all the tangible and intangible resources that the company has at that particular point in time.

While this inventory process may seem a bit mundane, it is absolutely critical to the process of identifying potential resources or capabilities that may provide a set of sustainable competitive advantages for the organization. As this is the first step in developing a sustainable competitive advantage, it is important to develop as complete a list as possible, encompassing the entire breadth of knowledge within the management team. This list may be quite long and should include absolutely everything that the company possesses now if it is already in business or, in the case of a new venture, that it may possess at the time it begins to conduct business.

Identifying the intangibles often presents the greatest challenge for managers and their key advisors or employees. We tend to think of our companies in terms of the products or services they provide or the customers they serve because this is what we see happening on a day-to-day basis. On the one hand, this natural orientation is positive because it reflects a fundamental customer and value-creation orientation. On the other hand, we need to recognize that products, services, and satisfied customers are simply a manifestation of a set of underlying organizational resources and capabilities that the business is built upon (see Figure 6.6). Our previous insights on the importance of the support activities portion of the value chain and coordinating activities across the value chain (Chapter 5) argue for an examination that goes deeper than mere products or services. In identifying the intangibles it is important to continue to ask questions that drill down to the essential core of what the company is really all about and what it does particularly well. In our experience, by repeatedly asking a single penetrating question to probe deeper and deeper, the core resources of a firm are revealed. That question is: "What is the cause of this outcome?" Figure 6.7 provides a relatively straightforward illustration of the probing process that identifies important intangible resources. In this example, the management team has now identified a number of important, extraordinary resources that they believe ultimately contribute to superior performance in the marketplace. Here they see that their capability (the routines created by the new product development team) depends fundamentally upon their recruiting network that enables them to hire, a knowledge database they have developed over time, a particular manager with knowledge about managing fast-cycle teams, and a culture that rewards ideation. These intangibles, then, might be added to the company's developing list, which might resemble the list in Figure 6.8.

Figure 6.7
Process to Identify Core Intangible Resources

Question	Management Response	
What is one of your competitive advantages?	Our product uniquely fills an important need of an important customer.	
What is the cause of this outcome?	Our product development team is very good.	
What is the cause of this outcome?	The team is able to respond quickly to new customer needs we identify.	
What is the cause of this outcome?	They work extremely well together as a team.	
What is the cause of this outcome?	We recruited people who each had previous experience in high-performing new product teams.	They have developed a system and protocols for working quickly on new product ideas.
What is the cause of this outcome?	Our recruiting network is quite strong. We have HR expertise in hiring in this industry.	A knowledge database provides guidance on what works in product development. Senior manager with development team coordination experience and expertise. Culture that encourages ideas and experimentation.

Figure 6.8
List of Identified Resources

Tangible Resources	Intangible Resources
Building location	Industry experience
Equipment (list)	Contacts
Initial financing (equity or debt)	Previous experience in same type of business
Inventory	Education
Patents or patent pending	Unique knowledge of the industry (usually from previous research)
Software and systems for business	Skill set of founders and managers (presentation, innovation, team coordination, etc.)
Build out of facility (list detail)	Name and branding
	Recruiting network
	New product development knowledge database
	Organizational culture

Identifying ordinary and extraordinary resources and capabilities.
The lists of resources of the organization now serve as a foundation for the next step in the process. Management should break every tangible and intangible resource and capability into one of two categories—ordinary and extraordinary. The company will create a list of ordinary resources or capabilities that is very long and a much smaller list of extraordinary items. As stated earlier, each of the ordinary resources or capabilities should be evaluated very simply to determine if the company is meeting the median expectation in the industry.

More importantly, each of the potentially extraordinary resources should be individually evaluated using the five-point VRIST framework to determine if it is truly extraordinary or simply ordinary. Those that fail to pass all five steps should be categorized as ordinary. Those that pass through all five steps are the unique resources and capabilities that the company should plan to leverage in an effort to develop a competitive advantage that is sustainable. The ordinary resources that are identified should be managed and managed well, but since they are customary in the industry and provide no basis for advantage or sustainability, they need only the amount of effort and time necessary to achieve parity with the industry.

Leveraging Extraordinary Resource Positions

The result of this effort is the creation of a short list of truly extraordinary characteristics for the business. This process moves beyond the question of "why would a customer purchase from us?" which, as a broader question, encompasses all of the characteristics of the firm without regard to their ability to generate superior competitive position on a sustainable basis. Now the business can narrow its strategic focus to those areas that are most important to creating a sustainable advantage. These areas should receive the majority of the time, investment, development attention, and focus of the firm. Leveraging the extraordinary resource positions may be accomplished in one of three ways, which include the following:

1. *Extending the current business model into additional products or customer segments.* After building its unique method for selling books online, Amazon.com leveraged its developed Internet capabilities into other product segments. The broader-selection Web site offers value both to its consumer shoppers as well as its product supply partners.

2. *Replicating the resource or capability elsewhere in the organization to enhance the performance of the business.* Nimbus Technologies, which designs and manufactures electronics subassemblies, reproduced quality control (QC) procedures it developed on behalf of one client in the rest of its company's operations. The expansion of more effective QC across the company reduces costs to its clients and improves finished goods throughput.

3. *Developing complementary resources.* Inmar Enterprises came into existence as a manufacturers' coupon clearinghouse, processing

millions of coupons received by retail stores for manufacturers' products. They processed payments for the retailers and billed the manufacturers. Originally organized using low-cost labor in other countries, Inmar has since made technology investments to economize on processing fees and provides superior competitive market and user information reports and service to its retail and manufacturer clients.

An Illustration of the Process

A fairly high-end Web design business formed around three very talented and personable individuals. In short order the company hired many more people and grew to thirty employees. They offered quality Web design, hosting, and customer relationship tracking services at a premium price and in an industry that was in its infancy. After three years in business the company hit a point where their business seemed to stall. During the next nine months they noticed a slow, gradual but steady decline in new business. Discussions with clients and others in the business failed to point out any particular problem with the operation.

They decided to take a break and held a two-day retreat to think through the business. They began by placing everyone in a room and having them talk about every aspect of their business that served as a resource enabling them to compete in the industry. After a slow start the ideas flowed rapidly and a very, very long list was developed. A small part of that list is recreated in Figure 6.9 as an example.

The shock in the room was palpable as they realized that most of the areas listed, which had been unique to them just a few short years earlier, were now standard in their industry. This company had started out with

---

Figure 6.9
Internet Design Company Resources and Capabilities

Office space with desks, chairs, telephones, paper, writing utensils, cubes, and some offices
Computers for each employee
Computer servers for client hosting, including all electrical
Attractive reception area for clients, receptionist, magazines, etc.
Well-laid-out break area for employees with free soft drinks, coffee, and pleasant
    atmosphere
Real-time Web host tracking and reporting capability
Web design expertise, Including creative designers
Customer relationship experts on staff
Internet marketing experts on staff
Payroll system
Accounting, cost, budget, and time management systems
Project management systems and staff expertise
Account executives
Business cards, letterhead, logo, invoices, statements
Strong Web presence

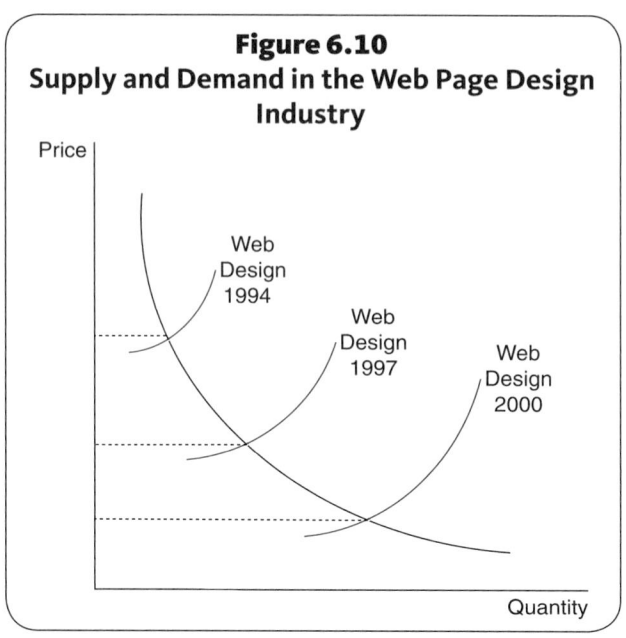

Figure 6.10
Supply and Demand in the Web Page Design Industry

Price

Web Design 1994

Web Design 1997

Web Design 2000

Quantity

three individuals working out of a rented house with two computers, one telephone, no letterhead, and just a plan for designing Web pages. Creating and hosting Web pages had developed as a result of a client's request for the service. As is the case in many industries, this industry had benefited from upward trajectory and sophistication of readily available software and hardware technology. So as the Internet became increasingly ubiquitous through the 1990s, and as the barriers to entry to Web designing became relatively inconsequential (a PC and widely available software), the supply of competing firms grew dramatically. Pricing dropped precipitously, as an increasing number of firms competed for what was essentially moving toward a commoditized type of service. Figure 6.10 illustrates the changes occurring in this industry during a time when the supply of Web design firms expanded significantly.

A careful examination by the company found that they were relying upon resources or capabilities at their company that had now become commonplace and standard in the industry. This being the case, they had become simply average in their competitive space and were being outcompeted by new businesses offering comparable services at a lower price. This should be a clear lesson that durability is not infinite. What was extraordinary at one time will become ordinary at some point, as competitors continue efforts to imitate, substitute, and invent their own value-creating practices. As durable advantages dissipate, uniqueness declines, opening the door for competitors to create the same value in the same ways or equal value in different ways.

The most important list to create and regularly update is the list of extraordinary resources or capabilities at the foundation of the business. This list is usually quite small, but in it are the seeds of the success. The Web design management group carefully considered what was at the root of their ability to attract business, and developed the new list in Figure 6.11.

Each of these potentially extraordinary resources or capabilities was then subjected to the resource-based analysis, using the VRIST framework, to try to determine which might truly have the capacity to provide a competitive advantage. While one might disagree with their analysis, the important lesson here is that there is both art and science involved in determining key sources of competitive advantage. The science of the process revolves around: 1) understanding of which resources are tangible and which are intangible; 2) using the VRIST framework to divide those resources and capabilities into ordinary and extraordinary for the industry in which the company competes; and 3) deciding to focus attention on extraordinary resources, and investing only as necessary in ordinary resources to maintain competitive parity. The art of the process is a matter of judgment of degree, discretion, and experience. The company's final chart appears in Figure 6.12.

In this exercise the team decided that two of their potentially extraordinary resources or capabilities were truly a foundation for developing their competitive advantage, and so the company set about the process of developing a strategic approach that focused on these areas. In turn, this approach prompted them to redefine the industry segment they were targeting as client firms that required high-quality designs quickly. It also prompted a refocusing internally on advanced development of these targeted capabilities,

---

Figure 6.11
Resources and Capabilities That Appeared to Be Extraordinary

Strong client base of Fortune 500 firms
Well-known brand name—winner of several national awards
Located in a very desirable location with relatively low cost of living
Unique Web development system that saved 70% of the time needed when compared to standard Web development
History of successful Web page designs
Talented team that worked as a cohesive unit

Figure 6.12
VRIST Evaluation of Resources

Resource	Valuable?	Rare?	Is It Difficult to Imitate?	Is It Difficult to Substitute?	Is It Difficult to Trade?
Strong client base of Fortune 500 firms	Yes	Yes	No	Yes	Yes
Well-known brand name	*Yes*	*Yes*	*Yes*	*Yes*	*Yes*
Desirable location with low cost of living	Yes	Yes	No	No	Yes
Unique development system saving 70% of time	*Yes*	*Yes*	*Yes*	*Yes*	*Yes*
History of successful designs	Yes	No	No	No	Yes
Talented team that worked as a cohesive unit	Yes	No	No	No	Yes

and a shifting of time and investment away from practices that merely supported ordinary Web design efforts.

CHAPTER SUMMARY

This chapter was devoted to an examination of the resources and capabilities of businesses in order to determine those that provide the opportunity to earn superior returns. The resource-based view of competitive advantage is an important supplement to industry and competitive analysis because it enables any business to consider its uniqueness and the sustainability of its unique position. A sequential process was developed that incorporated the following items: 1) develop a listing of all resources and capabilities; 2) divide that list between those that are tangible and those that are intangible; 3) divide those resources and capabilities into two additional categories of ordinary and extraordinary for the industry in which the company competes; 4) take those resources that are clearly ordinary and establish a process by which they will all be done, done well, but no better than the median expectation in the industry; 5) evaluate those that appear to be extraordinary based upon the VRIST framework as follows:

    a. Valuable
    b. Rare
    c. Imitation
    d. Substitution
    e. Tradable

and finally, 6) analyze the means to leverage extraordinary resource positions through the value chain in the industry. Extraordinary resources and capabilities provide the foundation for entering markets with products and services, and for earning superior returns versus competition on a sustainable basis.

There are additional issues for businesses to consider in using the resource-based framework for developing its strategy. We highlight a few of these here:

1. How do businesses develop a resource position to begin with? Almost without exception, every new venture begins as simply an idea about a potential opportunity, and the prospective entrepreneur possesses no assets or resources that can be claimed by the new venture he or she might start up. Thus a very real dilemma for the prospective entrepreneur is how to create something out of nothing.

2. What kinds of resources should be developed or invested in? At any stage of a business's development, managers face choices about the application of their time and the limited financial capital they may have backing their efforts. So what should be the priority of focus in the resource development process?

3. All businesses confront specific and identifiable types of strategic challenges over time as they develop through stages. Is there a resource development path that businesses should follow to respond to these widely experienced strategic challenges?

4. Like any kind of organizational asset, resources and capabilities can become obsolete over time. How should businesses respond in their resource development efforts to dynamic changes in industry conditions, evolving competition, and the general obsolescence of previously developed resource positions?

We will explore some of these critical issues in Chapter 8.

KEY TERMS

Capabilities (p. 177)

Causal ambiguity (p. 173)

Extraordinary resources (p. 166)

Historical conditions (p. 173)

Intangible resources (p. 165)

Intellectual property protection (p. 169)

Ordinary resources (p. 165)

Resource-based analysis (p. 179)

Social complexity (p. 174)

Tangible resources (p. 164)

SHORT ANSWER REVIEW QUESTIONS

1. What is your conclusion about a resource/capability that meets all five criteria in the VRIST framework?

2. Explain which resources should be processed through the lens of resource-based analysis.

3. Broadly defined, what are the types of resources that may be employed by a business?

4. What are the ways that extraordinary resources can create value for a business?

5. Ordinary resources must meet what criteria for the organization to be successful?

6. How do ordinary resources impact the competitive advantage of a business?

7. How is the VRIST framework used to the advantage of a business?

8. How are tangible resources used in business?

GROUP EXERCISES

1. Your group has decided to start a new business. You see an opportunity to open up a drive-in movie theater. With the dramatic rise in gas prices, people are not traveling very far and they are looking for a great bargain. You plan to charge only $8 per car. What ordinary resources will you need? What might you add to this business that could be extraordinary?

2. Using the VRIST framework, evaluate the extraordinary resources/capabilities that you listed in Question # 1. Which resources/capabilities provide the company with a real opportunity for a sustainable competitive advantage? Why?

3. Have the group do an Internet search on Wal-Mart. What elements of the business does the group believe make Wal-Mart unique? Process those items through the VRIST framework. Which ones hold up as potentially providing Wal-Mart with a sustainable competitive advantage?

REFERENCES

[1] http://www.classiccarclub.co.uk/; http://www.driveaclassiccar.com/; http://www.pistonheads.com/ doc/; Kurczewski, Nick. 2004. Old-car itch? Here's a club to scratch it. *New York Times*. Nov. 21 Section 12: 1; Arends, Brett. 2005. Car club concept lets renters drive dream. *Boston Herald*. January 13. Finance: 30; O'Grady, Sean. 2005. Club together to benefit from a classic experience. *The Independent*. June 8. Motoring Features; Heintz, Nadine. *Inc.* 2005. February: 52.

[2] Alvarez, S. A., and Busenitz, L. W. 2001. The entrepreneurship of resource-based theory. *Journal of Management* 27(6): 755–775; Barney, J. B. 1991. Firm resources and sustained competitive advantage. *Journal of Management* 17(1): 99–120; Grant, R. M. 1991. The resource-based theory of competitive advantage: Implications for strategy formulation. *California Management Review* 33: 114–135; Penrose, E. T. 1959. *The theory of the growth of the firm*. New York: John Wiley & Sons; Peteraf, M. A. 1993. The cornerstones of competitive advantage: A resource-based view. *Strategic Management Journal* 14: 179–191.

[3] Ghemahat, P. 1991. *Commitment*. New York: Free Press.

[4] Hall, R. 1993. A framework linking intangible resources and capabilities to sustainable competitive advantage. *Strategic Management Journal* 14(8): 607–619.

[5] Barney, J. B. 1991. Firm resources and sustained competitive advantage. *Journal of Management* 17(1): 99–120.

[6] http://www.forbes.com/2003/02/26/billionaireland.html.

[7] Polanyi, M. 1967. *The tacit dimension*. Garden City, NJ: Anchor Books.

[8] Kogut, B., and U. Zander. 1992. Knowledge of the firm, combinative capabilities, and the replication of technology. *Management Science* 3(3): 383–396.

[9] Quinn, J. B. 2005. Leveraging intellect. *Academy of Management Executive* 19(4): 78–94.

[10] There has been much discussion in the strategy literature about the relationship between resources, capabilities, and core competence. The definitions of these terms are somewhat different depending on the authors. The argument that resources lead to capabilities, which can

be leveraged in multiple ways, captures the sense of the collection of authors. Coyne, K. P., S. J. D. Hall, and P. G. Clifford. 1997. Is your core competence a mirage? *McKinsey Quarterly* 1: 41–55; Porter, M. 1996. What is strategy? *Harvard Business Review.* Nov–Dec: 61–78; Prahalad, C. K., and G. Hamel. 1990. The core competence of the corporation. *Harvard Business Review.* May–June: 79–91.

[11] Wingfield, N. 2008. Apple daydreaming: Report predicts move toward home devices. *Wall Street Journal.* May 22: D1.

[12] Teece, D. J., G. Pisano, and A. Shuen. 1997. Dynamic capabilities and strategic management. *Strategic Management Journal* 18: 509–533.

Strategy at the Business Level

LEARNING OBJECTIVES

1 *Compare and contrast business-level strategies available to organizations, and describe how they create competitive advantage.*

2 *Examine the underlying drivers that enable a company's choice of business-level strategy to be successful.*

3 *Analyze when outsourcing makes strategic sense.*

Airbus[1]

Airbus may have one of the most complex business models in the world. Airbus is the commercial airline subsidiary of EADS (European Aeronautic Defense and Space Company), which emerged in 2000 from the link-up of the German DaimlerChrysler Aerospace AG, the French Aerospatiale Matra, and CASA of Spain. EADS employs almost 113,000 people at more than seventy production sites, primarily in France, Germany, Great Britain, and Spain as well as in the United States and Australia. The company uses more than 1,500 suppliers based in more than thirty countries.

The company attempts to lead the industry with innovative aircraft and aircraft systems. Airbus successfully flew the first of its super jumbo A380 planes in 2006. The A380 is the largest flying commercial aircraft in the world. Holding the view that the industry will experience significant growth in international travel, the Airbus design is driven by the need to move large numbers of people between large cities worldwide. This view of the future led to the $12 billion development program for the aircraft.

At the same time that Airbus has been trying to lead in innovative aircraft, they have also been trying to cut costs to maintain their competitive position relative to Boeing in the production of midlevel aircraft. This very price-sensitive portion of the market is where more than 40 percent of all purchases of jets exist, and where Airbus worked hard to become the market leader, overtaking Boeing in total orders in 2001. That record was broken in 2006, when Boeing orders once again exceeded those at Airbus.

The company's efforts at cost containment are countered substantially by having to appease four government entities who vehemently attempt to maintain both subassembly and assembly operations in their countries. This stretches the communication systems and creates infighting with the organization, hindering its ability to compete in the market.

Innovation and cost containment: Attempting to accomplish either of these objectives would be daunting for a single company in such a brutally competitive market. Attempting to do both at the same time can be a recipe for a strategy disaster.

The company began feeling the impact of conflicting strategic initiatives when they announced a set of major delays in the delivery of the double-decker A380. Complications with the addition of customer-requested upgrades, a miscalculation of the market demand for such huge aircraft, inconsistencies across the multicountry operations, and a simple case of losing focus led to numerous aircraft order cancellations, numerous contract penalties, and an increase in the total cost of the A380 program by an estimated $2.5 billion.

Airbus made the decision to continue to complete the A380 program while at the same time initiating a new $15 billion program to create a competitor to Boeing's Dreamliner midsized aircraft for the price-sensitive midrange market. The company continues to try to satisfy multiple customer segments using multiple products that are both innovative and lower cost than Boeing. Losses at the organization threaten to dramatically reduce its ability to continue to bring out new aircraft.

Questions

1. How do sets of activities required for a strategic approach based on innovation differ from activities required for a low cost approach?
2. Around what concept might you suggest they refocus the company?
3. Which strategic approach seems to be most consistent with the company's resource positions?

LOGIC OF BUSINESS-LEVEL STRATEGIES

It is now time to step back a bit and look at strategy from a broader perspective. In the book so far we have developed a set of techniques for evaluating how and whether a firm has created a sustainable competitive advantage. Starting with an examination of the external environment in which a business operates (Chapter 4), we used the five forces, key success factors, and strategic maps to identify the conditions in which the business must operate. Next, two very effective and practical techniques for completing an internal analysis were examined—value chain (Chapter 5) and resource-based analysis (Chapter 6). Now we are ready to coalesce these ideas and analytical frameworks together to talk about specific strategic approaches that any company may take.

All organizations are observed at a point in time. At any point that we decide to examine them it is much like standing in a river. There is both a past and a future to that company and it continues to flow through us as we attempt to create a new future. Once we have developed our understanding of the market and the company, an overarching decision must be made as to how we will proceed. The significant part of this entire discussion that has yet to be discussed is the overarching question of *how* a firm competes with other companies. Over the years a framework has developed suggesting that successful companies must use one of five generic or **business-level strategies**. Any company not pursuing some form of these types of strategies will likely not develop competitive advantage and above-average returns.

These strategies lay out the highest level approach to a business. While they are extremely valuable as communication tools and a useful framework for making decisions, they are nonetheless significantly rich, quite complex, and a real challenge to manage effectively. Basic business-level strategies have been a bedrock component of many a company strategy and are used as a rallying point for consistency in organizing value chain activities and evaluating sustainability using resource-based analysis. Deciding upon a business strategy approach assists management in their efforts to have everyone in the organization moving in the same direction. Companies may be tempted to vary their approaches to the marketplace in reaction to other competitors, the shifting environment, the beliefs of new top management team members, stakeholders, and/or recent financial performance. However a consistent business strategy approach over a long period of time is a recipe for strong performance. A host of strategic management research has confirmed that selecting and following a distinct, overarching business-level strategic approach improves company performance.[2] Your ability to not only understand and apply this framework, but also to be able to explain both its best use and limitations, will put you in a stronger position in whatever company you go to work for following graduation.

In the 1980s strategy was given a significant boost as a means for systematically enhancing performance through the work of Michael Porter and his initial description of a set of "generic" strategies: "Competitive advantage grows fundamentally out of value a firm is able to create for its buyers

Business-level strategies
A term for strategic approaches at the highest, most straightforward level. Often referred to as "generic strategies."

that exceeds the firm's cost of creating it. Value is what buyers are willing to pay, and superior value stems from offering lower prices than competitors for equivalent benefits or providing unique benefits that more than offset a higher price."[3] These generic strategies have been applied at the business-unit level and have thus come to be referred to as business-level strategies.

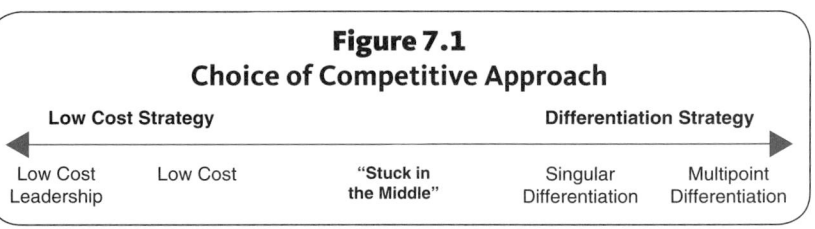

Figure 7.1
Choice of Competitive Approach

Low Cost Strategy — Differentiation Strategy

| Low Cost Leadership | Low Cost | "Stuck in the Middle" | Singular Differentiation | Multipoint Differentiation |

Reflecting these ideas, the most prevalent framework used by strategists suggests that competitive advantage can be achieved when firms employ one of two basic approaches: **low cost** or **differentiation**. Ordinarily we think of these approaches as polar opposites from each other, such as what Figure 7.1 suggests. Either a company seeks to cut costs versus competitors while offering a competitive level of benefits to customers, or it seeks to enhance the benefits it provides to customers versus competitors while maintaining a competitive level of cost. Within many industries we recognize that there are often several competitors appearing to pursue a low-cost strategic approach. However, usually only one company will, in fact, occupy THE **low-cost leadership** position. For instance Dell, the computer giant headquartered in Texas, has developed a competitive advantage over the past several decades by focusing on being the low-cost leader in their market space. Dell completely reinvented the value chain for personal computers and squeezed costs out of every conceivable area in the company. The most visible of these efforts to consumers is their direct sales strategy, which first used only the telephone and then subsequently combined that approach with the Internet to bypass the traditional retail system. This not only had the advantage of enhanced personal contact and cost containment, but allowed Dell to change the flow of goods through the value chain by allowing customers to customize their computers rather than buying stock computers on the shelf at a store. Dell further pressed suppliers of parts and components to locate and operate their own supply distribution centers next to Dell's assembly facilities, so that Dell was not required to incur the costs of carrying raw materials inventories. In contrast, Hewlett Packard acquired Compaq and has sought a low-cost position based largely on scale in manufacturing efficiency, a very different set of activities and method compared to Dell. As competitors such as HP have closed the cost gap, Dell announced that they believe both their supply chain and manufacturing areas can continue to be improved. Michael Dell stated, "I think you are going to see a more streamlined organization, with a much clearer strategy."[4] We note with interest that Dell is straying from their competitive strength with their recent decision to begin selling standard PCs in Wal-Mart stores. Pursuing a new sales channel will be a challenge and decidedly more expensive.

Similarly, there are usually several companies competing in the differentiation spectrum. Sometimes a competitor's success can be created by a single point of competitive differentiation, such as Qualcomm's targeted research

Low cost One of the generic strategies available to companies. It implies a broad market approach where the company rigorously reduces costs and expenses in an effort to lower the overall cost of operations below their competitors.

Differentiation One of the generic strategies available to companies. It implies a broad market approach where activities performed by the company provide sufficiently differentiated value to allow the company to obtain economic returns, generally through higher pricing.

Low-cost leadership Of the companies that pursue a low-cost generic strategy, one company will enjoy the lowest cost structure. This company has the strongest competitive position among low-cost strategists, since it enjoys greater pricing flexibility and can more easily weather industry conditions that compress profit margins.

and development resulting in its patented CDMA cell-phone transmission technology. Other competitors seek to develop multiple points of differentiated competitive advantage, in order to make competitive imitation less likely. Apple's iPod business combines elegant product design, proprietary copy protection software that inhibits piracy and file sharing, a slick Web interface for any type of computer, and an unparalleled digital music catalog. Any one of these features present significant challenges to competitors, while the combination affords Apple a huge, sustainable competitive advantage.

In Figure 7.1 we see a wide space between the low-cost and differentiation approaches. This has long been believed to be a sort of strategic "no man's land." Companies that find themselves simultaneously doing a bit of low cost and a bit of differentiation have often been called "**stuck in the middle**."[5] This is because they are trying to compete in multiple ways against companies that more single-mindedly dedicate resources and manage their value chains toward one of the "pure" generic strategic approaches. If Dell were to challenge Apple computer as an innovator (differentiator), for example, it would need to invest large sums in research and development. This might dramatically reduce its ability to maintain a low-cost position. That type of change would be both difficult and expensive, most likely leading Dell to a position of being stuck in the middle. Today Dell spends less on R&D than does Apple despite the fact that Dell is four times the size of Apple.[6]

Another important decision that companies must make when they select their business-level strategic approach is about the **market scope** that they intend to compete in. As suggested by Figure 7.2, a company can either compete broadly or narrowly.[7] Broad strategic approaches are pursued across multiple customer segments, broad geographical territories (even global; e.g., Staples in office supplies retailing and distribution or Arcelor-Mittal in steel), and often involve providing a variety of products or services to meet multiple needs or desires. In contrast, narrow strategic approaches tailor offerings of specific products or services to particular customer segments or limited geographic territories, and do so to the exclusion of a broader approach.[8] Regal Entertainment Group and Cinemark Holdings are national companies, operating theaters across the United States that show movies appealing to all ages and demographics. In contrast, Cinema Latino operates theaters in only four cities and focuses exclusively on Hispanic populations, showing movies subtitled or dubbed in Spanish and serving Hispanic foods at the concession stands. Ryanair provides low-cost passenger airline travel throughout Europe, while Wizz Air focuses on low-cost air travel exclusively in and out of Eastern European countries.

When the choice about competitive approach is combined with the choice about competitive scope, the result is the

Stuck in the middle A condition where a company simultaneously pursues both a differentiation and a low-cost strategy. The result is most often expenses that are too high and a product that does not command a premium price.

Market scope The degree to which a company competes broadly or narrowly within an industry. Differences in geography, customer segments, and user needs can describe broad versus narrow scope.

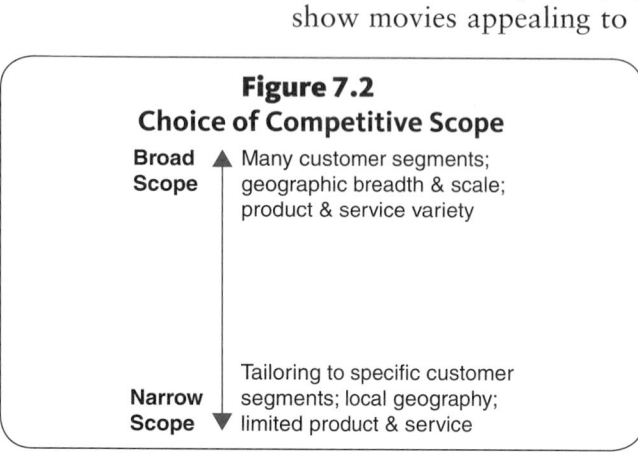

Figure 7.2
Choice of Competitive Scope

Broad Scope ▲ Many customer segments; geographic breadth & scale; product & service variety

Narrow Scope ▼ Tailoring to specific customer segments; local geography; limited product & service

simple array of generic strategies illustrated in Figure 7.3. Across the top are the broad low-cost and differentiation strategies. The approaches that pursue a narrow scope—whether low cost or differentiation—are commonly referred to as *focused* strategies.

You will notice that a fifth business-level strategy, called the "integrated low-cost and differentiation" strategy, has been added in the center of Figure 7.3. This approach is reflected in companies that seek to provide exceptional benefits while at the same time using a reasonably competitive cost structure. Though we mentioned the possibility of getting stuck in the middle when pursuing both low cost and differentiation simultaneously, there have been some recent developments in the field and evidence from industries that suggest that combinations are plausible under certain circumstances. It is a higher risk approach, and we will return to discuss this further later in this chapter.

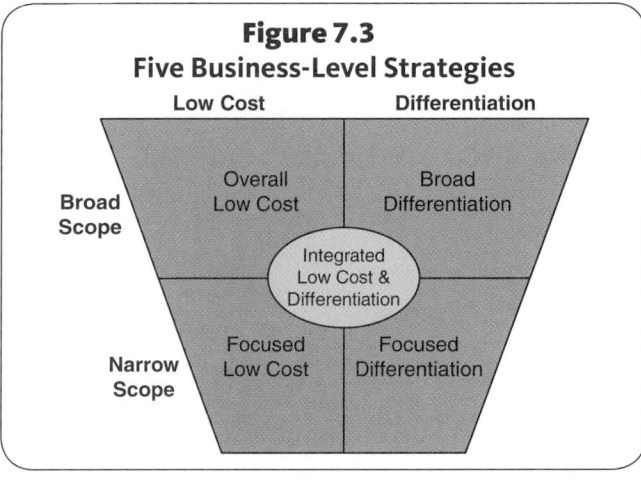

Figure 7.3
Five Business-Level Strategies

Connecting Business-Level Strategies with Superior Performance

The point of employing a business-level strategy is that it is generative of competitive advantage, and competitive advantage is supposed to result in above average returns or superior performance. We can see why this is the case by referring to Figure 7.4 and comparing each strategy to an average performing company in an industry. The other competitor in the industry earns a level of profits based upon an average cost structure and an average level of pricing charged for the benefits provided by its goods or services. The company pursuing the low-cost strategy seeks to lower its costs while providing roughly the same level of benefits as the average competitor and charging roughly the same prices. In Figure 7.4 the low-cost strategy shows that superior profitability is achieved when the company successfully reduces its cost structure. The company pursuing the differentiation strategy seeks to provide enhanced

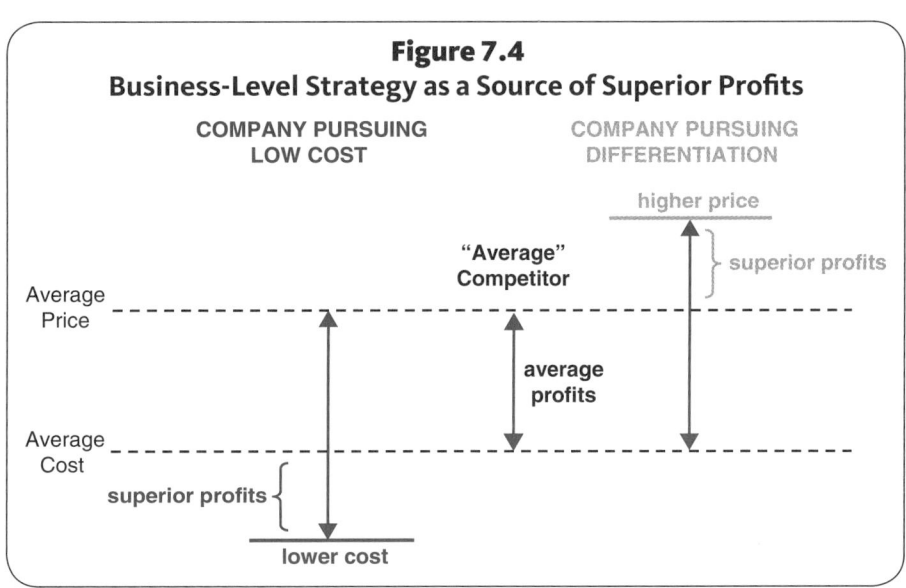

Figure 7.4
Business-Level Strategy as a Source of Superior Profits

benefits to its customers while maintaining roughly the same cost structure as the average competitor. With enhanced benefits that are valued in the market, it should be able to charge higher prices than the average competitor, and thus earn higher profits. While not shown in the figure, the integrated low cost/ differentiation strategy seeks to earn higher profits by slightly lowering its costs while slightly elevating the benefits provided and its prices.

If the diagram in Figure 7.4 reminds you of Figure 5.12 on value creation in Chapter 5, "Value Chain," it is not a coincidence. As we have already suggested, business-level strategies are closely tied to the value chain and value creation. Consistency of purpose across value chain activities can result in either the lowering of costs (and possibly prices) or the enhancement of benefits with the possibility of charging higher prices. Achieving this consistency of purpose requires strong understanding of the resources and integrated sets of value chain activities that contribute to cost reduction or value enhancement so that they can be proactively managed.

Important Caveats!

There are three important cautions that need to be understood before we go on to examine each of the business-level strategies in detail. Each of these cautions represents crucial conditions upon which the success of a strategy rests.

1. **Parity conditions.** All of the efforts made to pursue a business-level strategy will be wasted effort if the company does not achieve **parity** on other conditions that are valued by the marketplace. Differentiation on some dimension is an advantage only if other expected values are also delivered, and only if costs are roughly equivalent with those of competitors. It is very difficult to claim that your business is a five-star restaurant if the health rating on your establishment is a "C." The expectation in the industry is now an "A" rating, and your competitors will all be seeking to accomplish this rating. If the only way to achieve this five-star status is to spend exorbitantly on location, fixtures, salaries and wages, and advertising, then above-average profits may not materialize. Costs that are significantly more as a result of differentiation must be countered with a price that exceeds the cost differential, so long as the market values the additional points of differentiation and consumers are willing to pay the price. Cost leadership is an advantage only if there is comparability amongst the products/ services with its competitors. Remember the old axiom "you get what you pay for." Many companies have come and gone over the years by providing a product or service at a significantly reduced price, but were based on a low-cost structure that resulted from skimping on essential features or quality that customers have come to expect. Packard Bell, a now-defunct manufacturing company that sold inexpensive PCs, was renowned for its poor customer service. In the 1990s "as the market moved from novice buyers to second-time buyers, many experienced consumers shied away from

Parity Though companies compete on cost or some dimension of differentiation, they must maintain relative equality with other companies on other dimensions that are valued in the marketplace. Without reasonable parity on other valued conditions, the lowest-cost competitor or most-effective differentiator on some dimension may not succeed.

Packard Bell, citing its reputation for shoddy quality and indifferent service and support."[9] The effectiveness of each strategy assumes that all of the ordinary aspects expected of competitors in the industry are adequately delivered by the company.

2. **Evolution of customer expectations.** Pursuing one business-level strategy does not mean ignoring the positive aspects of other approaches. "A firm should always aggressively pursue all cost reduction opportunities that do not sacrifice differentiation. [Similarly] a firm should also pursue all differentiation opportunities that are not costly."[10] Importantly, as time goes by, customer expectations about valued product or service characteristics will tend to escalate. Therefore, pursuit of a business-level strategy requires the company to continually refine its own approach as well as ensure it maintains parity on other evolving conditions.

3. **Evolution of competition.** A business that operates in an environment where competitors are slow to react allows the well-designed and well-funded business to thrive until such time as competitors wake up or move to catch up. Formerly unsophisticated industries—such as dry cleaning, lawn care, and veterinary services—left large openings for a single well-designed competitor. Banfield, The Pet Hospital, was founded in 1955 in Portland, Oregon, and developed a reputation for bringing human-quality medical practice to pets. In 1990 PetSmart, recognizing an opportunity to bring consistency of practice on a nationwide scale, asked Banfield to join with them to build veterinary clinics in its stores nationwide. Today there are over 500, and Banfield is adding pet hospitals to PetSmart stores at the rate of 80 per year.[11] In intensely competitive industries other companies will likely cause obsolescence of a company's competitive position more quickly, and will push the envelope of customer expectations (and therefore the parity conditions) quite rapidly. Wal-Mart has doggedly pursued low costs in all parts of the operations for years. Wal-Mart executives love to tell stories about how they fly coach, share hotel rooms, and take advantage of free pens from hotels to save costs![12] Yet recently they have found their margins pressured as they attempted to move their operations into more high fashion and new technology. Wal-Mart's overall operating costs have risen sharply. In 2006 their total expenses rose to 18.4 percent of sales, an increase of nearly two percentage points in the last five years, while one of their main rivals—Target—has seen their expenses rise less than 1 percent over the same period of time, to 21.8 percent.[13] Wal-Mart still has an advantage, but that advantage appears to be slipping.

Parity conditions and their evolution—either through normal customer growth or through competitive dynamics—make the management of a business-level strategic approach more complex.

Wendy's International was founded in 1969 and now has more than 6,600 outlets worldwide. The company has always sought to differentiate itself from the rest of the industry with easy customer customization of sandwiches, unique offerings (the square hamburger and the Frosty), as well as their stated focus on some of the highest-quality food products in the fast food industry. The corporate offices felt that Wendy's was suffering a sales loss because cash strapped consumers were avoiding their stores. They invested in a 99¢ Super Value Menu and pushed franchisees to continually increase the number of such offerings on the menu to draw in traffic. One franchisee laid out the problem. "The differentiation of Wendy's from the other [fast-food] concepts was the fact that we were recognized as being the quality player," says Dave Norman, chief financial officer of Crofton, Maryland-based DavCo Restaurants Inc., which operates 161 Wendy's. "For us to compete at that 99-cent threshold, we either have to give away food . . . or we have to damage our quality image because we cannot purchase the quality commodities."

QUESTIONS

1. Should Wendy's continue as a differentiator or try to pursue a low-cost approach?

2. How might Wendy's differentiate in this market?

3. What would switching to a low-cost approach mean for the business?

4. What would you recommend to the board of directors and why?

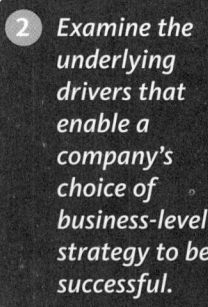

2 *Examine the underlying drivers that enable a company's choice of business-level strategy to be successful.*

DRIVERS OF BUSINESS-LEVEL STRATEGIES

A business-level strategy can best be thought of as the overarching philosophy of value creation within the company. Each element of the value chain displayed in Figure 7.5, along with each of the interrelationships between elements will yield more value if it is targeted at supporting a single approach. Similarly, resource-based investments that are all geared toward one type of strategy allow the firm to take advantage of both the organizational learning cycle and consistent application approach that is possible with a steady message to all employees. In contrast, companies that are inconsistent within their value chains or resource-based investments will find themselves working at cross-purposes internally, presenting themselves to the marketplace with conflicting approaches, and will likely find themselves moving toward a "stuck in the middle" position—doing neither one well. Friendster was the first social networking site, starting up in 2002, predating both MySpace and Facebook, yet the business flamed out early in the United States due to internally inconsistent approaches to the marketplace. According to founder Jonathan Abrams, each of the top executives hired by the company "came to Friendster with strong ideas about how to make the company as big as possible as fast as possible. . . . 'Everybody had their own agenda.' The result was a kind of corporate schizophrenia."[15] Management of the company lost sight of what values social networking site users sought and became involved in several competing initiatives that were based upon entirely different and incompatible strategic differentiation approaches, while competitors honed in carefully and consistently on these dimensions and succeeded wildly.

Business-level strategies rely on internal consistency in activities across the company's value chain, in order to successfully pursue a single approach. Once the decision on a strategic approach has been made, then it should be applied with rigor *all* across the organization. In the next sections we explore important drivers of each of the business-level strategies, and draw attention to the relationship between each strategy and the value chain.

Figure 7.5
Business-Level Strategies Rely on Internal Consistency within the Value Chain

Low-Cost Strategy

Creating and maintaining a low-cost position requires the organization to systematically lower its costs throughout its operations, such that the margins for that business exceed those of its competitors. The Vanguard Group was founded in 1974 as an investment company that single-mindedly focused on a low-cost position. Founder John C. Bogle reasoned that if his asset managers matched market investment performance in the long term with the lowest costs and the lowest charges to his clients, then the company's returns would consistently exceed the market averages. Their initial Vanguard 500 Index has risen to the second largest mutual fund in the United States, with 2007 assets of over $117 billion. In every facet of the business, they concentrate on lowering costs: returns are distributed directly to individual investors rather than through intermediary brokers, they advertise very little, have pleasant but not elegant offices, and formalize cost containment as a key component of the annual bonus. Vanguard has positioned itself as a no-load, low-cost friend to investors.[16]

There are several conditions under which the pursuit of a low-cost strategy may be more appropriate and hold a greater potential for success. One way to think about these conditions is to refer back to the five forces analysis (Chapter 4) to understand how each industry force might impact the low-cost approach.

- **Rivalry.** When there are few opportunities to differentiate one's product or service offering (because such values are not appreciated by buyers), then standardization of product/service features is accompanied by highly competitive pricing. When there is standardization of products or services among competitive rivals, the low-cost competitor will tend to fare better because the company with the low-cost structure will enjoy a higher profit margin.

- **Buyers and Suppliers.** When buyers and suppliers have strong bargaining power and are able to exact economic concessions from competitors, the company with the lowest cost structure is able to fare better. In addition, if buyers experience low switching costs, the low-cost competitor has the greatest flexibility to reduce pricing in order to keep and attract buyers.

- **New Entrants and Substitutes.** Other companies outside the industry may seek to offer products and services that provide a challenging price/value relationship. Given a set of values the company currently provides buyers, a low-cost position offers flexibility to reduce prices and offset any perceived advantages that other companies may offer.

There are several factors that can lead to a low-cost position. These include: 1) economies of scale; 2) capacity utilization; 3) experience curve; 4) product/service design; 5) process innovation (value chain design); and 6) internal value chain coordination.

Economies of scale. Economies of scale are realized as unit costs drop while quantities produced each period grow larger, as illustrated in Figure 7.6. As firms increase their production (be it a product or service), many are able to attain significant cost savings as a result of being able to spread fixed and indirect costs over a greater number of units. This is especially important for companies competing in industries in which significant fixed investment is necessary, such as steel and automobile manufacturing or for a fuel refinery. Cost reductions through scale often occur because of the specialization of activities and the knowledge creation of assembly lines that are possible when seeking to produce large quantities.

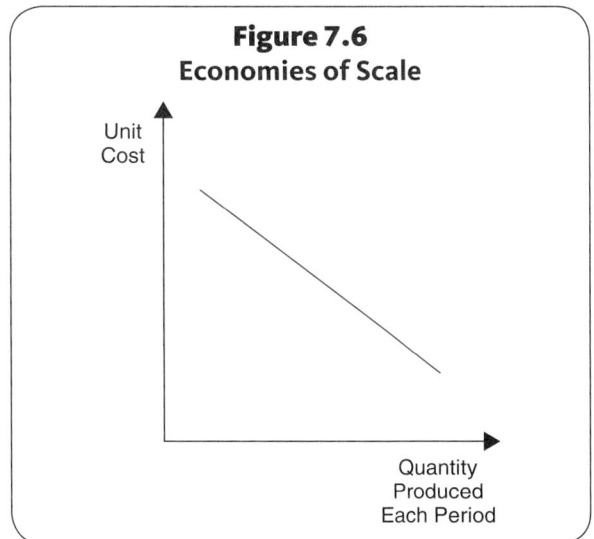

Figure 7.6
Economies of Scale

Unit Cost

Quantity Produced Each Period

Capacity utilization. Capacity utilization is closely related to economies of scale. Scale economies result from the cost savings associated with production through large facilities; however, costs are particularly sensitive to the ability of companies with large facilities to fully utilize them. If they are not fully utilized, then the fixed-cost burden of the facilities is spread across fewer units produced, and any possible scale benefits are lost. It is difficult to project sales and to match capacity to those numbers. However, companies that pursue a low-cost strategy as their overarching approach constantly evaluate this area in order to maximize their investment. There are many industries where fixed costs are significant and profits are highly dependent upon small fluctuations in demand. The dramatic turnaround in the airline industry in 2006–2007 was a direct result of a reduction in the number of available seat miles (the standard measure of capacity in the industry) at the same time that airline passenger traffic was increasing. The result was much higher fleet utilization. As we all know, this focused effort was trumped by a dramatic increase in the cost of fuel—an unforeseen environmental impact that changed the cost structures of the entire industry. Capacity of the big three domestic automobile manufacturers (GM, Ford, Chrysler) far exceeds demand for their vehicles, creating significant cost and competitive pricing problems. Each continues to shed capacity in order to reduce unused fixed costs.

Experience curve. As organizations gain greater experience over time in producing a product or a service—called the **experience curve**—employees usually learn how to perform many functions quicker, cheaper, and with fewer mistakes. A company that takes this general tendency and translates it into a systematic approach of improvement can yield significant gains in experience. The whole movement toward a Six-Sigma approach has been aimed at systematically looking at every facet of the organization, reducing redundancies, eliminating variation, and sharing best practices. It is one of a number of systems used to increase the capability and improve the communication within organizations. This experience curve, illustrated in Figure 7.7, has been observed in a wide variety of industries (e.g., bottle caps, refrigerators, long distance calls, insurance policies[17]), and is a well-understood process by which companies achieve significant cost savings associated not with the cost of their raw materials but with their internal abilities.

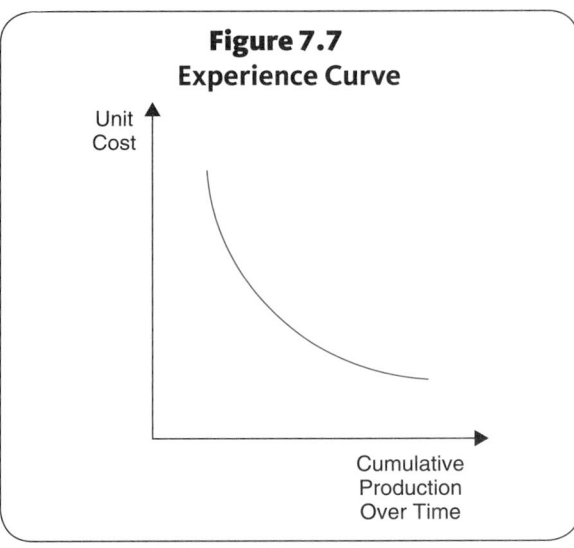

**Figure 7.7
Experience Curve**

Product/service design. The fundamental design of a product or service may be the single most important area in developing cost savings. Rather than looking for uniqueness from a customer perspective, a low-cost strategic approach is focused upon design simplicity, easy manufacturing, simple sourcing of raw materials, and inexpensive packaging. The product/service low-cost approach must be both systematic and systemic. That is, the company must carefully examine every available aspect of the product or service element, taking absolutely nothing as given and fixed. Simultaneously the company must build the process across the value chain, from input to delivery, in a manner that keeps costs as low as possible. As a new entrant in the very tough airline business, Southwest Airlines sought to provide a true low-price alternative to the major airlines. Their approach demanded that they be the lowest cost operation in the business. Every aspect of the business was examined individually for cost savings, and the whole organization was examined to ensure a consistent fit and approach throughout the business enterprise. The company purchases only one style of Boeing aircraft. This, by itself, makes gate operations and mechanical servicing more consistent and faster. In addition, every pilot and flight attendant is capable of filling in on a moment's notice. They have historically avoided reserved seating in order to speed up passenger boarding. Their employees accept a lower wage to work at a fun organization that doesn't lay people off, in part made possible because senior managers of the company do not collect obscene salaries or work in plush offices. A low-cost approach to design permeates every part of the business.

Experience curve
Reductions in cost per unit that are achieved through greater cumulative production over time.

Process innovation (value chain design). A new process that radically speeds up assembly, design, or delivery can yield dramatic cost savings that are not enjoyed by your competitors. The ability of an individual firm to change those processes in a manner that creates new efficiencies can be a key to great cuts in costs. In its development of the long-range 777 aircraft, Boeing scrapped the traditional design/build process and completely reinvented it. Moving entirely to an electronic process, the 777 was designed digitally in virtual space, and all 3 million parts for each $150 million airplane were sourced electronically among 3,000 suppliers worldwide. Then-CEO Phil Condit claimed that they bet the company on this bold new initiative,[18] which shaved eighteen months and more than $1 billion off the new plane's development, and which is now being used in next-generation aircraft design projects.

The ability to outmaneuver competitors by the use of speed in a business can provide significant cost savings while providing customers with something of value. France's automaker Renault determined it needed to rapidly produce a new car for a market that was demanding a compact, fuel-efficient car. The company put all the functions in automobile development under one roof, reporting to one leader, and slashed the development time in half. The Twingo was delivered in eighteen months, well ahead of their competition, at a sharply reduced developmental cost.[19]

Internal value chain coordination. Regardless of how costs are wrung out of the individual activities and functions within a company, the ability to reduce costs through the interrelationships between value chain activities is another crucial element in a low-cost strategy. For example, when Human Resources is able to staff individual positions within activity areas that create best fit within those units, costs are reduced for the whole company. Earlier we mentioned efforts made by both Southwest and Boeing to reduce costs. Southwest hires employees based upon their friendliness and enthusiasm, which enhances the customer interface and reduces subsequent customer complaints. Boeing staffed "design-build" teams for the new 777 airplane, putting together pilots, mechanics, assembly plant supervisors, and computer designers with both customers and suppliers. Companies that involve all parts of the organization in parallel to improve the development and handoff of products or services can speed up the whole process, avoid later-stage technical problems, and wring costs out of the system in both the short and long run. With recycling of products moving to center stage in society, some companies have utilized their R&D, production, distribution, and customer service operations to jointly develop products that can be easily recycled. This has actually led to significant cost savings and has put those companies well ahead of their competitors who might be forced into heavy investments to catch up. HP has spent considerable effort designing their PCs and their ink cartridges for easier recycling and reuse. The result has been a dramatic lowering of production costs, which allowed them to develop a customer service from something that has traditionally been the purview of production. "In 2005, HP recycled more than 70,000 tons of product, the equivalent of about 10% of company sales and a 15% increase from the year before. And it collected more than 2.5 million units (in excess of 25,000 tons) of hardware to be refurbished for resale or donation."[20]

Value Chain and Low-Cost Strategy

The low-cost generic strategy can be an extremely effective means of attaining superior profits. How might it be put into place and what are the interrelationships that are involved? Using the value chain, let's look at a detailed example. Ryanair is the dominant low-cost carrier in Europe today.[21] Founded in 1985, it almost died within the first five years by trying to provide a range of services, including a business class and a frequent flyer program, using a variety of small aircraft flown to and from Ireland. The airline accumulated over £20 million in losses. The company was recapitalized in 1990 with a new mantra to be *the* low-cost airline, and they make no apologies for their rigorous approach to the revised strategic direction. Figure 7.8 diagrams their value chain and highlights key low-cost-producing activities in each cell. Because of their efforts across its entire value chain, Ryanair enjoys a low-cost advantage in Europe that is larger than the advantage that Southwest Airlines enjoys in the United States.[22]

Risks Associated with Low-Cost Strategy

No generic strategy is without risks. This is because each involves significant investments, learning, development, and refinement across the company's entire value chain—a complex and time-consuming management undertaking. Here we outline several risks associated with the pursuit of a low-cost strategy.

Low-cost strategy versus low-cost leadership. As suggested in Figure 7.1, in most industries there may be a number of companies pursuing a low-cost generic strategy. It may be that some companies pursuing this strategy can, in fact, generate returns that are superior to the industry averages because they have managed to create cost structures that are superior to average competition. However, in any market there can be one—and only one—low-cost *leader*. Low-cost leadership is at the endpoint of the continuum in Figure 7.1 and represents the most powerful competitive position among companies pursuing a low-cost approach. Every other business is simply a wannabe low-cost leader, chasing the well-heeled, well-focused, low-cost leader. This can be a recipe for failure over the long run. Witness the rise of Wal-Mart in discount retailing during the 1980s. Its low-cost structure allowed it to *price* lower than Kmart's *costs,* so that in markets where the two companies were competing head-to-head, Wal-Mart could price low and still earn profits while Kmart would lose money.[24] Wal-Mart's low-cost structure helped drive Kmart into bankruptcy.

This should not be confused with the ongoing and important need to lower costs. In many (but not all) cases, the effort to lower costs may be a very appropriate approach. If you are operating a very high-end restaurant and are approached with the "opportunity" to lower your costs by using paper napkins (even extraordinary, high-end paper napkins) rather than cloth napkins, you are wise to forgo that savings as it would negatively impact the customers you are trying to attain. On the other hand, if you could find a means to clean the napkins at half the current costs, you would be unwise not to take advantage of the opportunity. We point this out because the intent and drive is at least as important as the action. Employees as a whole make thousands of

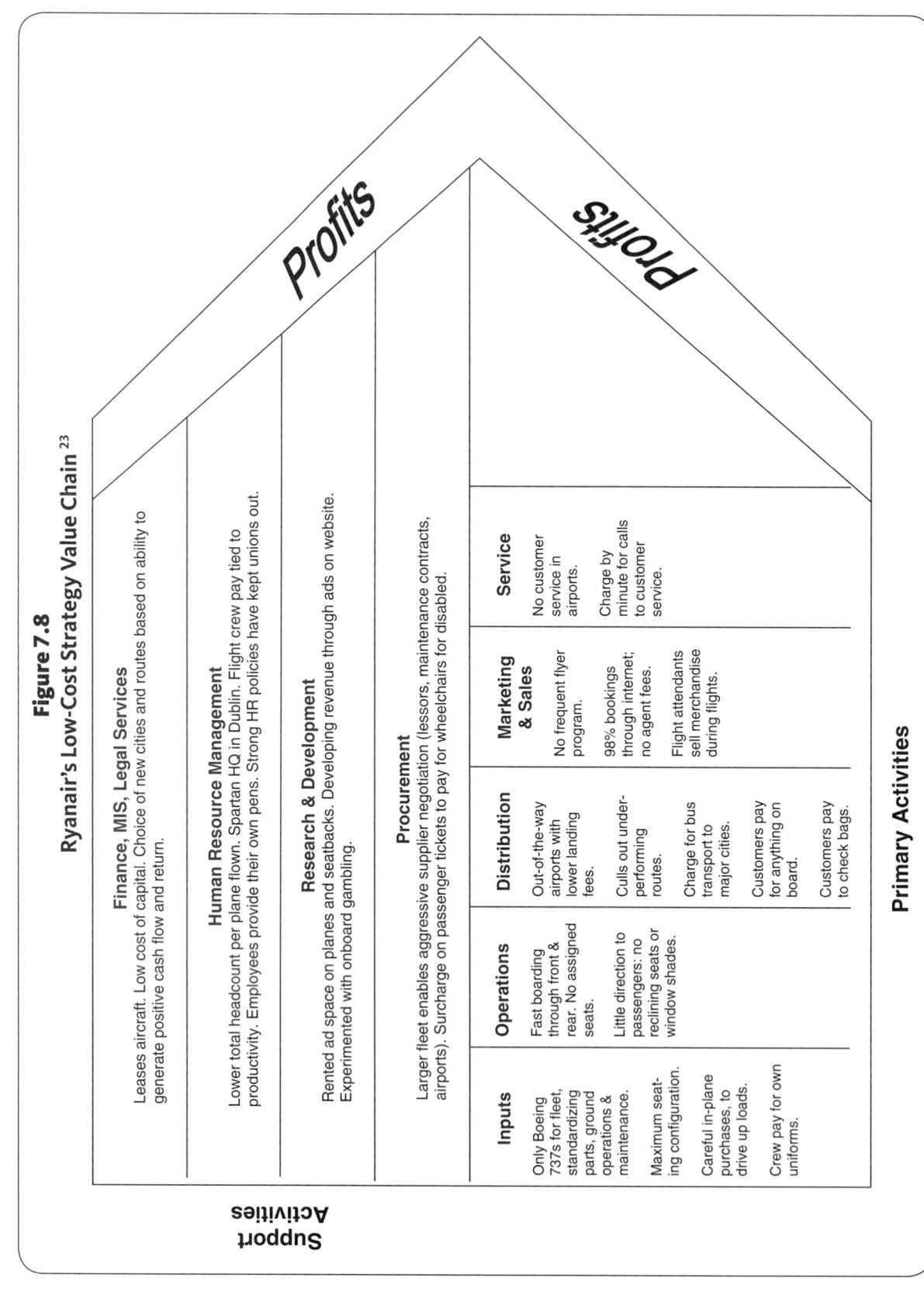

Figure 7.8
Ryanair's Low-Cost Strategy Value Chain [23]

Support Activities

Finance, MIS, Legal Services

Leases aircraft. Low cost of capital. Choice of new cities and routes based on ability to generate positive cash flow and return.

Human Resource Management

Lower total headcount per plane flown. Spartan HQ in Dublin. Flight crew pay tied to productivity. Employees provide their own pens. Strong HR policies have kept unions out.

Research & Development

Rented ad space on planes and seatbacks. Developing revenue through ads on website. Experimented with onboard gambling.

Procurement

Larger fleet enables aggressive supplier negotiation (lessors, maintenance contracts, airports). Surcharge on passenger tickets to pay for wheelchairs for disabled.

Inputs	Operations	Distribution	Marketing & Sales	Service
Only Boeing 737s for fleet, standardizing parts, ground operations & maintenance.	Fast boarding through front & rear. No assigned seats.	Out-of-the-way airports with lower landing fees.	No frequent flyer program.	No customer service in airports.
Maximum seating configuration.	Little direction to passengers: no reclining seats or window shades.	Culls out under-performing routes.	98% bookings through internet; no agent fees.	Charge by minute for calls to customer service.
Careful in-plane purchases, to drive up loads.		Charge for bus transport to major cities.	Flight attendants sell merchandise during flights.	
Crew pay for own uniforms.		Customers pay for anything on board.		
		Customers pay to check bags.		

Primary Activities

Profits

Wendy's continued to push their value meal offerings and then decided to roll out a breakfast offering to half their operating units within the next year. In addition they announced that they would drive sales by pushing four areas of the business; 1) emphasizing stronger marketing; 2) more new products; 3) sharper store operations; and 4) better relationships with franchisees. With the addition of an activist investor on their board, the company began pursuing the idea of selling the company. The investor has little faith that the company executives have a coherent strategy for the firm and are just reaching out using the same methods as their competitors.

QUESTIONS

1. How will selling the company improve its strategy?
2. Which strategic initiatives should Wendy's pursue and which should they drop?
3. What are the implications of offering a breakfast menu for a low-cost generic strategy?
4. Is Wendy's history one of being a low-cost leader?
5. What would you recommend to the board of directors and why?

decisions every day and they should always be encouraged to consider which of their actions will be the best fit given the company's strategic approach. A focus on low cost as a strategic approach is quite different from the cost savings that still allow for parity in the customers' perception.

Price is not a strategy. A low-price approach is often confused with a low-cost strategic approach. Price by itself is not a strategic factor, since prices can be changed instantaneously without strategic investments. It is relatively easy for any competitor to try and use low price as a customer attraction, or to instantly match another company's price, and yet without actually having the low-cost operation to back it up, low price is a certain means of achieving lower returns. Pricing is tactical, while managing to a low-cost position is very strategic.

Customers do not value the benefits derived from low costs. Often a company will use its low-cost position to reduce prices in order to make its products or services more attractive and drive up sales volume. However, in some situations and at some points in time customers may not be interested in cost- and price-based benefits, but instead may have significantly greater appreciation for other product or service characteristics and the benefits they convey. Many low-cost companies introduced MP3 players into the marketplace in the early 2000s, yet the market continues to embrace the Apple iPod despite its higher price.

Cost positions can be imitated over time. Technology, greater access to global markets, and the greater ease of forming alliances and joint ventures make it possible for competitors to more easily imitate the cost structure of low-cost companies. Companies pursuing a low-cost position must be constantly on guard against the evolution of competitive positions, and must continue to reinvest resources to further protect low-cost positions.

Differentiation Strategy

Differentiation is perhaps the most widely utilized generic strategic approach. This is because there are virtually unlimited methods by which a company can attempt to uniquely create value for customers. As with the low-cost strategy, effective differentiation requires a company to systematically organize its activities throughout its value chain in order to deliver superior value and thus command higher prices. Ferrari has always held out a reputation for extraordinary performance vehicles that have a standard twelve-to-eighteen-month waiting list. While Porsche produces more than 100,000 cars a year, Ferrari produces fewer than 6,000. The company carefully manages its value chain in order to create the value that customers prefer. In research and development the company applies Formula 1 technology to production cars, and has conducted advanced aerodynamic studies in its own wind tunnels. It does not rely on competitive market suppliers for key components such as aluminum, but instead operates its own specialist aluminum production arm. Every vehicle is assembled and customized by a staff that is required to spend years in training before being "allowed" to join the production line.[26] Employees are so dedicated to the company and its culture that it was named in 2007 as the best place to work in Europe.[27] The price premium Ferrari commands is directly related to the operation of its value chain. Neither speed nor standardization is a critical component in an industry where both are valued on an almost religious level.

There are several conditions under which the pursuit of a differentiation strategy may be more appropriate and hold a greater potential for success. We again refer back to the five forces analysis to understand how each industry force might impact this strategic approach. The key point for each of these forces is that downstream customer markets must embrace variety within the industry for a differentiation strategy to be successful.

- **Rivalry.** When diversity and variety exists among customers and their needs, then strategic variety is possible within an industry. So long as all buyers do not uniformly demand a common or standardized set of features or benefits, differentiation is a realistic and practical option for competitors.
- **Buyers.** If buyer concentration does not exist and consequently buyers have little power, then cost/price relationships may become less influential in the buying process.
- **Suppliers.** Suppliers may still exert bargaining power on competitors, but as long as diversity of needs exists among buyers and there is no standardization or commoditization occurring within the industry, higher costs from suppliers may be offset by higher prices charged that support the kind of value chain investments in differentiation.
- **New entrants and substitutes.** Effective differentiation often shields competitors from new competition presented by new entrants and possible substitutes. Unique value chain and resource investments designed to create differentiated value should be difficult to imitate.

There are several drivers of an effective differentiation strategy. These include: 1) product and service features; 2) psychographic and cognitive benefits; 3) process innovation (value chain design); and 4) internal value chain coordination. Here we briefly explore each of these drivers.

Product and service features. Most products and services are clearly delineated by their unique features relative to the competition. These features create the opportunity to attract new customers, make existing customers more loyal, and provide the foundation for charging a premium price that offsets the costs of differentiation. There are three dimensions of product/service features that help create an effective differentiated strategic position:

1. **Characteristics that respond to customer needs.** People buy products and services to fulfill their needs and desires, and they will balance the "performance" of their purchases against the prices they pay. The price/value relationship—between the higher prices paid for products or services and their performance—is the basis upon which customers will respond to efforts to differentiate. Performance dimensions that are judged by customers tend to be the kinds listed in Figure 7.9.

> **Figure 7.9**
> **Product & Service Performance Dimensions**
>
> - Effectiveness in intended use
> - Physical characteristics (e.g., color, size, shape, etc.)
> - Variety
> - Quality
> - Safety
> - Consistency
> - Convenience (location, ease of access)
> - Immediacy
> - Complementarity with other products (e.g., cell-phone synching with computer)
> - Speed
> - On the cutting edge

CarMax made the process of car buying and selling easy, allowing consumers to avoid the hated car salesman rat race at most car dealerships. Their no-haggle system allows consumers to buy and sell cars in a very objective process without having to negotiate.

Many travel agencies found their business plummeting as online reservation systems became popular and convenient. Now some agencies not only book airlines, but also book hotels, arrange tours, set up restaurant reservations, arrange for child sitters and guarantee an entire trip against unforeseen weather or sickness. The packaging of formerly separate services has allowed them to survive and charge a premium price compared to the stock agencies.

In Chapter 1 we described the opportunity recognition and value creation imperatives that drive today's strategy. Attempting to stay on the cutting edge of product and service characteristics is one manifestation of these imperatives that we regularly observe. For example, in 2006 Lexus designed a system that allowed a car to automatically perform a parallel park. In 2007 Microsoft introduced Surface, a 30-inch display in a tablelike form factor, which uses cameras to sense objects, hand gestures, and touch to turn an ordinary tabletop into a vibrant, interactive computer screen.

2. **Integrity of the product or service.** Before they purchase, customers increasingly evaluate the prospects of long-term satisfaction

with a company's product or service. Historical defect ratings and repair histories factor into automobile and other purchase decisions. Automobile manufacturers go to great lengths to assure prospective buyers about these important dimensions. Intuit guarantees the integrity of its TurboTax software, agreeing to pay for any tax bills resulting from errors in its program. Attesting to consumer interest in product integrity before buying, Consumer Reports saw an 11 percent increase in its revenue in 2006, with a nearly 25 percent increase in visits to its Web site.

3. **The use of quality inputs.** Many of the performance dimensions mentioned previously can be achieved, in part, through sourcing quality inputs from suppliers. This could mean the use of Intel chips in the assembly of laptops, or the staffing of biotech company R&D departments by hiring top Ph.D. candidates from the premier university biochemistry programs. In contrast, inferior quality inputs can contribute to poor performance characteristics as well as loss of product integrity. The highly successful Motorola Razr cellphone was hobbled early in its introduction by a faulty component from one of its suppliers, prompting the company to recall many phones and suspend sales until the problem could be corrected.[28] In 2007 pet food manufacturers in the United States discovered that Chinese suppliers of the ingredient wheat gluten were spiking its protein count by adding melamine, a poisonous chemical, which resulted in the deaths of hundreds of pets.

Psychographic and cognitive benefits. Customers gain value from companies that go beyond physical or operational characteristics of the products and services they buy. Psychographic and cognitive identification with a company and its products or services is difficult to create, but can be extremely valuable once the connection is made. One of the reasons that Chrysler was so successful in its 1980s introduction of the first minivan was that it used psychographic consumer research to better understand the image that young mothers had of themselves and their needs. Traditional demographic research could not reveal the developing market for a new type of vehicle, nor could the usual trends in sedan or truck sales.[29] There appear to be three sources of this type of value creation:

1. **Marketing and advertising.** One of the significant means by which companies can differentiate themselves in a visible and unique manner is with an effective advertising campaign. There is perhaps no other single item of as much importance in differentiation as that of brand. The ability to create a brand that has instant recognition and instant reference to the product/service sold allows the business to draw in customers more easily than their competitors as well as charge more. Google, Target, Outback Steakhouse, Apple, WD-40, and Sony are among the most recognized brands in the world. Each is well embedded in their customers' minds and connotes an exacting message as to what may be obtained. Apple computer with their

two spokespersons ("Hi, I'm a PC" and "Hi, I'm an Apple" who actually resemble Bill Gates and Steve Jobs) has allowed Apple to point out in a humorous and compelling manner the stark differences between an Apple and other computers. Earlier in its corporate life the famous Macintosh ad titled "1984," which aired only once during Super Bowl XVIII, permanently established Apple computers as leading-edge, break-the-rules machines. Your professors in marketing and strategy will help you understand that the "cola wars" fought for years between Coca-Cola and Pepsi have hinged almost exclusively on "lifestyle" advertising as a means of developing very different images about the two arch-competitors.

2. **Responsiveness to customers.** How many times have you been put on hold when you call a toll-free airline reservation number, or find that the customer service agent you finally reach is unable to help you because of "company policy"? We can whistle George Gershwin's *Rhapsody in Blue* from memory because we have heard it so many times while waiting on the United Airlines phone lines. Responsiveness to customers can make or break a company's image, as well as the desirability of buying or recommending its products or services. Some companies have engineered the customer interface to actually enhance the perceived benefit, presenting alternatives and ideas in advance to customers before they are even requested. Amazon.com presents book and music recommendations to customers who return to their Web site, based upon analysis of the customer's previous buying patterns.

3. **Corporate reputation.** Beyond the immediate experiences that customers have with a company's products and services, advertising, and customer service, a company's corporate reputation can facilitate or impede the creation of differentiated value to the customer. Mentioned earlier in this book in the chapter on value chain, Newman's Own enhances its relationship with customers who buy its food products through its sponsorship of camps for terminally ill children and its support of other charitable causes. Trust in the abilities of a company can be an important factor in the purchase decision, and has the ability to allow one company to outperform others in their industry. The Betty Ford Clinic has developed a powerful reputation as a premier facility not only for the breaking of addictions, but also for its ambiance and confidentiality. Reputations are built on skills and experience, and they can lead to extraordinary returns for the business. In contrast, when the Exxon Valdez spilled oil in Alaska, the company's reputation was sullied, and to this day some customers refuse to buy gas through Exxon's retail gas stations.

ETHICS

Process innovation (value chain design). The drivers of differentiation mentioned previously demonstrate that this strategic approach, like the low-cost approach, depends upon supportive activities within each cell of the value chain (see Figure 7.10). In addition, reconfiguring the value chain in a manner

Figure 7.10
Differentiation Strategy

Differentiation based on	Requires value chain excellence in
Product or service characteristics	Marketing research, R&D, Operations
Product or service integrity	Operations, Manufacturing control
Quality inputs	R&D, Procurement
Marketing & advertising	Marketing research, Creative marketing
Responsiveness to customers	Customer service, Administration
Corporate reputation	Administration

that differs from the competition has the ability to provide unique value. In confronting the growing trend to dine away from home at restaurants, competitors in the supermarket industry have reconfigured their value chains to better meet the needs of their customers. This includes preparation of fully cooked meals in their deli operations, so that customers on their way home from work can conveniently pick up high-quality meals ready to just heat up and eat at home. Many chains have also developed online ordering systems, where store personnel select and bag the desired groceries and deliver them to the customer curbside at an appointed time. The extremely competitive child care business has usually been considered a commodity business where companies seek to drive down costs, provide basic services, and minimally meet state licensing requirements. Bright Horizons discovered gold when they forged relationships with Fortune 500 employers, set up child care centers in or next to corporate headquarter office buildings, paid higher salaries, and incorporated learning centers within their facilities.[30]

Internal value chain coordination. The ability to achieve effective differentiation relies not only on consistency of activities within the value chain toward the intended point(s) of differentiation, but also on continuous coordination of these activities across the company. Figure 7.10 demonstrates that many of the drivers of differentiation rely on combinations of value chain activities. This recognizes, as is the case with the low-cost strategy, that an action taken in one department or function of a company can have a ripple effect throughout the company. A substitution of ingredients brought in by purchasing can dramatically effect whether consumers like the taste of a product. A change in package size by marketing to accommodate more information will impact production line machinery and how packages might fit into cases for shipping. A change in administrative policy about repairs and defects can reshape how customers view a company when they talk to customer service agents. We could go on with many such descriptions of coordination effects at a very specific and practical level. What examples can you think of that illustrate the critical connections between parts of the value chain?

On a grander scale, consistency and coordination of activities, in fact, define the differentiated approach that a company takes. Kodak has been fighting for its life as the film industry has moved to a largely digital environment. A company that traditionally earned returns through its photographic paper and processing businesses, Kodak has had to dramatically remake itself and find an effective differentiated approach to distinguish it from competitors such as Canon and Sony, who embraced the digital medium much earlier on. Within the last five to seven years Kodak has developed cameras, printers, and Internet-based printing services for consumers. A tremendous effort in research and product development resulted in a new line of products, while sales needed to forge new relationships with electronics retailers and marketing needed to reshape what Kodak stood for in the minds of consumers. Every aspect of the company's value chain for this business needed to be tightly integrated for the company to survive the death of film.

Value Chain and Differentiation Strategy

For the differentiation strategy to succeed, we have again stressed the importance of the value chain perspective. Let's look at another comprehensive example to see how it might be put into place and the interrelationships that are involved. Starbucks started business in 1971 as a roaster and seller of whole coffee beans in the Pike Place Market in Seattle.[31] Purchased by one of their former employees, Howard Schultz re-imagined the business along the designs of the Italian coffee shops he visited. Selling premium coffee in a relaxing setting where the coffee preparer (the barista) would know your name and your preferences would allow the business to charge premium prices and differentiate it from the vast number of competitors (including at that time mostly home brewing). Their consistent approach to a differentiation strategy throughout the value chain becomes obvious when we look at what they have done. Figure 7.11 diagrams their value chain and highlights key differentiation activities in each cell. The company has grown to 9,400 U.S. locations and another 3,700 stores in thirty-eight foreign countries; its revenue in 2006 increased by 22 percent over the previous year and net income increased by 11 percent.

In the past two chapters we have talked extensively about extraordinary resources and the unique importance of intangible resources and capabilities. One of those crucial intangibles is the means by which organizations coordinate activities across elements of the company. Another is the overall fit that the company achieves between activities within the organization's value chain. Starbucks began losing this fit by failing to see the interrelationships.

The company began a long move to install machines capable of creating any coffee combination. This move made the process faster and more consistent, but at the cost of the sights and sounds so crucial to the original Starbucks experience. The new machines were so large that they cut off conversation between the baristas and the customers, loosening the bond between them. Other moves that were inconsistent included the offering of hot lunch sandwiches and packaging the coffee beans in sealed bags. These decisions to streamline operations and generate additional revenue negatively impacted the customer in-store experience, which had been central to Starbucks' value creation efforts for years. Alignment between the functions of the organization is more critical than the specific choices made at most organizations. Something that makes perfect sense in isolation may be a crushing hit to the armor of the company.

LEADERSHIP

Risks Associated with Differentiation Strategy

Like the low-cost strategy, the differentiation strategy is subject to several risks. In addition to the parity caution offered earlier, several of the risks associated with a differentiation strategy are outlined as follows.

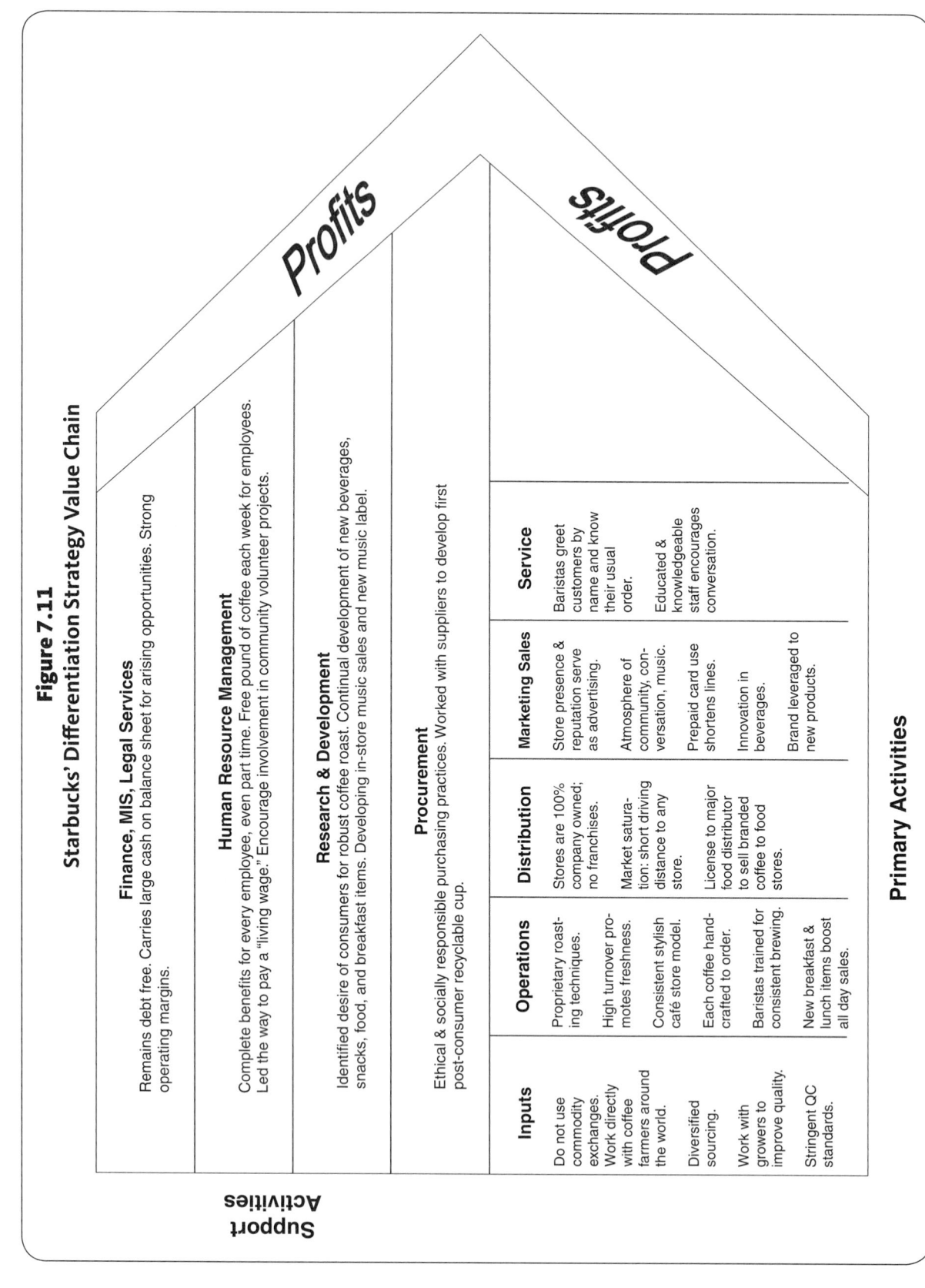

Figure 7.11
Starbucks' Differentiation Strategy Value Chain

Support Activities

Finance, MIS, Legal Services
Remains debt free. Carries large cash on balance sheet for arising opportunities. Strong operating margins.

Human Resource Management
Complete benefits for every employee, even part time. Free pound of coffee each week for employees. Led the way to pay a "living wage." Encourage involvement in community volunteer projects.

Research & Development
Identified desire of consumers for robust coffee roast. Continual development of new beverages, snacks, food, and breakfast items. Developing in-store music sales and new music label.

Procurement
Ethical & socially responsible purchasing practices. Worked with suppliers to develop first post-consumer recyclable cup.

Inputs	Operations	Distribution	Marketing Sales	Service
Do not use commodity exchanges.	Proprietary roasting techniques.	Stores are 100% company owned; no franchises.	Store presence & reputation serve as advertising.	Baristas greet customers by name and know their usual order.
Work directly with coffee farmers around the world.	High turnover promotes freshness.	Market saturation: short driving distance to any store.	Atmosphere of community, conversation, music.	Educated & knowledgeable staff encourages conversation.
Diversified sourcing.	Consistent stylish café store model.	License to major food distributor to sell branded coffee to food stores.	Prepaid card use shortens lines.	
Work with growers to improve quality.	Each coffee hand-crafted to order.		Innovation in beverages.	
Stringent QC standards.	Baristas trained for consistent brewing.		Brand leveraged to new products.	
	New breakfast & lunch items boost all day sales.			

Primary Activities

Product differentiation is not a strategy. In your marketing classes you have probably learned about product differentiation as an effective marketing tool—new sizes, flavors, colors, varieties, hours of operation, and so on. From the strategy point of view, however, mere product or service differences are not the basis for competitive advantage since these types of characteristics can generally be easily duplicated or imitated. Effective strategic differentiation has to do with the activity sets within and across the value chain. In this view product differentiation is a manifestation of something deeper within the organization. The strategic view of differentiation places a premium on processes that identify emerging customer needs and desires, and how a company organizes its activities in order to deliver the values that customers appreciate. Companies that focus their greatest attention on mere product differentiation may perform poorly over the long run.

Customers do not value the benefits derived from differentiation. Do you use all the functions that are embedded in your cell phone? In some situations and at some points in time customers may not be interested in differentiation activities that result in product and service features, but instead may have significantly greater appreciation for other dimensions. For example, in the desktop and laptop computer industry customers are most interested in standardization at a competitive price. Standardization is important for software compatibility, the use of "plug and play" peripheral devices, and ease of repair if a machine crashes. Price is important because the nature of technology trends have led customers to come to expect falling prices over time. While engineers and technical developers may value aesthetic and multifunctional designs, the technology-push capabilities of machines often exceed the desires and needs of customers.[32]

Differentiation positions can be imitated over time. When a company has developed a valued differentiation position that is insulated from competition, it enjoys an advantage over competitors and can earn superior profits. Competitors will not be unaware of what's going on, and will seek to imitate the value(s) that the company is creating and delivering to customers. Once again, with the advent of technology, greater access to global markets, greater access to financial capital, and the ability to more easily form alliances and joint ventures, in time competition will usually discover ways to become more competitive once again. Companies pursuing a differentiation approach must be constantly on guard against the evolution of competitors, and must continue to invest resources to further their positions.

Focus Strategies

A variation on the two primary business-level strategies of low cost and differentiation is based on the breadth of approach. Whereas a low-cost or a differentiation approach is a broad market strategy, a **focus** strategy takes each into a unique segment of the market. Segmentation possibilities are virtually unlimited, but each is usually aimed at a very small part of a larger market. Within the focus approach, companies can pursue either a low-cost or a differentiation strategy, thus in practice this is referred to as a cost focus

Focus A subset of the two main generic strategies of differentiation and low cost whereby the company pursues a narrow targeted market, geographic area, and/or particular customer group.

or a differentiation focus. The obvious implication here is that by segmenting the market, a company is able to exploit an inconsistency between the needs of that particular market and the overall market.

In-N-Out Burger has longed reigned supreme in the fast-food burger market of the western United States, catering to a clientele that loves fast food but wants the highest quality product they can get. At In-N-Out everything is made fresh to order. There are no microwaves or freezers. Customers can watch french fries being made from hand-diced, fresh, whole potatoes and the shakes being made from real ice cream.[33] They have narrowed their focus both geographically and by customer group. Their food is neither inexpensive nor fast when compared to the traditional fast food competitor.

Focus strategies are most appropriate under a limited set of circumstances. First, the segment in which the company seeks to focus is not as important to other companies pursuing broad strategic approaches. Pursuing a focused strategy is best accomplished by avoiding head-to-head competition with a larger company that usually possesses deep pockets and great resolve to succeed. This can occur either because the segment is too small for the larger competitor to pay attention to, or the incremental investment by the large competitor to tailor its approach sufficiently to address the segment is greater than the estimated return it might earn. Second, the segment or niche is large enough and presents sufficient growth opportunity for the focused strategy company. The possibility for organic growth within a company's market niche is more attractive than having to leverage value-chain and resource investments into unfamiliar territory. Finally, the pursuit of a focus strategy is most appropriate for companies with constrained resources that cannot effectively operate on a broad-strategy scope.

It may not surprise you that start-up companies, young companies, and family businesses usually pursue focus strategies. Why do you suppose this is true? These types of companies ordinarily do not have the depth and breadth of resources that allow them to pursue broad markets. Instead, they rely on a very narrow set of resources, which in turn are the foundation for a relatively specific capability or set of value-creating activities (recall Figure 6.5 in the last chapter). Broadening into different markets or segments usually requires access to fairly significant financial resources, which many of these types of companies do not enjoy. We will return to this topic of strategic challenges of growth and expansion that many companies experience, in Chapter 8.

The biggest risk to the focus strategy is that competitors pursuing a broad strategy will decide to drill down into this more narrow market space. Narrow markets or segments are places where larger, broad-strategy competitors can find additional sources of growth while at the same time leveraging their existing value chains and developed resources. In addition, the growth of the more-focused strategy company may entail ultimately confronting broader markets or segments more directly.

Integrated Low-Cost/Differentiation Strategy

A great deal of attention has been paid lately to a variation on these business-level strategies where companies purport to borrow elements from both the

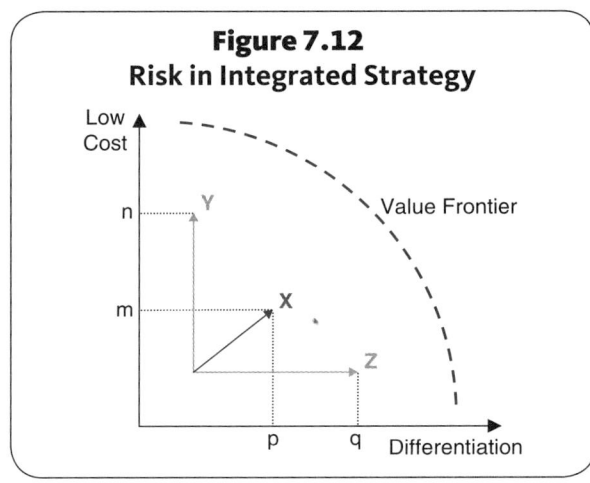

Figure 7.12
Risk in Integrated Strategy

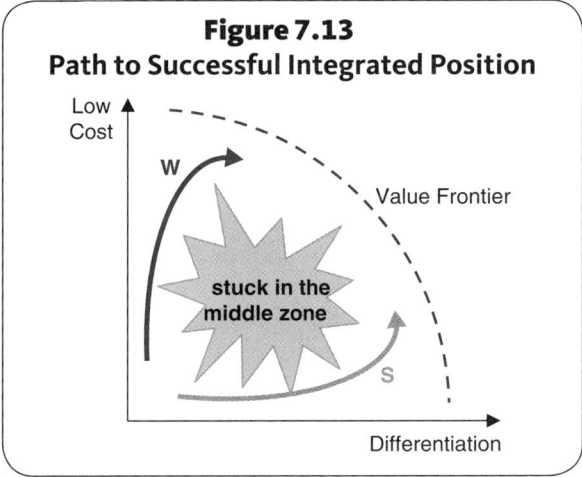

Figure 7.13
Path to Successful Integrated Position

low-cost and differentiation approaches. Yet this strategy runs a great risk of leaving the company that employs it "stuck in the middle." Let's examine the approach in two ways.

First, imagine three equally resource-endowed companies competing in an industry in which there exists strategic variety (i.e., in which both low-cost and differentiation strategic approaches may succeed). In Figure 7.12 we plot the estimated trajectories of companies X, Y, and Z as they seek to reach the "value frontier" (the boundary of optimal possibilities combining both low cost and high differentiation). Company X, which pursues the integrated strategy, faithfully applies its resources and is able to accomplish level m in the low-cost spectrum and level p in the differentiation spectrum. Yet company Y is single-mindedly focused on low cost, applies all its resources in that pursuit, and accomplishes level n in lowering its costs. This makes sense, because they are applying all of their resources and efforts against lowering costs, while company X is fragmenting its efforts against two different directions. Similarly, company Z is pursuing differentiation with single-minded focus and accomplishes level q. Unless company X has somehow uniquely identified a special market that appreciates the combination of moderately low cost and moderate differentiation, all else being equal the company will be outcompeted by companies that pursue the pure generic strategies. Management of X is following an integrated strategy right into a stuck-in-the-middle position, from which it may be difficult to recover.

How is it possible for companies to successfully pursue an integrated strategy, then? One possibility is that a company single-mindedly pursues a pure generic strategy, develops competitive advantage, generates superior returns, and then uses those superior returns to develop the integrated strategy and competitive position. This is illustrated in Figure 7.13, where a company avoids the zone of being stuck in the middle by moving away from a pure strategy only after it has sufficiently developed its position. Here company W has fully developed its low-cost position, and is now using its superior returns to develop a differentiated position as well. Company S has moved up the differentiation path, and is now seeking to lower its costs as an added source of competitive advantage.

This looks simple; however, the problem of developing competitive advantage based upon two different approaches simultaneously can be severe, even for highly successful companies. In 2006–2007, for example, Wal-Mart sought to bring more fashionable clothing lines into its discount retail stores. The clothing lines did not sell well, causing huge inventory overstocks throughout the company's U.S. stores, and resulted in lower store sales growth than expected. This prompted write-offs from their income statement, and caused problems for suppliers upstream when the company cut subsequent orders. Wal-Mart has long been known for its low-cost strategy, which is supported throughout every activity in its value chain. To succeed in differentiating itself, in addition to low cost, the company would need to significantly enhance capabilities across its value chain that would support this new approach. The new approach requires: marketing research that identifies and understands fashion trends, buyers who can source goods on dimensions other than low cost and acceptable quality, new (usually more expensive) methods of display and merchandising in stores, the attraction of different types of customers who are interested in more fashionable clothing, and more. When a company has been consistently and successfully operating in one mind-set for decades, it is very difficult to begin operating differently throughout its value chain. Like any strategic initiative, embarking on a strategy takes time using appropriate resource development.

The same comments can be made about attempts to move from a highly differentiated position toward a position that also embraces lower costs— company S in Figure 7.13. As we mentioned earlier in this chapter, during 2005–2006 Starbucks sought to increase the speed and efficiency of its store operations by moving away from handcrafted beverage preparations to machine-assisted preparations. In their stores machines were installed that automatically ground the beans and brewed the coffee for their lattés and other specialty coffees. On February 14, 2007, founder Howard Schultz wrote an impassioned letter to all Starbucks employees about their recent shift in strategy, titling the letter "The Commoditization of the Starbucks Experience," something which he claims has resulted in declining performance and opened the door to competitive threats:

> Over the past ten years, in order to achieve the growth, development, and scale necessary to go from less than 1,000 stores to 13,000 stores and beyond, we have had to make a series of decisions that, in retrospect, have lead to the watering down of the Starbucks experience, and, what some might call the commoditization of our brand.
>
> Many of these decisions were probably right at the time, and on their own merit would not have created the dilution of the experience; but in this case, the sum is much greater and, unfortunately, much more damaging than the individual pieces. For example, when we went to automatic espresso machines, we solved a major problem in terms of speed of service and efficiency. At the same time, we overlooked the fact that we would remove much of the romance and theatre that was in play with the use of the La Marzocca machines. This specific decision became even more damaging when the height of the machines,

which are now in thousands of stores, blocked the visual sight line the customer previously had to watch the drink being made, and for the intimate experience with the barista. This, coupled with the need for fresh roasted coffee in every North America city and every international market, moved us toward the decision and the need for flavor locked packaging. Again, the right decision at the right time, and once again I believe we overlooked the cause and the affect of flavor lock in our stores. We achieved fresh roasted bagged coffee, but at what cost? The loss of aroma—perhaps the most powerful nonverbal signal we had in our stores; the loss of our people scooping fresh coffee from the bins and grinding it fresh in front of the customer, and once again stripping the store of tradition and our heritage?

Having provided sufficient warning about the dangers of the integrated low-cost/differentiation approach, we should also recognize that there are some shining examples of companies that have successfully gone down this path. Toyota is a company that readily comes to mind. It has not only achieved tremendous success through differentiation in design, development, and manufacturing of a range of vehicles that deliver value to customers. It has also achieved a singularly lower cost structure than its chief competitors, enabling the company to price lower and still earn healthy returns. No wonder Ford, GM, and Chrysler continue to struggle!

OUTSOURCING, STRATEGY, AND THE VALUE CHAIN

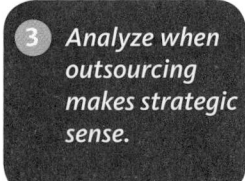

3 *Analyze when outsourcing makes strategic sense.*

The connections we have made throughout this chapter between business-level strategies and the value chain allow us to gain further insight on the process of **outsourcing**, which has become prevalent among all kinds of businesses over the last fifteen to twenty years. In Chapter 5, you will recall, we mentioned that outsourcing possibilities are occasionally identified through the value chain analysis. Outsourcing is a process through which a company depends on another organization to perform activities in its own value chain. For example, Nike outsources manufacturing of its athletic shoes to production companies in the Far East that have lower labor costs and can produce shoes less expensively than in the United States. Wal-Mart relies on other companies to manage the stocking and restocking of certain kinds of specialty merchandise within Wal-Mart's stores, instead of having that merchandise flow through Wal-Mart's own sophisticated distribution system. Why would a company outsource any of its activities? How does outsourcing work to improve a company's strategic approach to its industry? Under what conditions should a company refrain from outsourcing? We tackle these important questions in this section.

ETHICS

From a strategic leadership perspective there are two primary reasons that a company might decide to outsource some activity or set of activities: 1) to enhance strategic position in the marketplace, and 2) to offload activities in which they do not have any special competence and which do not contribute to its strategic position. Generally there are fairly straightforward situations that

Outsourcing When another organization is employed to perform a business process or service that is part of the company's value chain.

may fall into the first category. Small pharmaceutical companies often form joint ventures with larger companies in order to take advantage of their well-developed sales and marketing operations. In this case the outsourcing of marketing and sales can contribute to significantly greater buyer awareness and perceived legitimacy for the company. Toshiba discovered that their customers value extremely fast turn-around times when their Toshiba computers break down and require authorized repairs. The company farmed out repair operations to trained UPS employees at the Kentucky hub of United Parcel Service, which also picks up and redelivers the machine. Avoiding the extra steps of delivery and pickup to Toshiba itself, Toshiba customers receive repairs at least two days sooner and Toshiba's relationship with customers has been strengthened.[34]

The second reason—offloading nonessential activities—is more complicated for companies to determine. As we have illustrated in this chapter and in the earlier chapter on the value chain, management of the value chain to the internally consistent pursuit of a generic strategic approach is a complex undertaking. If we simply look at the variety of activities occurring in each cell of the value chain, as well as the coordination required among cells and the connections made upstream and downstream with suppliers and customers (Figures 7.8 and 7.11), we begin to see how monumental a challenge this can be. For this reason, not every company is—or should be—capable of managing and performing every one of the activities in its value chain. Our discussion in Chapter 6 on resource-based analysis helps us arrive at the same conclusion. Most companies develop and pursue unique resources and competitive excellence in a limited number of arenas; it is what they become especially good at, and what they become known for doing well. If in addition they attempt to manage and perform activities in which they have no unique capabilities or that do not leverage their resource positions, then they may be overextending themselves into activities that do not contribute to developing competitive advantage.

It is simple to see that this is the case in some examples, but more difficult in others. For example, every business generates volumes of garbage each day (even in this digital age). Part of conducting business effectively requires that they "take out the garbage;" however, few companies will actually haul their waste to the landfill. Instead, they outsource this to a local company. It makes sense, since hauling garbage is generally not central to what companies do. However when activities become more central to what a company does strategically, the challenge of deciding whether to outsource or not becomes much greater. On what basis does Nike decide to have other companies manufacture its shoes, and why would Wal-Mart entertain having other companies manage what happens within their own retail stores?

It may be easier to tackle this question from the other side—that is, when is it *inappropriate* to outsource activities? There appear to be several conditions that describe when outsourcing may damage or hinder a company's strategic efforts:

Loss of control over costs or differentiation values. Having another organization perform important value chain activities can damage the company's strategic efforts if, by using the outsourced organization, the company loses control over key values that are central to its strategy. In 2000 toy retailer Toys"R"Us signed a ten-year agreement that made Amazon.com the exclusive online retail outlet for Toys "R" Us toys, games, and baby products. Unfortunately, Toys "R" Us was unable to control the "look" of its merchandise on the Amazon site, nor prevent the introduction of other toys through Amazon's zShops partners.[35]

In contrast, Ryanair outsources aircraft maintenance to another company. Ryanair does not possess an internal set of resources or capabilities to actually perform aircraft maintenance; the company's expertise is in managing such areas as route selection, flight operations, customer-centric employee hiring, on a low-cost basis. Yet through long-term contracts they achieve low-cost maintenance performed by the other organization, while still retaining the rights to review and make changes to how maintenance is performed. So in this case outsourcing to a low-cost third party supports their generic strategy of low cost, but does so without the company having to relinquish control over that important yet standard dimension of the business.

Disruption of coordination and linkages in the value chain. Earlier we argued that the coordination and linkages that exist among elements in a company's value chain are the greatest sources of competitive advantage. This is because they are intangible and extremely difficult to imitate. When outsourcing breaks one of these important coordinating bonds, the company may be less well-insulated from competition.

Hollowing out the core. In the 1990s "business process reengineering" became the latest business fad to talk about in the classroom. Much of the reengineering had to do with outsourcing, and some companies were so enamored with the perceived benefits that they outsourced most of their activities. Individually, each activity may not seem strategically important. Yet often combinations of activities, and especially the coordinating linkages that exist between them, may be central to what a company does well. So any attempts to outsource should consider not only the activities by themselves, but the system and context in which those activities exist.

Competitive learning. In some instances, a competitor may gain greater insight into a company's internal value chain by observing which activities have been outsourced. Not only might the competitor learn more about the outsourced operation, because it will be more visible to outsiders, but they may be able to develop insights about what activities remain inside the company as constituting its strategic core.

Figure 7.14 presents a decision tree for outsourcing activity that summarizes the preceding discussion. In order to gain the benefits of outsourcing without incurring some of the problems that can accompany these efforts, companies will occasionally engage in either vertical or horizontal acquisitions in order to own another company that can perform an important set of activities. Acquiring another

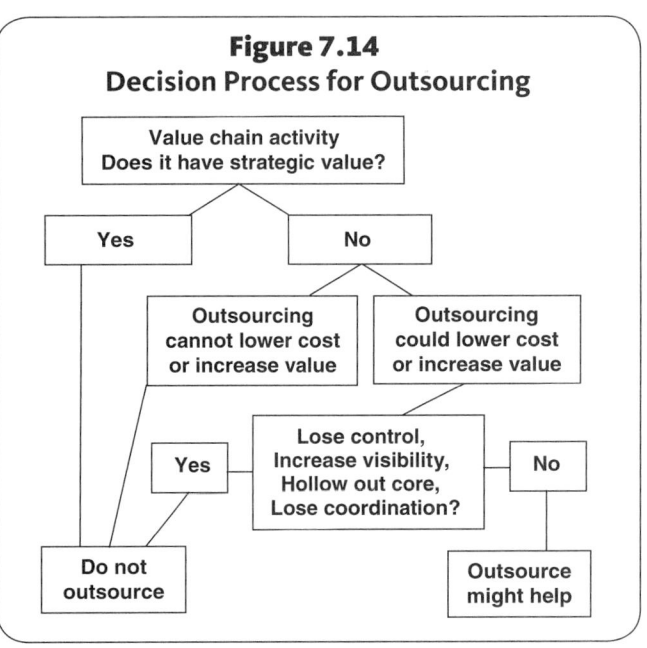

**Figure 7.14
Decision Process for Outsourcing**

company can ensure control over the process and minimize competitive learning; however, acquisitions present their own sets of issues. We will cover mergers and acquisitions more completely in Chapter 10.

CHAPTER SUMMARY

In this chapter we have examined the business-level (sometimes referred to as generic) strategies of low cost and differentiation as well as the variations of both focus strategy and integrated cost/differentiation strategy. These strategies lay out the highest-level approach to a business strategy and are extremely valuable as communication tools and a quick decision process methodology in the design of effective decisions. These strategies are used as a rallying point for organizations and as a means to evaluate consistency in various approaches when using value chain and resource-based analysis. Furthermore, these generic strategies have been a bedrock component of many a company strategy, and your ability to not only understand and apply this system, but also to be able to explain both its best use and limitations will put you in a stronger position in your organization.

Although several companies in an industry may attempt a low-cost approach, there can really be only one low-cost leader in a market. The low-cost leader has the opportunity to make significant returns by taking advantage of its relative cost structure. All others may find themselves undercut by the leader and discover that it is difficult to prosper under challenging market circumstances. On the other hand, a differentiation strategy has virtually unlimited variations in approach. Multipoint differentiators inherently enjoy greater security in their strategic positions than do single-point differentiators. In this chapter we presented a number of important criteria for differentiation to work. For both the low-cost and differentiation approaches, it is essential for companies to achieve parity on other competitive dimensions that are valued in the market. Much like we discussed in Chapter 6, there are ordinary and extraordinary resources. All of the ordinary resources must be present and leveraged at the average expectation of the industry.

Finally, a focus approach is simply a segmentation of the market and/or geography that, if effectively executed, leads to a low-cost focus or a differentiation focus. The integrated low-cost/differentiation strategy is intuitively appealing, yet it appears to be a risky approach that even very successful companies find difficult to balance. By attempting to compete against other companies that are more single-mindedly concentrating on a pure low-cost or differentiation approach, the integrated strategy company risks getting stuck in the middle.

The value chain plays a central role in understanding how business-level strategies are put into practice. The generic strategy represents a philosophy of competing that should translate to mutually supportive activities in every cell of the company's value chain, producing a consistent approach to the market across the company. Assessing whether or not a value chain activity is central to strategy, and whether third-party organizations can perform the activity at a lower cost or higher value-added, provides a guideline for companies on outsourcing.

KEY TERMS

Business-level (generic) strategies (p. 192)

Differentiation (p. 193)

Experience curve (p. 201)

Focus (p. 213)

Low cost (p. 193)

Low-cost leadership (p. 193)

Market scope (p. 194)

Outsourcing (p. 217)

Parity (p. 196)

Stuck in the middle (p. 194)

SHORT ANSWER QUESTIONS

1. How does consistency of effort across the value chain play a role in attaining extraordinary returns?
2. Under what circumstances would a focused, differentiation approach be most likely to allow a business to attain extraordinary returns?
3. Why is parity an important concept in the application of generic strategies?
4. Under what circumstances would a focused, low-cost approach be most likely to allow a business to attain extraordinary returns?
5. What strategy would you recommend for a new business being started by a small team of entrepreneurs?
6. Under what circumstances would a differentiation approach be most likely to allow a business to attain extraordinary returns?
7. How are generic strategies used in the day-to-day running of a business?
8. Under what circumstances would a low-cost approach be most likely to allow a business to attain extraordinary returns?
9. How does a firm become "stuck in the middle"?
10. What are the five business-level strategies available to organizations?
11. What issues must businesses keep in mind as they try to simultaneously be low cost and differentiated?
12. What are the three important conditions that must be kept in mind when considering the application of business-level strategies?

GROUP EXERCISES

1. Take two companies in the same industry that compete with each other in seemingly different ways. For example, Ford and BMW or Nordstrom and Kohl's. Using information from their annual reports and business stories that you can find on the Internet, attempt to map out their generic strategies and how their value chains support that approach.
   a. Do they appear to be consistent across their value chain activities?
   b. What unique resources do they seem to be using to separate themselves from their competitors?

2. Take a single industry such as the airline or grocery industry. Map out where the top ten competitors are using the Five Business-Level Strategies Map as shown in Figure 7.3.
   a. Are all five approaches being utilized in the industry?
   b. Map each of these firms based upon their five-year performance. How are they doing?
3. Periodically companies attempt to change their business-level strategy (usually due to significant changes in the environment). What cautions would you advise a business contemplating such a move? Can you name a company that has done just such a thing in the past five years?

REFERENCES

[1] http://www.airbus.com; http://www.eads.com; Lunsford, J., & D. Michaels. 2006. Bet on huge plane trips up Airbus. *Wall Street Journal*. June 15: A1/A11; Michaels, D. 2007. Airbus proves to be albatross to EADS. *Wall Street Journal*. January 18: A13; Michaels, D. 2006. Airbus launches A350 sales push but tempers hope. *Wall Street Journal*. December 5: A9.

[2] Porter, M. E. 1985. *Competitive advantage*. New York: Free Press; Porter, M. E. 1996. What is strategy? *Harvard Business Review* 74(6): 61–78; Veliyath, R., & E. Fitzgerald. 2000. Firm capabilities, business strategies, customer preferences, and hypercompetitive arenas: The sustainability of competitive advantages with implications for firm competitiveness. *Competitiveness Review* 20(1): 56–83; Thirnhill, S., & R. E. White. 2007. Strategic purity: A multiindustry evaluation of a pure vs. hybrid business strategies. *Strategic Management Journal* 28(5): 553–561.

[3] Porter, M. E. 1980. *Competitive strategy*. New York: Free Press; Porter, M. E. 1985. *Competitive advantage*. New York: Free Press.

[4] Lee, L., & P. Burrows. 2007. Is Dell too big for Michael Dell? *Business Week*. February 12: 33.

[5] Porter, M. E. 1985. *Competitive strategy*. New York: Free Press.

[6] Lee, L. 2006. It's Dell vs. the Dell way. *Business Week Online*. February 23, 17.

[7] Porter, M. E. 1985. *Competitive strategy*. New York: Free Press.

[8] Porter, M. E. 1996. What is strategy? *Harvard Business Review* 74(6): 61–78.

[9] Armstrong, L. 1996. The numbers are crunching Packard Bell. *Business Week*. December 30: 46.

[10] Porter, M. E. 1985. *Competitive advantage*. New York: Free Press, 20.

[11] http://www.banfield.net/about/mission.asp. http://www.petsmart.com/banfield/index.shtml.

[12] Fishman, C. 2006. *The Wal-Mart effect*. New York: Penguin Group.

[13] McWilliams, G. 2007. Wal-Mart's radio-tracked inventory hits static. *Wall Street Journal*, February 15: B1.

[14] http://www.wendys-invest.com/wendys.php; Arndt, M. 2006. Out, damned trans fats. *Business Week*. July 31: 12; Adamy, J. 2007. Why no. 3 Wendy's finds vanilla so exciting. *Wall Street Journal*. April 6: B1.

[15] Chafkin, M. 2007. How to kill a great idea. *Inc*. June: 85–91.

[16] Perold, A. F. 1998. *The Vanguard Group, Inc. – 1998* Boston: Harvard Business School Publishing. 9-299-002. https://flagship.vanguard.com/VGApp/hnw/content/Home/WhyVanguard/AboutVanguardWhoWeAreContent.jsp; Lim, P. 2007. How the biggest funds fared. *U.S. News & World Report*. January 15, 142 (2): 73; Maiello, M. 2005. The un-Vanguard. *Forbes*. September 19, 176(5): 182–186.

[17] Grant, R. M. 2005. *Contemporary strategy analysis*. Malden: Blackwell Publishing.

[18] The development of the Boeing 777. 1998. Public Broadcasting System.

[19] Capell, K. 2007. Glaxo mimics carmaker to speed vaccine. *BusinessWeek Online*. April 5: 16.

[20] Woellert, L. 2006. HP wants your old PCs back. *BusinessWeek*. April 10: 82–83.

[21] http://www.ryanair.com/site/EN/about.php; Wal-Mart with wings. *BusinessWeek Online*, November 17: 13; Sullivan, W. 2007. Flying on the cheap. *U.S. News and World Report*. March 6: 47.

[22] Serpen, E. 2006. *Key performance measures*. Presentation at 3rd annual Managing Airline Operating Costs Conference, London.

[23] http://www.ryanair.com/site/EN/about.php; Wal-Mart with wings. *BusinessWeek Online*. November 17: 13; Sullivan, W. 2007. Flying on the cheap. *U.S. News and World Report*. March 6: 47; Davy. 2004. Fare wars: A history lesson. *European Transport and Leisure*. February 16, Davy: Dublin.

[24] Ghemwat, P. 1986. *Wal-Mart stores' discount operations*. Boston: Harvard Business School Publishing, 9-387-018.

[25] http://www.wendys-invest.com/wendys.php; Arndt, M. 2006. Out, damned trans fats. *BusinessWeek*. July 31: 12; Adamy, J. 2007. Wendy's to discuss strategic review with investors. *Wall Street Journal*. May 16: B17; Adamy, J. 2007. Wendy's considers possible sale. *Wall Street Journal*. April 26: A2.

[26] Kahn, G. 2007. How to slow down a Ferrari: Buy it. *Wall Street Journal*. May 8.

[27] http://www.greatplacetowork-europe.com/best/lists.php?year=2007&idListName=eu&detail=0&order=companies.

[28] Motorola moves beyond RAZR glitch. 2006. http://www.forbes.com. May 31.

[29] West G. P., & J. O. deCastro. 2001. The Achilles heel of firm strategy. *Journal of Management Studies* 38(3): 417–442.

[30] Brown, R. 2001. How we built a strong company in a weak industry. *Harvard Business Review* 79(2): 51–57.

[31] http://www.starbucks.com; Adamy, J. 2007. Starbucks chairman says trouble may be brewing. *Wall Street Journal*. February 24: A4; Text of Starbucks memo. 2007. *Wall Street Journal Online*. February 24.

[32] Christensen, C. M. *The innovator's dilemma*. Boston: Harvard Business School Publishing.

[33] http://www.in-n-out.com/history.asp.

[34] Friedman, T. L. 2005. *The world is flat*. New York: Farrar, Straus, and Giroux.

[35] M. Wolk. 2006. *Toys R Us wins suit against Amazon.com*. http://www.msnbc.com, March 2.

Life Cycle Dynamics and Corporate Strategy

Competition today operates in rough-and-tumble, dynamically changing environments in which companies face a continuously changing set of circumstances. This is what we referred to in Chapter 1 as the need for opportunity recognition and value creation capabilities. This next section of the textbook takes us deep into the actual practice of strategy in this kind of dynamically changing marketplace.

Competing today can be like getting onto a rollercoaster—moving from slow to fast very quickly, with rapid rises and possibly precipitous descents. When dynamic changes occur in the marketplace in the form of an evolving industry, they have an impact on types of value creation that can be successful and on the need to continuously embrace new opportunities for future growth. Companies also evolve through stages, and must address unique strategic challenges that parallel their evolution. Once again there are implications for building resources and for configuring the company's value chain in order to succeed. In Chapter 8 we will explore how industry life cycles and company life cycles offer context and insight for the formulation and implementation of strategy. As companies evolve they inevitably confront the possibility of operating internationally. This chapter also explores dimensions of international strategy.

Many executives refer to today's business climate as hypercompetition, which we will discuss in greater depth in Chapter 9. Here, competitive dynamics play a central role in the success of a company's strategy. Competing successfully in markets today is akin to performing well in the Xbox game Halo 3: it requires performing well on straightforward executional aspects, anticipating and preempting "metagaming" patterns that competitors employ, and cooperating with other important players in the environment. Chapter 9 deals with competitive actions and responses, and how these impact the formulation and implementation of a company's strategy.

Many companies today view the growth challenge as one that necessitates moving *beyond* the existing business into other types of businesses. They do this through mergers and acquisitions, which is the subject of Chapter 10. The chapter provides perspective on why it is so difficult to engineer successful diversification of this sort—meaning why it is a challenge to provide positive returns to shareholders. Managing a diversified company—one that operates in multiple industries—presents its own unique strategic management challenges and decisions. So this chapter considers the nature of strategic management from a different perspective, that of senior executives at corporate headquarters.

Welcome to the real world, as we explore Life Cycle Dynamics and Corporate Strategy!

Life Cycles

LEARNING OBJECTIVES

1. Explain the stages of an industry life cycle and their impact on business strategy.

2. Analyze the strategy implications of competing in fragmented or consolidated industries.

3. Utilize organizational life cycle stages and the kinds of problems and resources issues that businesses experience in each to proactively recommend value creation activities.

4. Decide which strategy issues associated with being a first mover and pursuing business renewal apply given the resource position of a particular company.

5. Explain when a company should expand internationally and what approach it should take for doing so.

Invention of MP3 Players[1]

On July 27, 1997, an event occurred that changed your life, and it dramatically changed the trajectories of several industries that you know so well. On that day Don Katz invented a gadget to play "Motion Picture Experts Group Audio Layer 3" files, now commonly known as MP3 music files. His company, Audible, sold a few thousand of the gadgets. Ten years later nearly 40 percent of U.S. households own devices that play MP3 music files.

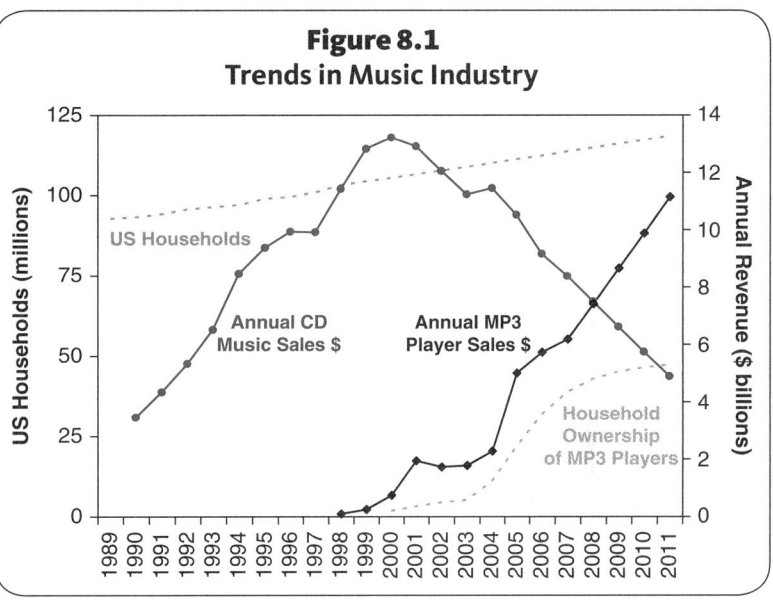

Figure 8.1
Trends in Music Industry

The introduction of the MP3 has changed the course of musical history and the nature of commercial music industries. Though the U.S. household population continues to grow at a steady pace, the advent of MP3 technology led to the start-up and rapid growth of an entirely new industry around digital music players. Whereas Sony had long been associated with portable music players through its Walkman franchise, new companies entered this market space—often for many different reasons. Samsung entered to leverage its capabilities in electronic entertainment devices, as did Diamond Multimedia with its Rio player. SanDisk introduced its Sansa line of players in order to occupy product space where its flash drive technology could be applied. The iPod represented an elegant next step in the evolution of Apple's innovative approach to digital technology for the consumer. Microsoft introduced the Zune because the company wants to occupy a central position in the digital home. Figure 8.1 shows the historical and estimated ownership and sales of MP3 players.[2]

Paralleling the start-up and growth of the MP3 player industry has been the devastating decline of the recorded music industry. Compact disks replaced LPs way back in the 1980s as a consequence of new technology introduced at the time. CD sales peaked at over $13 billion annually in 2000, just after the first MP3 player was introduced, but have been in steep decline ever since. Music labels such as Warner, EMI, Sony, and Universal find it

more difficult to support musicians, as the economics of producing and marketing a new CD has grown worse. In the prosperous years it would not be uncommon for a Number 1 CD to sell 500,000–600,000 copies each week, but now the best CDs sell only 60,000 per week, prompting agents for musicians to claim that "CDs have become little more than advertisements for more-lucrative goods like concert tickets and T-shirts."[3]

The decline in CDs has also had a cascading effect on other related industries, too. Longtime music retailer Tower Records, which had been in business for forty-six years and at one point had 800 stores nationwide, was liquidated in 2006. With the loss of independent music retailers, more powerful retailers like Wal-Mart now represent roughly 65 percent of music retail sales and are putting more price and margin pressure on music labels. Whereas Tower Records used to stock 100,000 titles, big box stores like Wal-Mart and Best Buy carry only 10,000–20,000 titles, emphasizing fast-selling hits. Wal-Mart recently decided to cut back the size of its CD department in order to make room for other fast-selling merchandise. Genres of music such as classical, jazz, and hip-hop will now experience even greater challenges in reaching consumers

Case continued from page 227

effectively. In addition to cashing in on sales of MP3 players as an offset to declining CD sales, big retailers like Best Buy, Wal-Mart, and Amazon.com have also started music download sites.

Questions

1. What steps would you take to address decline if you were in charge of strategy at a music label company such as EMI?

2. What challenges do you think MP3 player manufacturers are facing now, as their industry is experiencing phenomenal growth?

3. MP3 player household penetration is estimated to level out by 2011. If you were in charge of strategy at an MP3 player manufacturer, what steps would you take to address the maturing of your business?

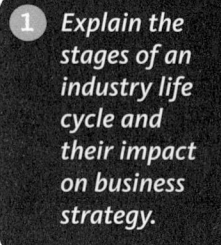

❶ *Explain the stages of an industry life cycle and their impact on business strategy.*

INDUSTRY LIFE CYCLES

One of the most exciting facets of the study of business and strategy is the nature of industry change. Many years ago the Austrian economist Joseph Schumpeter described "creative destruction" as a process that every industry experiences: they start up often based on some new entrepreneurial insight or innovation, attract new entrants, grow, begin to mature, and then a shakeup occurs that either launches renewed growth or thrusts the industry into decline. It's a "life cycle" that has been observed time and time again across dozens of types of industries.

Life Cycle Stages

An industry's evolution through a complete life cycle is fundamentally driven by two factors: new knowledge about how to create value and growth in demand (Figure 8.2). New knowledge about creating value forms the basis for any new industry to begin with—whether it be the application of modular manufacturing and assembly to democratize the automobile (Henry Ford), the use of durable-stitched material to sell the first pair of "blue jeans" (Levi Strauss), the creation of a new low-cost distribution method for retailing general merchandise (Sam Walton), or figuring out how to encode and play music digitally. However, new knowledge alone, without growth in demand, would lead only to faddish products and services and short-lived industry categories such as Beanie Babies, Pet Rocks, Pogs, Cabbage Patch dolls, or disco music. Growth in demand occurs because the sort of value creation resulting from an innovation is substantive and has long-lasting appeal to a wide audience of potential users. The potential for broad appeal attracts new entrants to an industry because they see the possibilities of earning profits, and they remain there to compete because of continued growth in demand.

But the growth of companies and the entrance of new competitors eventually leads to a saturation of demand. At this point an industry will experience one of two possible paths. Either there will be a renewed burst of growth because new, innovative knowledge developed within the industry provides

> **Figure 8.2**
> **Determinants of Industry Evolution**
> New knowledge about value creation
> Growth in demand

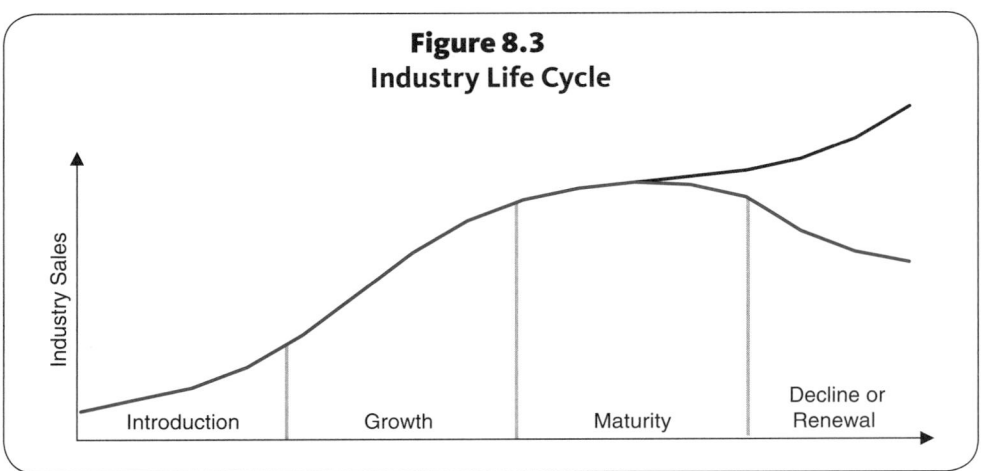

Figure 8.3
Industry Life Cycle

Industry Sales (vertical axis)

Introduction | Growth | Maturity | Decline or Renewal

the opportunity to create even greater value and attract new customers, or new knowledge that leads to innovation in some other economic sector will enhance the power of substitutes to draw off customers because of compelling price/value propositions, leading to the industry's decline. The evolution of most industries therefore follows a familiar pattern involving four stages, such as those illustrated in Figure 8.3. We typically describe the stages as the introduction, growth, maturity, and decline (or renewal). Each stage of the industry life cycle tends to exhibit its own defining characteristics that have implications for the type of strategic approach that might be successful.

Introduction stage. You would not expect to see a lot of competitors populating an industry at its infancy. Almost by definition, in the introduction stage of an industry there will typically be a very small number of companies dipping their toes in the waters of a type of business that has never been tried before. Sometimes there is just one such "new entrant," often referred to as a first mover. **First-mover advantage** refers to a sustainable competitive advantage that is achieved by being the first company to enter a new industry or industry segment, and we'll address it in more depth later in this chapter. Companies that are these first movers have the widest possible strategic choice. Innovation results in a wide variety of products or services being offered, primarily because early entrants are trying to determine which bundle of characteristics or approaches will create the greatest perceived value for the consumer. These companies are not only figuring out if customers will buy their offerings and which segments of customers might buy, but also which suppliers present the best opportunity for success. Consequently, value creation in the introduction stage is often occurring internally through product design as well as externally in relationship-building both upstream and downstream.

Growth stage. Industries move into a growth stage when the kind of value created begins to engender broader demand. Still experiencing the entrance of new companies seeking to profit from the potential, most industries will also begin to experience some corporate exiting by companies that are unable to successfully adapt to what is usually a growing degree of **standardization** of

First-mover advantage
The sustainable competitive advantage that is sought by being the first company to enter a new industry or industry segment.

Standardization
An industry condition in which customers begin to appreciate a standard set of features and benefits or products or services.

products or services. Although Sony essentially created the home VCR market in the 1980s with its Betamax technology, VHS technology became the industry standard and Sony finally withdrew the Betamax from the market (albeit stubbornly). As demand continues to increase, competitors focus on achieving scale to serve a broad swath of customers or markets while reliably and consistently delivering what customers value. There is still an opportunity for innovation and an effective differentiation strategic approach during the growth stage; however, increasing standardization opens the door for a low-cost leadership strategic approach. Because of the focus on standardization and achieving scale and scope, value can be created internally through process as well as externally by working to develop broad downstream customer relationships. Some consolidation begins to occur among industry participants, enabling a small number of competitors to more rapidly increase size and scale.

Maturity stage. Industries mature when demand begins to slow down. In contrast to the 1970s and 1980s when soft drink per capita consumption grew by 50 percent in a fifteen year period, moving into the 1990s per capita consumption remained relatively flat. Maturity is also experienced when a high level of customer saturation is reached, meaning there are relatively few new customers to bring into the industry. The U.S. cell phone market is beginning to experience this now (Figure 8.4),[4] as the industry is approaching 90 percent penetration among U.S. households. When these conditions occur, competition becomes fierce since one of the only routes to growth is to take market share away from other companies. **Commoditization** typically occurs in mature industries, when customers no longer really value innovation and new doohickeys but instead expect a standard set of features that increasingly incorporates the best of the market-tested capabilities. In turn this leads to less opportunity for differentiation-based advantage and more-intense cost competition among companies, often resulting in a shake-up among competitors and exits from the industry by those who are unable to compete effectively under such onerous conditions. Value creation at this stage is largely focused internally on cost efficiency. The availability of low-cost labor in other countries has led to outsourcing production by many U.S. companies in order to remain cost-competitive, as well as to large numbers of exits of U.S. companies from some industries such as furniture and textiles. Many of the exits occur through mergers and acquisitions when businesses are sold to competitors and other corporate buyers, and the result is a small number of large industry powerhouses.[5]

Decline stage. At some point an industry will evolve beyond the maturity stage, and one possible direction is decline. An industry will begin to decline either

Commoditization
An industry condition in which a standard set of features and benefits is required for any serious competitor, and in which such features and benefits are readily available from a variety of suppliers. These conditions lead to low-cost competition.

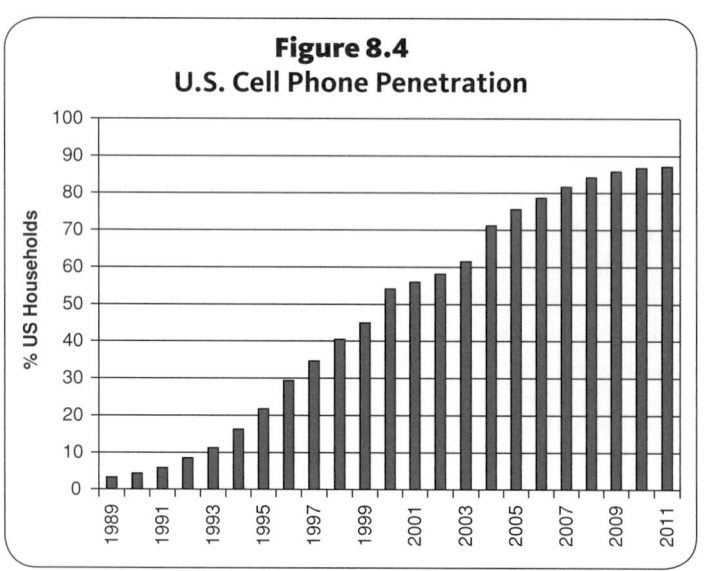

Figure 8.4
U.S. Cell Phone Penetration

because other substitute industries provide a more compelling combination of price and value, but ordinarily decline occurs because innovation in some other sector has made obsolete the value proposition that the industry had historically created. Figure 8.5 provides examples of industries thrust into decline because of innovations elsewhere. As end users flee to products and services offered in other industries, the declining industry experiences overcapacity. Companies seek to shed assets and engage in cost cutting in order to survive, and this often involves greater consolidation through horizontal mergers and acquisitions in order to gain greater control over remaining productive capacity, costs, and pricing. The value chain focus of companies in declining industries is primarily on internal operations in order to achieve cost control.

Figure 8.5
Declining Industries & Their Causes

Declining Industry	Innovation Elsewhere
Passenger trains	Automobile, airplane
Photo finishing	Digital camera
Network television	Cable broadcasting
Door-to-door sales	Internet
Public libraries	Online book sellers
Tobacco	Medical research
VHS tapes	DVDs
Video rental stores	Internet video services/Cable pay per view
Rivets	Welding

Renewal stage. The alternative to decline is renewal, where innovation *within* the mature industry leads to the opportunity to once again acquire new customers, new markets, and additional business from existing customers. Although one or two competitors in a mature industry might find ways to jack sales by courting niche arenas within the industry, renewal of the entire industry really depends on **reconfiguring the industry value chain** in one of several ways (Figure 8.6). These include the following:

Figure 8.6
Reconfiguring Industry Value Chain

Redefine industry boundaries
Disaggregate blocks of industry activity
Redefine value
Shift to complements

- **Redefine industry boundaries.** Broadening the definition of the boundaries to an industry enables its participants to generate new business by developing new sets of value-adding activities. In the 1950s the railroad freight industry was at a mature stage. Companies that survived the shakeout and participated in the industry's renewed growth broadened their industry definitions beyond purely "railroad freight" to "freight," which caused them to focus more carefully on how trucking companies and barge freighters operated. The broader industry focus resulted in the definition of a new set of key success factors that the railroad companies paid attention to, which in turn prompted a reconfiguration of their value-adding activities.[6] Approaching saturation in the cell phone market (Figure 8.4), cell phone companies are broadening their industry definition by enabling their users to surf the Web, take pictures, download music, instant message, check their e-mails and a variety of other services, no matter where they are or what they are doing. These kinds of efforts require companies to develop new supply-side relationships, develop new internal

Reconfiguring industry value chain A strategic approach that calls for changing the usual sets of relationships across the industry value chain.

capabilities, and cultivate new customer user groups—essentially reconfiguring the industry value chain from end-to-end.

- **Disaggregate blocks of value chain activity.** By considering how and where value is actually created in an industry value chain, companies may identify new opportunities through disaggregating sets of activities usually combined together that represent "how things are done." In the mature dry cleaning industry, for example, the typical retail store combines three value chain activities—management, operations, and customer service. New opportunities are being created, however, when dry cleaning chains unbundle this typical suite of activities and place customer service desks remotely in the lobbies of corporate office buildings, where customers can conveniently drop off and pick up their laundry. Placing the customer interface closer to the customer by separating it from operations helps change the usual configuration of value-creating activities in the industry. Similarly, supermarkets have unbundled their customary deli operations (mix, cook, serve) to allow customers to pick up fully assembled, prepackaged dinners made with fresh ingredients that need only be heated up at home. Instead of fully cooking meal items in advance and keeping them warm until the shopper is in the store, this new unbundling of activities captures customers who want freshly cooked meals but not the guilt of going out to restaurants.

- **Redefine value.** Redefining industry boundaries leads to the identification of new key success factors and therefore to new value chain activities, and disaggregating blocks of activities can also lead to new ways to create value. A third possibility is to redefine an existing value that is at the heart of the industry, leading to a new configuration of activities. Locked in fierce competition with Coca-Cola in the 1990s, Pepsi embarked on a program that centrally redefined its low-cost approach; its "10X" program changed the focus of the business from "cost per can of soda produced" to "cost per satisfied customer." The new cost concept not only included the manufacturing cost of the product, but also its retail delivery truck schedules to ensure no out-of-stocks occurred, its vending machine technology to provide transmitted data alerts when cans in the machine were running low, enhancing its customer service center operations, and other activities that were part of the customer value creation effort.

- **Shift to complements. Complements** are products or services that have a positive effect on the value of a company's own products or services. Apple's iPod business complements its iTunes business. Video games sold by Microsoft, Nintendo, and Sony all complement the value of the base game unit offered by each company, since the value of the base unit is zilch unless there are a variety of game applications that can be played on it. Disney became successful in theme parks, and more recently in cruise vacations, because of its studio creativity

Complements Products or services that have a correlation relationship with, and can affect the value of, a company's own products or services. For example, iTunes and iPod.

Figure 8.7
Industry Life Cycle Stage Characteristics

Stage	Introduction	Growth	Maturity	Decline	Renewal
Type of demand	Experimenters, early adopters	Broad penetration	Mass market	Traditionalists, loyal core	New customers, new segments
Competition	Few new entrants	Entrants & exits, consolidation	Shakeout, exits	Overcapacity, exits	
Strategy	Differentiation	Differentiation, low cost appearing	Low cost, focused differentiation	Low cost	New differentiation
Value creation	Innovation, variety	Scale & access to markets Process: standardization, consistency & reliability	Commoditization, cost efficiency	Cost cutting, asset reduction	Leverage core value chain capabilities
Value chain focus	Choices: internal & upstream or downstream	Extend & refine: internal, downstream	Survival: internal	Survival: internal	Reconfigure: redefine industry, redefine value, disaggregate, complements

and film success. As these examples suggest, generating renewal in a mature industry through a shift to complementary products or services relies on core characteristics of the companies involved but also requires new configurations of value chain activities to extend these core characteristics into related—but different—industries.

Figure 8.7 summarizes the characteristics of industry life cycle stages we have just discussed.

Length of Industry Life Cycle Stages

Lately it appears as if the business world has sped up, suggesting that industries evolve through at least the earlier life cycle stages fairly rapidly. Rapid progress has been the norm for consumer technology-based industries that we're more familiar with, such as compact disks or video cassette recorders and tapes, each of which moved from inception to peak to significant decline within a period of less than twenty years. Yet this is not always the case. Figure 8.8 illustrates the time periods associated with the rise and maturity of four different technologies that are central to our lives today.[7] The Internet and the personal computer are being adopted sooner after each was invented, but surprisingly

Best Buy's CEO, Richard Schulz, has been in the home electronics retailing business for over forty years. Following a tornado's destruction of one of his small audio components stores in Minnesota in 1981, he accidentally discovered that a larger market existed for electronics retailing when he ran a "tornado sale" in 1981 to liquidate vast quantities of merchandise. Taking advantage of the increased disposable income of "baby boomers" who loved rock and roll and could now afford to buy stereo equipment, and of skyrocketing demand for home VCRs, in 1983 Schulz changed his chain's name to Best Buy. Commissioned sales people "took a more proactive role" in assisting shoppers in the store, and retail prices often reflected the desire of the sales staff to earn high commissions. The chain expanded to twenty-four stores by 1987 and generated $240 million in revenue. By 1989 Best Buy had grown to nearly 100 stores.

Expansion of the consumer electronics retailing industry continued to be driven by new technology coming to market, such as innovative waves of personal computers and peripherals, compact disks, and larger televisions. Like Best Buy, other chains were also growing larger. In 1989 Best Buy nearly went bankrupt after a price war initiated by one of its large competitors. Schulz decided to modify his retail store model by increasing its square footage to generate more floor selling space, providing wider aisles, displaying a wider variety of merchandise; ending commissioned sales to take pressure off the salesperson-shopper relationship; and focusing on a low-margin high-turnover economic model. As the first "big box" discount electronics retailer, the combination was a hit with consumers and suppliers.

QUESTIONS

1. Describe how Best Buy's moves reflected changes in the industry's developments.

2. As the electronics retailing industry matures and competition becomes especially fierce, what methods of creating value would you recommend they pursue?

3. How does a company know what stage of its life cycle the industry is in?

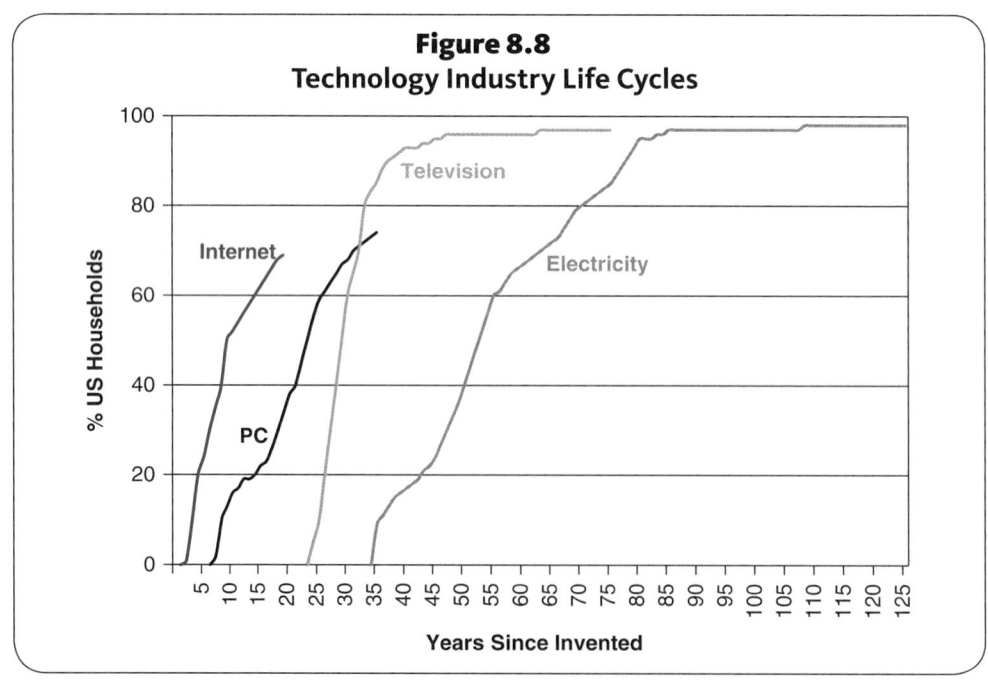

Figure 8.8
Technology Industry Life Cycles

not at a steeper rate of adoption than was television or even electricity in the home. It is still true that not all new industries grow up as quickly as some of these recent trends. Biotechnology, for example, has been around for nearly twenty years, has received considerable venture capital and corporate funding. Yet biotech industry sales are still considered in their infancy. Three factors work to stretch out the time it takes for a new industry to evolve beyond an introductory stage into growth: speed of commercialization, affordability, and the existence of complementary infrastructures. Biotech is a case where commercialization takes a long time due to complex research and government regulation, and where each new biotech application can cost tens of millions of dollars to develop. Cable television was developed in the 1960s, but until the physical infrastructure of cable lines strung through communities was developed, there was no way to deliver the signal broadly.

FRAGMENTED AND CONSOLIDATED INDUSTRIES

2 *Analyze the strategy implications of competing in fragmented or consolidated industries.*

Industry life cycle models ordinarily portray consolidation beginning to occur during the growth stage and then gaining in prominence as an industry moves into and through the mature stage. This is because standardization—and then commoditization—become valued competitive dimensions as an industry evolves. It is often true that larger companies with scale can achieve better standardization of features at lower costs and therefore compete more successfully. This is not always how the story goes, however, and we briefly mention here two other strategic possibilities in industry evolution. The first is how to compete in consolidated industries without benefiting from scale and a low-cost structure. The second is how to compete when industries mature without consolidation ever occurring, that is, in fragmented industries.

Consolidated Industries

Focused differentiation is one strategic approach that can succeed in a consolidated industry where the values of standardization and low cost tend to prevail. The department store industry is in a mature phase, now dominated by a small number of national chains, for example when Federated and May merged and then rebranded nearly all the combined stores as Macy's (Figure 8.9). The increased size of Macy's provides improved buying power with suppliers, achieves economies of scale in managing operations, and results in greater consistency in retail execution from store to store across the chain—values on which most department stores compete. Yet Saks Fifth Avenue occupies a highly focused differentiated position in this market, by carrying high-end merchandise, investing in expensive store fixtures, pampering customers, and (no fooling)

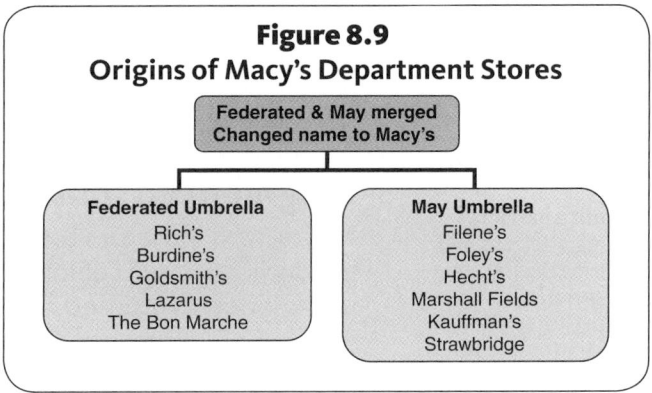

Figure 8.9
Origins of Macy's Department Stores

Federated & May merged
Changed name to Macy's

Federated Umbrella	May Umbrella
Rich's	Filene's
Burdine's	Foley's
Goldsmith's	Hecht's
Lazarus	Marshall Fields
The Bon Marche	Kauffman's
	Strawbridge

charging higher prices to pay for these luxurious value chain enhancements.

For competitors to succeed in consolidated industries without following the standardization and low-cost recipe, one of several conditions must exist (Figure 8.10). Although size confers the previously mentioned advantages of scale and efficiency, it also creates **mobility barriers**. For large companies with a portfolio of dedicated resources targeted at one type of competition, it is difficult to go after another business segment that would require a different set of resources and capabilities that are difficult to develop or imitate. Size may also present potential anti-trust concerns, since as we read in Chapter 4 the regulatory authorities are keen on preventing any one company from commanding too much market power. Dedicated sets of resources and traditional ways of doing business also cause large competitors to be blind to new opportunities afforded by niche positions within their industries, allowing other companies to gain traction and develop defensible positions. IBM considered— but then rejected—the opportunity to get into the personal computer business in the 1970s. Its entire value creation system was designed for mainframes and customized corporate software applications, and management could not imagine computing occurring in any way other than how it had traditionally been done. Of course, this opened the door for Apple. Finally, because consolidated industries are often characterized by cost/price competition, it suggests that many companies— especially those that do not in fact own the low-cost leadership position—may be experiencing profit margin pressure along with low growth. Such companies can be short on financial resources (cash on hand, access to inexpensive capital), which can prevent them from going after another more differentiated competitor.

The brewing industry provides an interesting example of how to compete successfully in a consolidated industry. Through the 1970s and 1980s the domestic beer industry experienced increasing consolidation with only three major domestic breweries remaining: Anheuser Busch, Adolph Coors, and Miller Brewing. Along the way, though, came the microbrews that have been so successful over the last twenty years (e.g., Sam Adams, Fat Tire, Saranac), defined as breweries with less than 15,000 barrel brewing capacity per year. Microbrews involve higher-cost ingredients, shorter production runs, longer aging, more expensive packaging, lower sales volume unsuitable for mass distribution—all characteristics that the major breweries were ill equipped to pursue because of their focus on the high-volume, low-cost method of competing with each other. The big three were blind to this new niche market emerging within the industry, and their resource investments and capabilities prevented them from pursuing it.

Fragmented Industries

Mobility barriers
Strategic actions and resource investments that prevent competitors in the industry from imitating the company.

Fragmented industries pre sent an entirely different picture. These are industries in which few large companies have emerged, and consequently where the HHI index, or concentration ratio (see Figure 4.13), is extremely low. In the 1990s, for example, there were 33,000 retail stores offering dry cleaning services in the United States, yet the two largest companies in the industry had only 360 stores and 180 stores, respectively. Industries remain fragmented because either 1) there are no mobility or entry barriers to insulate a company from competitive duplication, enabling easy entrance to the industry, or 2) value creation is largely dependent on local labor or conditions for a significant portion of its cost and competitive market position. These two reasons illustrate that fragmentation is the antithesis of consolidation, which depends on barriers to forestall competition and on advantages gained through scalable dimensions of the value chain. Because they behave much more like perfectly competitive markets, in fragmented industries the opportunity to earn superior profits is very small.

A successful strategic approach will involve reconfiguring the industry value chain, usually by unbundling or disaggregating its normally combined parts, into a new system that creates added value and cannot be easily imitated. For example the day-care industry has long been characterized by small neighborhood facilities, low-wage staff, poor benefits, high turnover and thus "barely adequate" child care services.[8] Bright Horizons, which solved the fragmentation problem to become the world's leading provider of child care, hired quality employees and developed rich experience programs, then used the quality care value to seek corporations as customers. By establishing child care centers in corporate office buildings and staffing them with quality staff, the company created value for corporations that are viewed as better supporting their own employees who have young children. Staples, Office Depot, and Office Max all participated in the **industry roll-up** of the highly fragmented office supplies market, previously populated by thousands of small independent shops across the country. Each chain unbundled the combined value chain activities at each individual store, and created new value through specialized investments at the corporate level in information systems, procurement expertise, large stores, and retail location modeling.

These examples might suggest that fragmented industries largely exist downstream at the "retail" level, but this is not always the case. Fragmentation can characterize the upstream supply side, as well. As the automobile manufacturing industry grew, for example, suppliers of parts and subsystems that were assembled into finished cars remained fairly fragmented. Other than minor design differences among competing automobile brands, a piston is a piston is a piston, and many machine shops manufactured pistons that were then incorporated into engines. An opportunity existed to create more consistent quality and provide better control and governance over the supply chain, and thus original equipment manufacturers (OEMs) came into being.[9] OEM companies acquired and consolidated many smaller contract manufacturers, as well as managed additional outsourced manufacturing, creating organizational and quality control values needed by the end users (Figure 8.11).

Industry roll-up
The consolidation of an industry when many small fragmented competitors are combined into a larger company.

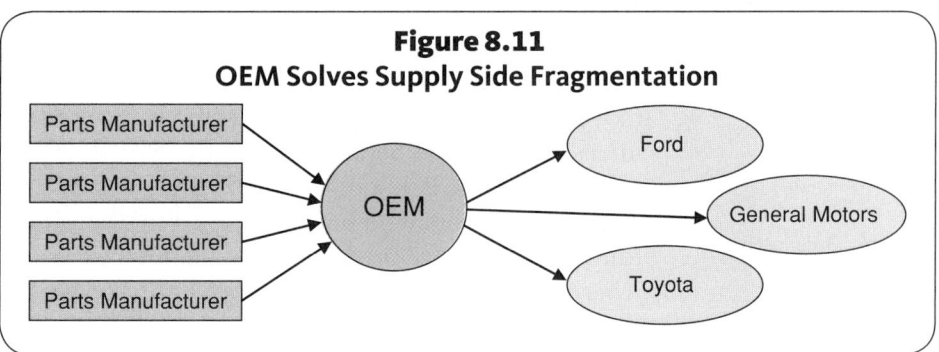

Figure 8.11
OEM Solves Supply Side Fragmentation

Parts Manufacturer
Parts Manufacturer
Parts Manufacturer
Parts Manufacturer
OEM
Ford
General Motors
Toyota

ORGANIZATIONAL LIFE CYCLES

In addition to the industry life cycles, firms also face challenges associated with what is known as the organizational life cycle. Like the industries in which they compete, companies also go through stages of development. As a company starts up, it first goes through a conception stage where the idea for the new business is further fleshed out and the strategic approach to the market is developed. Then the company actually "goes to market" in the commercialization stage, developing a customer base and achieving initial sales. If things go well, the company enters the growth stage as the customer base and geographic nature of the business expand. At some point a maturity stage will be reached, at which time the company's business growth begins to flatten out. The pattern of growth in sales that illustrates a company's stage of development (Figure 8.12) is familiar because it has been witnessed over and over again, so much so that venture capitalists often refer to it as the "hockey stick" curve.

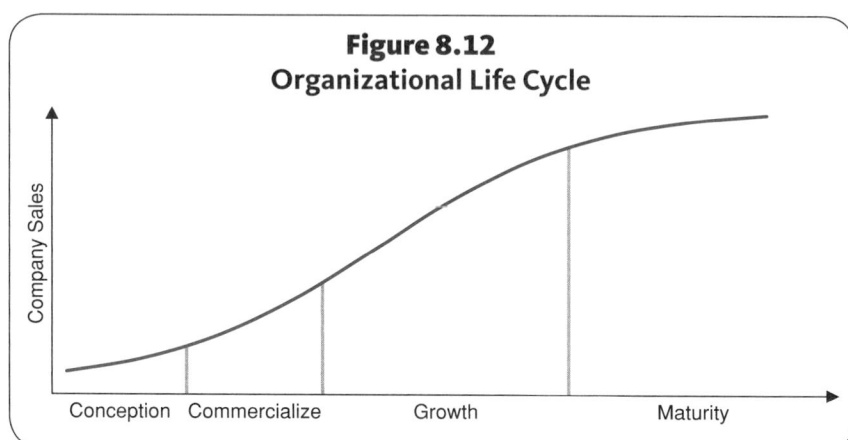

Figure 8.12
Organizational Life Cycle

The organizational life cycle concept is useful because it highlights two separate but related issues. Each stage of the organizational life cycle tends to exhibit its own characteristic problems and issues that have implications for the focus of management attention, the development of functional areas of the company, and the development of strategic resources appropriate for the problems encountered. These are the more pressing, shorter-term dimensions that determine a company's success in its present circumstances. But there are also strategy issues that are crucial to the longer-term success of the company, and these manifest themselves at different parts of the cycle.

Life Cycle Stages and Functional Area Issues

Conception. This first stage of a company's development is marked by a focus of the founders on three important elements that the business will require to move forward. First they must have a product or service that works, and so an intense effort is put behind the research and development function. This is often informal and experimental, usually involving a small number of product developers or engineers who have been recruited specifically for this task. Second, the founders must develop a clear articulation of their market entry strategy. This is where some of the insight about both industry analysis and the previous discussion in this chapter about industry stages can come in handy. Entering a mature market populated by large incumbent competitors presents a considerably different strategic problem than entering an early-growth industry where strategic variety exists and no company has achieved a dominant position. The strategic approach selected can have an impact on the product/service development effort, for example including more bells and whistles if the industry analysis indicates these could be effective strategically. Third, the founders must seek financial capital so that they are able to support the business appropriately when they do enter the market. Raising capital depends on having both an effective product or service and a clearly articulated market entry strategy. Few sophisticated investors would support a new venture unless a clear understanding of the competitive set and the strategic positioning had been developed, even if the product or service was phenomenal.

The key problems for companies in the conception stage are putting the right people with the right knowledge in place. Completion of the product or service development requires specialized technical knowledge. Science-based companies (such as biotech or medical device manufacturers) must also develop scientific procedures and protocols at this stage, so some formalization of the research and development process may be required. The articulation of strategy requires bringing in people who understand the market and the type of business, and raising capital requires tapping into social networks through which knowledgeable financial partners can be recruited. From a strategic resources point of view, the success of the company at this stage depends on the extent to which the founders can leverage their own knowledge about a market opportunity into these kinds of technical knowledge, human, and social resources.

Commercialization. Having invented something, the company must figure out how to consistently make it or provide it in some quantity. New food product companies are often based on a recipe cooked on a stove, but translating the stovetop recipe to a manufacturing quantity of, say, 15,000 pounds at a time is a challenge that must be met. It makes no sense to manufacture 15,000 pounds or more unless the company has customers to sell it to, so marketing and sales programs now need to be developed. Of course, these efforts should be consistent with the overall strategic approach that the company has previously developed. When manufacturing begins and sales are generated, a need develops for administrative systems of reporting and control.

The key problems that commercialization-stage companies confront have to do with these production and market start-up issues. Discrete organizational functions like manufacturing, marketing, sales, and finance ordinarily come into being at this point. The existence of "departments" containing these functions requires an organizational structure with lines of authority and the allocation of decision-making authority. Hiring the right people for the new functional areas becomes important, so that at this point a human resources position or department is also created. Greater complexity results from the combination of resources that have now been assembled to conduct business.

The company's performance at this stage depends on its ability to attend carefully to the myriad of organizational and operational details that make market entry efforts a success. Manufacturing procedures, marketing efforts, and effective selling approaches should be documented and reviewed, so that the company can make corrections that are needed or amplify on methods that are working. So in the face of greater organizational complexity at this early stage, it is important for companies to articulate carefully what works so that it can be reproduced.

Growth. With market acceptance and the existence of demand for the kind of value the company has created, it will experience a period of growth. This is an exciting time for any company; however, it can also be a time when great pains are experienced because growth exposes flaws in the system the business has so far developed. For example, to sell in vast quantities requires production in vast quantities. So the scale-up issue from the previous stage is compounded: instead of how to go from 0 to 15,000 pounds, now the challenge is how to go from 15,000 to 150,000 pounds (or more). Often this type of scale-up requires significant investment in physical facilities. The addition of facilities generates additional manufacturing process and efficiency issues, because the effective integration of large new production capacity does not magically happen overnight. Sales and marketing take on a much more central role in most organizations at this stage, since growth is often driven by the efforts of these functions. Internal conflict may arise, because sales and marketing are focused on selling more while manufacturing is having problems scaling up to produce more. Often manufacturing wants to go slower, while sales and marketing have the pedal to the metal—often promising more than manufacturing can consistently produce and deliver. This is precisely what occurred during late 2007 when Nintendo's manufacturing division could not keep up with the demand created by the company's marketing efforts for the Wii, resulting in significant out-of-stocks at retailers across the United States during the peak holiday sales period. Nintendo encouraged retailers to provide prospective buyers with "rain checks" for when manufacturing would have stock back in stores in February. One CNN news commentator noted, "There is nothing like the squeal on Christmas morning when the kid opens up the box and finds an IOU."[10]

Growth-stage companies are often constrained on all types of resources, so organization and planning take on added importance. Growth can be developed through a number of ways—existing customers buying more frequently, new customers added, and new territories opened up for sale. Management needs to make decisions about focusing limited resources on the best opportunities, not fragmenting efforts across the company. The resource problem facing companies at this stage is how to coordinate what has become very complex very quickly. Whereas in the previous stage the advice for the company was to make all the steps and procedures explicit so that best practices could easily be repeated throughout the company, now companies need to routinize activities so that employees tacitly understand what to do and can execute best practices without direction or supervision. Now companies also need to achieve greater cross-department coordination that does not require constant senior management involvement.

Maturity. At some point following tremendous growth, the maturity stage sets in. It happens to nearly every business. This is not necessarily connected with industry maturity; it may be that the particular products or services provided by the company have achieved customer saturation even though the industry is still growing, or that the kind of value appreciated by customers in an evolving industry no longer match the kind of value created by the company. As growth in revenue slows down, growth in profitability will depend upon greater efficiencies and cost reduction. Internal controls become more important, and the roles of the accounting and finance functions become more central to managing for enhanced financial performance. The company at this stage must also find ways to maintain previous growth momentum and market position, which typically involves developing extensions to the product/service or introducing a second-generation line of products/services.

Most companies in the maturity stage have become highly organized using a functional structure, and are characterized by bureaucratic operating principles. These structural characteristics are useful for monitoring and exerting cost control over operations, in order to improve the profitability of the existing business. But the challenge of developing new business will often require building additional resources and competencies. So the essential resource challenge for companies in the mature stage is to develop secondary or complementary resource positions, beyond those that led to their initial path of success.

Figure 8.13 summarizes the characteristics of organizational life cycle stages we have just discussed, including the problems encountered in each stage, the importance of functional areas of the company, and the resource challenges.

Figure 8.13
Organizational Life Cycle Stage Characteristics

Stage	Conception	Commercialization	Growth	Maturity
Dominant problems	Innovation effort Strategy design Raising capital	Startup production Hiring Systems	Scale-up production Marketing & sales Chaos & pace Loss of culture Organization	Profitability Internal controls Future growth
Functions important to address problems	R & D	Manufacturing Information Systems	Manufacturing Marketing Sales	Finance Accounting
Resources development challenge	Leveraging founders' knowledge to develop additional resources	Combining resources; Making explicit the processes that work so everyone understands	Coordinating resources; Making routine the processes that work so they can be performed without direction	Developing secondary or complementary resources
Important resources	Knowledge Human Social capital Technology	Human Organizational	Financial Organizational Physical	Knowledge Technology

With added competition from Circuit City and Wal-Mart, and with the U.S. economy falling into a recession in 2001–2002, Best Buy experienced a slowdown in its internal sales growth rate. In 2000 they reported that "same-store sales" (sales in stores open at least one year) had increased 11.1 percent, but in 2001 this had dropped to 4.9 percent and then to only 1.9 percent in 2002. In 2003 CEO Richard Schulz introduced a new customer-focused concept known as "Customer-Centricity." The new customer-centric approach involved: 1) careful customer segmentation research to better understand who were their most profitable customers and the purchasing behaviors of this group; 2) careful geographic and demographic research to better understand specifics of customers living near their stores; and then 3) creating store merchandise and marketing programs tailored at the local level to these specific customer targets. The types of merchandise stocked in stores therefore varied by location, and customers of each store began to receive personalized marketing and promotional mailings. This was in stark contrast to the models used by their competitors, which involved stocking the same merchandise in every store while employing broad-based general advertising. These new efforts enabled Best Buy to increase same-store sales rates, and to enhance gross profit margins through opportunistically charging higher prices.

QUESTIONS

1. Do you think Best Buy's initiatives were in response to industry life cycle or organizational life cycle issues? Why?

2. Since Best Buy moved first into this new way of cultivating the customer, would there have been any advantage for Circuit City to try the same thing then?

4 *Decide which strategy issues associated with being a first mover and pursuing business renewal apply given the resource position of a particular company.*

STRATEGY ISSUES IN STAGES

There are a few strategy issues that do not fit neatly into the box of generic business-level strategies (Chapter 7), but instead are more appropriately considered in the context of the organizational life cycle. These are "special situations" in strategy. They include first-mover strategy in the earlier stage, managing fast growth in the growth stage, and in the later stage the renewal strategies for the existing business.

First-Mover Strategy

A first-mover strategy describes the decision to enter a new market or industry space before any other company has done so. It is about creating a brand new business in a brand new market, so it is really about a particular strategic approach for the earliest stage of a business at the earliest stage of an industry.

In our experience students tend to believe there is a certain cachet associated with being first into a new market space, as if getting there first is always the ticket to a sustainable strategic position. Let's be clear that this is not always the case. There are plenty of examples illustrating that the company that moved first into a new market space was not the eventual "winner" in the ensuing competition (Figure 8.14).[11] So we need to be clear about both the advantages and disadvantages of pursuing a first-mover strategy.

There are two kinds of advantage that can accrue to first movers: **timing advantage** and **size advantage**. Any kind of sustainable competitive advantage rests on the ability of the company's to use timing or size to create barriers to entry to the industry, or barriers to mobility when other companies enter the industry.

Possible advantages due to timing can be a consequence of any of the following four dimensions:

Figure 8.14
First-Mover Winners & Losers

Industry	First Mover	Winner
Disposable diaper	Procter & Gamble	Procter & Gamble
Instant camera	Polaroid	Kodak
Jet airline	De Haviland	Boeing
MP3 player	Diamond Multimedia	Apple
Personal computer	Xerox	IBM
VCR	Sony	Matsushita
Web browser	Netscape	Microsoft

- **Standard setting.** The company hopes to be able to set an industry standard as a result of entering first, thereby requiring other companies to follow design specifications that are created by the company. This is risky, because user tastes and preferences are difficult to predict before they have had a chance to spend time with a product. Superior quality products are not always the standard that emerges (e.g., Betamax versus VHS tapes).

- **Installed base and buyer switching costs.** By entering first, the company expects to develop a large base of users who become functionally and/or emotionally attached to their product or service, "locking them in" and making it difficult for them to switch to competitors. Microsoft is pursuing this approach with its Xbox 360, which has an installed user base significantly exceeding either Nintendo or Sony. Programmers want to write game software for the platform that will deliver the greatest economic rewards, so that now more games are being written for Xbox. This feeds back on consumers who want to buy game platforms that have the most (and coolest) games written for it.

- **Reputation.** Where product performance or quality is difficult to determine prior to buying and there are no major price differences, customers will defer to the company with the strongest reputation. The first mover has a chance to build reputation before others gain traction. This is an approach that e*Trade Securities adopted early in its entry into the discount online trading industry, in which the technological trading capabilities of competitors were perceived as being nearly identical but where trust in handling personal investments is paramount.

- **Preemption.** First movers can lock in sources of supply and thus lock out competitors. The clearest example is when McDonald's

Timing advantage
One of the possible benefits of first-mover status when entering a new industry. Timing advantages tend to build customer loyalty through setting standards, building reputation, and achieving customer lock-in.

Size advantage One of the possible benefits of first-mover status when entering a new industry. Size advantages tend to produce favorable cost structures and network effects.

is first to locate on the busiest corner of a high-traffic intersection; once it owns the land, no other company can occupy that spot. For a period of time in the 1980s Pepsi had an exclusive supply relationship with the popular artificial sweetener NutraSweet, which enabled Pepsi to develop a consumer franchise for its diet soda before Coca-Cola was able to.

It is possible to develop competitive superiority due to size advantages that can accrue to first movers. These include:

- **Scale.** When cost per unit declines with larger production volumes in each period, the company that generates a higher volume of business sooner can enjoy cost—and presumably pricing—advantages. See Figure 7.6 and discussion.
- **Experience curve.** The longer it has done something, the more efficient a company becomes because it has the chance to apply its learning to improve its methods of operation. See Figure 7.7 and discussion.
- **Scope.** If a first mover is able to broaden its procurement of goods and services faster than other competitors, it should be able to develop stronger bargaining power with suppliers and lower costs more quickly as a result.
- **Network.** When a company can more quickly achieve size, its buyers may derive greater value as a result of the presence of other buyers. AOL Instant Messenger and Facebook are only as strong as their networks of users (imagine how often you would visit Facebook if its network had only 100,000 active users instead of 59 million).

This is a fairly compelling list of advantages (Figure 8.15). But there are also some significant disadvantages from pursuing a first-mover strategy, and these challenge the conventional wisdom that first-mover status confers sustainable advantage over the long run:

- **Pioneering costs.** It is expensive to carve out a new business in a new industry space. The costs of pioneering include the R&D, building new infrastructure, and educating customers about what the heck you're trying to do. After all, it is a new business in a new industry, so no one has seen it before. Competitors coming in to the market space later on can build on the knowledge gained from your company's efforts, and can generally affect a market entry at a lower cost. The economic benefits to being first must somehow overcome the economic costs of getting there first, and this usually cannot be evaluated up front. Therefore, there is greater risk involved for the first mover.

Figure 8.15
First-Mover Advantages & Disadvantages

Timing Advantages	Size Advantages	Disadvantages
Standard setting	Scale	Pioneering costs
Installed base & user switching costs	Experience curve	Technology uncertainty
Reputation	Scope	Demand uncertainty
Pre-emption	Network	Inertia

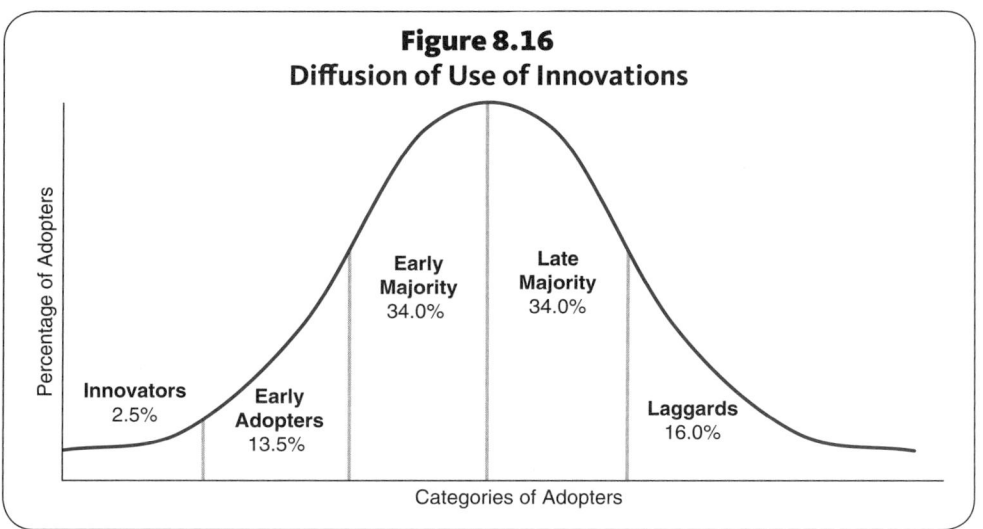

Figure 8.16
Diffusion of Use of Innovations

Percentage of Adopters

Innovators 2.5%

Early Adopters 13.5%

Early Majority 34.0%

Late Majority 34.0%

Laggards 16.0%

Categories of Adopters

- **Technological uncertainty.** As is illustrated by the Betamax story and other examples from Figure 8.14, "it ain't over til it's over." [12] You may be first in to the market with sweet technology that is superior on many fronts, but customers are unpredictable. In fact, it is often the case that pioneers in a market are banking on advanced technology of some sort. However, the early consumers are usually the "innovators" and "early adopters," and are in many respects not comparable to the mass market that will eventually follow (see Figure 8.16).

- **Demand uncertainty.** First movers typically have to make significant investments in specific manufacturing methods and other aspects of infrastructure, long before they know if sufficient demand will exist or even if the technology and standards are what will be preferred over the long run.

- **Inertia.** Having entered the market first and then discovered that different standards or technologies are taking off, many companies are still reluctant to modify their approaches. Sometimes this is based on a "sunk cost" argument that extols continuing on because of past spending, and sometimes it is based on the naïve belief that things will get better if they simply "try harder" and do "more of the same." Managers and product developers are often emotionally attached to their ideas, resistant to change even in the face of evidence that other approaches are preferred.

Fast Growth

Imagine the challenges you would face if your college workload (credit hours, amount of reading and homework) increased by 15 to 20 percent or more in every year! The volume and pace of activity picks up dramatically in any fast-growing organization, and it is not uncommon to find middle level managers putting in sixty- to seventy-hour weeks just to keep on top of current activity. During fast growth the company not only experiences a dramatic increase in customer volume, requirements from suppliers, extended operations, and more internal paperwork flow, but also attention from competitors who observe what is going on and who likely have vested interests in forestalling further growth. It is often tempting to "throw bodies" at the problems of work overload, so that some of the chaos that typically reigns can be balanced across more people. Most organizations experience a loss of "culture" during this phase because in the midst of pressure to grow and frenetic activity, employees often lose sight of what it was that bound them together originally. The real possibility exists that employees will spend inordinate amounts of time putting out the most immediate "fires" as opposed to focusing on the best long-term moves for the company.

This is why fast-growth organizations need to ensure consistency with the original strategy, vision, and mission. Vision and mission—which we discussed in Chapter 3—become critical during times when other forces try to pull the company in many different directions simultaneously. Refocusing on the business-level strategy that first propelled the fast-growth company into its current "predicament" is also called for. Here the importance of coordination across the value chain is critical, so that despite frenetic activity, each functional area of the company is pulling in the same direction and mutually supporting each other.

Fast-growth companies often find themselves challenged to implement the right kind of organizational structure to support their strategic approach. What works for companies that are mature or even growing at a normal rate, however, often does not work in fast-growth situations. Earthlink founder Sky Dayton had planned to sign up twenty to thirty new users a week to his new "dial-up" Internet service back in 1995, but found this new Internet offering was so popular that his company was fielding calls from thousands of interested users a week. He claims it was impossible to create an organizational structure that worked effectively, since the structure created one day was inundated within weeks. Therefore, he cycled between organizing and coping, organizing and coping, but made sure that he and his team considered organization on a regular basis as the company continued to grow. We'll talk more about structure in Chapter 11, where we will emphasize the point that structure goes hand in hand with strategy.

Renewal Strategies

We turn now to one of the special situations that a company encounters after it has entered the mature stage of the organizational life cycle. In today's dynamic markets it is seldom the case that a mature company can continue on indefinitely without its base business beginning to erode away. Once again, this type of erosion could be occurring—not because the entire industry is in a state of decline—but because other industry and competitive conditions are obsoleting the value the company's business was originally designed to deliver. At first the mature stage presents itself as a decelerating rate of growth, then growth flattens out, then finally it begins to actually decline year over year. Some kind of renewal effort is called for.

Occasionally some will discuss renewal as the reinvigoration of an existing line of business within the company, such as developing new customers or markets for the products or by encouraging existing customers to buy more frequently. These are actually steps that companies take during the company's growth stage, in order to prolong growth and lengthen the entire life for a particular line of products or services.

But here we are referring to the renewal of the company, and the goal of renewal in the *organizational* life cycle is to regenerate growth of the company. Organizational renewal can happen in one of two ways: 1) expansion through the development and introduction of new businesses, or 2) expansion through the acquisition of other businesses. Because an entire chapter of this textbook is devoted to corporate strategy and the acquisitions of other companies (Chapter 10), we comment here on factors that impact the ability of a company to successfully expand by diversifying into internally developed new businesses. There are four critical factors that organizational renewal efforts depend upon:

- **Opportunity recognition capabilities.** One of the resources that companies in the twenty-first century need to develop is foresight about new market opportunities to move into, which matches up with one of the two strategic imperatives we mentioned in Chapter 1 of this textbook (opportunity recognition). Better anticipation of emerging market trends usually calls for a set of internal organization processes, research methods, and communication that are different from what hierarchy and bureaucracy tend to produce. Being able to rapidly take advantage of new opportunities identified also calls for "speed-to-market" capabilities that are different from those needed for managing an existing line of business. We mentioned earlier the need for mature-stage companies to develop secondary or complementary resources so that they can effectively identify emerging opportunities.

- **Platform innovation.** Instead of focusing on a series of discrete new business opportunities, many companies today—especially those in industries where research and development costs can skyrocket—seek to focus on platform innovations. A platform represents a base upon which several promising new lines of business can be developed. For example one nanotechnology research group is focusing on the integration of nanostructures into devices for light gathering, a platform that can be developed into high-performance lighting systems for the home, office, and transportation sector uses. When a company such as Microsoft introduces a "developer application toolkit" for its Xbox game hardware (specifications for developers to use in writing applications to work with the hardware), the toolkit essentially represents a kind of platform off which dozens and dozens of new products can be developed. Platform development represents a more efficient way of making R&D investments, since it promises multiple possible outcomes from a singular direction.

- **Optioned investments in innovation.** There has been great debate over the years about the type of innovation effort that is more fruitful for companies—incremental or radical innovation. Innovation that is incremental tends to build slowly on previously developed technical knowledge about products or services. This type of approach can be useful in lengthening a product's life and forestalling organizational decline, but in a maturing business it does not usually present a solution to aggressively build company sales growth. In contrast, radical innovation is the type characterized by tremendous departures from existing technical knowledge, with potentially highly advanced results and payoffs. The flip side of radical innovation is high risk and greater volatility of results from research and development efforts: bigger potential payoffs, but bigger opportunities for failure as well. The solution for many companies has been to adopt an **options** approach, making small investments in a series of internal new business development initiatives and then evaluating whether further funding is warranted for each based upon the development milestones each effort achieves. Management that makes such option investments essentially adopts a portfolio approach to managing innovation, and the portfolio can include both radical and incremental efforts.

- **Culture and incentives.** As suggested earlier in the discussion of the characteristics of mature-stage companies, bureaucracy and formalization reign. These are not organizational characteristics that support a culture of innovation. Some time ago Rosabeth Moss Kanter described "rules for stifling entrepreneurial efforts" inside an organization (Figure 8.17).[13] Senior management must reengineer the organizational structure and incentive systems to

Options An investment approach that places a small initial bet on an initiative, with the opportunity to invest further if the initiative makes favorable progress and reaches positive milestones.

Figure 8.17
Rules for Stifling Entrepreneurial Efforts Inside a Company

1. Regard any new idea from below with suspicion—because it's new, and because it's from below.
2. Insist that people who need your approval to act first go through several other levels of management to get their signatures.
3. Ask departments or individuals to challenge and criticize each other's proposals. That saves you the job of deciding; you just pick the survivor.
4. Express your criticisms freely, and withhold your praise. Let them know they can be fired at any time.
5. Control everything carefully. Make sure people count anything that can be counted, frequently.
6. Assign to lower level managers, in the name of delegation and participation, responsibility for figuring out how to cut back, lay off, move people around, or otherwise implement threatening decisions you have already made. And get them to do it quickly.
7. Above all, never forget that you—the higher ups—already know everything important about this business.

encourage experimentation and innovation and to avoid punishing such efforts that do not succeed. Chapter 11 will offer greater insight on structure and systems that provide the appropriate kind of environment for encouraging innovation.

INTERNATIONAL STRATEGY

5 Explain when a company should expand internationally and what approach it should take for doing so.

Throughout this textbook we have consistently referred to how globalization impacts the kind of dynamic competitive environment that confronts companies in the twenty-first century. Globalization affects companies in many ways, some positively and some negatively. The fact that we now live in a "global village" makes it easier for foreign competitors to compete against us, since they now have significantly better access to information, technology, financial capital, and alliance partners. This makes nearly every industry more perfectly competitive, since barriers to entry are more easily skirted and new entrants make themselves known and felt. These conditions also create more varied competition, so that the type of "strategic space" that we evaluate when we use strategy maps (Chapter 4) is populated with many types of companies competing on a variety of strategic dimensions. Domestic companies with deep pockets can more easily form alliances abroad, resulting in downward-spiraling cost structures and prices—creating less margin for error (and less margin for profit!). In addition, your company can more easily outsource to save costs or focus on core activities, and can therefore more easily manage outsourced efforts using advanced technologies. So competition has thus become more complex, and it has become increasingly difficult to "own" or control a sustainable space on the playing board. But globalization can also work for us, since this dynamic presents opportunities for our business to expand internationally, too, in the same ways.

For these reasons the potential for growth through an international strategy draws significant attention from management, and from strategy professors. There are entire courses in business schools that are devoted to international strategy or management, and we could devote many more pages to this broad topic. We encourage interested students to consult additional resources on related issues such as the risks of conducting business internationally (political, economic, cultural),[14] factors affecting national competitiveness,[15] different methods for expanding (e.g., from minimally exporting to establishing new subsidiary operations),[16] ethical issues in international business,[17] and ideas about competing in emerging countries such as China.[18]

However, we want to be very clear that international expansion does not automatically follow from the fact that the world is now a global marketplace. International expansion is but one method of growth or renewal for a company, among others we have already identified in this chapter. As with any new strategic initiative, the decision to expand internationally must be made for the right reasons at the right stage of development, and must account for the value creation capabilities and resources that a company has developed and can leverage. We will focus our discussion of international strategy on these important dimensions in this section.

Motivations to Expand Internationally

Among the many reasons for companies deciding to expand internationally, four stand out as the most compelling from a strategic point of view (Figure 8.18). The first two—seeking growth and achieving synergies with existing value chain capabilities—reflect the kind of rationale discussed earlier in this chapter about growth and progress during stages of a company's organizational life cycle. Seeking revenue growth is usually the most obvious reason suggested. Yet the decision to expand into international markets must be compared to expanding into other domestic markets, or to introducing new products or services into existing or new domestic markets. The unique challenges presented by international markets, mentioned briefly earlier—political, economic, and cultural risks—make this type of expansion more uncertain than simple domestic expansion. Yet it is often the case that international markets experience more favorable economic conditions than domestic—such as higher growth rates, very large potential customer base, and stronger economies with better customer purchasing power. See Figure 8.19 for international market comparisons. These are very good reasons for considering such expansion, and are central to why so many companies today are carefully evaluating the growing Chinese market.

Similarly, growth is easier to come by if the methods used to generate that growth are identical to existing methods. If expansion into international markets can take advantage of a company's internal value chain, or build easily upon its foundation of extraordinary resources and capabilities (Figure 6.6), then the risks of such expansion are significantly reduced. Leveraging the value chain and capabilities may lead to greater efficiencies through increased manufacturing scale or market scope, or may simply extend with minimal risk a successful differentiated strategic position from the domestic market such as quality or reputation. The Classic Car Club, which we profiled at the beginning of Chapter 6, moved into the United States from its United Kingdom domestic market because the United States presented a large untapped market *and* the move could build on the company's resource foundation (of knowledge about exciting cars, and refined routines for handling such rentals). In contrast, in its international expansion plans Wal-Mart has repeatedly discovered that the local conditions encountered in other countries (e.g., Brazil, Germany, Japan) do not allow the company to perfectly translate its successful U.S. business model elsewhere.

A third reason to consider expanding internationally is to spread risk. When a company's revenue base is significantly related to the status of the domestic economy, then its entire business is subject to a systematic risk that it cannot manage. Different countries, of course, experience different

---

Figure 8.18
Reasons for International Expansion

New geographic revenue opportunities
Leveraging existing value chain & resources
Spreading risk
Achieving location advantages

Figure 8.19
2008 Regional Economic Comparisons

	United States	European Union	China & Japan
Population (millions)	299	480	1442
Share of World GDP	21.3%	23.1%	16.9%

economic conditions and rates of growth, and so expansion can help smooth out revenues and earnings. If a company that sells only domestically procures raw materials or other supply inputs from abroad, then it could fall prey to exchange rate fluctuations when its home market currency declines on the international exchange. In this case it might make sense to expand in order to generate sales revenue abroad, and thus take advantage of the increased value of foreign currencies. The U.S. domestic automobile manufacturers (GM, Ford, and Chrysler) have found most of their profitable growth in markets outside North America over the last few years. We will return to the question of spreading risk in Chapter 10 when we discuss diversification.

ETHICS

The first three reasons have essentially dealt with reasons to expand revenue-generating efforts into other international markets. The fourth reason listed in Figure 8.18 has to do with the process of value creation—that is, where and how does a company produce its products or services? Establishing production operations in international markets can make sense when such efforts take advantage of local conditions that enhance a company's value creation efforts. For this reason apparel and shoe companies establish facilities or outsource manufacturing in countries in which wage rates are much lower than those paid domestically. They hopefully do this without sacrificing either quality or company image—that is, maintaining parity on other competitive dimensions that are valued. The Maytag division of Whirlpool Corporation sources standardized dishwasher motors from China and Mexican-manufactured wiring harnesses for its dishwashers, but then assembles the final products in Tennessee. They say they want to build cost-competitive machines but also "stay as close as possible to the end market and avoid shedding American jobs."[19] Some steel companies mine iron ore in Brazil and then ship it to Trinidad to convert to iron carbide, since Trinidad has inexpensive natural gas to run their blast furnaces.

Leveraging Value Chain and Resources

As suggested by the preceding discussion and the Best Buy vignette, a central consideration in international strategy is if and how the company's value chain and resource position might be leveraged. This issue becomes of increasing importance as companies seek to expand further and further into international markets. Should the company adopt the same approach in South Africa as in Brazil? Should the company establish new manufacturing facilities abroad at the same time it establishes new sales offices? How much coordination is needed between operations in different countries? How does senior management ensure that such coordination is occurring? As we can see, the decision to expand abroad raises a number of questions that are materially different from the decision to expand our reach from Baltimore to Denver.

To answer these fundamental questions we can refer back to value creation once again. Here we ask two value chain questions that are related to the two basic business-level strategies of differentiation and low cost:

1. Where in the value chain is value created?
2. What is the pressure for efficiency in the value chain?

By 2001 Best Buy achieved $15 billion in revenue and net income of $396 million through 419 stores open in the United States. Over the next seven years CEO Richard Schulz took the company into international markets through a combination of acquisitions and opening new stores abroad. The first market the company entered outside the United States was Canada, where they acquired an existing chain (Future Shop) and began opening Best Buy stores. Future Shop gave the company an immediate presence in the Canadian market and allowed them to leverage their U.S.-based capabilities such as their supply chain and administrative functions. The new Best Buy Canada stores they built then took advantage of their merchandising techniques and advertising prowess.

In 2007 Best Buy acquired a 75 percent interest in Five Star, one of China's largest appliance and electronics retailers, with a contractual option to acquire the remaining 25 percent in several years (subject to Chinese government approval). This initial foray into a very different consumer market was designed "to increase our knowledge of Chinese customers and obtain immediate retail presence" in the market. The company opened its first Best Buy store in Shanghai in 2007, and plans to open eight more in 2009. They are also now laying plans to open new stores in both Mexico and Turkey.

QUESTIONS

1. With overall company sales continuing to grow so quickly, why did Best Buy decide to expand into international markets?

2. Why did they choose Canada, China, Mexico, and Turkey as markets to expand into?

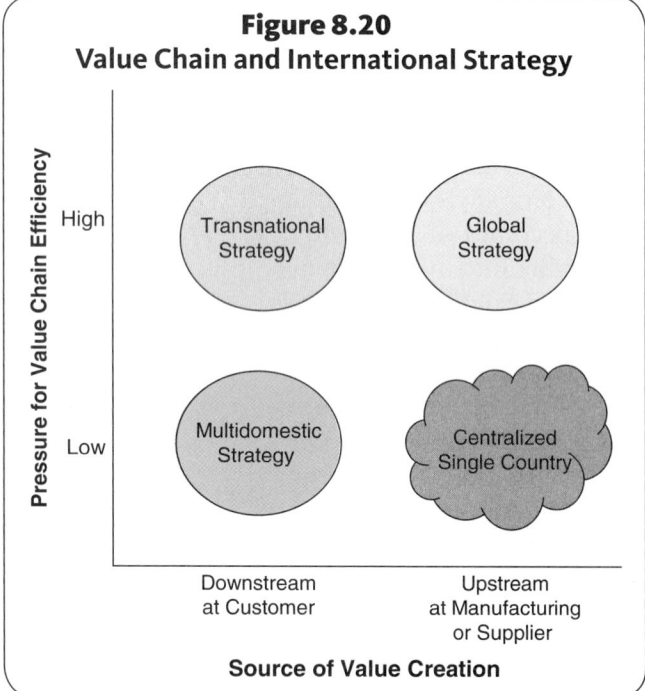

Figure 8.20
Value Chain and International Strategy

Pressure for Value Chain Efficiency

High — Transnational Strategy — Global Strategy

Low — Multidomestic Strategy — Centralized Single Country

Downstream at Customer — Upstream at Manufacturing or Supplier

Source of Value Creation

The answers to these questions help us determine the type of international strategy the company should seek to develop, and there are four types that are revealed. Figure 8.20 provides a useful visual guide for this discussion.

We will start at the upper right of Figure 8.20, and move counterclockwise looking at each type. When value is created upstream, closer to manufacturing or the supply side of a business, it is far less important for companies to make a series of discrete investments in each country in which it seeks to do business. Those types of in-country investments are not necessary, since they do not dramatically impact value creation. When there is significant pressure in the competitive market for efficiency, such as when pricing is competitive and low costs can be generated by manufacturing scale or scope, then the company should pursue a *global strategy*. Here the company produces a similar product or service for all international markets, and seeks to do so through a combination of facilities investments that optimize costs. Steel is a marvelous example of this type of approach. The location decisions for steel manufacturing plants seek to optimize the inbound transportation costs of raw materials and the outbound transportation costs of finished products. Arcelor-Mittal and other global steel companies have created networks of strategically located facilities to accomplish this goal in a cost-competitive commodity industry. This example demonstrates how a global strategy approach requires significant and complex integration and coordination capabilities by the corporation. Many automobile manufacturers have been searching for decades for a "world car," one that could be sold in all nations without being modified to local conditions. Ford has been going after this for decades, first with the Taurus, then in the 1990s with an unnamed model, and finally in 2008 with the Fiesta. Hope springs eternal! Unfortunately, automobile manufacturing is quite unlike steel or other commodities; consumer variation in preferences across countries and cultures is significant.

Where there is significant pressure on value chain efficiency, but where value creation must also account for local contexts, then a company is apt to follow a *transnational strategy*. As the name implies, the company's efforts are geared toward producing in a way that bridges across national boundaries in order to gain the efficiencies dictated by the competitive market. However, the pressure to deliver values that are appreciated differentially by local market customers necessitates flexible manufacturing or production—the kind that can tailor aspects of the product or service to local cultures. Many food manufacturing firms follow this type of approach: basic brand research and development is centralized at headquarters, but then brand flavor and size adjustments, packaging in foreign languages, production, and specialized distribution arrangements are tailored to local countries and cultures. Most automobile manufacturers are actually closer to this type of strategic approach today, seeking as much efficiency and low cost as possible by centralized, scale-efficient manufacturing facilities. But such facilities are still able to respond to local, or at least regional, differences around the world.

A *multidomestic strategy* is appropriate when there is little pressure for efficiency in value creation and where value creation occurs very close to the customer. In this approach a company sets up an operation in each country it enters, so that it can respond directly to the specific needs of customers in that country. While there will always exist competitive pressure to reduce costs and garner efficiencies, these conditions do not represent critical facets for successfully competing. There is little strategic coordination across borders with this type of strategic approach, since each country places its own unique demands on the company. Any type of strategic decision authority centralized at headquarters may in fact hinder quick response to emerging in-market situations. Therefore you would ordinarily find that companies pursuing a multidomestic approach would set up offices in each country with fully staffed functions across the board. Multidomestic strategy has historically emerged where there are significant differences in countries presented by culture or government regulation. This used to be the case across Western Europe, but with the advent of the European Union and the euro currency, such barriers to transnational or global approaches have been somewhat dissipated.

The three types of international strategic approaches we have discussed are the most prevalent. The fourth type—what we call *centralized single country strategy*—does not occur very often anymore in the twenty-first century. Here a company essentially produces and sells out of one centralized operation for the entire world. It would make sense when there is little need to respond to local conditions and when there is little competitive pressure to wring efficiencies out of the value chain. Although these conditions may have described global competition in the 1950s and 1960s, before modern globalization and global competitive dynamics took hold, there are few instances today when this approach can make sense. Specialized pharmaceutical drug manufacturing is one example, where a company's small niche product is patent protected. Here there is no need to set up more than one manufacturing facility and competition is effectively eliminated because of the patent. French wine used to represent this type of approach, but now we can buy very high-quality cabernets and merlots from California, Australia, and many other wine-growing regions. Moreover, customers today are typically demanding greater customization, and competitors are always putting pressure on efficiency. It is for this reason that we put this type in a cloud in the figure—today it is only a type of international situation that companies could dream about encountering!

Figure 8.21 provides a summary of the characteristics of these four international strategy approaches.

Figure 8.21
Four International Strategy Approaches

Strategy	Characteristics	Example
Global	Value added in upstream activities Efficiency through scale and scope is competitively important Only minor country-to-country variations Requires strong integration and coordination Location decisions important	Arcelor-Mittal steel
Transnational	Value added downstream near customer or user Efficiency through scale and scope is competitively important Variations across countries are meaningful Headquarters involved in strategy formulation, country offices in implementation and tactics	Kellogg's cereals McDonald's
Multidomestic	Value added downstream near customer or user Little or no pressure on efficiency Variations across countries are significant Country offices responsible for strategy formulation, implementation, and tactics	MTV in Europe
Centralized Single Country	Value added in upstream activities Little or no pressure on efficiency Occurs mainly where markets are protected or government controlled	Specialized pharmaceuticals Hollywood movie studios

CHAPTER SUMMARY

In this chapter we have explored the defining characteristics of industry life cycle stages, and assessed their potential impact on company strategy. The five stages are introduction, growth, maturity, decline, and renewal. Strategic variety can exist in an industry in its earlier stages. But increasingly as the industry grows toward maturity, standardization and then commoditization privilege low-cost strategic approaches. When an industry enters decline, renewal efforts are largely focused on either redefining the boundaries of the industry, reconfiguring industry activities, or redefining values that have been important in the industry. All three directions prompt the creation of new value chain activity sets.

Strategy effectiveness is also dependent on the organizational life cycle context. Organizations experience four different stages of development: conception, commercialization, growth, and maturity. Companies experience different kinds of problems at different organizational life cycle stages, and consequently have different strategic resource needs for each.

Unique strategic issues are highlighted by considering the organizational life cycle. These include the nature of first-mover advantage in the early stage of a company's development. There are both advantages and disadvantages from moving first into a market, and business history provides evidence of both successes and failures by companies adopting this approach. Fast growth presents a unique context that emphasizes the importance of vision, mission, and strong coordination across the internal value chain. The mature stage of company development highlights the need for renewal, which can occur by diversifying either new through internally developed businesses or through acquisition. Internal new business development depends on opportunity recognition capabilities and a series of structural and incentive system departures from how mature companies typically operate.

Finally, we considered international strategy. Moving into international markets is a decision to grow or expand that should be considered against other alternatives for growth. Often there are good reasons to expand internationally, especially if foreign markets present significant revenue enhancing possibilities or opportunities to leverage the company's value chain and the resources. Four types of international strategy are described, where each depends on where value is actually created in the value chain and the extent to which there is competitive pressure on the value chain to be efficient. These four types include global strategy, transnational strategy, multidomestic strategy, and centralized single-country strategy.

KEY TERMS

Commoditization (p. 230)

Complements (p. 232)

First-mover advantage (p. 229)

Industry roll-up (p. 237)

Mobility barriers (p. 236)

Options (p. 248)

Reconfiguring industry value chain (p. 231)

Size advantage (p. 243)

Standardization (p. 229)

Timing advantage (p. 243)

SHORT ANSWER QUESTIONS

1. Explain why a first mover is so successful.
2. International value creation opportunities are best under what circumstances?
3. How does a fragmented industry offer opportunities for expansion?
4. Why do companies seek to grow internationally?
5. Why do industries consolidate?
6. What unique issues does fast growth require management to address?
7. Where are the value creation opportunities in a consolidating industry?
8. Why is renewal so difficult to achieve for established organizations?
9. Explain why a new product tends to follow a life cycle.
10. How do companies initiate a pattern of continuous renewal?
11. How do life cycle stages affect the decision process of businesses?
12. How is being a first mover also dangerous for an organization?

GROUP EXERCISES

1. Using your knowledge of the latest and greatest gadgets to hit the market, map out the life cycle of a particular product. How fast will it traverse the entire cycle? How many competitors do you predict will enter the market and when? What would you recommend to management knowing that this cycle will most likely play out? What should the company do when the product moves into decline?

2. Over the years a number of formerly fragmented industries have gone through a rapid period of consolidation that changed the dynamics of the industry. Select at least two industries that you and your group believe are ripe for consolidation. What avenues do you think are available for the current players in this industry? How will consolidation change the business model they use? Will consolidation open other opportunities in the industry?

3. You have recently been hired as the head of strategy for a rapidly growing chain of computer repair shops. The company provides on-site service for all laptop and desktop computers, guaranteeing all repairs within a twenty-four-hour period. The CEO has announced a decision to expand internationally and has asked you to develop the best methodology for making this a reality. How will you organize the company going forward? What critical issues seem to have the highest potential for derailing the expansion? What industries would you look to for examples?

REFERENCES

[1] The Doors. 1967. When the music's over. *Strange Days*. Elektra Records: New York.

[2] Data based on Mintel Reports, Recording Industry Association of America (RIAA), U.S. Department of Commerce, and authors' estimates.

[3] Smith, E. 2007. Sales of music, long in decline, plunge sharply. *Wall Street Journal*. March 21, A1.

[4] Mintel Reports and authors' estimates.

[5] Deanes, G. K., F. Kroeger, and S. Zeisel, S. 2002. The consolidation curve. *Harvard Business Review*. December: 20–21.

[6] Barr, P. S., J. L. Stimpert, and A. S. Huff. 1997. Cognitive change, strategic action, and organization renewal. *Strategic Management Journal* 13(5): 15–36.

[7] Cox, W. M., and R. Alm. 1996. The economy at light speed: Technology and growth in the information age and beyond. *1996 Annual Report, Dallas Federal Reserve Bank*. Dallas: Federal Reserve Bank.

[8] U.S. Department of Labor. http://www.doleta.gov/SGA/sga/99-006sga.htm.

[9] Bitran, G. R., S. Gurumurthi, and S. L. Sam, 2006. Emerging trends in supply chain governance. Massachusetts Institute of Technology working paper. Cambridge, MA.

[10] CNN Headline News. 2007. December 18.

[11] Teece, D. 1987. *The competitive challenge: Strategies for industrial innovation and renewal*. Cambridge, MA: Ballinger.

[12] Attributed to Yogi Berra. Who else!?

[13] Kanter, R. M. 1985. *The change masters*. New York: Free Press.

[14] Bartlett, C. A., and S. Ghsoal. 1998. *Managing across borders: The transnational solution*. Boston: Harvard Business School Press; Jacques, L. L., and P. M. Vaaler. 2001. The international control conundrum with exchange risk: An EVA approach. *Journal of International Business Studies* 32: 813–832; Rodriguez, P., K. Uhlenbruck, and L. Eden. 2005. Government corruption and entry strategies of multinationals. *Academy of Management Review* 30(2): 383–396.

[15] Porter, Michael E. 1990. *The competitive advantage of nations*. New York: Free Press.

[16] Westhead, P., M. Wright, and D. Ucbasaran. 2001. The internationalization of new and small firms. *Journal of Business Venturing* 16: 333–358.

[17] Kolk, A., and R. V. Tulder. 2004. Ethics in international business: Multinational approaches to child labor. *Journal of World Business* 39: 49–60.

[18] Arnold, D. J., and J. A. Quelch. 1998. New strategies in emerging markets. *Sloan Management Review* 40(1): 7–20; Prahalad, C. K. 2005. *The fortune at the bottom of the pyramid*. Upper Saddle River, NJ: Wharton.

[19] Aeppel, T. 2003. Three countries, one dishwasher. *Wall Street Journal*. October 6: C5.

Competitive Landscape

LEARNING OBJECTIVES

1. *Design and execute plans for developing competitor intelligence.*

2. *Use industry and company trajectories to evaluate an industry environment.*

3. *Evaluate and select the appropriate techniques for predicting competitor intelligence.*

4. *Describe tactical methods for responding to competitors.*

5. *Discuss the conditions under which cooperation can be an effective competitive approach.*

Nearly forty years old, video gaming is a $30 billion dollar industry dominated by three main competitors—Sony, Nintendo, and Microsoft. Over the years these competitors have released system after system aimed at the same hard-core gaming market of boys and young men. Sony released the PlayStation and then the highly successful (over 100 million units sold) Playstation2. Nintendo released the marginally successful GameCube and Microsoft released the Xbox.

The pace of competitive pressure has intensified in this industry. By any measure, game console manufacturers have stepped up the frequency with which they introduce new consoles that take advantage of newer technology such as memory, chipsets, and networked computing. In the last seven years eight new or updated game consoles have been introduced—the most in any comparable period of the industry's history.

The competitive focus of the industry has recently been on the suppliers of game software as much as it has been on attracting customers to buy game consoles. A highly successful game launch, netting hundreds of millions for the successful video game producer, also attracts and retains console customers. *Halo 3*, for example, sold $170 million in the first twenty-four hours after its introduction, becoming the best-selling video game of all time and attracting many new buyers to the Microsoft Xbox 360 platform.

Microsoft was the first to release the latest round of gaming systems opting for a significantly beefed-up capability and an add-on HD-DVD player. The Xbox 360 came into the market more than a year ahead of the other two companies.

Sony decided to take their gaming machines to a new level by creating a unit that would form the hub of a media center in any household. Betting billions of dollars on the unit, they developed the PlayStation3, which had a Blu-ray drive at its core (a technology standard that is owned by Sony). The PS3 has a Web-browser, wireless Internet capability and a significant hard drive for downloading both music and movies.

Nintendo had always been the king of the handheld units with its GameBoy series as well as the new DS series, but their more recent game consoles lagged the other two companies. Rather than going head-to-head with who could pack more in their system, Nintendo decided to approach the market in a completely new way. They utilized energy-saving chips and a standard optical disk player, which allowed Nintendo to release the new system for hundreds of dollars less than their competitors. Figuring that they could get the hard-core gamers with great games like Zelda, Nintendo sought to build a very simple unit that would attract the nongamer. The Wii was the result. The Wii uses a revolutionary controller that simulates the action on the screen. The user can get a workout while playing many of the games. Arguably the most successful new game system release in history, the Wii has drawn in millions of nongamers, including for the first time large numbers of women and older users.

Questions

1. Do you believe that this newer approach has sustainable potential for Nintendo?
2. How might Sony and Microsoft respond to this challenge?
3. These companies have taken completely different paths
   a. Microsoft—High-end Game Console
   b. Sony—Media Center Hub
   c. Nintendo—Nongamer Game Console
   d. What forecasting techniques might you use to know where this industry will head over the next 5–15 years?

COMPETITOR INTELLIGENCE

Through the first eight chapters of this text we have focused our efforts on developing a sound foundation for strategy development. That foundation has included: 1) having a deep understanding of the competitive environment: 2) a solid knowledge of the relationship between strategy and performance; 3) an ability to use value chain and resource-based analysis to develop a set of sustainable competitive advantages that lie within the capability set of the organization; and 4) the development of a vision and mission for the organization. In addition we have discussed how to employ generic strategies and most recently how those strategies might be modified given varying conditions in the marketplace. As we pointed out in Chapter 8, strategy is not developed in a vacuum and its actual execution is most certainly not done in a vacuum. It is incumbent upon business executives to not only react to competitors, but much more importantly to predict how those same competitors might react to moves that our business initiates. The dynamism of competition creates tremendous uncertainty for the strategist, which amplifies the importance of anticipating the intentions and estimated moves of competitors. This chapter is about the development and use of competitive intelligence, as well as the application of techniques to predict, respond to, and even preempt competitor moves.

This chapter is much more about **tactics** than about strategy. Recall from Chapter 1 that strategy is about longer-term moves, significant resource investments that pay out over time, and a focus on sustainability and long-term performance. Subsequently in Chapters 2 and 4 we explored how financial statement analysis and industry analysis can reveal patterns of financial resource investments, strategic positions, and intentions of competitors. In contrast when we take up the topic of competitive dynamics, we are interested in the more immediate moves, countermoves, and responses of competitors to both changes in the industry environment as well as our own company's initiatives. Grand master chess players are known to think strategically about how their opponents will move eight to ten turns from now; in this chapter we want to think tactically about how they will move over the next one to three turns. Short-term tactics will (or should) be consistent with long-term strategy, so the previous work we have done in understanding strategic dimensions of competitors is certainly helpful here.

Tactics Dealing with short-term competitive moves and countermoves, as opposed to long-term direction, investments, and performance.

INDUSTRY CHARACTERISTICS AND TRAJECTORIES

Prior to examining the individual attributes of companies, it is important to recognize that competitive dynamics fundamentally relate to the types of conclusions we can draw from industry analyses in our discussion in Chapter 4. One important characteristic of an industry is how benign or hostile it is. While it is generally understood that a benign environment provides companies with significant opportunity primarily because of less intense competition, many companies operate in intensely competitive environments and must seek to prosper in hostile conditions. We will briefly examine the characteristics of each and then tie that analysis to strategies that appear to provide the best opportunity for sustainable advantage.

Benign Environments

Benign environments are characterized by the following: 1) market demand exceeds market supply; 2) generally high gross profit margins; 3) low competitive intensity—meaning no one competitor controls a high proportion of the market; 4) high customer loyalty; and 5) a general market and customer tolerance of management miscues.

Studies in this area have suggested that benign environments reward differentiators. As you may remember from our discussion of business-level strategies in Chapter 7, differentiation exists on one end of the generic strategy continuum. In benign environments customers are looking for unique product or service characteristics, high levels of product or service quality, and often rely on a substantial amount of educationally oriented advertising in order to make purchase decisions.[2] Once a company secures a customer base in this type of industry environment, customers tend to remain loyal, and competitors do not vigorously attack established positions. In this type of environment, therefore, we would not generally expect competition to directly assail our company's product or market position.

Hostile Environments

Hostile environments are characterized by the following: 1) slow growth, flat revenue, or even declining revenue; 2) frequent price wars; 3) high competitive intensity—meaning that one or a few competitors control a substantial portion of the market; and 4) a focus on cost containment by competitors. Hostile environments also occur where technological change is rapid, coming either from developments outside the industry or from suppliers or internal R&D. This is certainly the case in video gaming, where advances in memory, chip design, and software programming have led to fairly rapid obsolescence of platforms and games.

Whereas benign environments tend to exist at the earlier stages in an industry life cycle, hostile environments seem to engage once an industry approaches maturity. Referring to Chapter 8, a low-cost strategic approach seems to provide organizations the best opportunity for a sustainable advantage. In hostile environments, companies that seem to perform best have product lines that leverage a core set of resources and capabilities (so that they can concentrate on a tight fit within their organization), a broad market approach to maximize their geographic reach, sophisticated process technology, and purchasing advantages relative to their competitors.[3] These factors tend to support the low-cost management dimension that is elevated in importance under these conditions.

In the 1990s strategy professor Richard D'Aveni coined the term "hypercompetition" to describe a perceived new reality in industry dynamics. This view of the competitive environment argues that traditional competitive

Benign environment
Characterized by:
1) market demand exceeds the market supply; 2) generally high gross profit margins; 3) low competitive intensity—meaning no one competitor controls a high proportion of the market; 4) high customer loyalty; and 5) a general tolerance for management mistakes.

Hostile environment
Characterized by:
1) very slow growth; 2) continuous price wars; 3) high competitive intensity—meaning that one or a few competitors control a substantial portion of the market; and 4) a focus on cost containment by competitors.

responses are insufficient when the new realities of the marketplace—better information, global reach, access to capital—mean that the dynamic of competition is speeding up. This view suggests that the only real competitive advantage is that of speed. The rapid creation of new competitive advantages that either neutralize or make obsolete the advantages of competitors is the new core capability of successful organizations.[4] Sun Tzu would have certainly agreed with this approach to dealing with competitors, as he found virtually no advantage to measured responses and saw only positive consequences to the use of speed. Apple released the iPod in October 2001, and it rapidly became the gold standard for audio players. As industry competitors scrambled to match the capability of the original iPod, Apple successively released various versions aimed at specific points in the consumer market. iPod Nano, iPod Mini, iPod Touch, and iPod Shuffle all crushed the competitors' ability to respond because before competitors could match the existing product, Apple had released the next version. In hypercompetitive markets companies seek to stay ahead of their competitors by constantly destroying the old fabric and creating new rules of the game.

In these types of hostile or hypercompetitive environments we might, therefore, predict that key competitors will make a couple different types of moves. First, we can expect them to continue working on their own cost structures, in order to be price competitive or to offensively engage further in price wars. This means our company must continue its efforts to manage to lower costs, and often we will need to carefully **benchmark** how we are doing relative to competitors on this dimension. Secondly, we might anticipate that competitors will tend to introduce new products and services into larger customer and geographic segments, in order to gain efficiencies and disrupt the status quo.

Industry Trajectories

We learned in Chapter 4 how strategic mapping can be used to bring together information about competitors in a format that is both visual and compelling. Competitive maps take a variety of forms, but the most popular strategy execution maps track the primary competitors in comparison to each of the key success factors in the industry. A rigorously maintained set of maps showing current relative positions as well as historical trending for each company can be especially useful for analyzing competitive moves. We noted how historical trajectories in "strategic space" in a strategy map are an excellent indicator of future intention. Referring back to Figure 4.22, for example, if we were to predict the kinds of competitive moves that Dell might make in the future—based purely upon its past positions in a map that compares innovation versus unit cost—we would expect the company to continue to make investments that would lower its unit costs further. These might include pressing suppliers further, reorganizing its assembly operations, and possibly seeking additional distribution outlets for its existing products in order to increase scale. In fact, in 2008 Dell announced that it would begin selling PCs in retail stores.

Benchmark A process through which a company compares its own process and structure to that of other organizations. Companies most often benchmark directly against competitors. Occasionally, benchmarking will be done against other unrelated companies that have a "best in class" process. For example, General Mills examined how NASCAR pit crews organize for pit stops in order to better understand how to implement rapid cereal production line changes.

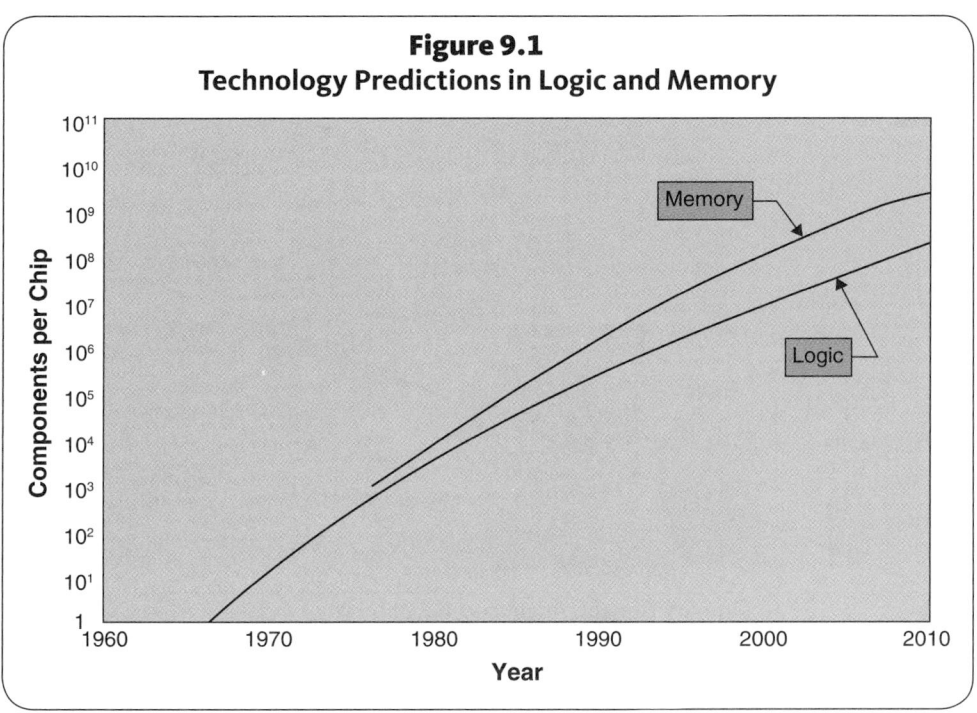

Figure 9.1
Technology Predictions in Logic and Memory

A second kind of industry trajectory prediction can also be extremely useful in anticipating possible new moves by competitors. In this case what we are interested in is not so much what competitors will do based upon past historical trends, but what all competitors must do based on the evolution of customer preferences and supplier technologies. In 1965 Intel co-founder, Gordon Moore, predicted that the number of transistors that could be inexpensively placed on a circuit board would double roughly every two years. From that prediction, which has been actually observed in practice to occur roughly every eighteen months, many have been able to predict the advent of new devices that utilize advancing technological capability. StorageTek was started up by three IBM employers who followed "Moore's Law" in the tape disk storage industry; it rapidly became a Fortune 500 company. Figure 9.1 shows a mid-1990s Moore's Law projection for memory and logic technologies, which many technology companies have used to anticipate when they (and their competitors) might be able to introduce new products incorporating advanced elements.

General predictions can also be made by carefully evaluating the evolution of customer preferences and demands. As we have stated throughout this textbook, a better understanding of what sort of value will need to be created in the future provides a company with an important roadmap of areas it needs to invest in, and likely presages what competitors will also be thinking about. Figure 9.2 shows the evolution of customer preferences in the cell phone handset market.[5] Strategy professor Richard D'Aveni points out that this type of mapping should have enabled competition to predict that the "ultra premium" segment would emerge and that Apple would be expected to drop its price to below the "expected" price line—both of which occurred.

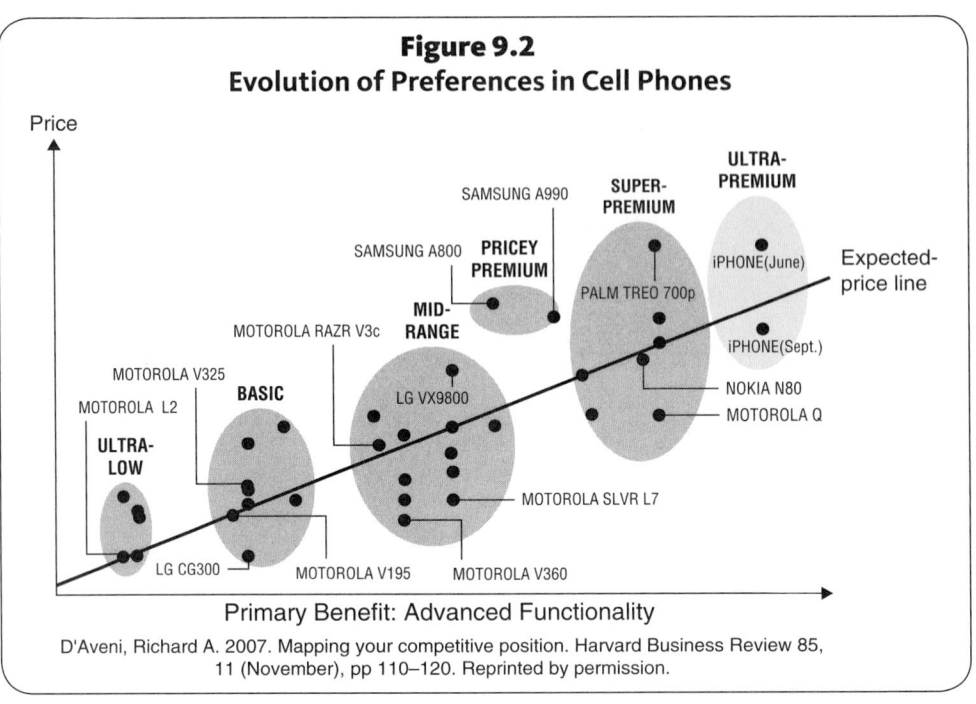

Figure 9.2
Evolution of Preferences in Cell Phones

D'Aveni, Richard A. 2007. Mapping your competitive position. Harvard Business Review 85, 11 (November), pp 110–120. Reprinted by permission.

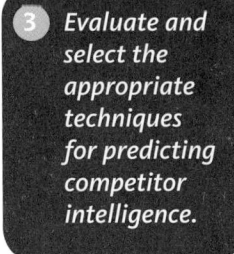

PREDICTING COMPETITIVE MOVES

As we can see from the previous discussion, some general characterizations about the industry environment can help us make general predictions about what competitors might be contemplating. We can, however, develop more specific and detailed information about key competitors in our industry. Competitive intelligence and the knowledge that such intelligence provides about competitors is the first step available for dealing with the competitive dynamism inherent in any industry. Fortunately, we have a number of tools available that allow for effective classification and use for competitor prediction. These include: 1) classifying organizations based upon their relative position in the industry; 2) examining internal competitor characteristics; and 3) scenario analysis.

Classifying Organizations

The first technique available for examining potential competitor moves is to attempt classifying organizations based on their past behavior. In many ways past behavior is one the best predictors of future actions and reactions, whether we are talking about organizations or individuals in our lives. There are many techniques available to classify organizations such that we can better understand and predict their strategic intentions and their likely reactions to moves by other companies. One of the best supported and best developed techniques is a classifying system developed some years ago by Raymond Miles and Charles Snow.[6] Their system suggests that every company in an industry can be classified into one of four categories: 1) **Prospector,**

Prospector A company that tends to view the industry from their own perspective and that of the customer rather than being concerned with the competition. They are usually leaders of change in the industry with little concern for the effects or impacts of other organizations.

2) **Defender**, 3) **Analyzer**, or 4) **Reactor** (Figure 9.3). The first three are all sustainable and viable postures for a company to take in an industry. The fourth type (Reactor) is unsustainable and companies that do not move from a reactor position are likely to fail as independent organizations. It is generally believed that each type is represented in every industry.

Figure 9.3
Four Ways to Classify Companies
Prospector
Defender
Analyzer
Reactor

Most companies do not fall cleanly into any one category, but are most likely to predominantly fall within one category. The lines between the categories are a bit fuzzy, so we look for overarching patterns in behavior to assist us in classifying the company. Let's take a look at each position.

Prospector. A prospector organization is one that tends to view the industry from its own internal perspective and that of its customer base rather than being concerned with the competition. Prospectors are usually leaders of change in the industry with little concern for the effects or impacts of other organizations. They are generally quite willing to cannibalize their own market position with something new and are thorough collectors of detailed information about customers and customer needs. A prospector organization is relatively inefficient primarily because it views control and cost-cutting efforts as counter to its primary objectives of organic growth and the opportunity to change the industry.

Apple computer has been a frame-breaking prospector organization, especially during the times that Steve Jobs has served as CEO of the company. The introduction of the Apple II PC, the Macintosh, the iPod, iTunes, the MacAir and the iPhone, just to name a few groundbreaking products and services simply changed the nature of each industry that the company entered. Google created a platform that was simple to use and very intuitive for the user by means of a new algorithm for ranking Web site importance. Their approach to this segment of the Internet changed the very way in which Internet searches occurred and forced other companies to develop better methods.

Prospector businesses pursue an aggressive stance aimed at identifying new ways to satisfy customers, new means to extend their reach, and a creative desire to lead rather than follow. A prospector organization is unlikely to directly react to a move by a competitor. It will release its latest product or service on its own schedule and simply presume that it is what the market was looking for. These organizations rarely lower prices or make new market entries as a result of moves by a competitor.

Defender. At the opposite end of the continuum is a defender organization. Defender organizations are intensive rather than extensive. That is, they usually focus on a limited number of key criteria, analyze their costs, and rigorously defend their competitive position against all competitors or potential competitors. A defender is geared toward protecting its current position and maximizing market share. This type of organization spends very little on new product or service development, is highly efficient, and is structured in its policies and procedures.

Defender A company that is intensive rather than extensive. That is, they usually focus on a limited number of key criteria, analyze their costs, and rigorously defend their competitive position against all competitors.

Analyzer A company that is somewhere between Prospectors and Defenders. Analyzer organizations generally take one of two forms. In the first form, there are parts of the company that behave like a defender and parts that behave like a prospector. The second form of Analyzer Company tends to swing somewhat seamlessly from Prospector to Defender without a significant negative impact on the organization.

Reactor A company that reacts (albeit very, very slowly) to conditions in the competitive environment. This is an unstable form of organization and one that is not destined to last very long.

The retailing icon Sears was once a prospector as it spread across the United States and became a one-stop shop for middle America. However, with the advent of other large specialized retailers it changed to a defender model as it sought to focus its efforts and protect what it perceived as its turf. American Airlines has historically erected rigorous defenses against any new airline in its perceived competitive space. Microsoft's historic focus has been on market share and domination in PC software. Defender organizations such as these will react swiftly and with an intensive attack to any move by a competitor that it deems threatening or even potentially threatening. They will lower prices, offer coupons, change formulas, pressure suppliers, or run what would constitute an attack advertisement to counter the move by a competitor.

Analyzer. Somewhere in between these two more extreme forms of organizations are analyzers. In analyzer organizations parts of the company behave like a defender while other parts of the company behave like a prospector. Usually an artifact of the way the organization formed and grew, this two-part stance within a company is quite expensive to maintain. While one part of the company performs the sophisticated customer analysis and develops products or services that will directly address the customer regardless of whether it cannibalizes its current product offering, another part of the organization is intensively examining competitors and trying to milk every dollar out of its current product or service portfolio. General Electric and Samsung are among a class of diversified conglomerates that have generally utilized this market-by-market approach.

Reactor. Reactor organizations perform as the name implies, by essentially reacting (often very slowly) to conditions in the competitive environment. This is usually an unstable form of organization and one that is not destined to last very long because it tends to be buffeted by the forces in the environment rather than making proactive, effective moves. It then has a choice—either to adapt and move to one of the other three models or collapse as an independent entity.

Defunct organizations such as Eastern Airlines, Montgomery Ward, and Gino's are classic examples of what happens to reactor organizations that refuse to change.

Starting in the late 1990s McDonald's (a company we generally praise for their incredible strategy execution capability today) had fallen into this mode. They were under attack from health groups, suffering from the consequences of a film documentary called *Super Size Me* (where one man ate super-sized meals at McDonalds morning, noon, and night for a month), were ineffectively responding to growth by their competitors, and lost perspective on their own competitive resources and capabilities. Same-store sales were dropping, and to the company's credit they sensed that they were in a precarious strategic position. It took a strong new management team to shake up the organization and move them into a more defined analyzer role, where utilizing the combination of prospector and defender they have flourished for the past five years. Portions of the company had always exhibited prospector aspects—the first fast food operation to serve breakfast, the introduction of the Happy Meal for children, and the creation and funding of the Ronald McDonald House charity. More recently, though, they have exhibited defender characteristics—the move into premium coffee service to bring back customers lost to Starbucks' U.S. stores, a rigorous value meal selection, advertising aggressively, and seeking to buy up and hold potential real estate sites for store growth.

It is important to understand the value and use of this Prospector, Defender, Analyzer, Reactor system as a means of insight into competitive dynamics. The ability to effectively classify organizations allows us to make relatively accurate predictions about how specific companies will respond to changes in the industry. This classification system also provides insights into how competitors view the industry. This systemization can augment the general kinds of predictions we make based upon industry characteristics, discussed previously. As an example, we might be preparing to release a brand new product that we believe has the potential to change the market. In the competitive analysis we would not be very concerned about the reactions to our new product release from prospector organizations, since they are usually focused on their own initiatives. Defender competitors are a significant concern, since they might view a new introduction as a competitive threat and therefore may actively work to defeat it. A company should consider devising effective tactics to deal

Strategic Moves
Nintendo, Part 1

In a bid to attract the hard-core gamer, Nintendo announced that the Wii (their highly successful game console for the nongamer) would soon add some high-end, serious gamer titles, including Capcom's Monster Hunter and two new titles in the Final Fantasy Crystal Chronicles series. Nintendo CEO Satoru Iwata told a packed house at this announcement that [Nintendo would] "tear down the wall" between games for ordinary consumers and the hard-core community.[1]

Sony responded to the announcement by dropping the price on the PlayStation3 and saw their sales soar. In fact, after the change in pricing, the PlayStation3 outsold the Wii in Japan for the first time in a year.

QUESTIONS

1. How should Microsoft and Sony respond to Nintendo?
2. How could you predict the moves by Nintendo's CEO?
3. Should Microsoft and Sony imitate the new controllers that Nintendo uses?
4. Would this fit with a long-range view of the industry?

with predicted competitor response. Analyzer companies are a bit of a wild card; each must be examined for its history and current position. We would be far less concerned about a potential response from reactor organizations, which have previously demonstrated nonthreatening responsive behavior in the market.

Characteristics of Competitor Companies

Classifying organizations as Prospector, Defender, Analyzer, or Reactor allows us to narrow the list of organizations that need further examination. A second means of evaluating competitor moves is significantly more detailed than the previous rough categorizations. In this analysis we will consider a number of internal competitor characteristics as they might impact our organization. These include: 1) understanding management patterns; 2) relative market position; 3) financial situation; and finally 4) several means of gathering competitor intelligence.

Understanding management patterns. Another very effective technique in the analysis of competitive dynamics is the observation and evaluation of patterns by competitor CEOs and their top management teams. Sun Tzu would argue that the general who never changes his pattern of battle is highly susceptible to a crushing defeat. All of us have patterns in our behavior. When those patterns become easily predictable, we expose ourselves to potential harm. Many CEOs are aware of this problem and work diligently to address it by changing up approaches and seeking new solutions. However, when times get tough, there is a tendency to return to base patterns of behavior. Those patterns, when effectively observed and utilized, provide competitive insight.

"Chainsaw" Al Dunlap became famous as a CEO for his single-minded approach to corporate profit. He took over troubled companies with the same approach—fire thousands of employees, dramatically cut back on all new spending and rigorously attack all current spending. This was his system and he executed it at companies including Scott Paper, Crown-Zellerbach, and finally at Sunbeam. Knowing his approach to business and his universal "game plan" for success, competitors were able to take advantage of the turmoil in his companies. Some top management teams have the same standard reaction to new competitive threats, making them easy to predict and therefore easier to work around.

Many organizations maintain business analysis units that have as their task (among others) the job of developing competitor profiles. Changes and responses are noted to build an effective "map" of predicted moves. Much like playing chess with someone over and over, it becomes fairly easy to predict his or her response to certain moves and therefore to use that information to beat that person in the game. Earl Weaver, the very successful Baltimore Orioles baseball team manager who won six division titles, assiduously studied the tendencies of opposing managers to know when they would steal bases, put on hit and run plays, and employ other tactical facets of the game.

Relative market position. The market position of competitors and their desire to impact that position is an important aspect in predicting competitor movement and reaction. As companies become entrenched in an industry, they work to establish their "claim" to a competitive space. A company that believes its market space is being encroached upon will often make dramatic moves to maintain competitive supremacy. The ability to predict these moves is available with a deep understanding of how each company perceives its relative position. This can easily be seen with some very visible organizations. Microsoft's view of themselves as the controller of the PC desktop led to their desire to dominate everything tied to the desktop. It should have been no surprise later on that their desire to move into the Web browser part of the industry was triggered as a reaction to the moves made by upstart Netscape to infiltrate the PC desktop.

On the other hand, companies that find themselves in a strong competitive position in a market will often ignore widely available information and miss opportunities that end up costing them their business. DEC was the king of minicomputers in the late 1970s and early 1980s, posting astounding returns in their industry. They held so strongly to the notion that minicomputers were their competitive advantage that they simply missed the PC revolution. The CEO at the time (Ken Olsen) noted the failure later when he observed that "we had 6 PCs in-house that we could have launched in the late '70s. But we were selling so many [minicomputers], it would have been immoral to chase a new market."[7]

The difference we see between these two examples—both dominating companies in their own spheres—has to do with the attitude of management of the company about the kind of business it is in and its "ownership" of a market or beliefs that it should control a market.

Financial situation. Firms that find themselves in a situation where their returns are not as they anticipated are more likely to react in unpredictable ways. As long as a company is growing and making industry average returns or better, it is likely to maintain its current competitive approach, believing that it will continue to deliver results. Unfortunately, if these returns slip or go negative, then predicting their actions becomes more difficult. Sun Tzu reminds us that an army with no retreat available will fight to the last and fight with everything available. Competitors that get into this situation need to be closely watched for industry-damaging behaviors.

We can observe this behavior happening right now in the U.S. automobile industry. The "big three" in Detroit—General Motors, Ford, Chrysler—have all been losing money for some time. Their initial approach was to cut prices in order to move unsold cars off dealer lots and keep assembly operations going. Unfortunately, cutting prices is not the way to move to profitability. It is the rare organization that can cut its way to success. Price wars generally damage the market by removing future customers, generating the need for even greater cost savings, and opening the door for better-organized foreign competitors who have lower cost structures.

Gathering Competitive Intelligence

Having classified each competitor as Prospector, Defender, Analyzer, or Reactor and having dug deeper into the competitor organizations by evaluating their internal processes, we need to discuss in very practical terms how detailed competitor information can be gathered.

Sun Tzu wrote more than 2,000 years ago that "The means by which enlightened rulers and sagacious generals moved and conquered others, that their achievements surpassed the masses, was advance knowledge."[8] Advance knowledge can be an extraordinary resource, because there are few means that improve performance like knowing exactly what a competitor is planning to do. In virtually every sport or competitive activity, being able to predict how a competitor might react or how they will act can dramatically change the outcome. General George Patton was a prolific reader of military history and military strategy. He understood not only that there were patterns to success, but that particular generals had their own approach to victory. Having studied the tactical battle books written by General Rommel and used by most German tank commanders, Patton would set up his battle plans to take advantage of the patterns laid out in Rommel's books. The same type of intelligence is often just as easily available in business.

In 2001 Hewlett Packard announced its intention to acquire Compaq Computer, and at the time then-CEO Carly Fiorini acknowledged that combining the two companies into a single organization would take at least three years. Knowing this, computer companies from IBM to Dell took advantage of HP's distraction to profit from their relative positions in the PC industry. HP performance suffered significantly during this time period.

It is relatively rare to have books written by a competitor or to have such a clear announcement of distraction as that made by HP available to guide the direction of your company. Fortunately, there are a number of other techniques for gathering and utilizing specific competitor intelligence (Figure 9.4). These include: 1) media stories services; 2) suppliers; 3) former employees; and 4) conferences and speeches.

All of these techniques allow us to drill down from the higher-level analysis performed in Chapters 2 and 4 as well as the overarching classifications we have talked about earlier in this chapter. For instance, utilizing our STEEPG approach we may have determined the overarching nature of an industry we wish to enter. The Five Forces analysis provided us with insight into the key characteristics of that industry, and an analysis of a specific competitor's financial statements allowed us to reconcile their actual strategy with their stated strategy. We then reclassified each direct competitor into their strategic posture (Prospector, Defender, Analyzer, or Reactor) and determined their

---

Figure 9.4
Methods of Gathering Competitive Intelligence

Media stories evaluation
Suppliers
Former employees
Conferences & Speeches

---

patterns of behavior. We now wish to delve deeply into those competitors that seem most likely to impact any new strategic move.

Media stories evaluation services. For as long as news has been reported, there have been businesses that accumulate and report on that information. A **clipping service** provides a complete, detailed record of all available public information about any particular company, area, person, or situation. This information is publicly available and could therefore be collected by anyone. In general such news gathering or clipping services companies will provide a more complete look at a particular subject or company, because they synthesize and interpret the volume of material they collect.

Hiring a clipping service to maintain information on a particular competitor is a common practice. The costs of these services are usually based upon the level of detail that the client desires, the breadth of outlets that need to be researched, and the type of media that the client would like to review. In the not-too-distant past, these services would develop binders full of newspaper articles, magazine reference, videotapes from local news reports, audio tapes of speeches or radio broadcasts, and any press releases from the target company. Today this is all provided on the Web with a secure Web site provided to the client.

Suppliers. A tremendous source of information is often available from suppliers that would like to have or already conduct business with a company. Just as the supply chain is often a great source of information and inspiration for new ideas and materials, suppliers will often discuss what competitors are doing. There may be many reasons for mentioning what competitors do, and these can include: 1) share cutting-edge technology or raw materials that can be useful to buying companies, 2) demonstrate a willingness to work with a customer, 3) create a more competitive group of customers seeking to buy so that their combined demand exceeds supply, possibly resulting in the ability to charge higher prices, or possibly 4) to simply vent frustration with a competitor. Start-up company Championship Foods, mentioned earlier in Chapter 4, learned how to reduce its cost of putting chili into glass jars by engaging in lengthy conversations with one of the manufacturers who supplied glass jars for Ragu spaghetti sauce. The same company learned what other chili seasonings manufacturers were up to when discussing its business with its spices and seasonings suppliers. We should be careful to note here that this may be a two-way street: just as your company learns about competition from your suppliers, so too will they learn about you through the same channels.

Former employees. Over the years, in virtually every endeavor from business to the military to the intelligence services, no one source of information has been as valuable as the information gathered from people who used to work for a competitor. This type of information gathering usually falls into three categories: 1) disgruntled former employees,

Clipping service
Provides a complete, detailed record of all available public information about any particular company, area, person, or situation.

2) people currently employed by the competitor, and 3) former employees paid as "consultants."

ETHICS

Job postings draw in many people, and they can (and do) draw in employees of the competition who are frustrated with their current employer. The interview process with these individuals can yield substantial information about competitors and can be captured and disseminated. An employee hired from a competitor provides unique insights into the cultural approaches and specific tendencies that may provide a competitive advantage. In some cases, new employees are subject to confidentiality agreements from their previous employers, which need to be respected.

Conferences and speeches. Senior managers are regularly asked to make speeches at various events and will often participate in presentations at conferences. While the text of a speech can be viewed with the assistance of a good clipping service, the context, Q&A session, and the interaction after a speech can best be gleaned in person. The value of conferences is much the same. Senior managers present new ideas, serve on panels, and provide after-meal comments at a number of conferences throughout the world. Even though these are generally open forums, the level and detail of thought provided can sometimes be quite insightful.

Scenario Analysis

The previous sections help all companies deal with the competitive nature or their industries as they exist today and in the near-term future. A final consideration for dealing with the competitive nature of an industry is the utilization of long-range planning tools.

A very interesting predictive approach that has been developed over the past thirty years is **scenario analysis**. The technique requires an organization to consider potentially dramatic shifts in its business environment over a set time frame, and to then map out a set of actions that it can begin to take if the warning signs of those shifts begin to appear.

Consider Figure 9.5, which shows oil price increases over the previous decade. To the shock of many organizations, oil went from less than $30 per barrel to over $120 per barrel, and then back to under $50 per barrel in a seven-year period of time. What if oil were to reach $200 per barrel? What would the impact of $200 oil have on an organization's transportation infrastructure, cost of goods, and the ability of customers to buy a product? Scenario analysis allows companies to plan out potential vectors for their organization as the environment changes, to have considered those actions long before they arrive, and to identify markers along the way that signal that a particular path is coming true to prediction. Response scenarios are dramatically improved if organizations have had the opportunity to consider and prepare for potential futures.

Turmoil can trigger crisis in the life of any organization. Alan Greenspan recalled his concerns for the stability of the banking system in the hours after September 11, 2001, in his 2007 book *The Age of Turbulence.* Stuck on an airplane being forced to return to Zurich as all U.S. airspace

Scenario analysis
The technique allows organizations to consider dramatic shifts in their business model. The organization then maps out a set of actions that it can begin to take if the warning signs begin to appear along the path of a particular scenario.

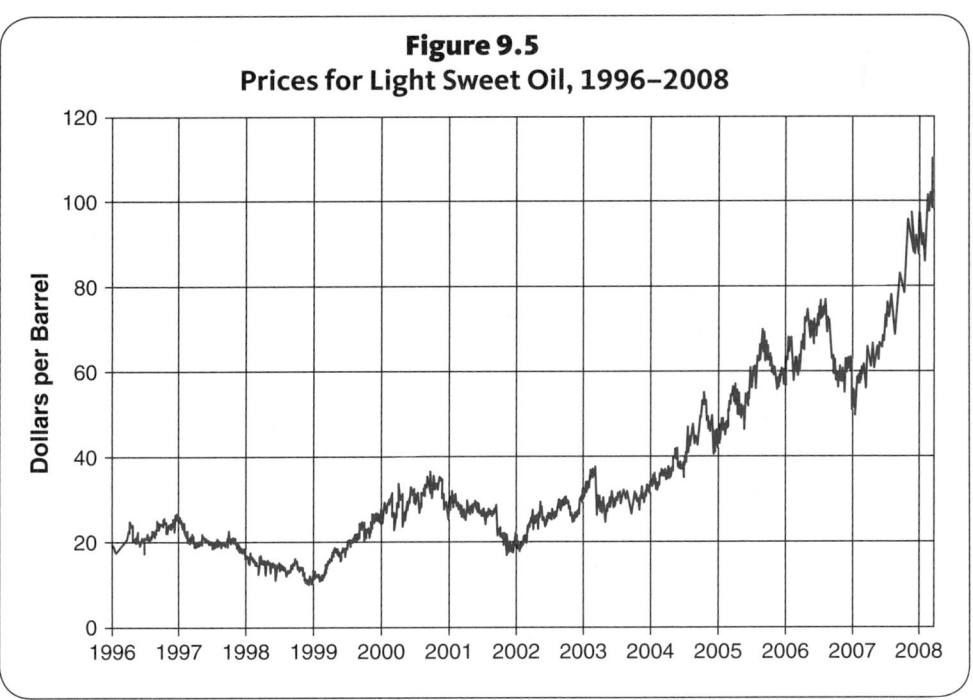

Figure 9.5
Prices for Light Sweet Oil, 1996–2008

was closed to civilian air traffic, he knew that there were well-understood plans that should be engaged if a scenario like this one played out. Arriving back in Zurich, he was relieved to hear that all the emergency plans had already been enacted and the Federal Reserve banking system was stabilized.[9]

Crisis scenarios are certainly a part of this planning process, as is consideration of the logical paths that may transpire in the next one to two decades. Indeed, scenario planning usually uses a time frame that goes from five to twenty-five years. Not knowing exactly how an industry will reach the next plateau does not mean that planning will not be of great assistance. In the airline industry it seems relatively easy to predict that at some point in the future all passengers will be able to stay connected with the Internet and make phone calls before, during, and at the end of a flight (whether or not the rest of us abhor the thought of all those loud cell-phone conversations when we are stuck on a four-hour flight in the seat next to Bill the Blowhard). This scenario has been forecast for the past decade or more. Knowing this might lead some airlines to build in a capability for all future airframe purchases or develop an effective system for charging new fees for the service. It might lead airlines to invest in systems that broadcast signals from the ground or utilize satellite-based technologies. As the day of reckoning approaches (and partial systems are now being installed), those airlines that had planned out their paths would be checking off the milestones and would have developed an effective set of tactical maneuvers to take advantage of the coming capability.

Strategic Moves
Nintendo, Part 2

Following their tremendous success with the Wii, Nintendo decided to pursue a part of the market that had never been approached before. Using a new platform that gamers would stand on while playing games in combination with their highly successful motion-oriented hand controller, Nintendo released the WiiFit.

The graphics continued to be only the most elementary and the exercises involve little more than balance and side-to-side movement. The Wii platform measures weight and balance to provide gamers with a workout in their own home using animated trainers.

The unit has been one of the most successful releases of a gaming device in the history of the industry.

QUESTIONS

1. How would you design a strategic map of Nintendo and its direct competitors Microsoft and Sony?
2. What type of potential scenarios would you suggest to Nintendo's CEO for future planning?
3. Why haven't Microsoft and Sony imitated the Wii?

The result of this type of process should be a holistic look at the environment, competitors, and potential paths that appear probable. Within each path, the company can (and should) apply its unique resources in order to engage in moves to be taken if a particular path begins to appear more plausible.

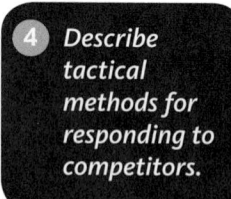

4 *Describe tactical methods for responding to competitors.*

TACTICAL AND STRATEGIC RESPONSES

Companies establish their *strategic* position by considering the value chains and unique resources they employ relative to the industry in which they compete. While we have examined the patterns of resource investments and value-creating activities that a company should engage in given its vision and strategy, we must also recognize that there are a set of *tactical* actions that may be more or less appropriate when taking into account the moves of a competitor. Competitors will react to our company's activities, and we need to be prepared to react to competitive activities. In this section we will address a set of responses to types of competitive moves.

Tactical responses are those that organizations pursue as a matter of course in dealing with regulators, stakeholders, and direct competitors. These include, from most passive to most active: 1) Acquiesce, 2) Compromise, 3) Avoid, 4) Defy, and 5) Manipulate. Figure 9.6 outlines the tactics associated with each of these response styles:

Figure 9.6
Response Styles and Tactics

Response Styles	Tactics	Descriptions[10]
Most passive (Acquiesce)	Habit Imitate Comply	Following invisible, taken-for granted norms Mimicking institutional models Obeying rules and accepting norms
Passive (Compromise)	Balance Pacify Bargain	Balancing the expectations of multiple constituents Placating and accommodating institutional players Negotiating with stakeholders
Neutral (Avoid)	Conceal Buffer Escape	Disguising nonconformity Disengaging Changing goals, activities, or playing fields
Active (Defy)	Dismiss Challenge Attack	Ignoring explicit norms and values Contesting rules and requirements Assaulting the sources of pressure
Most active (Manipulate)	Co-opt Influence Control	Importing influential constituents Shaping values and criteria Dominating constituents and processes

Organizations respond to tactical moves with varying degrees of aggression based upon history, personality, or position in the market. These tactical approaches are the traditional business responses to a threat.

A more complex set of approaches is called for when a threat is truly strategic and may impact the long-term performance of a company. When faced with a significant strategic threat, strategy research suggests that there are five fairly effective response types that are available (Figure 9.7), each of which we describe next.[11] Much of the capacity to engage in these responses falls upon each company's ability to spot a threat early.

Figure 9.7
Competitive Responses to Strategic Threats

Containment
Shaping
Absorption
Neutralization
Annulment

Containment is an approach that is best engaged in at the earliest stages of a competitor's entry into a market with a game-changing product or service. Existing companies will engage in a series of moves, including: locking in customers, raising switching costs (Chapter 4), filling the distribution channels to eliminate unused capacity, launching blocking brands, and making announcements that de-legitimize the company or its approach. Early in the MP3 revolution, for example, established record labels attempted all of these approaches in an effort to slow down the adoption of this new music standard.

Shaping is undertaken as the competitive threat develops and the containment strategies are no longer providing sufficient protection for the established organization. Here a threatened company will engage in moves that include co-opting the threat by purchasing the threatening organization itself, or forming a group to influence them through setting broad standards and creating accepted and acceptable practices within the industry. Another method used is to become involved with the threatening organization, such as through a strategic alliance, in order to have influence over its development. Shaping has also been called competitive cooperation, or *coopetition,* which we will address in the final section to this chapter.

Absorption is when it is clear that the competitive threat is likely to succeed and the prior approaches have not allowed the threatened companies to control the process. Threatened companies in this situation turn to responses that usually involve some sort of acquisition of the new competitor. Microsoft has engaged this approach on numerous occasions, as the control of the desktop and the development of applications software has moved increasingly to the Internet. Microsoft has specifically turned to acquiring new companies in the area of mobile communications. They have acquired companies such as Powerset, YaData, and Danger, spending more than $2 billion in 2008.[12]

Neutralization is generally engaged in when the competitive threat had not been truly appreciated earlier on and has now spread too widely to be contained, shaped, or absorbed. In this instance, threatened companies turn to very aggressive means of attack, including: 1) using legal action, 2) giving away the benefits offered by the new competitor for free, or 3) engaging in a process of continuously improving existing products. The Recording Industry Association of America used the courts to shut down the renegade Napster, which was seriously (and illegally) impacting the industry sales model. This successful effort forced other Napster-like companies to cease operations or try to stay so small that the RIAA would not seek sanctions against them. In confronting the onslaught of Netscape in the late 1990s Microsoft developed and gave away its Internet Explorer browser software at no charge. Why buy Netscape when you could get another effective browser for free? Netscape Communications did not last long as an independent company. Since then Microsoft has also engaged in serious and sustained upgrades to its Windows operating system—with new embedded applications such as music and video players as well as other digital media management tools—in order to neutralize the competitive impact of independent application development competitors.

Annulment is the last response left when all the other techniques have failed and the threatened company is in danger of being swamped by the new approaches. The threatened companies are left with only two responses. They can attempt to leapfrog the new company's approach or they can attempt to sidestep the new approach by changing the fundamentals of the industry. Gillette has a long history of leapfrogging their competition with the release of newer and more technologically advanced razors.

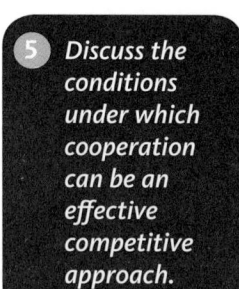

5 *Discuss the conditions under which cooperation can be an effective competitive approach.*

COOPERATION

A final category of competitive response that has received a substantial amount of attention most recently is the concept of cooperation with competitors. Both tactical and strategic, there are two occasions when cooperation between competitors may be useful. The first is when competition is unusually destructive. We mentioned earlier the very destructive price wars that are currently in vogue in the automobile industry. This has been experienced many times before in many different industries: prices are lowered by one manufacturer, triggering the lowering of prices by other competitors, resulting in the same volume of business for each competitor but now at a lower price (and lower profits). Fare wars in the airline industry have been rampant for nearly thirty years since deregulation of the industry. The problem for competitors is that it is illegal to collude on competitive tactics such as pricing and markets. This is the classic Prisoner's Dilemma problem you have probably heard about in previous courses. If all companies refrain from engaging in destructive tactics, then all companies are better off; but if one company fails to refrain, then all must jump into the fray. Our colleague Robert Grant humorously suggests that the Mafia has solved the problem of the individual who acts out of line and damages the rest of the "industry." Giving in—or confessing, in the case of the gangster—ultimately results in an untimely demise.[13]

The real solution to this type of problem where cooperation is needed is not easy, though. In some cases it never occurs, and competitors continue on in their mutually destructive ways. In some cases the competitors intuitively try to adopt a "multiple period" perspective, which deflects attention from the immediate need to generate added business volume through short-term tactics. Where industries are populated by companies that adopt this latter approach, there tends to emerge one or two companies who become "price leaders" or leaders in some other tactical dimension. Their behavior then "signals" what is acceptable to the rest of the industry.

Signaling is not just important in making tactical moves that other competitors will then follow. It also represents a means through which a company can *prevent* competitors from initiating destructive tactics. When a company repeatedly matches its competitor's tactics, action for action, time and time again, it sends a signal to the competitor and the rest of the industry that destructive tactical behavior will always be met with opposing force. In this way a company tacitly creates a cooperative situation in an industry, without formally cooperating.

The second type of occasion when cooperation with a competitor has advantages is when this type of collaboration can lead to developments that exceed the capacity of any one company. This situation results in the formation of **strategic alliances** with competing companies. Some time ago the automobile makers foresaw the need to have truly revolutionary battery technology. They did not want to leave this effort to chance, they did not want to embark on a development path where their direction would not become the accepted industry standard, and they did not want to deal with one powerful supplier that could control one of the most significant cost items in a car of the future. The automobile manufacturing companies formed the Advanced Battery Consortium (ABC) to cooperatively develop this critical component. New opportunity recognition in many industries will therefore involve the

Strategic alliance
A joint venture or partnership formed with other companies (sometimes competitors) in order to develop a new technology, process, or other type of strategically important resource.

use of cooperation for the development of new technologies or new capabilities that can be beneficial to all competitors.

Strategic alliances should not be lightly entered into. Each party to an alliance must have a clear understanding of what its resource investment obligation to the alliance is to be, as well as what its estimated benefit will be. In this way, it can more accurately assess whether participation in the alliance makes sense. Far too many alliances have been entered into over the years where participating companies have not fully appreciated what their investments would need to be or what they would get out of the results produced by the allied effort. Alliances will usually require the development of a new set of resources or capabilities to be properly managed and to derive the greatest value from the relationship. An effective alliance involves more than simply managing the effort as if it is the same as an internally managed department or project. Typically, the fullest value of an alliance is realized when multiple functions within a company are involved. We discovered earlier that achieving consistency and coordination across the internal value chain is one of the most difficult facets of strategic management, and this makes effective alliance management a real challenge. Management must therefore carefully consider the dedication of time and commitment to resource-building that such efforts will inevitably involve.

CHAPTER SUMMARY

This chapter aimed to examine the intricacies of strategy in the context of real competitors and the environment in which they operate. The ability to track and predict competitive moves (both proactively and reactively) provides one of the best tools in the running of a successful business.

We first examined the industry conditions under which companies must make their strategic moves. Industries may generally be classified as either benign or hostile, and can often be characterized as hypercompetitive. We looked at the conditions that describe each characterization, and the unique approaches that research has suggested are successful in these circumstances.

We next observed that improving our ability to predict competitive moves relies upon our ability to drill down more carefully into the nature of specific organizations. To do this we can classify organizations into one of four categories:

1. Prospectors
2. Defenders
3. Analyzers
4. Reactors

We also looked at internal competitive company characteristics that offer insights into their potential actions and reactions. These included: management team behavior patterns, relative market positions, and financial conditions. Information sources of competitive intelligence include: 1) Media reports through evaluative clipping services, 2) suppliers, 3) former employees, and 4) conferences or speeches by key executives of competitors. Scenario analysis was reviewed as another tool for companies to map out its own strategic moves over a very long period of time based on alternative scenarios for the future.

We examined competitive responses and actions based upon ordinary and strategic threats to the organization. Ordinary threats are traditionally addressed with one of five tactical approaches including: 1) Acquiesce; 2) Compromise; 3) Avoid; 4) Defy; and 5) Manipulate. Strategic threats are addressed with different approaches that are categorized as: 1) Containment; 2) Shaping; 3) Absorption; 4) Neutralization; and 5) Annulment.

Finally, we took a look at cooperation and strategic alliances as an increasingly important component of strategy in the twenty-first century.

KEY TERMS

Analyzer (p. 265)

Benchmark (p. 262)

Benign environment (p. 261)

Clipping service (p. 271)

Defender (p. 265)

Hostile environment (p. 261)

Prospector (p. 264)

Reactor (p. 265)

Scenario analysis (p. 272)

Strategic alliance (p. 277)

Tactics (p. 260)

SHORT ANSWER QUESTIONS

1. How does a company's financial position impact its strategic choices?
2. Why can't a company remain in a Reactor mode and still be a profit generator?
3. How should absorption be used as a response to an innovative new entry?
4. Provide an example of a Prospector organization (separate from the examples in the text) and explain how it reacts to its competitors.
5. What competitive tactics should Starbucks employ with the encroachment of McDonald's into the premium coffee business?
6. How would you characterize a hostile environment?
7. How would a scenario analysis assist the airline industry going into 2030?

8. How would a benign environment impact the strategic choices of an organization?

9. How would you collect competitive intelligence on a group of competitors?

GROUP EXERCISES

1. Select a well-known company in the Fortune 500. Using publicly available information, put together an analysis of the CEO who runs that organization. What are his or her strategic tendencies? How might he or she react to an encroachment by a competitor? Has this CEO been consistent in his or her behavior?

2. Using the same company that you selected in #1, create a strategic map with as many aspects examined as you can locate.

3. Select an example company from the past week in the *Wall Street Journal* that is under attack from a substantial new competitor or new process. Using the tactics defined in the chapter, what would you recommend as a strategy for that company?

REFERENCES

[1] Edward, C. 2006. Game definitely not over., *Business Week Online*. November 16: p. 11; Hall, K. 2007. Nintendo: Calling all players. *Business Week Online*. October 11: p. 24; Bremner, B. 2007. Nintendo storms the gaming world. *Business Week Online*. January 29: p. 21; Edwards, C. 2006. Nintendo Wii: One ferocious underdog. *Business Week Online*. November 26: p. 10.

[2] Covin, J., D. Slevin, and M. Heeley. 1999. Pioneers and followers: Competitive tactics, environment, and firm growth. *Journal of Business Venturing* 15: 175–210.

[3] Ibid.

[4] D'Aveni, R. 1994. *Hypercompetition: Managing the dynamics of strategic maneuvering.* New York: Free Press.

[5] D'Aveni, R. 2007. Mapping your competitive position. *Harvard Business Review*. November: 1–10.

[6] Miles, R. E., and C. C. Snow. 1978. *Organizational strategy, structure and processes.* New York: McGraw-Hill Book Company.

[7] The dark side of DEC's rebound. 1984. *Business Week*. January 30: 51–53.

[8] Sun Tzu. *The Art of War*. 1983 edited translation by James Clavell. New York: Delta.

[9] Greenspan, Alan. 2007. *The age of turbulence*. New York: Penguin.

[10] Oliver, C. 1990. Determinants of interorganizational relationships: Integrations and future directions. *Academy of Management Review* 15: 241–265; Oliver, C. 1991. Strategic responses to institutional processes. *Academy of Management Review* 16: 145–179.

[11] D'Aveni, R. 2002. The empire strikes back: Counterrevolutionary strategies for industry leaders. *Harvard Business Review*. November: 5–12.

[12] http://en.wikipedia.org/wiki/List_of_companies_acquired_by_Microsoft_Corporation.

[13] Grant, R. 2005. *Contemporary strategy analysis*, 5th edition. New York: Blackwell Publishing.

Strategy at the Corporate Level

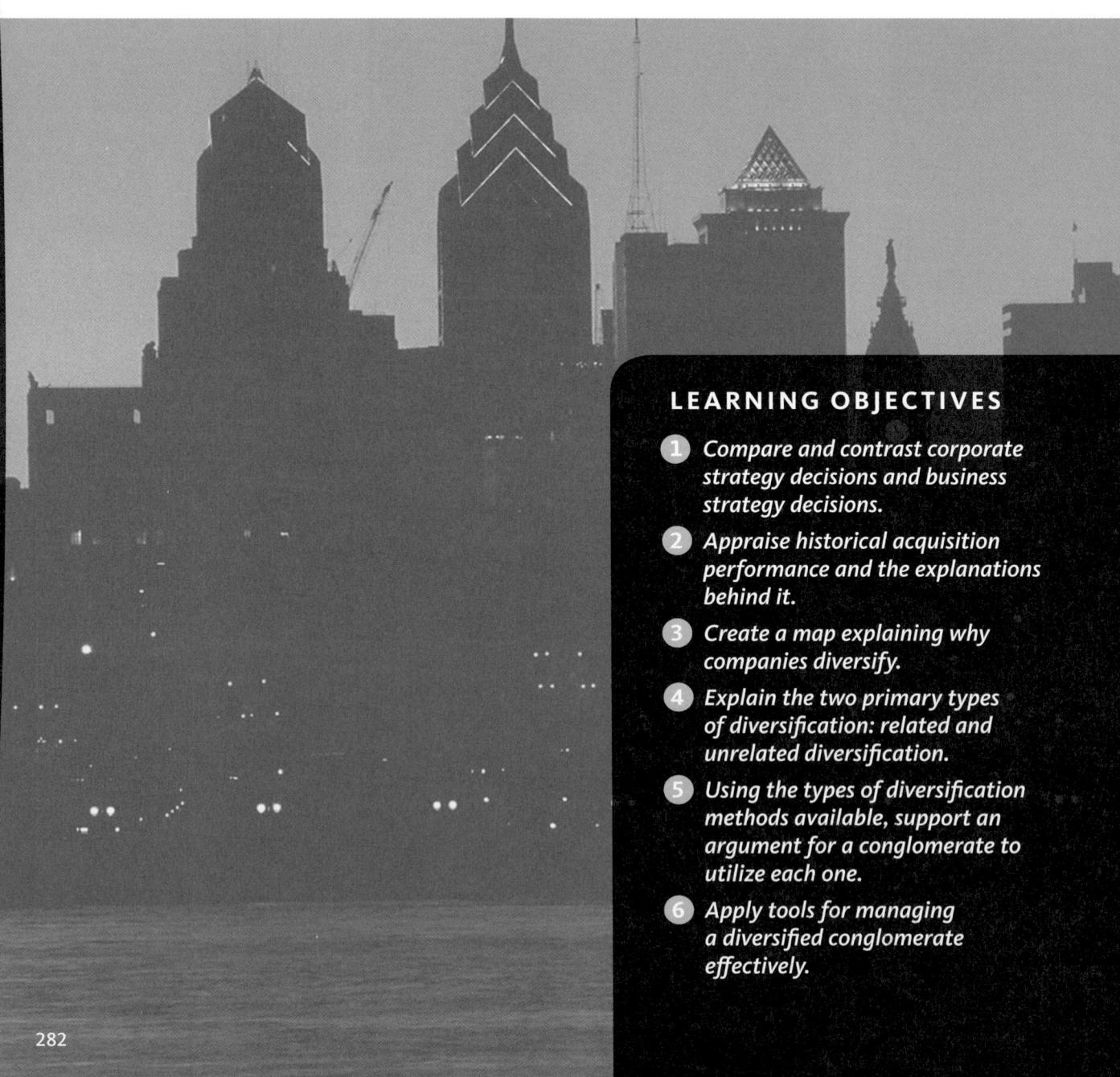

Internet Advertising[3]

In the span of just over one month in 2007, the following acquisitions were announced in the business press.

April 14, 2007. Google today announced that it would purchase Internet ad services company DoubleClick for $3.1 billion. Representing a stunning increase in DoubleClick's valuation from only $1.1 billion in 2005, Google's price tops overtures made by Microsoft to buy the company. Complementing Google's efforts to develop greater revenue from Internet advertising, the acquisition will put competitive pressure on Yahoo! for whom Internet advertising has been a traditional strength.

April 30, 2007. Yahoo! today agreed to purchase the remaining 80 percent of Right Media that it does not already own for $680 million. Right Media operates an online ad exchange, where buyer and sellers of Internet ads can find each other and execute transactions more efficiently. Yahoo! believes the exchange business will enhance its revenue from nonpremium Internet ads. Just prior to the acquisition announcement, DoubleClick announced plans for its own exchange.

May 18, 2007. WPP Group, a traditional advertising agency, announced that it would acquire 24/7 Real Media for $649 million. The company offers ad serving, targeting, tracking, an analytics platform, as well as search marketing capabilities and a global network of specialized Web sites that engage their target audiences with precision and transparency. 24/7's stock price has risen over 31 percent since Google announced its acquisition of DoubleClick; WPP's announced purchase price of $11.75 per share represents a premium of 37 percent over the company's mid-April stock price.

May 18, 2007. Microsoft today announced its intention to acquire aQuantive for $66.50 a share, or about $6 billion, which represents a whopping 85 percent premium over yesterday's closing price for the company. aQuantive is a holding company for several online advertising businesses. Their systems help advertisers, ad agencies and Web publishers manage and serve up online ads. Its Internet ad network also buys and resells large blocks of online ad space to advertisers. Recently aQuantive expanded internationally, opening up shops in Europe and Asia.

Questions

1. Why was there a sudden flurry of acquisitions within an industry? Is this coincidence? Are the 2nd, 3rd, and 4th moves really well thought out?
2. Why do companies pay such large premiums for the companies they acquire? Is it possible for the acquiring companies to earn a return on their investment?

CORPORATE STRATEGY VERSUS BUSINESS STRATEGY

For most of this book we have focused on strategy as it relates to managing a single business. Industry analysis, value chain, generic strategy, life cycles, and competitive moves: all fundamentally relate to how a company formulates its strategy for a particular type of business and competes in an industry with its products or services. When a company operates in only one line of business, the discussion stays in the realm of **business strategy**. As the opening vignettes to this chapter illustrate, however, companies often move beyond a single business by acquiring other similar or related businesses and by acquiring completely unrelated businesses. When a company owns multiple companies and/or operates in multiple lines of business, then we move into the realm of **corporate strategy**. Here, senior executives must make decisions about managing *sets* of businesses. Recall from Chapter 1 that one of our five critical questions defining the field of strategy is: "What is the nature of strategy in a multibusiness firm?"

Corporate strategy involves making decisions about issues that rise above—but also take into account—the decisions made at the business strategy level. Corporate strategy decision domains include the following areas (Figure 10.1):

Figure 10.1
Domain of Corporate Strategy

- Deciding which industries to enter and exit
- Defining a strategic business unit
- Establishing business unit investment priorities
- Effecting resources and management transfers
- Structuring the corporation

Business strategy The types of decisions made and direction created for a single business.

Corporate strategy The types of decisions made and direction created for a corporation that operates multiple lines of business.

Strategic business unit (SBU) The organization of a set of businesses that share identical or very similar strategies or strategic challenges.

Deciding which industries to enter and exit.

At the corporate strategy level executives contemplating growth through internally developed new businesses or acquisitions will evaluate the industries in which these new businesses would exist. Remember in Chapter 4 we concluded that industry structure can enhance or impede the ability of a participating company to earn above-average returns? It usually makes more sense to enter an industry where prospects for profits are strong. In addition, companies that have previously diversified will periodically reevaluate the wisdom of continuing in a particular industry. Diversified companies often decide to divest a business because they determine that its industry is no longer sufficiently attractive.

Defining a strategic business unit.
When a company owns and operates many different lines of business, management must decide how to organize the portfolio of businesses. The concept of the **strategic business unit (SBU)** captures the idea that a set of businesses that share very similar challenges or strategies can be effectively combined and managed as a single unit. General Electric competes with hundreds of products and services across literally dozens of industries; the company has been doing this for decades. Today, however, they have organized all of their business into six important groups and within each group are strategic business units. Within the GE Commercial Finance group, for example, there are four SBUs, each of which

combines multiple lines of business that confront similar issues and challenges. Defining strategic business units and which lines of business should be within them can be an extraordinary challenge for corporate strategists, especially in organizations such as GE or Illinois Tool Works that operate hundreds of types of businesses.

Establishing investment priorities. The diversified corporation usually engages in a budgeting process in which divisions or SBUs seek corporate investment to further develop their businesses. Corporate management must decide how to judge the merits of requests for additional capital investment by SBUs and how to allocate available capital among competing requests. The process effectively makes the corporate headquarters operate much like a bank, doling out resources based upon estimated output and return measures. Developing an effective set of evaluative criteria and creating a means of analyzing competing requests is a critical issue for corporate strategy decision makers.

Making resource and management transfers. Many corporations decide to acquire companies that are somewhat related to their existing lines of business. This is done to take advantage of anticipated synergies that might exist between the newly acquired company and the existing business or to establish a foothold in another promising area. When this happens, corporate management needs to determine how best to infuse the new company with the unique resources and learning from its existing business, as well as how to take advantage of what is special about the acquired company within the existing businesses. Facilitating this sharing of resources can be exceedingly difficult for a variety of reasons, which we will return to in the following discussion about capturing synergies. The corporate office must also implement appropriate management changes to align the new company with the corporation. Such moves may ultimately have the added benefit of developing managers with a broader experience across the entire organization.

How to structure the corporation. To accomplish all of this, corporate management must determine the type of structure that will be most effective for this complex set of businesses. Neither a traditional functional organization nor the hierarchy of a typical single-line business will generally work for a multiple-business corporation. Marketing management for Platinum Master Cards and marketing management for Lightspeed computerized tomography scanners (both business lines of GE) are worlds apart and each requires a completely different set of skills! Corporations employ a variety of structures to accomplish coordination, sharing, control, and management. This topic will be discussed in detail in Chapter 11, "Strategy and Structure."

HISTORICAL PERSPECTIVES

Developing a deep understanding of corporate strategy is important for students of strategy because diversified corporations are a significant part of the business landscape in the United States and around the world. Rarely does a week go by that the *Wall Street Journal* does not report on yet another corporate merger or buyout. The diversified company has become increasingly important in the U.S. economy. Figure 10.2 illustrates merger and acquisition (M&A) activity over the last forty-five years in the United States. Until the mid-1980s, although the number of M&A deals rose and fell, the total value of such deals remained fairly constant. Since the early 1990s both the number of transactions and their value has grown dramatically; in 2006 the value of all U.S. mergers and acquisitions exceeded $1.5 trillion.

The reasons for M&A activity over the years have changed. Until the 1960s many corporations had grown through internally generated new business within their own industries, or had completed horizontal diversification in order to own and manage other companies that were very similar to their core business. However, by the late 1960s many U.S. corporations found it increasingly difficult to grow because of maturing domestic markets, greater foreign competition in the United States, and concerns about antitrust enforcement since industry concentration ratios had increased in many domestic industries (see discussion in Chapter 4).[4] Therefore they sought to fuel growth by getting into new industries outside their **dominant business**. The era of **conglomerates** took shape, during which corporations acquired many types of companies that were completely different from what had

Dominant business
A company in which 70–95 percent of revenue comes from a single business.

Conglomerate A corporation that owns a large number of businesses that are different sizes and operate in different industry sectors.

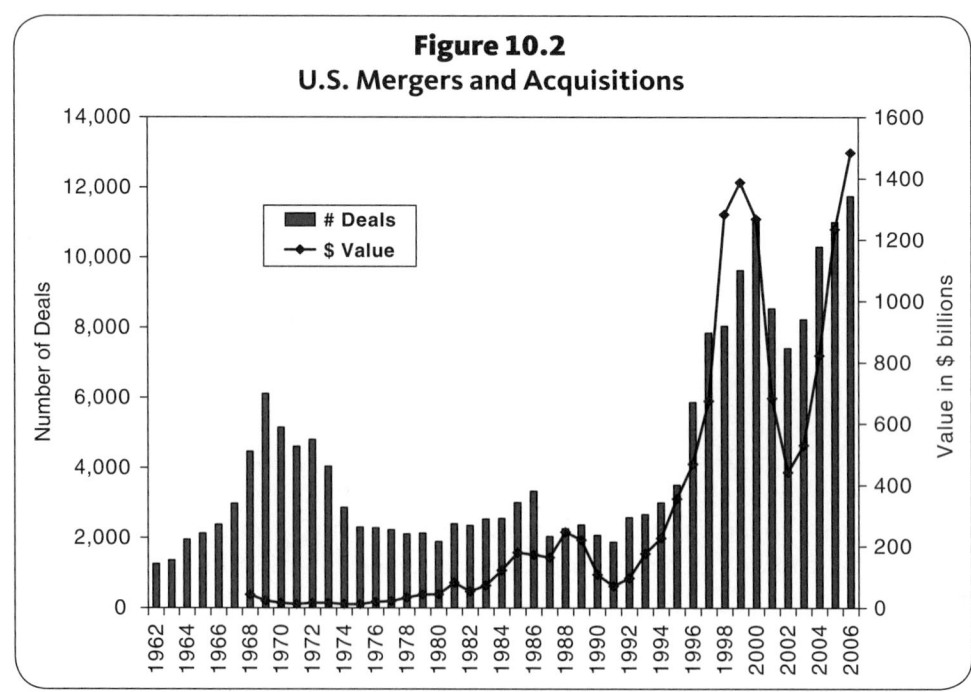

Figure 10.2
U.S. Mergers and Acquisitions

Source: Mergerstat.

originally been their dominant business. If you think of a conglomerate in its usual definition—"rock composed of fragments varying from small pebbles to large boulders in a cement"[5]—then you have a picture of what conglomerate corporations were like. Textron, Gulf + Western, ITT, Litton Industries, and General Electric are corporate names often associated with conglomerates. In fact, during the 1960s GE competed in twenty-three of the twenty-six industries defined and tracked by the Commerce Department,[6] with forty-six different operating divisions and 190 departments.

Conglomeration continued into the early 1970s as the largest corporations grew even larger. One business reporter, believing the trend toward monster-size corporations would not abate until virtually all companies were owned by only a few giant corporations, was prompted to write an article titled "The Day They Couldn't Fill the Fortune 500."[7] By 1974 the complexion of the U.S. economy had changed significantly from twenty-five years earlier. Figure 10.3 shows how diversified the Fortune 500 had become during this period of time. In 1949 over 40 percent of the largest corporations operated in only a single business, and 70 percent operated in a single business or were predominantly in a single industry. By 1974, in contrast, 64 percent of the largest companies were diversified and operating in multiple industries.[8]

By the 1980s large, widely diversified firms were experiencing significant difficulties in the sound and profitable management of such a breadth of businesses. What goes up must come down—or so we are led to believe. Corporate activity during the 1980s was characterized by efforts to dismantle conglomerate firms and redeploy their assets more effectively and efficiently. With a more permissive antitrust environment under President Reagan's administration, and with financial innovations such as **junk bonds** and **leveraged buyouts (LBOs)**, conglomerates began to shed unrelated businesses in order to become more focused in their portfolio of businesses.[9] By 1988,

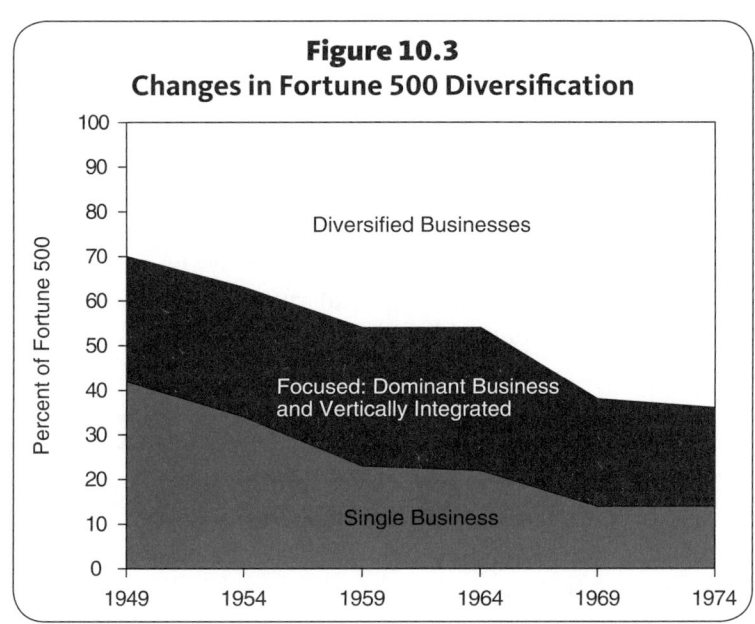

Figure 10.3
Changes in Fortune 500 Diversification

Junk bond High-yield debt that is rated below investment grade at the time of purchase. These bonds have a higher risk of default, but typically pay higher yields than better quality bonds in order to make them attractive to investors. Typically issued by businesses that are unable to secure investment grade financing.

Leveraged buyout (LBO) A process where a company is bought primarily using debt. Typically engineered by management of the company, or by private equity firms.

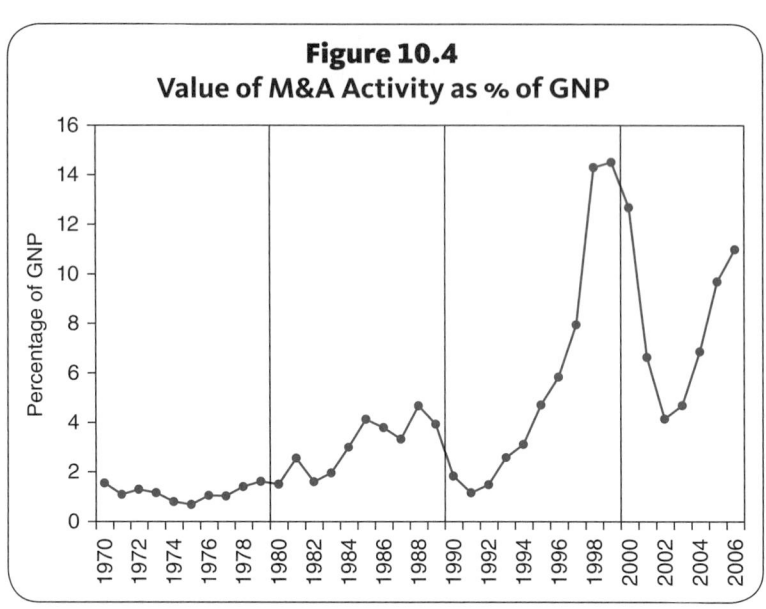

Figure 10.4
Value of M&A Activity as % of GNP

Source: Mergerstat and U.S. Dept. of Commerce.

Private equity firm
Private (nonpublic) corporations or partnerships that use their financial resources to engineer buyouts and acquisitions of other companies.

SPAC Special Purpose Acquisition Company. Empty-shell firms that promise to buy businesses with the proceeds of their initial public stock offerings.

CLO Collateralized Loan Obligation. Large pool of bank loans bundled together by financial services firms and sold off to investors in slices, with the goal to spread default risk "an inch deep and a mile wide."

when the value of deals peaked during the decade (Figure 10.2), 63 percent of acquisitions involved cash or debt (as opposed to using equity). LBOs were the talk of the town on Wall Street; the most exciting deal was the frenzied $25 billion LBO of RJR Nabisco in 1988, subsequently chronicled in a popular book titled *Barbarians at the Gate*.[10] If you enjoy corporate finance, backroom politics, soap opera, and drama, this book is a must-read page-turner!

The 1990s witnessed the escalation of M&A activity to a point never before experienced in the U.S. economy. Increasing globalization and more intense competition provided the impetus for firms to grow larger. The soaring stock market and a continuation of the restrained antitrust environment enabled firms to use their own highly valued shares of stock to acquire companies that were related to lines of business they were already in. The confluence of these factors led to a dollar volume of deals that exceeded 14 percent of the U.S. gross national product (Figure 10.4). After the recession in the early 2000s and the corresponding decline in diversification activity, M&As resumed their rise once again. In the most recent phase this activity is being assisted by the growth of **private equity firms** and by the advent of innovative financing methods such as **SPACs** (special purpose acquisition companies) and **CLOs** (collateralized loan obligations).[11]

3 *Create a map explaining why companies diversify.*

MOTIVATIONS FOR DIVERSIFICATION

We saw in Chapter 8 that companies experience different stages and strategic considerations in the course of their development. After a company has started up and then gone through the commercialization and growth stages, the challenges of managing a mature business set in. As a company matures

ONE OF THE WORST DEALS EVER?[12]

On January 17, 2006, Boston Scientific secured a deal to acquire Guidant Corp. In a follow-up investigative report published in *Fortune,* the deal was characterized as "a roller-coaster tale of bet-the-franchise corporate brinkmanship, miscalculation, and overreaching. It is a stark lesson in how the single-minded pursuit of victory can blind even brilliant execs to the true costs of a deal." Boston's $80 per share bid for Guidant beat out Johnson & Johnson's $71 offer after multiple rounds of bidding in which the "bad blood" that had existed between Boston and J&J manifested itself in "gladiatorial" combat.

J&J had originally bid to acquire Guidant because it saw opportunities for significant growth through Guidant's pacemakers and defibrillators in the medical products industry. J&J competed in this industry and wanted to broaden its product lines. Boston Scientific also saw a similar opportunity for growth through related acquisition. The marriage of Boston's Taxus drug-coated stent business and Guidant's promising new stent products and proprietary stent implantation technology also made a potential merger quite attractive.

Boston's winning bid was the eighth bid entertained by Guidant's board of directors. After earlier J&J bids had been viewed favorably by the Guidant board, Boston's CFO Larry Best is claimed to have announced to his internal team, "We need to make a bid that ends this, to swing for the fences." Best was viewed as a "mercurial street fighter" who "doesn't like to lose." The final Boston bid was $27.2 billion, valuing Guidant at $80.03 per share, representing a PE ratio of 64.6 and a premium of 40+ percent over its share price before the first J&J bid. The bid was paid in part with newly issued Boston shares, which increased its share count by 80 percent and diluted Boston shareholders. Part of the bid price was paid with cash, requiring Boston to borrow $6.5 billion on which it pays in excess of $300 million annually in interest.

Since the deal was consummated, Boston has been plagued with poor performance. Guidant was forced to recall stents due to poor quality control; the FDA warned Boston about its manufacturing facilities, preventing approval for new products. Drug-coated stents, in general, also received negative publicity from the health-care community. These factors interfered

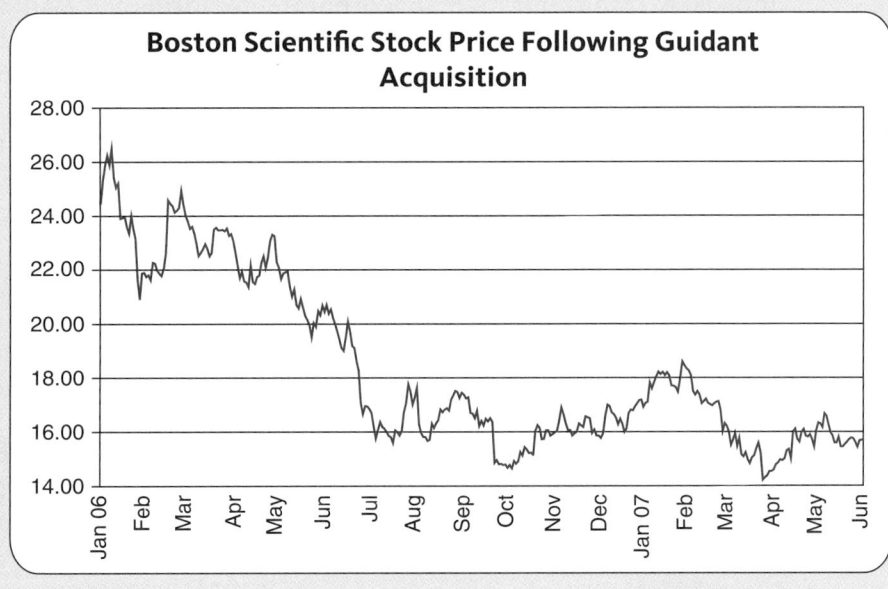

Boston Scientific Stock Price Following Guidant Acquisition

(continues)

with Boston's efforts to increase Guidant sales so that now, with the interest that Boston pays on the acquisition debt, the Guidant business is contributing nothing to the company's earnings. Boston's share price, which was at $24 when the bid was accepted, has dropped 34 percent into the mid-teens. Larry Best insists the acquisition will pay off and that success should be judged in three to four years, not based upon short-term hiccups. CEO Jim Tobin has "no doubt" that the company will eventually realize the deal's potential.

QUESTIONS

1. Without divesting itself of Guidant's business, what would you recommend to the Boston Scientific board of directors that the company should do to improve its business?

2. How might the company be structured to avoid the operational errors it seems to be incurring?

3. Where are the synergies in this combined business?

and its sales growth starts to flatten out, the strategic option to diversify is often considered by senior management. When a company diversifies by acquiring another company, there is usually a core logic that is operating. The company sees potential competitive advantage that might be attained with the combination. Through the application and sharing of corporate resources, the acquiring company believes that it will be able to assist the acquired company to become much more than it could have been if it had remained independent, or much more than it could have been if it had been acquired by another company. So the core logic of diversification through acquisition is usually that "we can do something special for and with them, and as a result our overall corporate performance will be significantly improved." It's also often the case that acquiring companies have something to gain from the acquired company, such as new technology or new capabilities. Here the logic is "they can do something for us."

There tend to be four primary motivations for diversifying a company, which include: 1) seeking growth, 2) market entry, 3) seeking market power, and 4) spreading risk. Within each of these primary motivations are sets of underlying reasons, and we briefly discuss each below.

The desire to continue growing a company generally heads the list of motivations to diversify, and this motivation to grow through diversification can occur for various offensive or competitively defensive reasons.

GROWTH
- Better external opportunities
- Acquire new capabilities
- Response to intensifying competition
- Avoiding decline & takeover
- Benefits to management & employees
- Managerial capitalism

Better external opportunities. Corporate management will come to believe that they have exhausted their opportunities to sustain strong growth rates through their customary internal actions. They may not see any exciting new products in their development pipeline, they may believe that they have saturated their current channels of distribution, or they may have expanded geographically as far as they possibly can with existing products or services. It may be that large markets or segments no longer exist in their core business that can satisfy the level of growth a company desires (remember that as a company grows in size, it will require larger increments of new revenue in order to sustain a given percentage rate of growth). Or it may be that the cost of expanding further within an existing business domain appears to be prohibitively expensive. To try to change an established organization so that it can generate a significant number of innovative ideas can be difficult, time consuming, and fraught with uncertainties that appear overwhelming. In these cases companies will typically search for external opportunities to fuel growth, and will consider acquiring another business that meets their acquisition criteria.

Acquire new capabilities. Expansion into new products or industries may require new capabilities and resources that the company does not possess. As we discussed in Chapter 9, a company may gain access to new capabilities through alliances or joint ventures with other companies. Yet the acquisition of another business and its inherent capabilities allows the parent company to own and control new resources and capabilities, as well as prevent access to them by competitors.

Oracle is a prime example of these first two reasons for growth through acquisition. The company was known historically for its database software; however it was clear that the industry was maturing. So they began to acquire other companies in business application software, financial services, and telecommunications. Over a three-year time period Oracle acquired more than twenty-five software application companies, as well as major purchases of PeopleSoft and Siebel Systems. Acquisition represented a quick route to maintain Oracle's historical growth rates, but was also required because Oracle systems developers did not possess the skills or capabilities required to enter other software application categories.[13]

Response to intensifying competition. As competitors become larger and more powerful, companies are often prompted to acquire other businesses in order to maintain a competitive position. Acquiring another business can generate benefits of size, reduce the company's dependence on its limited array of products and services, and reduce dependence on specific geographic markets or customer segments. In 2007, organic grocer Whole Foods sought to acquire Wild Oats Markets, another organic grocer, in order to counter the growing competition in organic foods from conventional supermarkets such as Kroger, Supervalu, and Wal-Mart. The argument was that the two organic grocers would save on overhead costs and would allow the combined company to more effectively compete for customers through advertising and retail location.

Avoiding decline and takeover. As internally generated growth of a company begins to slow down, management typically comes under pressure from investors and the stock market to continue generating attractive returns. This kind of slowing growth can occur for any number of reasons: the overall market is maturing, competitors are increasingly effective, the company's strategic approach is increasingly ineffective, or the overall complexity of the corporation makes it difficult to manage effectively. If revenue growth is slowing, improving returns can happen only through cutting costs, and cutting costs can only go so far before interfering with a company's competitive strategy in the marketplace. Lackluster revenue growth and inadequate investor returns paint a target on the backs of senior management, since they are responsible for performance. If the problem of growth in returns is not resolved, the business may become ripe for a **takeover**, in which another company buys the business and replaces the management team to make necessary changes. Senior managers therefore look at acquisitions and other diversifying moves as an effort to arrest decline and forestall the possibility of any sort of takeover.

Benefits to management and employees. Attempts to grow through acquisition occur for reasons sometimes unrelated to what is actually best for the company itself. Employees and (especially) senior managers derive benefits from working in larger organizations. Compared to smaller companies, in larger organizations there are usually greater opportunities for advancement in position and responsibility while compensation also tends to be higher. For senior management, incentive programs that include bonuses and stock options tend to become more lucrative in larger companies, and can be a powerful inducement to create growth for growth's sake. In this sense, big is beautiful, and getting bigger may be more attractive to employees for personal reasons.

The idea that important strategic decisions for a company might be made in order to personally enhance members of management highlights what is known as the **agency** issue. Corporate officers and managers are duty bound to act in the interests of shareholders, yet personal incentives may corrupt this straightforward charge. This is one of the reasons that controls are put in place by boards of directors and stockholders. We will return to these issues of governance in Chapter 12.

Managerial capitalism. The last two ideas suggest that something other than the basic economics of a business and its industry can affect whether and how managers pursue growth—that, in fact, managers may pursue growth based on their own personal needs, interests, and aspirations. Building on this idea, Robin Marris long ago suggested that managers trade their desire for growth against fear of takeover.[14] In his model of "managerial capitalism" corporate managers seek growth in ways that go beyond economic justification, until such time as they have assembled more than they can effectively and coherently manage. We will see further evidence of nonrational thinking about mergers and acquisitions in our following discussions.

ETHICS

Takeover A process where a large group of shareholders vote in new members to the board of directors, with the result that the new board can make changes in the company's management.

Agency Where an individual (such as a corporate officer) acts on behalf of someone else (such as a shareholder).

The quest for greater market power is a companion motivation to the quest for growth. Market power refers back to some of the dimensions of industry analysis that we covered in Chapter 4. Here a company seeks to attain a position in the industry that enables it to earn superior returns, through one of several ways.

MARKET POWER
- Gains in pricing authority
- Increasing bargaining power
- Forbearance—keep competitors at bay

Gains in pricing authority.
A company that grows larger in its industry by horizontally acquiring one of its competitors can develop size advantages it previously did not enjoy. These include greater economies of scale in its operations, as well as savings through the integration of identical support activities in its value chain (such as combining R&D, purchasing, and human resource functions). Together, these cost savings create greater flexibility in establishing prices for products and services. Most industries have price leaders and price followers; however, the price leaders tend to be the larger companies with the better cost structures.

Increased bargaining power.
Because they command a greater percentage of sales in an industry, larger companies will often enjoy enhanced bargaining power when they deal with both suppliers and customers. This is one reason that the Federal Trade Commission originally decided to oppose the Whole Foods—Wild Oats combination mentioned previously, because the combined company would have what is thought to be too much power to demand lower prices from small organic suppliers as well as greater power to command premium prices (without significant competition) with consumer shoppers.

Mutual forbearance—keeping competitors at bay.
Mutual forbearance is defined as "the ceding of control of one product or geographic market to a competitor in exchange for that competitor's acquiescence in another market."[15] This means that, in order to keep a competitor out of its industry (or at least less aggressive) and maintain its competitive superiority, a company might acquire a company in another industry in which that same competitor is active. It is sort of a "tit for tat" approach: if you do this to me, I'll do it to you. For example, to slow down Gillette's entry into the disposable pen market, which was BIC's primary market, BIC decided to enter the disposable razor blade market, which was Gillette's hallowed ground. As was pointed out in Chapter 1, this type of "attack" is taken directly from Sun Tzu, who suggested that attacking something of value to the enemy will cause them to reconsider attacking you. Although in this example BIC entered razors through internal development, many examples of mutual forbearance exist through acquisitions into an industry. In 2008 Microsoft bid to acquire Yahoo! to compete more aggressively in the online advertising business. This would likely prompt Google to devote much greater attention and resources to this battle, since it is central to Google's revenue stream, and by doing so draw Google's attention and resources away from its efforts to develop software applications that compete with Microsoft.

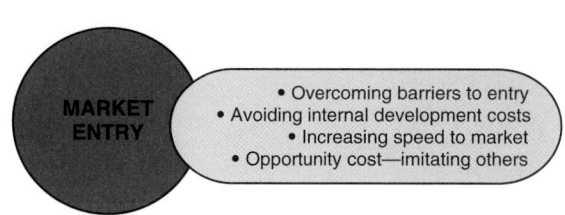

MARKET ENTRY
- Overcoming barriers to entry
- Avoiding internal development costs
- Increasing speed to market
- Opportunity cost—imitating others

Companies often seek to enter industries outside of where they currently operate. They plan to accomplish this type of diversification through acquisition, rather than through internal development, for a number of reasons that relate to cost and speed.

Overcoming barriers to entry. The competitors in most industries seek to raise entry barriers to keep the flow of new entrants to a minimum, thus better preserving their own stakes in the industry's profits. Barriers to entry can be both significant and expensive—whether they involve building scale-efficient manufacturing facilities, developing broad distribution, or creating brand awareness through advertising and promotion. Acquiring an existing company in a new industry does an end-run around the costs of breaking through the entry barriers because the company takes advantage of an existing industry player who already holds the resources needed to be a competitor. Breaking into the sports drink market with a new product line would have been a difficult and slow road for Quaker Oats to pursue; instead they purchased Gatorade (at a somewhat outrageous price) and immediately became an important player in the industry.

Avoiding internal development costs. Similarly, through the acquisition of a going concern in an industry, the acquiring company can avoid the costs and uncertainty of developing products or services internally. Buying a company means taking over an existing business with defined suppliers and a customer base. Therefore most of the uncertainty that is usually associated with any type of new product development effort is also avoided.

Increasing speed to market. If analysis reveals that another industry is attractive, acquiring a company in that industry enables the acquiring firm to begin operating more quickly than would be the case if it developed its own products or services internally. Acquisitions often close within six to twelve months, whereas effective new product development efforts can take many years.

Opportunity cost. Finally, a "bandwagon" effect sometimes happens when a leading company in one industry makes an acquisition in another industry, encouraging competitors to make similar acquisitions. In the 1990s, pharmaceutical manufacturer Merck acquired generic drug distributor Medco, and shortly afterward a number of Merck's competitors also snatched up drug distribution companies. One of the vignettes at the beginning of this chapter portrayed the flurry of acquisitions in the Internet ad industry by major software manufacturers within about a one-month period of time. In each of these cases the first acquisition prompted other firms to consider the opportunities they might be missing if they stayed on the sidelines. This kind of bandwagon effect usually occurs when the industries involved are undergoing dynamic changes, revealing new possibilities for value creation through a new combination achieved by acquisition.

The final motivation for diversification has to do with spreading risk. Every company experiences

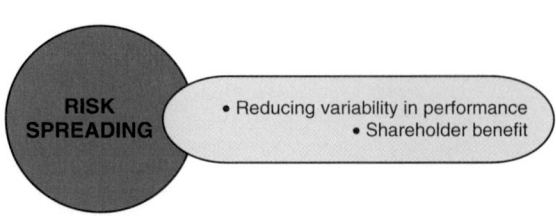

RISK SPREADING
• Reducing variability in performance
• Shareholder benefit

two kinds of risk. These are the **systematic risk** that is associated with macro-economic forces (forces that affect everyone in the economy), and the **unsystematic risk** that is associated with its particular line of business. You have no doubt run into these terms in finance classes you have taken previously, because they are both involved in calculating the beta (β) of a company's stock. Companies which diversify can reduce their unsystematic risk by acquiring other companies whose lines of business offset performance variations in the company's own business. In Figure 10.5 Company A's business fluctuates, such as might be the case when A manufactures hot chocolate mix, which is primarily sold in colder months or in mostly northern states. During the warm months A must reduce employment because seasonal sales are low, but may still find that it loses money because of high fixed overhead costs associated with its underutilized plant during that time. So during the summer its revenue and profits decline, as suggested by curved line A in Figure 10.5. When it files its quarterly reports with the SEC, the investment community responds to unprofitable quarters by selling stock, and its stock price declines. So Company A decides to acquire Company B, which manufactures popsicles sold primarily in the warm months and the southern states. After the acquisition, A combines the two manufacturing operations so that consistent employment and better plant utilization can be maintained. Administrative, marketing and sales efficiencies work to lower other costs as a percentage of revenue. Since revenue and profits do not now fluctuate widely, the company may report more consistently profitable quarters throughout the year. Shareholders of A benefit from the smoothed-out revenues and earnings the company now achieves.

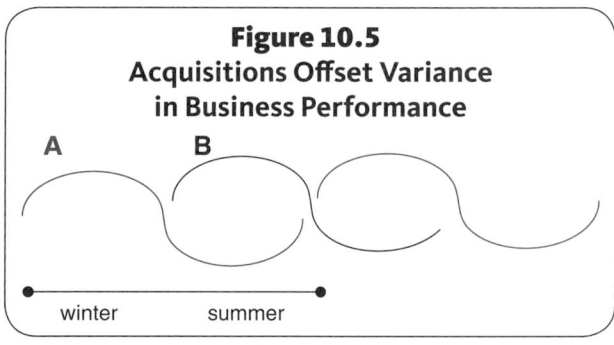

Figure 10.5
Acquisitions Offset Variance in Business Performance

Why couldn't shareholders in Company A simply buy shares of Company B to accomplish the same level of risk spreading? In this case Company B's business also fluctuates considerably during a year and across geographies. So shareholders of A, who also invest in B would simply be buying another company with a fair degree of unsystematic risk. However, by putting together the lines of business the fluctuations associated with the combined company are reduced,[16] and shareholders thus benefit from a stock price that should be more stable over time.

Systematic risk Risk associated with macro-economic forces.

Unsystematic risk Risk associated with a particular business.

TYPES OF DIVERSIFICATION

In Chapter 8 we covered a range of options that companies have at their disposal for growing their businesses—including introducing new products within their industry, expanding into new geographic regions or internationally, or forming alliances or joint ventures. Because this chapter deals with corporate strategy (managing multiple lines of business), we have more or less focused on the acquisitions route at this point. We have to recognize,

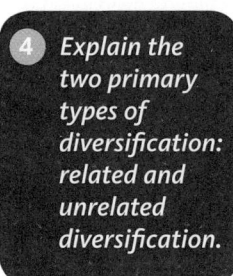

4 Explain the two primary types of diversification: related and unrelated diversification.

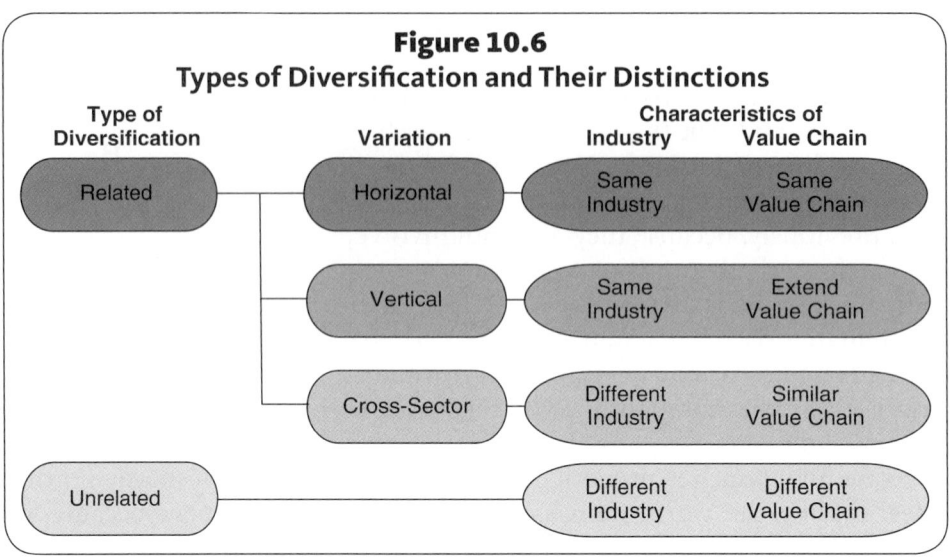

Figure 10.6
Types of Diversification and Their Distinctions

Type of Diversification	Variation	Characteristics of Industry	Value Chain
Related	Horizontal	Same Industry	Same Value Chain
	Vertical	Same Industry	Extend Value Chain
	Cross-Sector	Different Industry	Similar Value Chain
Unrelated		Different Industry	Different Value Chain

however, that companies may still diversify into new businesses through internal development efforts or through joint ventures and alliances, in addition to acquisition. As discussed in the preceding section, diversifying through acquisition can offer some advantages over these other methods. These advantages relate to control of resources and capabilities, overcoming entry barriers, avoiding internal development costs, and increasing speed of entry.

Regardless of how a company diversifies, there are distinctions in the type of diversification that a company engages in. These distinctions can be described in terms of the combinations of industry similarity and value chain similarity (Figure 10.6). The primary types of diversification fall into two well-known categories: **related diversification** and **unrelated diversification**.

Related Diversification

As the phrase implies, related diversification means that there is some dimension of similarity between the corporation and the company it seeks to acquire. Related diversification can be divided into three variations: 1) horizontal, 2) vertical, and 3) cross-sector. **Horizontal diversification** occurs when a company enters another business in the same industry and essentially employs the exact same value chain as is used in its core business. Earlier we mentioned how Whole Foods acquired Wild Oats Markets during 2007. These two organic foods grocery store chains draw upon the same suppliers, operate in the same fashion at retail, and seek to attract the same types of customers. In 2008 InBev, one of the largest European beer companies, acquired Anheuser-Busch in order to establish a worldwide distributor of beer. Black & Decker, the 100-year-old manufacturer of power tools for homeowners and the construction trade, acquired Vector Products, which manufactures battery chargers, jumpstarters, and other equipment for the automotive market. Since many of the Vector products are sold in traditional

Related diversification
A merger or acquisition where there is some similarity of industry and/or value chain between the corporation and the company it seeks to acquire.

Unrelated diversification When a corporation enters a new business in a different industry from that in which it currently operates *and* does not expect to achieve any value chain synergies through the combination.

Horizontal diversification
Acquisition of a company that operates in the same industry using the same value chain.

hardware store channels of distribution, Black & Decker is able to leverage its resources and capabilities in tool manufacturing and sales distribution to significantly expand the presence and impact of the Vector line.

Because horizontal diversification extends a company's influence further into an industry in which it is already operating, acquisitions of this sort tend to draw the attention of regulatory authorities. Acquiring companies in the same industry may lead to significantly enhanced market power, through which the resulting combination may exert undue influence upstream on suppliers or downstream on customers, in the form of pricing demands or other requirements. InBev announced plans to cut $1.5 billion from Anheuser-Busch's cost structure partly by reducing the number of independent distributors and reducing payments to those distributors that remain.[17] From our earlier discussion in Chapter 4 on industry analysis, we know that the Federal Trade Commission and the Department of Justice are interested in preventing combinations that lead to excessive market power for just these reasons. This is why the FTC objected to Staple's acquisition of Office Depot and Whole Foods' acquisition of Wild Oats Markets.

Occasionally companies will engage in **vertical diversification**, in which they enter new businesses in the same industry but which occupy different positions up or down the value chain. Vertical acquisitions ordinarily occur when a company wants to continue operating in its own industry, where it has deep knowledge and capabilities, but wants to exert greater control over some part of the industry value chain. When Disney decided to enter the cruise line business, it could have simply licensed its name and the use of its characters to another company that already operated in this business. Yet Disney believed that the quality of the customer experience is at the heart of the company, and that delivering an exceptional experience is a critical part of their strategy. Monitoring how another company accomplished this on their behalf would have been incredibly difficult and would have subjected the company to a significant downside risk that the Disney image might be tarnished. So, in entering this business they decided to enter vertically, by building and operating their own cruise ships and cruise line reservation service.

Vertical diversification also occurs when companies seek to gain greater control over sources of supply in their value chains. You have probably been advised by your university to back up your files in case the hard drive on your computer fails and you lose those term papers you have been working on (it's probably more important to you to back up your MP3 and picture files!). Western Digital manufactures internal and external hard drives used for this purpose, and their drives are often sold in electronic stores like Best Buy and Circuit City. In 2007 the company acquired Komag for nearly $1 billion. Komag manufactures the rotating disks that serve as the storage media inside the drive box you buy. The acquisition was made so that Western Digital could better keep pace with technological developments and cost changes in the manufacturing of this important component, allowing them to be more competitive with Seagate Technology. Said John Coyne, CEO of Western Digital, "This acquisition puts us in a position to be in greater control of our own destiny."[18]

Vertical diversification Acquisition of another company upstream (supplier) or downstream (buyer) in the value chain of the same industry in which the corporation operates.

Cross-sector diversification describes the situation when a company enters a completely new industry but intends to utilize a value chain that is very similar to that employed in their core business. The Philip Morris Company decided to apply its branded marketing and sales capabilities for cigarettes to the categories of beer and soft drinks, resulting in the acquisitions of Miller Brewing and the 7-Up Company in the 1970s. Long known for its razor blades, Gillette acquired Duracell in 1996, believing that its value chain capabilities in innovation, marketing, and retail sales management could be effectively brought to bear to improve the Duracell battery business. In a further twist of corporate combinations, Procter & Gamble subsequently acquired Gillette in 2005. Although P&G already operated in many different industries (paper products, personal care items, cleaning agents, etc.), acquiring the Gillette lines of business could also be considered cross-sector diversification because they expected to leverage their existing value chain capabilities by entering new industries. In discussing the acquisition, CEO A. G. Lafley claimed that Gillette was "one of our biggest growth opportunities, and served to provide…a balanced mix of businesses, brands, markets, and customers provide flexibility to deliver results reliably, in good times and challenging times alike."[19] It becomes apparent that P&G viewed the Gillette acquisition not only as a means of generating future growth through entry into new markets, but also as a means to spread risk—three of the motivations for diversification mentioned previously.

Why Related Diversification Is Supposed to Succeed

Corporate performance is expected to improve because diversification takes advantage of synergies that are believed to exist between the corporation and the company it is seeking to acquire. Each of the types of diversification discussed previously illustrates how related diversification builds upon or leverages aspects of the corporation's existing value chain (Figure 10.7).

Three forms of "fit" offer the opportunity for synergistic gains from an acquisition. Synergies may spring from **market fit**, in which the corporation takes advantage of external value chain relationships with customers or suppliers in order to improve the competitive position and business of the acquired company. When Cisco Systems acquires another company, for example, advanced planning allows Cisco to add the acquired company's products onto its own price list the very first day the new company is officially part of

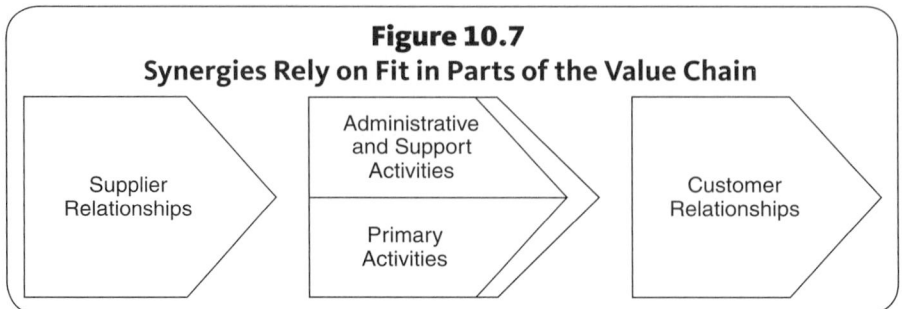

Figure 10.7
Synergies Rely on Fit in Parts of the Value Chain

Supplier Relationships

Administrative and Support Activities

Primary Activities

Customer Relationships

Cross-sector diversification Acquisition of a company in a different industry, but which employs a similar value chain.

Market fit When a corporation can take synergistic advantage of relationships with suppliers and/or customers in making an acquisition.

the Cisco family. In this way the Cisco sales organization can immediately begin selling the new company's products on a much broader scale. Procter & Gamble expected to significantly expand the Duracell and Gillette product lines throughout their worldwide organizations, selling these products to wholesale and retail accounts that P&G already had relationships with.

Operational fit occurs where the corporation is able to combine similar primary value chain activities, such as manufacturing facilities, transportation systems, or warehousing operations. In 2007 XM Satellite Radio Holdings proposed a merger with Sirius Satellite Radio, its chief competitor. The two companies, competing aggressively with each other and both losing money as a result, would expect to combine significant aspects of their nearly identical broadcasting operations and eliminate duplicate operational activities. E*Trade Financial and TD Ameritrade also engaged in merger talks during 2007, believing that "uniting both company's [sic] accounts on a single computer system" would eliminate duplicate computer operations and minimize the cost of adding new customers.[20]

The third type of fit is the kind of **management fit** that occurs when synergies might be realized in the administrative and support activities of the value chain. Combining procurement and purchasing functions can lead to increased bargaining power with suppliers and with the shippers who deliver raw materials and other inputs to the company's primary activities locations. Research and development efforts can be enhanced either through the streamlining that can occur when redundancies are eliminated or through the access to new types of technical knowledge, processes, or patents that result from combining two companies. Other corporate support functions, such as finance and legal, can also be made available to acquired companies and thereby further reduce redundancies. Perhaps most importantly, the more sophisticated knowledge possessed by management about how to successfully build a business and compete can be leveraged into a newly-acquired division.

Just as there are three fit sources of synergies in related diversification, there are three types of synergistic benefits that related diversification efforts can lead to: scope, economizing, and leverage (Figure 10.8). **Scope** is created when the corporation is able to broaden its product line or broaden its customer base by virtue of an acquisition. Scope provides immediate performance benefits in the form of higher sales revenue. It also provides immediate opportunity for sales revenue growth, such as the type that Procter & Gamble or Cisco count on, by expanding distribution into existing channels of distribution.

So many of the merger and acquisition deals announced in the newspapers trumpet the synergies to be gained from **economizing**. Economizing refers to the cost savings accomplished by operating the combined companies more efficiently. Occasionally efficiencies are created by combining

Figure 10.8
Sources and Results of Synergies

Sources of Synergies	Results of Synergies
Market fit	Scope
Operational fit	Economizing
Management fit	Economizing; Resources Leverage

Operational fit When a corporation is able to combine similar primary value chain activities.

Management fit When a corporation can take synergistic advantage of administrative and support activities of the value chain in making an acquisition.

Scope Ability to broaden a product line or a customer base achieved through an acquisition.

Economizing Cost savings accomplished by operating combined companies more efficiently.

separate manufacturing operations into a large, scale-efficient plant. More often than not, however, efficiencies are realized through layoffs and workforce reduction of redundant and duplicate jobs. This kind of economizing strikes white collar workers in support and administrative activities as often as it does blue collar workers in manufacturing and service jobs in the primary activities sector of the value chain. Arguments for economizing have become so prevalent as justification for acquisitions that *Fortune* magazine offered a wry view about the usual meaning of synergies (Figure 10.9).[21]

Both scope and economizing present more objective, more obvious benefits of related diversification. Consequently, corporate actions immediately following an acquisition tend to be focused on developing these more immediate economic benefits. However, the cost of making an acquisition in order to diversify is seldom paid back through these types of benefits alone. The return on investment in related diversification will usually occur when the corporation develops the benefits of **resources leverage**. Leverage does not occur through merely combining; it occurs through the extension and application of corporate resources to the newly acquired company. If we think back to the discussion of resources and the value chain in Chapters 5 and 6, we will recall that the dimensions of the value chain that are most valuable are those that have to do with "the coordination and linkages that exist between and across elements of a company's value chain." This is because they are unobservable to competition and extremely difficult to reproduce. The resource-based arguments of Chapter 6 would call these "extraordinary" resources, ones that provide the opportunity for sustainable advantage. Other intangible resources include management knowledge. The greatest performance benefits that accrue to corporations that diversify relatedly through acquisitions should therefore come from the extension, or leverage, of these extraordinary resources into the newly acquired company. Because coordinating mechanisms within a corporation are often tacit and buried in routines or culture, they are less obvious and more complex, and therefore it can be extremely difficult to leverage them effectively. We will return to this point in the next section when we discuss the evidence on diversification performance.

Unrelated Diversification

Unrelated diversification occurs when a corporation enters a new business in a different industry from that in which it currently operates *and* does not expect to achieve any value chain synergies through the combination. Unrelated diversifiers are usually referred to as either *conglomerates* or as **holding companies**. Conglomerates such as GE operate multiple lines of business under one corporate name. In contrast, holding companies own other companies, or at least own the majority of the voting shares of other companies so that they may control management and operations by influencing or electing their

Resources leverage
The benefits that develop through the extension and application of corporate resources to a newly acquired company.

Holding company
Corporation that owns the majority of voting shares of other companies, but that allows the other companies to operate as independent entities.

board of directors. On the other hand, they allow the other companies to operate as relatively independent entities. Warren Buffet's holding company Berkshire Hathaway owns forty-eight subsidiary operating companies that compete in seventy-three different businesses, and the company continues to aggressively manage its portfolio of companies. Kohlberg Kravis Roberts and other private equity firms also operate as holding companies, owning shares and controlling the companies but not actually participating in the active management of the business of these companies.

If unrelated diversification is not intended to improve corporate performance through capturing synergies, then what is the reason for this type of corporate behavior? Unrelated diversification is supposed to succeed because of the exceptional financial expertise that the acquiring corporation brings to the table. The senior management in these organizations usually excel in identifying undervalued companies, financially distressed firms with strong business fundamentals, and companies that have significant growth prospects if they can gain access to financial capital. With the injection of corporate financial capital, as well as a strong corporate governance system to ensure effective monitoring of the performance of acquired companies, unrelated diversifiers expect that corporate performance will be buoyed by above-average performance of their acquisitions.

The astute student will recognize that these types of unrelated diversification transactions are apt to occur primarily when there are certain types of financial market imperfections. In some cases financial markets may look unfavorably at an entire industry, in which case the stock price of a company that has particularly strong fundamentals or prospects may get "unfairly" beat down. Corporations that identify these "diamonds in the rough" can provide the financial capital that the companies cannot gain access to through financial markets. Another issue may be that the costs of raising either equity or debt capital is prohibitively expensive in financial markets, whereas the corporate holding company's transactions costs for providing capital are significantly lower.

DIVERSIFICATION PERFORMANCE

5 *Using the types of diversification methods available, support an argument for a conglomerate to utilize each one.*

Even though mergers and acquisition activity is a huge economic force, the evidence is mixed as to whether these diversification efforts actually enhance the performance of corporations. Corporations engage in diversification in order to derive corporate benefits from bringing a new business into the corporate family. Ultimately, these moves should provide enhanced returns to shareholders of the corporation.[22] Yet a variety of sophisticated studies over the years conclude that diversification is nearly as likely to destroy shareholder value as it is to create shareholder value. One popular study from the early 1990s examined 150 deals that exceeded $500 million, finding that shareholder value was eroded 50 percent of the time, while shareholder value was only created 17 percent of the time. In the rest of the cases (33 percent) there was little change in shareholder value.[23] A more recent study examined the results of dozens of sophisticated analyses and arrived at a similar conclusion.

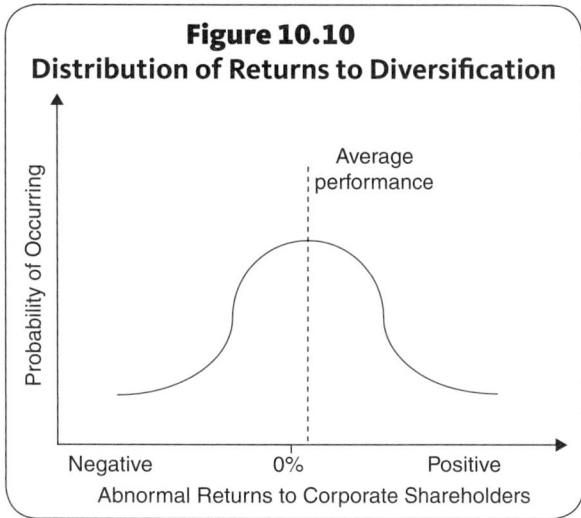

Figure 10.10
Distribution of Returns to Diversification

Probability of Occurring

Average performance

Negative   0%   Positive

Abnormal Returns to Corporate Shareholders

This study finds that shareholders of *acquired* firms make out exceedingly well. However the benchmark-adjusted return to shareholders of corporations that do the acquiring "is close to zero...[and] the distribution of corporate returns is wide—which means that many buyers in M&A transactions should prepare to be disappointed."[24] Figure 10.10 illustrates this conclusion: negative abnormal returns to shareholders are nearly as likely as are positive abnormal returns, and the average level of returns is marginally above zero. The conclusion, then, is that acquisitions on average produce slightly positive returns but those efforts subject shareholders to high volatility.

There is some limited evidence that management experience in making acquisitions tends to produce better corporate returns. For corporations that have been down the acquisition path at least six times, abnormal positive shareholder returns are created 72 percent of the time; zero or negative returns occur only 28 percent of the time.[25] We suppose this is a better story than the 50/50 chance of enhanced performance mentioned previously. However the ability to accomplish even this modest feat comes at the expense of multiple costly business mistakes.

What type of diversification do you think would produce better returns for corporations: related or unrelated? Once more, the story is somewhat mixed. You might think that corporations that diversify relatedly, capturing synergies by taking advantage of similarities in industries and value chains, would tend to perform better than would corporations that acquire completely unrelated companies. One study reports that moderate related diversification can enhance performance versus single-business firms, but that moving into unrelated businesses leads to poor performance.[26] Corporations that move beyond being a single-business firm can better utilize assets through scale and scope advantages, and economize through combining value chain activities. Yet the ability to effectively manage many different types of businesses becomes increasingly difficult as a corporation moves into unrelated businesses. That kind of complexity can contribute to poor performance. The effectiveness of diversification efforts depends on a number of critical factors.

Factors Affecting Acquisition Performance

In speaking about successful diversification through acquisition, someone once declared that it is like having a baby: "easy to conceive, but hard to deliver." It is pretty easy for corporate managers to imagine how great a combination of companies can be. Unfortunately, there are a number of factors that are critical to engineering successful acquisitions, both individually and collectively. Figure 10.11 lists the range of factors that corporate managers must pay attention to if they want to increase the likelihood that their diversification moves will produce positive returns for their shareholders. Some of these are relatively obvious but deserve brief mentioning anyway; some of them are not so obvious.

Attractive industries. In Chapter 4 we learned how various forces can cause a particular industry to be more or less competitively attractive. Less attractive industries are those in which competition begins to resemble perfect competition—where standardization of products or services is highly valued, growth has slowed, profit margins are razor thin, and companies that do well are those that have truly superior cost positions. These conditions often characterize mature industries, as we read about in Chapter 8, and they present tough environments for any company. Some industries may involve onerous conditions like significant government regulation, as in health care or medical products and services. In contrast, more attractive industries are those that are experiencing growth, and where strategic variety can exist. Since industry attractiveness impacts the opportunity to earn above-average returns, it stands to reason that diversification efforts should take advantage of industry context.

Strategic rationale. The more successful acquisitions are those that spring from well-defined acquisition target criteria that relate to the strategy of the corporation or its existing business units. Acquisitions are occasionally pursued because corporate managers concentrate more on the opportunity that a target company presents, rather than its consistency with existing strategy. Establishing criteria for acquisitions that mirror the corporation's strategy narrows the field of potential target companies to those that offer the greatest possibilities for economizing, scope, and leverage.

Cisco Systems, a leading supplier of networking equipment and network management for the Internet, has been particularly successful in its string of acquisitions because it specifies strategic criteria before it ever engages in a search for target companies. These criteria include:

- must be complementary technology,
- that can be sold using Cisco's existing sales force,
- and serviced by Cisco's existing customer support organization,
- and which leverage Cisco's resource base.

Although you may think of eBay as a purely online auction Web site, the company's business has grown phenomenally because of its acquisitions of PayPal, Shopping.com, Skype, StubHub, StumbleUpon.com, and other businesses. Although to the casual observer it may not be clear why eBay has decided to enter into so many different types of businesses, management has articulated a very clear view about their acquisitions. As Figure 10.12 illustrates, the company says that "where we play" are three related domains of Internet commerce, and the companies they acquire will enhance the corporation's ability to integrate across these domains.[27]

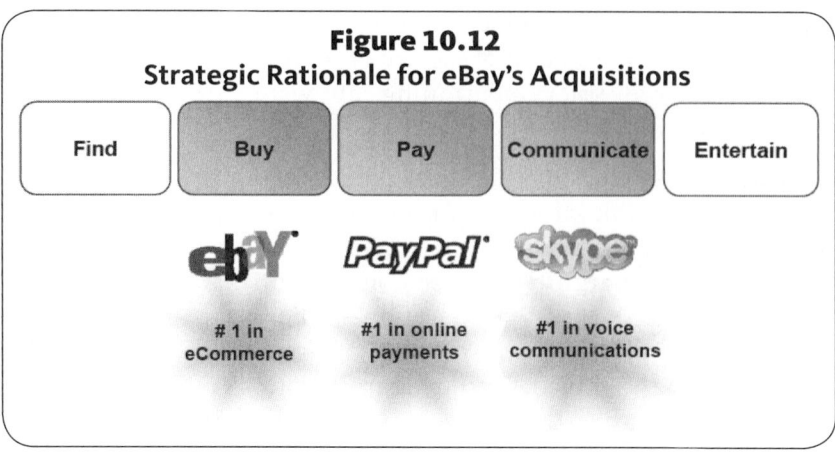

Figure 10.12
Strategic Rationale for eBay's Acquisitions

| Find | Buy | Pay | Communicate | Entertain |

1 in eCommerce   #1 in online payments   #1 in voice communications

Occasionally a corporation discovers it has acquired a company that needs to employ a very different strategy in the marketplace. This is what occurred when Gillette purchased the Duracell business. Gillette's core razors and blades business was built on a highly differentiated approach, and they believed they could leverage their differentiation capabilities into the battery business. However, the battery market was in transition, where what was becoming increasingly valued in the marketplace was low cost and price—a set of strategic management disciplines that Gillette did not possess.

Do the due. Corporate acquisition teams often fail to complete a thorough due diligence process. In due diligence every aspect of a targeted company's external and internal dimensions, as well as its potential fit with the corporation, should be exhaustively investigated. This includes the target company's markets, customers, suppliers and competitors, its internal operations, its people, its culture, and more. Due diligence includes analysis that carefully identifies where and how opportunities for scope and economizing exist through the potential acquisition, and how the management and cultural fits between the two companies can leverage the corporation's resources and competencies.

Acquisitions are plagued by poor due diligence, which manifests itself in two important ways. First, many acquisition efforts simply fail to follow a rigorous process. This leads to statements such as the following by QVC's chairman Barry Diller when he contemplated acquiring CBS in 1994: "Sure there are some (synergies) here for sure. I don't know where they are yet. To say that now would be an idiot's game."[28] When there is poor due diligence, acquiring companies make the mistake of assuming that synergies exist and can be captured. Second, even when the due diligence process is followed, some acquisition analysis teams focus on the more obvious of the potential economic benefits—scope and economizing—while devoting significantly less effort to the more difficult and complex area of leverage through management, administrative systems, resources, and culture. GE Capital's John Lanier comments on this failure, claiming that errors during the due diligence process are rarely due to faulty technical analysis: "The reason why the prognosticated value fails to appear in many cases is that people fail to pay enough attention to cultural factors. That is why many acquisitions flounder—because of the people side, the soft side. That is the reason for failure in three out of five cases."[29]

Capturing synergies. Identifying potential synergies leading to scope, economizing, and leverage is one thing; actually capturing them is quite another. Combining sales organizations and operations to accomplish scope and economizing is difficult enough. It is often unclear how to leverage the intangibles of the corporation—value creation routines, resources, capabilities—to the advantage of the acquired company.

Integrating cultures usually leads the list of reasons why synergy is so difficult to achieve. Corporations that acquire companies try to avoid a "winners and losers" or "conquerors and conquered" mentality, but often these feelings persist in the post-acquisition phase anyway. In addition, the clashing of very different cultures can make any synergistic effort fail miserably. Perhaps the best known clash of cultures occurred when America Online (AOL) acquired Time Warner in 2001 for $103.5 billion. AOL was a hip, knowledge-based Internet company run by freewheeling young people tuned in to the new digital age, whereas Time Warner was a traditional asset-based media company (magazines, books, studios, cable television) run by old school managers who made money the "old-fashioned way." After five years of trying, management of the combined company finally gave up trying to push synergy across two such different enterprises.[30]

In an effort to exert control over newly acquired companies, corporations often install new rules and regulations, routines, procedures, and corporate managers in the acquisition. Inadequately communicated as to why these actions are taken, they are either misunderstood by employees of the acquired company or serve to reinforce the "conquered" feeling. It is also difficult to start changing the ways one acts on a day-to-day basis, so the implementation of new systems and procedures often requires the "new" employees to take time away from the business itself in order to attend to the "administrivia" forced on them from the new corporate owners.

In combination, the clash between cultures and the installation of new systems leads to serious problems in achieving the synergies that the corporation had hoped for. One study quantified the negative impact of acquisitions on employees in acquired companies (Figure 10.13).[31] Presumably a corporation acquires a company because it believes the employees of the company have accomplished something worthwhile that the corporation can build upon. When employee morale and productivity suffer, and when employees resign, it is difficult at best to achieve the hoped-for leverage.

Acquisition premiums. Due to the opportunities for scope, economizing, and resources leverage in an acquisition target, corporate executives generally believe a target company is worth more than how financial markets value that company. They

Figure 10.13
Workforce Impact of Acquisitions

Decrease in employee productivity	17%
Decrease in employee morale	41%
Increase in unwanted turnover	25%
Increase in desirable turnover	33%
Increase in retirements	25%

are therefore willing to pay more than the current stock price for the target company. Between 1978 and 1990 the average premium paid over a company's stock price immediately preceding an acquisition announcement was 34 percent.[32] After the excesses of the late 1990s stock market Internet bubble, one would think sanity might return to the corporate suite, but in fact in the early 2000s acquisition premiums increased to an average of almost 40 percent over a target company's stock price three months prior to acquisition.[33] These premiums make it very difficult for a corporation to produce a positive return for their shareholders. Students can use a spreadsheet to calculate this very simply: to break even on a 35 percent premium would require the corporation to increase the acquired company's ROE by 10 percentage points (say, from 14 percent to 24 percent) in the second year, and then to maintain that increase for the next seven years. Such increases would call for significant short-term improvement in some combination of the ratios that make up ROE (profitability, asset productivity, or financial leverage—see Chapter 2), all very difficult to pull off.

> **Figure 10.14**
> **Reasons for Acquisition Premiums**
>
> Poor due diligence
> Synergy trap
> Bidding wars
> Hubris & ego of CEO
> Bandwagon effects

Why are corporate executives willing to pay so much to acquire other companies? Figure 10.14 lists the most compelling reasons behind this behavior. Poor due diligence is right at the top of the list (literally). Poor due diligence leads to what is known as the "synergy trap," in which executives justify ever-higher acquisition prices because of synergies they think they will be able to find and capture. Then we witness bidding wars occurring with some regularity, such as what happened between Boston Scientific and J&J profiled earlier in this chapter. In 2007 Tom Tom and Garmin, the two leading manufacturers of GPS tracking devices, engaged in a bidding war for electronic mapmaker Tele Atlas. Tom Tom finally bid 41 percent higher than its initial bid earlier in the year, at a level representing an 81 percent premium to Tele Atlas's shares before the initial bid.[34] Executives become emotionally tied to acquiring a particular company, so that in the face of competitive bidding they are willing to increase the stakes. Often the egotistic personalities of corporate executives play a hand in this. Supreme self-confidence—some call it hubris—leads executives to believe that they can accomplish nearly anything. "Almost all of us believe ourselves to be in the top 20 percent of the population when it comes to … managing a business."[35] This tendency is also evident in the Boston Scientific–Guidant acquisition, where CFO Larry Best didn't want to lose and believed that the management team could make the acquisition work at even higher prices. Occasionally, we observe a bandwagon effect happening, where an acquisition is made "because everyone else is doing it" and because "we don't want to get left behind." The rash of Internet advertising firm acquisitions during 2007, profiled at the beginning of this chapter, is an example of this type of corporate behavior.

Loss of focus. It is not uncommon to find corporate management so caught up in the process of trying to effectively integrate two businesses to capture synergies that they pay less attention to the core business of both the corporation and the acquired company. In 1997, for example, Boeing and McDonnell Douglas merged to create a larger commercial aircraft manufacturer and the largest defense contractor. Unfortunately, the problems of integrating McDonnell Douglas into Boeing led Boeing executives to "take their eyes off the ball," and Boeing soon experienced serious problems in managing its own aircraft assembly operations. In turn this led to a dramatic management shake-up, but more importantly it led to an opportunity for Airbus to gain additional business and challenge Boeing's status as the worldwide leader in the commercial aircraft industry.

Accelerating growth is tough. When companies spend so much energy trying to attain synergies, when they spend so much effort seeking to combine different cultures, when they lose focus on their core businesses, it becomes difficult to accelerate the growth of the acquired company. Employees worry about their jobs and new procedures, suppliers worry about their contracts, and customers become unsettled. Accelerating revenue growth under ordinary conditions is difficult because of competition, but under these circumstances accelerating growth becomes an extraordinary challenge. In fact, the evidence is that most acquiring companies fail to accelerate growth (Figure 10.15).[36]

> ### Figure 10.15
> ### Success in Accelerating Growth
> **Change in Revenue Growth %**
> | | |
> |---|---|
> | Slowed down | 19 |
> | No change | 64 |
> | Accelerated | 12 |

As we mentioned before, accelerating growth of the acquired company is one of the most important challenges that management of the corporation faces, since the economic success of acquisitions ordinarily depends more on revenue growth than it does on cost savings. Where there is little revenue growth, then management is under tremendous pressure to cut costs drastically in order to achieve the desired return on the premium price it paid for the acquisition. Cutting costs—often by shedding jobs—can simply complicate further efforts to merge two companies. On the other hand, the pressure to cut costs is significantly reduced where revenue growth has been accelerated, as is suggested in Figure 10.16.[37] While holding costs constant, accelerating revenue growth of the acquired company will deliver enhanced cash flows to the corporation. The most successful acquisitions are those which economize, create scope, *and* leverage resources in order to accelerate growth and cut costs. These are companies that operate in the upper right corner of Figure 10.16, creating value for their shareholders through the acquisition.

Post-acquisition efforts. A few lessons about post-acquisition efforts have been learned by observing companies that have an enviable track record in making successful acquisitions, such as Cisco Systems and General Electric. Although

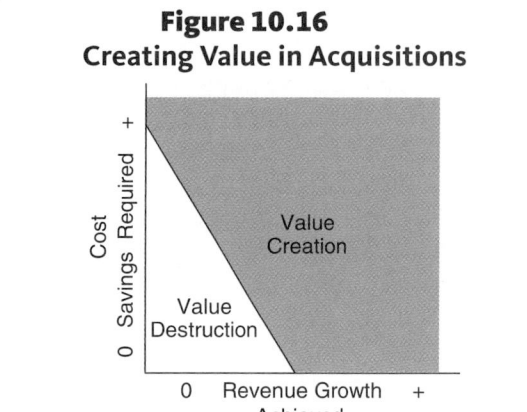

Figure 10.16
Creating Value in Acquisitions

every acquisition situation offers a unique context, the following steps seem to enhance the odds of success:

- **Immediately establish an integration team.** The team should be jointly formed with members from both the acquiring and the acquired company.
- **Ensure that senior management of both companies are visibly involved.** Involvement by senior management of the corporation signals that the acquisition is important, while involvement by senior management of the acquired company signals that the perspective of the acquired is critical.
- **Give accountability to the integration team, and also provide them authority and resources to effect changes.** Nothing is worse than constituting a team that can only advise and wait for a decision to be rendered. This slows the integration process down, and signals that senior corporate management really holds all the cards after all.
- **Have a human resources transition plan and team in place the day the acquisition becomes official.** In order to avoid the kind of turnover mentioned earlier, it is helpful to make HR resources available to employees of the acquired company to answer questions and calm concerns.
- **Implement a system that provides financial controls and operational indicators.** While strategic responsibility for the integration is shifted

---

Strategic Moves
Boston Scientific, Part 2

ONE OF THE WORST DEALS EVER?[38]

Two-and-a-half years after completing the acquisition of Guidant Corporation, Boston Scientific was continuing to suffer from the deal. On top of massive cuts and continuing restructuring charges related to the deal, the company was also being impacted by the entry of a new, very powerful competitor.

Medtronic received approval from the FDA to sell its coated stent in the U.S. market starting in 2008. In the first quarter of its release to the market, Medtronic's share went from zero to 26 percent.

In April 2008, Boston Scientific announced that it was going to divest itself of what it referred to as "noncore" businesses and lay off 2,300 employees in an effort to cut expenses by over $500 million a year. They also announced that the integration of Guidant was complete and the company was poised to move forward.

QUESTIONS

1. Examine the company Web page and determine what is core and what is noncore for Boston Scientific.

2. Given the discussion in the earlier section, what preacquisition advice would you have given to the Boston Scientific senior managers before they acquired another company?

3. Do you agree with the way Boston Scientific is proceeding to digest this acquisition? If not, what specifically would you recommend they do now and why?

to the integration team, it must be clear that financial performance is the overarching goal of the corporation. A system of operational indicators will provide valuable feedback to both the integration team and corporate management if problems are cropping up.

- **Communicate early and often.** Employees of both the acquired company and the corporate parent don't want to be left in the dark about what is going on or how things are going. Building on the discussion in Chapter 3 on vision and mission, communicating with employees helps to align their day-to-day actions with the goals of the company. The corporation should also have a proactive plan to communicate with suppliers and customers.

MANAGING THE CORPORATE PORTFOLIO

6 Apply tools for managing a diversified conglomerate effectively.

The advent of companies that were highly diversified in the 1960s and 1970s created a new management problem that had really not been experienced previously. How do you manage such a variety of different types of businesses? How does corporate management establish investment priorities among subsidiary operations? On what basis does corporate management decide to prune the portfolio, weeding out companies that no longer seem to have real promise to contribute to corporate performance?

Portfolios Management Tools

In response to these evolving challenges, two consulting firms developed methods of evaluation that became very popular tools used by diversified corporations. These include the GE Business Development Matrix developed by McKinsey & Co. and the BCG Growth Share Matrix developed by the Boston Consulting Group. We'll discuss each briefly because you will undoubtedly run into these at some point after you have graduated. However we'll also mention a few of the limitations of portfolio tools, since they do not reflect more contemporary thinking about strategic management.

GE business development matrix. Figure 10.17 presents an example of this matrix developed specifically for General Electric. Each operating division is plotted on the chart using metrics that assess the attractiveness of its industry and the operating division's strength. Market attractiveness is determined by many of the same factors we discussed in Chapter 4 on Industry Analysis. A rating for the strength of the division is developed after assessing factors such as brand strength, market share and market share growth, cost position and margins relative to competitors, innovation strength and technological capability, quality, management strength, and other dimensions. As was the case when we measured key success factors and created strategic groups maps in Chapter 4, one needs to carefully quantify factors and avoid pure judgment or "guesstimates," in order to get an objective picture of the operating divisions. By convention, the size of a circle represents the size of the industry

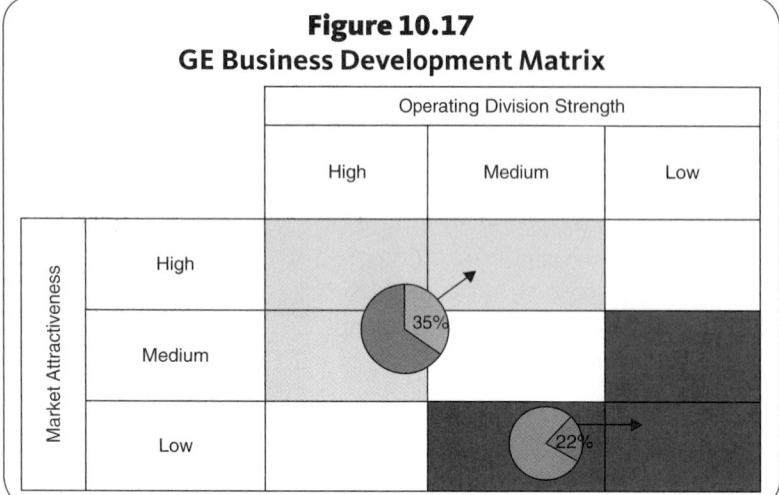

Figure 10.17
GE Business Development Matrix

in which the business unit operates, and the "pie slice" within each circle represents the market share of the business unit. The arrows represent the direction the business unit is expected to move in the future.

The lightly shaded cells in the figure represent areas of opportunity for the corporation because divisions that are in these cells or headed into these cells are strong business units operating in attractive industries. These are divisions that the corporation would want to invest in. On the other hand, the divisions that are in or headed into the darker shaded cells are those with weaker business strength operating in less attractive markets. These divisions might be candidates for divestiture, since continued investment in them might not pay off.

BCG growth share matrix. By far the most popular tool in the 1970s and 1980s for assessing portfolios of companies under a corporate umbrella was Boston Consulting Group's Growth Share Matrix (Figure 10.18). The BCG matrix contains only four cells, but here the operating divisions are measured and plotted along the dimensions of industry growth rate and relative market share (share relative to largest competitor). One of the reasons the BCG matrix is so well known is

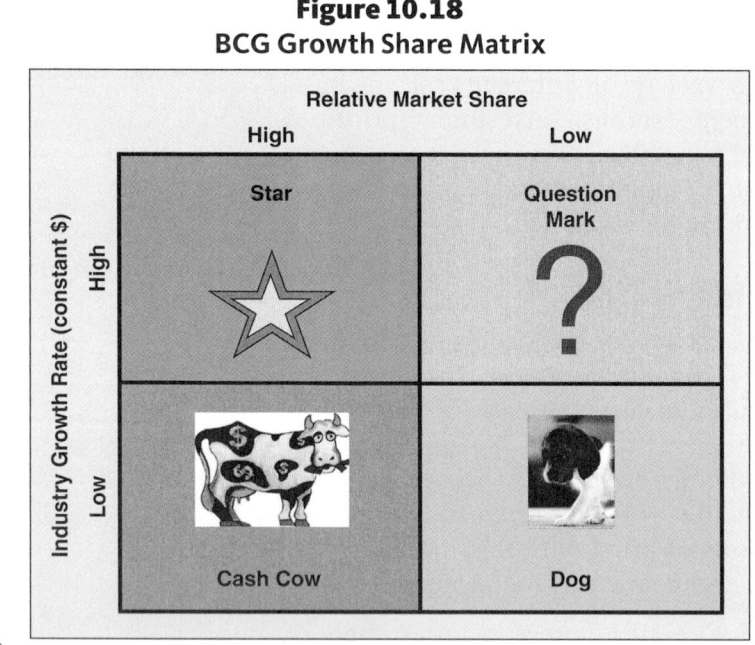

Figure 10.18
BCG Growth Share Matrix

because each cell is labeled according to its cash flow characteristics and needs. Where the division has a high relative market share in a growing industry, it is a "star" and merits investment by the corporation. Where the division has a high market share but is in a low-growth industry, it is called a "cash cow"; it should not receive major corporate investment. Instead the corporation should "milk the cash cow," using cash the operating division generates to fund other more promising divisions. A "dog" is a division that is a candidate for divestiture: low share in a low-growth industry. The only way to grow that kind of a business would be to steal share from stronger rivals, which would require a huge investment and is typically a risky move. In the upper right corner is the "question mark," because it is unclear what to do with businesses that fall in this low share-high industry growth quadrant. To gain market share in a growth industry would require growth faster than the rest of the industry, which means taking market share from competitors. Divisions that exist in this quadrant are thus likely to require large injections of capital from the corporation.

Drawbacks of portfolio techniques. While these two methods for arraying a corporation's businesses do provide a comprehensive picture and are relatively easy to understand, there are a number of drawbacks that users of the tools should be aware of. Most importantly, neither method draws upon the dimensions of competitive advantage that have been emphasized throughout this book: value chain, extraordinary resources, core competence. Earlier in this chapter we described how GE organizes its multiple lines of business into strategic business units, since they acknowledge that there are strategic characteristics that are shared across businesses that compete in different industries. The GE and BCG matrices are static, not necessarily accounting for whether or how strategically important resources in one business could be leveraged into others. In addition, if an operating division is in one of the uncolored cells in the GE matrix, or is a cash cow or question mark in the BCG matrix, there is no straightforward advice that corporate managers may take from the analysis. It is not clear whether investment in the question mark businesses will result in market share growth. Even cash cows may be costly to fortify and defend if competition grows more intense (which often happens in low-growth industries).

Finally, the BCG matrix critically depends on an underlying assumption that high market share is always related to superior profitability. Following this assumption, BCG advice has usually been to expand product lines and sales territories in order to develop experience curve economies (see Chapter 7), which would result in lower unit costs and presumably higher profits. We now know that enhanced profitability is *sometimes* related to higher market share, but this relationship is certainly not *always* the case. Market share can be "bought," such as when companies invest in a business at a rate higher than makes economic sense for long periods of time. Additionally, efforts to support larger market shares, such as building additional manufacturing capacity to achieve scale efficiency—especially if pursued by competitors who are also aware of the BCG matrix—may result in industry overcapacity, leading to poor asset utilization, higher unit costs, and lower profitability. The domestic automobile manufacturing industry in the first decade of the 2000s is a dramatic, striking example of the economic dilemma that occurs when a number of competitors build more capacity than they can productively use. Overcapacity, combined with stiff competition from foreign-owned manufacturers, leaves each of Detroit's "Big 3" struggling for their very survival.

Restructuring

The waves of conglomeration and acquisitions seen in the United States and global economies over the last few decades have ordinarily been followed by periods of restructuring. As in baseball, amusement parks, and life, "what goes up often comes down." Corporations that have diversified too much or too broadly through acquisitions often find they have difficulty managing the resulting complexity and experience performance declines. Such corporations then engage in restructuring, through which they seek to improve performance by divesting undesirable businesses.

Typically, restructuring efforts will involve what is known as **downscoping**.[39] Through downscoping a corporation reduces its level of diversification and strategically refocuses on core businesses where the synergies of scope, economizing, and leverage are more evident and more easily realized. In 2007, for example, VeriSign announced that it would sell off ten of its fifteen business units. The financial community on Wall Street had criticized the company for poor financial performance due to over-acquiring into fields unrelated to its core Internet name registry and e-commerce security businesses. Analysts had seen little synergy among its wide array of technology businesses, beat down the company's share price, and forced the resignation of the CEO who had acquired all these businesses between 2004 and 2006. William A. Roper Jr., the new CEO, indicated that "with so many divergent businesses and teams fighting for resources, the company had lacked a coherent focus."[40] Pruning out these less-related divisions allowed the company to focus.

Downscoping can also involve selling a part of a company in order to achieve better strategic focus. Nike sold its Starter footwear and apparel brand, removing this line from its Nike-branded items. As part of a new strategic thrust, Nike had acquired Starter in 2004 in order to capture low-end shoe markets, and it sold Starter-branded products primarily at Wal–Mart. Later recognizing that succeeding in the downmarket shoe segment required different strategic capabilities that were inconsistent with the Nike-branded business, the company made the decision to downscope.

Another cause for restructuring is when *some* of the parts are worth more than the whole (which is in contrast to the usual synergistic argument that the *sum* of the parts are worth more than the whole). In 1994 Ralston Purina spun off its breakfast cereals business into a new company named RalCorp. Management of the new company could pay attention strictly to the cereal business and not be distracted by the much larger pet food business, which was Ralston Purina's core focus. Consequently, the RalCorp cereal business performed much better, and the new company's stock price rose from $15 per share to $23 per share in a little over a year.[41] Ralston Purina shareholders who received shares of RalCorp would never have seen this kind of rise with the cereal business buried inside a pet food company.

Similarly, in 2007 General Electric's CEO Jeffrey Immelt discovered that financial markets placed a significantly higher value on the Saudi Basic Industries plastics business it sold than had GE's own management. Realizing $11.6 billion in the sale of the business (which was 45 percent higher than internal valuations placed on the business), it has sparked consideration as to whether GE is too diversified and holds other assets that are also undervalued.[42]

Often restructuring efforts such as those described here are undertaken not only to improve the corporation's performance, but also to smooth relations with large activist shareholders. Activist shareholders—such as T. Boone Pickens, Rupert Murdoch, and Carl Icahn—accumulate large blocks of corporate stock and then command management and board attention when

Downscoping When a corporation reduces its level of diversification and strategically refocuses on core businesses where the synergies of scope, economizing, and leverage are more evident and more easily realized.

they point out the need to do something about underperforming businesses or divisions. If existing management does not improve the performance of the underperforming business or sell it off, the possibility exists that the large shareholders will persuade other shareholders to join them in an attempt to take over control of the company.

Deciding What and How to Unload

The idea of gaining more strategic focus through restructuring begs the question of what businesses to divest. Referring back to the BCG Growth Share Matrix (Figure 10.18), we could simply sell off the "dogs." However, as we described in that earlier section, this tool provides insight only on the market share characteristics of businesses and not on their strategic importance. So management needs to develop another set of criteria to help guide decision making on divestitures.

Divestiture, of course, is simply the reverse of acquisition. This simple insight suggests that management can use many of the same decision criteria for divesting that guide their thinking about acquiring:

- Is the industry still attractive?
- Is there a strategic rationale for holding onto a particular business?
- Are there scope, economizing, and leverage synergies that are possible with other businesses in the corporate portfolio?
- Do opportunities still exist to grow the business?
- Will the invested capital that the business requires enhance the corporate ROE?
- Is the value of the business greater as part of the corporate family, as an independent business enterprise, or as part of some other corporation's portfolio of businesses?

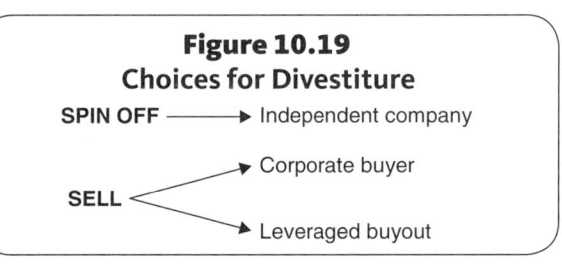

Figure 10.19
Choices for Divestiture

SPIN OFF ⟶ Independent company

SELL ⟨ Corporate buyer
Leveraged buyout

If the answer to any of these questions is "No," then the business under scrutiny is a candidate for divestiture.

There are generally three ways to divest a company (Figure 10.19). As Ralston Purina did with RalCorp, the corporation can **spin off** the business into a new independent company. Corporate shareholders receive shares in the newly formed enterprise, and a new board of directors is created. Spin-offs will generally favor corporate shareholders when the new company has a strong competitive position in its industry and the industry environment is attractive.

The other two ways of divesting are by selling a business, either to another corporate buyer or through a leveraged buyout. Most typically, another corporation will be the buyer for a business that is being sold, and that corporation will entertain the same set of acquisition criteria that we discussed earlier (Figure 10.11). During 2007 Kraft Foods decided to downscope by

Spin-off Divestiture in which a corporation creates a new company out of one of its businesses. The new company has its own shares of stock and shareholders, and its own board of directors. Typically, shareholders of the corporation will receive newly issued shares out of the spin-off company at its organization.

selling off its Post Cereals business, which would allow Kraft to focus its management attention and resources on faster growing brands. The buyer for Post Cereals was RalCorp, earlier spun out of Ralston Purina; the acquisition would increase RalCorp's sales by 50 percent and create a larger, more credible player in the cereal business.

Leveraged buyouts occur when the management of a company uses debt financing to buy the company from its corporate parent, and then continues to run the company. LBOs occur when management of the business sees greater potential in the business than does the corporate parent, or when the corporate parent is unable or unwilling to provide corporate financial resources that would be necessary to take advantage of the potential that exists. Extremely popular in the United States in the 1980s, LBOs surged in Europe in 2007–08, fed by well-functioning capital markets abroad and the rising purchasing power of the euro. Yet the success of LBOs depends on interest rates, since the "leverage" in the phrase indicates that the companies are purchased using large amounts of debt. High interest rates tend to depress LBO activity and make consummated transactions very risky. The success of LBOs also depends critically on both cutting costs and accelerating revenue growth (Figure 10.15), since interest payments on the debt create onerous conditions for management if the business does not improve.

CHAPTER SUMMARY

Whereas business strategy concerns itself with management of a single business, corporate strategy involves the management of sets of businesses. Corporate strategists must make decisions about which industries to enter and exit, how to combine businesses that are strategically related, how to establish investment priorities among a portfolio of businesses, how to achieve synergies among related businesses, and whether to acquire or divest businesses. These are important decision domains because the economic landscape of the United States has been dominated by diversified corporations for nearly fifty years.

Corporations diversify beyond a single business for a variety of reasons. They seek to grow, to develop market power, to enter new markets more rapidly, and to spread risk—all in an effort to enhance corporate financial performance.

Diversification is either related or unrelated. Unrelated diversification depends on financial market imperfections, in which case corporate financial expertise presents an advantage over market-based transactions. Related diversification depends on similarities in industry and value chain conditions between the corporation and its intended acquisition. Synergies that take advantage of these similarities are of three types: scope, economizing, and leverage. Leverage is the most challenging to achieve, but also the most rewarding if achieved.

Successful acquisitions hinge on the following factors:

- selecting attractive industries
- being guided by a well-articulated strategic rationale
- conducting due diligence, examining in very specific terms where synergies can be captured
- not paying a huge premium to acquire a company
- post-acquisition steps that enhance the integration of the companies

Due diligence and a well-articulated plan to capture synergies will help corporations avoid the loss of focus and the difficulty in accelerating growth that often occurs after the acquisition is completed. Refusing to pay outrageous premiums reduces the urgency to cut costs that management often feels is necessary, and instead leads to concentration on creating scope and leverage synergies that accelerate revenue growth.

Corporate strategists also make divestiture decisions in efforts to restructure the corporate portfolio. Downscoping involves divesting a business in order to focus more carefully on the strategically related businesses at the core or the corporation. Divestiture may also unlock economic potential of businesses that might fare better under different ownership.

KEY TERMS

Agency (p. 292)

Business strategy (p. 284)

CLO (p. 288)

Conglomerate (p. 286)

Corporate strategy (p. 284)

Cross-sector diversification (p. 298)

Dominant business (p. 286)

Downscoping (p. 312)

Economizing (p. 299)

Holding company (p. 300)

Horizontal diversification (p. 296)

Junk bond (p. 287)

Leveraged buyout (LBO) (p. 287)

Management fit (p. 299)

Market fit (p. 298)

Operational fit (p. 299)

Private equity firm (p. 288)

Related diversification (p. 296)

Resources leverage (p. 300)

Scope (p. 299)

SPAC (p. 288)

Spin-off (p. 313)

Strategic business unit (SBU) (p. 284)

Systematic risk (p. 295)

Takeover (p. 292)

Unrelated diversification (p. 296)

Unsystematic risk (p. 295)

Vertical diversification (p. 297)

Short Answer Questions

1. How about an unrelated company?
2. Discuss the different types of diversification.
3. What issues would you discuss if you were approached about an opportunity to buy a related company?
4. What considerations should a business make prior to divesting a business entity?
5. How do diversified companies decide which business areas to divest?
6. How would you use the GE Business Development Matrix?
7. What are the critical questions that each company should ask itself before embarking on a course of diversification?
8. What information does the BCG Matrix provide?
9. Why do companies choose to diversify?
10. What can management do to improve the odds of success in an acquisition?

Group Exercises

1. Take a look at the *Wall Street Journal* for the past week. What mergers and acquisitions have been announced? Based on your analysis, how successful will this M&A be? What would you recommend they do in the short term?
2. General Electric has announced that they will be divesting businesses over the next few years. Take a look at the companies that they have divested in the past year. How have those businesses performed since leaving the GE fold?
3. One of the more significant functions in a company that is an active acquirer is the analysis of which companies to acquire. Pick a company that actively acquires other companies (e.g., 3M, Intel, Microsoft, GE) and develop a short list of potential target companies for them to approach. How much would you pay for such an acquisition? Why? Where are the opportunities for the acquiring firm?

References

[1] 2007. Warner Music still considers EMI serenade. *Wall Street Journal*. June 5: C1.

[2] Brat, I. 2007. Turning managers into takeover artists. *Wall Street Journal*. April 6: A1.

[3] Berman, D. K., K. J. Delaney, and R. A. Guth. 2007. Google to pay $3.1 billion for Web firm DoubleClick. *Wall Street Journal.* April 14: A3; Delaney, K. J. 2007. Yahoo! agrees to pay $680 million to take control of Right Media. *Wall Street Journal.* April 30: A3; Rose, J., and S. McGrath. 2007. WPP to buy 24/7 Real Media as appeal of Web-ad firms rises. *Wall Street Journal.* May 18: B3; Guth, R. A., K. J. Delaney, S. Vranica, and E. Steel. 2007. With big buy, Microsoft joins online-ad flurry. *Wall Street Journal.* May 19: A1; 2007. Truth in advertising. *The Economist.* May 27: 70.

[4] Nissan, E., and J. Caveny. 2005. Aggregate concentration in corporate America: The case of the Fortune 500. *International Journal of Applied Economics* 21(1): 132; Yellen, J. L. 1998. Testimony before Senate Judiciary Committee. June 16. Washington, DC. http://clinton2 .nara.gov/WH/EOP/CEA/html/19980616.html.

[5] Definition from *Webster's New Collegiate Dictionary.* 1974. Springfield, MA: G. and C. Merriam Company.

[6] Using 2-digit industry codes under the Standard Industrial Classification (SIC) system.

[7] Tobias, A. 1976. March 3, 1998: The day they couldn't fill the Fortune 500. *New York.* December 20: 63. Three weeks after this article was published, *New York* was acquired by media mogul Rupert Murdoch.

[8] Rumelt, R. P. 1982. Diversification strategy and profitability. *Strategic Management Journal* 3: 359. The data presented in this article are from a sample of the largest firms listed annually by *Fortune.*

[9] Markides, C. 1992. The economics of de-diversifying firms. *British Journal of Management* 3: 91.

[10] Burrough, B., and J. Helyar. 1990. *Barbarians at the gate.* New York: HarperCollins.

[11] Ng, S., and H. Sender. 2007. Behind buyout surge, a debt market booms. *Wall Street Journal.* June 26: A1. More than half the loans behind buyouts in 2006 were resold to investors as CLOs.

[12] Burton, T. M. 2006. Boston Scientific faces pivotal test after victory in fight for Guidant. *Wall Street Journal.* January 26: A1; Hensley, S. 2006. How Boston Scientific beat J&J. *Wall Street Journal.* January 26: C1; Rappaport, M. 2006. After Guidant deal, a case of seller's remorse. *Wall Street Journal.* October 23: C3; Tully, S. 2006. The [second] worst deal ever. *Fortune.* October 16: 102.

[13] Vara, V. 2007. Oracle results reflect successful acquisitions. *Wall Street Journal.* March 21: B3; Vara, V. 2007. Oracle's profit shows acquisition spree is paying off. *Wall Street Journal.* June 27: A3.

[14] Marris, R. 1999. *Managerial capitalism in retrospect.* New York: Palgrave Macmillan.

[15] Golden, B., and H. Ma. 2003. Mutual forbearance: The role of intrafirm integration and rewards. *Academy of Management Review.* 28(3): 479.

[16] Technically, the covariance between the company's returns and market returns would be reduced, leading to a lower beta.

[17] Foust, D. 2008. Looks like a beer brawl. *BusinessWeek.* July 28: 52–53.

[18] Clark, D. 2007. Western Digital purchase shows disk-drive dilemma. *Wall Street Journal.* June 29: B5.

[19] Procter & Gamble 2005 Annual Report.

[20] Craig, S., and D. K. Berman. 2007. TD Ameritrade in merger talks with E*Trade. *Wall Street Journal*. August 22: A1.

[21] Boyle, M. 2001. Better start saving those pennies. *Fortune*. April 30: 186.

[22] Returns or the investors in the corporation can be measured in several ways, including the following in increasing order of rigor: 1) Did the share price of the corporation rise after the acquisition? 2) Did the corporation's return exceed a comparable benchmark in which they might otherwise have invested, for example an S&P 500 index? 3) Are corporate shareholders better off after the acquisition than they would have been if it had not occurred? This third test is difficult to assess in practice because there is no way to know what might have happened if a deal was not struck.

[23] Sirower, M. 1997. *The synergy trap*. New York: Free Press.

[24] Bruner, R. 2004. Where M&A pays and where it strays: A survey of the research. *Journal of Applied Corporate Finance* 16(4): 63–76.

[25] M. Sirower, op. cit.

[26] Palich, L. E., L. B. Cardinal, and C. C. Miller. 2000. Curvilinearity in the diversification-performance linkage: An examination of over three decades of research. *Strategic Management Journal* 21(2): 155–174.

[27] Swan, B. 2007. eBay presentation at Merrill Lynch Internet Software and Service Conference. February 17. New York. http://files.shareholder.com/downloads/ebay/194914530x0x75856/c3e92e6e-19f6-4c15-b0e7-fa02a9c36bcc/eBay_MerrillLynch_Feb07_FINAL_web.pdf.

[28] Quoted in Mueller, D. C., and M. L. Sirower. 2003. The causes of mergers: Tests based on the gains to acquiring firms' shareholder and the size of premia. *Managerial and Decision Economics* 24(5): 373–391.

[29] Knowledge@Wharton. 2001. The right way—and some wrong ways—to make an acquisition. General Electric Corporation. http://www.ge-cef.com.

[30] Karnitschnig, M. 2006. After years of pushing synergy, Time Warner Inc. says enough. *Wall Street Journal*. June 2: A1.

[31] Towers Perrin. 2004. HR rises to challenge: Unlocking the value of M&A. http://www.towersperrin.com/tp/getwebcachedoc?webc=HRS/USA/2004/200412/TPTrack_MA.pdf.

[32] Mueller and Sirower, op. cit.

[33] William Blair & Company. 2004. Presentation to the board of directors of Johnson Outdoors. http://www.secinfo.com/d14D5a.166Mw.d.htm.

[34] Singer, J., and A. Ewing. 2007. Tom Tom escalates bid war for digital mapper. *Wall Street Journal*. November 8: B4.

[35] Lovallo, D. P., and O. Sibony. 2006. Distortions and deceptions in strategic decisions. *McKinsey Quarterly*. February: 19–29.

[36] Bekier, M. M., A. J. Bogardus, and T. Oldham. 2001. Why mergers fail. *McKinsey Quarterly* 4: 6–10. Based on a sample of more than 160 acquisitions made during 1995–1996.

[37] Ibid.

[38] Kamp, J. 2008. Boston Scientific net falls hurt by charges, stent sales. *Wall Street Journal*. July 22: B6; Twitchell, E. 2008. Recovering from heart failure. *Smart Money*. April: 29.

[39] Hoskisson, R. E., and M. A. Hitt. 1994. *Downscoping: How to tame the diversified firm.* New York: Oxford University Press.

[40] White, B. 2007. VeriSign to slim down, sharpen its focus. *Wall Street Journal.* November 14: A12.

[41] Forest, S. A., G. Burns, and G. DeGeorge. 1995. The whirlwind of breaking up companies. *BusinessWeek.* August 14: 44.

[42] Cox, R., and D. Cass. 2007. Placing value on GE's Parts. *Wall Street Journal.* May 22: C14.

Implementation

In this last section of this book we will examine one of the most crucial and yet most difficult areas of the field—managing strategy implementation. In the previous three sections we have laid out the foundations of the field and its importance to organizations, developed a means for analyzing the competitive landscape and developing a strategy, and discussed a number of contextual situations for putting strategy into practice with a deep understanding of competitor's reactions. The chapters in Section D tackle areas that must be addressed for the organization to successfully implement all of this great effort that you have now formulated. A well-developed strategy that is right for the market and provides a competitive advantage is of little value if it is not implemented effectively. In fact, evidence suggests that many failures to obtain competitive advantage are the result of good strategy that is just implemented poorly.

In Chapter 11 we will examine how to structure the organization for success. There is a reason that organizations exist—to accomplish what cannot be accomplished by a single individual. When we have more than one person doing the work, questions immediately arise about who does what, who reports to whom, who makes decisions, who should be getting certain kinds of information, how people elsewhere in the company are to know what is going on, how we know that others are doing what they are supposed to do, and more. Structuring the organization in response to these types of questions is not only crucial to our strategy, it is the means by which we accomplish it. Simply stated, the more effectively the company is organized, the more likely it is that its performance will meet our expectations for superior performance. As we have done in previous chapters, we will look at this first from a broad level and then dig down deeper into the details. We incorporate some of the best thinking in consulting practices and solid academic research to provide you with a practical understanding and some very useful techniques.

In Chapter 12, we examine the methods for translating the ideas and practices from the preceding chapters into methods through which important strategic activities can be monitored and therefore managed. Developing measures of performance that can be used by everyone in the organization, along with the effective use of strategy monitoring techniques, such as the balanced scorecard, enables a company to become a learning organization that can respond to changes in the competitive environment and thus outperform its competitors.

Structure

LEARNING OBJECTIVES

1. *Explain how strategy is implemented through a company's structure.*

2. *Construct a map of the types, characteristics, and outcomes of the most common means of structuring organizations.*

3. *Appraise an organization and decide which groups constitute the core.*

4. *Analyze and explain the type of mechanisms used to coordinate the activities in an organization.*

5. *Evaluate whether the structure of an organization aligns it effectively with its strategy.*

Electrolux[1]

Founded in the early 1900s with a single vacuum cleaner, Electrolux today sells more than 40 million products in 150 countries. The company produces and sells appliances such as vacuums, dishwashers, washing machines, and various cookers under such well-known names as Electrolux, Eureka, and Frigidaire. The company employs 60,000 people. As can be seen by the following organization chart, Electrolux has structured the company around the type of products they offer (Major Appliances, Floorcare/Small Appliances, and Professional Indoor Products). Furthermore, since their Major Appliances group has been the main business for so long, that operation has evolved into three divisions, which are organized by geographic location (Europe, Asia Pacific & North/Latin America).

Beyond the operating divisions, the company has created four head office staff functions under the executive. They are Finance, Legal, HR, and Communication/Branding.

There are many ways to structure a company such that the strategic priorities of the business are supported. In the company's most recent annual report Electrolux states that they are transforming from a "production-focused industrial company to an innovative, market-driven company that builds on consumer insight." They go on to say that they are in the midst of a complete restructuring program, which will involve moving more than half of their production locations to low-cost countries. Furthermore they plan to increase the number of new product entries and to double their R&D investment. The new innovation effort includes a new Head of Consumer Innovation, Johan Hjertonsson, who "believes it will take many, many years to complete the transformation. 'Once you are on this quest,' he says, 'it is a continuous journey rather than a race.'"

Questions

Electrolux is making a significant change in their business model and may need to reexamine the organization structure to see if it still fits the new direction.

1. What is your reaction to the current Electrolux organization structure?
2. Why does the company mix geographic divisions with product group divisions?
3. If you were developing an appliance business, how would you organize the business?
4. Does their current structure provide them any competitive advantage?
5. Who should Johan Hjertonsson, the new Head of Consumer Innovation, report to?

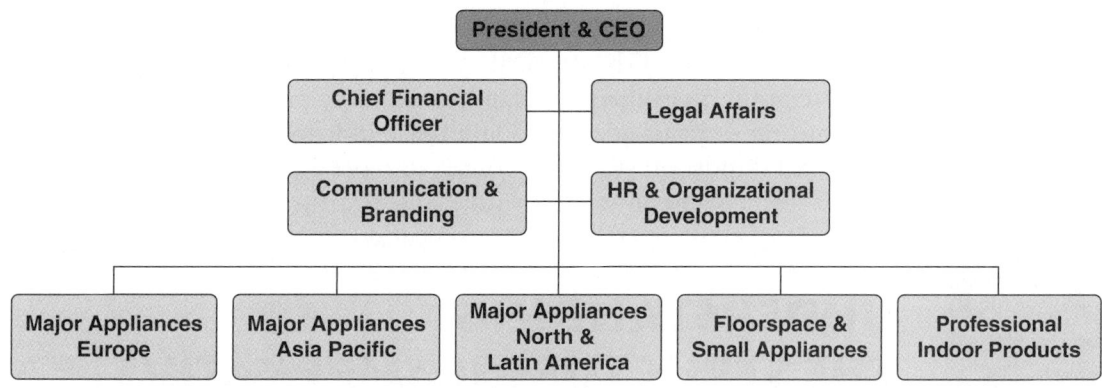

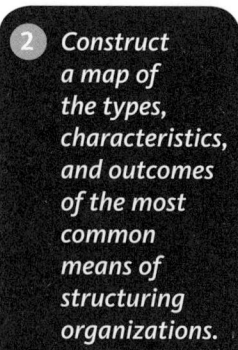

1 *Explain how strategy is implemented through a company's structure.*

ALIGNING STRATEGY AND STRUCTURE

We have spent a considerable portion of this text learning how to create the optimal strategy for an organization. This has included analyzing the competitive environment, developing a unique competitive advantage, a means to communicate that advantage, as well as what types of businesses we should be involved with. We now turn our attention to implementing our strategy. The topic of structuring an organization is as old as the study of business itself. At its most fundamental level we are faced with an absolutely pivotal question: How do we orchestrate ten people, or ten thousand people, in an organization such that they are all moving in the same direction and that this direction is consistent with the company's strategy? Coordinating the activities of even a few people is challenging. However it gets increasingly difficult as three impactful factors work against the organization. Those are: 1) the number of people working in the company increases; 2) employees are increasingly dispersed geographically; and 3) the business becomes more multidimensional with different products, services, and operating divisions.

Let's actually consider the case of an orchestra as an example of coordination. Each musician has a specific instrument and role to play in providing the audience with the very finest performance. The conductor provides the overall coordination, but cannot and does not play the individual instruments. Instead, each musician is expected to be an expert in playing a particular instrument, reading the music, reacting to the musicians around them, as well as being able to follow the direction of the conductor. The structure employed by a typical orchestra is referred to as a simple structure, as there is only one person to whom all the players "report." Yet there is effective coordination because all the musicians can see the conductor and simultaneously hear all the notes being played by the other musicians. By convention the coordinating mechanism for everyone has been distilled down to a universally understood metric—the musical note on a sheet of paper. What if the conductor was not present, or what would happen if the sheet music was lost by the airline when the orchestra traveled to its next concert site? What if the musicians were dispersed between rooms throughout the building, or were in different buildings and sent audio tracks in as a broadcast that was then somehow mixed on stage in real time? What if the musical composition called for improvisational playing by certain instruments located in different places? How would you structure an orchestra to accommodate these innovative and eclectic approaches, and what kinds of systems would you need to coordinate geographically distant—and sometimes innovative and improvisational—efforts? These are the kinds of challenges that strategic leaders in every organization face.

UNDERSTANDING THE STRUCTURING IMPERATIVE

Deciding how to structure an organization is perhaps one of the most visible components in effectively implementing a strategy developed for a company. It is much more than deciding who works for whom, although that is a crucial element. Structuring the company formalizes who is responsible and accountable for decision making, how important information is channeled within the company (and where channels may impede information flows), how budgets and resources are provided, how procedures and controls will be implemented, and how the company believes its organization of activities can enable it to outcompete its competition. Together, these characteristics of structure describe how the company's strategy will be implemented.

The answers to these questions become increasingly complicated as organizations expand and grow. Alfred Chandler, who first described "strategy" as it relates to companies (we mentioned him in Chapter 1), observed this complexity in his study of four large U.S. companies.[2] Expansion through new products and new markets pushes organizations to grow larger, with the usual result that individuals with strategic responsibility tend to become increasingly removed from day-to-day operations. At the same time field units and people on the operating level tend to become increasingly specialized and therefore separated from other operational units. This creates a new set of problems: coordinating disparate departments and workgroups, communication between the groups, creating the understanding of a common set of goals across the entire organization, and ensuring that day-to-day operations are actually consistent with overall direction.

The complexity that Chandler observed in aligning strategy and structure can be described by three structural facets of organizations: specialization, centralization, and formalization (Figure 11.1). Specialization occurs as companies grow, hire more people for functional areas such as marketing or production, and need to create greater efficiency or effectiveness of activities within these areas. When departmental specialization occurs, then issues of centralization come up—whether important decisions are made centrally by the head office or by others in the newly formed departments and divisions. Additionally, the more companies rely upon departments and divisions, the more formalization of rules and procedures usually takes the place of informal "seat of the pants" methods for making sure everyone is on the same page.

> **Figure 11.1**
> **Structural Facets of Organizations**
> - Specialization
> - Centralization
> - Formalization

The conflicts created by specialization, centralization, and formalization are a major issue in both large and small organizations. When growth necessitates the formation of departments or groups, removed as they are from easily interacting with each other, it is unfortunately not uncommon for individual departments to come to believe that their own activities are the *raison d'être* of the company and to create their functional-level plans and goals in isolation from the rest of the organization. The accounting department's goal in a manufacturing company is not to create a world-class public accounting operation (however laudable that effort may seem); it is to accurately track and report on the internal activities of the company. Human Resources' goal in the same company is not to demand every employee's participation in semiannual benefit program information sessions; it is to effectively support the hiring, retention, and growth needs of the employees of the company.

Sometimes this may require progressive new systems, sometimes not. Engineering's goal is not to create a world-class R&D lab with every cutting-edge device available; it is more likely to be the development of functional products that meet the needs of the company's consumers in the most desirable manner possible. The fragmentation that can exist requires attention from management.

So with the advent of departments, divisions, and groups that specialize come both centralization and formalization. Strategic decision making becomes the province of management in the central office to ensure that there is one consistent approach throughout the company, and formal rules and procedures are instituted to make sure all the departments are coordinated with that approach. This sounds good in the sense that the complexities created by growth and expansion may be resolved. Yet the combination of these three facets makes it exceedingly difficult for companies to excel at the two strategic imperatives we have discussed throughout this book: opportunity recognition and value creation. Value creation occurs more easily when various parts of the value chain are more aligned, where their respective activities are well-integrated with the rest of the company. When separate departments are created and formal rules and procedures are instituted, this type of synthesis is more difficult to achieve. Similarly, opportunity recognition capabilities often depend on cross-functional efforts, which also become more difficult with separation, centralization, and formalization. When centralization and formalization are prevalent, the kind of experimentation and flexibility that is important in trying to take advantage of new opportunities is reduced.

Communication, Coordination, Control

These ideas lead us to the fundamental issues that lie at the heart of the alignment of organizational structure with strategy—which are communication, coordination, and control. As we earlier described in Chapter 5 on the Value Chain, a business is nothing more than an organized system of activities that creates value.

The structure of the business should be aligned with the strategy in order to support the system of activities. So the core structure question is how it can be used to facilitate communication, coordination, and control. By working to facilitate and improve these three Cs (Figure 11.2), the structure can enhance the system of value-creating activities.

> **Figure 11.2**
> **Three Cs of Systems**
> **C**ommunication
> **C**oordination
> **C**ontrol

Communication. Effective communication is central to any organization structure. Think about how often it seems that one part of a company has absolutely no idea what another part is doing. Have you ever called an airline to get a fare quote, and then called back again later only to receive a completely different quote? How often have you heard someone say "I didn't get the memo"? What's the effect on a company whose differentiation strategy involves new product introductions, if the manufacturing plant manager is only interested in producing the existing products 24/7? What do you suppose employees think and talk about when a new CEO or vice president is hired? How long does it take someone in management to approve a budget request for a new development project, or to OK a special price reduction for an important customer who has been enticed by an aggressive competitor? These questions point out that communication must be effective up, down, and across the organization.

The business strategy lays out the logic of how value will be created (e.g., through low cost or a specific type of differentiation). This logic must be communicated throughout the company, so that employees understand it and their efforts can be coordinated. This is accomplished partly through ongoing efforts to embed the vision and mission (Chapter 3), but this is also accomplished through everyday communications and information that flow through the formal channels created by structure. It is difficult to strike the right balance between overwhelming employees with information and ensuring that they are kept well-informed, in tune with their areas of specialization, and the overall direction that the senior management wants to go. Because communication systems are even more sophisticated than they have ever been and we are in an instantaneous information-rich society (memos, reports, e-mails, text messages, blogs, video downloads, video conferencing, etc.), the danger of overwhelming individuals (such that they then ignore important information) is much greater now than in the past.

Organizational communication is more than just downloads from senior management up high. In addition, the organization needs a system through which employees can pass critical information back up to senior decision makers, as well as across departmental boundaries. Upward flows of information can provide better perspective on the sources of core competence within the company, and how activities supporting the strategic logic can be improved upon. Lateral flows between departments or divisions, without having to go up a chain of command and back down again, can improve organizational response to competitive threats and new opportunities.

Coordination. Central to effective strategy is the coordination of activities across the value chain, which achieves consistency of effort throughout the organization. We know quickly when organizations have failed to coordinate their activities. The Boeing 787 launch has been repeatedly delayed because the company failed to properly coordinate suppliers with the assembly operation, aggressive sales efforts, and the rigorous testing schedule required by the Federal Aviation Administration. Disaster relief for Hurricane Katrina victims was delayed so long because of inept coordination by the U.S. government's FEMA office that George W. Bush's presidential standing and effectiveness was significantly damaged. We have also witnessed examples of coordination excellence. Recall from the last chapter, for example, how Cisco Systems makes sure that an acquired company's products are listed on the Cisco's price list the day the deal closes so that its salespeople can immediately start selling them.

Control. Creating, maintaining, and managing an effective system of control allows senior management to implement the vision, mission, and strategy as designed. While we will discuss control in significantly more detail in

Chapter 12, it is important to note here that structure performs one of the key control functions for strategy implementation. Structure not only provides the means to share certain information in an organized fashion. It also provides the opportunity to identify areas where there are problems, so that corrective action can be taken.

We can see that the issues of coordination, communication, and control are highly related to the decision about how to structure a company. We want to be careful that any structure we put into place provides formal recognition to the kinds of coordination and communication that are most important for the company's strategy to be successful, and to the ways in which control must be exercised. We will see in a few minutes that there are a variety of ways to be thinking about this.

Prior to moving to structure, however, we think that managers should develop a better understanding of what type of activities need to be structured and how they might be coordinated to most effectively support strategy. There are three critical aspects to examine:

1. What are the key organizational components of the company's business?
2. What coordinating mechanisms are available for use with these components?
3. What types of structures might work best for a company's chosen strategy?

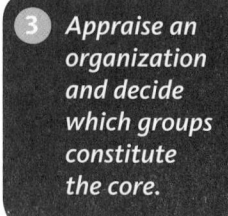

3 *Appraise an organization and decide which groups constitute the core.*

ACTION STEPS

Core The group or groups that are directly responsible for competitive advantages that the firm enjoys.

Techno structure Those groups who are advice givers and policy makers to the core.

Staff support All other groups who are not core and not advice givers/ policy makers.

KEY ORGANIZATIONAL COMPONENTS

Every part of a business must be coordinated to some extent; however, as much as some people may not want to admit it, there are parts of an organization that are simply more critical to the overall success of a company than others. Understanding the elements of an organization is a crucial first step to structuring. In general, the parts of any organization (excluding top management) may be divided into three components: 1) **Core**, 2) **Techno Structure**, and 3) **Staff Support**.[3] We want to emphasize the universal nature of this part of structuring. Regardless of the type of organization (public or private, profit or nonprofit, domestic or international), the size of the organization or its age, these three parts of the company are central to any structuring or restructuring effort (Figure 11.3).

The Core

What part of the business is most crucial to its success with consumers? What area or areas of the company are therefore at the strategic core of the business? The core group or groups are those most central to generating the competitive advantage that the firm enjoys. Developed in our earlier chapters on Value Chain and Resource-Based Analysis, the areas of the business that are most responsible for the competitive advantage of the business are the areas that should receive the lion's share of management time, attention, resources, and focus. The activities in other parts of the business, while still important, are then viewed as providing support to and servicing the strategic center of the company in the core.

An example can illustrate what we mean by the core. If we were running an upscale restaurant known for its top-rated cuisine, it would be relatively obvious that the chefs would be the core of the business. This is the primary reason that customers come to eat there. As managers, we mistakenly placed primary focus on the wait staff, then critical decisions might be made in support of the wait function—such as about when the food would be delivered and how it would be presented—that may compromise the efforts of the chefs. This may seem a bit obvious, but it is also a central aspect of competitive advantage.

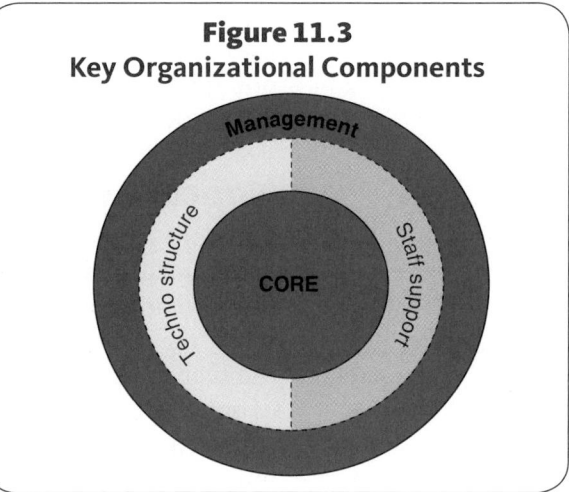

Figure 11.3
Key Organizational Components

Management
Techno structure
Staff support
CORE

Many years back, Bennigan's introduced a lunch deal where your meal was free if it took longer than 10 minutes to deliver it to your table from the time of order. In this case, we hope it is obvious that customers were not coming to the restaurant because of its supreme quality food; they were coming because of the service promise. Whether consciously or not, Bennigan's placed its waitstaff at the strategic core, and it was the table-serving process that provided the competitive advantage for the firm. It was the waitstaff that had to make the promise happen, both by getting the order to the kitchen and by getting it back to the table. Everything the company did was oriented around the facilitation of rapid order-taking, rapid food preparation, and rapid table-waiting. An acceptable quality of food was assumed to be an orthodox feature, and simply had to meet (but not exceed) average expectations in this case.

Don't mistake from this discussion that other areas of the company are not important—they are. They are just not the core reason that customers give the company their business. Reflecting the previous discussion on ordinary resources (Chapter 6) and competitive parity (Chapter 7), all other functions within the organization must be done and done well, but the company need not perform those tasks any better than the median for the industry. That is, all the other jobs—like the chefs, hostess, table cleaners, dishwashers—need to be done for the business to function. If any one of these areas fails to perform, then the business can be damaged such that the core cannot deliver on the customer promise. Secondly, they must do their jobs well. That is, they must perform in a manner that does not negatively impact the customer or the core. The dishes must be clean, the food must be satisfactory, and the host or hostess must be pleasant and efficient. Finally, although these noncore activities must be done well, there is no strategic benefit in outperforming the rest of the industry. Since resource allocation is a fundamental decision to make in strategic management, companies must decide where to concentrate their limited resources. Tying together your knowledge of resource-based advantages and the value chain, you can see that any resources applied toward improving an orthodox part of the organization such that it exceeds the industry norm is wasteful and will not lead to superior competitive and financial performance. Similarly, resources not applied to the core are missed opportunities for developing and sustaining competitive advantage.

Noncore Functions

Noncore functions of the business can be classified into two quite distinct areas: techno structure and staff support. The techno structure consists of those groups whose activities provide advice and policy input to the core, while the staff support consists of all other groups (other than the core and the techno structure) who carry out work of the organization. In the earlier example of Bennigan's, where the waitstaff was core, the chefs would be categorized as techno structure, since their advice and food preparation policies must be considered crucial to the operation. For instance, the waitstaff may want the burgers put on the plate immediately to meet the 10-minute deadline, but the chefs are required to cook the burgers to a standard temperature prior to serving the customers. The chefs have bounds to their policy making and advice giving. They are bounded by their scope of their operational responsibility; however, their positions put them in a higher "orthodox" category as they have influence on the core.

In contrast, we might categorize the table cleaning crews as staff support because they neither provide advice nor establish any policy that might affect the core. Their job is to effectively and efficiently bus and clean so that the tables can be reset for the next customer. Staff are not in a position to advise the core on how plates should be arranged to make their work easier or set a policy for how long it is before they clean a newly abandoned table.

The relationship between the core and either techno structure or staff support is not a two-way street. While input and advice from the techno structure and staff often establish boundaries within which core activities occur, the demands of the strategic core exert a profound influence that completely shapes both the techno structure and the staff support. In the case of a fast-service restaurant like Bennigan's, the core premise of the business may demand that the kinds of meals prepared by the kitchen are only those that can be prepared quickly. Food ingredients and other supplies may be purchased and delivered in premeasured quantities that facilitate rapid preparation. Fast service also requires a certain amount of support staffing at the lunch hour to ensure that tables are turned around and dirty dishes are washed quickly in order to be ready for the next customers.

This division of activities allows all types of organizations to function more smoothly as everyone more implicitly understands their relative contributions in a system that is focused on a specific method and process of value creation. Effectively developed and communicated, it allows for far fewer disputes that must be resolved by senior management. The operation is more focused on the sustainable competitive advantage of the organization.

Think about the groups that make up a typical commercial airline: pilots, flight attendants, gate agents, maintenance workers, baggage handlers, reservation specialists, not to mention the back office operations of accounting, payroll, IT, policies and procedures, purchasing, human resources, training, etc.

What group is core at a typical airline?

What difference might it make if we defined different parts of an airline as the core? Remembering that the core group is primarily responsible for the areas of the company in which value creation occurs, what if we define the pilots as core? Do you know who your pilots are on a commercial flight? Would it make a difference if you could actually understand the announcement at the beginning of a flight regarding who your pilots are for the flight? Do you choose your airline or flight based upon the pilots for that flight? Would you pay more for a particular pilot team?

The pilots of commercial airlines in the United States are typically in the techno structure of the company. In many ways they personify what it means to be techno structure. They must do their job and do it well; furthermore, they provide advice to the core and help set policies. Pilots can and do decide whether the planes are flight worthy and make hundreds of decisions about how the flight proceeds; however, they make no decisions about the type of plane flown, what gate it will fly out of, what the scheduled departure time is, and what city the flight is headed toward. If you make no decisions about which airline to fly based upon who the pilots are, if suppliers provide resources regardless of who the pilots are, and if management plans flights assuming that they will be able to staff the plane, then the pilots cannot be core to the function of the airline.

QUESTIONS

1. A similar analysis could be applied to every single group that was mentioned at the beginning of this section. So, what group is responsible for the unorthodox?

2. Does it vary by airline?

3. Why do you fly a particular airline?

COORDINATING MECHANISMS

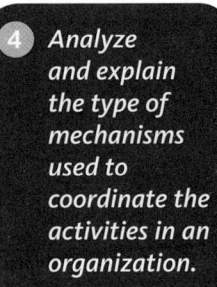

4 Analyze and explain the type of mechanisms used to coordinate the activities in an organization.

Once the organization has been divided into the groups of activities that comprise the core, techno structure, and staff support, then decisions must be made about how to coordinate the work of each group. In other words, the first step is to distinguish among critical value adding activities and the next is to decide the most appropriate means of coordinating their activities. There are five relatively common methods for coordinating work, and within virtually every organization we typically find all five in use. Using a combination of coordinating mechanisms gives the organization an opportunity for the best fit, but will lead to one of the ultimate goals of good structure design, that of reducing layers of hierarchy to their bare minimum. Fewer layers in a company generally translates into swifter and more accurate transmission of important information both to and from the apex of the business (CEO and top management team), and thus generally leads to higher quality strategic decisions.

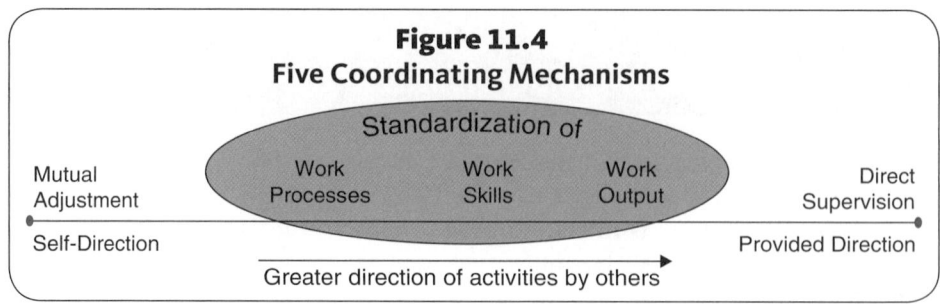

Figure 11.4
Five Coordinating Mechanisms

Standardization of

Mutual
Adjustment

Work
Processes

Work
Skills

Work
Output

Direct
Supervision

Self-Direction

Provided Direction

Greater direction of activities by others

Five effective coordinating mechanisms were outlined by Henry Mintzberg almost thirty years ago, and they have since been developed and modified over the years to fit the practice of business.[4] They are:

1. Mutual Adjustment
2. Standardization of Work Processes
3. Standardization of Work Skills
4. Standardization of Work Output
5. Direct Supervision

These five mechanisms really represent a continuum from self-direction of the activities of a group to total direction of all aspects of the activities by a single authority within the company (Figure 11.4). Some units are best coordinated by mutual adjustment, while others by work skills. Even within smaller departments, there is sometimes the need to use multiple techniques, as for instance when we have technicians and administrative staff within the same unit.

We should point out here that coordinating is not the same as evaluating. Virtually everyone within an organization will have their performance measured in some form, and that form usually takes place as some type of output measure. Here we are talking about how to structure and coordinate efforts, not how to measure the effectiveness of those efforts. None of these coordination methods negate the need for effective performance measures that are tied to the overall performance of the organization.

Mutual Adjustment

The best possible coordination method is **mutual adjustment** because virtually 100 percent of each employee's effort is devoted to moving the company forward. Under mutual adjustment, everyone knows everything that is happening in the organization and simply adjusts their work patterns for the conditions at hand. When used within departments, these groups require a relatively small number of folks who all understand the goals and work collaboratively to accomplish those goals.

In a small organization where everyone works within the same room, this type of coordination method can be easily used. Take the packing operation at a typical UPS retail store. Various packages arrive during the day and must all be boxed correctly and prepared for shipping. A group of employees, each

Mutual adjustment
A method of coordination where every individual knows everything that is happening in the organization and adjusts his or her work pattern for the conditions at hand.

of whom is trained in all aspects of the operation, can mutually adjust to one another in order to handle the flow and get what needs to be completed prior to the shipping time. Many entrepreneurial firms use mutual adjustment as their operations begin and every member of the team is expected to do what needs to be done without a "supervisor" to coordinate their movements.

In class, we often use the example from the movie *Apollo 13* where a dozen or so engineers were brought into a room to design a carbon dioxide filter out of spare equipment that happened to be in the capsule. There were no supervisors in the room and each person knew that if they didn't get it designed within the next three hours that the astronauts would die in space. They did not have the time to establish a supervisor and have that person coordinate their efforts, nor were they sure exactly how they would even design the unit. These are perfect conditions for using mutual adjustment as a coordination method.

With mutual adjustment, almost no time is wasted in meetings, preparing status reports, or duplicating others' efforts. This coordination method provides the highest percentage of time devoted to work effort available. It seems to work best in the following situations:

1. Where there is a small group of people,
2. Where the tasks are either very well known such that everyone is cross-trained on all the jobs, or
3. Where the means to success is uncertain and a strong degree of innovation will be required.

Standardization of Work Processes

As the number of employees grows and mutual adjustment is no longer viable as a means of coordination, companies will look to one of three standardization criteria. Using these criteria, literally hundreds or more employees can be effectively managed without reverting all the way to direct supervision. Using **standardization of work processes** requires a deep understanding of the work involved such that a supervisor can manage the processes rather than the employees. To a certain extent and without impugning the potential that any one employee may have upon an organization, employees are seen as somewhat interchangeable when this coordination method is employed. In an automobile manufacturing plant, engineers have meticulously designed the system so that a frame enters at one end of the plant and a car emerges from the other end. Each process along the way has been designed to be done in a particular order and in a particular way for the overall product to be a success. Supervisors walk the line looking to see if the processes are being followed and trying to improve the processes along the way. The actual employee is evaluated on his or her ability to perform the process as designed.

At virtually every organization of any size, there are parts of the business that can be designed into a process. For those areas, the process itself becomes the focus and the employees are measured against the process. Using this system, the number of employees reporting to a single supervisor can be

Standardization of work processes
A method of managing large numbers of employees based upon the processes that they perform.

dramatically increased. Each supervisor can manage larger numbers when the processes are well designed and implemented. Furthermore, this coordination method works for both manufacturing as well as service companies. In most banking operations tellers are expected to follow a very strict protocol for taking deposits and distributing money. Tellers are measured upon their ability to follow the procedures that have been set, and deviation from those procedures—even when no loss occurs—is negative performance.

Blackjack dealers at a casino are another prime example of standardized work processes. Each dealer is required to shuffle in a particular manner (and that method is actually different at different casinos), pay the winners in a particular order, make change with a standard process, and so on. Dealers are evaluated on their adherence to process.

Standardization of Work Skills

Once again, as we move away from our ability to use mutual adjustment and prior to resorting to direct supervision, there are groups within the company where it is simply inappropriate to attempt a routinized process operation. Where possible (and when standardization of work processes is not practical), we can use **standardization of work skills** as a basis for coordination. This is especially so for groups whose skill sets are well understood in the wider market. Traditionally, this was only done for groups of employees who held valid, well-recognized, national, or international certifications. These might include, for example, CPA (Certified Public Accountant), CMA (Certified Management Accountant), CFA (Certified Financial Analyst), JD (Law—often with bar exam passage as an additional criteria), MD (Medicine—again, most often with Board certification), PE (Professional Engineer), Plumber and Electrician (requiring completion of both the exam and journeyman work time), CLU (Chartered Life Underwriter—Insurance Industry), among others. Through their organizations and professional associations these groups tend to self-police (or so they are supposed to) and typically require ongoing maintenance of activity and education. These groups of people can be managed in large numbers with the expectation that they have certain fundamental skills.

In practice, this coordination technique has been extended by a number of companies to include detailed training and certification within their organizations. For example, General Electric has been on a campaign since 1995 to certify employees in Six Sigma (an efficiency and management control system) and indeed that certification has become an important criterion for promotion within the company. The level, complexity, and importance to the organization elevates GE's training efforts well above the typical quick-hit training session so prevalent at most organizations.

The value of standardized skills includes a common nomenclature among the members, a common base knowledge set, and an understanding of the responsibilities expected by someone who holds that particular designation. Using this method of coordination, the manager hires only those individuals with the requisite qualifications and leans on the expectations of the certifying organization to provide a baseline for performance. Performance beyond

Standardization of work skills A method of managing large numbers of employees based upon their skill sets as established by some externally validated means.

that baseline is what is measured and evaluated within individual company human resources systems.

Standardization of Work Output

For those groups where standardization of work skills or processes is not applicable, and yet when the group is still too large or scattered to utilize mutual adjustment, one means of coordination exists prior to reverting to direct supervision. Those employees can be coordinated via **standardization of work output**. There are many groups where the other coordinating techniques are simply not appropriate. How do you coordinate the activities of a sales staff? What makes a great salesperson? There is no standard set of skills, nor any outside society that can certify a salesperson as having achieved any level of sophistication within their profession. Furthermore, there is simply no one best way to sell something. Companies that have tried to apply a rigorous methodology to a sales call or sales cycle have found themselves marginalized by other players in the market who discover more effective methods.

Working with a large automobile dealer operation on the east coast, we were struck by the complete dissimilarity of the three top salespeople. One was an outgoing, loud, bear of a person who knew very little about cars but loved to talk with people. He turned many people off, but his manner was really loved by others and his sales numbers were the best in the entire multistate operation. The next person (with sales just barely behind the first person) was a quiet, professional woman who would wait and watch potential car buyers looking for clues as to their real needs. The third salesperson (again with numbers barely below the first two) was a bit of a slob who simply knew everything there was to know about cars. He was a classic "car guy." There were no processes that were the same between them and no common background on which to hang a skill set. They each worked in his or her own manner toward the objective of selling as many cars as possible in a month for as much money as could be made on each sale. The company used output measures (more than 29) to measure their performance. Output measures that are well crafted allow a manager the ability to track a majority of performance using a spreadsheet or computer. Discrepancies can be dealt with as they impact the output measures.

Care in developing the output measures such that they include the balanced nature of the business is critical. Furthermore, when employees are coordinated through output measures, it is important to have a well-established ethical code of conduct. In this way the company explicitly jettisons any kind of "ends justify the means" mentality. We will further discuss the establishment of important output measures in Chapter 12 on control and performance.

Direct Supervision

Although mutual adjustment may be the preferred means of coordination, some situations move organizations toward **direct supervision** as a coordination method. The first situation is when the group working together simply

ETHICS

Standardization of work output
A method of managing large numbers of employees based upon a well-developed set of output measures that in combination provides insight into the performance of the employee.

Direct supervision
Every person is coordinated via a direct supervisor and coordination flows into and from that supervisor.

gets too big or too scattered for them to be able to effectively mutually adjust. Classic symptoms of this problem situation include products that are mis-shipped, a production line misses its targets, a backlog is created in the operation, or employees voice complaints regularly about lack of coordination. Poor coordination among employees demands that a more directed coordination approach be adopted.

Direct supervision is necessary when standardization of work processes, skills, and outputs are also ineffective in achieving the kind of coordination that is necessary. Direct supervision is called for when an organization's strategic approach requires that work 1) be done in a certain way, 2) be done by employees with specific skills sets, and 3) result in a highly predictable and consistent output. Under these circumstances none of the standardization methods, by themselves, would be sufficient for what the company needs. For example, Johnson & Johnson's Alza pharmaceutical division manufactures implantable and transdermal drug delivery systems for personal use. Manufacturing these devices must follow FDA-approved methods, must be done by certified technicians, and absolutely must result in a consistently safe and effective final product since patients' lives are at risk. This type of business leaves no room for flexibility, and must be subject to direct supervision.

Another situation that may call for direct supervision is when cost control is of paramount competitive concern. The risk in striving to become the low-cost leader is that a company may not actually develop the leadership position; a lower cost rival may outcompete it through aggressive pricing. In the early 2000s Dell achieved the low-cost leadership position in the personal computer business through a variety of value chain activities, including direct supervision of its PC assembly operations. In these types of assembly operations where strict control is required in order to drive down unit costs, information flows and coordination typically run through a supervisor or manager who is able to see the whole picture at once and immediately take any corrective actions needed in case a problem comes up.

Unfortunately, ego is occasionally the driving force behind direct supervision. There are many managers and owners who feel they must be "in charge." They demand to be the focal point through which all work flows, and as such they become the control point in the operation. Although managing an organization for strategic excellence often requires a delicate balancing effort between coordination and control, these types of managers opt for control as their means of coordination.

These examples illustrate that there are very appropriate times and places for using this traditional method of coordination. In general, this is a default pattern of coordination and should be used as a last resort. In other words, it should be used only if one of the other four coordination methods is ineffective.

Strategy and Coordination

The previous discussion implies that a certain type of coordination is appropriate for a certain type of strategic approach. A deep understanding of the core areas of a company and what means might work best for their coordination

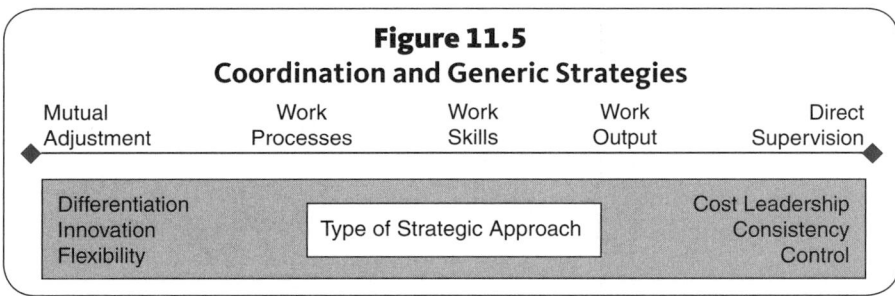

Figure 11.5
Coordination and Generic Strategies

Mutual Adjustment	Work Processes	Work Skills	Work Output	Direct Supervision

Differentiation Innovation Flexibility	Type of Strategic Approach	Cost Leadership Consistency Control

provides good insight into an organizational structure that can enhance and support strategy. There are many ways to define the core by combining up groups of employees and then deciding on a set of coordination methods. Remember we stated earlier that a company uses a variety of different forms of coordination for the various groups it has identified. So there is simply no "perfect answer" to this process; it is at least as much art as it is science.

Yet we can offer some general guidelines for the mixture of strategy and coordination (Figure 11.5). Where a company's strategy depends increasingly on cost leadership, consistency of output, or significant control over aspects of the product or service production process, the method of coordination

Strategic Moves
Commercial Airlines in the United States, Part 2

Earlier we considered which groups might constitute the core of a commercial airline. What if senior management decided to make the pilots the core of a new airline? How might this be effectively implemented? If pilots were core, then the company might need to educate customers to make their airplane purchase decisions because of the pilots. Simply claiming that we had the best, most experienced pilots would probably not be sufficient. The strategy of the organization would need to be focused upon the pilots and we would need to structure it appropriately. We could design the Web page to highlight the pilots that would be in charge of each flight: their flight experience, a rating provided by passenger feedback (regarding takeoff, landings, information provided in flight, etc.), their pictures on the Web, etc. In other words, we would make the pilots not only more accountable to their customers, but more accessible to the customer decision making. If we were right to make them core, then the industry might have to scramble to catch up with an important new

criteria of travel. As the industry tried to catch up, we could focus on pilot pay, benefits, scheduling, ego (from the heightened attention), and work conditions to attract the best pilots to our airline. Our company could gain a first-mover advantage by building the reputation as the airline that not only does everything that the other airlines are doing (the orthodox), but we put only the best in the front seats that should matter the most to you.

QUESTIONS

1. How might these pilots be managed and why?
2. Would you use an output-based system, a process system, or a skill-based system?
3. Which would be most appropriate given their new role as the core of the airline?
4. Referring back to the resource-based approach, could we achieve competitive advantage and superior financial performance with our new organizational plan?

will tend toward the direct supervision end of the spectrum. The company values a strict, disciplined approach to the conduct of its business and discourages employees from acting independently. This is an organization that is more machine-like, with all the parts working tightly in synch. In contrast, where innovation and flexibility are desirable—often hallmarks of a company seeking a differentiation approach—coordination will tend toward the mutual adjustment end of the spectrum. Here employees are increasingly able to investigate new information they receive and respond to new ideas, making decisions on their own for the benefit of the company.

5 *Evaluate whether the structure of an organization aligns it effectively with its strategy.*

TYPES OF ORGANIZATIONAL STRUCTURE

Having examined the individual parts of the company and determined which parts of the organization are core, which fit into techno structure, and which are more appropriately staff support, each area needs to be examined to determine the best means of coordinating its activities using the techniques outlined in the previous section. Combining like-oriented groups allows for a common coordination method to be used and improves the patterns of communication and the types of information that are important in managing the strategy of the company. However, we must now specifically examine exactly how we can apply our understanding of components and coordination to the development of an effective structure. It is one thing to be able to state with some clarity which groups are which and how you will coordinate their activity; it is quite another to develop that into a functioning hierarchical structure for the overall management of the company. That is the focus of this section.

While there are many variations on how to structure an organization, most evolve from five basic types. We will examine each of these by building on our understanding of the core and the appropriate methods for coordination. But we should also pay attention to the two strategic imperatives of value creation and opportunity recognition within organizations. The five structures we will discuss below are 1) Simple; 2) Functional; 3) Divisional or Multidivisional; 4) Matrix; and 5) Adhocracy.[5]

Simple Structure

The simple structure appears just as its name implies. It usually develops organically as an organization has grown larger, with many of its "legs" being created originally as individuals or small groups. Each group has now become larger, and the company has reached the stage where it requires more formal coordination. In a simple structure all areas of the company report to a single person. The pure form of the simple structure is referred to as a flat organization structure such as the one in Figure 11.6.

A simple organizational structure provides most of its value in rapid response and leans heavily on the capability of the single head of the organization. The company's business is not organized by functions, by products,

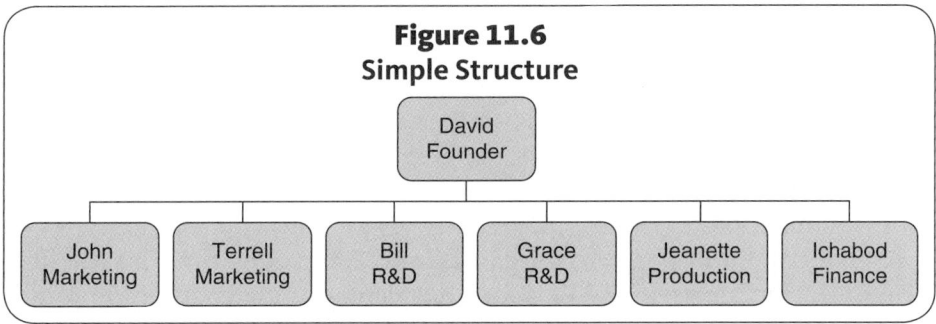

Figure 11.6
Simple Structure

David
Founder

| John Marketing | Terrell Marketing | Bill R&D | Grace R&D | Jeanette Production | Ichabod Finance |

or by geography; as Figure 11.6 illustrates, multiple individuals from the same functional area may report to the leader. There is little to filter information; coordination is straightforward, and involves strong person-to-person managerial abilities. While it requires the leader to be knowledgeable about a variety of functions, the structure is nonetheless easily understood. Since the "distance" is short between operating managers and the location of decision making at the leadership level, this structure allows for rapid opportunity recognition and quick changes to adapt to the market conditions. On the other hand, the company is limited by the capability of the person in charge as well as by the resource constraints of having to manage an increasing number of people and issues. Increasing complexity makes it more difficult to maximize each employee's contribution as the time the manager can spend with each employee is reduced. When a manager has six managers reporting to him or her, there are twenty-one different person-to-person relationships that exist within the group, and over 275,000 possible paths through which information could be communicated between group members.

A **simple structure** is usually best under one of four conditions: 1) single product (or function) organization; 2) a new organization; 3) one trying to maintain an entrepreneurial orientation; and 4) a crisis organization.

The first condition where a simple structure works very effectively is a company that is a single product (or function) organization dealing in a relatively dynamic environment where reaction time is at a premium. Interestingly, this would include many organizations in the retail sector. A typical, locally owned restaurant has all of the employees reporting to a single owner regardless of their function. Employees such as the cooks, waitstaff, cleaning staff, and hostess all report to a single individual. The ability to make a quick decision to please a customer or react to changing conditions is a hallmark of the simple structure. Value is created in these organizations by having almost instant access to a decision maker. It is said that in retail all profits are made in the moment. A simple structure allows the company to maximize this responsiveness.

A second condition is a new organization. New organizations start with one person or a small number of people and as new people are hired they report directly to the founders. There is no need to complicate the communication system with a structure that negatively impacts the ability of the founders to make quick decisions.

Simple structure
A method of organizing a company in which all areas of the company report to a single person. The pure form of the simple structure is referred to as a flat organization.

A third condition is a firm that is trying to maintain an entrepreneurial orientation tied to the founder or leader of the organization. By flattening the organization, the company is able to rely on the entrepreneurial approach of the founder and his or her unique skills/insights. There are some individuals who possess an amazing capability in this regard, and a simple structure allows this person to use these talents to direct the actions of the organization.

A final condition is a crisis organization. At various times in the life of an organization a crisis may develop that demands swift attention and the focused efforts of everyone in the company. Just such a condition has been faced by companies like Dow Chemical (the Bhopal cyanide leak), Tylenol (the tampering and poisoning of their products), Coors (an investigation by CBS News' *60 Minutes* reporters), NASA (the *Apollo 13* crisis) and others. A crisis is best handled with a swift response, few or no layers of hierarchy, an ability to quickly respond to the slightest change, and the ability to unilaterally clear communications that come from all points in the organization. The simple structure allows the company to quickly react and deal with a crisis, returning to their former structure after the crisis has passed.

Functional Structure

As organizations develop they generally find that particular functions of the company are becoming either quite large, quite important to the mission of the organization, and often quite scattered geographically. One means for bringing a measure of control to this situation is to form the organization into functions. This **functional structure** generally divides up the company based upon their functional areas of expertise such as procurement, accounting/finance, marketing, and IT. Interestingly, this often follows an approach to business structure where groups are clustered together that perform a similar or related sets of activities. Often a functional structure will include grouping similar to those in the basic value chain diagram (Chapter 5). This can be advantageous when applying various coordination methods, since functional groups can generally have their work coordinated with similar methods. For example, managing the legal department with standardization of work skills is relatively easy. The company can require every employee to have a law degree, and if they wish, can extend the capability by having each attorney also pass the bar exam in that state. The nonlawyers in that area are most likely staff support and can be managed by standardization of work outputs or processes, depending upon the requirements of the organization. Functional structures are effective organizational forms under one of the following three conditions: 1) growing business activity or volume; 2) public or governmental organization; 3) large, mass-production organization.

A growing volume of business usually parallels the need for an organization to develop specialization and greater efficiency. These can be accomplished through structure and coordination. Businesses tend to grow because they have developed a unique and inimitable method for creating value; often this method will rely upon sets of specialized functional activities, as well as coordination across functions. At some point the company realizes that they

Functional structure
A method of organizing a company that divides up the company based upon their functional areas of expertise.

need to have a structure that supports the type of specialization that will lead to an improving strategic position, and management also realizes the need to exert greater control over related processes and procedures that are evolving. As it grows, a company also tends to add employees simply because of the higher volume of transactions and activity. The growth in size and the need to better manage specialization often leads companies to adopt a functional structure.

High-speed Internet service provider EarthLink is a marvelous example of just this process of growth and organization. Started up by Sky Dayton in 1994, EarthLink experienced phenomenal growth in the mid-1990s after Netscape's Internet browser software was introduced and consumers became aware that this thing called the Internet existed "out there" somewhere.[6] Dayton started off with a simple structure in his company—just himself and three other managers working together. However, as subscriptions to the Internet service skyrocketed, he learned that he needed to move from the chaos of the growing business to greater control afforded by a functional structure that included marketing, engineering, customer service, and finance.

Cheltenham Borough Homes is a not-for-profit management company that manages, maintains, and rents homes in the United Kingdom.[7] This organization has developed a functional structure as illustrated in Figure 11.7. In this case the business has been split almost directly along the value chain lines for a services organization. Notice that the right side of the chart under the Vice President for Resources consists of the support value chain functions (Finance, Information Systems, HR, and in this case Corporate Governance). The left side of the chart under the Vice President for Service Delivery consists of the primary value chain functions for this organization's value creation (Investment and Asset Management, Property Services, Safer Estates, Neighborhood Services, and Community Involvement). These functional areas are dramatically different in size and are not organized in this manner in order to balance the organization. Rather, this type of organization structure has a number of benefits including a focus upon the strategic approach of the organization. The structure formally elevates services as constituting the core, enabling greater attention on each of these services as well as the flow of important information and resources to support them.

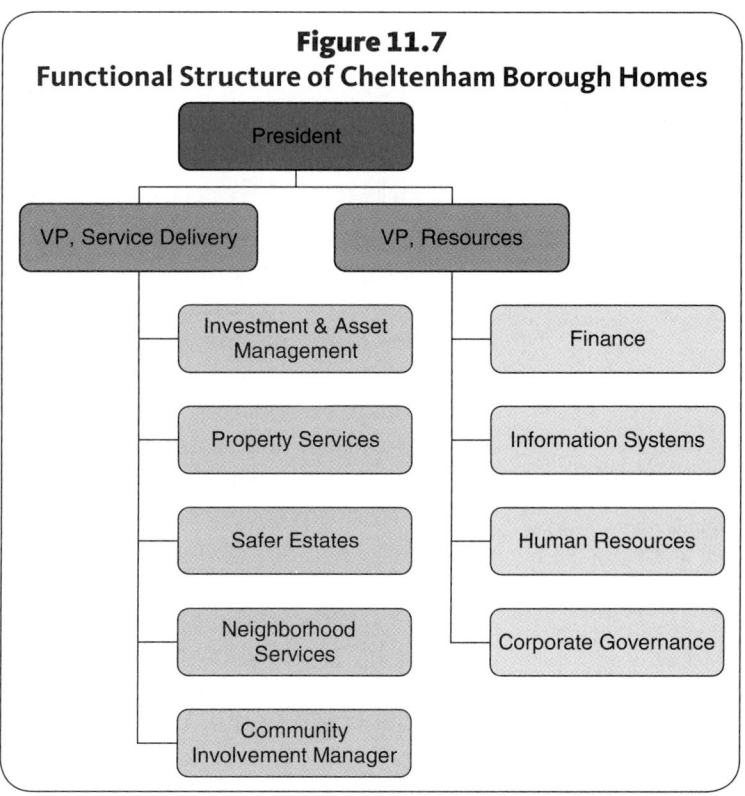

Figure 11.7
Functional Structure of Cheltenham Borough Homes

A second condition in which a functional organization is particularly effective is the typical public service operation of governmental agencies. As control is more important than efficiency, these organizations tend to be molded along lines of specialization. In fact, specialization is prized within a fairly bureaucratic framework. The negative to the functional structure becomes increasingly clear in this scenario, that of communication. Communication between functions then requires endless meetings and groups specifically designed to achieve coordination between the activities of different groups.

The third condition where a functional structure makes strategic sense is in a large mass production organization. Developed for efficiency in producing a product, these organizations tend to form functional specialties in order to tightly manage available skills and resources. As some mass production organizations stagnate in sales growth, they refocus their efforts on efficiency and cost reduction. As long as the company is in a single line of business or a dominant business, then the functional structure provides the company an opportunity to take advantage of efficiencies and provides the organization some level of sophistication in the development of expertise within functional areas.

A classic type of functional organization chart is that of integrated circuit developer Seiko NPC Corporation (Figure 11.8).[8] Each segment is comprised of functional specialists who each report to a department head. Each of these department heads reports directly to the president.

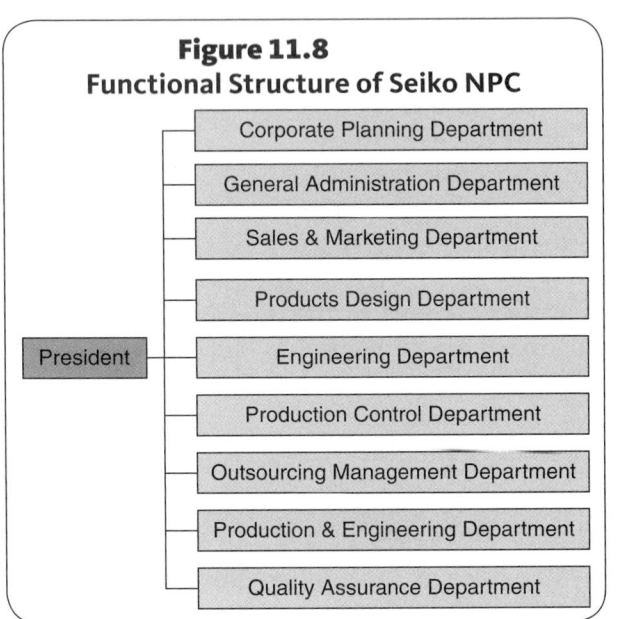

Figure 11.8
Functional Structure of Seiko NPC

- Corporate Planning Department
- General Administration Department
- Sales & Marketing Department
- Products Design Department
- Engineering Department
- Production Control Department
- Outsourcing Management Department
- Production & Engineering Department
- Quality Assurance Department

President

Divisional Structure (Multidivisional)

The **divisional structure**, also known as the **multidivisional structure** or "M-form," is traditionally used as companies develop and/or acquire completely separate lines of business. That is, as the company diversifies it establishes different operating divisions within the overall company. While it is common for most organizations to initially accommodate diversification through an existing functional structure, as diversification continues and greater complexity arises, most corporations move to some form of a multidivisional structure.[9]

M-Form corporations can be structured in a variety of ways. Figure 11.9 shows one that is organized by lines of business. However, other forms are possible. The major divisions of Boeing are organized by a combination of product line and customer segment (Figure 11.10). Other companies organize by geographic region. Coca-Cola is largely organized by geographic regions (Africa, Eurasia, European Union, Latin America, North America, Pacific), and within each region are complete capabilities for production of soft drinks, marketing, and sales that can respond adeptly to the region's unique culture and conditions.

Divisional (multidivisional) structure A method of organizing a company that divides up the organization into discrete companies (or semiautonomous divisions) within the overall company. These divisions generally contain all the elements of an independent company.

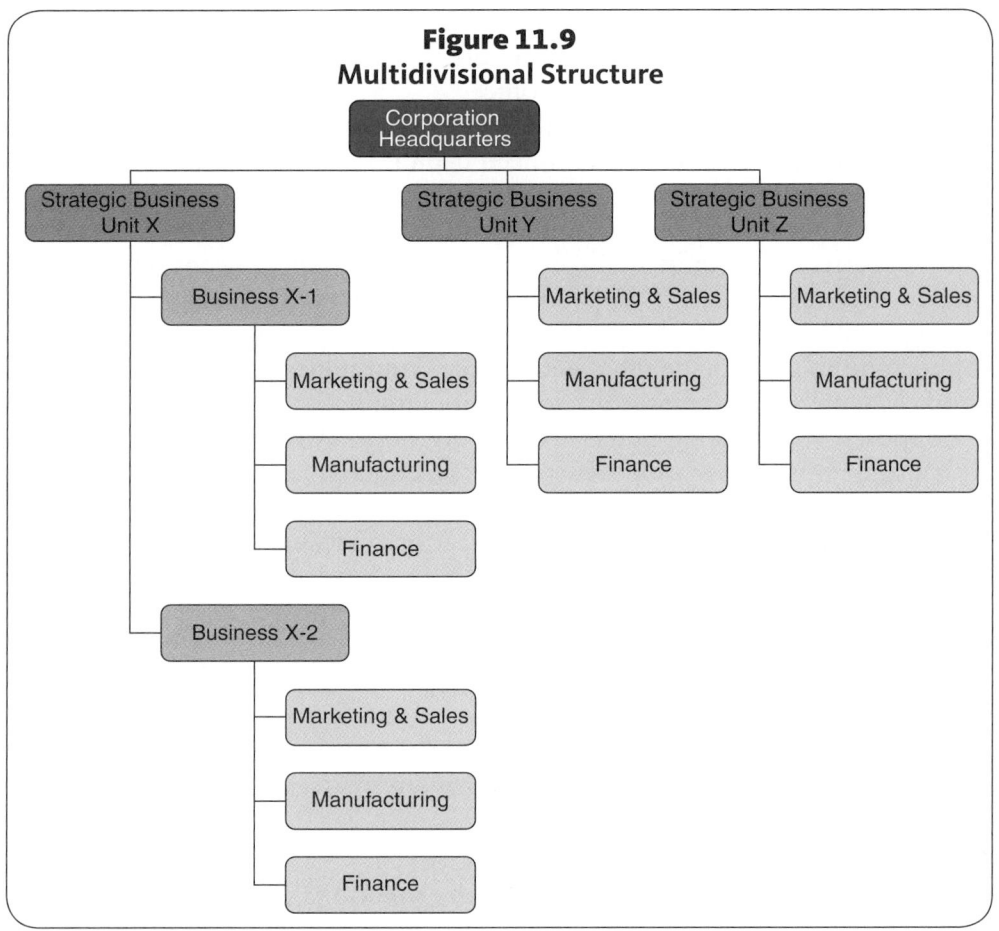

Figure 11.9
Multidivisional Structure

Corporation Headquarters

Strategic Business Unit X

Strategic Business Unit Y

Strategic Business Unit Z

Business X-1
- Marketing & Sales
- Manufacturing
- Finance

Business X-2
- Marketing & Sales
- Manufacturing
- Finance

Strategic Business Unit Y
- Marketing & Sales
- Manufacturing
- Finance

Strategic Business Unit Z
- Marketing & Sales
- Manufacturing
- Finance

Quite unlike the functional structure, each operating division consists of a fully functioning entity in which every area of its value chain is contained within the operating division. In turn, the divisions then often structure their individual operations using a functional structure (Figure 11.9). In most diversified corporations there are also sets of staff functions at the headquarters level; however those are usually responsible for setting overarching company policies and initiatives, for performing financial and accounting analysis for the divisions, and for managing the flow of resources and information between the divisions. The headquarters office of the corporation usually exercises control over divisions using financial performance output measures and comparing each division to the others for resource allocation purposes. In some cases under this structure the headquarters operation might also exercise considerable strategic control. This is apt to occur when a company is pursuing a global strategy, meaning value is created upstream in manufacturing and supply networks (Chapter 8), yet the divisional structure is organized geographically by region so that sales and marketing can

Figure 11.10
Boeing M-Form Divisions

Customer
- Commercial Aircraft
- Integrated Defense Systems
- Phantom Works (aerospace)

Product Line
- Boeing Capital (financial services)
- Shared Services (design services)

be handled locally. Here the regional division offices are clearly important, yet the primary strategic value creation occurs through arrangement and activities orchestrated through the corporate office.

Value creation is found within the capabilities of the structure itself. The individual divisions or companies need capital in order to pursue their markets. This capital is often more easily and more cheaply obtained through the internal corporate headquarters than through external financial markets. Furthermore, as an individual profit center, each entity is constantly seeking to maximize its own division's returns. The entire division is focused on the returns for that division and is in a better position to seek out new opportunities and pursue them with vigor. Communication between the divisions is usually problematic as each is directing its efforts within its division as opposed to pursuing goals of other divisions. An attempted solution to this problem is the creation of strategic business units (SBUs) that combine groups of related divisions or companies under a single office which reports to the corporate headquarters. If interactions between divisions is crucial for success and yet the organization wishes to have each division be nimble within its own market, then an SBU structure improves that coordination with another layer of management (Figure 11.9).

Hitachi is a classic multidivisional organization that is almost 100 years old, displaying a mix of functional divisions and SBUs.[10] Developed to effectively handle a broad array of businesses, this M-form structure (Figure 11.11) has functioned well for this company for many years.

Matrix Structure

Dissatisfied with the ineffectiveness of the functional structure for multiple lines of business, but frustrated with decentralizations and the dispersion of control apparent in the multidivisional structure, the **matrix structure** was developed to attempt to address both efficiency and effectiveness across diverse businesses. This form is no longer quite as fashionable as it once was, and yet there are a number of organizations that continue to use it despite its numerous negatives. The matrix organization has a dual structure such that each employee in the organization has both a functional home as well as a divisional home (in some cases this structure is used where each employee has a product home and a geographic home). The functional home is their area of specialization and their divisional home is the focus of their work flow.

As organizations grow they tend to add functional specialists to handle the increasing volume, complexity, and information needs of the company. In the normal ebb and flow of business, some parts of the organization end up with functional groups that become too large for the volume of business in that division, while others have significant needs that can't be quickly met through hiring. Furthermore, existing employees develop a knowledge base about a company that helps make them effective more quickly than brand new employees hired from the outside. All of this combines to suggest the matrix organization, in which functional specialists could be reassigned to lines of business where the work was most needed.

Matrix structure
A method of organizing a company that utilizes a dual structure such that everybody in the organization has both a functional home as well as a divisional home.

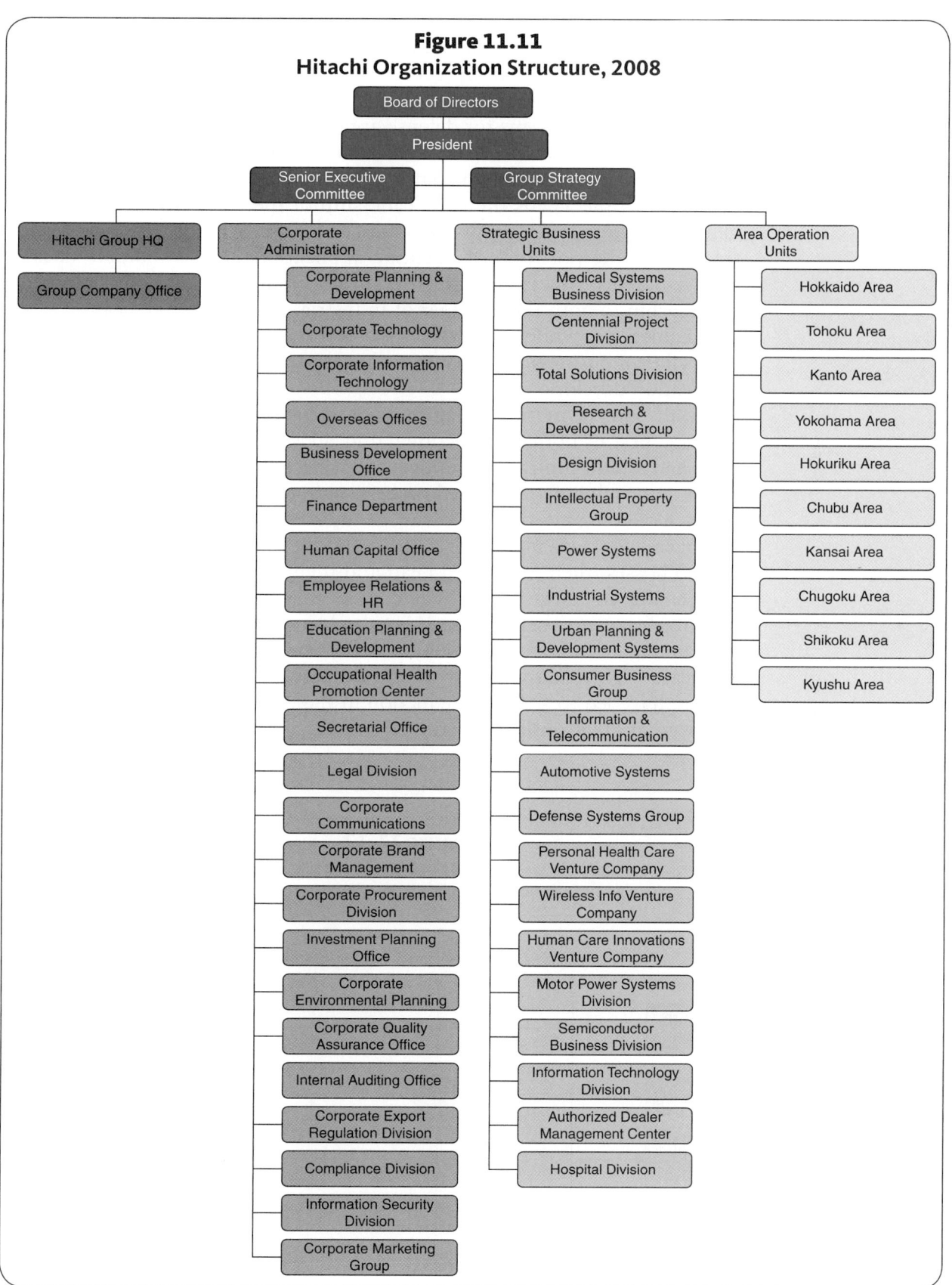

Figure 11.11
Hitachi Organization Structure, 2008

Board of Directors

President

Senior Executive Committee

Group Strategy Committee

Hitachi Group HQ
- Group Company Office

Corporate Administration
- Corporate Planning & Development
- Corporate Technology
- Corporate Information Technology
- Overseas Offices
- Business Development Office
- Finance Department
- Human Capital Office
- Employee Relations & HR
- Education Planning & Development
- Occupational Health Promotion Center
- Secretarial Office
- Legal Division
- Corporate Communications
- Corporate Brand Management
- Corporate Procurement Division
- Investment Planning Office
- Corporate Environmental Planning
- Corporate Quality Assurance Office
- Internal Auditing Office
- Corporate Export Regulation Division
- Compliance Division
- Information Security Division
- Corporate Marketing Group

Strategic Business Units
- Medical Systems Business Division
- Centennial Project Division
- Total Solutions Division
- Research & Development Group
- Design Division
- Intellectual Property Group
- Power Systems
- Industrial Systems
- Urban Planning & Development Systems
- Consumer Business Group
- Information & Telecommunication
- Automotive Systems
- Defense Systems Group
- Personal Health Care Venture Company
- Wireless Info Venture Company
- Human Care Innovations Venture Company
- Motor Power Systems Division
- Semiconductor Business Division
- Information Technology Division
- Authorized Dealer Management Center
- Hospital Division

Area Operation Units
- Hokkaido Area
- Tohoku Area
- Kanto Area
- Yokohama Area
- Hokuriku Area
- Chubu Area
- Kansai Area
- Chugoku Area
- Shikoku Area
- Kyushu Area

Perkin Elmer was founded in the 1930s based on the interests of its two founders in astronomy and precision optics. Over the years its core optics research led the company into a variety of different lines of businesses, including optical systems for defense applications, lasers, and medical imaging technologies. The company's most famous endeavor was grinding and polishing the primary mirror that is central to the operation of the Hubble telescope. In the 1970s the new leadership of the company implemented a matrix structure, such as that illustrated in Figure 11.12, in order to better manage the portfolio of scientific applications across multiple lines of science-based businesses. In this organization employee B had a reporting relationship to both the manager of Industrial Optics and the head of Optical Engineering, while employee C was responsible to the Analytical Instruments line of business manager as well as the scientist who oversaw software application development.

In theory, the matrix structure would provide a diversified organization with the best of both the functional and divisional forms. Resource allocations and establishing annual budgets between lines of business and functions can become a highly politicized process with negotiated solutions developed through ongoing meetings involving heads of divisions, functions, and senior management. More importantly, the reality of the structure is that reporting to two bosses (their functional head and their line of business head) proves problematic for most people. The conflict that inevitably arises in devoting time to the requirements of each boss reduces effectiveness. The difficulties in planning and budgeting, together with the natural tendency of employees to please a particular boss or to choose between the wishes of competing bosses, have led to a drastic reduction in the number of companies that use this type of organization structure.

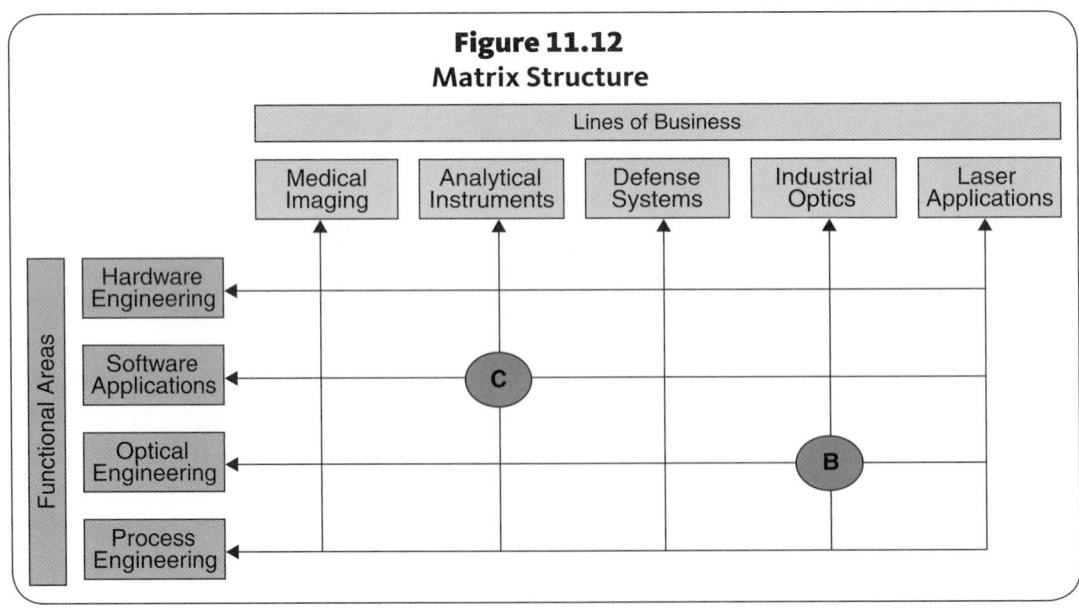

Figure 11.12
Matrix Structure

Adhocracy

A very special set of organizational circumstances might lead to the creation (or perhaps recognition) of an organizational form with little formal structure that can take advantage of mutual adjustment as a coordinating mechanism. In business organizations that can utilize an **adhocracy** there are no true supervisors and everyone in these groups function with a single goal in mind (Figure 11.13). This form is most effective and yields the best effect under the following conditions: 1) when the means to task accomplishment is unknown, but the goal is well understood; 2) when the duration of the task is well defined; and 3) when creativity is the most prized outcome.

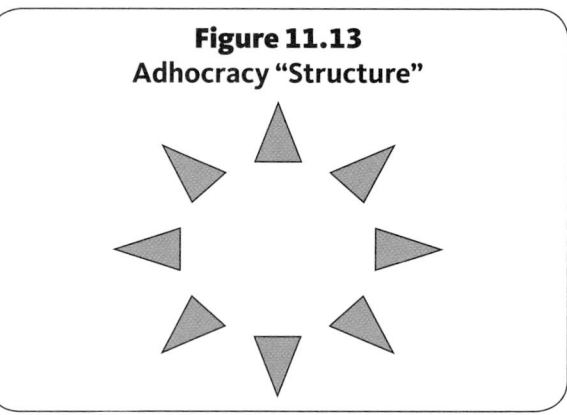

Figure 11.13
Adhocracy "Structure"

Means of task accomplishment is unknown. When the methods and outcomes are well known and repeatable, then a process can be developed and taught. In situations that are new to the organization, however, an adhocracy may provide the best structural solution. In this structure there are no supervisors and every person on the team mutually adjusts off of each other in order to attain the goal. Many small project teams are formed to find a way to accomplish some new need of the organization. For instance, a well-known shirt manufacturing company had to decide whether to accept a new order that would double the number of shirts produced during a year, but did not want to sharply increase its staff because they were uncertain as to whether they would get a reorder the following year. The company put together a small team to devise a means of accommodating the order while maintaining staffing at the current levels and not unduly taxing the current staff. They determined that a bonus system dramatically rewarding those employees who could increase their output and were willing to work extra hours in the short term would be a viable solution. The pay system solution, the communication approach to the employees, its impact on the organization, and the schedule for the implementation plan were put together over a two-day period by a team of six people.

Special effect teams that work on a movie are another classic example. The script may call for visuals that have never been previously filmed, and it is the special effect team's charge to bring those visuals to life for the director. These folks are not effectively managed in the same manner as a programmer; instead they are told what the outcome should look like and given free reign to find a means to create the scene for filming.

Duration of task is well defined. A second situation when an adhocracy structure works well is when the amount of time available prior to a decision is very well defined and usually very short. When groups have a very short time frame to accomplish their task, then an adhocracy structure helps to facilitate the best returns for the company. There is an old saying that the task will expand to the time allotted for its completion. Task success can be greatly enhanced with the use of an adhocracy.

Adhocracy A method of organizing usually used within portions of the organization rather than the entire organization. There are no supervisors, and everyone in the group operates organically toward a well-defined goal.

Creativity is most prized. When the creativity of the solution is the most important outcome need of a group effort, then the use of an adhocracy structure is most likely to yield the best result. Not relying on any one individual to filter the solutions and having everyone understand the need for a speedy solution lends itself to an approach that eschews bureaucracy.

The most critical components of an adhocracy structure are to: 1) maintain the equality in the group; 2) ensure that all have a complete understanding of the goal and any relevant time frames; 3) isolate the group from the rest of the company; and 4) free the group from any formal reporting criteria. All four of these criteria can be easily seen in the making of a large budget movie (providing the director and producer are sufficiently accommodating). The *Apollo 13* example from earlier in this chapter is an excellent example of an adhocracy in practice.

CHAPTER SUMMARY

In this chapter we looked at the very sensitive and yet critical process of structuring an organization. First we learned that organizational structure must inevitably change as organizations expand, grow, and mature. "Structure follows strategy." Structure can either help or hinder the implementation of strategy, so strategic managers must carefully think through the type of structure that helps the most.

Three facets of structure include specialization, centralization, and formalization. These may present inherent conflicts in effective strategy implementation, and may be especially troublesome for companies seeking to address the two strategic imperatives of opportunity recognition and value creation. The issues presented to managers considering the right type of structure include effective communication, coordination, and control.

We looked at the three areas of any company's organization:

1. The Core—the group or groups most responsible for the company's sustainable competitive advantage.
2. The Techno Structure—those groups that are advice givers and policy makers.
3. The Staff Support—those groups that are not core, and not advice givers or policy makers for the organization. These groups are responsible for the orthodox of the company.

Fundamentally these are the three parts of any company that must be organized by senior management to focus the organization on those areas where they have the potential to develop a sustainable competitive advantage.

Once these areas have been identified, then each group of employees needs to be organized by the most appropriate and effective means of coordinating work. The five coordinating methods are:

1. Mutual Adjustment
2. Direct Supervision
3. Standardizing Processes

4. Standardizing Skills
5. Standardizing Outputs

All five coordinating mechanisms generally exist in every organization.

We then examined the different types of structures that organizations can use, and how the coordinating mechanisms aligned with those overarching structures.

The five types of organizational structure:

1. Simple
2. Functional
3. Divisional or Multidivisional
4. Matrix
5. Adhocracy

KEY TERMS

Adhocracy (p. 347)

Core (p. 328)

Direct supervision (p. 335)

Divisional (multidivisional) structure (p. 342)

Functional structure (p. 340)

Matrix structure (p. 344)

Mutual adjustment (p. 332)

Simple structure (p. 339)

Staff support (p. 328)

Standardization of work output (p. 335)

Standardization of work processes (p. 333)

Standardization of work skills (p. 334)

Techno structure (p. 328)

SHORT ANSWER QUESTIONS

1. What would you suggest to a manager who wants to increase the effectiveness of the communication within the company?
2. Why is direct supervision a structure of last resort?
3. What must you keep in mind if you wish to utilize an adhocracy?
4. Provide several examples where standardization of work processes might work the best in an organization.
5. Faced with a crisis in your organization, what structure might you suggest the company employ? Why?
6. Under what conditions would mutual adjustment be the best system to apply to a particular group?
7. Under what circumstances would you suggest that an organization consider a divisional or multidivisional structure?
8. List what groups might constitute the techno structure of a bank.

9. How does a functional structure assist an organization that has grown from an entrepreneurial venture?
10. What groups are core to a company?
11. What type of coordination method might you suggest for the payroll group of a large insurance company?
12. How does structure affect strategy?
13. Explain how output measures are used to direct employee efforts.

GROUP EXERCISES

1. With the exception of new ventures, all businesses are operating under some type of established structure. Select three *Fortune 500* companies and, using their Web pages, annual reports, and available public material, attempt to piece together their organizational design.
    a. What do you think of the design that is in place?
    b. Does the structure align with their mission/vision/strategy?
    c. Pick a particular area within the company that you believe needs a change. What would you change and why?

2. Select a local business that you are very familiar with as a customer.
    a. What group or groups constitutes their core? techo structure? staff?
    b. How are these aligned from your perspective?
    c. What do you believe is the company's sustainable competitive advantage?
    d. How does the structure align with your assessment in "c"?

3. Grocery stores are quite varied in their approach to the customer. Select three competitor grocery stores in your area.

    a. What are the differences in their competitive approach?
    b. Given your answer in "a," how would you structure each company?
    c. Create a chart with the grocery stores across the top and the following categories down the side—Core, Techno Structure, Staff, primary organizational form as it exists, suggested organizational form. Evaluate each.

REFERENCES

[1] http://www.electrolux.com; 2006 Electrolux Annual Report; Sains, A., and S. Reed. 2006. Electrolux redesigns itself. *BusinessWeek*. November 27: 13–15; Sains, A., S. Reed, and M. Arndt. 2006. Electrolux cleans up. *BusinessWeek*. February 27: 42–43.

[2] Chandler, A. D. 1962. *Strategy and Structure*. Cambridge, MA: MIT Press.

[3] Adapted from Mintzberg, H. 1979. *The structuring of organizations*. Englewood, NJ: Prentice Hall.

4 Ibid.

5 Ibid.

6 In telling the story of his start-up efforts, Sky Dayton discovered that there were no businesses anywhere in all of Southern California with the word "Internet" in their company names as late as 1993.

7 http://www.cheltborohomes.org/libraries/templates/page.asp?URN=2225.

8 http://www.npc.co.jp/en/general/chart.html.

9 Chandler, A. D. 1962. *Strategy and structure*. Cambridge, MA: MIT Press.

10 http://www.hitachi.com/about/corporate/organization/index.html.

Control and Performance

LEARNING OBJECTIVES

1. Translate strategy into functional area goals and activities using the keys to implementation control.

2. Develop effective metrics for the control and growth of the organization.

3. Describe the differences between the models used for implementing a strategic plan.

4. Name the core responsibilities of strategic leadership.

McDonald's[1]

McDonald's was a one-store business in San Bernardino, California, run by brothers Dick and Mac McDonald. In 1954 Ray Kroc convinced them to let him open several more restaurants based on their process-based business formula. The astounding success of the company is a testament to tenacity and a striving for perfection in a business that primarily sells hamburgers, sodas, and french fries.

During the next forty-plus years, McDonald's grew to a worldwide organization with more than 31,000 restaurants in 118 different countries. McDonald's was the first fast food chain to have a drive-thru window (1975); offer breakfast (1977); and create whole product categories such as the Happy Meal (1979) and the Chicken McNugget (1983).

The elimination of a corporate program for the evaluation of stores, a focus on international expansion and a lack of focus on the nuts and bolts of the core business set off a terrible sales decline in the mid to late 1990s. This was accelerated by a rapid growth in competitors, dramatic improvements in competitors' processes, a set of international crises, a focus on healthy eating, and the release of the film *Super Size Me,* which took direct aim at McDonald's as the purveyor of an unhealthy lifestyle.

In January 2003, McDonald's reported their first-ever quarterly loss ($343 million). Same-store sales (a critical metric for store health), which had been stagnant for the past ten years (not a good sign) fell for fourteen straight months through the first quarter of 2003. The company's rating amongst consumers ranked it last among seventy fast food chains measured that same year. McDonald's was in trouble.

Jim Cantalupo (newly re-minted CEO in 2003) came out of retirement to fix the company, after having been with the company in various capacities for more than twenty-eight years. He developed an approach that was back to basics.

He focused on the McDonald's brand by systematically eliminating or reducing the importance of other brands the company had picked up during the years. These included: Chipotle, Boston Market, Fazoli's, Donato Pizzeria, and Pret a Manger. He cancelled big IT initiatives started by his predecessor and virtually halted the new store building program.

His next step was to determine what the key value drivers were for the company. The company looked to its foundation with Ray Kroc, who had restated in his autobiography what a consulting company previously concluded. "The basis of McDonald's success is serving low-priced value oriented product fast and efficiently in clean and pleasant surroundings." Cantalupo said "Those are the greens fees; unless you execute (those basics) you go nowhere."

So McDonald's had its marching orders. The only question left was would they be able to execute the strategy? Quite honestly, most analysts were quite skeptical and openly predicted his ouster in the next eighteen months.

Questions

1. Do you believe that this approach was the best one for McDonald's to take at the time?
2. How would you organize the company to implement this approach?
3. How would you suggest they measure success?
4. Will their efforts provide them any competitive advantage?

LEADERSHIP

KEYS TO IMPLEMENTATION CONTROL

Far too much time, money, effort, and goodwill is devoted to the development of an effective strategy for its implementation to be ignored or handed off to lower-level employees as something beneath the attention of senior management. Having worked through the process of strategy design and development, it is now time to implement all that has been decided. This can best be done by approaching the issue as a process that simultaneously provides control and yet ensures that the performance of the organization is tied to the mission.

There are a number of methods that exist for coordinating the implementation of strategy. However, all of them begin with metrics. In this chapter we will examine the development of metrics (measures of performance) and then discuss three of the most popular implementation approaches: 1) the balanced scorecard, 2) the value-driver-action model, and 3) the 7-S framework.

Prior to that discussion it is critical that you understand that there are five overall keys to implementation control. These should be kept in mind as you read on, and should be the characteristics by which all your implementation efforts are considered.

Key #1—Fit

There is no more important concept to keep in mind than that of fit. The complete alignment of the company's strategy, structure, and value chain is crucial to its success. Companies are difficult to align and there are many aspects, both formal and informal, that need to be dealt with in order to attain fit. Imagine a Google where every employee was required to be in his or her cubicle by 8 A.M. and the dress code was a business suit. Or you walk into a bank branch where there is trash on the floor and the tellers don't seem to have a handle on how to do simple math. Have you recently called the 800-number for a company that distinguished itself in the marketplace through its customer service—only to find that you are kept on hold for twenty minutes waiting for an operator who ultimately does not have the authority to correct the error the company originally made? How might a company such as Apple Computer perform if it was led by a rigid, bureaucratic leader whose entire goal was organizational efficiency? These simple examples point out the most elementary aspects of the need for fit.

Key #2—Clear and Compelling Objectives

Implementation is a process of attempting to get everyone in the organization moving in the same direction. It is an effort to focus all the energy of the organization toward achieving a set of objectives. This is far easier to do if the objectives are not only clear to all the employees of the company, but also if every employee feels that he or she has the ability to truly contribute to that achievement. Far too often companies have a very general objective to grow sales or to increase profitability, which are simultaneously uninspiring and remote. People who not only understand a compelling set of objectives, but also how they can contribute to their success, will pour out their energy and ability in an attempt to achieve them. We should break down every high-level objective within a company into definable metrics that are relevant and important to employees, in order to help the company achieve its goals.

Key #3—A Single Company Currency

One of the quickest ways to dismantle an effective plan is to provide different employees with different types of performance incentives, resulting in internal conflicts and inconsistent actions. Most reward systems are based upon some metric that would be representative of strong performance, whether it is bonuses, merit pay increases, stock options, stock grants, ESOP plans, and the list goes on. Virtually every type of "currency" has been tried. However, one of the tried and true success factors in effective strategy implementation has been for companies to reward as many people as possible in the organization using the same "currency." Jack Welch talked at length about the success at General Electric as he shifted more and more people over to a system where they were rewarded with General Electric stock. Individual bonuses still existed, but they were just a very small part of the compensation package as was any reward tied to the particular part of the company that person was working for within the General Electric family.[2] The financial rewards were primarily tied to the success of the parent company stock, and it was that single currency system that helped focus employees in a widely disparate conglomerate on a single overarching financial performance goal.

Key #4—Top-Management Involvement

Implementation has been regarded by some as that dirty business that is "operational," not "strategic," and therefore beneath the role of senior management. Absolutely nothing could be further from the truth. A well-designed strategy that is not effectively implemented is useless. One of the most important functions of the executive is seeing that strategy is executed well. Larry Bossidy (retired CEO of Honeywell and Allied Signal) and Ram Charan stated in their book (*Execution: The Discipline of Getting Things Done*) that execution is: "…a central part of a company's strategy and its goals and the major job of any leader in business.…"[3]

Key #5—Resource Allocation

Strategy implementation is about action and the commitment of resources. A strategic plan that does not include a commitment of resources is doomed from the start. The concept of resources is broad and includes people, finances, plant and equipment, knowledge, time, and support, among others. One of the best ways to see if a company is truly committed to its stated strategic plans is to look at its resource allocations. A mismatch suggests either a lack of consistent follow-through in the management of the strategy, or alternative and competing priorities that are not aligned with the stated direction. Both situations are a recipe for disaster.

Keep these five overarching keys to successful implementation in mind as you read this chapter. These principles should help in organizing what is inherently a messy and difficult part of strategic management.

The refinement of an overarching strategy into a workable program is a process of continuous improvement and of iteration. Refer back to Figure 1.6 in Chapter 1, in which we discussed the "feedback" arrows suggesting that what managers observe and learn about implementation efforts through structuring and internal control provides guidance for how to go back and modify the strategic approach. Separating Strategy Formulation from Strategy Implementation and Evaluation (Figure 1.6) is something of an artifact arising from how strategy concepts have historically been taught in a logical and sequential fashion. In practice, though, they are combined and continuous, constituting what many refer to as the "learning organization."

2 *Develop effective metrics for the control and growth of the organization.*

METRICS

Strategy implementation is focused on defining what constitutes success, the means to get there, and the ability to measure its achievement. The development of metrics is both a key to that process and simultaneously difficult to achieve. Metrics should be tied to the overall goals of the organization and then translated by management to the most basic levels of the company. Virtually all of the efforts in the company should be tied to an overarching set of corporate metrics. Work effort that is not related directly to one of the goals of the organization should be eliminated, outsourced, or minimized.

That said, the development of metrics is made much easier with the understanding that all companies have to balance their work effort toward the simultaneous movement forward on a number of fronts. One of the key challenges in strategic management is the effective implementation of the wide variety of activities that constitute the essential value chain.

A company that singly focuses on its financial performance will probably distort the actions of their employees toward a "whatever yields returns must be good" approach that leads to embarrassing and debilitating scandals like those at Tyco and Enron. A single focus upon market share, for example, can produce excesses that lead to unprofitable distortions where sales are maintained by cannibalizing profit, quality, or other critical areas, much as what happened at Gateway Computers through most of the past decade. Effective strategy implementation adopts the basic premise of a balanced need across multiple domains of the business; strategy implementation must build upon and reflect the tenets of value chain and the complexity of the company's resources and capabilities.

In Chapter 2 we discussed in some detail how performance measures may be used to discern the strategy in use within a company. In reference to the role of the top management, we pointed out that companies deal with a multitude of stakeholders who have complex and diverse wants from the organization. Therefore all companies must have measures of performance that are both quantitative and qualitative. We now want to extend this performance measurement perspective and apply it inside the company as a means of focusing employee effort.

Every company has (or should have) a unique mission and a unique means of competing. Therefore it is crucial that the metrics of the company be unique to its mission. ROE is a good general measure of performance across an industry, but says precious little about how a particular company is achieving its individual mission internally. The mission goals of your organization are the means by which you hope to draw in increasing numbers of customers returning to you an increasing economic profit. Therefore, metrics should meet the following criteria (Figure 12.1):

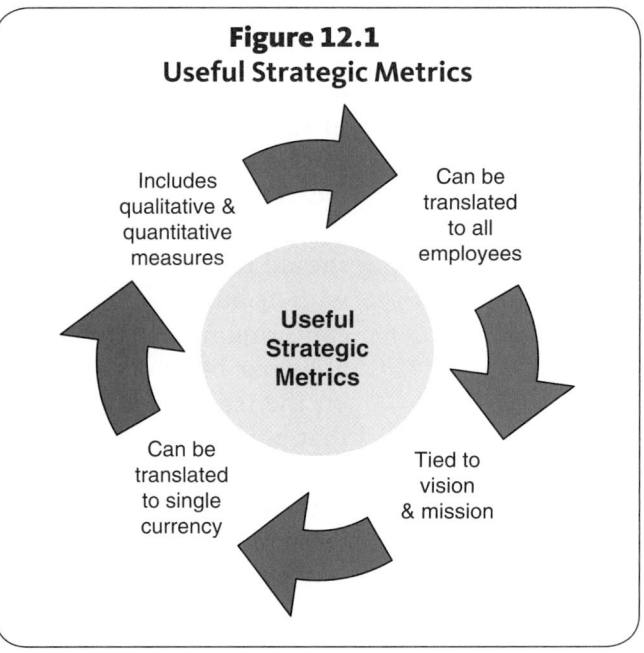

Figure 12.1
Useful Strategic Metrics

1. Be tied to the overall mission/vision of the organization
2. Be composed of both quantitative and qualitative measures of performance
3. Can be translated to all levels of employees within the organization
4. Can be ultimately translated to a single corporate "currency"

Metrics Tied to the Mission/Vision

The most fundamental issue regarding the creation of useful metrics is ensuring that they are tied directly to the mission and vision of the company. It is relatively easy for a company to get caught up in the development of easily measured, but generally unhelpful measures of activity and/or performance. The mission statement for the organization should provide the guidance for the kind of value the company seeks to create, and therefore the types of metrics that will provide guidance on how well the company is creating value.

Consider the mission statement points for the Coca-Cola Company:[4]

- **To Refresh the World** . . . in body, mind, and spirit.
- **To Inspire Moments of Optimism** . . . through our brands and our actions.
- **To Create Value and Make a Difference** . . . everywhere we engage.

This mission statement suggests that there is a set of values that the company seeks to create in its business. These include the psychological and physical benefits of consuming its beverage products, the creation of a relationship with stakeholders that transcends mere consumption of food products, and a substantive contribution to communities and populations with which the company engages. If these values do indeed reflect the mission of Coca-Cola as a company, then it is incumbent upon the senior management to initiate activities that directly support the implementation of these values. In turn, management will need to develop metrics that will allow them to track these activities and evaluate their progress toward achieving the value creation they envision.

The point here is that the metrics that a company decides to employ should reflect the mission and the strategic approach the company is taking with its business. If the company is pursuing a differentiation approach, then capturing information about efforts to reduce costs will be unproductive in allowing top management to understand whether progress is being made on the true strategic agenda. Unless "brand image" is a key success factor that parallels "low cost" in being able to effectively compete in an industry, then precious management time, attention, and resources might be used up gathering data on the effectiveness of a company's advertising campaign or the reputational effect of its product logo.

We have already discussed basic financial measures, such as ROE, as a comparative measure of performance in Chapter 2. However, the kinds of metrics we refer to for implementation are those that guide the internal activities of the business in order to maintain strategic consistency, and that allow senior management to understand whether the company is making positive progress in the pursuit of its strategic goals.

Recall from Chapter 1 that strategic management has to do with making substantive decisions affecting every area of the company, the results of which may not be apparent for a long period of time (in some cases years). Between the time an important strategic decision is made and the time when the results of that decision are clearly apparent in the form of enhanced economic returns, senior management must somehow gain insight as to whether the company is actually making progress. Creating insightful performance metrics allows senior management to assess progress, to enhance initiatives that are working well, and to change those that are not. Thus an interim set of metrics provides a means for senior management to exert strategic control.

Measures of Performance

Companies should develop a list of performance measures that are a mix of both **quantitative metrics** and **qualitative metrics**. All performance measures need to account for two aspects: 1) The current state of the measure and 2) a means for ensuring that the measure is comparable to competitors. The current state of the measure requires that we need to establish where the metric is at the present time so that we can measure its relative movement going forward. In general, absolute measures of increase are not nearly as valuable as are relative measures. If the organization has determined that an important criteria for the success of the company is high quality (for example, when uniquely high quality is an effective differentiator in the market), then it might create a new metric that measures defects. This gives the organization

Quantitative metrics
Numerically based measures of firm success.

Qualitative metrics
Measures of success that are descriptive and relative rather than point-specific.

three important issues to deal with. The first is the establishment of the current defect rate. Taking a random sample of products over some period of time (created in a scientific manner so that it can be replicated in the future), the firm should establish the current average defect rate as well as the range of defects experienced. Secondly the firm must decide by what denominator they will divide the defect rate, such that they can compare their performance to the industry. Comparing the raw number of defects produced by a small shop and a multinational business is not of much value unless we can equalize the measure. Defects per thousand products produced, defects per employee, defects per volume shipped are among those that will provide valuable insight into the metric and the changes in that metric. Finally, the same average defect rate should be calculated, estimated, or researched for each of the company's direct competitors.

With quantitative performance metrics, averages are often used; however, they are not nearly as important a measure of performance improvement as is range. The average defect rate across all production shifts may be 10 per thousand produced, but the defect rates vary by production shift, sometimes as low as 5 per thousand and sometimes as high as 50 per thousand. The variation in a metric is therefore an extraordinarily powerful measure of performance improvement, since it highlights one of the most compelling issues in managing toward the strategic improvement of a company.

Assume that the defect rate is 10 for every thousand products produced (we are keeping the numbers simple for illustration, realizing that a defect rate of 10 in a thousand is ordinarily a recipe for disaster in most companies). After significant efforts at reducing this rate the company is pleased to announce a 20 percent improvement to 8 per thousand. What those numbers don't show is the range of defects, and this would illustrate what customers will actually experience and more importantly what will matter to them. If the range per thousand moves from 5 to 100 defects beforehand but now runs from 3 defects to 200 defects, it shows that nominal improvements in the average defect rate have come at the expense of greater volatility (Figure 12.2). This

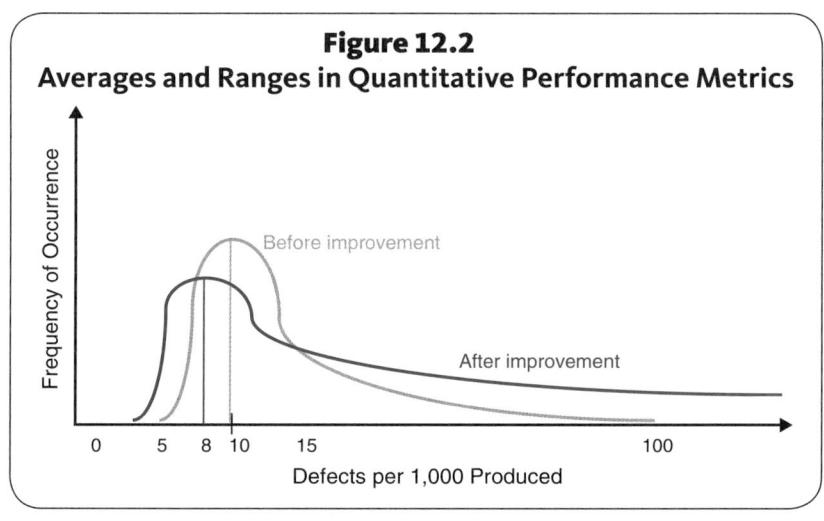

Figure 12.2
Averages and Ranges in Quantitative Performance Metrics

subjects the customer—and the company's reputation—to higher risk. A narrowing of the range without an improvement in the average is arguably much better for the organization because consistency is the hallmark expectation of most customers.

Quantitative metrics that reveal progress toward strategic performance need not be those which can only be measured by observing operations and calculating hard, factual numbers. Perceived quality is an area where this could be utilized, for example. Rather than a specific quantified measure of quality such as the defect rate, the business decides that an important measure is the customer's perception of quality. Regardless of actual defect or customer complaint rates this may be a much better measure, especially when you consider the problems that the big three automakers have had trying to convince customers that they have equaled their foreign competitors in terms of quality. Utilizing a survey methodology, the company contacts its customers periodically and asks them to rank the quality of the products it produces as well as those of its competitors. There is a relatively simple set of questions that will allow a company to create a comparative chart of perceived quality. This data can then be collected on a regular schedule, such that progress toward particular quality goals can be assessed (Figure 12.3).

Qualitative measures are just as important as quantitative measures. Qualitative data collection requires that the management team resist the temptation (and it is a strong one) to quantify everything. Results from surveys, focus groups, call reports from the sales force, input from the customer service lines, trends in complaints or compliments are all ripe for quantification, losing valuable perspective that cannot be captured numerically. Qualitative metrics involve reading between the lines of numerical response data that are

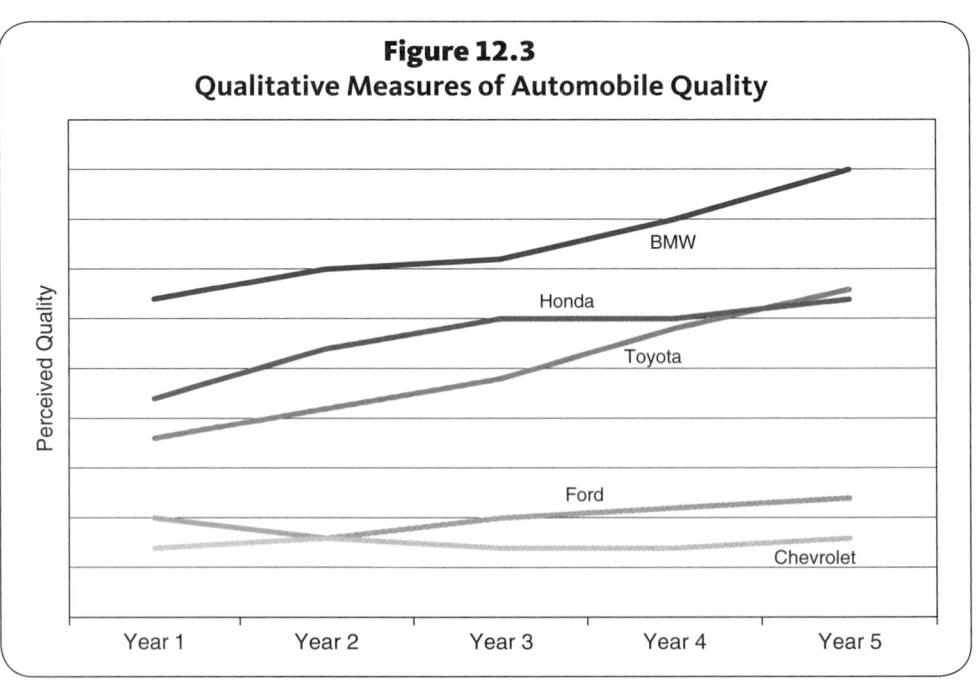

Figure 12.3
Qualitative Measures of Automobile Quality

gathered, asking open-ended questions, and interpreting responses for which there are no clearly defined categories.

For example, although field sales reports may indicate that physicians are seeing pharmaceutical company representatives on a timely basis, they feel that the sales calls are not particularly helpful. Further interviews may reveal that physicians are not receiving as much technical detail on new products as they would like. This suggests better training of the salespeople, the provision of more technically oriented literature, or possibly the creation of a company Web site strictly for physician use. This should lead the company to consider a measure of performance that is not a number, but a perception from a physician's point of view. After changes are made at the pharmaceutical company, follow-up interviews yielded fewer and less derisive negative comments about the information received in sales calls.

Consumer products companies often use focus group research, engaging small groups of consumers in deep conversations, to better understand how consumers think about and use their products. The results from these explorations provide a much deeper insight into new advertising messages

Strategic Moves
Ford Motor Company, Part 1

One of the true classic companies in the United States, Ford Motor Company, is one of the largest automobile producers in the world. Founded by Henry Ford and eleven business associates in 1903, Ford Motor Company pioneered the moving assembly line where workers remained in place performing the same job on each and every automobile that came down the line. Henry Ford's vision was to produce automobiles that everyone could afford. Over the next 100-plus years, Ford grew its line of automotive labels to include Ford, Lincoln, Mercury, Mazda, and Volvo. Despite this proud heritage, Ford Motor Company has been struggling for many years with multiple issues, including enormous legacy costs (retirement benefits to former employees), high labor costs (another historic distortion fostered by decades of contentious labor relations with their unions), a slow response to changes in the environment (gas price increases and changing consumer desires), as well as a slow response to new competitive challenges (non U.S. automakers).

These changes left Ford losing billions of dollars each year. The company needs to work its way out of those problems. They announced a new strategic plan dubbed "The Way Forward." As stated in the Annual Report, "Our goal is simple—to build more of the products that people really want and value. Exciting new products that reflect the needs of today's and tomorrow's customers, with striking designs that are safer, more fuel efficient, and offer even greater value. That includes an expanded commitment to small cars, more crossovers, and more capable and fuel efficient trucks."[5] With this, they have spelled out exactly where they want to go. Developing a set of both qualitative and quantitative metrics would be an important first task.

QUESTIONS

1. What metrics would you suggest?
2. If you had to keep it to seven or fewer metrics, which would be most important?
3. Focusing on the qualitative side of the issue, how might you evaluate such concepts as "exciting new products," "needs for tomorrow's customers," or "striking designs"?

and possible new product extensions. A qualitative evaluation would include the impressions the focus group leaders had while observing the group rather than the number of times that X was said. The "sense" of customers is a key means of guiding a company.

Metrics Translated to Functional Levels

As we have suggested previously, the overarching goals for the organization must become the guideposts for everyone in the company. This requires the creation of a set of metrics for every manager and every employee that guides their daily activities, such that the accomplishment of the activities is directly related to the overall organizational value creation objectives. This means there are three additional implications for the creation of metrics that maximize the opportunity for effective strategic control in addition to the use of both quantitative and qualitative metrics (Figure 12.4): balance, the right metric for the right level, and connecting performance incentives with metrics. These four elements constitute the **characteristics of effective metrics**.

> **Figure 12.4**
> **Characteristics of Effective Metrics**
> Quantitative & qualitative
> Balanced across functions
> Appropriate for the function or level
> Connected to incentives

Balance. We have suggested that important metrics may be gathered about production operations, sales effectiveness, employee training, marketing and advertising, and other activities in the company. This is a key element in implementation as strategy involves coordinated and consistent effort across every area of a company. If a differentiation advantage is sought, this might translate not only to lower defect rates in manufacturing operations, but also the acquiring of raw materials from top-notch suppliers, the creation of superior packaging, the development of a unique advertising campaign, and the cultivation of a special customer segment. For this company to truly succeed in its differentiation strategy, metrics should be developed to indicate how well each of the functional areas or departments responsible for these efforts is succeeding. As we discussed in earlier chapters on the value chain (Chapter 5) and generic strategies (Chapter 7), the coordination, consistency of approach within and across an organization, and fit is often at the heart of superior performance.

Appropriate for the functional level. The metrics created for each employee or level must be related to activities that are under the control of that employee or level. Each metric is supposed to guide the conduct of certain activities or functions. What sense would it make to establish a metric for an individual or group that in part is determined by activities beyond the control of that individual or group? Not only would this potentially lead to frustration by employees who cannot fully control outcomes they are made responsible for, but it also leads to poor feedback to management regarding the sources of problems if a metric is not progressing as was desired.

Characteristics of effective metrics There are four elements to high-quality metrics. They must be: 1) both quantitative and qualitative; 2) balanced across functions: 3) be appropriate for the function or level; and 4) be connected to incentives.

Distilling down higher-level value creation goals into activity-based metrics at the functional, group, or individual level is truly a challenge for management. This essentially challenges management to develop a **causal logic** about why things work the way they do. For example, one manager might believe that quality, as defined by minimizing defective products shipped can be best achieved by ensuring that assembly line workers: 1) have undergone training to enhance their production skills and capabilities; 2) are evaluated at their individual stations at a certain piece rate per minute; and 3) who then place personal signatures on products to certify their adherence to quality standards. The same kind of causal logic can be applied to every area of the company that is mission-critical in pursuing a particular strategic approach.

Establishing appropriate metrics for each functional level fosters greater control over strategy outcomes by creating the opportunity for organizational learning, as well as an understanding of when and where to take corrective actions if something is not working as planned. This is because the company can more closely monitor progress on the critical activities that are tied directly to the strategy of the business, and can make changes more quickly if progress is not apparent. In Figure 12.5 a company has the cause-effect logic of A, where a certain activity taken in one of its departments will lead to an expected outcome at the departmental level that supports the company's stra-

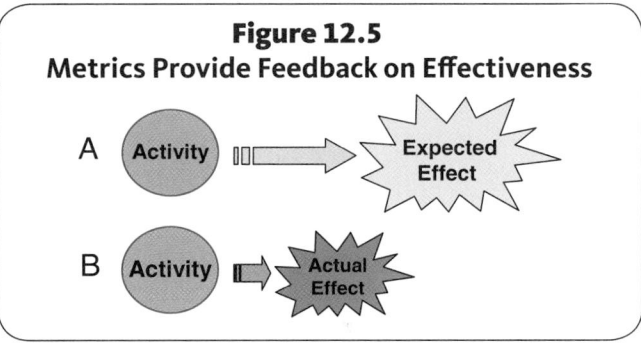

Figure 12.5
Metrics Provide Feedback on Effectiveness

A Activity → Expected Effect

B Activity → Actual Effect

tegic approach. Yet what the company actually experiences is B, where the outcome is less than stellar. By collecting outcome metrics on this important activity-effect relationship, the company might learn that its causal logic is flawed. The company then responds in one of two ways: either it needs to strengthen the activity in order to achieve the desired outcome, or it needs to engage in a different activity to achieve the outcome. Either way, the early insight the company gains on this very specific activity level increases the likelihood that the company can make necessary changes in order to enhance its strategy. This is a fundamental element in the creation of a learning organization.

Metrics connected to incentives. Creating a company where everyone is dedicated to the same set of goals is most successful if the organization can connect everyone's pay, bonuses, and/or incentive rewards to the metrics they are personally responsible for.

One of the most traditional means for public companies to attempt this connection has been to use stock options (the option to purchase x number of shares of stock at a fixed price with the hope that when exercised, the stock will be worth substantially more) as a reward for corporate financial performance. The theory has been that this will focus executive attention on profitability and ROE (which will drive up stock prices), and thereby

Causal logic An assessment of why things work the way they do.

encourage them to do whatever it takes to get the stock price above their option level. Even as some companies have increased the participation in stock option programs to include lower levels of management, its connection with what lower level managers actually do and can control is suspect at best. Stock prices rise and fall for a whole variety of reasons that may or may not have anything to do with their actions. Furthermore when stock options are underwater (a term used to describe options that are priced substantially above the current market price of the stock), there is little to motivate performance.

Since the metrics that are developed to monitor and control performance have a clear connection with the company's strategy, they should also have a clear and discernible effect on the company's financial performance. When metrics are developed, therefore, it should be made clear to employees exactly how their own individual efforts contribute to both strategic objectives and financial performance goals. The best performing organizations are those that connect the efforts of employees to these overarching objectives and goals.

As we discussed in Chapter 3, one way to accomplish this is to communicate the vision and mission of the company to all employees. Here we are suggesting ways to put that connection into practice, making sure that when employees successfully perform activities that are mission-critical, they participate in the financial rewards that accrue from that success. If the focus of the company is on quality, then achieving certain stretch quality standards should result in economic rewards for everyone. If corporate success is tied to the simultaneous achievement of three values (as in Coca-Cola), then success in those areas (as measured by stretch metrics) should enable contributing employees to share in the financial rewards that result. Stretch metrics are measures that really push the organization to achieve something of true significance. Sun Tzu admonished leaders to distribute the profits of war to everyone involved in order to incentivize their continued efforts. The currency of the business must be available to everyone in the company, not just the senior management team.

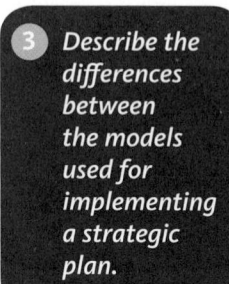
3 *Describe the differences between the models used for implementing a strategic plan.*

DEVELOPING A STRATEGY IMPLEMENTATION PLAN

Now that we have introduced and described the nature of performance metrics that enable senior management to monitor and control performance, we need to see how we can put these ideas into practice. The rest of this chapter is devoted to examining three practical approaches for creating an implementation plan that bridges the divide between lofty strategic objectives and the day-to-day activities of employees. Translating strategy into action is the core of strategy implementation. There are a number of tools available for this purpose. We will examine three of those tools: 1) Balanced Scorecard; 2) Value-Driver-Action Model; and 3) 7-S Framework.

Balanced Scorecard Model

Introduced in the 1990s, the **balanced scorecard**[6] presents one practical (and very visible) approach to connecting strategy to action. This approach allows top management the ability to monitor progress toward overarching organization objectives and identifies those areas that are not meeting expectations. The central notion of the balanced scorecard is that financial measures of performance are the *result* of a variety of activities that people in the company engage in, not the cause. This is a point we made in the very first chapter of this textbook. Therefore, managers need to examine and manage the activities that will ultimately contribute to financial performance. This central idea is, once again, entirely consistent with the nature of strategic management itself. That is, strategy has to do with sustainable long-term performance. Those that try to connect today's action's to today's financial performance find that the data is quite misleading, and can lead to inappropriate decisions. So one of the main purposes of the balanced scorecard is to connect short-term actions and investments with long-term financial and competitive performance.

There are three dimensions of the balanced scorecard model that are important to understand. The Balanced Scorecard is: 1) driven by strategy, 2) used to address the cause-and-effect logic across four levels of the organization, and 3) used to delineate both lead and lag metrics.

The first dimension reflects the earlier discussion, that every metric developed must fundamentally reflect the strategic approach of the business. If we were to consider two restaurants in the fast food business, one pursuing a low cost leadership approach and one pursuing a differentiation approach, we would expect to see that the metrics used by one would be very different from the metrics used by the other. Not unlike the observation from Chapter 2 that a company's financial statements should reflect the nature of its market strategy, the set of metrics in a balanced scorecard should also mirror the company's strategy.

Second, the model incorporates four different levels of any organization, which are connected in a cause-and-effect fashion (Figure 12.6). Success in one perspective leads to success in the next perspective. In the Learning & Growth Perspective, management considers the skills and competencies that the company develops in employees, as well as the facilitating systems,

Balanced scorecard
An implementation method that considers a wide variety of stakeholders in the "performance" of the company.

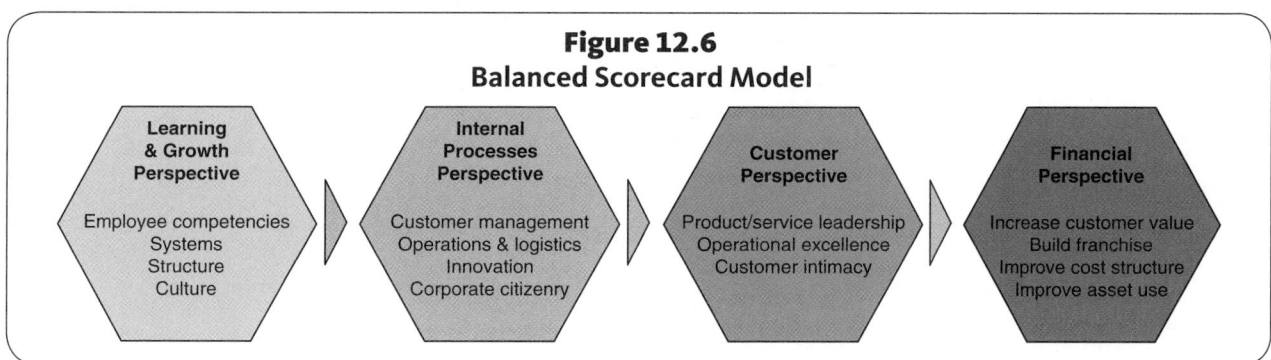

Figure 12.6
Balanced Scorecard Model

Learning & Growth Perspective	Internal Processes Perspective	Customer Perspective	Financial Perspective
Employee competencies Systems Structure Culture	Customer management Operations & logistics Innovation Corporate citizenry	Product/service leadership Operational excellence Customer intimacy	Increase customer value Build franchise Improve cost structure Improve asset use

structure, and culture in which employees do the work of the company. If management provides the right structure, builds the right culture, and provides the right kind of training for employees, this should contribute to strong performance in the Internal Processes Perspective. In turn, excellence in internal processes regarding innovation, production, and customer management systems should enable the company to deliver new and better products or services to customers and to develop strong, enduring relationships with customers. Finally, the successes achieved in the Customer Perspective should roll up into strong performance in the Financial Perspective. The challenge for management is to create a set of metrics that provides insight on the extent to which the company is making positive progress in each of the subdimensions of the four perspectives that is specific to their organizational goals. Similar to the cause-effect logic illustrated in Figure 12.6, close ongoing attention to these specific metrics enables management to monitor progress and make changes when necessary.

The third dimension of the balanced scorecard model involves the development of both **lead metrics** and **lag metrics**. Lag metrics are results that we would hope and expect to observe for each of the subdimensions in any one perspective. These are results that we cannot directly change. For example, in the Customer Perspective we may have a goal to acquire new customers, but the decision to buy from our company is up to the customer, not us. Customer acquisition is therefore a lag metric, but there are actions that our company can take that will impact this metric—for example, increasing sales call frequency or increasing the sales training of our salespeople. These are actions that we can take—that we can directly affect—and they represent lead metrics that we can also measure. Figure 12.7 provides examples of lead and lag metrics in the Customer Perspective.

You might recognize that the balanced scorecard fundamentally reflects an important theme of strategic management that is carried throughout this textbook. Competitive advantage has to do with creating value through sets of well-coordinated activities across the company's entire value chain.

Lead metrics Represent the observable actions of employees that we hope will lead to the results we are ultimately trying to achieve.

Lag metrics Represent the results that we would hope and expect to observe for each of the subdimensions in any one perspective of a balanced scorecard.

> ## Figure 12.7
> ## Examples of Lead and Lag Metrics in the Customer Perspective
>
> | Lead | Lag |
> |------|-----|
> | % orders filled immediately | Customer acquisition |
> | % on-time delivery | Customer retention |
> | Customer survey feedback | Share of customer's total purchases |
> | Number of sales calls per period | Ranking by customers vs. competition |
> | Hours of sales training per sales person | % of sales from new products |
> | Number of special customer requests filled | % of product line carried |

Similarly, the balanced scorecard focuses attention on strategically important activity sets and how these, in combination, work toward superior financial performance.

Value-Driver-Action Model

It is important to recognize the contribution of the balanced scorecard to the ability of organizations to implement their strategy. Forcing organizations to simultaneously consider multiple facets of the organization and to codify those into measurable outcomes has made a significant impact in the ways in which some organizations manage and perform. On the other hand, the balanced scorecard model requires management to think about its organization using the four perspectives, which does not often resemble the way organizations are structured or the way in which managers think about their value chain activities. So for many managers, the balanced scorecard may be like asking a right-handed batter to bat left-handed: you know what to do, but you are definitely not practiced at it and it therefore is very difficult, if not impossible, to use.

An alternative to the balanced scorecard is what we refer to as the value-driver-action model. This model builds more directly off the key ideas that managers use when they consider formulating strategy. Where strategy implementation can more transparently take advantage of strategy formulation ideas and perspectives, the formulation effort can be more easily accomplished. Like the balanced scorecard, this model also focuses on the needs of the individual company and its unique resource-based advantages.

The design of an effective value-driven-action plan has five components:

1. Identifying key value drivers that will lead to a competitive advantage for the business.
2. Outlining the position the company wants to occupy from the perspective of how customers, suppliers, employees, and other stakeholders experience the company.
3. Translating desired stakeholder experience to business/market position.
4. Creating a list of actions to be taken, both short-term and long-term, that answer the question what must we do now to ensure success?
5. Developing metrics (both quantitative and qualitative) that measure progress toward the accomplishment of each value driver.

Key value drivers. The first and most critical element is the identification of the **key value drivers** for the organization. These can be identified from three sources:

- The list of key success factors (KSFs) developed through industry analysis (Chapter 4)
- The resource-based analysis that pinpoints extraordinary resources (Chapter 6)
- The vision and mission statements (Chapter 3)

Key value drivers
Those elements of the organization that provide the company with the best opportunity for success in their industry.

One of the goals of industry analysis that we discussed in Chapter 4 was the identification of key success factors—those three to five competitive dimensions that are critical to succeeding in an industry. Through resource-based analysis (Chapter 6) managers should also be able to draw conclusions about the extraordinary, advantage-producing resources that the company possesses. Finally, the aspirations of the company may extend beyond the immediate industry environment and immediate resource endowments, and so critical dimensions for creating value over the long run might be identified with reference to the company's vision and mission statements.

The key value drivers for the company therefore arise out of some combination of current industry demands, current company capabilities, and future company aspirations. It is usually the case that current demands and current organizational capabilities dominate the list of value drivers that management decides upon. There is no absolute "right answer" when it comes to establishing the drivers, but the choice of drivers will make a significant difference in the results of the overall implementation plan.

Earlier in this chapter we noted that the mission elements of Coca-Cola were: 1) to refresh the world in body, mind, and spirit; 2) to inspire moments of optimism through their brands and actions, and 3) to create value and make a difference everywhere they engage. Coca-Cola, which competes in an industry where scale, innovation, and global presence are critical, also has significant and extraordinary resources in brand marketing, international management, and bottler relations, among others. Together this combination of mission elements, industry requirements, and company capabilities should form the basis for identifying the value drivers for the business.

Desired stakeholder experiences. Articulating desired statements from the point of view of stakeholders anchors the second section of an effectively developed strategy implementation plan using the value-driver-action model. Within each key value driver there will be a set of statements that the company aspires to hear from its stakeholders, which would indicate that the company has sincerely met its goals. It is relatively easy to develop a set of statements relating to a particular value. Done well, the statements capture the value driver's overall concept. These might include such statements as "I really like drinking Dasani water because it tastes so clean," (retail customer) or "I get the best prices without ever going out of stock on a product that sells quickly through my stores," (retail store owner) or "We love investing in Coca-Cola because of the environmental efforts they have initiated" (shareholders). Again, there is no right or wrong with these statements; they are a reflection of the way we want to see the value drivers manifest themselves with our stakeholders. In effect, they tell a story that we want to hear about our company, product, or service.

Translating experience to position. Having established the statements that we are looking to achieve from our stakeholders, the company must translate each statement into a particular business or market position.

Strategic Moves
Ford Motor Company, Part 2

Consistent with the desire to develop a strategic planning document, five different groups of graduate students were asked to put together a strategy implementation plan for Ford Motor Company. Each independently formed their own list of Ford Motor Company value drivers as listed below:

Team	Key Value Drivers
Team A	1) Value 2) Brand Focus 3) Mass Production 4) Fast Follower
Team B	1) Pricing 2) Reliability 3) Innovation 4) Driving by Customers 5) Efficiency
Team C	1) Brand 2) Innovative Heritage 3) Quality
Team D	1) Brand Clarity 2) Customer Focus 3) Agility & Efficiency 4) Trucks 5) Innovation
Team E	1) Innovation 2) Quality 3) Operational Excellence 4) Ford Family 5) Bold

As stated previously, there is no single best way to establish the Key Value Drivers for an organization. However, the choice of value drivers will significantly change the design of the overall document and therefore the overall success of the organization. There are similarities in the Value Drives that were chosen, but hopefully you can see that some of these drivers would take the company down a completely different path than others. A focus on the Ford Family (Team E) will take the company down a path that might include a number of nameplates, while a focus on Trucks (Team D) might lead to a minimization effort in new car design.

QUESTIONS

1. What stakeholder statement would you write to align with the key value drivers?

2. Would you establish different value drivers for Ford Motor Company?

These translations identify the key areas that the company must move to from where it currently exists. In 2007, the Associated Press released an article detailing how all water is not the same. They found that "potassium, for example, may give water a sweet taste. Silica may impart silkiness. Calcium can give the water a lactic taste some people find refreshing. Others enjoy the cleansing quality of water with high sodium content."[7] If Coca-Cola would like to achieve the desired stakeholder statement "I really like drinking Dasani water because it tastes so clean," then its laboratory food scientists might need to develop new, leading-edge techniques for purifying and fortifying bottled water, which, in fact, they did. Similarly, the desired shareholder experience of wanting to invest in the company because of its environmental efforts might prompt management to establish a goal of becoming the leading beverage company in the recycling of plastic containers.

This latter example points out the possible disconnect between a targeted business or market position (based upon desired stakeholder experiences) and a company's existing resources and capabilities. Which resources, capabilities, structures, or programs must we have to increase the chances that our stakeholders will, in fact, make the statements related to each value driver? Of course, it is not possible for a company to instantly become a leader in recycling, because of the significant investments required in science, infrastructure, manufacturing, customer relations, and other important value chain dimensions. Thus, part of the benefit of translating desired experiences to targeted business positions is examining what can be done immediately and what will require significant long-term investment.

Actions list. Implementation is often driven by the earliest of actions. An effective and motivating plan allows everyone in the company to get started on their efforts immediately. The third piece of the value-driver-actions model consists of distilling the desired stakeholder perspective goals down into specific sets of actions. Starting with each statement listed in the stakeholder experience section, a list of actions that must be started now should be developed. There are two kinds of actions that are identified in this phase: 1) actions that immediately address stakeholder experiences taking advantage of existing resources, and 2) actions to build new resources to address stakeholder experiences and long-term aspirations.

If Coca-Cola wishes to develop water that has a "clean, refreshing taste," then a plausible immediate action might consist of a series of lab-developed examples along with a series of customer-focused tasting sessions. The effort to achieve a clean, refreshing taste is one that the organization will constantly be trying achieve. Individuals have different tastes and what constitutes clean and refreshing might change as new competitors enter a market.

Metrics. Finally, we come back to developing metrics that afford the opportunity to monitor and control progress toward strategic goals. Each metric should tie directly to the stakeholder statement made for that value driver. Companies often have crossover metrics that align several value drivers. The initial effort will most likely lead to a long list of metrics. Prior to publishing

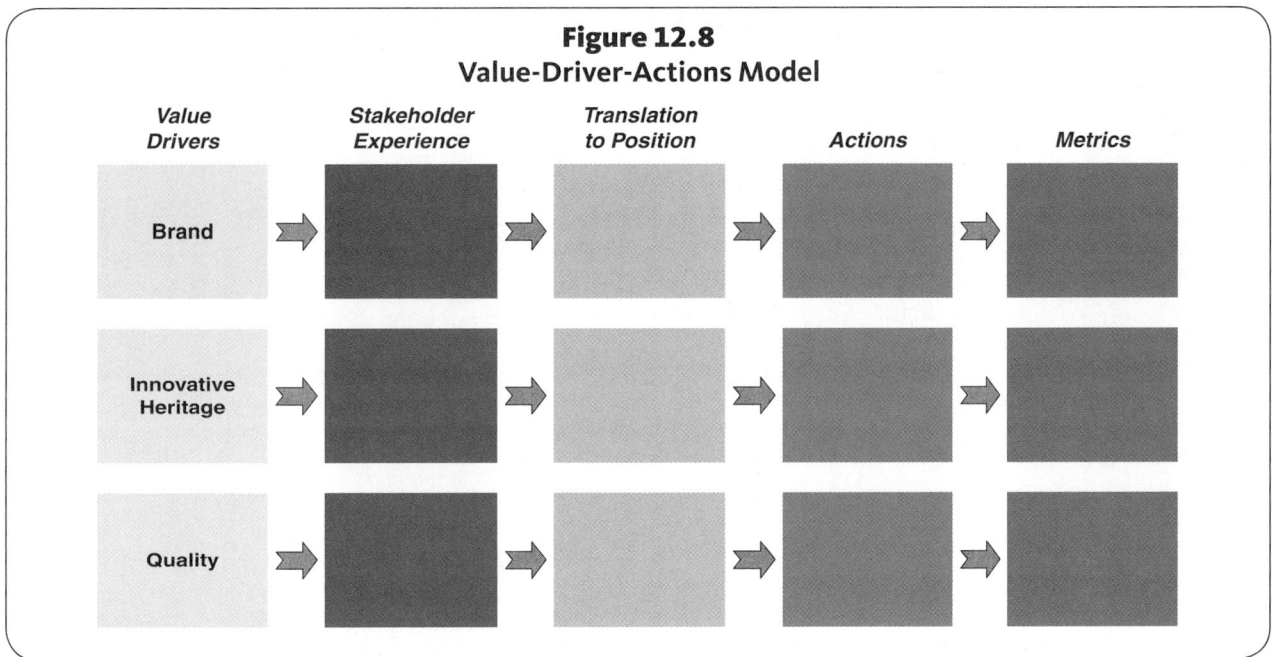

Figure 12.8
Value-Driver-Actions Model

Value Drivers	Stakeholder Experience	Translation to Position	Actions	Metrics
Brand				
Innovative Heritage				
Quality				

the chart for everyone in the company, these metrics will need to be consolidated. The core of the plan is the ability to drive everyone in the organization toward the same set of measurable goals.

Coke might consider a qualitative metric comparing the refreshing taste of Dasani as compared to their competitor offerings where the desire is to have Dasani score well above their competitors. Another effective metric for the shareholder statement might be a quantitative assessment of the five- and ten-year stock performance of Coke relative to other companies with equivalent risk portfolios. Again, since this is an important statement for Coke, they would want to see this metric be substantially above their competition.

Putting all of this together is the final step. Ideally, this entire plan can be seen on a single page that can be shared with everyone in the company. The chart might look something like the one in Figure 12.8. The science of strategy implementation is the development of a set of metrics and immediate plans that are all focused on the value drivers for the organization. The art of strategy implementation is the actual terms used and focus desired by senior management.

The 7-S Framework

The third tool available for turning strategy into action is one of the most consistently useful frameworks available. The **7-S framework** was developed nearly three decades ago by McKinsey & Co.[8] Intentionally using alliteration to help aid memory, the technique helps us align the functions of an organization. Most strategists split the seven S's into the hard S's (so called because they are relatively easy to find in writing) and the soft S's

7-S framework
A method for examining the various aspects of the organization in such a way that some alignment can be achieved. Elements include strategy, structure, systems, style, skills, staff and superordinate goals (shared values).

Strategic Moves
Ford Motor Company, Part 3

Value Drivers	Stakeholder Experience	Translation to Position	Actions to Take Now	Metrics
Value	1. "I always feel like I'm getting the most bang for my buck" with Ford. 2. "Buying a Ford is straightforward, no haggling, no 'cash on the hood' rebates." 3. "When I sell my Ford, it feels like I'm getting a good return."	1. List price = sales price. 2. No haggle sales process. 3. Develop classic popular designs to ensure high retained value. 4. Reduce cost structure significantly to best in class.	1. Reduce management and employees as a result of efficiencies below to achieve best in class cost. 2. Change incentive structure and sales process. 3. Revamp designs where needed to classic timeless designs.	1. # of cash rebates lowest in industry. 2. Avg discount off list/Industry Avg discount off list. 3. Residual prices highest in peer group. 4. # Consumers Choice awards for value. 5. Production cost/model compared to peer group.
Brand Focus	1. "My family has always owned Fords and we believe in buying American Ford vehicles...it's a tradition." 2. "My job is to produce the best new Ford Back to the Future truck or car on the road." 3. "Ford's repositioning strategy has combined the best of brand loyalty and preference." 4. "People understand what we stand for—simply a Ford with the focus on consistency and reliability."	1. The company immediately divests itself of other competing or distracting brands (Lincoln and Mercury). 2. Narrow Ford's selection to typify its heritage: Ford F-Series, mid-sized SUV (combining the best of the Explorer and Expedition), sporty Mustang and smaller, entry-level sedan (combining best of the Escape and Fusion). 3. Ford offers only four colors: Ford Black, Ford Blue, Ford Red, and Ford White. Develop each of the four colors as a distinct new color only offered on Fords. 4. Develop a unique "Back to the Future" integrated marketing campaign that creates the "buzz" and "call to action" to compel consumers to buy a new Ford.	1. Locate a buyer for non-Ford brands. 2. Develop a timeline for selling down the existing Ford inventory. 3. Hire a new advertising and public relations firm to begin developing message and planning marketing/advertising campaign. 4. Plan an Analysts' Day to introduce Wall Street analysts to the new "Ford—Back to the Future" strategy.	1. Survey consumers to determine the orthodox and unorthodox for a new Ford vehicle, interior and exterior. 2. Ratio of customer complaints to total customer touch points (e.g., online feedback, service questionnaires, post-purchase surveys, car show customer research). 3. Number of Ford's purchased in the U.S./Total number of cars/trucks purchased in the U.S. 4. Number of Ford trucks purchased in the U.S./Total number of Trucks purchased in the U.S. (Same metrics for SUVs, sports cars that compete with the Mustang and smaller sedans at entry price points).

| Mass Production | 1. "Ford has brought back the workmanship and quality."
 2. "I know my job is to make vehicles every day and understand the impact of lost time if the line is down."
 3. "Ford has succeeded in accurately matching market demand with their manufacturing capacity."
 4. "Our plants now achieve 85% efficiency and utilization." | 1. Design engineering team leaders spend one week a month working in design related manufacturing plant to understand capabilities and build designs toward automation and efficiency.
 2. Review all facilities for core competency related to automation and high efficiency, including manufacturing personnel at all levels.
 3. Develop list of which of these facilities match up to remaining product lines of Trucks/SUVs, Mustangs, 500s, and Focus.
 4. Analysis of Fords 5-year market demand and match production plants to this capacity. | 1. Idle all outdated/ substandard mfg facilities by 2010 to have only 20% reserve capacity above market demand projections.
 2. Update facilities by 2010 to automate toward the mass production of Trucks, Mustangs, 500s, and Focus.
 3. Reduce manufacturing complexity and costs: <br> a) Reduce colors to Red, Blue, White, Black <br> b) Implement defined 3-tier level of options— Trucks: X (standard), XL (upgraded), XLT (loaded)
 c) Implement 2 motor (standard and premium) and 2 transmission options | 1. Efficiency of plant/ Efficiency of all plants.
 2. Overall efficiency of all plants/Estimated efficiency of competitors plants.
 3. Production capacity/ Production demand.
 4. Production capacity by model type/Industry model market demand.
 5. Overall Ford capacity/ Overall market capacity.
 6. Overall Ford capacity Overall market demand. |

(continues)

Strategic Moves
Ford Motor Company, Part 3 (continued)

Value Drivers	Stakeholder Experience	Translation to Position	Actions to Take Now	Metrics

Fast Follower	1. "Ford offers the technologies and options that I would expect from a great car company, I especially like the all-wheel drive and I am looking forward to experiencing the new hybrid derivatives that I have heard about."
	
	2. "The technology we install in our cars is market proven and therefore very reliable."
	
	3. "Ford is able to offer the latest mainstream technology without a major technology driven R&D investment."
	
	4. "By keeping a close eye on the market we only adopt proven technology solutions for our cars."
		1. Design and engineering teams monitor the trends of new technologies; They adopt the best technologies after market acceptance and the economies of scale have driven down the cost.
		
		2. Track "cutting edge" producers and types of vehicles they are selling add systems and technologies based on 1st/2nd-year market sales.
		
		3. Identify 3rd party subsystems that can be quickly incorporated into existing and future designs.
			1. Put a system into place to track competitor's products and technologies (engine, safety, electronics, alternative fuels, amenities . . .)
			
			  a. As new technologies are introduced quickly measure the market acceptance rate.
			  b. Identify a vendor for the technology and track subsystem cost.
			
			2. Once vendors are identified begin designing into new models and determine if the new system can be added to existing models.
			
			3. As price declines begin offering the new technology.
				1. Features offered on Ford products/Features offered in each product class.
				
				2. For each technology: Number of models offering the new technology/Total number of industry models offering the technology.
				
				3. Customer feedback received requesting individual features/technologies.

One group (Team A from Part II) developed the chart above as a complete strategy implementation chart.

QUESTIONS

1. What do you think about the chart as developed?
2. What changes would you make to the chart?
3. Do the metrics meet your expectations for the company as laid out in the value drivers and mission?

(named because they are more difficult to pin down in an exact manner). The entire framework is oriented around the concept of fit. The better each of the seven fit together, the better the organization performs. The Seven S's are:

HARD S's	SOFT S's
Strategy	Style
Structure	Staff
Systems	Superordinate Goals (Shared Values)
	Skills

Hard S's

Strategy. This is the written set of statements that constitutes the strategic direction of the company. This formulation is the compilation of most of what we have discussed in this text. It is the examination of the value chain, resource-based advantages, and design of the organization such that it can compete effectively with the company's competitors. The strategy is the means by which the company intends to be successful.

Structure. The formal and informal organization of the company. Most often seen as the written organization chart, students of this text should view this as the design of the organization, which was discussed in significant detail in Chapter 11. That design is a combination of knowing: 1) what constitutes the core, techno structure, and support staff of the organization; 2) how you will coordinate their activities; and 3) what organizational structures you will use. The informal organization simply recognizes that within any organization, there is an unwritten, informal structure through which much of the work of the organization actually gets done. The structure should be designed to support the strategy. Therefore, as we mentioned previously, the core of the organization is that group or groups most responsible for the sustainable competitive advantages outlined in the strategy.

Systems. While often thought of as the information technology systems of the company, this is but the beginning of what constitutes the systems of the company. Having designed an effective strategy and aligned the structure such that it supports the strategy, it is incumbent upon senior management to align the systems of the company such that they support both the strategy and the structure. Quality control systems, performance review systems, human resources systems, and policies and procedures are all amongst the systems that need to be considered. Aligning the systems such that they support the new structure is a critical step in implementation. Little will happen if the systems do not provide the new information needs of the company. Changing the systems of an organization can be quite traumatic as they have usually been developed over a long period of time, and employees are accustomed to them. That said, a new strategy and structure demands a reevaluation of all the systems of the organization. What can be eliminated? What needs to be done to support the new core functions? What new metrics must be gathered? Systems support the organization and its goals, providing the critical link between a strategy that is desired and a structure that is trying to implement that strategy.

Soft S's

Style. The symbolic behavior of the organization starts at the top of the organization. The way that employees treat each other, the dress code, and the approach to the work day are all elements of the organization's style. The CEO and the top management team of the company set the style that constitutes acceptable behavior. This element is based in action and has little to do with what is said. An organization that is fundamentally built upon freedom of expression, creativity, and taking chances can be enhanced by a CEO like Steve Jobs who embodies those style elements and can be crushed by a CEO like John Scully whose style was corporate control and formality oriented. The alignment of style with the desired strategy, structure, and systems of a company has the ability to propel the organization forward.

Staff. Staffing is an examination of the means and processes for bringing in new employees as well as the processes inherent in getting them to be productive for the company. New employees take time to start really providing value to the organization. Staffing is about shortening that time and aligning the process with the rest of the company.

Too often employees are brought in with no formal means of incorporating their efforts into the organization. They learn the nomenclature, practices, and people via an informal, ad hoc system that makes early contribution to success virtually impossible. Arthur Andersen & Co. was the storied accounting firm that had this process down to a science. Every employee started their career at the Andersen school in Illinois. They learned about the processes, practices, and expectations in a high-pressure, fast-paced program that made them quickly valuable to the organization.

Superordinate Goal (Shared Values). These are the overarching goals of the organization. In practice this is usually manifested in the vision and mission of the company, representing the focus of the company and its reason for existence. Aligning the vision and mission of the company with the strategy would seem to be obvious. As we discussed extensively in Chapter 3, this is an important element in guiding the practices of every employee, every day of the week.

Skills. These are the dominant skills of the organization, and dictate what is most important in creating value for that particular organization. These are similar to what we referred to as core competence in Chapter 5. Within the same industry, we often see a wide variety of skill sets depending upon the overarching goals of the company. One insurance company might determine that deep knowledge of insurance is a core skill for their company. They might require everyone to study insurance and be certified in the area. Another insurance company might decide that the core set of skills is customer service. They would set their training program up to establish customer service skills as those that should permeate the entire organization.

Strategic Moves
McDonald's—The Rest of the Story[9]

One of the amazing success stories in strategy implementation, McDonald's utilized everything we have discussed in this chapter to create their "Plan to Win." That plan (now in its third generation) put the entire implementation effort onto a single page, in a format that allows everyone in the organization to understand the keys to success and how they will measure those keys.

McDonald's originally established their Key Value Drivers and what those drivers meant as:

Key Value Driver	Meaning
Our People	Well-trained, friendly people are key to providing *I'm Loving It* Service.
Our Products	Our menu features the choice and variety that consumers enjoy eating often.
Our Places	The comfort and convenience of our restaurants attract customers.
Our Prices	Through our products and restaurant experience, we deliver value to customers.
Our Promotions	"Forever Young" and engaging, our brand connects with people around the world.

Each of these drivers was converted into stakeholder statements such as:

Key Value Driver	Stakeholder Statement
Our People	"A simple smile makes me feel welcome . . . it's the perfect start to my meal . . . it's the reason I love McDonald's."
Our Products	"What do I want from a restaurant? Good food and good choices. That's why I go to McDonald's."
Our Places	"McDonald's is a cool place where everyone can relax. I'm comfortable here, and my friends and I know we're always welcome."
Our Prices	"Whether I have a lot or a little to spend, McDonald's always offers great taste at a great value."
Our Promotions	"I love McDonald's. I can eat great food, play, and get a fun toy. I guess that's why my mom loves McDonald's too."

The company listed out their critical success factors and "must do now" actions before designing a set of metrics so that they could measure success. We show the metrics from the first value driver as an example.

Key Value Driver	Metrics
Our People	Training & Development—$$ Investment, number of graduates from Hamburger University; new platforms for career development. Great Place to Work—Rated in 100 Best Companies to Work For. Diversity Initiatives—McDonald's trains more minorities and women than any other U.S. employer: 40% of owner/operators and more than 50% of workforce is women and minorities. McPassport—A program of employee training and certification that allows free movement throughout the EU.

Overarching metrics included items such as return to shareholders, new product launches, store growth, dividend growth, etc. By virtually any measure available—whether sales, same-store sales, stock price, returns, etc.—McDonald's has executed with precision.

Another insurance company might decide it is all about sales and sales skills. They would organize around the salespeople and emphasize sales skills as the dominant skills of the organization.

Putting together the entire 7-S framework for a company is significantly more art than it is science. It is important to consider all of the elements when designing the implementation plan. Effective strategy implementation means bringing together all the elements of the 7-S framework together in the implementation of the strategy. It is another form of a balanced approach being employed to improve the success of an organization.

One interesting approach for incorporating both the 7-S framework and the implementation plan is to utilize the seven S's in the formation of the metrics for the organization, requiring that at least several metrics touch each of the seven areas of the company.

The effort at aligning the organization provides the information flow necessary for a learning organization. Company-designed metrics provide information that is focused on the resource-based advantages of the business and that provides the feedback to start the process over again with new insight. Insight is provided not only on the true capabilities of the company, but also exposes new opportunities for the organization. This opportunity recognition is the starting point for achieving a sustainable competitive advantage.

FedEx had long viewed itself as an overnight delivery service that specialized in the process of package movement. The company received continual praise for their operation and the service that they provided to business. Over the years, more and more competitors were able to approach their service levels causing the key value drivers for FedEx to start changing. The process of continually formulating and implementing strategy allowed them to see that one of their key value drivers was providing services to people for whom speed and last-minute quality handling were a priority worth paying for. FedEx bought Kinkos and dramatically expanded their hours, service offerings, and tie to the FedEx operation.

The other significant advantage of an effective implementation effort is the effect that it has on speed with which the business can move in new directions. Well-designed metrics allow for an early warning system within the company. That agility provides the key source of competitive advantage in dynamic markets.

The model that we discussed in Chapter 1 is a dynamic model that has continual feedback for the decision makers in an organization. Designing and implementing strategy is a process, not an event.

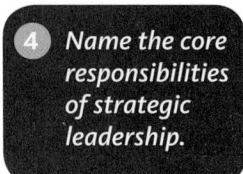

4 *Name the core responsibilities of strategic leadership.*

STRATEGIC LEADERSHIP

As a conclusion to our discussion of effective strategy implementation, we briefly mention the critical role played by strategic leadership. In fact, every step along the way in this textbook we have been highlighting points where strategic leadership is important. It is the responsibility of the senior management team to bring together all of the strategic management functions so that the business can develop sustainable competitive advantages and earn superior returns. These core responsibilities of strategic leadership can be summed up in the following list:

- **Establish vision, mission, goals.** Leadership is at its core about guiding the total business forward in a manner that has the potential to be extraordinary. Designing an appropriate vision and mission is at the heart of this effort.
- **Build senior management team.** Identifying, recruiting, and hiring the best people to lead a particular company and a particular point in time is crucial for success.
- **Establish structure for communication, coordination, and control.** The structure of the organization is wholly dependent upon the strategy that has been designed.
- **Exert control over direction.** Using a performance monitoring system ensures effective strategy implementation.
- **Establish a code of ethics for conduct and decision making.**

- **Evaluate, decide, act.** Decision making about value chain, resources allocation, type of strategy, growth, and implementation are the province of successful leaders.
- **Rational decision making.** Strategic moves are not decided on a whim or based upon personal egos or desires. Effective strategy requires excellence in deep, revealing analysis. This can then be married to intuition and perspective that comes from personal experience.
- **Establish top-management team process that challenges assumptions, surfaces alternatives.** The strategic imperatives of opportunity recognition and value creation demand nothing less.
- **Establish culture that matches personal leadership style.** A culture that reflects the values of the leader and is in harmony with the leader's actions will prove to be a powerful driving force for the organization.
- **Motivate through incentives and rewards aligned with goals.** Establish a system that rewards employees when their individual accomplishments contribute to organizational goals.

Guiding an organization through the combination of dynamic challenges from the general environment, aggressive competitors, demanding customers, and other stakeholders is a complex process. It is a process that demands the application of both science and art. A deep understanding of the science of strategy and its application has been the goal of this book. The art of strategy is the art of strategic leadership. You will become the strategic leaders of tomorrow, and we hope this book helps you to succeed.

CHAPTER SUMMARY

This chapter focused on the issues involved in internal control and performance, which is a challenging part of strategy implementation. We began the chapter by discussing five keys to control and performance systems:

1. Fit
2. Clear and Compelling Objectives
3. A Single Company Currency
4. Top-Management Involvement
5. Resource Allocation

We reviewed the development of different types of metrics, because any system of control and performance must be based on definable dimensions that can be measured. Any metric must meet four conditions:

1. Be tied to the overall mission/vision of the organization
2. Be composed of both quantitative and qualitative measures of performance
3. Can be translated to all levels of employees within the organization
4. Can be ultimately translated to a single corporate "currency"

Next we reviewed three frameworks for monitoring and evaluating performance. These systems allow management to evaluate whether short-term progress toward long-term strategic goals is positive, or if corrective actions are called for:

1. Balanced scorecard model, which examines execution through four perspectives:
   - Learning and Growth
   - Internal Process
   - Customer
   - Financial
2. Value-driver-action model, which is directly translatable to an individual organization's strategic direction and consists of five parts:
   - Value Drivers
   - Stakeholder Experience
   - Translation to Position
   - Action
   - Metrics
3. The McKinsey 7-S framework, which consists of three hard and four soft S's:
   - Strategy
   - Structure
   - Systems

- Skills
- Style
- Superordinate Goals (shared values)
- Staff

KEY TERMS

7-S framework
  (p. 371)

Balanced scorecard
  (p. 365)

Causal logic
  (p. 363)

Characteristics of
  effective metrics
  (p. 362)

Key value drivers
  (p. 367)

Lag metrics (p. 366)

Lead metric (p. 366)

Qualitative metrics
  (p. 358)

Quantitative metrics
  (p. 358)

SHORT ANSWER QUESTIONS

1. What types of statements constitute good stakeholder statements?

2. What issues should be addressed in the alignment of style?

3. How do we determine the key value drivers for an organization?

4. What four criteria constitute the soft S's in the 7-S framework?

5. How does the value-driver-action method differ from the balanced scorecard method?

6. How are key stakeholder statements translated into action plans?

7. Why do we start with the learning and growth part of the model?

8. What is a qualitative metric and how should it be used in the organization?

9. How do the elements in the balanced scorecard work with each other?

10. How would you recommend corporate metrics be translated to individual employee metrics?

11. What is a balanced scorecard?

12. How do metrics guide the organization?

13. What elements would you consider to be critical for effective implementation?

14. What criteria should you use when designing good metrics?

15. Why is strategy implementation so important to a company?

GROUP EXERCISES

1. Select a large, well-known consumer company that is of interest to you and your group members.
   a. What are the key value drivers for this company?
   b. Given those drivers, what statements would you like to hear from stakeholders for each of the value drivers?
   c. How might you measure whether the company was successfully achieving those stakeholder statements?

2. Take a look at one of the big overnight package delivery companies such as FedEx, UPS, or DHL. They each need a balanced scorecard for their organization and each of those scorecards should be quite different. Select one of those companies and develop a balanced scorecard for the company based upon publicly available information.

3. A new salon has approached you about their business and would like help in designing a 7-S framework for their new business idea. Design a 7-S for this business.

   > The mission of this organization is: "Everything for the body."

   > They plan to be the largest salon in the state of Illinois, with hairstylists, manicurists, massage therapists, tanning facilities, a huge 50 foot by 120 foot saltwater warm bathing area, sauna facilities, yoga facilitation, meditation classes, and Pilates. There will be a personal attendant for each customer and the customer will be truly pampered. A large office staff will be required, a day care facility for the children, a high-end artsy restaurant will be on-site for the patrons, and everything will be cutting edge with each patron only having to press their thumbprint to gain access to an area or pay for their purchases!

REFERENCES

[1] Grainger, David. 2003. "Can McDonald's cook again?" *Fortune.* April 14, 147(7): 40–47; Horovitz, Bruce. 2003. It's back to basics for McDonald's. *USA Today.* May 20. http://www.usatoday.com, http://www.mcdonalds.com/corp/about/mcd_history_pg1.html.

[2] Welch, Jack, and John Byrne. 2001. *Jack: Straight from the gut.* Warner Books. New York.

[3] Bossidy, L., and R. Charan. 2002. *Execution: The discipline of getting things done.* New York: Crown Business.

[4] http://www.thecoca-colacompany.com/ourcompany/mission_vision_values.html.

[5] http://www.ford.com/doc/2006_AR.pdf.

[6] Kaplan, R. S., and D. P. Norton. 1992. Balanced scorecard: Measures that drive performance. *Harvard Business Review* 70(1): 71–80; Kaplan, R. S., and D. P. Norton. 1996. Linking the balanced scorecard to strategy. *California Management Review* 39(1): 53–79.

[7] Kayal, Michele. 2007. Top beverage. The Associated Press in *The Winston-Salem Journal*. November 5: D1.

[8] Waterman, Robert H., Thomas J. Peters, and Julien R. Phillips. 1980. Structure is not organization. *Business Horizons*. June: 14–26; Waterman, Robert H. 1982. The seven elements of strategic fit. *Journal of Business Strategy* 2(3): 69–73.

[9] McDonald's Corporation—2006 Annual Report.

Glossary

7-S framework A method for examining the various aspects of the organization in such a way that some alignment can be achieved. Elements include strategy, structure, systems, style, skills, staff, and superordinate goals (shared values).

A

Activity-based costing A managerial accounting method used to assign all direct and indirect costs to a particular activity.

Adhocracy A method of organizing usually used within portions of the organization rather than the entire organization. There are no supervisors, and everyone in the group operates organically toward a well-defined goal.

Agency Where an individual (such as a corporate officer) acts on behalf of someone else (such as a shareholder).

Analyzer A company that is somewhere between Prospectors and Defenders. Analyzer organizations generally take one of two forms. In the first form, there are parts of the company that behave like a defender and parts that behave like a prospector. The second form of Analyzer Company tends to swing somewhat seamlessly from Prospector to Defender without a significant negative impact on the organization.

B

Balanced scorecard An implementation method that considers a wide variety of stakeholders in the "performance" of the company.

Benchmark A process through which a company compares its own process and structure to that of other organizations. Companies most often benchmark directly against competitors. Occasionally, benchmarking will be done against other unrelated companies that have a "best in class" process. For example, General Mills examined how NASCAR pit crews organize for pit stops in order to better understand how to implement rapid cereal production line changes.

Benign environment Characterized by: 1) market demand exceeds the market supply; 2) generally high gross profit margins; 3) low competitive intensity—meaning no one competitor controls a high proportion of the market; 4) high customer loyalty; and 5) a general tolerance for management mistakes.

Business strategy The types of decisions made and direction created for a single business.

Business-level (generic) strategies A term for strategic approaches at the highest, most straightforward level. Often referred to as "generic strategies."

C

Capabilities Sets of tightly integrated activities, organizational skills, and internally developed routines that rely on extraordinary resources and that allow the company to create value in a fashion superior to other companies.

Causal ambiguity A condition that exists when the link between a business's resources and its competitive advantage are poorly understood.

Causal logic An assessment of why things work the way they do.

Characteristics of effective metrics There are four elements to high-quality metrics. They must be: 1) both quantitative and qualitative; 2) balanced across functions; 3) be appropriate for the function or level; and 4) be connected to incentives.

Clipping service Provides a complete, detailed record of all available public information about any particular company, area, person, or situation.

CLO Collateralized Loan Obligation. Large pool of bank loans bundled together by financial services firms and sold off to investors in slices, with the goal to spread default risk "an inch deep and a mile wide."

Commoditization An industry condition in which a standard set of features and benefits is required for any serious competitor, and in which such features and benefits are readily available from a variety of suppliers. These conditions lead to low-cost competition.

Common stock returns Take into account both the dividends paid by a company to its shareholders as well as increases in the price of the shares.

Common-sized statements A method of financial analysis that facilitates comparisons between different-size companies. For income statements set revenue for each company equal to 100 percent, and for balance sheets set each side of the balance sheet to 100 percent.

Complements Products or services that have a correlation relationship with, and can affect the value of, a company's own products or services. For example, iTunes and iPod.

Concentration ratio The percentage of market share in the industry owned by the largest firms.

Conglomerate A corporation that owns a large number of businesses that are different sizes and operate in different industry sectors.

Core The group or groups that are directly responsible for competitive advantages that the firm enjoys.

Corporate strategy The decisions made and the direction provided for managing multiple business units under a single corporate umbrella.

Cross-sector diversification Acquisition of a company in a different industry, but which employs a similar value chain.

D

Defender A company that is intensive rather than extensive. That is, they usually focus on a limited number of key criteria, analyze their costs, and rigorously defend their competitive position against all competitors.

Differentiation One of the generic strategies available to companies. It implies a broad market approach where activities performed by the company provide sufficiently differentiated value to allow the company to obtain economic returns, generally through higher pricing.

Direct supervision Every person is coordinated via a direct supervisor and coordination flows into and from that supervisor.

Divisional (multidivisional) structure A method of organizing a company that divides up the organization into discrete companies (or semiautonomous divisions) within the overall company. These divisions generally contain all the elements of an independent company.

Dominant business A company in which 70–95 percent of revenue comes from a single business.

Downscoping When a corporation reduces its level of diversification and strategically refocuses on core businesses where the synergies of scope, economizing, and leverage are more evident and more easily realized.

E

Economic logic The means by which the successful company seeks to generate a return that is greater than what competitors earn and greater than its cost of capital.

Economic profit The residual income above and beyond normal profit that accrues to owners, deriving from the prowess of management in planning, supervision, and control.

Economizing Cost savings accomplished by operating combined companies more efficiently.

Equifinality Multiple means to achieve success.

Executional drivers Performance and cost dimensions of activities that are derived from the execution of the business activities—involving people, systems, routines, culture, and coordination—and usually have a fairly important learning dimension to them.

Exogenous forces Forces outside the control of the business.

Experience curve Cost reductions per unit produced that are based upon cumulative production over time (in contrast to economies of scale, in which unit cost reductions are associated with volume during a fixed time interval).

Extraordinary resources Those resources or capabilities that are believed by the management of a business to be simultaneously rare, durable, relatively nonsubstitutable, nontradable, and valuable.

F

First-mover advantage The sustainable competitive advantage that is sought by being the first company to enter a new industry or industry segment.

Five-forces model A model originally created by Michael Porter to examine the various aspects of the competitive environment. The model consists of new entrants, substitutes, suppliers, buyers, and rivalry.

Focus A subset of the two main generic strategies of differentiation and low cost whereby the company pursues a narrow targeted market, geographic area, and/or particular customer group.

Frederick Taylor Father of the "science of work" time and motion studies that helped identify more efficient production processes and ideas about structure and hierarchy.

Functional structure A method of organizing a company that divides up the company based upon their functional areas of expertise.

H

Historical conditions The ability to develop unique resources often depends on the time and place in which the business began operations.

Holding company Corporation that owns the majority of voting shares of other companies, but that allows the other companies to operate as independent entities.

Horizontal diversification Acquisition of a company that operates in the same industry using the same value chain.

Hostile environment Characterized by: 1) very slow growth; 2) continuous price wars; 3) high competitive intensity—meaning that one or a few competitors control a substantial portion of the market; and 4) a focus on cost containment by competitors.

I

Idiosyncratic Unique to the company (and hopefully of value), which cannot be reproduced by a competitor or imitated very easily.

Incumbent firms Established firms in the industry.

Industry analysis Means by which we examine whether the nature of competitive forces makes an industry attractive or unattractive.

Industry roll-up The consolidation of an industry when many small fragmented competitors are combined into a larger company.

Intangible resources Those resources/capabilities that are not physical in nature, including such things as relationships with key suppliers/businesses, the culture of the organization, the history of the business to date, and perhaps most importantly, the skills of the founders.

Intellectual property protection A legal means of protecting those tangible and intangible assets that are unique to the organization. This is accomplished through patents, copyrights, trademarks, and trade secrets.

J

Junk bond High-yield debt that is rated below investment grade at the time of purchase. These bonds have a higher risk of default, but typically pay higher yields than better quality bonds in order to make them attractive to investors. Typically issued by businesses that are unable to secure investment grade financing.

K

Key success factors (KSF) "Rules of thumb" for doing business in an industry that reflect the structural conditions of the industry.

Key value drivers Those elements of the organization that provide the company with the best opportunity for success in their industry.

L

Lag metrics Represent the results that we would hope and expect to observe for each of the subdimensions in any one perspective of a balanced scorecard.

Lead metric Represent the observable actions of employees that we hope will lead to the results we are ultimately trying to achieve.

Leveraged buyout (LBO) A process where a company is bought primarily using debt. Typically engineered by management of the company, or by private equity firms.

Long-range planning A traditional approach to planning used before 1980 that often simply extrapolated into the future what the company had done well in the past.

Low cost One of the generic strategies available to companies. It implies a broad market approach where the company rigorously reduces costs and expenses in an effort to lower the overall cost of operations below their competitors.

Low-cost leadership Of the companies that pursue a low-cost generic strategy, one company will enjoy the lowest cost structure. This company has the strongest competitive position among low-cost strategists, since it enjoys greater pricing flexibility and can more easily weather industry conditions that compress profit margins.

M

Management fit When a corporation can take synergistic advantage of administrative and support activities of the value chain in making an acquisition.

Market capitalization The market value of outstanding shares of stock. Stock price multiplied by all outstanding shares.

Market fit When a corporation can take synergistic advantage of relationships with suppliers and/or customers in making an acquisition.

Market scope The degree to which a company competes broadly or narrowly within an industry. Differences in geography, customer segments, and user needs can describe broad versus narrow scope.

Matrix structure A method of organizing a company that utilizes a dual structure such that everybody in the organization has both a functional home as well as a divisional home.

Metrics Qualitative and quantitative measures that allow the firm to measure the effectiveness of its business strategy.

Michael Porter Leading proponent of the move from long-range planning to strategy. His two early books on the subject, *Competitive Strategy* and *Competitive Advantage,* described competitive strategy as "positioning a business to maximize the value of the capabilities that distinguish it from its competitors."

Mission statement A brief statement that summarizes how and where the firm will compete in the present.

Mobility barriers Strategic actions and resource investments that prevent competitors in the industry from imitating the company.

Monopoly A situation where a single firm virtually constitutes the entire industry.

Mutual adjustment A method of coordination where every individual knows everything that is happening in the organization and adjusts his or her work pattern for the conditions at hand.

N

NAICS code (North American Industry Classification System) Generated by the U.S. government in an effort to gather, track, and publish data on specific industries (http://www.census.gov/epcd/www/naics.html).

Normal profit The minimum return earned by a company that is necessary to attract and secure the owners' inputs. Generally defined as the cost of equity capital multiplied by the amount of shareholder equity.

O

Operational fit When a corporation is able to combine similar primary value chain activities.

Opportunity recognition The critical need in business to identify and exploit where the market is heading.

Options An investment approach that places a small initial bet on an initiative, with the opportunity to invest further if the initiative makes favorable progress and reaches positive milestones.

Ordinary resources Those resources or capabilities that are required just to be considered a business in an industry.

Outsourcing When another organization is employed to perform a business process or service that is part of the company's value chain.

P

Parity Though companies compete on cost or some dimension of differentiation, they must maintain relative equality with other companies on other dimensions that are valued in the marketplace. Without reasonable parity on other valued conditions, the lowest-cost competitor or most-effective differentiator on some dimension may not succeed.

Perfect competition A situation of little or no differentiation between competitors and one in which there is virtually perfect information available to market participants.

Private equity firm Private (nonpublic) corporations or partnerships that use their financial resources to engineer buyouts and acquisitions of other companies.

Profit pool Generally the amount of profit available in the industry in a particular period of time.

Prospector A company that tends to view the industry from their own perspective and that of the customer rather than being concerned with the competition. They are usually leaders of change in the industry with little concern for the effects or impacts of other organizations.

Q

Qualitative metrics Measures of success that are descriptive and relative rather than point-specific.

Quantitative metrics Numerically based measures of firm success.

R

Reactor A company that reacts (albeit very, very slowly) to conditions in the competitive environment. This is an unstable form of organization and one that is not destined to last very long.

Reconfiguring industry value chain A strategic approach that calls for changing the usual sets of relationships across the industry value chain.

Related diversification A merger or acquisition where there is some similarity of industry and/or value chain between the corporation and the company it seeks to acquire.

Resource-based analysis An approach to an organization that examines its current resources and capabilities in an effort to find those that will provide the company with sustainable value-generating competitive advantages.

Resources leverage The benefits that develop through the extension and application of corporate resources to a newly acquired company.

S

Sarbanes-Oxley Act (SOX) The legislative initiative enacted in 2002 that imposes stiff new demands on companies and their auditors to ensure that published financial statements are accurate.

Scenario analysis The technique allows organizations to consider dramatic shifts in their business model. The organization then maps out a set of actions that it can begin to take if the warning signs begin to appear along the path of a particular scenario.

Scope Ability to broaden a product line or a customer base achieved through an acquisition.

Simple structure A method of organizing a company in which all areas of the company report to a single person. The pure form of the simple structure is referred to as a flat organization.

Size advantage One of the possible benefits of first-mover status when entering a new industry. Size advantages tend to produce favorable cost structures and network effects.

Social complexity Resources that may result from a socially complex phenomenon, something that cannot be systematically managed or influenced.

Social contract Implied relationship between businesses and the communities in which they operate.

SPAC Special Purpose Acquisition Company. Empty-shell firms that promise to buy businesses with the proceeds of their initial public stock offerings.

Spin-off Divestiture in which a corporation creates a new company out of one of its businesses. The new company has its own shares of stock and shareholders, and its own board of directors. Typically, shareholders of the corporation will receive newly issued shares out of the spin-off company at its organization.

Staff support All other groups who are not core and not advice givers/policy makers.

Stakeholders Individuals or groups who have an interest in or an influence on the business and operations of a company. They fall into two categories—internal stakeholders and external stakeholders.

Standardization An industry condition in which customers begin to appreciate a standard set of features and benefits or products or services.

Standardization of work output A method of managing large numbers of employees based upon a well-developed set of output measures that in combination provides insight into the performance of the employee.

Standardization of work processes A method of managing large numbers of employees based upon the processes that they perform.

Standardization of work skills A method of managing large numbers of employees based upon their skill sets as established by some externally validated means.

Strategic alliance A joint venture or partnership formed with other companies (sometimes competitors) in order to develop a new technology, process, or other type of strategically important resource.

Strategic business unit (SBU) The organization of a set of businesses that share identical or very similar strategies or strategic challenges.

Strategic decisions Strategic decisions exhibit five characteristics: 1) are relevant to ill-structured and nonroutine situations; 2) significantly affect the subsequent actions of the entire organization; 3) involve a significant commitment of resources; 4) are difficult to reverse both economically and politically; and 5) are easily identified with the success or failure of the organization.

Strategic group A group of businesses competing for virtually the same customers in virtually the same manner.

Strategic management The process through which strategy is developed, executed, and evaluated. There are typically four stages of the strategic management process: analysis, formulation, implementation, and evaluation.

Strategy The overall concept for how a company organizes itself and all its activities in order to conduct business successfully, out-perform competitors, and deliver superior returns to its shareholders.

Strategy map A two-dimensional map showing where competitors are positioned using a quantitatively defined set of criteria.

Structural drivers Performance and cost dimensions of activities that are derived from the strategic choices made about the underlying economic logic and structure of the business—such as the scale and scope of its operations, the complexity of its products or services, and its use of technology.

Stuck in the middle A condition where a company simultaneously pursues both a differentiation and a low-cost strategy. The result is most often expenses that are too high and a product that does not command a premium price.

Substitutes Products or services that perform the same function or meet the same need as the products or services in the industry under study, but which are produced using different raw materials and inputs.

Sun Tzu Author of *The Art of War,* an ancient Chinese book on military strategy.

Superior performance As used in the field of strategy, refers to performance outcomes that exceed the average for the industry in which the company competes.

SWOT analysis A form of analysis, resulting in a listing of a company's strengths, weaknesses, opportunities, and threats. It is a static view of the company at a particular point in time.

Systematic risk Risk associated with macro-economic forces.

T

Tactics Dealing with short-term competitive moves and countermoves, as opposed to long-term direction, investments, and performance.

Takeover A process where a large group of shareholders vote in new members to the board of directors, with the result that the new board can make changes in the company's management.

Tangible resources Physical assets such as equipment, buildings, land, furniture, human resources, money, and patents.

Techno structure Those groups who are advice givers and policy makers to the core.

Timing advantage One of the possible benefits of first-mover status when entering a new industry. Timing advantages tend to build customer loyalty through setting standards, building reputation, and achieving customer lock-in.

TOWS matrix A matrix that arrays a company's strengths and weaknesses against its opportunities and threats, providing general direction.

U

Unrelated diversification When a corporation enters a new business in a different industry from that in which it currently operates *and* does not expect to achieve any value chain synergies through the combination.

Unsystematic risk Risk associated with a particular business.

V

Value capture When a company creates value by acting in ways that its competitors cannot or will not act.

Value chain An approach that emphasizes that a company is an organization of interrelated activities designed to create value for stakeholders, and that the derivation of superior performance is better understood by focusing on what a company actually does.

Value chain analysis A method that identifies value-creating activities in a company, categorizes them into important subsets, develops information to understand how the activities create value and what their costs are, and pinpoints opportunities for enhanced value creation and cost reduction. It is a dynamic view of a company's activities.

Value creation The primary goal of strategy. The profitable aspect of a transaction that results from an exchange of goods or services.

Vertical diversification Acquisition of another company upstream (supplier) or downstream (buyer) in the value chain of the same industry in which the corporation operates.

Vision statement More compelling and overarching than the mission statement, an image of the organization in the future that motivates employees to focus their actions toward a common point.

Company and Name Index

Friedman, Milton, 55

Friendster, 198–199

G

Garmin, 306

Gates, Bill, 55

Gateway, 123–125

Gault, Stanley, 21*f*

General Electric, 150, 170, 173, 266, 284, 287, 309–310, 312, 316, 334, 355

General Motors, 22*f*, 82, 269

Gillette, 276, 293, 298, 304

GlaxoSmithKline, 82, 134*f*

Google, 61, 160, 283, 293

Grant, Robert, 277

Great Lakes Aviation, 135*f*

The Greenbrier Resort, 142, 154

Greenspan, Alan, 272–273

Guidant Corp., 289–290, 308

H

H&R Block, 78*f*

Hackensack University Hospital, 152

Halliburton Co., 72

Harvard University, 144*f*

Henry V, 65

Hewlett Packard, 102, 122, 123–125, 193, 202, 270

Hitachi, 344, 345*f*

Hjertonsson, Johan, 323

Host Marriot, 78*f*

I

IBM, 236

Immelt, Jeffrey, 150, 312

InBev, 296–297

In-N-Out Burger, 214

Intel, 113, 263

iPhone, 264*f*

J

JetBlue Airlines, 35*f*–36*f*, 135*f*

Johnson & Johnson, 134*f*, 289, 336

J.P. Morgan Chase, 73

K

Kanter, Rosabeth Moss, 248

Katz, Don, 227

Kavanaugh, David, 163

Kavanaugh, Phil, 163

Kennedy, John F., 66–67

Kmart, 203

Kodak, 144, 210–211

Kohlberg Kravis Roberts, 301

Kohl's, 48

Kraft Foods, 313–314

Krispy Kreme Doughnuts, 169

Kroc, Ray, 353

L

Lafley, A. G., 298

Lanier, John, 304–305

Lena Pope Home Inc., 69, 78

LG, 264*f*

Liberty Media, 6

Lincoln, Abraham, 90

M

Macy's, 235

Marriott, 40

McDonald's, 169, 178, 266–267, 279, 353, 377

McDonnell Douglas, 307

McKinsey & Co., 309, 371

Medtronic, 80, 308

Merck, 74, 134*f*, 294

MGM Mirage, 78*f*

Microsoft, 20*f*, 39, 68*f*, 91, 149, 259, 266, 269, 274, 276, 283, 293

Miles, Raymond, 264

Mintzberg, Henry, 64

Moore, Gordon, 263

Morita, Akio, 79

Motorola, 264*f*

Mt. Tabor High School, 86

N

Napster, 276

NASCAR, 148

Nestlé, 40

Netflix, 12, 144*f*

Netscape, 20*f*

Newman, Paul, 172*f*

Newman's Own, 39

New York Times, 77

Nike, 217, 312

Nimbus Technologies, 182

Nintendo, 240, 259, 267, 274

Nokia, 264*f*

Norman, Dave, 198

Northwest Airlines, 35–36

Nucor, 144*f*

O

Olsen, Ken, 269

Oracle, 291

Oxford Health Plans, 68*f*

P

Packard Bell, 196

Palm, 264*f*

Parker, Doug, 35

Parker Hannifin, 73, 75

Pathmark, 17–18

Patton, George, 270

Peery, Richard, 173, 174–175

PepsiCo, 145, 170, 232

Perkin Elmer, 346

Pets.com, 21*f*

PetSmart, 197

Pfizer, 134*f*

Philip Morris Co., 298

Pinnacle, 135*f*

Plexus, 152

Porter, Michael, 24, 103, 192–193

Subject Index

7-S framework, 371, 375–376, 378

A

Absolute cost advantages, of new business, 106

Absorption, 276

Access to distribution, for new business, 106

Access to inputs, for new business, 106

Acquisition, as diversification, 288–309

Actions list, 370

Action steps, long-term effects of, 42–48

Activity-based costing, 148

Adhocracy structure, 347–348

Advantage, competitive, 10–13, 41–44

Agency issue, 292

The Age of Turbulence, 272–273

Airline industry
    average returns of, 135*f*
    and capacity utilization, 200
    competition in, 35
    key organizational components of, 331, 337
    operating characteristics of, 52
    scenario for, 273
    See also individual airlines, e.g., American Airlines

Alliances, strategic, 277–278

Analysis, 9–10, 27–28, 28, 272–273
    See also Five-forces analysis

Analyzer organization, 266

Annulment, 276

Appropriateness, of metrics, 362–363

Arab oil embargo (1973), 22–23

The Art of War, 19, 20*f*, 21*f*, 22*f*

Asset productivity, ROE ratio of, 42–43

Automobile industry, 22–23, 200, 277–278

B

Backward integration threat, 112

Balance, in metrics, 362

Bandwagon effect, 294–295, 306

Barbarians at the Gate, 288

Bargaining power, gains in, 293

BCG Growth Share Matrix, 310–311

Benchmark, 262

BHAG, 67

Bidding wars, 306

"Big, Hairy, Audacious Goal", 67

Bottled water industry, 370

Brewing industry, 236

Budget process, and long-range planning, 22

Business-level strategy
    consistency in, 198–199
    and customer expectations, 197
    and differentiation, 206–211
    and evolution of competition, 197

G

Gaming industry, 259, 261

Gas prices, shortages, 23

GE Business Development Matrix, 309–311

Global forces, in industry, 100*f*

Global strategy, 252–253

Goals, of mission statements, 76

Good to Great, 44

Government organizations, performance in, 40–41

Government regulation, and new business, 108

"Green" organizations, 25, 38, 40

Growth, in business, 229–230, 292, 307

H

Herfindahl-Hirschman Index (HHI), 111*f*

Historical conditions, and resources, 173

Holding companies, 300–301

Horizontal diversification, 296–297

Hypercompetition, 7, 261–262

I

Idiosyncratic activity, 151

Implementation
    balanced scorecard model for, 365–367
    defined, 10
    keys to, 354–356
    metrics for, 356–364
    of strategy, 28–29
    value-driver-action model for, 367–368, 370–371

Incentives, and metrics, 363–364

Incumbent firms, 103

Industry
    analysis of, 93
    attractiveness of, 117, 309
    boundaries of, 97, 126
    capacity in, 114–115
    consolidated, 235–236
    defining, 95–99
    external analysis of model, 85–86
    five forces analysis of, 103–117
    forces affecting, 99–103
    fragmented, 236–237
    growth rate in, 114

International, 249–254
    life cycle stages of, 228–241
    market share loss in, 24
    roll-up, 237
    signaling in, 277
    trajectories of, 262–263

Installed base, of users, 52

Integrity, of product, service, 207–208

Intellectual property protection, 169

International strategy, 250, 251–254

Introduction, stage of, 229

Investment, within corporations, 285

J

Junk bonds, 287

K

Key success factors
    competitive analysis of, 121–122
    as competitive factor, 117–119

Key success factors (*continued*)

    identifying, 119–120

    identifying threats, 134

    as industry rules, 94–95

    and strategic mapping, 122–126

Key value drivers

    of Ford Motor Co., 369, 372–374

    of McDonald's, 377

    as priority, 378

    sources of, 367–378

L

Lag metrics, 366–367

Leadership

    among competitors, 277

    and communication, 326

    and coordination, 336

    human resources and, 202

    and implementation control, 354, 371

    low-cost, 193

    in middle management, 25–26

    and reactor vs. analyzer roles, 266

    and restructuring, 311

    in society, 39

    strategic, 378–379

    for SWOT analysis, 136

    using resources, 177, 183

Lead metrics, 366–367

Leveraged buyouts (LBO), 287, 314

Life cycles

    commercialization of, 239–240

    conception of, 238–239

    first-mover strategy in, 242–245

    growth of, 240, 245–246

    industry, 228–235

    length of, 233–235

    maturity of, 240–241

    organizational, 238

    renewal strategies in, 246–249

    stages of, 228–233

Long-range planning, 22

Long-term orientation, 13–14

Low-cost strategy

    conditions for success of, 199–200

    and differentiation integration, 195, 214–217

    leadership in, 193, 195

    vs. low-cost leadership, 203, 205

    risks of, 203, 205

    and value chain, 203, 204*f*

M

Management involvement, 355

Management patterns, 268

Managerial capitalism, 292–293

Mapping, strategic, 122–126, 262–263

Markets

    analysis of, 90–93

    capitalization of, 44

    fit for, 298–299

    relative position of, 269

    scope of, 194

Matrix structure, 344–346

Maturity, stage of, 230

Merger and acquisition (M&A) activity, 286–287, 288

Metrics

    development of, 356–357, 370–371

    of Ford Motor Co., 372–374

Post-acquisition efforts, 307–309

Preferences, customer, 264*f*

Pricing authority, gains in, 293

Prisoner's Dilemma, 277

Private equity firm, 288

Product differentiation, for new business, 107

Profit, profitability

    metric of, 17–18

    normal vs. economic, 41

    pool, 103, 105

    potential for, 93

    See also Return on equity (ROE)

Prospector organization, 265

Q

Qualitative metrics, 360–362

Quality input, 208

Quantitative metrics, 358–360

R

Rationale, for businesses, 11

Reactor organization, 266–267

Recycling, 202

Related diversification, 296–300

Renewal, stage of, 231–233

Renewal strategy, 246–249

Reputation, corporate, 209

Research and development (R&D), 121–122

Residual income, 41

Resource-Based Analysis 179–186

Resources

    allocation of, 355–356

    and capabilities, 176–179

    identifying, 181*f*, 182

    intangible, 165

    and international strategy, 251–254

    leverage for, 300

    leveraging, 182–183

    ordinary, 165–166

    tangible, 164

    See also Extraordinary resources

Responses, tactical and strategic, 274–276

Responsiveness, to customers, 209

Restructuring, 311–314

Retaliation, to new business, 108

Return on equity (ROE)

    analyzing, 42–43

    and common stock returns, 44

    and market capitalization, 44

    metric of, 17–18

    as performance indicator, 41–42

    questions on, 50

    and sales revenue growth, 43–44

Revenue growth, 43–44

RFID technology, 112

Risk, of diversification, 294–295

Rivals, rivalry, 115, 199, 206

ROE. *See* Return on equity (ROE)

Role models, 79

Roll-up, industry, 237

S

Sales revenue growth, 43–44

Sarbanes-Oxley Act (SOX), 102

Satellite radio industry, 5

tied to business-level strategy, 196

and value capture, 151–154

and value creation, 149–151, 152–154

See also Value chain analysis

Value chain analysis

characteristics, costs of, 156–158

identifying activities for, 155–156

identifying improvements for, 158

internal vs. external, 134–136

of Microsoft, 133

opportunity recognition in, 153–154

of pharmaceutical industry, 134

results of, 154–155

and SWOT, 136–142

in travel industry, 133, 143

See also Value chain

Value creation, 149–151, 152–154, 344

Value creation imperative, 7–8, 12

Value-driver-action model, 367–368, 370–371

Vertical diversification, 297

Vision

communicating, 78–80

defined, 64

developing, 67–69

horizons for, 66–67

and mission, activities, 64*f*

need for longer term, 24–25

statement of, 62–63, 64–67

Volume, and suppliers, 113

VRIST framework, 167–171, 179–180, 185f

W

Wealth of Nations, 90